Second Edition

ORGANIZATIONAL ETHICS

To my colleagues

Second Edition

ORGANIZATIONAL ETHICS

A Practical Approach

CRAIG E. JOHNSON
George Fox University

Los Angeles | London | New Delhi
Singapore | Washington DC

Los Angeles | London | New Delhi
Singapore | Washington DC

FOR INFORMATION:

SAGE Publications, Inc.
2455 Teller Road
Thousand Oaks, California 91320
E-mail: order@sagepub.com

SAGE Publications Ltd.
1 Oliver's Yard
55 City Road
London EC1Y 1SP
United Kingdom

SAGE Publications India Pvt. Ltd.
B 1/I 1 Mohan Cooperative Industrial Area
Mathura Road, New Delhi 110 044
India

SAGE Publications Asia-Pacific Pte. Ltd.
33 Pekin Street #02-01
Far East Square
Singapore 048763

Acquisitions Editor: Lisa Cuevas Shaw
Editorial Assistant: Mayan White
Production Editor: Astrid Virding
Copy Editor: April Wells-Hayes
Typesetter: C&M Digitals (P) Ltd
Proofreader: Sally M. Scott
Indexer: Gloria Tierney
Cover Designers: Anupama Krishnan and
                 Candice Harman
Marketing Manager: Helen Salmon
Permissions Editor: Karen Ehrmann

Printed in the United States of America

Library of Congress Cataloging-in-Publication Data

Johnson, Craig E. (Craig Edward), 1952-

Organizational ethics : a practical approach / Craig E. Johnson. — 2nd ed.

p. cm.
Includes bibliographical references and index.

ISBN 978-1-4129-8796-7 (pbk. : acid-free paper)

1. Business ethics. 2. Corporate culture. 3. Ethics. I. Title.

HF5387.J645 2012
174′.4—dc23   2011027016

This book is printed on acid-free paper.

11 12 13 14 15 10 9 8 7 6 5 4 3 2 1

Contents

List of Case Studies

Acknowledgments

Writing this text would have been impossible without assistance at every stage of the project. Editor Lisa Cuevas Shaw called for a significant revision of the original version of the book—*Ethics in the Workplace: Tools and Tactics for Organizational Transformation*—and provided valuable guidance. During the writing process, student employees under the direction of Kelly Borror gathered books and photocopied materials. Rebecca Jensen provided editing assistance. At the same time, she kept the Doctor of Business Administration program running smoothly so I could focus more attention on writing. Faculty in the George Fox School of Business provided feedback on case studies, and students enrolled in my Ethics in the Workplace and Business Ethics classes were the first to try out cases, self-assessments, and other chapter material. My colleagues around the university have given me a greater appreciation of what it means to live in an ethical community.

Three reviewers offered helpful critiques on the earlier version of this text. I have incorporated their insights whenever possible into this revision. The editorial and production staff at Sage skillfully guided me through the final publication stages.

I am grateful to all the individuals and groups named above. Thanks, too, to my wife, Mary, who is all too aware of the demands that writing makes on my time but supports my efforts nonetheless.

Finally, I want to acknowledge the ethics scholars whose research and analysis provide the foundation of this book. Their continuing efforts make me optimistic about continued progress in the study and practice of organizational ethics.

Introduction:
The Case for Studying
Organizational Ethics

"It's just us today. Campbell called in ethical."

SOURCE: © Matthew Difee 11/25/2002 The New Yorker Collection/www.cartoonbank.com.

E vidence for the importance of organizational ethics is all around us. Scarcely a day goes by without revelations of a new organizational scandal. We read and hear about ethical failures in every sector of society—business, education, social service, environmental, entertainment, military, religious, government. Here is just a small sample of the prominent organizations accused of immoral behavior:

- Countrywide Mortgage, Washington Mutual Savings: Fraudulent home loans
- Toyota: Delayed recall of defective vehicles
- Galleon hedge fund: Insider trading
- National Football League: Player misconduct; disregard for player safety
- Boys & Girls Clubs of America: Excessive executive pay and travel expenses
- BP: Safety lapses, inadequate response to environmental disaster on the Gulf Coast
- Johnson & Johnson: Manufacture of defective medicines; secret product recall
- British Parliament: Misuse of public funds for personal projects
- Harvard Medical School: Conflicts of interest involving faculty members employed by drug companies
- Siemens International: Systematic bribery to win foreign contracts
- Bell, California: Exorbitant pay for city officials
- Merck: Marketing a painkiller that greatly increased the risk of heart attack
- The Catholic Church: Sexual abuse by clergy in the United States, Europe, and South America
- Army Intelligence, the National Guard: Prisoner abuse in Iraq and Afghanistan
- Palm Beach County, Florida: Widespread corruption
- Peanut Corporation of America: Shipping tainted peanut products
- AIG: Using federal bailout funds for executive bonuses and lavish retreats
- Massey Energy: Safety violations leading to a West Virginia mine explosion
- U.S. Congress: Failure to report personal income; misuse of campaign funds; sexual misconduct

We all pay a high price for unethical organizational behavior. Offending organizations suffer damaged reputations; declining revenues, earnings, donations, and stock prices; downsizing and bankruptcy; increased regulation; and civil lawsuits and criminal charges. Their members may lose their jobs, see their retirement savings shrink, and end up doing jail time. Outsiders who have a stake or interest in the fallen organization also suffer. For example, patients who take drugs with undesirable side effects face a higher risk of death; neighbors of a polluting manufacturing plant must live with environmental damage; investors who are victimized by fraud see their net worth decline; needy citizens must do without important services when taxpayer funds are wasted. In addition, society as a whole suffers because trust in many of our basic institutions is lost. According to a 2010 survey conducted by the public relations firm Edelman U.S., 46% of Americans said they trusted business, down from 54% in 2009. This percentage was lower than the worldwide business trust rating of 56%.[1] U.S. banks received the lowest business trust score, with just 25% of respondents expressing trust in the financial sector (16% of British subjects reported that they trusted their banks). Government fared even worse than business in the survey—only 40% of U.S. residents trust their political institutions. The nation's composite-trust score, which is made up of its business, government, nonprofit, and media ratings, ranked near the bottom of the 23 countries surveyed.

Preventing significant harm is one reason why organizational ethics is worth your time and attention; the fact that you will constantly be faced with ethical choices is another. As a member of an organization, you will make ethical decisions almost daily. Some are obvious, like whether or not to clock in for a coworker or to lie to customers. Yet even routine decisions involving hiring, accounting, planning, purchasing, manufacturing, and advertising have an ethical dimension. Consider the supermarket produce buyer who decides which fruits and vegetables to sell in her local stores. She must weigh several ethical considerations when making these determinations. For example: Should she stock only organic products? Should she use suppliers who treat their workers poorly? Should local growers be given priority over distant producers even if the cost is higher? Is price a more important consideration than quality, or vice versa? Should she use her bargaining power to take advantage of growers, or should she negotiate agreements that benefit all parties?

Not only will you continually make ethical choices, but those decisions can also determine your success or failure in your career. Technical skills alone are not enough to guarantee you a productive future. For instance, accountants at the now defunct Arthur Andersen accounting firm had all the proper professional certifications. But in order to keep their clients happy and to generate consulting revenue, they signed off on fraudulent financial statements at Waste Management, the Baptist Foundation of Arizona, Sunbeam, Enron, and WorldCom. In the end, the company, which was one of the world's largest and most respected accounting firms, failed.[2] Business ethics professor Lynn Paine argues that moral thinking is "an essential capability for effective managers and organizational leaders."[3] She contrasts moral reasoning, which is concerned with ethical principles and the consequences of choices, with strategic or result-based thinking, which focuses on reaching objectives, such as increasing revenue, finding new distributors, or manufacturing products. Though distinct, these two strands of reasoning intertwine. As a manager making strategic choices, you ought to consider important moral principles and weigh potential ethical consequences or outcomes. If you don't, your organization (like Arthur Andersen) may lose the right to operate in a modern society. Conversely, you must be a good strategic thinker in order to make wise moral decisions. You have to understand marketing, production, and organizational design, for example, in order to implement your ethical choices.

There's one final reason that you should focus on understanding ethics in organizations: You have a duty to do so. I believe that when we enter organizations as managers, workers, or volunteers, we assume the ethical burden of making them better places. *Organizational Ethics: A Practical Approach* is designed to help us carry out that task. But as we take on that responsibility, we need to clear up some misunderstandings that serve as barriers to ethical change. I call the first of these myths "There's nothing to it." Those who fall victim to this misconception believe that changing ethical performance is easy. They are seriously mistaken. Acting morally can be a tough task, as you probably discovered when you tried to do the right thing in the face of peer pressure or were punished for telling the truth. At times, you will be called upon to put aside your self-interest to meet the needs of others, to stand alone, and to endure criticism. You could risk losing your job because you "aren't a team player" or because you have to bring organizational wrongdoing to the attention of outside authorities (see Chapter 9). Further, ethical decisions are complex and often lack clear answers. They may require choosing between what appear to be two "rights" or two "wrongs."

The second myth is "It won't do any good." This myth comes out of widespread cynicism about organizations and stands at the opposite end of the spectrum from the first misconception. According to this perspective, change is too hard, not too easy. The individual can have little impact on the ethical climate of an organization. Organizations are too complicated and have lives of their own. Even people with high personal moral standards leave their scruples at the door when they go to work. They end up following company dictates, no matter how immoral.

This misconception contains an element of truth. Situational pressures are important determinants of ethical or unethical behavior. In recognition of that fact, a great deal of this text is devoted to ways we can reshape the ethical climates of our groups and organizations. There is little doubt that many of us do act contrary to our personal convictions due to outside pressures. However, this myth overlooks the fact that organizations are the products of choices. Organizations become embroiled in scandals because individuals and groups decide to lie, steal, abuse their positions and power, and cover up crimes. The same members who create and sustain unhealthy practices, values, and structures can develop more productive alternatives instead. Granted, your ability to make significant systemwide changes will be limited if you are a college graduate entering your first job. Nevertheless, you do have the power to manage your own behavior, and your coworkers will note how you react to ethical issues. Your influence will likely grow over time, as those with undergraduate and graduate degrees generally end up in management positions. If you question the ability of one person to make a difference, consider former Supreme Court Justice Sandra Day O'Connor. She started life on a cattle ranch in Arizona that had no electricity or running water. O'Connor graduated third in her class from Stanford Law School, but major West Coast law firms refused to hire her or offered her only secretarial positions. She finally landed a job at a county attorney's office by offering to work for free. Later, she went to work as an assistant attorney general and was elected majority leader of the Arizona state senate. She then served on state and federal appellate courts before Ronald Reagan appointed her to the Supreme Court in 1981, where she became the first female Supreme Court justice. During her last 10 years on the bench, she voted with the majority in more than three quarters of court rulings that were decided by a 5–4 margin. For example, she cast the deciding vote in reaffirming *Roe v. Wade* (which permits abortions), in stopping the Florida recount in the 2000 presidential election, and in supporting affirmative action in the University of Michigan's law school admissions. Based on her pivotal role in these decisions, one observer noted: "We are all living now in Sandra Day O'Connor's America."[4]

The third myth is "Too little, too late." Proponents of this view (including some university faculty) argue that our ethical values and standards are determined in childhood. Studying ethics in college or on the job is a waste of time, if that's the case. If we don't have strong values by the time we are adults, course work will do little good.

Research does not support this argument, as we'll see in Chapter 3. Psychologists have established that moral development, like physical and psychological development, continues beyond childhood.[5] Discussing ethical issues in the classroom, in fact, increases moral reasoning abilities all the way through graduate school. Most of us, whatever our stage in life, can point to ways in which our views have changed over a period of years on such moral issues as the death penalty, cloning, gay marriage, stem cell research, and recycling.

The fourth myth is labeled "Been there, done that." Proponents of this view argue that current excitement about organizational ethics is just a fad. They note that right now organizational ethics is a "hot" topic; interest in the subject will dissipate as our memory of recent scandals fades. These critics have a point. Discussion of organizational ethics did peak during such earlier scandals as Watergate, the My Lai Massacre, the Iran-Contra affair, the Sears auto repair scandal, and the failure of the savings and loan industry in the 1980s. Ethical talk subsided as time passed. Yet ethics is not a fad. Popular attention may shift to other concerns, but as the recent spate of scandals demonstrates, moral decision making is more important than ever. An Ethics Resource Center survey found that fraud is common in all types of organizations. According to the survey, 56% of business employees reported observing unethical conduct, as did 57% of those in the government sector and 55% in the nonprofit sector.[6]

The fifth and final myth I've entitled "We can't afford it." The argument here is that adopting high ethical standards is too costly. Adherents believe that ethical organizations can't compete in the modern marketplace. Groups that do the right thing, such as refusing to bribe foreign officials to gain contracts, lose out to less scrupulous competitors. Proponents of this view also point out that unethical behavior often goes undetected and that good intentions by themselves are no guarantee of organizational success.

There is no doubt that ethical behavior can be costly. Unethical behavior often does go unpunished, and careful planning and execution must back lofty goals. However, there is evidence that ignoring ethics is more costly than pursuing ethics. Business ethicists report that more often than not, it pays to be ethical. High moral standards and outstanding performance frequently go hand in hand. Many ethical strategies and actions—empowering employees, creating a sense of shared mission and values, demonstrating concern, telling the truth, rewarding moral behavior—can improve employee commitment and productivity. The productivity of the entire organization improves as a result. In addition, there is evidence that organizations that strive to be good citizens are frequently (but not always) more successful. Winners of the prestigious Baldrige Performance Excellence award, for instance, must demonstrate ethical and social responsibility. Companies adopting the Dow Jones Sustainability Index (DJSI) standards for social and environmental performance reported higher gross profit margin and higher return on investment than similar, non-DJSI firms.[7]

A Practical Approach to Organizational Ethics

For the study of organizational ethics to make a positive difference to us, to our organizations, and to society as a whole, we must put our knowledge to work. That calls for an applied or practical approach. A practical approach to organizational ethics is founded on the premise that we can develop our ethical expertise just as we develop our abilities to manage, to do cost accounting, and to oversee operations. University of Notre Dame psychologist Darcia Narvaez argues that we can master the knowledge and skills that can help us behave more like moral experts. She points out that ethical authorities, like experts in other fields, think differently from novices.[8] First, they know more about the ethical domain. Their networks of moral knowledge are more developed and connected than those of beginners. Second, they see the world differently from novices. While beginners are often overwhelmed by new data, those with expertise can quickly identify and act on the relevant information, such as what ethical principles might apply in this situation. Third, experts have different skill sets. They are better able to define the moral problem and then match the new dilemma with previous ethical problems they have encountered. "Unlike novices," Narvaez says, "they know *what* information to access, *which* procedures to apply, *how* to apply them, and *when* it is appropriate."[9] As a result, they make better moral decisions faster and automatically.

Experts become expert by learning in situations that reward the behaviors that lead to success in that domain, building on the knowledge of previous generations, and putting forth sustained effort. A professional violinist, for example, spends years taking lessons, completing classes in music theory, practicing hours daily, and performing in recitals and concerts. You must follow similar strategies if you want to become less of an ethical novice and more of an ethical expert. Learn in a well-structured environment, where correct behaviors are rewarded and where you can interact with mentors and receive feedback and coaching. Master both moral theory and skills. Familiarize yourself with ways in which previous experts have dealt with moral problems and why some choices are better than others. Gain experience so that you'll not only get better at solving ethical problems but can better explain your choices. Finally, practice, practice, practice. You will have to put in the necessary time and concentrated effort. Ethical progress takes hours of practice wrestling with moral dilemmas.

Organizational Ethics: A Practical Approach incorporates all of the developmental components outlined by Narvaez. The book is designed for use in a college or university classroom where ethical knowledge and behaviors are encouraged and professors and classmates provide feedback. In the chapters to come, you will be introduced to the insights of ethical experts both past and present, and you will see how some behaviors are more effective than others. The text supplies plenty of opportunities for you to practice your problem-solving abilities and to defend your decisions. You'll be provided with lists of steps or actions that you and your organization can take. Cases provide opportunities to apply what you've read, and the Self-Assessment in each chapter measures your (or your leader's or organization's) performance on an important behavior, skill, or concept. The Takeaways section at the end of each chapter reviews important concepts and their ramifications for you and your organization. The Application Projects ask you to engage in further reflection, analysis, and implementation. Some of these activities can be completed on your own; others require group participation.

Wright State University business ethics professor Joseph Petrick outlines three types of competencies you need to develop during your study of business and organizational ethics. (See Ethics in Action 0.1 for a detailed look at these competencies.) They can serve as a yardstick by which to measure your ethical progress. *Cognitive decision-making competence* means demonstrating the "abilities to recognize, understand, analyze, and make responsible judgments about moral matters" in business and other organizational contexts.[10] *Affective prebehavioral disposition competence* encompasses ethical emotions, attitudes, and motivations. Becoming more of an expert in organizational ethics should not only improve your problem-solving abilities, it should also encourage you to develop your character and increase your motivation to follow through on your choices. *Context management competence* involves the managerial skills needed to build ethical organizational environments. You need to help create ethical settings that encourage members to demonstrate their cognitive and affective competence. You should also be able to encourage your organization to meet the needs of stakeholders, protect the environment, honor the rights of overseas workers, and so on. Each of these sets of competencies—intellectual, emotional/motivational, managerial— is addressed in this text. In the chapters to come, you'll learn how to develop your ethical reasoning, ethical character, and motivation as well as your ability to shape your organization's ethical climate. You can chart your progress by completing the Self-Assessment on the next page. Complete the instrument now to determine your current level of ethical competence. At the end of the text and your course, take the instrument again and compare the two sets of scores to measure your ethical development.

ETHICS IN ACTION 0.1 ETHICAL COMPETENCIES

Cognitive Decision-Making Competencies

1. *Moral awareness:* Perceiving and discerning the ethical dimensions of an organizational issue; sensitivity to stakeholders.

2. *Moral understanding:* Mastering the conceptual foundation to understand ethical conflicts and dilemmas.

3. *Moral reasoning and dialogue:* Participating in ethical argumentation and discussion; taking a reasoned stance on an ethical issue.

4. *Moral complexity resolution:* Balancing the trade-offs that must be made when making ethical choices; arriving at sound moral conclusions and implementing them.

Affective Prebehavioral Disposition Competence

1. *Moral sensitivity/emotional virtue:* Expressing concern and caring about potential victims of organizational decisions; cultivating honesty, love, and other virtues while avoiding immoral motivations, such as greed, jealousy, and hate.

2. *Moral courage/moral virtue:* Acting on personal convictions by persevering and overcoming obstacles and adversity.

3. *Moral tolerance/sociopolitical virtue:* Tolerating and respecting opposing views.

4. *Moral imagination/intellectual virtue:* Stepping back from the situation at hand to critique and evaluate; cultivating and appreciating that which is ethically desirable.

(Continued)

(Continued)

Context Management Competence

1. *Responsible management of the organizational compliance and ethics context:* Designing, implementing, and improving formal and informal ethics systems; punishing immoral conduct while rewarding ethical actions.

2. *Responsible management of the corporate governance context:* Knowing how the system is governed and using this knowledge to create a corporate governance system that supports ethical behavior.

3. *Exercising business citizenship to influence the institutionalization of ethically supportive, extraorganizational contexts in the domestic and global environments:* Systematically promoting global organizational citizenship; partnering with outside organizations to promote human welfare and to preserve the environment.

SELF-ASSESSMENT

Instructions: In the survey below, indicate how strongly you agree or disagree with each statement. Each item is designed to measure one of the ethical competencies described in the chapter.

Organizational Ethics Survey

(Circle only one response for each statement.)

	Strongly Agree	Agree	Neither Agree nor Disagree	Disagree	Strongly Disagree
1. I recognize (perceive) ethical issues (as distinct from economic and legal issues) in business that affect multiple stakeholders inside and outside the firm.	5	4	3	2	1
2. I understand how regularly engaging in ethical business practices strengthens my character (readiness to act ethically) and sustains my humanity.	5	4	3	2	1
3. It is important to tolerate diverse and even opposing moral perspectives and to creatively imagine ways to morally improve solutions at work.	5	4	3	2	1

	Strongly Agree	Agree	Neither Agree nor Disagree	Disagree	Strongly Disagree
4. I care about the impact of business actions on those affected by them, and I am determined to continually improve the morality of business practices.	5	4	3	2	1
5. I understand the multiple factors (results, rules, character, and context) to be considered in making responsible ethical judgments through moral reasoning.	5	4	3	2	1
6. I understand how my business philosophy and management/work style influence and reflect my value priorities with regard to expected business behavior.	5	4	3	2	1
7. Ethical business leaders are expected to elevate the moral development of their followers and their work culture/climate.	5	4	3	2	1
8. Corporate governance leaders are morally accountable for managing business integrity capacity as a strategic asset to enhance or protect organizational reputation.	5	4	3	2	1
9. Business should be held to triple bottom line accountability (for economic, social, and ecological performance) to respect current and future generations of multiple stakeholders.	5	4	3	2	1
10. Ethical business leaders should develop their organizational compliance and ethics systems to sustain a morally supportive work context.	5	4	3	2	1
11. Ethical business leaders should exercise positive influence in their firms' external socio-political-legal-ecological environments, both domestically and globally, to sustain a morally supportive external context for responsible business citizenship.	5	4	3	2	1

Cognitive competence: Items 1, 2, 4, 5, 6

Affective prebehavioral competence: Items 3, 4, 7

Managerial competence: Items 9, 10, 11

SOURCE: Petrick, J. A. (2008). Using the business integrity capacity model to advance business ethics education. In D. L. Swanson & D. G. Fisher (Eds.), *Advancing Business Ethics Education* (pp. 103–124). Charlotte, NC: Information Age Publishing, p. 117. Reproduced with permission of Information Age Publishing in the format Textbook via Copyright Clearance Center.

Defining Organizational Ethics

The first step toward mastery is to define the field of study. In the case of organizational ethics, that means identifying the unique characteristics of organizations and determining what sets ethical choices and actions apart from other forms of decision making and behavior. Organizations consist of three or more people engaged in coordinated action in pursuit of a common purpose or goal. They function as socially constructed, structured, interconnected systems.[11] Let's look at the elements of this definition in more detail.

Three or More People. The presence of three or more persons sets the stage for the formation of organizations, allowing for the development of structure, coalitions, shared meanings, and so forth. Organizational membership is generally voluntary, which sets organizations apart from families. We choose the organizations we want to join; we don't choose the family we are born into.

Coordination of Activities. Completion of any complex task, whether making a film, repairing a highway, or starting a health club, requires the coordination of people and units. Coordination, in turn, produces synergy. *Synergy* denotes the way in which organizations are greater than the sum of their parts. The achievements of an organization as a whole are much greater than could be reached by a collection of individuals working on their own.

Goal Directed. Organizations don't form by chance. Instead, they are intentionally formed to meet specific needs and to serve specific purposes, such as educating elementary school children, developing and selling automobiles, passing legislation, and combating crime. These objectives focus the collective energies of members.

Socially Constructed. Organizations are human creations shaped through the collective decisions and actions of their members. The socially constructed nature of organizations is particularly apparent in their cultures. No two organizations are exactly alike. Every group has its unique way of seeing the world and its own culture, developed through shared meaning and experiences. New employees often undergo a form of culture shock as they move into an organization with different language, customs, and attitudes about work and people.

Structured Interaction. The word *organization* frequently conjures up images of organizational charts, policy manuals, discipline policies, articles of incorporation, and other official documents. Bureaucratic organizations, in particular, do their best to leave nothing to chance, spelling out everything from how to apply for sick leave and retirement benefits to the size of office cubicles. They also specify in detail the management of such tasks as processing auto insurance payments and registering students. However, some of the most important elements of structure aren't formalized. Communication scholars, for instance, study communication networks, which are patterns of messages sent between individuals and organizational units. These networks may have little resemblance to the flow of information outlined in the official organizational chart.

Roles and hierarchy are two particularly important aspects of structure. Roles are sets of expectations, responsibilities, and duties associated with organizational positions. Failure to meet role expectations generates sanctions in the form of criticism, reprimands, lower wages, and termination. Hierarchy grants certain individuals and groups more power, status, and privileges. These differences in status and power are part of every interaction between organizational members. The degree of structure helps set organizations apart from groups. Groups, too, have three or more members, may be goal directed, and delegate various roles. Nonetheless, they lack many of the formal elements (written policies, job descriptions, job titles) common to organizations.

Interconnectedness (Systems). Organizations function as interconnected systems. Consider all the departments involved in the introduction of a new product, for instance: research and development, design, purchasing, production, marketing, finance, human resources. The success of the product introduction depends on each division doing its part. Marketing can do an effective job of promoting the new item, but first purchasing must secure the necessary components at the right cost, and production must meet manufacturing deadlines. Because organizations function as systems, a change in any one component will influence all the others. A new accounting system, for example, will change the way every department records expenses, books revenue, and determines profits.

Ethics involves judgments about the rightness or wrongness of human behavior. To illustrate this point, I've collected definitions of the term *ethics* from a variety of sources. Notice how each highlights the evaluative nature of ethical study and practice.

> "Ethics is concerned with how we should live our lives. It focuses on questions about what is right or wrong, fair or unfair, caring or uncaring, good or bad, responsible or irresponsible, and the like."[12]

> "[Ethics includes] the principles, norms, and standards of conduct governing an individual or group."[13]

> "Ethical judgments focus . . . on degrees of rightness and wrongness, virtue and vice, and obligation in human behavior."[14]

> "Ethics refers to the rules or principles that define right and wrong conduct."[15]

> "Ethics can be defined as the values an individual uses to interpret whether any particular action or behavior is considered acceptable and appropriate."[16]

> "[An ethical act or decision] is something judged as proper or acceptable based on some standard of right and wrong."[17]

Some scholars make a distinction between ethics and morals, drawing in part on the origins of each word.[18] *Ethics* comes from the Greek term *ethos,* meaning "custom," "usage," or "character." *Moral* is derived from the Latin *mos* or *moris,* meaning "conduct" or "way of life." From this perspective, ethics has to do with the systematic study of general principles of right and wrong behavior. Morality and morals, on the other hand, describe specific, culturally transmitted standards of right and wrong ("Thou shall not steal"; "Treat your elders with respect"). Maintaining this distinction is becoming more difficult, however. Both ethics and morality involve decisions about right and wrong. When we make such evaluations, we draw upon universal principles as well as upon our cultural standards. Further, scholars from a number of fields appear to use the terms *ethics* and *morals* interchangeably. Philosophers interested in ethics study moral philosophy, for example, whereas psychologists examine moral reasoning, and educators promote moral education. For these reasons, I use the terms synonymously in the remainder of this text. You, of course, are free to disagree. You may want to engage in a class discussion about whether these two concepts should be integrated or treated separately.

Organizational ethics applies moral standards and principles to the organizational context. Organizations are well suited for ethical analysis because, as we've seen, they are the products of conscious, goal-directed behavior. Whatever form they take (small, family-owned restaurants; community-based nonprofits; large, multinational corporations; international relief agencies), all employers share the common features described above. These shared elements mean that members in every type of organization face some common ethical temptations and dilemmas. Further, a common body of theory, principles, strategies, and skills can be used to address these moral challenges.

I am convinced there is much to be gained in looking at ethical problems and solutions across organizational boundaries. No matter what particular type of organization we belong to, we can learn from the experiences of others in different settings. Knowing how corporate managers communicate important values, for instance, can be useful to those of us who work in the federal government. If we work in business, we can gain important insights into empowering employees from watching how nonprofit executives recruit and motivate volunteers. The case study below describes one ethical issue that is now faced by nonprofit groups as well as businesses.

CASE STUDY 0.1

Nonprofit Executive Compensation: How Much Is Too Much?

Corporations aren't the only organizations accused of paying their executives too much and providing them with outlandish perks. Lawrence Small, the former chief executive of the Smithsonian Institution in Washington, D.C., saw his pay jump from $536,000 to $915,000 between 2000 and 2007. He traveled by private, chartered plane and took nearly 10 weeks of vacation a year. His deputy was absent from the Smithsonian one quarter of her workdays while serving on other boards, which earned her about $10 million in outside income. Combined compensation for executives at the National Veterans Business Development Corporation amounted to more than 22% of the money Congress appropriated to the organization to help veterans. The group's leaders also spent over $5,000 for two meals at a steakhouse. Senators criticized the Boys & Girls Clubs for paying its president nearly $1 million a year while spending over $4 million on travel expenses for 350 staff members. The president and CEO of Philadelphia public radio station WHYY earns more than the heads of the Public Broadcasting System, National Public Radio, and many commercial stations.

The Internal Revenue Service has tightened restrictions on nonprofits in light of the compensation scandals. Nonprofits are now required to reveal executive salaries greater than $150,000 and to disclose amounts spent on housing allowances, expense accounts, chauffeurs, bodyguards, and first-class air travel. Board members can be hit with penalties if pay packages are considered too generous. However, the IRS waives the penalties if the board can establish that the compensation package is comparable to those paid by other, similar charities.

It is easy to see why the IRS is increasing its oversight of nonprofit executive compensation. Money spent on salaries and travel often means less money available for helping the poor, educating children, supporting the arts, healing the sick and other causes. A number of Boys & Girls Clubs were also forced to close, for example, even as the parent organization's CEO took home $1 million in compensation. Then, too, tax-exempt organizations are supposed to serve the public good, not take advantage of the tax code to enrich their leaders. Society expects nonprofit executives to be motivated by service, not pay. According to the director of the Nonprofit Leadership and Management program at the University of San Diego, "There is a moral obligation for nonprofits to compensate their top staff in a way that is respectful of their mission."[1] Some donors are fighting back, refusing to support organizations led by highly paid executives. Critics of WHYY distributed bumper stickers with a red circle and slash over WHYY with the words "Its CEO makes over $400,000. Do you?"[2]

Greater IRS scrutiny and donor protests will not end the debate over nonprofit executives' salaries. That's because more and more charities are adopting strategies traditionally associated with businesses, such as hiring MBAs, conducting market research, advertising, and jettisoning unproductive activities. Those groups that operate in a more businesslike fashion may experience a dramatic increase in revenues and programs, increasing their outreach and enabling them to better fulfill their mission. However, nonprofits that adopt a business model can end up bidding against businesses (and other nonprofits) when recruiting talented executives. For example, the Los Angeles County Museum of Art lured a new director from the Dia Art Foundation in New York by offering him a $1 million annual compensation package. Said the museum's major donor, "We wanted him and we had to induce him to leave where he was, and the financial package was a major part of that inducement. It's a market. You've got to be competitive."[3]

Many board members argue that high-performing nonprofit executives deserve what they make. According to the chairman of the Museum of Modern Art in New York, which paid its director $2.7 million in salary, housing allowance, and other benefits in 2008, "If you are lucky enough to have the best executive in the field, you should compensate the person accordingly...because if you want your organization to be well run, you've got to find the person who can accomplish it."[4]

Discussion Probes

1. How much is too much when it comes to nonprofit executive compensation? What standards do you use to make this determination?

2. How should nonprofit pay levels be set?

3. Should managers at charities be expected to work for less than their colleagues in corporations? Why or why not?

4. Should nonprofit groups operate like businesses? What are some of the potential benefits of doing so? The potential dangers?

5. If you discovered that the leader of your favorite charity was receiving a very high salary and benefits package, would you stop supporting that group?

Notes

1. Kosseff, J. (2004, March 14). Charity Inc. *The Oregonian,* p. A11.
2. Davis, C. (2008, November 9). Pay package awarded to WHYY chief questioned. *The Philadelphia Inquirer,* p. A01.
3. Pogrebin, R., & Taylor, K. (2010, April 26). Pulling the reins (a bit) on hefty salaries for cultural executives. *The New York Times,* p. C1.
4. Pogrebin & Taylor.

Sources

Inzie, S. (2010, March 13). Senators critical of salary expenses, perks at Boys & Girls Clubs. *The Washington Post,* p. A05.
Olson, E. (2008, December 30). A nonprofit for veterans is faulted on spending. *The New York Times,* p. B3.
Pogrebin, R. (2007, June 21). Smithsonian ex-chief criticized in report. *The New York Times,* p. E1.
Spector, M., & Banjo, S. (2009, March 27). Currents: Pay at nonprofits gets a closer look. *The Wall Street Journal,* p. A9.

Looking Ahead

Organizational Ethics: A Practical Introduction is a significant revision of *Ethics in the Workplace: Tools and Tactics for Organizational Transformation.* The book has been reshaped to capture what readers liked most about the earlier version: its practical focus. It is significantly longer than the first edition and now includes chapters on negotiation, followership, and key organizational functions. An additional case has been added to the end of each chapter. A new feature, Ethics in Technology, addresses the ethical issues raised by computers, video cameras, electronic sensors, and other technologies playing increasingly important roles in the organizational setting.

Several features found in *Ethics in the Workplace* are found in this text as well. First, this is a book about the practice of ethics in all sorts of organizations (not just businesses) for the reasons cited earlier. Second, the text retains its interdisciplinary focus. In recent years, a significant number of social scientists have begun to examine ethics in the organizational setting. I cite findings from the fields of management, moral psychology, communication, marketing, human resources, finance, and social psychology, in addition to philosophy. This research is cited in the chapter endnotes as well as in the comprehensive References section at the end of the book. Third, my goal is to write in a reader-friendly style in order to make the discussion of ethics less intimidating. Fourth, I don't hesitate to reveal my biases. You are likely to take issue with some of my conclusions. I hope you do. Discussion and dialogue are essential to the learning process.

Fifth, *Organizational Ethics: A Practical Approach* is organized around levels or layers of organizational behavior, like its predecessor. Part I lays the groundwork. Chapter 1 concludes this introductory section by introducing ethical theories and principles frequently used in ethical problem solving. Part II, "Practicing Individual Ethics in the Organization," examines individual motivations and decisions. Chapter 2 surveys personal moral development, including character development. Chapter 3 describes moral reasoning, decision-making processes, and formats. Part III, "Practicing Interpersonal Ethics in the Organization," looks at the moral issues raised by our connections to other organizational members. Chapter 4 outlines an ethical framework for interpersonal communication. Chapter 5 addresses questions of power and influence in organizational settings. Chapter 6 examines the practice of ethical negotiation. Part IV, "Practicing Group, Leadership, and Followership Ethics," focuses on the ethical dilemmas that are part and parcel of organizational groups and teams (Chapter 7), as well as the leadership and followership roles (Chapters 8 and 9). Part V, "Practicing Ethics in Organizational Systems," examines organizations as integrated units. Chapter 10 outlines strategies for building ethical organizations. Chapter 11 describes ways to manage common ethical issues in marketing, finance/accounting, and human resources. Chapter 12 discusses tactics for promoting social responsibility and global citizenship.

ENDNOTES

1. Malone, S. (2011, January 25). Trust in business tumbled in 2010: Survey. *Reuters.* Retrieved January 27, 2011, from http://www.reuters.com/article/2011/01/25/; Edelman Trust Survey Executive Summary 2011. Retrieved from http://www.edelman.com/trust/2011/

2. Barbara Toffler provides an in-depth look at what went wrong at Arthur Andersen in Toffler, B. L., & Reingold, J. (2003). *Final accounting: Ambition, greed, and the fall of Arthur Andersen.* New York: Broadway Books.

3. Paine, L. S. (1996). Moral thinking in management: An essential capability. *Business Ethics Quarterly, 6*(4), 477–492, p. 477.

4. Lemonick, M. D., & Novak, V. (2005, July 11). The power broker. *Time,* p. 31. See also: Thomas, E., Taylor, S., Jr., Murr, A., Wingert, P., Clift, E., & Meadows, S. (2005, July 11). Queen of the center. *Newsweek,* pp. 24–31.

5. Kohlberg, L. A. (1984*). Essays on moral development: Vol. 2. The psychology of moral development: The nature and validity of moral stages.* New York: Harper & Row; Rest, J. R. (1993). Research on moral judgment in college students. In A. Garrod (Ed.), *Approaches to moral development* (pp. 201–211). New York: Teachers College Press.

6. Wright, A. D. (2008, May). Survey: Nonprofits fall short on ethics. *HR Magazine, 53*(5), p. 24.

7. Foote, J., Gaffney, N., & Evans, J. R. (2010). Corporate social responsibility: Implications for performance excellence. *Total Quality Management, 21*(8), 799–812; Byus, K., Deis, D., & Ouryang, B. (2010). Doing well by doing good: Corporate social responsibility and profitability. *SAM Advanced Management Journal, 75*(1), 44–55.

8. Narvaez, D. (2006). Integrative ethical education. In M. Killen & J. G. Smetana (Eds.), *Handbook of moral development* (pp. 703–733). Mahwah, NJ: Lawrence Erlbaum.

9. Narvaez, D., & Lapsley, D. K. (2005). The psychological foundations of morality and moral expertise. In D. K. Lapsley & F. C. Power (Eds.), *Character psychology and character education* (pp. 140–165). Notre Dame, IN: University of Notre Dame Press, p. 151.

10. Petrick, J. A. (2008). Using the business integrity capacity model to advance business ethics education. In D. L. Swanson & D. G. Fisher (Eds.), *Advancing business ethics education* (pp. 103–124). Charlotte, NC: Information Age; Petrick, J. A. (2011). The measured impact of the transtheoretical model of educational

change on advancing business ethics education. In D. L. Swanson & D. G. Fisher (Eds.), *Toward assessing business ethics education* (pp. 335–360). Charlotte, NC: Information Age.

11. Newstrom, J. W., & Davis, K. (1993). *Organizational behavior: Human behavior at work* (9th ed.). New York: McGraw-Hill; Sims, R. R. (2002). *Managing organizational behavior.* Westport, CT: Quorum Books.

12. Jaska, J. A., & Pritchard, M. S. (1994). *Communication ethics: Methods of analysis.* Belmont, CA: Wadsworth, p. 3.

13. Trevino, L. K., & Nelson, K. A. (2004). *Managing business ethics: Straight talk about how to do it right* (3rd ed.). Hoboken, NJ: John Wiley, p. 13.

14. Johannesen, R. L. (2002). *Ethics in human communication* (5th ed.). Prospect Heights, IL: Waveland Press, p. 1.

15. Sims, R. R. (1994). *Ethics and organizational decision making: A call for renewal.* Westport, CT: Quorum Books, p. 5.

16. Ferrell, O. C., & Gardiner, G. (1991). *In pursuit of ethics: Tough choices in a world of work.* Springfield, IL: Smith Collins, p. 2.

17. Stanwick, P. A., & Stanwick, S. D. (2009). *Understanding business ethics.* Upper Saddle River, NJ: Pearson Education, p. 2.

18. Day, L. A. (2003). *Ethics in media communications: Cases and controversies* (4th ed.). Belmont, CA: Thomson/Wadsworth; Jarrett, J. L. (1991). *The teaching of values: Caring and appreciation.* London: Routledge; Johannesen (2002).

PART I
Laying an Ethical Foundation

1

Ethical Perspectives

Ethical theories are critical to personal and collective ethical practice. We will employ them repeatedly throughout the remainder of this text. Ethical perspectives help us identify and define problems, force us to think systematically, encourage us to view issues from many different vantage points, and provide us with decision-making guidelines. In this chapter, I'll introduce five widely used ethical approaches. I'll briefly summarize each perspective and then offer an evaluation based on the theory's advantages and disadvantages.

Resist the temptation to choose your favorite approach and ignore the rest. Use a variety of theories when possible. Applying all five approaches to the same problem (practicing ethical pluralism) is a good way to generate new insights about the issue. You can discover the value of ethical pluralism by using each theory to analyze Case

Studies 1.2 and 1.3 at the end of the chapter (see Application Project 7). You may find that some perspectives are more suited to these problems than others. Combining insights from more than one theory might help you come up with a better solution. At the very least, drawing from several perspectives should give you more confidence in your choice and better prepare you to defend your conclusions.

Utilitarianism: Do the Greatest Good for the Greatest Number

Many people weigh the advantages and disadvantages of alternatives when making significant decisions. They create mental balance sheets listing the pluses and minuses of each course of action. When it's a particularly important choice, such as deciding which job offer to accept or where to earn a graduate degree, they may commit their lists to paper to make it easier to identify the relative merits of their options.

Utilitarianism is based on the premise that our ethical choices, like other types of decisions, should be based on their consequences.[1] English philosophers and reformers Jeremy Bentham (1748–1832) and John Stuart Mill (1806–1873) argued that the best decisions (1) generate the most benefits relative to their disadvantages, and (2) benefit the largest number of people. In other words, utilitarianism is attempting to do the greatest good for the greatest number of people. *Utility* can be defined as what is best in a specific case (act utilitarianism) or as what is generally preferred in most contexts (rule utilitarianism). We can decide, for example, that telling a specific lie is justified in one situation (to protect a trade secret) but, as a general rule, believe that lying is wrong because it causes more harm than good.

Utilitarians consider both short- and long-term consequences when making ethical determinations. If the immediate benefits of a decision don't outweigh its possible future costs, this alternative is rejected. However, if the immediate good is sure, and the future good is uncertain, decision makers generally select the option that produces the short-term benefit. Utilitarians are also more concerned about the ratio of harm to evil than the absolute amount of happiness or unhappiness produced by a choice. In other words, a decision that produces a great amount of good but an equal amount of harm would be rejected in favor of an alternative that produces a moderate amount of good at very little cost. Further, the utilitarian decision maker keeps her or his own interests in mind but gives them no more weight than anyone else's.

Making a choice according to utilitarian principles is a three-step process. First, identify all the possible courses of action. Second, estimate the direct as well as the indirect costs and benefits for each option. Finally, select the alternative that produces the greatest amount of good based on the cost-benefit ratios generated in step two. Government officials frequently follow this process when deciding whether or not to impose or loosen regulations. Take decisions about raising rural highway speed limits, for instance. States have the option of maintaining the 55 mile-per-hour speed limit or selecting from a range of higher speeds. Raising speed limits produces immediate benefits—reduced travel and delivery times. Fewer motorists are tempted to break the law. These benefits, however, must be weighed against the short-term cost of greater fuel consumption and the long-term risk of higher fatalities. After balancing the costs and benefits, a great many states have opted to loosen speed restrictions.

Evaluation

Few could argue with the ultimate goal of utilitarianism, which is to promote human welfare by maximizing benefits to as many people as possible. We're used to weighing the outcomes of all types of decisions, and the utilitarian decision-making rule covers every conceivable type of choice, which makes it a popular approach to moral reasoning. Utilitarian calculations typically drive public policy decisions, such as where to set speed limits, for example. In fact, Bentham and Mills introduced utilitarianism to provide a rational basis for making political, administrative, and judicial choices, which they felt previously had been based on feelings and irrational prejudices. They campaigned for legal and political reforms, including the creation of a more humane penal system and more rights for women. Utilitarian reasoning is also applied in emergency situations, such as in the wake of the massive earthquake that hit Haiti in 2010. In the midst of such widespread devastation, medical personnel ought to give top priority to those who are most likely to survive. It does little good to spend time with a terminal patient while a person who would benefit from treatment dies.

Despite its popularity, utilitarianism suffers from serious deficiencies, starting with defining and measuring "the greatest good."[2] Economists define utility in monetary terms and use such measures as the gross national product to determine the greatest benefit. But the theory's originators, Bentham and Mills, define the greatest good as the total amount of happiness or pleasure, abstract concepts that are hard to quantify. Sometimes identifying possible consequences can be difficult or impossible as well. Many different groups may be affected, unforeseen consequences may develop, and so on. Even when consequences are clear, evaluating their relative merits can be challenging. Being objective is difficult because we humans tend to downplay long-term risks in favor of immediate rewards (see Case Study 1.1) and to favor ourselves when making decisions. Due to the difficulty of identifying and evaluating potential costs and benefits, Utilitarian decision makers may reach different conclusions when faced with the same dilemma. States have opted to raise highway speeds, but they don't agree on what the new limits should be. Some state legislatures determined that traveling at 65 miles per hour produces the greatest good; others decided that 70 or 75 miles per hour generates the most benefits.

Ironically, one of the greatest strengths of Utilitarian theory—its concern for collective human welfare—is also one of its greatest weaknesses. In focusing on what's best for the group as a whole, utilitarianism discounts the worth of the individual. The needs of the person are subjugated to the needs of the group or organization. This type of reasoning can justify all kinds of abuse. For example, a number of lawsuits accuse Wal-Mart of cheating individual employees out of overtime pay to cut labor costs for the greater good of the company.[3] Then, too, by focusing solely on consequences, utilitarianism seems to say that the ends justify the means. Most of us are convinced that there are certain principles—justice, freedom, integrity—that should never be violated.

CASE STUDY 1.1

Sacrificing the Future in the NFL

Athletes demonstrate how easy it is to ignore long-term consequences when making choices. They are all too willing to sacrifice their futures for immediate results. Competitors in a variety of sports, including baseball, track, cricket, soccer, rugby, cycling, tennis, ice hockey, and orienteering, have been suspended for taking steroids and other illegal performance-enhancing drugs. These substances have been linked to mood swings, liver damage, high blood pressure, heart disease, strokes, blood clots, and other dangerous side effects.

Professional football players appear particularly willing to sacrifice their health and longevity for temporary success. National Football League linemen, for example, are bulking up to land jobs. The number of players listed at over 300 pounds soared from 130 to 350 between 1996 and 2004, and 70% of this group is made up of offensive linemen. The dangers of drastic weight gain are just as real as those linked to steroids, though not as well publicized. A study conducted by *The New England Journal of Medicine* found that the rate of sleep apnea among NFL players is five times higher than among other males in the same age groups. Apnea victims suffer from repeated interruptions of breathing during sleep that can sometimes result in an irregular heartbeat. Over time, sufferers are more likely to experience high blood pressure and congestive heart failure. Apnea is believed to have contributed to the death of former Pro Bowl defensive lineman Reggie White, who died in his sleep at age 43. In addition to developing apnea, heavy players, like other heavy Americans, are much more likely to develop diabetes and suffer from strokes.

Injuries are a greater problem for football players than for athletes in most other sports. All professional football players face a 90% chance of permanent physical injury if they compete for three years, which may include brain damage. More than half of NFL players report suffering concussions on the field, with 25% reporting at least three. Multiple concussions have been linked to serious mental problems later in life. Former players are five times more likely than nonplayers to suffer from Alzheimer's disease or other forms of dementia. Former players with multiple concussions suffer depression at three times the rate of retired players not reporting concussions. Former Philadelphia Eagle running back Andre Waters committed suicide at age 44. An examination revealed that Waters had the brain of an 80-year-old suffering from Alzheimer's disease.

Why do football players risk their lives to further their careers? The macho culture of the sport plays a part. Football players are supposed to be tough and overcome injuries. In the past, concussions didn't generate much sympathy, because the damage they cause is hidden. However, most players likely put their futures on the line because the rewards are so great. Enhanced performance can literally mean millions of dollars in higher salaries and endorsement contracts, not to mention celebrity status. Bulking up and playing through pain and injuries allow football players to earn fortunes while playing the sport they love in front of adoring fans. Then, too, it's easy to discount future risks by rationalizing that "it won't happen to me" or to argue that the dangers don't outweigh the immediate payoffs. After all, earning a substantially higher salary now can guarantee a comfortable (if not luxurious) lifestyle for an athlete and his or her family after retirement. The trade-offs—a shorter life span, serious health problems, dementia, and chronic pain—appear to be worth the risk.

Fans and NFL coaches and owners have done their part to put players at risk. Ticket holders and television audiences want their teams to win now. If success takes a huge offensive line, then so be it. The violent nature of professional football has helped make it America's most popular sport, and the vicious hits most likely to cause concussions and other injuries make the highlight shows. Coaches, focused on victories so they can keep their jobs, have forced concussed players back into games. It took pressure from former players, Congress, and the medical community to get the NFL franchise holders to take the problem of concussions seriously. Now, players are not allowed to reenter games if they have suffered a concussion, and they cannot play again until given approval by a third party. Helmet-to-helmet hits are banned. Yet, the league is counting on players to report their own head injuries and those of other players' as well. Given the rewards for playing through injury, many players will keep quiet. Few will determine that the long-term risks outweigh the short-term benefits, as retired Arizona Cardinals quarterback Kurt Warner concluded. Warner felt good enough to come back to play another year but was worried about suffering another head injury (he suffered several during his career). "I've got the rest of my life in front of me," he said. "I've got seven kids I have to raise. Football is a great career. But you can't jeopardize your life for this game."[1]

Discussion Probes

1. Why do you think the NFL owners and league officials were slow to take the problem of concussions seriously?

2. What additional steps can the NFL take to reduce concussions and other injuries? What would be the potential costs and benefits of these steps?

3. How much responsibility does the public bear for putting players at risk? How can fans help protect the health of players?

4. Considering the damage done to its players, is it ethical to support the NFL?

5. Imagine that you are a professional football player. How far would you go to keep playing? Or imagine you are a professional athlete in one of your favorite sports other than football. How far would you go to improve your performance?

6. What, if anything, can be done to encourage football players to consider the long-term consequences of their choices?

7. What steps can you take to better balance long-term consequences against short-term rewards when you make ethical decisions?

Notes

1. Farmer, S. (2010, September 12). Concussions and the NFL: Hard knocks. *Los Angeles Times*, p. C1.

Sources

Adler, A., Underwood, A., Scelfo, J., Juarez, V., Johnson, D., Shenfeld, H., . . . Raymond, J. (2004, December 20). Toxic strength. *Newsweek*, pp. 44–52.
Crossman, M. (2007, June 25). Lost. *The Sporting News*, p. 12.
Ever farther, ever faster, ever higher? (2004, August 7). *The Economist*, pp. 20–22.

Hiestand, M., & Mihoces, G. (2004, December 29). Apnea common for NFL linemen. *USA Today*, p. 1C.

Mihoces, G. (2007, June 19). Concussions command NFL's attention. *USA Today*, p. 1C.

Saraceno, J. (2004, December 29). White's death sends message to super-sized NFL. *USA Today*, p. 12C.

Schwarz, A. (2007, May 31). Study of ex-N.F.L. players ties concussion to depression risk. *The New York Times*, p. A1.

Schwarz, A. (2009, December 3). New N.F.L. rule on concussions benches injured. *The New York Times*, p. A1.

Starr, M. (2004, August 16). A long jump. *Newsweek*, pp. 52–53.

Kant's Categorical Imperative: Do What's Right Despite the Consequences

Like the Utilitarians, German philosopher Immanuel Kant (1724–1804) developed a simple set of rules that could be applied to every type of ethical decision. However, he reached a very different conclusion about what those principles should be. Kant argued that moral duties or imperatives are *categorical*—they should be obeyed without exception. Individuals should do what is morally right no matter what the consequences are.[4] His approach to moral reasoning falls under the category of deontological ethics. Deontological ethicists argue that we ought to make choices based on our duty to follow universal truths, which we sense intuitively or identify through reason (*deon* is the Greek word for "duty"). Moral acts arise out of our will or intention to follow our duty, not in response to circumstances. Based on this criterion, an electric utility that is forced into reducing its rates is not acting morally; a utility that lowers its rates to help its customers is.

According to Kant, "what is right for one is right for all." We need to ask ourselves one question: Would I want everyone else to make the decision I did? If the answer is yes, the choice is justified. If the answer is no, the decision is wrong. Based on this reasoning, certain behaviors, like honoring our commitments and being kind, are always right. Other acts, like cheating and murder, are always wrong. Kant cited borrowing money that we never intend to repay as one behavior that violates what he called the *categorical imperative*. If enough people made such false promises, the banking industry would break down because lenders would refuse to provide funds.[5] That's what happened during the recent collapse of the U.S. housing market. A number of borrowers never intended to pay their home loans back, which helped generate a wave of foreclosures. Home loans then became much harder to get. Deliberate idleness is another violation of Kant's principle, because no one would exercise his or her talents in a culture where everyone sought to rest and enjoy themselves.

Kant also argued for the importance of "treating humanity as an end," or respect for persons, which has become one of the foundational principles of Western moral philosophy. Others can help us reach our objectives, but they should never be considered solely as a means to an end. We should, instead, respect and encourage the capacity of others to choose for themselves. It is wrong, under this standard, for companies to expose manufacturing workers to hazardous chemicals without their consent or knowledge. Managers shouldn't coerce or threaten employees, because such tactics violate freedom of choice. Coworkers who refuse to help one another are behaving unethically because ignoring the needs of others limits their options.

Respect for persons underlies the notion of moral rights. Fundamental moral or human rights are granted to individuals based solely on their status as persons. Such rights protect the inherent dignity of every individual regardless of culture or social or economic background. Rights violations are unethical because they are disrespectful and deny human value and potential. The rights to life, free speech, and religious affiliation are universal (always available to everyone everywhere), equal (no one has a greater right to free speech than anyone else, for instance), and cannot be given up or taken away.[6] (I provide one list of universal human rights in Chapter 10.)

Evaluation

Kant's imperative is a simple yet powerful ethical tool. Not only is the principle easy to remember, but asking if we would want our behavior to be made a universal standard should also prevent a number of ethical miscues. Emphasis on duty builds moral courage. Those driven by the conviction that certain behaviors are either right or wrong no matter what the situation are more likely to blow the whistle on unethical behavior (see Chapter 8), to resist group pressure to compromise personal ethical standards, to follow through on their choices, and so on. Recognizing that people are intrinsically valuable is another significant ethical principle. This standard encourages us to protect the rights of employees, to act courteously, to demonstrate concern for others, and to share information. At the same time, it condemns deceptive and coercive tactics. (See the Ethics and Technology feature on the next page for one set of computer guidelines based on treating others with respect.)

Critiques of Kant's system of reasoning often center on his assertion that there are universal principles that should be followed in every situation. In almost every case, we can think of exceptions. For instance, many of us agree that killing is wrong yet support capital punishment for serial murderers. We value our privacy but routinely provide confidential information to secure car loans and to order products online. Then, too, how do we account for those who honestly believe they are doing the right thing even when they are engaged in evil? "Consistent Nazis" were convinced that killing Jews was morally right. They wanted their fellow Germans to engage in this behavior; they did what they perceived to be their duty.

Conflicting duties also pose a challenge to deontological thinking. Complex ethical dilemmas often involve competing obligations. For example, we should be loyal both to our bosses and to our coworkers. Yet, being loyal to a supervisor may mean breaking loyalty with peers, such as when a supervisor asks us to reveal the source of a complaint when we've promised to keep the identity of that coworker secret. How do we determine which duty has priority? Kant's imperative offers little guidance in such situations.

ETHICS AND TECHNOLOGY

The Ten Commandments of Computer Ethics

The Computer Ethics Institute is a nonprofit organization dedicated to providing a "moral compass" for computer use. CEI is best known for its "Ten Commandments of Computer Ethics," which has been published in a number of books and articles. The first commandment, "Thou shalt not use a computer to harm other people," lays the groundwork for the remaining nine guidelines:

1. Thou shalt not interfere with other people's computer work. For example: overloading someone else's e-mail server box, spreading false rumors online, or forwarding material that distracts people from their computer tasks.

2. Thou shalt not snoop around in other people's computer files. For example: opening the work of coworkers, accessing resumes or tax forms from the network drive.

3. Thou shalt not use a computer to steal. For example: credit card numbers or trade secrets.

4. Thou shalt not use a computer to bear false witness. For example: sending anonymous spam, hiding one's identity while participating in online discussion groups.

5. Thou shalt not copy or use proprietary software for which you have not paid. For example: sharing copies of software, not registering shareware programs.

6. Thou shalt not use other people's computer resources without authorization or proper compensation. For example: doing freelance work on an employer's computer.

7. Thou shalt not appropriate other people's intellectual output. For example: papers, artwork, music.

8. Thou shalt think twice about the social consequences of the program you are writing or the system you are designing. For example: creating spyware programs that capture employee keystrokes or monitor e-mail.

9. Thou shalt always use a computer in ways that ensure consideration and respect for your fellow humans. For example: use the computer in ways that you would want it used toward you.

Sources

Goldsborough, R. (2000, January). *Tech Directions*, pp. 5–6.

The Ten Commandments of Computer Ethics. Computer Ethics Institute. Retrieved January 17, 2010, from http://computerethicsinstitute.org

SOURCE: The *Ten Commandments of Computer Ethics* were developed and published by Dr. Ramon C. Barquin.

Rawls's Justice as Fairness:
Balancing Freedom and Equality

Limited organizational resources make conflicts inevitable. There are never enough jobs, raises, corner offices, travel funds, laptop computers, iPads, and other benefits to go around. As a result, disputes arise over how to distribute these goods. Departments battle over the relative size of their budgets, for example, and employees compete for performance bonuses, promotions, and job titles. Participants in these conflicts often complain that they have been the victims of discrimination or favoritism.

Over the last third of the 20th century, Harvard philosopher John Rawls developed a set of guidelines for justly resolving disputes like these that involve the distribution of resources.[7] His principles are designed to foster cooperation in democracies. In democratic societies, all citizens are free and equal before the law. However, at the same time, citizens are unequal. They vary in status, economic standing, talents, and abilities. Rawls's standards honor individual freedom—the foundation of democratic cultures—but also encourage more equitable distribution of societal benefits. The theorist primarily focused on the underlying political structure of society as a whole. Nevertheless, his principles also apply to organizations and institutions that function within this societal framework.

Rawls rejected the use of utilitarian principles to allocate resources. He believed that individuals have rights that should never be violated no matter what the outcome. In addition, he asserted that seeking the greatest good for the greatest number can seriously disadvantage particular groups and individuals. This can be seen in decisions to outsource goods and services to independent contractors. Outsourcing reduces costs and helps firms stay competitive. Remaining employees enjoy greater job security, but some employees lose their jobs to outsiders.

As an alternative to basing decisions on cost-benefit ratios, Rawls argued that we should follow these principles of justice:[8]

Principle 1: Each person has an equal right to the same basic liberties that are compatible with similar liberties for all.

Principle 2: Social and economic inequalities are to satisfy two conditions: (a) They are to be attached to offices and positions open to all under conditions of fair equality of opportunity, and (b) they are to be to the greatest benefit of the least advantaged members of society.

The first principle, the *principle of equal liberty,* has priority. It states that certain rights are protected and must be equally applied to all. These liberties include the right to vote, freedom of speech and thought, freedom to own personal property, and freedom from arbitrary arrest. Invading employee privacy and pressuring managers to contribute to particular political candidates would be unethical according to this standard. So would failing to honor contracts, since such behavior would reduce our freedom to enter into agreements for fear of being defrauded.

Principle 2a, the *equal opportunity principle,* asserts that everyone should have the same chance to qualify for offices and jobs. Job discrimination based on race, gender, or ethnic origin is forbidden. Further, all citizens ought to have access to the training and education needed to prepare for these positions. Principle 2b, the *difference principle,* recognizes that inequalities exist but that priority should be given to meeting the needs of the disadvantaged.

Rawls introduced the concept of the *veil of ignorance* to support his claim that his principles should guide decision making in democratic societies like Great Britain, the United States, and Canada. Imagine, he said, a group of people who are asked to come up with a set of guidelines that will govern their interactions. Group members are ignorant of their characteristics or societal position. Faced with such uncertainty, these individuals will likely base their choices on the *maximin rule.* This rule states that the best option is the one whose worst outcome is better than the worst outcomes of all the other options. Or, to put it another way, the best choice is the alternative that guarantees everyone a minimum level of benefits.

Rawls argued that individuals standing behind the veil of ignorance would adopt his moral guidelines because they would ensure the best outcomes even in the worst of circumstances. Citizens would select (1) equal liberty, because they would be guaranteed freedom even if they occupied the lowest rungs of society; (2) equal opportunity, because if they turned out to be the most talented societal members, they would not be held back by low social standing or lack of opportunity; and (3) the difference principle, because they would want to be sure they were cared for if they ended up disadvantaged.

Evaluation

Rawls became one of the most influential philosophers of his time because he offered a way to reconcile the long-standing tension between individual freedom and social justice. His system for distributing resources and benefits encompasses personal liberty as well as the common good. Individual rights are protected. Moreover, talented, skilled, or fortunate people are free to pursue their goals, but the fruits of their labor must also benefit their less fortunate neighbors. Applying Rawls's principles would have a significant positive impact on the moral behavior of organizations. High achievers would continue to be rewarded for their efforts, but not, as is too often the case, at the expense of their coworkers. All of an organization's members would be guaranteed a minimum level of benefits, such as a living wage and health insurance. Everyone would have equal opportunity for training, promotion, and advancement. The growing gap in compensation between the top and bottom layers of the organization would shrink.

Rawls's theory addresses some of the weaknesses of utilitarianism outlined earlier. In his system, individuals have intrinsic value and are not to be treated as means to some greater end. Certain rights should always be protected. The interests of the organization as a whole do not justify extreme harm to particular groups and individuals.

Stepping behind a veil of ignorance does more than provide a justification for Rawls's model; it can also serve as a useful technique to use when making moral choices. Status and power differences are an integral part of organizational life. Nonetheless, if we can set these inequities aside temporarily, we are likely to make more just decisions. The least advantaged usually benefit when status differences are excluded from the decision-making process. We need to ask ourselves if we are treating everyone fairly or if we are being unduly influenced by someone's position or relationship to us. Classical orchestras provide one example of how factoring out differences can improve the lot of marginalized groups. Orchestras began to hire a much higher percentage of female musicians after they erected screens that prevented judges from seeing the gender of players during auditions.[9]

Rawls's influence has not spared his theory from intense criticism. Skeptics note that the theory's abstractness limits its usefulness. Rawls offered only broad guidelines, which can be interpreted in a number of different ways. Definitions of justice and fairness vary widely, a fact that undermines the usefulness of his principles. What seems fair to one group or individual often appears grossly unjust to others. Take, for example, programs that reserve a certain percentage of federal contracts for minority contractors. Giving preferential treatment to minorities can be defended based on the equal opportunity and difference principles. Members of these groups claim that they should be favored in the bidding process to redress past discrimination and to achieve equal footing with Whites. On the other hand, such policies can be seen as impinging upon the equal liberty principle because they limit the freedom of Caucasians to pursue their goals. White contractors feel that these requirements unfairly restrict their options. They are denied work when they believe they can provide better quality at lower cost than those given the work.

By trying to reconcile the tension between liberty and equality, Rawls left himself open to attack from advocates of both values. Some complain that he would distribute too much to the have-nots; others believe that his concern for liberty means that he wouldn't give enough. Further, philosophers point out that there is no guarantee that parties who step behind the veil of ignorance would come up with the same set of principles as Rawls. They might not use the maximin rule to guide their decisions. Rather than emphasize fairness, these individuals might decide to emphasize certain rights. Libertarians, for instance, hold that freedom from coercion is the most important human right. Every individual should be able to produce and sell as he or she chooses, regardless of the impact of his or her business on the poor. Capitalist theorists believe that benefits should be distributed based on the contributions each person makes to the group. They argue that helping out the less advantaged rewards laziness while discouraging productive people from doing their best. Because decision makers may reach different conclusions behind the veil, critics contend that Rawls's guidelines lack moral force, that other approaches to distributing resources are just as valid as the notion of fairness.

Confucianism: Building Healthy Relationships

China's emergence as an economic superpower has focused the attention of Western scholars on Chinese culture and thought. Ethicists have been particularly interested in Confucianism. Confucius (551–479 B.C.E.), the son of a low-level official, was born into a turbulent period of Chinese history. Wars, palace coups, and power struggles were common as the ruling Zhou dynasty collapsed into competing states. Confucius wanted to restore order and good government. He believed that the ideal society is based on series of harmonious, hierarchical relationships (starting in the family and extending all the way up to the pinnacle of government) marked by trust and mutual concern. Ideal citizens are individuals of high character who engage in lifelong learning and always strive to improve their ethical performance. Ideal leaders govern by setting a moral example.[10]

Confucius apparently served a brief period as a government minister but spent most of his life working outside the political system, offering his ideas to various rulers. After his death, a number of his disciples, most notably Mencius, spread his ideas; Confucianism gained a foothold in Korea, Japan, and Vietnam. The philosophy's most important guidebook, *The Analects,* is a collection of the founder's (Master's) sayings. Confucianism was adopted as the official state doctrine of the Han dynasty, but throughout Chinese history Confucian thought has undergone periodic attack, most recently during Mao's Cultural Revolution of the 1970s. However, since that time Confucius has regained his popularity. 300 Confucius institutes have been formed in 87 countries. Several highly successful businesses in mainland China, Taiwan, and Korea operate according to Confucian principles, including apparel maker Weizhan Group, Sinyi Real Estate, financial services conglomerate Pin An Insurance, and electronics giant LG.[11]

Several key components of Confucianism are particularly relevant for modern business and organizational ethics, starting with the philosophy's emphasis on relationships.[12] Confucius argued that humans don't exist in isolation but are social creatures connected to others though networks of relationships. Because organizations consist of webs of relationships, it is critical that these connections be based on trust and benefit all parties. Organizations must also establish relationships with other organizations, as in the case of a firm that moves into a new foreign market. This company must enter into agreements with shippers, suppliers, local distributors, banks, and other business partners in the new country. The firm's expansion plans will fail if its relational partners don't live up to their responsibilities.

Confucianism emphasizes that policies, norms, procedures and rituals—referred to as etiquette, or *li*—maintain relationships within and between organizations. These practices also prevent ethical misbehavior. It is easier to trust others if we operate under the same guidelines, and we are less likely to cheat or steal if there are clearly stated rules against such activities. (We'll take a closer look at the formal and informal elements of ethical culture in Chapter 10.) However, Confucius was quick to point out that rules and codes are not enough, by themselves, to maintain good relationships and ethical behavior. Individuals have a moral duty to take their roles and duties seriously. They should follow the Golden Rule ("Do not do to others what you do not want them to do to you") in all of their dealings.

Confucian thought puts a high priority on personal virtues or character because virtuous behavior is essential to maintaining healthy relationships and fulfilling organizational duties. (I'll have much more to say about virtues in the next chapter.) The most important Confucian virtue is that of humaneness or benevolence.

Benevolence goes beyond displaying compassion. It also means treating others with respect and promoting their development through education and other means. In addition to benevolence, the key virtues of Confucianism are honesty, trust, kindness, and tolerance. Virtuous people put the needs of others above their own. They seek the good of the organization as a whole and of the larger society. Consider profit taking, for instance. While they do not condemn profit, Confucian thinkers argue that profit should never take precedence over moral behavior or concern for others. The ideal person strives first for virtue, then for profits. In instructing the king, Mencius emphasized that commercial activities should serve the needs of society:

> Your majesty . . . What is the point of mentioning the word 'profit'? All that matters is that there should be benevolence and rightness . . . If the mulberry is planted in every homestead, then those who are fifty can wear silk; if chickens, pigs and dogs do not miss their breeding season, then those who are seventy can eat meat; if each field is not deprived of labor during the busy season then families with several mouths to feed will not go hungry . . . When those who are seventy wear silk and eat meat and the masses are neither cold nor hungry, it is impossible for the prince not to be a true king. (Mencius I, 3, I, A, 1, 1, A, 3)[13]

Finally, Confucians recognize the reality of status and power differences in society as well as in organizations. Individuals occupy various roles and levels in the organizational hierarchy, and humaneness demands that we treat every person, whatever his or her role or position, with love and concern. At the same time, Confucius recognized the important role played by those at the top of the hierarchy. Executive-level management plays a key role in establishing moral organizational climates by setting an ethical example and expecting ethical behavior from followers. For example,[14]

> The Master said, 'When a prince's personal conduct is correct, his government is effective without issuing orders. If his personal conduct is not correct, he may issue orders, but they will not be followed. (*Analects,* XIII, vi)

> The Master said, 'The superior man seeks to perfect the admirable qualities of men, and does not *seek to* perfect their bad qualities.' (*Analects,* XII, xvi)

Evaluation

Confucianism highlights the fundamental truth that organizations, economies, and societies are built on relationships. As the global economy grows, fostering ethical relationships will become even more important. People who never meet each other in person now conduct much of the world's business. Confucius offers a blueprint for fostering trusting, healthy relationships that we can put into practice. We need to institute rules and procedures that create ethical organizational climates. However, codes and policies are not enough. We have to develop personal character to equip us to take our duties seriously and follow the Golden Rule. Every person, no matter what that individual's status, is worthy of our respect and should be treated as we would want to be treated. Putting the interests of others ahead of our own concerns can keep us from taking advantage of them or pursuing profit above people. Confucian thought also recognizes that the leader shapes the ethical climate of the organization by setting a moral example.

The strengths of Confucianism can become weaknesses if taken too far.[15] Take the philosophy's emphasis on social connections, for example. Placing too much importance on relationships can undermine justice or fairness. Jobs and promotion in China often go to family members, friends, and associates instead of the most qualified individuals. In China, *guanxi*, which is the practice of favoring those with social connections, has led to corruption. Local and foreign firms try to establish *guanxi* through bribes to win public works contracts, commercial deals, and bank loans. Placing too much emphasis on hierarchy and submission to the collective good can foster authoritarian paternalism, where employees have little freedom but blindly submit to authority. In these organizations, leaders act as father/mother figures "who know best," and followers go along with their directives without protest. Critics also point out that pursuing harmony at any cost can suppress individual rights and silence dissent.

Altruism: Concern for Others

Altruism is based on the principle that we should help others regardless of whether or not we profit from doing so.[16] Assisting those in need may be rewarding (we may feel good about ourselves or receive public recognition, for example). Nevertheless, altruistic behavior seeks to benefit the other person, not the self. The most notable cases of altruism are those that involve significant self-sacrifice, as when a soldier jumps on a grenade to save the rest of his platoon or when an employee donates a kidney to another worker in need of a transplant. The word *altruism* comes from the Latin root *alter*, which means "other." Advocates of altruism argue that love of one's neighbor is the ultimate ethical standard.

Some philosophers argue that altruism doesn't deserve to be treated as a separate ethical perspective, because altruistic behavior is promoted in other moral theories. Utilitarians seek the good of others, Kant urges us to treat others with respect, and Confucius identified compassion as a key element in maintaining proper social relations. However, I believe that altruism deserves to be considered on its own merits and demerits. To begin with, altruism often calls for self-sacrificial behavior, which utilitarianism and the categorical imperative do not. Kant warns us never to treat people as a means to an end. Altruism goes a step further and urges us to treat people as if they *are* the ends. Then, too, there is significant debate over the existence of prosocial behavior. One group of evolutionary biologists believes that humans are conduits of "selfish genes." [17] For instance, they believe that anything we do on behalf of family members is motivated by the desire to transmit our genetic code. Some skeptical philosophers argue that people are egoists. Every act, no matter how altruistic on the surface, always serves our needs, such as helping others because we expect to get paid back at some later time.

In response to the skeptics, a growing of body of research in sociology, political science, economics, social psychology—and other fields—establishes that true altruism does exist and is an integral part of the human experience.[18] In fact, altruistic behavior is common in everyday life:

> We humans spend much of our time and energy helping others. We stay up all night to comfort a friend who has suffered a broken relationship. We send money to rescue famine victims halfway round the world, or to save whales, or to support public television. We spend millions of hours per week helping as volunteers in hospitals, nursing homes, AIDS hospices, fire departments, rescue squads, shelters, halfway houses, peer-counseling programs and the like. We stop on a busy highway to help a stranded motorist change a flat tire, or spend an hour in the cold to push a friend's—even a stranger's—car out of a snowdrift.[19]

Care for others appears to be a universal value, one promoted by religions the world over. Representatives from a variety of religious groups agree that every person deserves humane treatment, no matter what his or her ethnic background, language, skin color, political beliefs, or social standing (see Chapter 10).[20] Western thought has been greatly influenced by the altruistic emphasis of Judaism and Christianity. The command to love God and to love others as we love ourselves is the most important obligation in Judeo-Christian ethics. Since humans are made in the image of God, and God is love, we have an obligation to love others no matter who they are and no matter what their relationship to us. Jesus drove home this point in the parable of the Good Samaritan. In this tale, a generous businessman stops (at great risk to himself and his reputation) to befriend a wounded Jewish traveler—a person he could have considered his enemy. (See Ethics in Action 1.1 for another story that highlights the importance of loving one's neighbor.)

ETHICS IN ACTION 1.1 THE RABBI GOES TO HEAVEN

In Nemirov, a small town in eastern Europe not unlike the town where the now famous Tevye of *Fiddler on the Roof* fame lived, a story is told of a Chassidic rabbi, his devoted flock, and a skeptic. The people, of course, were very, very poor; the rabbi very, very holy; and the skeptic very, very unbelieving. The story is as follows: The people believed that each year, just prior to the Penitential Season marking the Days of Awe which began the Jewish New Year, their rabbi went to heaven. After all, the Jews, however poor, still needed to eke out some kind of a livelihood, even as they needed good health and good matches for their sons and daughters, and they believed that their rabbi went to heaven to intercede on their behalf. One day, a skeptic, a Jewish shoemaker from Lithuania, arrived in town, and on that day the Jews of the town were very happy because some time within the next twenty-four hours their rabbi was going to heaven, they said, to plead for them before the Throne of the Most High.

The skeptic called them foolish Jews for believing this. Not even Moses ascended to heaven, let alone a poor rabbi. Nevertheless, the skeptic was intrigued, so he decided to follow the rabbi, even to hide in the rabbi's house so that he would be able to see everything the rabbi did that day and thereby discredit the notions of the rabbi's foolish flock.

(Continued)

(Continued)

That evening, when the Jews of Nemirov journeyed to the river to symbolically rid themselves of their sins, their rabbi was not among them, nor was he in the house of prayer. "He must be in heaven," a congregant announced, and all of the others agreed.

Meanwhile the skeptic, hiding under the rabbi's bed, saw the rabbi dress himself in the clothing of a Polish peasant. On his feet he placed high boots, and on his head a woodsman's cap, and on his body a greatcoat. The rabbi then placed a sack in the inner pocket of the coat and tied a large leather belt about his waist. The skeptic could not imagine what was going on until the rabbi took hold of an axe. "For sure," thought the skeptic, "the rabbi knows I'm here, and he is going to kill me."

Instead, the rabbi put the axe in his belt, exited his small house, and walked deep into the woods. The skeptic followed and watched the rabbi fell a tree, chop it into logs, and then chop some of the logs more finely into sticks. The rabbi then bundled the wood and placed it into the large sack, which he took from his greatcoat. He then dragged the sack of wood even more deeply into the forest to a small hut where a poor widow lived.

The rabbi knocked on the door. "Who is there?" cried the widow. "It is Ivan," said the rabbi, "Ivan the woodcutter. I have heard that you are ill, and it is very cold, so I have brought you some wood." The woman opened the door and, from behind the tree where he was hiding, the skeptic heard the woman say, "I have no money to pay for wood." She coughed. "My son is looking for work in the next town, but he has found none," she said. The rabbi, alias Ivan, said, "He will find work soon; then you will pay. Plenty of time." The rabbi then entered the widow's hut. Through the window, the skeptic saw him light a fire, give the woman a crust of bread from his pocket, and then exit the house.

At daybreak, when the Jews were going to synagogue for morning prayers, they once again encountered the skeptic. "Well," one said to him, "our beloved rabbi went to heaven last night. Next year will surely be a little better for us. But you don't believe us, do you?" he asked.

Quietly, the skeptic said, "Yes, I do. He went to heaven, if not higher. In fact, I saw him do it."

Concern for others promotes healthy relationships like those described by Confucius. Society functions more effectively when individuals help one another in their daily interactions. This is particularly apparent in organizations. Many productive management practices, like empowerment, mentoring, and teambuilding, have an altruistic component. Researchers use the term *organizational citizenship behavior* to describe routine altruistic acts that increase productivity and build trusting relationships.[21] Examples of organizational citizenship behavior include an experienced machine operator helping a newcomer master the equipment, a professor teaching a class for a colleague on jury duty, and an administrative assistant working over break to help a coworker meet a deadline. Such acts play an important if under-recognized role in organizational success. Much less work would get done if members refused to help out. Take the case of the new machine operator. Without guidance, he or she may flounder for weeks, producing a number of defective parts and slowing the production process. Caring behaviors also break down barriers of antagonism between individuals and departments. Communication and coordination increase, leading to better overall results. You can determine your likelihood to engage in organizational citizenship behavior by completing the test in the Self-Assessment.

SELF-ASSESSMENT

Organizational Citizenship Behavior Scale

Instructions

Take the following test to determine your willingness to engage in altruistic behavior in the work setting. Respond to each item on a 5-point scale ranging from 1 (*never engage in this behavior*) to 5 (*nearly always engage in this behavior*). Reverse the scale where indicated, so that it ranges from 5 (*never engage in this behavior*) to 1 (*nearly always engage in this behavior*). Generate a total by adding up your scores. Maximum possible score: 80.

1. Help other employees with their work when they have been absent.

2. Exhibit punctuality in arriving at work on time in the morning and after lunch and breaks.

3. Volunteer to do things not formally required by the job.

4. Take undeserved work breaks. (Reverse)

5. Take the initiative to orient new employees to the department even though it is not part of the job description.

6. Exhibit attendance at work beyond the norm; for example, take fewer days off than most individuals or fewer than allowed.

7. Help others when their work load increases (assist others until they get over the hurdles).

8. Coast toward the end of the day. (Reverse)

9. Give advance notice if unable to come to work.

10. Spend a great deal of time in personal telephone conversations. (Reverse)

11. Do not take unnecessary time off work.

12. Assist others with their duties.

13. Make innovative suggestions to improve the overall quality of the department.

14. Do not take extra breaks.

15. Willingly attend functions not required by the organization but that help its overall image.

16. Do not spend a great deal of time in idle conversation.

SOURCE: From *Organizational Citizenship Behavior: The Good Soldier Syndrome* by Organ, D. W. Copyright © 1988 by Lexington Books. Reproduced with permission of Lexington Books in the format Textbook via Copyright Clearance Center.

The Ethic of Care

Altruism provides the foundation for the *ethic of care,* which developed as an alternative to what feminists deem the traditional, male-oriented approach to ethics.[22] The categorical imperative and justice-as-fairness theories, for example, emphasize the importance of acting on abstract moral principles, being impartial, and treating others fairly. Carol Gilligan, Nel Noddings, and others initially argued that women take a different approach (have a "different voice") to moral decision making that is based on caring for others. Instead of expressing concern for people in abstract terms, women care for others through their relationships and tailor their responses to the particular needs of the other individual. Subsequent research has revealed that the ethic of care serves as a moral standard for many men as well as for many (but not all) women.[23]

The ethic of care incorporates both attitude and action.[24] Caring individuals are alert to the needs of others. They value those who demonstrate care and concern as well as groups and societies that tend to the needs of their members. Care is also an activity.[25] To practice care, we must first recognize or be attentive to the needs of others. We then have to take responsibility for meeting those needs. Providing good care depends on having the right skills, such as listening, counseling abilities, and medical training. As caregivers, we should recognize that receivers of care are in a vulnerable position, and we must not take advantage of that fact.

Philosopher Virginia Held identifies five key components of the care ethic that separate it from other moral philosophies.[26]

1. *Focuses on the importance of noting and meeting the needs of those we are responsible for.* Most people are dependent for much of their existence, including during childhood, during illness, and near the end of life. Morality built on rights and autonomy overlooks this fact. The ethic of care makes concern for others central to human experience and puts the needs of specific individuals—a child, a coworker—first.

2. *Values emotions.* Sympathy, sensitivity, empathy, and responsiveness are moral emotions that need to be cultivated. This stands in sharp contrast to ethical approaches

that urge decision makers to set aside their feelings in order to make rational determinations. However, emotions need to be carefully monitored and evaluated to make sure they are appropriate. For instance, caregivers caught up in empathy can deny their own needs or end up dominating the recipients of their care.

3. *Specific needs and relationships take priority over universal principles.* The ethic of care rejects the notion of impartiality and believes that particular relationships are more important than universal moral principles like rights and freedom. For instance, the needs of our immediate coworkers should take precedence over the needs of distant employees or society as a whole (though we should be concerned for members of those groups as well). Most moral theories see ethical problems as conflicts between two extremes: the selfish individual and universal moral principles. The care ethic falls somewhere in between. Persons in caring relationships aren't out to promote their personal interests or the interests of humanity; instead, they want to foster ethical relationships with specific individuals. These relationships benefit both parties. Family and friendships have great moral value in the ethic of care, and care giving is a critical moral responsibility.

4. *Breaks down the barriers between the public and private spheres.* In the past, men were dominant in the public sphere while relegating women to the "private" sphere. Men largely made decisions about the exercise of political and economic power while women were marginalized. As a result, women were often economically dependent and suffered domestic violence, cut off from outside help. Previous moral theories focused on public life and ignored families and friendships, but the ethic of care addresses the moral issues that arise in the private domain. It recognizes that problems faced in the private sphere, such as inequality and dependency, also arise in the public sphere.

5. *Views persons as both relational and interdependent.* Each of us starts life depending on others, and we depend on our webs of interpersonal relationships throughout our time on Earth. These relationships help create our identity. Unlike liberal political theory, which views persons as rational, self-interested individuals, in the ethic of care individuals are seen as "embedded" in particular families, cultures, and historical periods. Embeddedness means that we need to take responsibility for others, not merely leave them alone to exercise their individual rights.

Adopting the ethic of care would significantly change organizational priorities. Employers would use caring as a selection criterion, hiring those who demonstrate relational understanding and skills.[27] Managers would be evaluated based on how well they demonstrated care and concern for employees. Organizations would help members strike a better balance between work and home responsibilities, provide more generous family leave policies, expand employee assistance programs, and so on. Those directly involved in caregiving—assisted-living attendants, nursery school teachers, hospice workers, home health caregivers—would receive more money, recognition, and status. Corporations would devote additional attention to addressing societal problems.

Evaluation

Altruism has much to offer. First, concern for others is a powerful force for good. It drives people to volunteer to care for the dying, to teach prisoners, to act as Big Brothers and Sisters, to provide medical relief, and to answer crisis calls. Clinical psychologist Kathleen Brehony found hundreds of cases of what she calls "ordinary grace"—average men and women doing extraordinary good on a daily basis.[28] She describes, for example, one 72-year-old woman who rises at 4:30 every morning to deliver food and clothing donations to poverty-stricken Native Americans in the Phoenix area. A retired Air Force physician reduces the isolation of chronically ill children around the country by providing them with computers.

Second, following the principle of caring helps prevent ethical abuses. We're much less likely to take advantage of others through accounting fraud, stealing, cheating, and other means if we put their needs first. (We'll return to this theme in our discussion of servant leadership in Chapter 7.) Third, altruistic behavior, as we've seen, promotes healthy relationships and organizations. There are practical benefits to acting in a caring manner. Fourth, altruism lays the foundation for high moral character. Many personal virtues, like compassion, hospitality, generosity, and empathy, reflect concern for other people. Fifth, adopting an ethic of care would make our workplaces more humane and provide caregivers with the rewards they so richly deserve. Finally, altruism is inspiring. When we hear of the selfless acts of Gandhi, Desmond Tutu, and the Rwandans who risked their lives to save their neighbors from genocide, we are moved to follow their example.

While compelling, altruism suffers from serious deficiencies. All too often, our concern for others extends only to our immediate families, neighbors, or communities.[29] Sadly, well-intentioned attempts to help others can backfire. They fail to meet the need, have unintended negative consequences, or make the problem worse. As we saw in the Introduction, a large proportion of the money donated to some charities pays for fund-raising expenses rather than for client services. Government agencies can create dependence by providing welfare assistance.

Altruism is not an easy principle to put into practice. For every time we stop to help a stranded motorist, we probably pass by several others who need assistance. Our urge to help out a coworker is often suppressed by our need to get our own work done or to meet a pressing deadline. Common excuses for ignoring needs include the following: (1) Somebody else will do it, so I don't need to help; (2) I didn't know there was a problem (deliberately ignoring a coworker's emotional upset or someone's unfair treatment); (3) I don't have the time or energy; (4) I don't know enough to help; (5) People deserve what they get (disdain for those who need help); (6) It won't matter anyway, because one person can't make much of a difference; and (7) What's in it for me? (looking for personal benefit in every act).[30] There's also disagreement about what constitutes loving behavior. For example, firing someone can be seen as cruel or as caring. This act may appear punitive to outsiders. However, terminating an employee may be in that person's best interests. For someone who is not a good fit for an organization, being fired can open the door to a more productive career.

The ethic of care often conflicts with the ethic of justice. Take the allocation of jobs and resources, for instance. The ethic of care suggests that job openings and organizational funds should go to those closest us to us—family, friends, acquaintances, coworkers. The ethic of justice holds that such determinations should be impartial, based on qualifications, not relationships (see our earlier discussion of Confucianism). Care and justice often clash in the legal system as well. Some advocate that jails should focus on rehabilitation; others (likely the majority) argue that the prison system should focus on punishment, seeing that criminals get the treatment they deserve. Case Study 1.2, "Is This Any Way to Run a Prison?" describes one nation that takes a caring approach to incarceration. You may find this approach unjust to victims and society.

CHAPTER TAKEAWAYS

- Mastering widely used ethical theories greatly enhances your chances of success as an ethical change agent.
- Each ethical perspective has its weaknesses, but each makes a valuable contribution to moral problem solving.
- Whenever possible, apply a variety of ethical approaches when faced with a moral dilemma. Doing so will help you generate new insights into the issue.
- Utilitarian decisions are based on their consequences. The goal is to select the alternative that achieves the greatest good for the greatest number of people. To apply Utilitarian principles, identify all the possible courses of actions, estimate the direct and indirect costs and benefits of each option, and select the alternative that produces the greatest amount of good based on the cost-benefit analysis. Utilitarian reasoning is common when making ethical choices, but identifying and weighing consequences can be difficult and this approach can disregard the interests of individuals and minority groups.
- Kant's Categorical Imperative is based on the premise that decision makers should do what's morally right no matter what the consequences. Moral choices flow out of a sense of duty and are those that we would want everyone to make. Always respect the worth of others when making ethical decisions. However, you may determine that there are exceptions to universal standards and that some moral duties may conflict with one another.
- Justice as Fairness Theory provides a set of guidelines for resolving disputes over the distribution of resources. Assure that everyone in your organization has certain rights like freedom of speech and thought, the same chance at positions and promotions, and receives adequate training to qualify for these roles. Everyone should be provided with minimum level of benefits, and excess benefits should go to the least advantaged organizational members. Try to make decisions without being swayed by personal or status considerations. Recognize, though, that organizational members will have different ideas about what is fair.
- Confucianism focuses on the importance of creating healthy, trusting relationships. You can help build such connections by establishing ethical organizational practices, taking your responsibilities seriously, following the Golden Rule, demonstrating humanity towards others, and seeking the good of others over you own interests. As a leader, set a moral example and expect ethical behavior from followers. Nevertheless, if taken too far, Confucian principles can lead to nepotism, authoritarianism, paternalism, and silencing dissent.
- Altruism seeks to benefit the other person, not the self. By making caring for others the ethical standard, you can encourage practices (empowering, mentoring, teambuilding, organizational citizenship behavior) that build trust and increase productivity. Altruism is difficult to practice, however, and it is not always clear what constitutes altruistic behavior.

- The ethic of care specifically rejects abstract, universal moral principles in favor of focusing on meeting the needs of specific individuals. You can encourage your organization to be more caring by hiring and evaluating employees based on their relational attitudes and skills, and by promoting caring policies like generous family leave and employee assistance programs. At times you will need to determine what should be given priority: care or justice.

APPLICATION PROJECTS

1. Reflect on one of your ethical decisions. Which approach(es) did you use when making your determination? Evaluate the effectiveness of the approach(es) as well as the quality of your choice. What did you learn from this experience?

2. Form a group and develop a list of behaviors that are always right and behaviors that are always wrong. Keep a record of those behaviors that were nominated but rejected by the team and why. Report your final list, as well as your rejected items, to the rest of the class. What do you conclude from this exercise?

3. Join with classmates and imagine that you are behind a veil of ignorance. What principles would you use to govern society and organizations?

4. How would your organization operate differently if it was governed by the ethic of care?

5. During a week, make note of all the altruistic behavior you witness in your organization. How would you classify these behaviors? What impact do they have on your organization? How would your organization be different if people didn't engage in organizational citizenship behavior? Write up your findings.

6. Write a case study based on an individual or group you admire for its altruistic motivation. Provide background and outline the lessons we can learn from this person or persons. As alternative, create a case study on an organization based on Confucian principles.

7. Apply all five ethical perspectives presented in the chapter to one or both of the Chapter End Cases. Keep a record of your deliberations and conclusions using each one. Did you reach different solutions based on the theory you used? Were some of the perspectives more useful in this situation? Are you more confident after looking at the problem from a variety of perspectives? Write up your findings.

CASE STUDY 1.2

Is This Any Way to Run a Prison?

Halden prison in Norway has all the amenities you would expect at an expensive resort and then some. Prisoners can take advantage of a sound studio, jogging trails, a "kitchen laboratory" for cooking classes, and two-bedroom homes for hosting their visiting families. They live in dormitory-style rooms complete with flat-screen televisions and mini-refrigerators. (There are no bars on the cells.) At Balstøy, another Norwegian prison, murderers, rapists, and other felons enjoy the beach, horseback riding, and tennis. They also grow organic vegetables and raise their own livestock for food.

The Halden and Balstøy prisons reflect the guiding principles of the Norwegian penal system. National leaders believe that repressive prisons do not work. They operate under the premise that treating inmates with respect and giving them responsibilities reduces the chances that they will end up back in jail. According to the Halden prison governor, "In the Norwegian prison system, there's a focus on human rights and respect. When they [inmates] arrive, many are in bad shape. We want to build them up, give them confidence through education and work and have them leave as better people."[1]

Caring relationships between staff and inmates are essential to carrying out the prison's system's mission. At Halden, prison guards don't carry guns, and they routinely eat meals and participate in sports with their charges. They strive to create a sense of family for inmates, who often come from poor home situations. Many staff members choose to work at the prison in order to transform lives. Said one, "Our goal is to give all prisoners—we call them our pupils—a meaningful life inside these walls."[2]

There is evidence that the Norwegian approach is effective. Within two years of release, 20% of Norway's prisoners end up back in prison. That compares favorably with rates in the United Kingdom and the United States, which range from 50 to 60%. Observers point out, however, that the imprisonment rate in Norway, a small, equalitarian, and prosperous country, is much lower than in the United States (69 per 100,000 compared to 753 per 100,000). Norway's total prison population is only 3,300, which makes it much easier to focus on rehabilitation.

Given the American public's determination to get tough on crime, it's not likely that the United States will adopt Norway's caring approach to prisons any time soon. However, Norway's model is worth considering. The current U.S. penal system is extremely expensive and has resulted in the highest incarceration rate in the world. Further, it doesn't seem to work, since so many released prisoners end up back in jail. Perhaps if more U.S. prisons emphasized rights, respect, and concern for inmates, the demand for additional jails would drop, and more ex-prisoners would reintegrate into society.

Discussion Probes

1. Could the Norwegian prison model work in the United States or other countries? Why or why not?

2. Is it fair to crime victims (and to society) to treat prisoners so well?

3. Do Norwegian prisons reward criminals for their bad behavior?

4. Should prisons focus on punishment or on rehabilitation?

5. Should prison staff develop caring relationships with inmates? Why or why not?

6. Do you think that the Norwegian prison model is ethical?

Notes

1. Adams, W. L. (2010, May 10). Postcard: Halden. A look inside the world's most humane prison. *Time,* p. 14.
2. Adams.

Sources

Fouche, G. (2009, October 19). Where convicts lead the good life. Globalpost. Retrieved January 11, 2011, from http://www.globalpost.com/dispatch/europe/091017/

Soares, C. (2007, September 4). Norwegian prisoners do organic porridge in world's first "green jail." *Belfast Telegraph.*

CASE STUDY 1.3

The Phantom Recall

Things were not going well for the company Johnson & Johnson in 2008–2009. Safety and effectiveness concerns forced the recall of several of the company's products, including over-the-counter medications, artificial hips, and contact lenses. Some of the company's drugs, for example, appeared to have been contaminated with bacteria and minute metal shavings. Many of the problems stemmed from quality control issues at two of its McNeil Consumer Health Care subsidiary plants, one in Puerto Rico and the other in Pennsylvania.

The House Committee on Oversight and Government Reform held hearings to investigate Johnson & Johnson's recall of 136 million bottles of liquid children's medicines, including pediatric Tylenol, Motrin, Zyrtec, and Benadryl. In the course of its investigation, the panel discovered that J&J had undertaken a secret or "phantom" recall of its adult pain reliever Motrin. The medicine in two lots of eight-pill Motrin tablet packets sold exclusively in convenience stores and gas stations was slow to dissolve. The pills posed no danger to consumers but needed more time to take effect, reducing the medication's potency. Instead of instituting a recall through the federal Food and Drug Administration (FDA), the company hired private contractors to visit stores and buy back the affected batches. They told the contractors not to provide any information to store personnel if questioned. One contractor, WIS International, instructed employees, "You should simply 'act' like a regular customer when making these purchases. THERE MUST BE NO MENTION OF THIS BEING A RECALL OF THIS PRODUCT!"[1] At the same time, officials at J&J told the FDA they were conducting an audit or field alert to determine how much defective Motrin remained on store shelves. If the defective batches weren't available for purchase, then a recall wouldn't be necessary. Several months passed before the firm initiated an official recall under pressure from the FDA.

As a result of the recall hearings, Representative Edolphus Towns introduced a bill giving the FDA the power to institute mandatory recalls, authority it currently lacks. The State of Oregon brought suit against J&J, citing 787 violations of state trade law and asking $25,000 for each packet sold to consumers. Oregon attorney general John Kroger hopes to keep medical companies from making secret recalls common practice. "It would be a disaster if these kinds of phantom recalls became an acceptable business practice," he said. "The real significance is to send a message to pharmaceutical companies and other companies that make medical products that they have to do proper recalls that give customers real notice."[2] The Oregon complaint also notes that while the pills posed no immediate health risk, consumers could have suffered from "a worsening of their pain, fever or inflammation symptoms" while waiting for the medications to take effect.[3] An FDA internal audit criticized the agency's handling of the Motrin recall. J&J may face federal criminal charges brought by the Justice Department at the request of criminal division of the FDA.

For its part, J&J claims it received verbal approval from the FDA to conduct a field alert instead of a full-blown recall and kept the agency informed during the process. While Johnson & Johnson CEO William Weldon admitted that buying its own products off shelves was a "mistake," the company argues that there is "no legal basis" for the Oregon suit. Said a company spokesperson, "McNeil's actions were consistent with applicable law and there was no health or safety risk to consumers associated with this limited recall."[4]

Discussion Probes

1. Were consumers hurt by purchasing and using the defective Motrin tablets?

2. Even if the phantom recall was legal, as J&J claims, was it ethical?

3. Would there ever be a circumstance that would justify a phantom recall?

4. Johnson & Johnson officials apparently determined that the benefits of the phantom recall outweighed the potential costs. Were they right?

5. What are the long-term consequences of the secret recall for J&J?

6. Should the FDA be given the authority to force companies to recall products?

Notes

1. Zaitz, L. (2011, January 13). State sues the maker of Motrin. *The Oregonian,* p. A8.
2. Zaitz, p. A8.
3. Singer, N., & Abelson, R. (2011, January 13). Oregon sues J. & J. in Motrin buyback. *The New York Times,* p. B3.
4. Singer & Abelson.

Sources

J&J loses its way with secret buy-up of defective drug. (2010, October 5). *USA Today,* p. 10A.

Rubin, R. (2010, October 1). FDA says recall of adult Motrin 'took too long': company hired contractor to buy up affected product. *USA Today,* p. 4A.

Singer, N. (2010, January 18). In recall, role model stumbles. *The New York Times,* p. B1.

Singer, N. (2010, May 28). F. D. A. weighs more penalties in drug recall by J.&J. unit. *The New York Times,* p. B1.

Singer, N. (2010, June 11). Johnson & Johnson seen as uncooperative on recall inquiry. *The New York Times,* p. B1.

Singer, N. (2010, June 12). More disputes over handling of drug recall. *The New York Times,* p. B3.

Zajac, A. (2010, October 1). J&J chief sees lapses in quality. *Los Angeles Times,* p. B4.

ENDNOTES

1. Material for this summary of utilitarian theory is drawn from the following sources: Barry, V. (1978). *Personal and social ethics: Moral problems with integrated theory.* Belmont, CA: Wadsworth; Bentham, J. (1948). *An introduction to the principles of morals and legislation.* New York: Hafner; De George, R. T. (1995). *Business ethics* (4th ed.). Englewood Cliffs, NJ: Prentice Hall, Chap. 3; Troyer, J. (Ed.). (2003). *The classical utilitarians: Bentham and Mill.* Indianapolis, IN: Hackett; Velasquez, M. G. (1992). *Business ethics: Concepts and cases* (3rd ed.). Englewood Cliffs, NJ: Prentice Hall, Chap. 2; West, H. R. (2004). *An introduction to Mill's utilitarian ethics.* Cambridge, UK: Cambridge University Press.

2. Hartman, E. (1996). *Organizational ethics and the good life.* New York: Oxford University Press, Chap. 2; Barry (1978); DesJardins, J. (2011). *An introduction to business ethics* (4th ed.). New York: McGraw-Hill; Velasquez (1992).

3. Fisk, M. C. (2008, December 24). Wal-Mart to settle 63 lawsuits over wages. *The Washington Post,* p. D01.

4. Kant, I. (1964). *Groundwork of the metaphysics of morals* (H. J. Ryan, Trans.). New York: Harper & Row; Christians, C. G., Rotzell, K. B., & Fackler, M. (1990). *Media ethics* (3rd ed.). New York: Longman; Leslie, L. Z. (2000). *Mass communication ethics: Decision-making in postmodern culture.* Boston: Houghton Mifflin; Velasquez (1992).

5. Graham, G. (2004). *Eight theories of ethics.* London: Routledge, Chap. 6.

6. Shaw, W. H. (2011). *Business ethics: A textbook with cases* (7th ed.). Boston, MA: Wadsworth.

7. Material on Rawls's theory of justice and its critics is taken from the following sources: Rawls, J. (1971). *A theory of justice.* Cambridge, MA: Belknap Press; Rawls, J. (1993). Distributive justice. In T. Donaldson & P. H. Werhane (Eds.), *Ethical issues in business: A philosophical approach* (4th ed., pp. 274–285). Englewood Cliffs, NJ: Prentice Hall; Rawls, J. (1993). *Political liberalism.* New York: Columbia University Press; Rawls, J. (2001). *Justice as fairness: A restatement* (E. Kelly, Ed.). Cambridge, MA: Belknap Press; Barry (1978); Blocker, H. G., & Smith, E. H. (Eds.). (1980). *John Rawls' theory of justice: An introduction.* Athens: Ohio University; Velasquez (1992); Mulhall, S., & Swift, A. (1992). *Liberals and communitarians.* Oxford, UK: Blackwell.

8. Rawls (2001), p. 42.

9. Gladwell, M. (2005). *Blink: The power of thinking without thinking.* New York: Little, Brown.

10. Wusun, L. (2010). *Getting to know Confucius—A new translation of the Analects.* Beijing: Foreign Languages Press; Cleary, T. (1992). *The essential Confucius: The heart of Confucius' teachings in authentic I Ching order.* San Francisco: HarperSan Francisco.

11. Weber, J. (2009). Using exemplary business practices to identify Buddhist and Confucian ethical value systems. *Business and Society Review, 114*(4), 511–540.

12. See, for example: Chan, G. K. Y. (2008). The relevance and value of Confucianism in contemporary business ethics. *Journal of Business Ethics, 77,* 347–360; Romar, E. J. (2002). Virtue is good business: Confucianism as a practical business ethics. *Journal of Business Ethics, 38,* 119–131; Confucius (2007). *The Analects of Confucius* (B. Watson, Trans.). New York: Columbia University Press; Romar, E. J. (2004). Globalization, ethics, and opportunism: A Confucian view of business relationships. *Business Ethics Quarterly, 14,* 663–678.

13. Lau, D. C. (1970). *Mencius.* New York: Penguin Books.

14. Lau, D. C. (1979). *The Analects.* New York: Penguin Books.

15. Ip, P. K. (2009). Is Confucianism good for business ethics in China? *Journal of Business Ethics, 88,* 463–476.

16. Batson, C. D., Van Lange, P. A. M., Ahmad, N., & Lishner, D. A. (2003). Altruism and helping behavior. In M. A. Hogg & J. Cooper (Eds.), *The Sage handbook of social psychology* (pp. 279–295). London: Sage; Post, S. G., Underwood, L. G., Schloss, J. P., & Hurlbut, W. B. (2002). General introduction. In S. G. Post, L. G. Underwood, J. P. Schloss, & W. B. Hurlbut (Eds.), *Altruism and altruistic love: Science, philosophy, and religion in dialogue* (pp. 3–12). Oxford, UK: Oxford University Press.

17. Post, S. G. (2002). The tradition of agape. In S. G. Post, L. G. Underwood, J. P. Schloss, & W. B. Hurlbut (Eds.), *Altruism and altruistic love: Science, philosophy, and religion in dialogue* (pp. 51–64). Oxford, UK: Oxford University Press; Batson et al.

18. Piliavin, J. A., & Charng, H. W. (1990). Altruism: A review of recent theory and research. *American Sociological Review, 16,* 27–65.

19. Batson et al. (2003), p. 279.

20. Kung, H. (1998). *A global ethic for global politics and economics.* New York: Oxford University Press.

21. Kanungo, R. N., & Conger, J. A. (1993). Promoting altruism as a corporate goal. *Academy of Management Executive, 7,* 37–49; Organ, D. W. (1988). *Organizational citizenship behavior: The good soldier syndrome.* Lexington, MA: Lexington Books.

22. Gilligan, C. (1982). *In a different voice: Psychological theory and women's development.* Cambridge, MA: Harvard University Press; Larrabee, M. J. (Ed.) (1993). *An ethic of care: Feminist and interdisciplinary perspectives.* New York: Routledge; Noddings, N. (2003). *Caring: A feminine approach to ethics and moral education.* Berkeley: University of California Press; Held, V. (2006). The ethics of care. In D. Copp (Ed.), *The Oxford handbook of ethical theory* (pp. 537–566). Oxford, UK: Oxford University Press.

23. Jaffee, S., & Shibley Hyde, J. (2000). Gender differences in moral orientation: A meta-analysis. *Psychological Bulletin, 126,* 703–726.

24. Held, V. (2004). Taking care: Care as practice and value. In C. Calhoun (Ed.), *Setting the moral compass: Essays by women philosophers* (pp. 59–71). Oxford, UK: Oxford University Press.

25. Tronto, J. C. (1993). *Moral boundaries: A political argument for an ethic of care.* New York: Routledge.

26. Held (2006).

27. Kracher, B., & Wells, D. L. Employee selection and the ethic of care. In M. Schminke (Ed.), *Managerial ethics: Management of people and processes* (pp. 81–97). Mahwah, NJ: Lawrence Erlbaum.

28. Brehony, K. A. (1999). *Ordinary grace: Lessons from those who help others in extraordinary ways.* New York: Riverhead Books.

29. Sorokin, P. A. (1954). *The ways and power of love: Types, factors, and techniques of moral transformation.* Boston: Beacon Press.

30. Kottler, J. A. (2000). *Doing good: Passion and commitment for helping others.* Philadelphia: Brunner-Routledge.

PART II

Practicing Individual Ethics in the Organization

2

Components of Personal Ethical Development

"Is it bad apples or bad barrels?" Observers sometimes ask this question when trying to account for organizational misbehavior or "rottenness." Do groups engage in immoral behavior because unethical individuals (the "bad apples") spoil those around them, or do unethical organizations (the "bad barrels") corrupt their employees? Truth is, *both* individual and contextual factors contribute to ethical failure.[1] That means we'll have to address both the person and the situation when attempting to improve the ethical performance of our organizations. While we could begin by examining the organizational barrel, I believe that we are better off starting with the apples. Before addressing the organizational context, we need to examine our limitations, personal mission, values, character, motivations, and moral reasoning. In this chapter, we'll identify the elements that should be part of any personal ethical development plan. In the next chapter, we will zero in on the process of moral reasoning and moral action.

Component 1: Facing the Shadow Side of the Personality

Personal change efforts should begin with a realistic self-assessment. In particular, we need to acknowledge our potential to do harm as well as good. Many of the causes of aggression, discrimination, and other destructive behaviors (competitiveness, hostility, prejudice) lie within the individual.

Psychotherapist Carl Jung introduced the shadow metaphor to account for those parts of ourselves that fall short of what we want to be and that we don't want to share with others.[2] These elements could be embarrassing ("I'm afraid of the dark"), socially unacceptable ("I'm bigoted"), or dangerous ("I'm filled with hostility"). In most cases, the shadow is considered a negative force, but it can fuel creativity and spontaneity.

Jung and others interested in the dark side of the personality have argued that ignoring this side of ourselves puts us at great risk. Repressing these impulses (anger, jealousy, rage, insecurity, pride) doesn't make them go away. According to Jung, "Mere suppression of the shadow is as little of a remedy as beheading would be for headache."[3] The shadow is likely to surface under stressful conditions. If you think of yourself as a caring person, for example, you may be surprised when you lash out at your family or roommates as homework begins to pile up. Under this stressful situation, the anger hiding in the shadow side of your personality might suddenly emerge. The same dynamic occurs in organizations when supervisors cope with their own fear of failure by making unreasonable demands on employees or when coworkers respond to their own insecurities by belittling members of other work teams.

Leaving the shadow side unattended also leaves us vulnerable to projection. In projection, we unconsciously transfer or project undesirable characteristics onto others. Jung believed that racial hatred is a projection of the shadow side of the personality, as when the Nazis cast their shadows on the Jews. Another sign of projection is reacting negatively when others reflect the very characteristics (selfishness, dogmatism, a critical attitude) we dislike in ourselves.

Confronting the shadow side of the personality brings many benefits. First, acknowledging that we have undesirable characteristics begins to break their hold over us. We can't master them until we admit that they exist. Second, facing the shadow side provides us with a clearer sense of who we really are. Third, knowing that we harbor destructive tendencies humbles us, making us more understanding of others. Fourth, we are less likely to project our shadow on others in the workplace, thus reducing the frequency of destructive behaviors and improving the ethical climate. Fifth, acknowledging our weaknesses can encourage others to do the same, building healthier work relationships.

There is no blueprint for controlling the shadow side of the personality. However, these tips can help you better manage the unpleasant aspects of the self.[4]

- Take personal responsibility for your actions. You are ultimately accountable for how you act. You have a choice as to how to respond to shadow forces.
- Determine if the negative images you have of others are the result of projecting your undesirable qualities on them. If so, address these negative characteristics in yourself.
- Learn from your mistakes. When your behavior contradicts your self-image, probe for the underlying reasons for your misbehavior. Determine how you can respond more appropriately in the future.
- Find a supportive partner. Create a trusting relationship in which you can explore your weaknesses with one another through listening and feedback.
- Accept criticism. Your critics (supervisors, coworkers, customers) can provide you with valuable insights into your weaknesses.
- Keep yourself out of harm's way. You may need to adjust your behavior or environment to keep from unleashing shadow forces. For example: If high stress levels at work are harming your relationships with your family and coworkers, you may need to reduce your hours or find another job.

In cases where you have fallen significantly short of your personal standards, you may need to forgive yourself. Self-forgiveness begins with acknowledging that you have done something wrong (lied, stolen company property, threatened a coworker) and taking steps to make things right with those you have harmed.[5] However, if even if others don't forgive you, you can still pardon yourself. In fact, refusing to forgive yourself denies your intrinsic worth and dignity as a human being. You must move beyond shame, guilt, and self-reproach if you are to interact effectively with others and to make better moral decisions in the future. Chances are that when you forgive yourself it will be easier to offer forgiveness and to ask for forgiveness from others.

Component 2: Discovering Vocation

Any strategy for personal ethical development ought to address the question "Where am I headed?" A number of authors suggest that we can best determine our life direction through understanding our vocation or calling. In popular usage, the word *vocation* refers to a job or occupation. However, the original meaning of the term was much broader. The English word is drawn from the Latin *vocare,* which means "to call" or "calling."[6] Discovering our vocation means determining our purpose in life. That purpose is based on a clear understanding of our unique skills, abilities, and desires.

For many of us, the work we do is essential to fulfilling our vocation. At times, however, the pursuit of vocation has little to do with paid employment. Some use the money they earn from their jobs to pursue their vocations (working with homeless youth, performing music, inventing, researching) in their spare time. Others, such as stay-at-home parents, retirees, and the voluntarily unemployed, follow their callings without earning a salary. Career experts suggest that we will play a variety of roles over our lifetimes, most of them nonwork related (e.g. child, student, citizen, home-maker, retiree). The prominence of each role will vary depending on our age and stage in life.[7] The student role is more important through our early twenties, for example, but we generally become more focused on work as we get closer to age 30. Retirement/homemaking will take priority after we end our careers. Vocation guides us as we carry out all of our roles, both work and nonwork related, no matter how young or old we are.

Finding our calling produces significant ethical benefits. One, when we are using our abilities and interests, we enjoy a feeling of personal satisfaction, or self-actualization. This sense of satisfaction increases our level of commitment and reduces the likelihood that we will poison the ethical climate of the organization. Two, having a clear direction makes us better stewards. Instead of wasting time and energy on tasks that aren't central to our purpose, we can focus on more meaningful projects that make effective use of our abilities. Three, vocation equips us for service to others. This outward focus is captured in writer Frederick Buechner's description of vocation as "the place where your deep gladness and the world's deep hunger meet."[8] Because we are more productive when pursuing our vocation, we are better able to serve others, whether as engineers, architects, graduate students, software developers, nursing home administrators, or scientists.

Discovering Your Personal Gifts

Philosophy professor Lee Hardy offers some practical advice for discovering how you can use your gifts to serve others in the workplace.[9] The first step is to determine your unique gifts. Pay particular attention to past experiences. Ask yourself these questions:

- What have I done and done well?
- What kinds of skills did I make use of?
- What kind of knowledge did I acquire?
- What kind of objects did I work with?
- In what capacity was I relating to others?
- Was I working in a position with a lot of freedom and responsibility, or was I working in a highly structured situation where my activity was thoroughly and carefully structured?

Hardy suggests that you try out a variety of jobs. Even if you don't like a particular position, you will learn from the experience. Identify your personality type (see Ethics in Action 2.1) and get feedback about your strengths and weaknesses from those who know you well.

ETHICS IN ACTION 2.1 HOLLAND'S PERSONALITY AND CAREER TYPES

John Holland, a professor emeritus at Johns Hopkins University, offers the following personality types on which career choices can be based.[1] These types are the product of both genetic background and experience. A child who has musically gifted parents may inherit the ability to recognize pitch and melody, for example. However, to become a professional musician, she will need plenty of practice and encouragement (lessons, attendance at concerts, special schools).

Holland identifies six patterns that impact career choices.

The Realistic Type

The Realistic person likes carefully structured, ordered activities that involve the use of objects, tools, machines, and animals. He or she acquires mechanical, electrical, agricultural, and other competencies in order to achieve goals. Sample professions: surveyor, mechanic.

The Investigative Type

An Investigative person seeks to observe and understand the physical and cultural world. Such an individual strives to acquire scientific and mathematical skills. Sample professions: medical technician, chemist, physicist.

The Artistic Type

An individual with the Artistic preference prefers unstructured activities that allow for the creation of art forms and new products. This type masters artistic skills that draw from music, art, drama, and language. Sample professions: artist, musician, writer.

The Social Type

Heredity and experience encourage the Social person to inform, train, and enlighten others. This requires the acquisition of interpersonal skills and knowledge along with a strong educational background. Sample professions: teacher, counselor.

The Enterprising Type

The Enterprising individual wants to reach goals and make money through others. As a result, he or she works on acquiring persuasive, interpersonal, and leadership competencies. Sample professions: salesperson, executive.

(Continued)

(Continued)

The Conventional Type

A Conventional individual gravitates to tasks that involve the systematic manipulation of data through keeping records, filing, analyzing numbers, and use of databases. This type focuses on developing clerical, computational, and computer skills. Sample professions: accountant, clerk.

SOURCE: Holland, J. L. (1997). *Making vocational choices* (3rd ed.). Odessa, FL: Psychological Assessment Resources. Reproduced by special permission of the Publisher, Psychological Assessment Resources, Inc., 16204 North Florida Avenue, Lutz, FL 33549, from *Making Vocational Choices, Third Edition,* copyright 1973, 1985, 1992, 1997 by Psychological Assessment Resources, Inc. All rights reserved.

NOTE: For a complete copy of Holland's career inventory, see Holland (1997).

Professor Hardy's second and third steps to finding vocation consist of identifying your specific concern for others and your interests. You may be concerned about the housing needs of immigrant populations, for instance, or environmental and educational problems. Your interests—like art, music, literature, bird watching, hiking, photography, film production, current events—can motivate you to develop skills and knowledge that later can be employed in service. For example, one of my colleagues was prompted by his boyhood hobby of collecting baseball statistics into pursuing a career as a professor of mathematics.

The final step is to find the right job fit. Locate a place where your gifts, concerns, and interests can be put to best use. According to Hardy, finding the right fit goes beyond matching your talents to the job description. It should also include an evaluation of the values and goals of the work setting. You may be well suited for a position (for example, a job writing copy for tobacco ads) yet refuse it on moral grounds. Research suggests that those who view their work as a meaningful calling, rather than as a means to earn money (a job) or as a way to advance (a career), report more satisfaction with their work and their lives, have more rewarding relationships at work, and are more likely to be committed to their teams and organizations.[10]

Barriers to Obeying Our Callings

Sadly, the call of vocation often falls upon deaf ears. Ambition is one significant barrier to obeying our callings. Following our heart's desires may put us in direct conflict with what the world defines as success. We may want to study art, protect wildlife, or teach, but our culture encourages us to pursue other objectives, like making money, getting promoted, and achieving status. Emory University professor Brian Mahan argues that to follow our vocation we must "forget ourselves on purpose."[11] After determining what is most satisfying and meaningful to us, we then need to discover what is preventing us from hearing its call. We can uncover our preoccupations by asking, "What is keeping me from living fully for the thing I want to live for?" Setting aside distractions enables us to acknowledge that pride and the trappings of success are constant temptations. By understanding their power, we can begin to break their hold over us. Then we are ready to respond to our life purpose.

Avoidance is another obstacle to vocation. Like the biblical figure Jonah, who headed in the opposite direction when God sent him to the city of Nineveh, many of us resist our call. We may do so out of a sense of caution, doubts about our own abilities, self-imposed limitations, or compliance with orders from authority figures. Resistance can take these forms:

- Waiting for just the right moment
- Analyzing the call to death
- Lying to ourselves
- Replacing one call with another, more socially acceptable one
- Sabotaging our own efforts
- Filling our lives with other activities[12]

In order to overcome resistance, we need to break free of our low self-esteem. Fortunately, our chances of success are much greater when we respond to a genuine call. That realization should make it easier to leave our self-doubts behind and move forward.

Component 3: Identifying Personal Values

Personal moral values are "desirable goals, varying in importance, that serve as guiding principles in people's lives."[13] Values drive a good deal of our decision making and behavior on the job, including how hard we work, how we treat coworkers and subordinates, how we evaluate performance, and so on. For example, those who put a high value on responsibility are rarely late to work and may show up even when they are sick. Those who place more value on enjoying life may skip work to go skiing or to the beach. We also use our values as standards to determine right from and wrong and to set our priorities.

Spanish economics and ethics professor Antonio Argandona argues that our personal value systems are likely to be inadequate or incomplete unless we consider the impact of our actions on other employees and on the organization as a whole.[14] He offers these suggestions for developing and analyzing personal values systems in an organizational context:

- Know the reasons for your actions. (Why do you do it?)
- Take into account the consequences of your actions for yourself. (How will you change if you act in this manner?)
- Consider the consequences of your actions on others. (What will happen to them if I act this way and encourage them to follow my example?)
- Aim to discover other people's needs and take them into account.

- Always strive to be guided by higher-order motives, moving beyond choosing between "good" and "bad" to choosing between "good" and "best."
- Help others know the reasons why they act.
- Help others know the effects of their actions on themselves and other people.
- Help others identify other people's needs and act to satisfy them.
- Eliminate any actions that may encourage others to act for selfish reasons.
- Trust others and communicate that trust.
- Always set an excellent example.
- Strive to understand other people's values.
- Do not rely exclusively on ethical instinct or intuition, but apply reason.
- Be able to generate a variety of alternatives.
- Don't get carried away by feelings, but employ logic when determining ethical priorities.

One way to identify or clarify the values you already have is by sitting down and generating a list. The odds are good that you'll have no trouble coming up with at least a few of your core values. Nevertheless, there may be some potentially important values that you overlook. For that reason, you may want to consider rating a list of values supplied by values experts. Hebrew University professor Shalom Schwartz developed one widely used value system. Schwartz argues that, due to the human condition, people around the world organize themselves around the same set of 10 universal values, described in the following Self-Assessment.[15] These values, in turn, can be grouped into four dimensions along two main axes. The first axis pits openness to change against conservation. Openness to change emphasizes stimulation, self-direction, and following personal interests; conservation is more concerned with tradition, conformity, and security. The second axis contrasts self-enhancement and self-transcendence. Self-enhancement means pursuing personal interests even at the expense of other people. Self-transcendence looks beyond selfish concerns to improve the welfare of others. Power and achievement are self-enhancement values; universalism and benevolence are self-transcendence values.

Value priorities change based on personal experiences and cultural differences. You are more likely to respect authority, for instance, if you grew up in a strongly religious family. Tradition and conformity often motivate behavior in collectivist cultures that seek to subordinate the individual to the group. Self-direction, hedonism, and stimulation tend to drive behavior in individualistic societies that encourage personal autonomy. Industrial psychologists report that values play a critical role in *person-organization fit*.[16] Person-organization fit describes the degree of compatibility between an employee and his or her work environment. Those who share values in common with their organizations have greater commitment and motivation, feel more successful, and experience less work stress and anxiety. They are also convinced that their organizations are more ethical.

Complete the Self-Assessment to determine your value priorities and those of your organization. If your rankings agree with those of the larger group, you are well fitted to your organization. As a consequence, your job satisfaction is likely to be high. You might have others in your work group complete the same inventory and then compare rankings. (See Application Project 4.)

SELF-ASSESSMENT

Schwartz's Value System

Take a few moments and rank the items below. Each value is described, along with sample behaviors produced by that value. These will serve as your anchor points. Next, rate each value according to its importance as a guiding principle in your life. Use a 9-point scale ranging from −1 (*opposed to my principles*) to 0 (*not important*) to 7 (*of supreme importance*). When you finish, you'll have a sense of how important each value is to you as well as how it rates in comparison to the other values on the list. Then, rank and rate the values for your work group or organization as a whole. Compare the two sets of scores. What do they reveal?

Power: Social status and prestige, control, or dominance over people and resources (social power, authority, wealth)
> *Behaviors:* Pressure others to go along with my preferences and opinions; choose friends and relationships based on how much money they have

Personal Rank _____ Rating _____ Organizational Rank _____ Rating _____

Achievement: Personal success through demonstrating competence according to social standards (successful, capable, ambitious, influential)
> *Behaviors:* Study late before exams even though I studied well during the semester; take on many commitments

Personal Rank _____ Rating _____ Organizational Rank _____ Rating _____

Hedonism: Pleasure and sensuous gratification for oneself (pleasure, enjoying life)
> *Behaviors:* Take it easy and relax; consume food or drinks even when I'm not hungry or thirsty

Personal Rank _____ Rating _____ Organizational Rank _____ Rating _____

Stimulation: Excitement, novelty, and challenge in life (daring, a varied life, an exciting life)
> *Behaviors:* Watch thrillers; do unconventional things

Personal Rank _____ Rating _____ Organizational Rank _____ Rating _____

Self-Direction: Independent thought and action—choosing, creating, exploring (creativity, freedom, independent, curious, choosing my own goals)
> *Behaviors:* Examine the ideas behind rules and regulations before obeying them; come up with novel setups for my living space

Personal Rank _____ Rating _____ Organizational Rank _____ Rating _____

Universalism: Understanding, appreciation, tolerance, and protection for the welfare of all people and for nature (broad-minded, wisdom, social justice, equality, a world at peace, a world of beauty, unity with nature, protecting the environment)

Behaviors: Use environmentally friendly products; make sure everyone receives equal treatment

Personal Rank _____ Rating _____ Organizational Rank _____ Rating _____

Benevolence: Preservation and enhancement of the welfare of people with whom one is in frequent personal contact (helpful, honest, forgiving, loyal, responsible)
  Behaviors: Agree easily to lend things to neighbors; keep promises I have made

Personal Rank _____ Rating _____ Organizational Rank _____ Rating _____

Tradition: Respect for, commitment to, and acceptance of the customs and ideas that traditional culture or religion provide the self (humble, accepting my portion in life, devout, respect for tradition, moderate)
  Behaviors: Observe traditional customs on holidays; show modesty with regard to my achievements and talents

Personal Rank _____ Rating _____ Organizational Rank _____ Rating _____

Conformity: Restraint of actions, inclinations, and impulses likely to upset or harm others and violate social expectations or norms (politeness, obedient, self-discipline, honoring parents and elders)
  Behaviors: Obey my parents; avoid confrontation with people I don't like

Personal Rank _____ Rating _____ Organizational Rank _____ Rating _____

Security: Safety, harmony, and stability of society, of relationships, and of self (family security, national security, social order, clean, reciprocation of favors)
  Behaviors: Refrain from opening my door to strangers; buy products that were made in my country

Personal Rank _____ Rating _____ Organizational Rank _____ Rating _____

SOURCE: Bardi, A., & Schwartz, S. (2003). Values and behavior: Strength and structure of relations. *Journal of Personality and Social Psychology, 29,* 1207–1220, p. 1211. Used by permission of Sage Publications.

Component 4: Developing Character

Character plays an important role in ethical decision-making and behavior. Your chances of making wise decisions and following through on your choices will be higher if you demonstrate the positive moral traits or qualities referred to as *virtues.* The notion that good people make good choices is the premise of virtue ethics. Virtue ethics is one of the oldest ethical traditions, dating back to the times of Plato, Aristotle, Confucius, and before.[17] In contrast to the rules-based theories presented in the last chapter, virtue theory highlights the person or actor instead of general ethical principles. Virtue ethicists note that ethical decisions are typically made under time pressures in uncertain conditions.[18] Individuals in these situations don't have time to weigh possible consequences or to select an abstract guideline to apply. Instead, they respond based on their character. Those with high (virtuous) character will immediately react in ways that benefit themselves, others, and the greater good. They will quickly turn down bribes, reach out to help others, and so on. (Read Case Study 2.2 to see character demonstrated under horrific conditions.)

Virtues are "deep-rooted dispositions, habits, skills, or traits of character that incline persons to perceive, feel, and act in ethically right and sensitive ways."[19] It takes a long time for such qualities to develop. Being virtuous increases sensitivity to ethical issues and encourages moral behavior. Further, virtues aren't bound by context. A virtue may be expressed differently depending on the situation (courage takes different forms in the boardroom and on the battlefield, for example). Nonetheless, a virtuous person doesn't abandon his or her principles to please others or act civilly to some people but not to others. Aristotle and Plato identified primary or cardinal virtues appropriate for the Greek city-state: prudence (discernment, discretion), justice (righteousness, integrity), courage (strength in the face of adversity), and self-restraint (temperance). Christians added faith, hope, and love.[20] Later, a number of other virtues, such as compassion, generosity, empathy, hospitality, modesty, and civility, were derived from the original seven.

Positive Psychology and Virtues

In recent years, virtues have also attracted the attention of positive psychologists. Positive psychologists take issue with the traditional approach of psychology, which tries to fix the weaknesses or deficiencies of people. They argue, instead, that it is more productive to identify and build on the strengths of individuals. Positive psychologists define virtues as morally valued personality traits. Introversion would not be considered a virtue because, although it is a personality trait, it is not considered ethically desirable or undesirable. Kindness, on the other hand, would be considered a virtue because compassion is honored in most cultures.[21] Positive organizational psychologists have identified six broad categories of character strengths, which share much in common with the lists of virtues described above. These character strengths include: (1) wisdom and knowledge—cognitive strengths that involve the acquisition and use of knowledge; (2) courage—emotional strengths that exercise the will to reach goals in the face of external and internal opposition; (3) love—interpersonal strengths that involve caring for and befriending others; (4) justice—civic strengths that make healthy community life possible; (5) temperance—strengths that protect against excess; and (6) transcendence—strengths that forge connections to the larger world and help supply meaning.[22]

Psychologist Augusto Blasi argues that moral character is organized around moral desires.[23] He distinguishes between the traits described above (which he refers to as lower-level virtues) and what he calls higher-order virtues. The higher-level traits make it possible to develop and exercise the lower-level traits. The first cluster of higher-order virtues centers on will power or self-control. Virtues of the will include perseverance, determination, and self-discipline. These qualities enable us to regulate ourselves when solving problems. Willpower is made up of a set of interlocking skills that include analyzing problems, setting goals, focusing attention, resisting temptations and distractions, and staying on task. The second cluster of higher-order traits is organized around integrity. Integrity traits reflect self-consistency—being true to one's word, being transparent and accountable, and so forth. Those who value integrity feel a sense of responsibility to do the right thing. (Turn to Case Study 2.3 for an example of someone who violated his integrity.) Blasi points out that willpower and integrity function independently of morality. For example, a thief can show a great deal of determination and perseverance in planning and executing a bank robbery, and an evil person may consistently engage in bad behavior. To become essential to moral character, self-control and integrity must be coupled with the desire to act ethically. (I'll have more to say about ethical motivation in the next section of the chapter.)

Direct Approaches to Character Development

Strategies for fostering character development can be classified as direct or indirect. Direct approaches are specifically designed to promote virtues. For instance, a number of schools offer character education programs.[24] The most effective character education efforts don't tell children how to behave but, instead, engage students in debate, dialogue, case studies, role-plays, self-evaluation, and problem solving. They introduce students to ethical issues suitable to their age and stage of development. Teachers model desired behaviors, and character education is central to the school's purpose and mission. For college and university students, experiential learning (particularly service learning) plays an important role in character development. Hands-on experience, coupled with reflection on those experiences, makes participants more sensitive to moral issues, broadens their perspectives, and increases their commitment to the community.[25] (Case Study 2.1 describes the efforts of one university to promote character development.)

Like educators, positive psychologists take a direct approach to character development.[26] The specific tactics they use vary depending on the particular virtue they want to build. For example, to foster optimism, they encourage clients to identify their negative thoughts ("I am a loser") and then convert them into more constructive thoughts ("I may have failed in this case, but I am successful in other activities"). To foster courage, they expose individuals to low-level threats and then expose them to progressively greater dangers. To foster humility, they encourage counselees to realistically assess their weaknesses as well as their strengths.

CASE STUDY 2.1

Character Development at West Point

The United States Military Academy at West Point takes character development very seriously. However, instead of focusing on punishing offenders after they violate the rules, the leaders at West Point take a more proactive approach, which begins with the selection process. When admitting students, admissions staff looks for a pattern of selfless behavior (for example, involvement in the Boy Scouts or Girl Scouts). They send all candidates a book about the academy's honor code. Those selected for admission go through a rigorous orientation and socialization process that addresses ethics and character. Carefully screened juniors and seniors mentor incoming cadets and are expected to lead by example. Character is emphasized in every activity, including intramural sports (it is possible to win a game and later lose it due to poor sportsmanship). Officer candidates are placed in active-duty Army units during the summer, where they are exposed to the challenges of leading but, at the same time, also take West Point values into the field. After graduation, some high-character alumni serve at West Point in instructor or administrative roles.

Cadets go through a developmental process to prepare them to make ethical decisions on the battlefield. They first become familiar with the 12-word Honor Code: "A cadet will not lie, cheat, steal, or tolerate those that do." They also master decision-making guidelines, such as the Three Rules of Thumb. The rules of thumb provide three questions to ask when making ethical choices: Does the action involve deception? Does it provide an unfair advantage? How would the cadet feel being on the receiving end of the action? These guidelines are supplemented with ongoing communication about ethical standards. Over time, cadets take on greater decision-making responsibility, such as when they are placed in Army units and when they are assigned to lead other cadets.

West Point's approach to discipline is particularly noteworthy. For decades, the academy expelled or otherwise silenced violators and hoped they would serve as an example to others. Now, academy leaders view violations as opportunities for personal development, believing that individuals can grow through these experiences. Those who break the honor code are assigned honors mentors, maintain an ethical-moral journal, write ethics cases, design and implement a developmental project, and create a developmental portfolio. The organization as a whole creates case studies based on past cadet violations as well as on wartime scandals, such as prisoner abuse at Abu Ghraib.

West Point officials admit that no character development program is 100% effective (sexual harassment and assault continue to be a problem at all the academies, for example). Nonetheless, the positive developmental strategies used at the academy provide a model that could be adopted for use at other schools as well as in businesses and nonprofit organizations.

Discussion Probes

1. What role should character play in the admissions process at colleges and universities?

2. Should all colleges and universities make character development an important component of their mission? Why or why not?

3. Should ethical violations be punished or treated as opportunities for personal development?

4. What are the strengths of the United States Military Academy character development program? What are its weaknesses?

5. What elements of the West Point character development program could be implemented at your college or university?

SOURCE: Offstein, E. H., & Dufresne, R. L. (2007). Building strong ethics and promoting positive character development: The influence of HRM at the United States Military Academy at West Point. *Human Resource Management, 46*(1), 95–114.

Indirect Approaches to Character Development

While the direct methods described above build character, virtues often develop indirectly as well, as a by-product or outcome of other activities. These indirect methods include developing habits, finding role models, telling and living collective stories, and successfully navigating the passages in our organizational lives.

Habits

According to Aristotle, we cannot separate character from action. We acquire virtues through exercising them: "Men [and women] become builders by building, and lyre-players by playing the lyre, so too we become just by doing just acts, temperate by doing temperate acts, brave by doing brave acts."[27] Good habits are voluntary routines or practices designed to foster virtuous behavior. Every time we engage in a habit (telling the truth, giving credit to others, giving to the less fortunate), it leaves a trace. Over time, these residual effects become part of our personality, and the habit becomes "second nature." In other words, by doing better, we become better. We also become more skilled in demonstrating the virtue. Practicing self-restraint, for instance, improves the ability to demonstrate self-restraint under pressure. Conversely, practicing bad habits encourages the development of vices that stunt character development. This was the case at Microsoft, according to some critics who claimed that chair Bill Gates and president Steve Ballmer did not appear ever to have admitted mistakes. When they faced an antitrust suit, this pattern repeated itself, damaging the reputation and standing of the company. The Microsoft executives were unrepentant and saw no reason to change their business practices even though the judge in the case ruled that they were monopolistic.[28]

Character-building habits include being honest in every transaction, no matter how small; never hiding the bad news from the boss; and treating every person with respect. Stephen Covey has described seven habits that characterize highly effective, ethical individuals.[29] Each habit incorporates knowledge ("what to do" and "why"), skill ("how to do") and desire ("want to do."). Covey and his colleagues have presented these principles to thousands of businesses, schools, and nonprofit organizations. You can use his list of habits as you strive to develop your character on the job.

Habit 1: Be proactive. Proactive people realize that they are in charge of their lives; they can choose how they respond to events. When faced with a career setback, they try to grow from the experience instead of feeling victimized by it. Proactive individuals also take the initiative by opting to attack problems instead of accepting defeat. Their language reflects their willingness to accept rather than to avoid responsibility. A proactive employee makes such statements as "Let's brainstorm some possible solutions" and "I can develop new sales leads." A reactive worker makes comments such as "My boss won't go along with that idea," "I can't learn the new software program," and "That's just who I am." Those with a proactive orientation also seek to expand the circle of people that they can influence.

Habit 2: Begin with the end in mind. This habit is based on the notion that "all things are created twice." First we get a visual picture of what we want to accomplish (a mental creation), and then we follow through on our plans (a physical creation). Inadequate mental creation is the cause of many organizational failures. Entrepreneurs fail to anticipate start-up costs, for instance, or to correctly identify markets for their products and services. On a personal level, if we're unhappy with the current direction of our lives, we can generate new mental images and goals, a process Covey calls *rescripting*. Discovering our vocation and identifying our values helps to isolate the results we want and thus control the type of life we create. Covey urges leaders to center their lives on inner principles such as fairness and human dignity rather than on such external factors as family, money, friends, or work.

Habit 3. Put first things first. Our time should be organized around priorities. Unfortunately, though, most of us spend our days coping with emergencies, mistakenly believing that urgent means important. Meetings, deadlines, and interruptions place immediate demands on our schedules, but other, less pressing activities, such as relationship building and planning, are more important in the long run. To be effective, we need to carve out time for significant activities by identifying our most important roles, selecting our goals, creating schedules that enable us to reach our objectives, and modifying plans when necessary. We can create space for important but not urgent items by learning to say no to requests that don't fit our priorities (see the "Ethics and Technology" box on the next page). We'll also need to delegate more, outlining the results we want but letting others determine the methods they'll use to achieve these objectives.

Habit 4. Think win–win. Adopt a win–win perspective that reflects a cooperative orientation to communication (I'll have more to say about cooperation in Chapter 9). Be convinced that the best solution benefits both parties. The win–win habit is based on these dimensions: character (integrity, maturity, and a belief that the needs of everyone can be met); trusting relationships committed to mutual benefit; performance or partnership agreements that spell out conditions and responsibilities; organizational systems that fairly distribute rewards; and principled negotiation processes in which both sides generate possible solutions and then select the one that works best.

Habit 5. Seek first to understand, then to be understood. Put aside your personal concerns to engage in empathetic listening. Seek to understand the other party, not to evaluate, advise, or interpret. Empathetic listening is an excellent way to build a trusting relationship. Covey uses the metaphor of the emotional bank account to illustrate how trust develops. Principled individuals make deposits in the emotional bank account by understanding the other person, showing kindness and courtesy, keeping commitments, clarifying expectations, demonstrating personal integrity, and sincerely apologizing when they make a withdrawal. These strong relational reserves help prevent misunderstandings and make it easier to resolve any problems that do arise. Being understood is also important. You can't enter into win–win agreements unless the other party understands your position.

Habit 6. Synergize. Synergy creates a solution that is greater than the sum of its parts and uses right-brain thinking to generate a third, previously undiscovered alternative. Synergistic, creative solutions are generated in trusting relationships (those with high emotional bank accounts) where participants value their differences. You can eliminate those negative forces—distrust, fear—that block change by creating a setting where it is safe to talk about these forces and to come up with an agreement.

Habit 7. Sharpen the saw. Sharpening the saw refers to continual renewal of your physical, mental, social or emotional, and spiritual dimensions. Care for your body through exercise, good nutrition, and stress management. Promote your mental development by reading good literature and writing thoughtful letters and journal and blog entries. Create meaningful relationships with others, and nurture your inner or spiritual values through study or meditation and time in nature. Renewal should be balanced, addressing all four elements of the self. Be careful not to focus your efforts entirely on one dimension (say, physical fitness) because you will neglect your mental, social, and spiritual development.

ETHICS AND TECHNOLOGY

Effective, Ethical E-Mail Habits

Technology, which was supposed to save us time and make us more efficient, often has the opposite effect. Such is the case with e-mail. Electronic communication has made it much easier to generate and deliver messages to mass audiences. Not only is automated spamming a growing problem, but e-mail has led to "emergent spamming." In emergent spamming, "thousands of individuals unwittingly and collectively overload some mailboxes." Examples of emergent spam include the thousands of résumés sent to personnel departments by job seekers and the flood of e-mail letters sent by constituents to politicians in response to pleas by special interest groups. Then, too, businesses send out ads to their e-commerce customers and partners, and business units feel compelled to send announcements or newsletters to everyone in the entire organization. Just deleting emergent spam takes time because first the recipient has to read enough of the message to determine if the e-mail is worthy of attention. To illustrate, if an employee receives 100 such e-mail messages daily and spends 20 seconds evaluating each one, this consumes 30 minutes a day. Reading courtesy announcements from other business divisions could take another 30 minutes out of the workday.

Institutional technology expert Peter Denning offers three suggestions for managing online communication that will free you up to fulfill your ethical responsibility to get your real work done. First, develop practices for evaluating your commitments. Use your personal mission statement or calling to determine whether an e-mail message is valuable or wasteful. Decline all unimportant commitments; anticipate problems and act on them before they become urgent crises. For example, raise an e-mail "red flag" with colleagues if you spot a possible issue, stating your concern about a policy, plan, or procedure that could prove problematic.

Second, develop a set of practices for evaluating your personal capacity. Make a spreadsheet to measure your current commitments or load against your ability to carry out your duties. List each commitment, record how many hours you devote each week to this responsibility, and identify other resources besides time that you need to fulfill this obligation. Add up the totals and determine which duties are not getting enough time and if you are overcommitted, spending far too much time on the job.

Third, develop a set of practices for coordination. All commitments are fulfilled through conversations with other people, many of them through e-mail. Keep track of online conversations and follow through on all promises—notify customers if something interferes with fulfilling promises, negotiate new deadlines as needed, and so on. Remember that other people are just as busy as you are and may decline requests by deleting e-mail. Ask for a few minutes of their time first, and then follow up with the main request.

These three sets of practices won't be enough to keep you from being overwhelmed by online communication unless you learn to say no to requests. If you can't say no to the boss, for example, come up with a counteroffer that promises what you can deliver; role-play saying no to colleagues. Denning concludes by noting that managing online commitments is part of being a professional. Meeting these commitments with coworkers builds trust and increases your capacity to influence others. Customers, too, appreciate it when you conduct business in a way that respects their time and honors your promises.

SOURCE: Denning, P. (2002, March). Internet time out. *Communications of the ACM*, pp. 15–18. Vol. 45:03, © 2002 ACM, Inc. Reprinted by permission.

Role Models

Virtues are more "caught than taught" in that they are often acquired through observation and imitation. We learn what it means to be courageous, just, compassionate, and honest by seeing these qualities modeled in the lives of others. Role models can be drawn from the people we know (managers, friends, teachers); historical figures; or contemporary political, business and military leaders. For example, those interested in careers in government can turn to a set of exemplars provided by the American Society for Public Administration.[30] These examples of virtue include Harvard W. Wiley, the chief chemist of the U.S. Department of Agriculture, who engineered passage of the Food and Drug Act in 1906; former U.S. comptroller general Elmer Stats (1966–1981), who used the General Accounting Office to root out corruption and inefficiency; William Ruckelshaus, the U.S. attorney general who refused to follow President Nixon's orders to fire the independent prosecutor investigating the Watergate scandal; former surgeon general C. Everett Koop, who fought against smoking and for treatment of AIDS as a medical, not moral, problem in the 1980s; and Marie Ragghianti, a Kentucky official who, in 1977, uncovered a scheme by the governor of Kentucky to sell paroles.

Government ethics expert David Hart argues that it is useful to differentiate between different types of moral examples or exemplars.[31] Dramatic acts, such as when

Captain Chelsey ("Sully") Sullenberger safely landed his plane on the Hudson River shortly after takeoff, capture our attention. However, if we're to develop worthy character, we need examples of those who demonstrate virtue on a daily basis. Hart distinguishes between moral episodes and moral processes. Moral episodes are made up of moral crises and moral confrontations. Moral crises are dangerous, and Hart calls those who respond to them "moral heroes." Tuvia and Zus Bielski are two such heroes. These two Belorussian brothers saved more than 1,000 of their fellow Jews from Nazi extermination squads by creating a hidden village in a forest. (More moral heroes are described in Case Study 2.2.) Moral confrontations don't involve physical danger, but they do involve risk and call for "moral champions." Researcher Jeffrey Weigand emerged as a moral champion when he revealed that the tobacco industry had suppressed evidence that smoking was harmful.

Moral processes consist of *moral projects* and *moral work*. Moral projects are designed to improve ethical behavior during a limited amount of time and require "moral leaders." A moral leader sets out to reduce gang activity, for example, to feed the victims of a famine, or to provide more affordable housing for low-income residents. In contrast to a moral project, moral work does not have a beginning or an end but is ongoing. The "moral worker" strives for ethical consistency throughout life. This moral exemplar might be the elementary school lunchroom supervisor who befriends her young diners or the retiree who faithfully delivers meals to shut-ins several times a week.

Hart believes that the moral worker is the most important category of moral exemplar because, as he points out, most of life is lived in the daily valleys, not on the heroic mountain peaks. Since character is developed over time through a series of moral choices and actions, we need examples of those who live consistent moral lives. Those who engage in moral work are better able to handle moral crises like war and genocide.

Stories

Narrative is one of humankind's primary tools for understanding the world. We tell stories, read stories, watch and read stories, think in story form, and star in our dream stories. Narratives not only help use make sense of the world, they also promote desired behavior.[32] The narratives told by our families, schools, and religious bodies are designed to impart values and to encourage caring, self-discipline, and other virtues. When we learn of the bravery of a distant relative, for instance, we get a better grasp of our family's heritage. At the same time, we are encouraged to follow his or her example in order to maintain the family name. A similar process unfolds in the organizational setting. The story of a coworker who went to extraordinary lengths to serve a customer inspires us to do likewise. (See Chapter 9 for more information on organizational stories.)

Character growth comes not only from hearing narratives but also from "living up" to our roles in the stories we share with others.[33] When we align ourselves with an organization, we become actors in its ongoing narrative. We should seek out organizations that will bring out the best in us or try to change the collective story of which we are a part.[34]

Literature can also enhance character development. Educator Stephan Ellenwood notes that literature mirrors the complexity of real life. Literature and biography introduce us to complicated individuals who, like us, must make judgments in specific situations. Wrestling with fictional moral dilemmas or reading about the struggles of historical figures can prepare us for the ethical issues we face both on and off the job. According to Ellenwood:

> Sound moral choices depend on reflection, taking time, and active communication about nuances, connotations, understandings, and implications. In that context literature is an especially rich resource for truly understanding moral issues because good authors attend carefully to details and complexity. Good stories do not provide quick fixes or simplistic solutions.[35]

When it comes to moral development, the best narratives are both vivid and vexing. Vivid stories introduce characters we care about; vexing stories place characters in ethical situations that are difficult and challenging.

Passages

Intense experiences—those that push us out of our comfort zones—play a critical role in character development. These crossroads events, called *passages,* often result in failure. Important passages include diversity of work experiences (joining a company, accepting a major new assignment); work adversity (significant failure, losing a job, coping with a bad boss); diversity of life experiences (living abroad, blending work and family into a meaningful whole); and life adversity (death or divorce, illness).[36]

All types of passages offer significant potential for character growth if we negotiate them successfully through a nine-step process:

Step 1: Learn resilience. Don't define yourself as a failure when things go wrong, but remain optimistic and self-confident. Learn from your mistakes.

Step 2: Accept personal responsibility. Don't blame others or the organization for problems. You can only learn and grow if you take personal responsibility.

Step 3: Reflect. When confronted with a life passage, ask yourself why this happened, whether you contributed to the event, how you might have acted differently, and how you could go back and change something you said or did.

Step 4: Seek support from your partner, family, friends, and professionals. Avoid isolating yourself, which can lock you into a negative mind-set. Instead, be vulnerable to others and seek out emotional support.

Step 5: Develop and use a professional network. Networks can be sources of information, advice, and insights. Take advantage of these connections by asking questions and seeking help.

Step 6: Seek refuge. Passages are intense, so take time to get away to a relaxing location or immerse yourself in an enjoyable activity like sports, meditation, or yoga. You'll have more energy and insights when you return.

Step 7: Gain perspective. Use the pain of a passage experience to step back and take a broader perspective. Putting some distance between yourself and immediate issues can help you put difficult experiences into context. A bad boss may not be so threatening if you step back and realize that you are not defined by your job, for instance.

Step 8: Retirement. Mastering a series of passages should provide you with the self-understanding and maturity you need to take on the next phase of life beyond work. This transition is much more difficult, though, if you have invested all your energies in your career.

Step 9: Pass on your experience. Take what you have learned and the character qualities you have developed, like empathy and authenticity, and use them to help others who are going through similar passages.

Component 5: Creating a Moral Identity

We are not likely to face our shadow sides, seek to discover our vocations, identify our values, or develop our character unless motivated to do so. A number of psychologists use the term *moral identity* to describe one powerful motivating force behind ethical behavior.[37] Those with high moral identity define themselves in terms of their ethical commitments. Moral principles and character traits are at the core of their being. They feel compelled to act in ways that are consistent with their self-definitions, demonstrating highly developed willpower and integrity virtues (see our earlier discussion) activated by a strong desire to do the right thing. For those with strong moral identity, to betray their ethical commitments is to betray themselves. They follow in the footsteps of Protestant reformer Martin Luther. When called upon to defend his radical religious beliefs in front of the Catholic hierarchy at the Diet of Worms, Luther declared, "Here I stand; I can do no other."

Moral exemplars like those described earlier have extremely high moral identities. Anne Colby and William Damon studied 23 contemporary moral exemplars and found no separation between these individuals' morality and core identity.[38]

> Over the course of their lives, there is a progressive uniting of self and morality. Exemplars come to see morality and self as inextricably intertwined, so that concerns of the self become defined by their moral sensibilities. The exemplars' moral identities become tightly integrated, almost fused, with their self-identities.[39]

Participants in the Colby and Damon study were very clear about what they believed and then acted (often spontaneously) on their convictions. Most drew their moral beliefs from religious faith or faith in a higher power. They had a positive approach to life and defined success as pursuing their life mission. Their moral commitments extended well beyond those of ordinary citizens. They were devoted to significant, far-reaching causes like feeding the world's poor children and campaigning for human rights.

Colby and Damon offer some clues about how we might develop a high moral identity like the exemplars in their study. They note that some in their sample didn't take on their life's work until their forties and beyond. This suggests that our moral identities can continue to develop well beyond childhood. The researchers also found that working with others on important ethical tasks or projects fosters moral growth by exposing participants to different points of view and new moral issues. We, too, can benefit by collaborating with others on significant causes, such as eliminating sexual slavery, building affordable housing for seniors, or fighting malaria. The key is to view these tasks not as a burden but as an opportunity to act on what we believe. Adopting a joyful attitude will help us remain optimistic in the face of discouragement.

Other scholars suggest that elements of the situation can prime or activate our sense of moral identity.[40] Organizations can enhance the moral motivation of their members by creating climates where close, cooperative relationships can flourish, by providing opportunities for moral discussion and reflection, by continuously emphasizing values and mission, and by encouraging ongoing involvement in the local community.

Component 6: Drawing Upon Spiritual Resources

Spirituality can play a significant role in our personal moral development as well as in the ethical development of our organizations. As we noted above, faith provides the foundation for the moral identity of many moral exemplars. Investigators have also discovered a number of links between spiritual values and personal and organizational performance. They report that spirituality enhances the following qualities:[41]

Ethical sensitivity	Commitment to mission, core values, and ethical standards
Moral reasoning	
Altruism	Organizational learning and creativity
Job satisfaction	Morale
Job involvement and commitment	Collaboration
Job effort	Loyalty
Quality of life	Trust
Employee well-being	Willingness to mentor others
Sense of community	Social support
Meaningfulness of work	Productivity and profitability

Given the relationship between spirituality and personal and collective performance, it's not surprising that there has been a surge of interest in spirituality in the workplace among both academics and practitioners. According to one survey, of the nearly 1,600 articles dealing with spirituality published in social science journals between 1991 and 2008, approximately 80% appeared after the year 2000. Of the books published on the topic over the past two decades, nearly half were written during the latest five-year period.[42] Thousands of Bible study and prayer groups meet in corporate settings. Spiritual seekers can find business and spirituality courses at a number of colleges and universities or attend conferences and seminars devoted to the subject. Tom's of Maine, Herman Miller, TD Industries, Medtronic, Bank of Montreal, and Toro are just a few of the companies that base their organizational cultures on spiritual values.

Organizational spirituality encompasses a number of themes or threads (see Ethics in Action 2.2). Duchon and Plowman offer one definition of workplace spirituality as "the recognition that employees have an inner life that nourishes and is nourished by meaningful work that takes place in the context of community."[43] The *inner life* refers to the fact that employees have spiritual needs (their core identity and values) just as they have emotional, physical, and intellectual wants, and they bring the whole person to work. *Meaningful work* describes the fact that workers are generally motivated by more than material rewards. They want their labor to be fulfilling and to serve the needs of society. *Community* refers to the fact that organization members desire connection to others. A sense of belonging fosters the inner life. It should be noted that religion and spirituality overlap but are not identical. Religious institutions encourage and structure spiritual experiences, but spiritual encounters can occur outside formal religious channels.[44]

ETHICS IN ACTION 2.2 WORKPLACE SPIRITUALITY: DEFINITIONAL THREADS

Self-actualization; self-fulfillment; self-awareness; self-consciousness; self-discovery

Wholeness, holism; integration; integrity; authenticity; balance; harmony

Meaning; purpose

Emotion; passion; feeling

Life force; energy; vitality; life; intrinsic motivation

Wisdom; discernment; courage; creativity

Morality; values; peace; truth; freedom; justice

Interconnectedness; interdependence; interrelationship; cooperation; community; teamwork

SOURCE: From Hicks, D. A., *Religion and the workplace: Pluralism, spirituality and leadership.* Copyright © 2003. Reprinted with the permission of Cambridge University Press.

Caring for the Soul

Spiritual values need to be nurtured. Psychotherapist and best-selling author Thomas Moore uses the phrase "caring for the soul" to describe the ongoing process of cultivating the inner emotional and spiritual self.[45] In an organizational setting, Moore says you can feed your soul through the following:

Intimacy (closeness and connection). Organizations foster intimacy through encouraging friendship, repeating the history of a business to foster employee attachment, opening up contact between departments, storytelling, creating a sense of family, and being sensitive to the community.

Creative work. Creativity is a drive or impulse that needs to be supported by allowing people to work in their own ways and by accepting their failures. Even routine tasks are creative because they produce products and profits, further careers, and generate new organizational structures.

Nature and beauty. Refreshment comes through encounters with nature, whether in the form of landscaping, interior design, a park, or the countryside. Nature is a provider of what every soul must have—beauty. Unfortunately, by focusing on success, the modern organization sacrifices beauty for efficiency. Colors, textures, and sounds are essential to the soul but are often forgotten in the rush to build drab, inexpensive, and efficient buildings. Stopping to contemplate beauty is seen as a barrier to progress instead of as a vital way to nourish the soul.

Spirituality. The term *sacred need* not be reserved solely for personal beliefs. Work can be dedicated to higher purposes, as we've seen. In addition, business activity is sacred because it has a dramatic impact on the lives of individual workers, the community, and the economy as a whole. Corporations attuned to the soul recognize that making a profit can work in harmony with other important values like concern for the poor and the environment. These groups establish a strong business identity and earn the trust of outsiders. (We'll take an in-depth look at organizational citizenship in Chapter 12.)

The Stages of Spiritual Transformation

Workplace spirituality expert Margaret Benefiel offers a five-stage model of individual spiritual transformation, depicted in Figure 2.1. Her model—based on the teachings of such prominent spiritual leaders as Buddha, Jesus, the Sufi mystic Rumi, Moses, Teresa of Avila, and Zen master Thich Nhat Hanh—highlights the fact that spiritual development is an ongoing process or journey and that spiritual progress is likely to have its ups and downs.[46]

Awakening is the first stage of Benefiel's model. The spiritual journey is usually triggered by a sense of dissatisfaction (a sense of emptiness, for instance), and seekers initially experience abundance, feeling a greater sense of connection and fulfillment. In the second stage, *transition*, employees discover that spirituality is not just about receiving, it's about personal transformation. Their initial sense of abundance and connection dries up. At this point, they may feel as though spirituality was just a passing phase and might give up on such practices as meditation and prayer. If they persist, seekers then move to the *recovery* stage. Here, they discover new ways of connecting with God or larger forces, realizing that spirituality is not about getting but about giving. Seekers let go of personal concerns and adopt new ways of relating to God, relationships, work, and community.

The *dark night* stage is a period of discouragement, in which God seems far away, and spiritual growth appears to have stopped. To move beyond this stage, seekers must

Figure 2.1 Individual Spiritual Transformation

FIRST HALF OF THE JOURNEY

SECOND HALF OF THE JOURNEY

Stage I Awakening	Stage II Transition	Stage III Recovery	Stage IV Dark Night	Stage V Dawn
Become aware of spiritual reality	Spiritual practices not "working"	Discover new way of relating to ultimate reality (e.g. God)	Spiritual practices not yielding transformation	Spiritual practices move beyond role to feeling "given" and responsive
Adopt spiritual practices	Disaffection with spiritual practices	Adopt new spiritual practices	Deeper core questions emerge	Self gets relativized to higher good
Seek connections with others on spiritual quest	Sense of isolation	Connectedness with others on spiritual path	Sense of isolation	Sense of connectedness with the universe
	Confusion			
Awareness of sacredness and glimpse of everyday life	Question following spiritual path	Identify worth with personal transformation	Deeper blocks to progress are manifested	Sense of alignment with transcendent power
	Frustration	Renewed awareness of daily sacredness	"Deep abyss"	New ways of making meaning emerge
		Renewed joy	"Is this the end?"	
Fullness	Emptiness	Fullness	Emptiness	Fullness

SOURCE: From Benefiel, M. (2005). The second half of the journey: Spiritual leadership for organizational transformation. *The Leadership Quarterly*, p. 733.

decide to seek God or transcendence for God's sake, not for the sake of the self. *Dawn* is the final stage, in which seekers surrender their egos and focus on the higher or greater good. Benefiel notes that only a few individuals permanently inhabit this final state. Seekers may briefly enter it and slip back, though the more often they reach the fifth stage, the longer they are likely to dwell in it.

Professor Benefiel argues that entire organizations go through similar stages of spiritual development. Like individuals, groups can transform themselves and become highly sensitive to spiritual goals and values. However, groups can expect to experience the same periods of spiritual growth and frustration as their members do. Knowing these personal and collective developmental paths can help us chart our individual and organizational spiritual progress. This knowledge should encourage us to persist during spiritually "dry" periods and to recognize that spirituality ultimately is other-serving, not self-serving.

Dealing With the Dangers of Organizational Spirituality

Despite its benefits, there are reasons to be cautious about incorporating spirituality into the workplace.[47] First, there is a danger of proselytizing, as managers and entire companies try to convert workers to their particular religious or spiritual doctrines. This can lead to coercion, favoritism, and discrimination. Second, not all members will feel comfortable with incorporating spirituality into the workplace and may consider it a personal issue or an invasion of privacy. Others may sense a threat to their power and status. The third problem is the risk of using interest in spirituality as a management tool to manipulate employees or of treating spirituality as the latest management fad. Because spirituality appears to enhance productivity, it is tempting for leaders to focus on spiritual values not because they speak to inner needs but to motivate employees to work harder. The fourth problem is scholarly skepticism about the topic of workplace spirituality. As an emerging field, organizational spirituality lacks a strong theoretical and research base. Even defining spirituality is difficult, as Ethics in Action 2.2 demonstrated.

There are ways to address the potential dangers of bringing spiritual concerns into the workplace. These include (1) accommodating the spiritual requests of all employees from all religious traditions; (2) respecting the spiritual diversity of employees; (3) making openness and respect for diversity the center of organizational attention, allowing all employees the freedom to express their values and feelings; and (4) acknowledging and knowing the entire employee (emotional, intellectual, and spiritual), recognizing that members bring their hearts and souls to work along with their minds and bodies.

Component 7: Directing Change From the Inside Out

University of Michigan management professor Robert Quinn offers an organizational change model that integrates many of the components of personal development.[48] For that reason, his Advanced Change Theory is a fitting conclusion to this chapter. Quinn argues that system-wide change starts from inside the individual and then moves outward. He contrasts his from-the-inside-out approach with more traditional change strategies that rely on telling (rational persuasion) or on forcing others to comply. Trying to change others from the outside in is both unproductive and unethical. Those targeted for change frequently resist and become locked into their current behavior patterns. Change agents then assume that the problem lies with the change targets. Instead of examining their own motivations and behaviors, they blame their audiences and treat them as objects standing in the way of progress.

Instead of imposing their will, change agents must model the change process. For instance, parents faced with rebellious teenagers often try to bring their children into line with additional rules and sanctions. A better approach would be for parents to examine their own attitudes, making sure that their love is unconditional, not based on their children's performance. Individuals in the organizational setting can start social change movements through their actions. When even one member of an organization changes, the whole system is affected. To demonstrate this principle, begin to treat an enemy at work as a friend. He or she must take notice and decide how to respond. More often than not, this individual's behavior will become less hostile, and the atmosphere of the group as a whole will improve.

Quinn offers these principles or "seed thoughts" that can help you succeed in producing organizational transformation:

Envision the productive community. We all carry mental images of human relationships. Often, these images reinforce the traditional, top-down organizational hierarchy. Visions of productive communities, in contrast, include the notion that members are inner directed, focus on the needs of others, and look beyond their self-interests. Transformational change agents practice higher-level moral reasoning by asking, What is the right thing to do? and What result do I want? (see Chapter 3).

First look within. Transformational change agents look inward. They make a "fundamental choice" to be true to their own values and calling. This choice provides a touchstone to return to when facing challenges and decisions. Because authentic change agents understand themselves, they avoid knee-jerk reactions to events. They realize that they can choose their responses to organizational conditions.

Embrace the hypocritical self. The presence of the shadow side of the personality means that few of us live up to our personal standards on every occasion. We keep silent when we should speak up, lie when we advocate the truth, impose our will when we proclaim the importance of empowering others. When challenged about our integrity gap, we become defensive. We either deny that anything is wrong or blame others for our failures. Recognizing personal hypocrisy can be a source of transformational power because we can make a conscious choice to rewrite our scripts or narratives. If we align the ideal and actual self, we model authenticity. Authenticity, in turn, attracts colleagues to the change movement.

Transcend fear. Many personal behaviors and organizational systems are driven by fear. We fear failure, disapproval from our friends and colleagues, and not living up to expectations. Organizations built on these fears encourage conformity through top-down authority systems, rules and regulations, and punishment of dissent and deviance. Transcending our fears requires separating ourselves from how others define us. This is easier when we have identified our vocation. Understanding our purpose makes us more internally driven and provides us with a greater sense of power. We then become change leaders who take risks to speak out, challenging traditions and widely accepted "truths."

Embody a vision of the common good. The most effective change agents act as living symbols, personifying the values of productive communities. Gandhi, for example, backed up his call for sacrifice by simple living. He made his own clothes and had little money. Martin Luther King, Jr., dreamed of a country in which his children would be judged by their character, not their racial background. He lived out this value by courageously facing beatings, jailings, and ultimately death. As ordinary change agents at any level of the organization, we can follow their example. We can decide to choose the collective interest over personal interest, bring uncomfortable topics out into the open, and listen to others in order to create a shared organizational vision.

Disturb the system. Organizations and other living systems are maintained by negative feedback. Any action too far outside the norm is treated as a problem and then controlled through punishment or other means. Successful change agents disrupt the system to overcome negative feedback. They know when and how to introduce new ideas and procedures that break members out of their old mind-sets and behavioral patterns.

Surrender to the emergent process. Those in a transformational state try to live out their message and focus on being in the right state of mind or being in order to promote change. The most effective transformational change agents have "bold-stroke capacity." They understand the system so well that they can alter it with just a single statement, question, or action. Former Coca-Cola CEO Roberto Goizueta performed such a bold stroke in the 1980s. At that time, Coke was locked in a market-share battle with Pepsi and losing. Goizueta found that the average per capita daily consumption of fluids around the world was 64 ounces; the daily per capita consumption of Coke was less than 2 ounces. He then asked, "What's our market share of the stomach?" This question greatly enlarged Coca-Cola's market, shifting the focus from beating Pepsi to winning a larger share of the total global consumption of fluids. Goizueta's bold stroke helped transform Coca-Cola from a stagnant company into one of the stock market's top performers.[49]

Entice through moral power. Powerful change agents put a high value on both tasks and persons. They pursue excellence and at the same time build strong relationships with others. Such individuals "do things for their own sake." They set their own goals, find satisfaction in the task, and evaluate their performance according to their own standards. Those who find their rewards in their work exert more control over the quality of their lives. They aren't trapped by circumstances but control their attitudes, seeing even a lousy job as an opportunity for personal growth and learning. Effective change agents also offer emotional and practical support to others who join the transformational movement.

CHAPTER TAKEAWAYS

- You need to acknowledge your potential to do harm as well as good. The shadow side of your personality contains the parts of yourself that are embarrassing, socially unacceptable, or dangerous. To confront your shadow side, take personal responsibility for your actions, learn from those times when your behavior contradicts your self-image, and adjust your behavior and your environment to keep from unleashing shadow forces. You may also need to forgive yourself when you fall short of your ideals.
- Discovering your vocation means determining your purpose in life, which is based on a clear understanding of your unique skills, abilities, and desires. Following your vocation produces greater self-fulfillment, makes you a better steward, and equips you for more productive service to others. To hear your call, you'll need to set aside ambition, distractions, and resistance based on fears and low self-esteem.
- Moral values serve as guiding principles that drive behavior and help us determine right from wrong. Be sure your values take into account the needs of others and the organization as a whole. You can clarify your values by generating a list or rating a list of values. If your principles agree with those of your organization, you will experience a better fit, helping you feel more committed to the group and more satisfied with your job.
- High moral character will better enable you to make wise ethical choices. Direct approaches to character building include formal character education programs and psychological interventions designed to develop specific virtues. You can also foster the virtues that make up character though such indirect means as (a) developing moral habits, (b) observing and imitating ethical role models, (c) telling and living collective stories, and (d) learning from passage experiences.
- Moral identity motivates ethical behavior. Those with high moral identity define themselves in terms of their ethical beliefs and feel compelled to act on those commitments. You can foster your moral identity throughout your life. Work with others on important ethical projects and join organizations that heighten your awareness of your ethical values.
- Spirituality can play an important role in your moral development and that of your organization. Organizational spirituality recognizes the importance of inner needs, meaningful work, and community. Nourish your soul through intimacy (closeness and connection), exposure to nature and beauty, and recognition of the sacred nature of work. You and your organization can expect to experience highs and lows on the road to spiritual transformation, which is focused on the greater good.
- When addressing spirituality in the workplace, don't impose one particular set of spiritual values but respect and foster religious and spiritual diversity.
- Organizational change can operate from the inside out, starting with the individual and spreading outward. Begin the organizational transformation process by modeling the desired behaviors instead of imposing them on others. Remember that, even as one person, you can bring about systemwide change.

APPLICATION PROJECTS

1. Analyze the life of a fallen leader. Which elements of the shadow side of the personality contributed to this individual's downfall? What do you learn from this person's failure that you can apply in your own life? Write up your findings.

2. Use the steps outlined in the chapter to identify a job that fits your vocation. Identify distractions that might be keeping you from hearing your call. Determine how you might put these pressures and preoccupations aside.

3. With classmates, create a list of six to eight virtues that you think are most important in the workplace. Present your list and defend your choices to the rest of the class.

4. Complete the Self-Assessment and reflect on the findings. What does this instrument reveal about your values and those of your organization? How do your values impact your behavior at work? What values conflicts do you have with coworkers? How good is the match between your values and those of your employer?

5. What habits do you want to develop? How will you go about developing them?

6. Analyze a popular television show from an ethical perspective. Identify the issues raised by the program, the values it promotes, and the virtues and vices demonstrated by the important characters.

7. Identify some key passages in your life. What have you learned from these experiences?

8. Develop a case study based on someone you consider to be an outstanding moral example. How does this person demonstrate character and high moral identity? What factors contributed to this person's moral development? What do you learn from this person's example that can help you develop your character and moral identity?

9. Choose two strategies for nurturing your soul and implement them on a daily basis for two weeks. Note any changes in your attitudes and behavior.

10. Chart your spiritual progress or that of your organization. What stage are you (or your organization) currently in? Why do you think you are at this level? What can you do to progress further? Record your conclusions and share them with someone you trust.

11. Test the Advanced Change Theory by engaging in more positive behavior toward a friend, family member, coworker, or fellow student. How does this person respond? How does your relationship change or improve? Record the results of your experiment.

CASE STUDY 2.2

Heroism in the Twin Towers

In the terrorist attacks of September 11, 2001, 1 hour and 42 minutes elapsed between the crash of the first plane into the North Tower of the World Trade Center and its subsequent collapse. During that period, from 8:46 a.m. to 10:28 a.m., the South Tower was also destroyed. What went on inside the towers during those 102 minutes? To find out, *New York Times* reporters Jim Dwyer and Kevin Flynn interviewed hundreds of survivors and rescue workers and examined masses of phone, radio, and e-mail transcripts. They report that 12,000 people were able to evacuate largely because office workers behaved calmly and civilly, guided by volunteer fire wardens who helped them file out.

Dwyer and Flynn also uncovered many cases where individuals banded together to help others. For example, fire commander Orio Palmer and his colleagues ran up to the 78th floor of the South Tower (the impact zone) to organize survivors and rescue an elevator car filled with people who had been trapped for 45 minutes. The building collapsed shortly after they arrived. In the North Tower, a "committee of the willing—self-selected civilians and self-assigned uniformed rescuers" stationed themselves at the mezzanine level to direct people away from the plaza, where pieces of the building were raining down.[1] A group of firefighters and New York Port Authority police were able to drag an overweight man to safety moments before the tower disintegrated.

One particularly heroic group, led by manager Frank De Martini and coworker Pablo Ortiz, was made up of members of the Port Authority's construction team. Housed on the 88th floor of the North Tower, these individuals first scouted for unblocked stairways on their level, removed debris, and organized the evacuation of other Port Authority workers. Then they headed to other floors, using crowbars to break through drywall and open stairway doors to help victims escape. At the 102nd minute, they were rescuing workers on the 78th floor. The construction team is credited with saving the lives of 70 people.

Reporters Dwyer and Flynn point out that De Martini's team was charged with overseeing remodeling projects, not emergency operations. However, group members wasted no time in reaching out to others, sacrificing their lives so that others could live.

And below 92, across all or parts of 10 floors, dozens of people had been unable to open doors or walk through burning corridors to the stairs and find their way past the rubble. Then help appeared. With crowbars, flashlights, hard hats, and big mouths, De Martini and Ortiz and their colleagues pushed back the boundary line between life and death.[2]

Discussion Probes

1. Why do some people act heroically in emergencies while others do not?

2. What character traits did the rescuers demonstrate?

3. How can we prepare ourselves to respond effectively and ethically to crises?

4. Have you ever faced an emergency situation? How did you react?

5. What ethical insights do you draw from the stories of the heroes of 9/11?

Notes

1. Dwyer & Flynn (2005), p. 240.
2. Dwyer & Flynn (2005), p. 88.

Source

Dwyer, J., & Flynn, K. (2005). *102 Minutes: The untold story of the fight to survive inside the Twin Towers.* New York: Times Books.

CASE STUDY 2.3

A Breach of Integrity

The high-tech world was rocked when Hewlett-Packard CEO Mark Hurd was fired in 2010 for filing false expense reports to cover up his relationship with a female contractor. Hurd had a reputation as a careful, meticulous, plain-speaking executive who emphasized the importance of integrity in his personal and business dealings. Jonathon Schwartz, former chief executive of Sun Microsystems, summed up the reaction of most observers: "I am shocked and surprised," he said. "That is not the Mark Hurd I worked with."[1]

Hurd joined Hewlett-Packard in 2005. His low-key style was a welcome change from that of his predecessor, Carly Fiorina, who acted more like a rock star than a CEO. Using a mix of fiscal discipline, cost cutting, and acquisitions (EDS, Palm, and 3Com), Hurd helped Hewlett-Packard become the world's largest technology company. The firm's stock price doubled on his watch, and annual company revenues rose from $80 billion to $130 billion. He was in the process of negotiating a three-year, $100 million extension to his contract when Jodie Fisher, a former contact employee who hosted company events, filed a sexual harassment suit against Hurd. Fisher, a former soft-porn film actress and reality show contestant, settled the suit out of court. (Both Hurd and Fisher denied having a sexual relationship.)

In investigating the harassment charges, the HP board discovered that the chief executive had lied on expense reports to cover up the fact he billed the company for expensive dinners, first-class airline tickets, and luxury hotel rooms for Fisher at the same time that employees were required to travel cheaply. Hurd offered to reimburse the company, but board members worried about his lapse of judgment and the possible public relations nightmare that could result when word got out that the CEO had developed a close relationship with a former porn actress. For his part, Hurd admitted, "There were instances in which I did not live up to the standards and principles of trust, respect and integrity that I have espoused at HP."[2] HP's stock price dropped 10% after news of Hurd's departure became public, costing investors $10 billion. Hurd left HP with a $12.2 million severance package. Board members extended a deadline to allow him to exercise options on additional HP stock.

Corporate governance expert Nell Minnow said that HP had no choice but to fire Hurd, since companies doing business with the government are obligated to apply ethics policies uniformly. If a midlevel employee would have been fired for fudging expense reports, then HP "had no other option" but to fire the chief executive.[3] Nevertheless, some observers criticized the board for being far too generous. After all, if Hurd deserved to be let go, they wondered, then why reward him? Others criticized HP for firing Hurd for such a minor infraction. Larry Ellison, chief executive of Oracle, blasted the HP board for "the worst personnel decision since the idiots on the Apple board fired Steve Jobs many years ago."[4] Ellison then hired Hurd, a close friend, triggering a lawsuit by Hewlett Packard, which feared that Hurd would reveal corporate secrets to his new employer. Ellison claimed that the "vindictive" suit would make it hard for the two firms, which both cooperate and compete, to work together in the future. HP later withdrew the suit when Hurd agreed to forfeit his stock options, worth an estimated $14 million. The SEC is investigating to determine whether Hurd revealed any inside information to Fisher about pending acquisitions during their friendship and whether he destroyed information on his computer.

Hurd may not last that long in his new position. Oracle founder and CEO Larry Ellison is known for ousting executives who want to share the spotlight, which contributes to his reputation as a "first-class SOB" and "a modern-day Genghis Khan who has elevated ruthlessness in business to a carefully cultivated art form."[5] Unless he is careful, Hurd may soon find himself out of a job again.

Discussion Probes

1. Can Hurd ever regain his reputation for integrity? How?

2. Was Hewlett-Packard justified in firing Mark Hurd?

3. What messages did HP send by providing Hurd with a generous severance package? By later suing Hurd?

4. Would you have hired Mark Hurd to be the leader of your company? Why or why not?

5. What were the risks to Oracle of hiring Hurd? Of engaging in a public feud with HP?

6. How do you account for the success of Ellison and other business leaders who apparently have significant character flaws?

Notes

1. Vance, A. (2010, August 7). Hewlett-Packard ousts chief for hiding payments to friend. *The New York Times*, p. A1.

2. Vance.

3. Nocera, J. (2010, September 11). H.P.'s blundering board. *The New York Times*, p. B1.

4. A case of Hurd labour. (2010, September 11). *The Economist*, p. 75.

5. Mandleson, R. (2010, November 8). Why it pays to be a jerk. *Canadian Business*, pp. 28–34.

Sources

The curse of HP. (2010, August 14). *The Economist*, p. 54.

Evangelista, B. (2010, September 21). Oracle's Hurd cedes options, settling HP suit. *San Francisco Chronicle*, p. D1.

Vance, A. (2010, December 21). S.E.C. is investigating Hurd's departure as chief of H.P. *The New York Times*, p. B4.

ENDNOTES

1. Trevino, L. K., & Youngblood, S. A. (1990). Bad apples in bad barrels: A causal analysis of ethical decision-making behavior. *Journal of Applied Psychology, 75,* 378–385; Trevino, L. K. (1986). Ethical decision making in organizations: A person-situation interactionist model. *Academy of Management Review, 11,* 601–607.

2. Mattoon, M. A. (1981). *Jungian psychology in perspective.* New York: Free Press; Hall, C. S., & Nordby, V. J. (1973). *A primer of Jungian psychology.* New York: New American Library.

3. Storr, A. (1983). *The essential Jung.* Princeton, NJ: Princeton University Press, p. 89.

4. Miller, W. A. (1981). *Make friends with your shadow.* Minneapolis, MN: Augsburg; Johnson, R. A. (1993). *Owning your own shadow: Understanding the dark side of the psyche.* San Francisco: HarperSan Francisco.

   5. Blustein, J. (2007). Doctoring and self-forgiveness. In R. L. Walker & P. J. Ivanhoe (Eds.), *Working virtue: Virtue ethics and contemporary moral problems* (pp. 87–112). Oxford, UK: Clarendon; Holmgren, M. R. (1998). Self-forgiveness and responsible moral agency. *The Journal of Value Inquiry, 32,* 75–91; Snow, N. E. (2003). Self-forgiveness. *The Journal of Value Inquiry 27,* 75–80.

   6. Rayburn, C. A. (1997). Vocation as calling. In D. P. Bloch & L. J. Richmond (Eds.), *Connections between spirit and work in career development* (pp. 162–183). Palo Alto, CA: Davies-Black.

   7. Super, D. E. (1990). A life-span, life-space approach to career development. In D. Brown, L. Brooks, & Associates (Eds.), *Career choice and development: Applying contemporary theories to practice* (2nd ed.). San Francisco: Jossey-Bass; Gouws, D. J. (1995). The role concept in career development. In D. E. Super & B. Sverko (Eds.), *Life roles, values and careers: International findings of the Work Importance Study* (pp. 22–53). San Francisco: Jossey-Bass.

   8. Buechner, F. (1973). *Wishful thinking: A theological ABC.* New York: Harper & Row, p. 95.

   9. Hardy, L. (1990). *The fabric of this world: Inquiries into calling, career choice, and the design of human work.* Grand Rapids, MI: Eerdmans.

   10. Stairs, M., & Galpin, M. (2010). Positive engagement: From employee engagement to workplace happiness. In P. A. Linley, S. Harrington, & N. Garcea (Eds.), *Oxford handbook of positive psychology and work* (pp. 155–172). New York: Oxford University Press; Wrzesniewski, A., McCauley, C., Rozin, P., & Schwartz, B. (1997). Jobs, careers, and callings: People's relations to their work. *Journal of Research in Personality, 31,* 21–33.

   11. Mahan, B. J. (2002). *Forgetting ourselves on purpose: Vocation and the ethics of ambition.* San Francisco: Jossey-Bass.

   12. Levoy, G. (1997). *Callings: Finding and following an authentic life.* New York: Three Rivers Press.

   13. Schwartz, S. H., & Sagiv, L. (1995). Identifying culture-specifics in the content and structure of values. *Journal of Cross-Cultural Psychology, 26,* 92–116, p. 93.

   14. Argandona, A. (2003). Fostering values in organizations. *Journal of Business Ethics, 45,* 15–28.

   15. Schwartz, S. H. (1994). Are there universal aspects in the structure and contents of human values? *Journal of Social Issues, 50,* 19–45; Schwartz, S. H. (1994). Beyond individualism/collectivism: New cultural dimensions of values. In U. Kim, H. C. Triandis, C. Kagitcibasi, S. Choi, & G. Yoon (Eds.), *Individualism and collectivism: Theory, method and applications* (pp. 85–119). Thousand Oaks, CA: Sage; Bardi, A., & Schwartz, S. H. (2003). Values and behavior: Strength and structure of relations. *Journal of Personality and Social Psychology, 29,* 1207–1220.

   16. De Clercq, S., Fontaine, J. R. J., & Anseel, F. (2008). In search of a comprehensive value model for assessing supplementary person-organization fit. *The Journal of Psychology, 142*(3), 277–302; Kristof-Brown, A. L., Zimmerman, R. D., & Johnson, E. C. (2005). Consequences of individuals' fit at work: A meta-analysis of person-job, person-organization, person-group, and person-supervisor fit. *Personnel Psychology, 58,* 281–343; Kristof, A. L. (1996). Person-organization fit: An integrative review of its conceptualizations, measurement, and implications. *Personnel Psychology, 49*(1), 1–49; Posner, B. Z. (2010). Another look at the impact of personal and organizational values congruency. *Journal of Business Ethics, 97,* 535–541; Coldwell, D. A., Billsberry, J., van Meurs, N., & Marsh, P. J. G. (2008). The effects of person-organization ethical fit on employee attraction and retention: Towards a testable explanatory model. *Journal of Business Ethics, 78,* 611–622.

   17. See, for example: Cooper, T. L. (1992). Prologue: On virtue. In T. L. Cooper & N. D. Wright (Eds.), *Exemplary public administrators: Character and leadership in government* (pp. 1–8). San Francisco: Jossey-Bass; Devettere, R. J. (2002). *Introduction to virtue ethics: Insights of the ancient Greeks.* Washington, DC: Georgetown University Press; McKinnon, C. (1999). *Character, virtue theories, and the vices.* Peterborough, ON: Broadview Press; Statman, D. (1997). Introduction to virtue ethics. In D. Statman (Ed.), *Virtue ethics* (pp. 1–41). Washington, DC: Georgetown University Press.

18. Johannesen, R. L. (2002). *Ethics in human communication* (5th ed.). Prospect Heights, IL: Waveland Press.

19. Johannesen (2002), p. 11.

20. Hart, D. K. (1994). Administration and the ethics of virtue. In T. C. Cooper (Ed.), *The handbook of administrative ethics* (pp. 107–123). New York: Marcel Dekker.

21. Park, N., & Peterson, C. M. (2003). Virtues and organizations. In K. S. Cameron, J. E. Dutton, & R. E. Quinn (Eds.), *Positive organizational scholarship: Foundations of a new discipline* (pp. 33–47). San Francisco: Berrett-Koehler.

22. Peterson, C., Stephens, J. P., Park, N., Lee, F., & Seligman, M. E. P. (2010). Strengths of character and work. In P. A. Linley, S. Harrington, & N. Garcea (Eds.), *Oxford handbook of positive psychology and work* (pp. 221–231). Oxford, UK: Oxford University Press. Seligman, M. E. P. (2002). *Authentic happiness: Using the positive psychology to realize your potential for lasting fulfillment.* New York: Free Press.

23. Blasi, A. (2005). Moral character: A psychological approach. In D. K. Lapsley & F. C. Power (Eds.), *Character psychology and character education* (pp. 67–100). Notre Dame, IN: University of Notre Dame Press; Lapsley, D. K. (2008). Moral self-identity as the aim of education. In L. P. Nucci & D. Narvaez (Eds.), *Handbook of moral and character education* (pp. 30–52). New York: Routledge.

24. Lockwood, A. L. (2009). *The case for character education: A developmental approach.* New York: Teachers College Press; Salls, H. (2007). *Character education: Transforming values into virtue.* Lanham, MD: University Press of America; Damon, W. (Ed.). (2002). *Bringing in a new era in character education.* Stanford, CA: Hoover Institution Press.

25. Brandenberger, J. W. (2005). College, character, and social responsibility: Moral learning through experience. In D. K. Lapsley & F. C. Power (Eds.), *Character psychology and character education* (pp. 305–334). Notre Dame, IN: University of Notre Dame Press.

26. See, for example: Emmons, R. A., & McCullough, M. E. (2003). Counting blessings versus burdens: An experimental investigation of gratitude and subjective well-being in daily life. *Journal of Personality and Social Psychology 84*(2), 377–389; Morris, J. A., Brothridge, C. M., & Urbanski, J. C. (2005). Bringing humility to leadership: Antecedents and consequences of leader humility. *Human Relations, 58*(10), 1323–1350; Tangney, J. P. (2005). Humility. In C. R. Snyder & S. J. Lopez (Eds.), *Handbook of positive psychology* (pp. 411–419). Oxford, UK: Oxford University Press; Carver, C. S., & Scheier, M. F. (2005). Optimism. In C. R. Snyder & S. J. Lopez (Eds.), *Handbook of positive psychology* (pp. 231–243). Oxford, UK: Oxford University Press; Luthans, F., Youssef, C. M., & Avolio, B. J. (2006). *Psychological capital: Developing the human competitive edge.* Cary, NC: Oxford University Press; Burke, R. J., & Koyuncu, M. (2010). Developing virtues and virtuous behavior at workplace. *The IUP Journal of Soft Skills, IV*(3), 39–48.

27. Aristotle. (350 B.C.E./1962). *Nicomachean ethics* (Martin Ostwald, Trans.). Indianapolis, IN: Bobbs-Merrill, Book II, p. 1.

28. Sison, A. J. G. (2003). *The moral capital of leaders: Why virtue matters.* Northampton, MA: Edward Elgar.

29. Covey, S. R. (1989). *The seven habits of highly effective people.* New York: Simon & Schuster. See also: Covey, S. R. (2004). *The 8th habit: From effectiveness to greatness.* New York: Free Press.

30. Cooper, T. L., & Wright, N. D. (1992). *Exemplary public administrators: Character and leadership in government.* San Francisco: Jossey-Bass.

31. Hart, D. K. (1992). The moral exemplar in an organizational society. In T. L. Cooper & N. D. Wright (Eds.), *Exemplary public administrators: Character and leadership in government* (pp. 9–29). San Francisco: Jossey-Bass.

32. Kirkpatrick, W. K. (1992). Moral character: Story-telling and virtue. In R. T. Knowles & G. F. McLean (Eds.), *Psychological foundations of moral education and character development: An integrated theory of moral development* (pp. 169–184). Washington, DC: Council for Research in Values and Philosophy.

33. MacIntyre, A. (1984). *After virtue: A study in moral theory* (2nd ed.). Notre Dame, IN: University of Notre Dame Press, p. 216. See also: Hauerwas, S. (1981). *A community of character*. Notre Dame, IN: University of Notre Dame Press.

34. O'Connor, E. S. (1997). Compelling stories: Narrative and the production of the organizational self. In O. F. Williams (Ed.), *The moral imagination: How literature and films can stimulate ethical reflection in the business world* (pp. 185–202). Notre Dame, IN: University of Notre Dame Press.

35. Ellenwood, S. (2007). Revisiting character education: From McGuffey to narratives. *The Journal of Education, 187*(3), 21–43, pp. 22–23.

36. Dotlich, D. L., Noel, J. L., & Walker, N. (2004). *Leadership passages: The personal and professional transitions that make or break a leader*. San Francisco: Jossey-Bass. See also: Moxley, R. S. (2004). Hardships. In C. D. McCauley, R. S. Moxley, & E. Van Velsor (Eds.), *Handbook of leadership development* (2nd ed., pp. 183–204). San Francisco: Jossey-Bass; Bennis, W. G., & Thomas, R. J. (2002). *Geeks and geezers: How era, values and defining moments shape leaders*. Boston: Harvard Business School Press.

37. Hardy, S. A., & Carlo, G. (2005). Identity as a source of moral motivation. *Human Development, 48,* 232–256; Blasi (2005); Lapsley (2008).

38. Colby, A., & Damon, W. (1992). *Some do care: Contemporary lives of moral commitment*. New York: Free Press; Colby, A., & Damon, W. (1995). The development of extraordinary moral commitment. In M. Killen & D. Hart (Eds.), *Morality in everyday life: Developmental perspectives* (pp. 342–369). Cambridge, UK: Cambridge University Press.

39. Colby & Damon (1995), p. 364.

40. Shao, R., Aquino, K., & Freeman, D. (2008). Beyond moral reasoning: A review of moral identity research and its implications for business ethics. *Business Ethics Quarterly, 18*(4), 513–540; Reynolds, S. J., & Ceranic, T. L. (2007). The effects of moral judgment and moral identity on moral behavior: An empirical examination of the moral individual. *Journal of Applied Psychology, 92*(6), 1610–1624; Lapsley (2008).

41. Oswick, C. (2009). Burgeoning workplace spirituality? A textual analysis of momentum and directions. *Journal of Management, Spirituality & Religion, 6,* 15–25.

42. Information on the benefits of workplace spirituality is taken from the following:

Craigie, F. C. (1999). The spirit and work: Observations about spirituality and organizational life. *Journal of Psychology and Christianity, 18,* 43–53.

Fairholm, G. W. (1996). Spiritual leadership: Fulfilling whole-self needs at work. *Leadership & Organization Development Journal, 17*(5), 11–17.

Garcia-Zamor, J. C. (2003). Workplace spirituality and organizational performance. *Public Administration Review, 63,* 355–363.

Giacalone, R. A., & Jurkiewicz, C. L. (2003). Right from wrong: The influence of spirituality on perceptions of unethical business activities. *Journal of Business Ethics, 46,* 85–97.

Giacalone, R. A., & Jurkiewicz, C. L. (2003). Toward a science of workplace spirituality. In R. A. Giacalone & C. L. Jurkiewicz (Eds.), *Handbook of workplace spirituality and organizational performance* (pp. 3–28). Armonk, NY: M. E. Sharpe.

Jurkiewicz, C. L., & Giacalone, R. A. (2004). A values framework for measuring the impact of workplace spirituality on organizational performance. *Journal of Business Ethics, 49,* 129–142.

Karakas, F. (2009). Spirituality and performance in organizations: A literature review. *Journal of Business Ethics, 94,* 89–106.

Mirvis, P. H. (1997). "Soul work" in organizations. *Organization Science, 8,* 193–206.

Rego, A., & Pina e Cunha, M. (2008). Workplace spirituality and organizational commitment: An empirical study. *Journal of Organizational Change Management, 21*(1), 53–75.

43. Ashmos, D. P., & Duchon, D. (2000). Spirituality at work: A conceptualization and measure. *Journal of Management Inquiry, 9,* 134–145, p. 137. See also Duchon, D., & Plowman, D. A. (2005). Nurturing the spirit at work: Impact on work unit performance. *Leadership Quarterly, 16,* 807–833.

44. Zinnbauer, B. J., & Pargament, K. I. (2005). Religiousness and spirituality. In R. F. Paloutzian & C. L. Park (Eds.), *Handbook of the psychology of religion and spirituality* (pp. 21–42). New York: Guilford.

45. Moore, T. (1995). Caring for the soul in business. In B. Defoore & J. Renesch (Eds.), *Rediscovering the soul of business: A renaissance of values* (pp. 341–356). San Francisco: Sterling & Stone. See also: Moore, T. (1992). *Care of the soul: A guide to cultivating depth and sacredness in everyday life.* New York: HarperCollins.

46. Benefiel, M. (2005). *Soul at work: Spiritual leadership in organizations.* New York: Seabury Books; Benefiel, M. (2005). The second half of the journey: Spiritual leadership for organizational transformation. *Leadership Quarterly, 16,* 723–747.

47. Karakas, F. (2009).

48. Quinn, R. E. (2000). *Change the world: How ordinary people can achieve extraordinary results.* San Francisco: Jossey-Bass. See also: Quinn, R. E. (1996). *Deep change.* San Francisco: Jossey-Bass.

49. Charan, R., & Tichy, N. (1988). *Every business is a growth business: How your company can prosper year after year.* New York: Random House.

3

Ethical Decision Making and Action

In making and implementing decisions, we put into practice widely accepted ethical principles, as well our vocation, values, character, and spiritual resources. This chapter focuses both on the how (the processes) and the how-to (the formats) of moral thinking and action. Our chances of coming up with a sound, well-reasoned conclusion and executing our plan are greater if we understand how ethical decisions are made and take a morally grounded, systematic approach to problem solving.

Components of Ethical Behavior

Breaking the process down into its component parts enhances understanding of ethical decision-making and behavior. Moral psychologist James Rest identifies four elements of ethical action. Rest developed his four-component model by asking, "What must happen psychologically in order for moral behavior to take place?" He concluded that ethical action is the product of these psychological subprocesses: (1) moral sensitivity (recognition); (2) moral judgment or reasoning; (3) moral motivation; and (4) moral character.[1] The first half of the chapter is organized around Rest's framework. I'll describe each factor and then offer some tips for improving your performance on that element of Rest's model.

Component 1: Moral Sensitivity (Recognition)

Moral sensitivity is the recognition that an ethical problem exists. Such recognition requires us to be aware of how our behavior impacts others, to identify possible courses of action, and to determine the consequences of each potential strategy. Moral sensitivity is key to practicing individual ethics. We can't solve a moral dilemma unless we know that one is present.

Empathy and perspective skills are essential to identifying and exploring moral issues. Understanding how others might feel or react can alert us to the potential negative effects of our choices and makes it easier to predict the likely outcomes of various options. For example, the central figure in the first scenario of Case Study 3.2, "Is It Better to Ask Permission or to Ask Forgiveness?" empathizes with neighborhood residents and understands their point of view. As a result, he realizes that he faces an ethical problem.

According to University of Virginia ethics professor Patricia Werhane, many smart, well-meaning managers stumble because they are victims of tunnel vision.[2] Their ways of thinking or mental models don't include important ethical considerations. In other words, they lack moral imagination. Take the case of the Nestlé Company. The European food producer makes a very high-quality infant formula, which the firm successfully marketed in North America, Europe, and Asia. It seemed to make sense for the company to market the formula in East Africa using the same communication strategies that had worked elsewhere. However, Nestlé officials failed to take into account important cultural differences. Many East African mothers could not read label directions, were so poor that to make the product last longer they over-diluted it, and used polluted water to mix it. In a society that honors medicine men, parents felt pressured to use the formula because it was advertised with pictures of men in white coats. As a result, many poor African mothers wasted money on formula when they could have breast-fed their children for free. Thousands of their babies died after drinking formula mixed with polluted water. Nestlé refused to stop its marketing campaign despite pressure from the World Health Organization and only quit when faced with a major boycott. Company leaders didn't consider the possible dangers of marketing to third-world mothers and failed to recognize that they were engaged in unethical activities.

To exercise moral imagination, managers and employees step outside their current frame of reference (disengage themselves) to assess a situation and evaluate options. They then generate creative solutions. Werhane uses Chicago's South Shore Bank as an example of moral imagination at work. In the early 1970s, a group of investors bought a failing bank in the impoverished South Shore neighborhood and began loaning money for residential restoration. Few people in the area qualified for traditional bank loans, so South Shore managers developed a new set of criteria. Loan officers gave credit to individuals of limited means who had good reputations. The bank prospered and, at the same time, the neighborhood became a desirable place to live. South Shore's morally imaginative owners and managers envisioned a profitable financial institution in a depressed, poverty stricken area. They disproved traditional "bank logic" by demonstrating that they could make money in a responsible manner under tough conditions.

Moral muteness, like lack of moral imagination, interferes with the recognition of moral issues. Managers can be reluctant to talk about their actions in ethical terms. They may want to avoid controversy or may believe that keeping silent will help them appear practical, efficient, powerful, and capable of handling their own problems.[3] Describing a situation in moral terms breaks this ethical code of silence. Such terms as *values, justice, immoral, character, right,* and *wrong* encourage listeners to frame an event as an ethical problem and to engage in moral reasoning.[4]

A number of researchers believe that elements of the ethical issue itself are key to whether on not we recognize its existence. They argue that problems or dilemmas differ in their degree of *moral intensity.* The greater an issue's moral intensity, the more likely we are to notice it. The components of moral intensity include the following six elements:[5]

1. *Magnitude of consequences.* The moral intensity of an issue is directly tied to the number of harms or benefits it generates. Moral dilemmas attract more attention when they have significant consequences. For example, denying someone a job because of his or her race raises significant ethical concerns; rescheduling an employee's vacation dates does not. A massive oil spill generates stronger condemnation than a minor one.

2. *Social consensus.* Moral issues are more intense if there is widespread agreement that they are bad (or good). Societal norms, laws, professional standards, and corporate regulations all signal that there is social consensus on a particular issue.

3. *Probability of effect.* Probability of effect is "a joint function of the probability that the act in question will actually take place and the act in question will actually cause the harm (benefit) predicted."[6] For example, selling a gun to an armed robber has a much greater likelihood of causing harm than does selling a gun to a law-abiding citizen.

4. *Temporal immediacy.* Issues are more intense if they are likely to generate harm or good sooner rather than later. That helps explain why proposals to immediately reduce social security benefits attract more attention than proposals to gradually reduce them over a long period of time.

5. *Proximity.* Proximity refers to social, cultural, psychological, or physical distance. We tend to care more about issues involving people who are close to us in terms

of race, nationality, age, and other factors; we care less about issues involving people who are significantly distant from us or significantly different from us.

6. *Concentration of effect.* Causing intense suffering violates our sense of justice and increases moral intensity. Thus, we are more likely to take note of policies that do severe damage to a few individuals than to take note of those that have minor consequences for large groups of people. For instance, cutting the salaries of 10 people by $20,000 each is seen as more problematic than reducing the salaries of 4,000 employees by $50 each.

Moral intensity has been correlated not only with moral sensitivity but also with the other components of Rest's model—moral judgment, moral motivation, and moral behavior.[7] Not only are decision makers more likely to recognize morally intense issues, but they also respond more quickly and appropriately. In addition, decision makers faced with intense issues are more motivated to follow through on their choices. However, investigators are still trying to determine if some components of moral intensity are more critical to problem recognition and resolution. At this point, magnitude of consequences and social consensus appear to have the strongest relationship to moral sensitivity. Individuals are most likely to notice ethical dilemmas if they generate significant harm and if there is widespread agreement that these issues have a moral dimension.

Tips for Enhancing Your Ethical Sensitivity

Engage in active listening and role-playing. The best way to learn about the potential ethical consequences of choices, as well as the likely response of others, is through listening closely to what others have to say. (See Chapter 4 for a closer look at the process of active listening.) Role-play can also foster understanding. Taking the part of another individual or group can provide you with important insight into how the other party is likely to react.

Challenge mental models or schemas. Recognize the dangers of your current mental models, and try to visualize other perspectives. Distance yourself from a situation to determine if it indeed does have moral implications. Remember that you have ethical duties that extend beyond your group or organization.

Be creative. Look for innovative ways to define and respond to ethical dilemmas; visualize creative opportunities and solutions.

Speak up. Don't hesitate to discuss problems and your decisions in ethical terms. Doing so will help frame arguments as ethical ones for you and your colleagues.

Crank up the moral intensity. Frame issues to increase their intensity and thus improve problem recognition. In particular, emphasize the size of the problem—how many people are affected, how much the company or environment will be damaged. Point out how even small acts like petty theft can have serious consequences. Also, highlight the fact that there is consensus about whether a course of action is wrong (illegal, against professional standards, opposed by coworkers) or right. As a group, develop shared understanding about the key ethical issues facing your organization.

Component 2: Moral Judgment

After determining that there is an ethical problem, decision makers then choose among the courses of action identified in Component 1. They make judgments about the right or wrong thing to do in this specific context.

Moral judgment has been studied more than any other element of the Rest model. There is far too much information to summarize it here. Instead, I'll focus on three topics that are particularly important to understanding how problem solvers determine whether a solution is right or wrong: cognitive moral development, unhealthy motivations, and cognitive biases.

Cognitive Moral Development

Before his death, Harvard psychologist Lawrence Kohlberg was the leading champion of the idea that individuals progress through a series of moral stages just as they do physical ones.[8] Each stage is more advanced than the one before. As individuals develop, their reasoning becomes more sophisticated. They become less self-centered and develop broader definitions of morality (see Ethics in Action 3.1).

ETHICS IN ACTION 3.1 STAGES OF MORAL DEVELOPMENT

Level and Stage	Content of Stage	
	What Is Right	Reasons for Doing Right
LEVEL 1: PRECONVENTIONAL		
Stage 1: Heteronomous Morality	To avoid breaking rules backed by punishment, obedience for its own sake, and to avoid physical damage to persons and property.	Avoidance of punishment; the superior power of authorities.
Stage 2: Individualism, Instrumental Purpose, and Exchange	Following rules only when it is in your immediate interest; acting for your own interests and needs and letting others do the same. Right is also what's fair, what's an equal exchange, a deal, an agreement.	To serve your own needs or interests in a world where you have to recognize that other people have their interests, too.

(Continued)

(Continued)

Level and Stage	Content of Stage	
	What Is Right	Reasons for Doing Right
LEVEL II: CONVENTIONAL		
Stage 3: Mutual Interpersonal Expectations, Relationships, and Interpersonal Conformity	Living up to what is expected by people close to you or what people generally expect of people in your role as son, brother, friend, etc. "Being good" is important and means having good motives, showing concern about others. It also means keeping mutual relationships with trust, loyalty, respect, and gratitude.	The need to be a good person in your own eyes and those of others. Your caring for others. Belief in the Golden Rule. A desire to maintain rules and authority that support stereotypical good behavior.
Stage 4: Social System and Conscience	Fulfilling the actual duties to which you have agreed. Laws are to be upheld except in extreme cases where they conflict with other fixed social duties. Right is also contributing to society, the group, or institution.	To keep the institution going as a whole, to avoid a breakdown in the system, or to fulfill a sense of personal obligation.
LEVEL III: POSTCONVENTIONAL, PRINCIPLED		
Stage 5: Social Contract or Utility and Individual Rights	Being aware that people hold a variety of values and opinions, that most values and rules are relative to your group. These relative rules should usually be upheld, in the interest of impartiality and because they are the social contract. Some nonrelative values and rights like *life* and *liberty* must be upheld in any society and regardless of majority opinion.	A sense of obligation to law because of one's social contract to make and abide by laws for the welfare of all and for the protection of all people's rights. A feeling of contractual commitment, freely entered upon, to family, friendship, trust, and work obligations. Concern that laws and duties be based on rational calculation of overall utility, "the greatest good for the greatest number."
Stage 6: Universal Ethical Principles	Following self-chosen ethical principles. Particular laws or social agreements are usually valid because they rest on such principles. When laws violate these principles, one acts in accordance with the principle. Principles are universal principles of justice: the equality of human rights and respect for the dignity of human beings as individual persons.	The belief as a rational person in the validity of universal moral principles, and a sense of personal commitment to them.

SOURCE: Kohlberg, L. A. (1986). A current statement on some theoretical issues. In S. Modgil & C. Modgil (Eds.), *Lawrence Kohlberg: Consensus and controversy* (pp. 485–546). Philadelphia: Falmer Press, pp. 488–489.

Pre-conventional thinking is the most primitive stage and is common among children. Individuals at Level I decide on the basis of direct consequences. In the first stage, they obey to avoid punishment. In the second, they follow the rules in order to meet their own interests. Stage 2 thinkers believe that justice is giving a fair deal to others: You help me and I'll help you.

Conventional (Level II) thinkers look to other people for guidance for their actions. They strive to live up to the expectations of family members and significant others (Stage 3) or recognize the importance of going along with the laws of society (Stage 4). Kohlberg found that most adults fall into Stages 3 and 4, which suggests that the typical organizational member looks to work rules, leaders, and the situation to determine right from wrong.

Postconventional or principled (Level III) thinking is the most advanced type of reasoning and relies on universal values and principles. Stage 5 individuals are guided by Utilitarian principles, seeking to do the greatest good for the greatest number. They recognize that there are a number of value systems within a democratic society and that regulations may have to be broken to serve higher moral purposes. Stage 6 thinkers operate according to internalized, universal ethical principles like the categorical imperative or justice as fairness. These principles apply in every situation and take precedence over the laws of any particular society. According to Kohlberg, only about 20% of Americans can be classified as Stage 5 postconventional moral thinkers. Very few individuals ever reach Stage 6.

Kohlberg's model has drawn heavy criticism from philosophers and psychologists alike.[9] Some philosophers complain that it draws too heavily from Rawls's theory of justice and makes deontological ethics superior to other ethical perspectives. They note that the theory applies more to societal issues than to individual ethical decisions. A number of psychologists have challenged the notion that people go through a rigid or "hard" series of moral stages. They argue instead that individuals can engage in many ways of thinking about a problem, regardless of their age.

Rest (who was a student of Kohlberg's) responded to these criticisms by replacing the hard stages with a staircase of developmental schemas. *Schemas* are general structures or patterns in our memories. We use these patterns or structures when we encounter new situations or information. When you enrolled in college, for example, you probably relied on high school experiences to determine how to act in the university classroom. Rest and his colleagues contend that decision makers shift upward, adopting more sophisticated moral schemas as they develop. Rest's group redefined the postconventional stage to make it less dependent on one ethical perspective. In their "neo-Kohlbergian" approach, the most advanced thinkers reason like moral philosophers.[10] Postconventional individuals look behind societal rules to determine if they serve moral purposes. These thinkers appeal to a shared vision of an ideal society. Such a society seeks the greatest good for the entire community and assures rights and protections for everyone.

Rest developed the Defining Issues Test (DIT) to measure moral development. Subjects taking the DIT respond to six scenarios and then choose statements that best reflect how they went about making their choices. The statements (which correspond to the levels of moral development) are then scored. In the best-known dilemma,

Heinz's wife is dying of cancer and needs a drug Heinz cannot afford to buy. He must decide whether or not to steal the drug to save her life.

Over 800 studies have been conducted using the DIT.[11] Among the findings:

- Moral reasoning ability generally increases with age.
- The total college experience, both inside and outside the classroom, increases moral judgment.[12]
- Those who love learning, taking risks, and meeting challenges generally experience the greatest moral growth while in college.
- Ethics coursework boosts the positive effects of the college experience, increasing moral judgment still further.
- Older students (those in graduate and professional school) gain a great deal from moral education programs.
- When education stops, moral development plateaus.
- Moral development is a universal concept, crossing cultural boundaries.
- There are no consistent differences between the moral reasoning of men and that of women.
- Principled leaders can improve the moral judgment of the group as a whole, encouraging members to adopt more sophisticated ethical schemas.

Destructive Motivations

No discussion of moral judgment is complete without consideration of why this process so often breaks down. Time after time, very bright people make very stupid decisions. Former President Bill Clinton illustrates this sad fact. By all accounts, Clinton was one of the country's brightest leaders. Not only was he a Rhodes scholar with a nearly photographic memory, but his former advisor, David Gergen, reports that Clinton could hold conversations with aides and visitors while completing the *New York Times* crossword puzzle.[13] Somehow, the former chief executive thought he could have sex with an intern and keep the affair quiet despite constant media scrutiny. Further, he didn't think he would suffer any serious consequences if word got out. He was wrong on both counts.[14]

The moral stupidity of otherwise intelligent people can be explained in part by the power of their destructive motivations. Three motivating factors are particularly damaging: insecurities, greed, and ego.

1. *Insecurities.* As we saw in the last chapter, low self-esteem and inner doubts can drive individuals to use others to meet their own needs, and insecure people fall into the trap of tying their identities to their roles. Those plagued by self-doubt are blind to larger ethical considerations and, at the same time, they are tempted to succeed at any cost.

2. *Greed.* Greed is more likely than ever to undermine ethical thinking because we live in a winner-take-all society.[15] The market economy benefits the few at the expense of the many. Professional sports are a case in point. Superstars like Kobe Bryant and LeBron James account for the vast majority of the payroll, while others sit on the bench making league minimums. Or consider the inequity of the salary structure at the Banana Republic clothing chain. The average employee at a Banana Republic store makes near minimum wage with no health benefits. Store managers do better, receiving

an adequate salary and benefits. Professionals working at the headquarters of Gap Inc. (the parent of Banana Republic) make several times the wages of local managers. Those at the top earn a fortune. Former CEO Millard Drexler engineered a $25 million pay raise in one year and left the company with $500 million.

A winner-take-all culture encourages widespread cheating because the payoff is so high. In addition, losers justify their dishonesty by pointing to the injustice of the system and to the fact that they deserve a larger share of the benefits. When greed takes over, altruism disappears, along with any consideration of serving the greater good.

3. *Ego.* Even the most humble of us tend to greatly overestimate our abilities (more on this shortly).[16] Unless we are careful, we can become overconfident, ignore the risks and consequences of our choices, take too much credit when things go well and too little blame when they don't, and demand more than our fair share of organizational resources. Inflated egos become a bigger problem at higher levels of the organizational hierarchy. Top managers are often cut off from customers and employees. Unlike the rest of us, they don't have to wait in line for products or services or for a ride to work. Subordinates tell them what they want to hear and stroke their egos. All these factors make it easier for executives to excuse their unethical behavior (outrageous pay packages, diversion of company funds to private use) on the grounds that they are vital to the organization's success. (The Self-Assessment provides some questions to help keep your ego in check.)

The formidable forces of insecurity, greed, and ego become even more powerful when managers and subordinates adopt a short-term orientation. Modern workers are under constant time pressures as organizations cut staffing levels while demanding higher performance in the form of shorter product development cycles, better customer service, and greater returns on investment. Employees are sorely tempted to do what is expedient instead of what is ethical. As ethics expert Laura Nash puts it, "Short-term pressures can silence moral reasoning by simply giving it no space. The tighter a manager's agenda is, the less time for contemplating complex, time-consuming, unpragmatic issues like ethics."[17]

Time-pressed managers lose sight of the overall purpose of the organization and fail to analyze past conduct. They don't stop to reflect on their choices when things are going well. Overconfident, rushed decision makers are only too willing to move on to the next problem. Eventually, they begin to make mistakes that catch up with them. In addition, short-term thinkers begin to look for immediate gratification, which feeds their greedy impulses.

The damage caused by rushing to judgment can be seen in the results of a study by Ohio State professor Paul Nutt.[18] Professor Nutt examined 400 poor organizational decisions over a period of 20 years, including construction of Euro Disney, Ford's failure to recall the Pinto, and NASA's decision to launch the Challenger space shuttle. Adopting a short-term perspective helps to account for many of the decision-making blunders he uncovered. Nearsighted decision makers (a) overlooked important ethical questions, (b) came to premature conclusions, (c) failed to consult with important stakeholders, (d) lacked a clear direction, (e) limited their search for information, (f) demonstrated little creativity, and (g) learned little from either their successes or their failures.

SELF-ASSESSMENT

Ego-Busting Questions

Apply the following questions to an important ethical decision you face. After you have answered these queries, summarize what this exercise tells you about the soundness of your moral reasoning.

- What is my intention?
- Have I invited and tolerated dissent?
- Have I rubbed elbows with subordinates? (With peers?)
- What have I omitted from my analysis?
- What if I get caught?
- Have I listened to other opinions? Can I tolerate hearing them directly, or only filtered through company communication channels?
- Did I address the facts? Precisely what value am I creating?
- At whose expense am I creating value?
- Have I articulated factual information in as objective and impartial a way as possible?
- Are my decisions or behavior having a negative impact on the relationships involved?
- Am I rewarding ego-dominant, relationship-destroying attitudes in others?
- Have I laughed at myself recently?

SOURCE: Nash, L. 1990, *Good intentions aside: A manager's guide to resolving ethical problems.* Boston: Harvard Business School Press, p. 212. Used by permission.

Cognitive Biases

Harvard professor Max Bazerman and his colleagues believe that unethical choices are more often the product of perceptual and cognitive biases than of unhealthy motivations. These unconscious distortions cause us to participate in or approve of "ordinary unethical behaviors" that we would normally condemn.[19] Examples of common biases include the following:

1. *Overestimating our ethicality.* When it comes to ethics, the majority of us have a "holier than thou" attitude.[20] We believe that we are more caring, loyal, fair, and kind than the typical person and are quick to condemn others for their moral failings. In addition, we predict that we will behave more ethically in the future than we actually do and believe that we have behaved more ethically in the past than we actually have.

2. *Forgiving our own unethical behavior.* We want to be moral and to behave ethically. So, when we behave in an unethical fashion, we feel a sense a sense of psychological tension, called *cognitive dissonance,* because our actions and self-images don't match. To relieve this distress, we either change our behavior or use a variety of tactics to excuse what we've done. One minimizing strategy is *moral disengagement.* In moral disengagement, organizational members convince themselves that their

questionable behavior was really morally permissible because (a) it served a worthy purpose; (b) it was driven by outside forces ("My boss told me I had to it."); (c) it did not have any damaging consequences; or (d) the victims had it coming (dehumanizing them).[21] Another strategy is *motivated forgetting.* We have selective recall, remembering events in a way that supports our decisions. In particular, we forget that we have violated moral rules. Permissive work environments (those that excuse immoral behavior) encourage moral disengagement and moral forgetting. However, reminding employees that ethical choices are important reduces the use of both tactics.[22]

3. *Overlooking other people's unethical behavior.* As noted above, we generally judge others more harshly than ourselves. But not always. There are times when we excuse others' unethical behavior.[23] We are tempted to forgive the ethical shortcomings of others when we benefit from their choices. Auditors at Arthur Andersen, for example, were motivated to overlook the accounting irregularities of Enron, WorldCom, Tyco, and other clients because they were earning consulting fees from those same groups. By the same token, we excuse the unsavory recruiting methods of the coach of our favorite basketball team if he or she has a winning record.

Observers are less likely to hold people and organizations accountable if they delegate unethical behavior, as in the case of a manager who avoids blame by assigning a project and then declaring that employees should complete it "by any means possible." Merck used an indirect approach to shift blame when it sold the cancer drug Mustagen to another pharmaceutical company. The smaller firm raised the price of the medication tenfold. While Merck kept manufacturing the product, it deflected public criticism toward the other company. Gradual changes also encourage observers to ignore unethical behavior. We are less likely to notice declines in moral standards if they occur slowly over time; this is referred to as the *slippery slope.* Overlooking minor infractions like taking change from the cash register can lead to ignoring more serious offenses like stealing equipment.

4. *Implicit prejudice.* Implicit prejudice is different from conscious forms of prejudice like racism and sexism. This type of bias comes from our tendency to associate things that generally go together, like gray hair and old age or pick-up trucks and blue-collar workers.[24] These associations are not always accurate (some young people go gray, and some blue-collar workers drive luxury cars). When it comes to personnel decisions, false associations discriminate against marginalized groups. For instance, those who hold unconscious gender stereotypes are less likely to hire women who demonstrate stereotypical "masculine" traits like independence or ambition for jobs requiring interpersonal skills and other stereotypical "feminine" qualities.

5. *Favoring members of our own group.* It's only natural to do favors for people we know who generally come from the same nationality, social class, religion, neighborhood, or alma mater as we do. We may ask the chair of the business department to meet with the daughter of a neighbor or recommend a fraternity brother for a job. Trouble is, when those in power give resources to members of their in-groups, they discriminate against those who are different from them.[25] A number of universities reserve admissions slots for the sons and daughters of alumni, for instance. Since Caucasians make up

the vast majority of college graduates at most schools, White applicants may be selected over more qualified minority students who are not the children of graduates.

6. *Judging based on outcomes rather than on the decision-making processes.* Employees are typically evaluated based on results, not on the quality of the decisions they make.[26] We determine that a choice is good if it turns out well, and bad if it generates negative consequences. However, just because a poorly made decision had a desirable outcome in one case doesn't mean that a similar decision won't turn out badly in the future. In fact, poor decision-making processes eventually produce bad (ineffective, unethical) results. Take the case of Arthur Andersen described earlier. The questionable practice of mixing auditing and consulting functions was accepted for years because it generated positive results—profits for Arthur Andersen and valuable advice for clients. Nevertheless, this arrangement eventually led to disaster as the firm's auditors lost their independence and signed off on faulty financial statements. (For a closer look at the importance of independence to financial professionals, see Chapter 11.)

Tips for Improving Your Moral Judgment

Stay in school. The general college experience (including extracurricular activities) contributes greatly to moral development. However, you'll gain more if you have the right attitude. Focus on learning, not grades; be ready to take on new challenges.

Be intentional. While the general college experience contributes to moral development, focused attention on ethics also helps. Take ethics courses and units, discuss ethical issues in a group, reflect on the ethical challenges you experience in internships.

Reject ethical pessimism. Ethical values and thought patterns are not set in childhood, as pessimists claim, but continue to grow and develop through college and graduate school and beyond.

Take a broader view. Try to consider the needs and positions of others outside your immediate group; determine what is good for the community as a whole.

Look to underlying moral principles. Since the best ethical thinkers base their choices on widely accepted ethical guidelines, do the same. Draw upon important ethical approaches like utilitarianism, the categorical imperative, and justice as fairness for guidance.

Acknowledge your dark side. Before coming to a conclusion, try to determine if your decision is shaped by feelings of self-doubt and self-interest as well as your need to feed your ego. If so, then reconsider.

Step outside yourself. We can't help but see the world through our own selfish biases. However, we have a responsibility to check our perceptions against reality. Consult with others before making a choice, consider the likely perspective of other parties (refer back to our earlier discussion of role-taking), and double-check your assumptions and information.

Keep your ego in check. Stay close to those who will tell you the truth and hold you accountable. At the same time, don't punish those who point out your deficiencies. Use the questions in the Self-Assessment as tools for breaking the ego barrier.

Take a long-term perspective. In an emergency (when lives are immediately at stake, for example), you may be forced to make a quick decision. In all other situations, provide space for ethical reflection and deliberation. Resist the temptation to grab onto the first solution. Take time to consult with others, gather the necessary data, probe for underlying causes, and set a clear direction. Adopting a long-term perspective also means putting future benefits above immediate needs. In most cases, the organization and its clients and consumers are better served by emphasizing enduring relationships. You may make an immediate profit by selling low-quality products, but customers will be hurt and refuse to buy again, lowering corporate performance.

Apply rational remedies to overcome your cognitive biases. Use the conscious strategies outlined in Ethics in Action 3.2 to avoid the traps posed by your unconscious biases.

ETHICS IN ACTION 3.2 RATIONAL REMEDIES FOR COGNITIVE BIASES

Don't overestimate your ethical abilities.

Prepare ahead of time (imagine how you will respond to questions, for example) so that you don't engage in unethical behavior under pressure.

Publicly commit to an ethical course of action, or make such a commitment to someone who is important to you. (This increases the likelihood that you will follow through on your choices.)

Recognize and resist your tendency to excuse your immoral actions.

Create organizational climates that punish unethical behavior.

Remind yourself and others of the importance of acting ethically (e.g., have students sign honor codes; post regulations and corporate values statements).

Don't be lenient toward others because you are benefiting from their unethical behavior.

Don't try to shift blame by delegating to others or excuse groups and individuals that take this approach.

Don't ignore even minor ethical infractions, which can lead to much more serious transgressions.

Put yourself in environments that challenge your implicit biases or stereotypes.

Audit your organization to determine if it is trapped by in-group biases; eliminate initiatives that perpetuate the tendency to admit, hire, and promote those of similar backgrounds. For example: alumni children admission programs, rewards for employees who recommend people they know for jobs at the organization.

Generate more equitable choices by pretending that you don't know what group you belong to when making decisions and by imagining how a policy change will impact different groups.

Evaluate the quality of the decision-making process, not the outcome; don't condemn those who make good-quality decisions only to see them turn out badly.

Component 3: Moral Motivation

After reaching a conclusion about the best course of action, decision makers must be motivated to follow through on their choices. Moral values often conflict with other important values like job security, career advancement, social acceptance, and wealth. Ethical behavior will only result if moral considerations take precedence over competing priorities.

Moral hypocrisy demonstrates how competing values can overcome our commitment to doing the right thing. In moral hypocrisy, individuals and groups want to appear moral but don't want to pay the price for actually behaving morally.[27] Self-interest overwhelms their self-integrity. For example, participants in experimental settings say that dividing pleasant tasks equally with a partner is the moral course of action. However, when they believe that their partners will never find out, subjects assign themselves the majority of pleasant tasks, in violation of their moral standard. The same pattern is repeated in real-life settings. Sellers often use privileged information to take advantage of purchasers. They might hide the fact that the car they are selling was in a serious accident or needs a new transmission. Companies may use public relations campaigns and marketing to maintain their ethical reputations while continuing to engage in unethical activities. Tobacco giant Philip Morris provides one example of corporate moral hypocrisy in action. The firm spent much more money publicizing its charitable contributions ($108 million) than it did on the charitable contributions themselves ($60 million).

People are more likely to engage in moral hypocrisy when there is a high cost for behaving ethically, when they can disguise their actions, and when they can easily justify their inconsistent behavior by claiming that they are acting out of self-defense or are serving the greater good.

Two factors, rewards and emotions, play an important role in ethical follow-through. It is easier to give priority to ethical values when rewarded for doing so. Conversely, moral motivation drops when the reward system honors inappropriate behavior.[28] Individuals are much more likely to act ethically when they are evaluated on how well they adhere to important values and when they receive raises, bonuses, promotions, and public recognition for doing so. On the other hand, they are motivated to lie, steal, act abusively, take bribes, and cheat when offenders prosper. At far too many mortgage companies, for instance, lending officers generated large commissions by lying to borrowers. They misled homeowners about the terms of their loans and steered them into loan products they couldn't afford. (Reward and performance evaluation systems will be discussed in more detail in Chapter 10.)

Emotional states are another significant influence on moral motivation. For example:[29]

- Positive affect (joy, happiness) makes individuals more optimistic and therefore more likely to live out their moral choices.
- Jealousy, rage, envy, and feelings of aggression have been linked to a wide variety of antisocial behaviors in organizations, including stealing, sabotage, revenge, lying, and unwarranted lawsuits.
- People in positive moods are more likely to help coworkers and others. In other words, feeling good leads to doing good.
- Helping others maintains positive feelings.
- Depression lowers motivation by lowering self-confidence and energy levels. In contrast, sadness may motivate individuals to repair their moods by doing what they believe is right.
- Guilty people are more likely than shamed people to try to rectify their wrongs through asking for forgiveness and making restitution.
- Feeling sympathy leads to more prosocial (altruistic) behavior toward both individuals and groups.

- Experiencing high personal stress reduces prosocial behavior.
- Anger and frustration often lead to aggressive behavior.
- Regulating moods can improve moral motivation. Those who recognize and modify their feelings increase the likelihood that they will carry through on their choices. For example, they put themselves in a better frame of mind by replacing angry thoughts with calmer ones and by engaging in behaviors (listening to music, reading, walking) that cheer them up.

Tips for Increasing Your Moral Motivation

Put moral integrity above moral hypocrisy. Reduce the cost of ethical behavior (reward whistleblowers instead of punishing them, for example). Put principle above self-interest. Promote transparency, which makes it harder to hide choices. For instance, make sure that both buyers and sellers, employees and management, have access to the same data. Reject the tendency to justify your unethical behavior by identifying the costs of your immoral choices. And take a hard look at yourself and your motivations, making sure that you are motivated by your moral standards and not solely by the desire to look good.

Seek out ethically rewarding environments. When selecting a job or a volunteer position, consider the reward system before joining the group. Does the organization evaluate, monitor, and reward ethical behavior? Are rewards misplaced? Are organizational leaders concerned about how goals are achieved?

Reward yourself. Sometimes, ethical behavior is its own best reward. Helping others can be extremely fulfilling, for example, as is living up to the image we have of ourselves as individuals of integrity. Congratulate yourself on following through even if others do not.

Monitor your emotions. Some emotions (happiness, optimism, joy, guilt) can have a positive effect on ethical implementation. Determine if your feelings (depression, anger, personal distress) are inhibiting your ability to carry out your ethical choice.

Regulate your emotions. Master your moods to bring them in line with your goals. Put a brake on destructive feelings; try to shift into a more positive frame of mind. (Case Study 3.1 provides you with a chance to apply tips from the first three components of Rest's model to an ethical dilemma.)

CASE STUDY 3.1

Managerial Decision

You are the plant manager of a chemical firm north of Midland, Michigan. The fumes from your plant are toxic and usually blow in a northeasterly direction into Ontario, Canada. The fallout from the fumes is killing the forests in the wind's path.

Your plant's employees are all partially handicapped. Yours is the only firm in the state that goes out of its way to hire the handicapped. Without these jobs, at least 300 of them could not find work elsewhere. The odds are 70–30 that 140 of the 300 would see their families break up. The cost of putting scrubbers in the smokestacks is prohibitive. The firm will shut down the plant as inefficient if the pollution has to be cleaned up.

You are 61 years old and one year away from retirement. You have no savings, since your spouse has severe allergies and takes care of your 30-year-old handicapped child. If the plant closes down, you will be terminated with a $100,000 lump sum retirement fee. If you can last until retirement, the firm will give you $35,000 per year for the rest of your life. The odds are 90–100 that your age and skills would not enable you to find another job in the area. Your spouse's allergies demand that you live in the area.

The Canadians have commissioned a scientific study that has arrived at the following conclusions:

1. Your plant alone is the major cause of forest devastation in a 100 square-mile area of Ontario.

2. The cost in lost timber is $100,000 per year. (The loss of jobs to your handicapped workers who probably could find other employment would cost them $1 million in wages per year.)

3. The odds are 80–20 that the 300 Canadians living in that wooded area of Ontario will have their lives shortened by five years if the pollution continues for six more months. About three of those Canadians will develop cancer because of the pollution (if it continues) and die painfully. All of the 300 Canadians in that area live in a religious commune.

The Canadians demand that you clean up or shut down. The U.S. government refuses to interfere. The firm's CEO says the decision is yours. Before recording your decision below, consider the following questions:

1. What factors make this a morally intense issue? How do these factors influence your perception of the situation?

2. What destructive motivations might influence your decision?

3. What cognitive biases could undermine your choice in this scenario?

4. What steps can you take to avoid these cognitive biases?

5. What role should emotions play in this decision?

Given that you must choose only one of the following options, which would you choose? Why? How do your answers to the five questions above influence your decision to keep the plant open or to close it?

1. Keep the plant open. _____

2. Shut the plant down. _____

SOURCE: Van Es, R., French, W., & Stellmaszek, F. (2004). Resolving conflicts over ethical issues: Face-to-face versus Internet negotiations. *Journal of Business Ethics 53*, pp. 171–172. Used by permission. (Questions not in the original source.)

Component 4: Moral Character

Carrying out the fourth and final stage of moral action—executing the plan—requires character. Moral agents must overcome active opposition, cope with fatigue, resist distractions, and develop sophisticated strategies for reaching their goals. In sum, they must persist in a moral task or action despite obstacles.

Persistence can be nurtured like other positive character traits (see Chapter 2), but it is also related to individual differences. Those with a strong will, as well as confidence in themselves and their abilities, are more likely to persist. So are individuals with an internal locus of control.[30] Internally oriented people (internals) believe that they have control over their lives and can determine what happens to them. Externally oriented people (externals) believe that life events are beyond their control and are the product of luck or fate. Because internals take personal responsibility for their actions, they are motivated to do what is right. Externals are more susceptible to situational pressures. As a consequence, they are less likely to persist in ethical tasks.

Successful implementation demands that persistence be complemented with competence. A great number of skills can be required to take action, including, for instance, relationship building, organizing, coalition building, and public speaking. Pulitzer Prize–winning author and psychiatrist Robert Coles discovered the importance of ethical competence during the 1960s.[31] Coles traveled with a group of physicians who identified widespread malnutrition among children of the Mississippi Delta. They brought their report to Washington, D.C., convinced that they could persuade federal officials to provide more food. Their hopes were soon dashed. The secretaries of agriculture and education largely ignored their pleas, and Southern senators resisted attempts to expand the food surplus program. The physicians were skilled in medicine, but they didn't understand the political process. They got a hearing only when New York Senator Robert Kennedy took up their cause. A highly skilled politician, Senator Kennedy coached them on how to present their message to the press and public, arranged special committee meetings to hear their testimony, and traveled with them to the South to draw attention to the plight of poor children.

Tips for Fostering Your Moral Character

Take a look at your track record. How well do you persist in doing the right thing? How well do you manage obstacles? Consider what steps you might take to foster the virtue of persistence.

Believe that you can have an impact. Unless you are convinced that you can shape your own life and surroundings, you are not likely to carry through in the midst of trials.

Master the context. Know your organization, its policies, and important players so you can better respond when needed.

Be good at what you do. Competence will better enable you to put your moral choice into action. You will also earn the right to be heard.

ETHICS AND TECHNOLOGY

Resolving Ethical Dilemmas Online

The advent of new forms of information technology like e-mail, web pages, and groupware means that discussions of ethical issues are increasingly taking place online instead of in person. There may be some advantages to resolving ethical dilemmas using computer-mediated communication channels. Asynchronous Internet discussions allow participants more time to formulate their arguments, to reflect on the statements of others, to reexamine their logic, and to change their tactics and strategies. Online discussants interrupt less and don't make as many highly emotional statements. To determine if online discussions can be as productive as face-to-face conversations, one group of investigators gave the "Managerial Decision" scenario in Case Study 3.1 to 20 pairs of face-to-face negotiators and 20 pairs of Internet negotiators. Of the Internet negotiations, 14 ended in agreement, while only 11 of the face-to-face negotiations ended successfully.

While initial research suggests that computer technology can enhance moral dialogue, investigators note that Internet discussions have significant drawbacks. It takes greater effort to write down thoughts than to say them out loud, and the chances of miscommunication are greater because there are no nonverbal cues to help receivers interpret messages. The conversation takes much longer and can lose its continuity as a result. Then, too, recipients may ignore e-mail messages.

As information technologies become even more popular, it will be increasingly important for researchers to identify the advantages and disadvantages of resolving ethical conflicts online. Such knowledge will help organizational members determine when and how to use information technologies when making moral choices.

Sources

Drake, B., Yuthas, K., & Dillard, J. E. (2000). It's only words—Impacts of informational technology on moral dialogue. *Journal of Business Ethics, 23*, 41–59.

Van Es, R., French, W., & Stellmaszek, F. (2004). Resolving conflicts over ethical issues: Face-to-face versus Internet negotiations. *Journal of Business Ethics, 53*, 165–172.

Decision-Making Formats

Decision-making guidelines can help us make better moral choices both individually and as part of a group or organization. Formats incorporate elements that enhance ethical performance while helping us avoid blunders. Step-by-step procedures ensure that we identify and carefully define ethical issues, resist time pressures, investigate options, think about the implications of choices, and apply key ethical principles. I'll introduce four decision-making formats in this the second half of the chapter. You can test these guidelines by applying them to the scenarios described in Case Study 3.2. You'll probably find one format more interesting and useful than the others. Which format you prefer is not as important as approaching moral problems systematically.

Kidder's Ethical Checkpoints

Ethicist Rushworth Kidder acknowledges that ethical issues can be "disorderly and sometimes downright confusing."[32] They can quickly arise when least expected, are usually complex, may lack a clear cause, and generally have unexpected consequences. However, Kidder argues that there is an underlying structure to the ethical decision-making process. Following his nine steps or checkpoints can help you cut through the confusion and generate a well-grounded solution.

Checkpoint 1: Recognize That There Is a Moral Issue. In this step, determine if there are ethical considerations in the situation that demand attention. Sort out genuine ethical issues from those involving etiquette, personal taste, or custom. I may be irritated at someone who burps at the next table at my favorite restaurant. However, such behavior is not morally wrong but rather a breach of etiquette or a reflection of cultural differences.

Checkpoint 2: Determine the Actor. Kidder makes a distinction between involvement and responsibility. Because we're members of larger communities, we're involved in any ethical issue that arises in the group. Yet we are only responsible for dealing with problems that we can do something about. I may think that police use excessive force in a neighboring town, but there is little I can do as a nonresident to address this issue.

Checkpoint 3: Gather the Relevant Facts. Become a reporter and gather important information—for example, the history of the problem, key actors, motives, what was said and who said it, patterns of behavior. Consider the future as well. What will be the likely consequences if the problem continues? The likely outcome of one course of action or another? The likely future behavior of those involved in the issue?

Checkpoint 4: Test for Right-Versus-Wrong Issues. Determine if there is any wrongdoing in the case. Four tests can be applied to make this determination: (1) The legal test asks if lawbreaking is involved. If so, then the problem becomes a legal matter, not a moral one. Resolution will come through legal proceedings. (2) The stench test relies on intuition. If you have a vague sense of unease about the decision or course of action, chances are it involves right-versus-wrong issues. (3) The front-page test asks how you would feel if your private decision became public by appearing on the front page of tomorrow's newspaper. If that thought makes you uncomfortable, then you had better choose another alternative. (4) The Mom test asks how you would feel if your mother or some other important role model got wind of your choice. Once again, if such a thought makes you queasy, you had better revisit your choice.

Checkpoint 5: Test for Right-Versus-Right Paradigms. If an issue doesn't involve wrong behavior, then it likely pits two important positive values against each other. These right-versus-right dilemmas generally fall into three categories or paradigms:

Justice versus mercy. Norms of fairness and equality often clash with the desire to extend mercy and forgiveness. Consider the dilemma of the professor who catches an honors student cheating on an exam. According to university regulations, the student should automatically receive a zero on the test, which would cost him his scholarship. The student then appeals to the instructor for partial credit. The professor wants to be fair to other class members who didn't cheat and to mete out the necessary punishment. Nonetheless, she feels sympathy for the student, who appears to be a first-time offender with a great deal to lose.

Short term versus long term. Short-term advantages often come at the expense of long-term benefits. For instance, shifting money from research and development into marketing may generate more immediate sales but undermine a company's future by cutting off the flow of new products and ideas. Ethical decision makers balance immediate needs against long-range consequences. The economic benefits of cutting timber in national forests, for example, must be weighed against the long-term costs to the environment.

Truth versus loyalty. This ethical tension pits our loyalty to friends, family, groups, and organizations against our desire to tell the truth. It arises when we have to determine whether to speak up or to lie to the boss to protect a coworker, to keep quiet about safety violations at the plant or to go public with our allegations, or to award a contract to a friend or to another supplier with a better bid.

Checkpoint 6: Apply Resolution Principles. Once the options or sides are clear based on Checkpoints 4 and 5, apply the ethical perspectives described in Chapter 2.

Checkpoint 7: Look for a Third Way (Investigate the "Trilemma" Option). Compromise is one way to reveal a new alternative that will resolve the problem. Both state and federal governments have used compromise to deal with the manufacture and marketing of cigarettes and alcohol. Many religious and public health groups want to ban these products, yet they are widely used by Americans. Government officials have tried to strike a balance that recognizes the dangers of smoking and drinking while allowing citizens to engage in these activities. Tobacco and alcoholic beverages can't be sold to minors, and there are limits to where they can be consumed.

The third way can also be the product of moral imagination. Setting up "pay for play" online music libraries is one such innovative concept. The music industry and millions of consumers have been locked in a legal and ethical battle over the downloading of copyrighted tunes for free. Now, listeners can get just the songs they want without violating copyright laws. Record producers, who have seen a steady decline in CD sales, are enjoying a new source of revenue.

Checkpoint 8: Make the Decision. Exhausted by wrestling with the problem, we may overlook this step. Yet no decision, no matter how well grounded, is useful unless it is put into action. Kidder argues that this step requires moral courage. Such courage, along with our ability to reason, sets us apart from the animal kingdom.

Checkpoint 9: Revisit and Reflect on the Decision. Return to the decision later, after the issue has been resolved, to debrief. Reflect on the lessons to be learned. In some instances, the problem can be shaped into a case or example that can be used in ethics teaching and training.

The Moral Compass

Harvard ethics professor Lynn Paine offers a four-part "moral compass" for guiding managerial decision making.[33] The goal of the compass is to ensure that ethical considerations are factored into every organizational decision. Paine believes that we can focus our attention (and that of the rest of the group) on the moral dimension of even routine decisions by engaging in the following four frames of analysis. Each frame or lens highlights certain elements of the situation so that they can be carefully examined and addressed. Taken together, the lenses increase moral sensitivity, making it easier for organizational members to recognize and discuss moral issues.

Lens 1: Purpose—Will this action serve a worthwhile purpose? The first frame examines end results. Proposed courses of action need to serve worthy goals. To come up with the answer to the question of purpose, we need to gather data as well as make judgments. Important subsidiary questions include these:

- What are we trying to accomplish? What are our short- and long-term goals?
- Are these goals worthwhile? How do they contribute to people's lives?
- Will the course of action we are examining contribute to achieving these goals?
- Compared to the possible alternatives, how effectively and efficiently will it do so?
- If this is not the most effective and efficient course, do we have a sound basis for pursuing the proposed path?

Lens 2: Principle—Is this action consistent with relevant principles? This mode of analysis applies ethical standards to the problem at hand. These guidelines can be general ethical principles, norms of good business practice, codes of conduct, legal requirements, and personal ideals and aspirations. We need to determine the following:

- What norms of conduct are relevant to this situation?
- What are our duties under these standards?
- What are the best practices under these standards?
- Does the proposed action honor the applicable standards?
- If not, do we have a sound basis for departing from these standards?
- Is the proposed action consistent with our own espoused standards and ideals?

Lens 3: People—Does this action respect the legitimate claims of the people likely to be affected? The third frame highlights the likely impacts of decisions. Identifying possible harm to stakeholder groups can help us take steps to prevent damage. Such analysis requires understanding the perspectives of others as well as careful reasoning.

- Who is likely to be affected, both directly and indirectly, by the proposed action?
- How will these parties be affected?
- What are these parties' rights, interests, expectations, and concerns?
- Does our plan respect the legitimate claims of the affected parties?
- If not, what are we doing to compensate for this infringement?
- Have we mitigated unnecessary harms?
- Are there alternatives that would be less harmful or more beneficial on balance?
- Have we taken full advantage of opportunities for mutual benefit?

Lens 4: Power—Do we have the power to take this action? The final lens directs attention to the exercise of power and influence. Answers to the first three sets of questions mean little unless we have the legitimate authority to act and the ability to do so. Subsidiary questions of power include these:

- What is the scope of our legitimate authority in view of relevant laws, agreements, understandings, and stakeholder expectations?
- Are we within our rights to pursue the proposed course of action?
- If not, have we secured the necessary approvals?
- Do we have the resources, including the knowledge and skills as well as tangible resources, required to carry out the proposed action?
- If not, do we have the ability to marshal the needed resources?

Paine uses the example of a failed product introduction to illustrate what can happen when organizational decision makers don't take moral issues into account. In the early 1990s, Lotus Development and Equifax teamed up to create a product called Lotus Marketplace: Households. This compact disc and software package was designed to help small businesses create targeted mailing lists from their desktop computers. For $695, purchasers could draw from a database of 80 million households (created from credit information collected by Equifax) instead of buying one-time mailing lists from list brokers. Businesses could then tailor their mailings based on income, gender, age, marital status, and lifestyle.

Criticism began as soon as the product was announced to the public. Many consumers didn't want to be included in the database due to privacy concerns and asked if they could opt out. Others worried that criminals might misuse the information— for instance, by identifying and then targeting upper-income single women. The system didn't take into account that information would soon be outdated and that data could be stolen. The two firms tried to address these issues by allowing individuals to remove their names from the list, strengthening privacy controls, and improving security. Lotus and Equifax failed to sway the public, and the project was scuttled. Equifax subsequently stopped selling credit information to marketers.

The Foursquare Protocol

Catholic University law professor and attorney Stephen Goldman offers another decision-making format designed specifically for use in organizational settings. He calls his method a *protocol* because it focuses on the procedures that members use to reach their conclusions.[34] Following the protocol ensures that decisions are reached fairly.

Protocol Element One: Close description of the situation. Ethical decision-making begins with digging into the facts. Goldman compares the process to how a physician generates a diagnosis. When determining what is wrong with a patient, the doctor gathers information about the patient's symptoms and relates them to one another to identify the problem. In the same way, we need to get a complete account of the ethical "patient," or problem. Gather data and identify the relevant facts. Take the case of a company determining whom to lay off in an economic downturn. Age, seniority, gender, and race are relevant considerations in making this decision.

Protocol Element Two: Gathering accumulated experience in similar situations. Doctors rely on their past experience when treating patients; organizational decision makers should do the same. Use important ethical principles but, at the same time, look to past experiences with similar problems. How did the organization respond to cases of sexual harassment in the past, for instance? Explore how other managers have responded to related dilemmas. To be fair, similar cases should treated the same way. Also consider how others will talk about your decision. Remember that how you respond to the issue will shape the group's ethical culture going forward. For example, if you excuse those who engage in sexual harassment now, you can expect more cases of harassment in the future.

Protocol Element Three: Recognize the significant similarities between the current problem and past ones. Identify the important differences between the current situation and past incidents. Some distinctions are insignificant, while others are critical. The ability to discern which is which separates average ethical decision makers from the really good ones. In the case of a layoff, there are significant differences between current and past labor laws. At one time, companies could hire and fire without regard for race, gender, and age. Now, state and federal laws prohibit discrimination. Strategies used in the past will not work in the present.

Protocol Element Four: Situating yourself to decide. Once the facts are gathered and sorted, it is time to make the choice. To "situate" yourself to make the decision, consider three factors. One, what, if any, self-interest do you have in the choice that might compromise your judgment? You might have a financial stake in a course of action, or you may be faced with disciplining an employee who is also a friend. Two, imagine that you are on the receiving end of your decision, which is likely to be costly to some groups. Consider how you would respond if you were to be laid off, for instance. Three, determine what your moral instincts are telling you to do. For example, does your "gut" tell you that it is wrong to lay off those with the longest tenure? That protecting the organization's diversity by retaining minority employees is the right thing to do? Use your instincts to test the choice you make through the application of ethical principles like utilitarianism.

The Five "I" Format

Remembering all of Kidder's checkpoints, Paine's subsidiary questions, or all the details of Goldman's protocol would be difficult without referring to a book or a handout. Sometimes, we need to make decisions without access to our notes. For that reason, I offer the easily memorized Five "I" Format as a guide. This approach incorporates elements of the first two models into the following sequence:

Identify the problem. Identification involves recognizing there is an ethical problem to be solved and setting goals. Describe what you seek as the outcome of your deliberations.

Will you be taking action yourself or on behalf of the group or organization? Developing recommendations for others? Dealing with an immediate issue or setting a long-term policy?

Investigate the problem. Investigation involves two subprocesses: problem analysis and data collection. "Drill down" to develop a better understanding of the problem. Determine important stakeholders as well as conflicting loyalties, values, and duties. Develop a set of criteria or standards for evaluating solutions. This is the time to introduce important ethical perspectives. You may decide that your decision should put a high value on justice or altruism, for instance. In addition to analyzing the issue, gather more information. Knowing why an employee has been verbally abusive, for example, can make it easier to determine how much mercy to extend to that individual. You will likely be more forgiving if the outburst appears to be the product of family stress (divorce, illness, rebellious children). There may be times when you can't gather more data or when good information is not available. In those cases, you'll need to make reasonable assumptions based on your current knowledge.

Innovate by generating a variety of solutions. Resist the temptation to reach quick decisions. Instead, continue to look for a third way by generating possible options or alternative courses of action that could reach your goals and meet your criteria.

Isolate a solution. Settle on a solution using what you uncovered during the investigation stage. Evaluate your data, weigh loyalties and duties, consider the likely impact on stakeholders, and match the solution to your ethical criteria. The choice may be obvious, or you may have to choose between equally attractive or equally unattractive alternatives. When it comes to decisions involving truth and loyalty, for instance, there is no easy way out. Lying for a friend preserves the relationship at the expense of personal integrity; refusing to lie for a friend preserves the truth but endangers the relationship. Remember that you are looking not for the perfect solution but for a well reasoned, carefully considered one.

Implement the solution. Determine how you will follow through on your choice. If you are deciding alone, develop an action plan. If you are deciding in a group, make sure that every team member knows her or his future responsibilities.

CHAPTER TAKEAWAYS

- Moral behavior is the product of moral sensitivity, moral judgment, moral motivation, and moral character. You'll need to master each of these components in order to make and then implement wise ethical decisions.
- You can enhance your ethical sensitivity through active listening, challenging your current ways of thinking, looking for innovative ways to solve problems, and discussing decisions in moral terms. Increase the moral intensity of issues by emphasizing their consequences and by pointing out that there is widespread agreement that they are problematic.

- Your moral judgment can be impaired if you look only to others for guidance or blindly follow the rules of your organization. Try to incorporate universal ethical principles into your decision-making process.
- Beware of major motivational contributors to defective decision-making: insecurities, greed, and ego.
- Recognize the unconscious cognitive biases that lead to unethical choices. These include (1) overestimating your ethicality, (2) forgiving your own unethical behavior, (3) overlooking other people's unethical behavior, (4) implicit prejudice, (5) favoring members of your own group, and (6) judging based on outcomes rather than on the quality of the decision-making process.
- You will be more likely to put ethical values first if you resist the temptation to engage in moral hypocrisy, if you are rewarded for putting moral considerations first, and if you monitor and regulate your emotions to create a positive frame of mind.
- To succeed at implementing your moral choice, you'll need to be both persistent and competent. Believe in your own ability to influence events, master the organizational context, and develop the necessary implementation skills.
- When making collective decisions, ensure that the process is democratic and fair. All those who will be governed by a course of action should have a voice in choosing it. Be prepared to challenge the validity of claims made by others and to defend the claims that you make.
- Decision-making formats can help you make better moral choices. Which format you use is not as important as approaching moral problems systematically. Kidder's ethical checkpoints can help you cut through the disorder and confusion surrounding ethical issues; the moral compass factors ethical considerations into every organizational decision; the foursquare protocol ensures that decisions are reached fairly; and the five "I" format offers a shorthand approach that incorporates elements of the first three sets of guidelines.

APPLICATION PROJECTS

1. Use the suggestions in the chapter to develop an action plan for improving your moral sensitivity, judgment, motivation, and character.

2. Select a moral issue, and evaluate its level of moral intensity using the components described in the chapter. Or choose an ethical dilemma that you think deserves more attention. What steps could you and others take to increase this issue's level of moral intensity?

3. Describe how your college career has influenced your moral development. What experiences have had the greatest impact?

4. Which of the cognitive biases described in the chapter poses the most danger to moral judgment? Defend your choice in a small group discussion.

5. Describe a time when you made an ethical decision in a group. Evaluate the group's discussion using the standards of discourse ethics.

6. Apply one of the decision-making formats to an ethical dilemma found at the end of the chapter or to another one that you select. Keep a record of your deliberations and your final choice. Then evaluate the format and the decision. Did following a system help you come to a better conclusion? Why or why not? What are the strengths and weaknesses of the format you selected? Would it be a useful tool for solving the ethical problems you face at school and work? Write up your findings.

7. Using the material presented in the chapter, analyze what you consider a poor ethical decision. What went wrong? Why? Present your conclusions in a paper or in a presentation to the rest of the class.

8. Develop your own set of guidelines for ethical decision-making. Describe and explain your model.

CASE STUDY 3.2

Scenarios for Analysis

Scenario 1: Is It Better to Ask Permission or to Ask Forgiveness?

Anselmo Escobar is the owner of Stately Homes, a small residential contracting firm. Stately Vistas is the company's biggest project yet. Escobar is anxious to begin building this new subdivision after a series of costly delays caused by a backlog in the city zoning office. He plans to remove nearly all the mature trees in the area so that he can build more homes and recoup his losses. However, the contractor knows this move will be unpopular with current residents, who believe that the trees enhance the neighborhood and improve property values.

Escobar is under no legal obligation to consult with the neighborhood association about his plans. Further, he fears that notifying neighbors might lead to additional delays. A successful protest could force Anselmo to retain some of the trees scheduled for removal. Yet, the builder feels uneasy about moving ahead without talking to neighborhood representatives. Taking unilateral action could generate negative publicity and increase opposition to future Stately Homes developments. More importantly, Escobar wonders about his responsibility to current residents. He knows that he would be upset if another contractor removed trees in his neighborhood without notifying anyone.

As he ponders what to do, Anselmo is reminded of the old saying, "It is easier to ask for forgiveness than to ask for permission." He is torn between consulting with the neighbors before removing the trees (asking for permission) and removing the trees and then dealing with the fallout (asking for forgiveness).

What should Escobar do?

Scenario 2: Unpaid Internships

College internships are often the key to landing a job after graduation. Recognizing this fact, 83% of all graduating students held field internships in 2008, up from just 9% in 1992. While many interns are paid for their labor, a great number are not. More companies are offering unpaid positions as they try to keep their costs down in a tough economy. Unfortunately, some employers take advantage of unpaid interns by requiring them to do menial labor like wiping down doorknobs and shipping packages.

The proliferation of unpaid internships has attracted the attention of federal and state officials in California, New York, Oregon, and elsewhere. Regulators have fined firms for using unpaid positions to violate labor and minimum wage laws. Businesses offering unpaid internships must meet several federal standards. For example, such positions must offer training similar to that received in a vocational school, cannot displace regular workers, and must provide "no immediate advantage" to employers. The criteria are strict enough that the interim director of the U.S. Labor Department's Wage and Hour Division believes that few firms qualify. "If you're a for-profit employer or you want to pursue an internship with a for-profit employer," she declares, "there aren't going to be many circumstances where you can have an internship and not be paid and still be in compliance with the law."

Internships will be much harder to find if state and federal officials have their way. This will have serious implications for the thousands of students who remain eager to take unpaid internships despite their disadvantages.

Should federal regulators lessen restrictions so that more companies can offer unpaid internships to students?

Sources

Greenhouse, S. (2010, April 4). Unpaid internships worry state and federal officials. *The Oregonian,* p. E3.
Mortenson, E. (2010, April 22). Unpaid internships may skirt rules. *The Oregonian,* p. B1.

Scenario 3: When the Good News Is Bad News

Employees and administrators at Kentucky College were excited to hear that the incoming freshman class was the largest in the small private school's history. Years of slumping enrollment had left the college, which depended heavily upon tuition dollars, strapped for cash. Now the school's leadership could add new staff, increase faculty salaries, and improve facilities.

Unfortunately, what was good news for the Kentucky College as a whole was bad news for some freshmen. There weren't enough rooms available to house everyone. New students were placed in study rooms and in double rooms that were converted to "triples" by adding an extra bunk bed. All students paid the same price for room and board regardless of their housing arrangements. A few freshmen complained, arguing that they should pay less because their living arrangements weren't equal to those of other students. The housing director refused their request. Less revenue would mean fewer repairs to dorms and apartments. In addition, he believed that conceding to such demands could set a bad precedent. Some dorms are older and more run down than others. Residents living in these facilities might also claim that they should pay less.

Was Kentucky College wrong to admit more students than it could house comfortably?

Was the housing director justified in refusing to reduce fees for those students forced to live in substandard conditions?

Scenario 4: Mercy for Margaret?

Receptionist Margaret Simpson was one of the first employees hired at T Rex Manufacturing when the company opened 20 years ago. The first 2 years of operations were difficult ones, and Simpson accepted late paychecks on more than one occasion to help keep the company afloat. For two decades she has been the face of the company to visitors and a friendly voice on the phone for suppliers and employees alike. Company president Gregg Smith often praises Margaret at employee meetings, citing her as an example of what the "T Rex family" is all about.

Sadly, Margaret's job performance has begun to slip. Over the past few months she has often been late to work and has become cold and distant. Outsiders and coworkers alike complain about how difficult the new Margaret is to deal with. They resent her rude comments and brusque manner. Earlier this month president Smith took the receptionist aside to confront her about her poor performance but to no avail. If anything, she is more unpleasant than ever. Smith did discover, however, that Simpson plans to retire in 3 years but that the value of her retirement savings plan has declined dramatically.

Smith knows that he must come to a decision about Margaret soon. In fact, she would have been fired earlier if she had been most any other employee. However, the T Rex executive knows that the choice is a difficult one given Margaret's loyal service, her age and lack of retirement savings, and his desire to foster a family-like atmosphere at the plant.

What action should Smith take?

ENDNOTES

1. Rest, J. R. (1994). Background: Theory and research. In J. R. Rest & D. Narvaez (Eds.), *Moral development in the professions: Psychology and applied ethics,* (pp. 1–25). Hillsdale, NJ: Lawrence Erlbaum; Rest, J. R. (1986). *Moral development: Advances in research and theory.* New York: Praeger.

2. Werhane, P. H. (1999). *Moral imagination and management decision-making.* New York: Oxford University Press.

3. Bird, F. B. (1996). *The muted conscience: Moral silence and the practice of ethics in business.* Westport, CT: Quorum Books.

4. Trevino, L. K., & Nelson, K. A. (2004). *Managing business ethics: Straight talk about how to do it right* (3rd ed.). Hoboken, NJ: John Wiley.

5. Jones, T. M. (1991). Ethical decision making by individuals in organizations: An issue-contingent model. *Academy of Management Review, 16,* 366–395.

6. Jones, p. 375.

7. See, for example:

Butterfield, K. D., Trevino, L. K., & Weaver, G. R. (2000). Moral awareness in business organizations: Influences of issue-related and social context factors. *Human Relations, 53,* 981–1018; May, D. R., & Pauli, K. P. (2002). The role of moral intensity in ethical decision-making: A review and investigation of moral recognition, evaluation and intention. *Business & Society, 41,* 84–117; Frey, B. F. (2000). The impact of moral intensity on decision making in a business context. *Journal of Business Ethics 26,* 181–195; Carlson, D. S., Kacmar, K. M., & Wadsworth, L. L. (2009). The impact of moral intensity dimensions on ethical decision-making: Assessing the relevance of orientation. *Journal of Managerial Issues, 21,* 534–551; McMahon, J. M, & Harvey, R. J. (2006). An analysis of the factor structure of Jones' moral intensity construct. *Journal of Business Ethics, 64,* 381–404; Singer, M., Mitchell, S., & Turner, J. (1998). Consideration of moral intensity in ethicality judgments: Its relationship with whistle-blowing and need-for-cognition. *Journal of Business Ethics 17,* 527–541.

8. Kohlberg, L. A. (1984). *The psychology of moral development: Vol. 2. The nature and validity of moral stages.* San Francisco: Harper & Row; Kohlberg, L. A. (1986). A current statement on some theoretical issues. In S. Modgil & C. Modgil (Eds.), *Lawrence Kohlberg: Consensus and controversy* (pp. 485–546). Philadelphia: Falmer Press.

9. Rest, J. R., Narvaez, D., Bebeau, M. J., & Thoma, S. J. (1999). *Postconventional moral thinking: A neo-Kohlbergian approach.* Mahwah, NJ: Lawrence Erlbaum; Trevino, L. K., & Weaver, G. R. (2003). *Managing ethics in business organizations: Social scientific perspectives.* Stanford, CA: Stanford University Press, Chap. 7.

10. Rest, Narvaez, Bebeau, & Thoma (1999).

11. See, for example: Rest, J. R., & Narvaez, D. (1991). The college experience and moral development. In W. M. Kurtines & J. L. Gewirtz (Eds.), *Handbook of moral behavior and development. Vol. 2: Research* (pp. 229–245). Hillsdale, NJ: Lawrence Erlbaum; Rest, J. R. (1979). *Development in judging moral issues.* Minneapolis: University of Minnesota Press; Trevino & Weaver (2003).

12. Not all studies reveal a relationship between education and moral reasoning. See: Loe, T. W., Ferrell, L., & Mansfield, P. (2000). A review of empirical studies assessing ethical decision making in business. *Journal of Business Ethics, 25,* 185–204.

13. Gergen, D. (2000). *Eyewitness to power: The essence of leadership.* New York: Simon & Schuster.

14. Sternberg, R. J. (2002). Smart people are not stupid, but they sure can be foolish. In R. J. Sternberg (Ed.), *Why smart people can be so stupid* (pp. 232–242). New Haven, CT: Yale University Press.

15. Examples of the "winner take all" society come from: Callahan, D. (2004). *The cheating culture.* Orlando, FL: Harcourt.

16. Messick, D. M., & Bazerman, M. H. (1996, Winter). Ethical leadership and the psychology of decision making. *Sloan Management Review,* pp. 9–23.

17. Nash, L. (1990). *Good intentions aside: A manager's guide to resolving ethical problems.* Boston, MA: Harvard Business School Press, p. 166.

18. Nutt, P. (2002). *Why decisions fail.* San Francisco: Berrett-Koehler.

19. Why your negotiating behavior may be ethically challenged—and how to fix it. (2008, April). *Negotiation, 11*(4), 1–5.

20. Epley, N., & Dunning, D. (2000). Feeling "holier than thou": Are self-serving assessments produced by errors in self- or social prediction? *Journal of Personality and Social Psychology, 79,* 861–875; Tenbrunsel, A. E., Diekman, K. A., Wade-Benzoni, K. A., & Bazerman, M. H. (2009). The ethical mirage: A temporal explanation as to why we aren't as ethical as we think we are. *Harvard Business School Working Paper No. 08–012.* Available at http://www.people.hbs.edu/mbazerman

21. Bandura, A. (1999). Moral disengagement in the perpetration of inhumanities. *Personality and Social Psychology Review, 3,* 193–209.

22. Shu, L. L., Gino, F., & Bazerman, M. H. (2009). Dishonest deed, clear conscience: Self-preservation through moral disengagement and motivated forgetting. *Harvard Business School Working Paper No. 09–078.*

23. Gino, F., Moore, D. A., & Bazerman, M. H. (2008, January). See no evil: When we overlook other people's unethical behavior. *Harvard Business School Working Paper No. 08–045.* Retrieved from http://www .people.hbs.edu/mbazerman

24. Banaji, M. R., Bazerman, M. H., & Clugh, D. (2003, December). How (un)ethical are you? *Harvard Business Review,* pp. 56–64; Bazerman, M. H., Chugh, D., & Banaji, M. R. (2005, October). When good people (seem to) negotiate in bad faith. *Negotiation, 8,* 3–5.

25. Banaji, Bazerman, & Clugh.

26. Gino, F., Moore, D. A., & Bazerman, M. H. (2009). No harm, no foul: The outcome bias in ethical judgments. *Harvard Business School Working Paper 08–080.* Available at http://www.people.hbs.edu/mbazerman

27. Batson, C. D., Collins, E., & Powell, A. A. (2006). Doing business after the fall: The virtue of moral hypocrisy. *Journal of Business Ethics, 66,* 321–335; Batson, C. D., Thompson, E. R., & Chen, H. (2002). Moral hypocrisy: Addressing some alternatives. *Journal of Personality and Social Psychology, 83,* 330–339. Batson, C. D., & Thompson, E. R. (2001). Why don't people act morally: Motivational considerations. *Current Directions in Psychological Science, 10,* 54–57; Batson, C. D., Thompson, E. R., Seuferling, G., Whitney, H., & Strongman, J. A. (1999). Moral hypocrisy: Appearing moral to oneself without being so. *Journal of Personality and Social Psychology, 77*(3), 525–537.

28. James, H. S. (2000). Reinforcing ethical decision making through organizational structure. *Journal of Business Ethics, 28,* 43–58.

29. Eisenberg, N. (2000). Emotion, regulation, and moral development. *Annual Review of Psychology, 51,* 665–697; Gaudine, A., & Thorne, L. (2001). Emotion and ethical decision-making in organizations. *Journal of Business Ethics, 31,* 175–187; Salovey, P., Hsee, C. K., & Mayer, J. D. (1993). Emotional intelligence and the self-regulation of affect. In D. M. Wegner & J. W. Pennebaker (Eds.), *Handbook of mental control* (pp. 258–277). Englewood Cliffs, NJ: Prentice Hall; Giacalone, R. A., & Greenberg, J. (Eds.). (1997). *Antisocial behavior in organizations.* Thousand Oaks, CA: Sage.

30. Trevino & Weaver (2003), Chap. 7.

31. Coles, R. (2001). *Lives of moral leadership.* New York: Random House.

32. Kidder, R. M. (1995). *How good people make tough choices.* New York: Simon & Schuster. For an example of how Kidder's model can be applied to ethical problems in one industry, see: Baker, S. (1997). Applying Kidder's ethical decision-making checklist to media ethics. *Journal of Mass Media Ethics, 12*(4), 197–210.

33. Paine, L. S. (2003). *Value shift: Why companies must merge social and financial imperatives to achieve superior performance.* New York: McGraw-Hill.

34. Goldman, S. (2008). *Temptations in the office: Ethical choices and legal obligations.* Westport, CT: Praeger.

PART III

Practicing Interpersonal Ethics in the Organization

4

Ethical Interpersonal Communication

Communication is a logical starting point for any consideration of ethical relationships because organizational partnerships are created through verbal and nonverbal messages. If we want to establish and maintain healthy relationships, we must adopt a moral stance toward our communication with others and master communication skills that foster ethical interactions and decisions.

Dialogue: An Ethical Framework for Interpersonal Communication

The outcome of any conversation is largely dependent upon the attitude we bring to the encounter. Consider how you respond to a request from a coworker whom you respect as compared to one whom you distrust, for instance. You're likely to be more friendly and helpful to the former than to the latter. The 20th-century German philosopher Martin Buber argued that our attitudes also set the moral tone for our conversations. He identified two primary human attitudes or relationships: I-It and I-Thou.[1] Communicators in I-It relationships treat others as objects. Centered on their own needs, they are not really interested in the ideas of their conversational partners. Participants in I-Thou (I-You) relationships, in contrast, treat others as unique human beings. They are genuinely committed to understanding the perspectives of their fellow communicators.

Buber identifies three types of communication that reflect varying degrees of interest in the self or the other. *Monologue* is self-centered, I-It communication. At its worst, monologue is characterized by deception, exploitation, coercion, and manipulation. *Technical dialogue* reflects a more neutral stance toward self and other. In this type of interaction, the focus is on gathering and processing information. *Dialogue* is the product of an I-Thou relationship. Dialogue occurs between equal partners who focus on understanding rather than on being understood. Together they create meaning.

All three forms of communication have their place in the organization. There are times when we legitimately engage in monologue to meet our needs, such as when we need emotional support. Technical dialogue enables us to get our work done, and we spend the vast majority of our time sending and receiving information-centered messages. However, dialogue has the most potential to build productive relationships and organizational communities. Entering into I-Thou relationships heightens self-esteem by reaffirming the worth of both parties, strengthens interpersonal bonds, and promotes understanding and learning. Yet, before we can pursue dialogue, we need to clear up some common misconceptions about this form of communication, clarify its unique characteristics, and identify the ethical demands dialogue makes of us.

Dialogue is frequently misunderstood. It is *not* merely venting one's feelings (that is a form of monologue). Successful dialogue focuses on what happens between communicators based on the meanings and understandings they jointly develop. For that reason, dialogue can't be forced, only encouraged, and it may occur infrequently. Communication scholar John Stewart urges us to "open a space" for dialogue.[2] Opening this space takes three elements. First, we need to develop the right competencies, including a willingness to engage in dialogue and to seek continuous improvement. Second, we should enter encounters with what Stewart terms a *default dialogue index*, which means we should employ behaviors associated with I-Thou communication, like committing ourselves to being good listeners and treating others with respect, even when engaged in technical dialogue. Third, when the other person appears open to engaging in dialogue, we need to take advantage of this opportunity.

Dialogue is not limited to friendly interactions between friends or intimates. Instead, dialogue is most powerful when acquaintances profoundly disagree but remain in an I-Thou relationship. Buber urged discussants to walk "a narrow ridge" between extreme positions, avoiding the temptation to take up residence in one opposing camp or another.[3] They should stand by their convictions while remaining open to the positions of others. Buber had this type of relationship with Mahatma Gandhi. The two disagreed about whether violence should be used against the Third Reich in World War II. Gandhi urged nonviolent tactics, while Buber (who suffered persecution as a Jew) was convinced that such strategies would not sway the Nazis. After the war, Buber believed that both Jews and Arabs should jointly develop the land of the Middle East. Finally, it should be noted that dialogue does not assume that all people are good. Buber recognized that every person has a dual nature that consists of good and evil. Engaging in dialogue is one way to nurture the positive dimension of persons.

Communication experts Kenneth Cissna and Robert Anderson outline the following as characteristics of interpersonal dialogue:[4]

Presence. Partners in dialogue are less interested in a specific outcome than in working with others to come up with a solution. Their interactions are unscripted and unrehearsed.

Emergent unanticipated consequences. Dialogue produces unpredictable results that are not controlled by any one party.

Recognition of "strange otherness." If dialogue is to flourish, discussants must refuse to believe that they already understand the thoughts, feelings, or intentions of others, even people they know well. Instead, they are tentative, continually testing their understanding of the perspectives of other group members and revising their conclusions when needed.

Collaborative orientation. Dialogue demands a dual focus on self and others. Participants concentrate not on winning or losing but on coming up with a shared, joint solution that preserves the relationship.

Vulnerability. Dialogue is risky because discussants open their thoughts to others and may be influenced by the encounter. They must be willing to change their minds and to be changed as persons.

Mutual implication. Speakers engaged in dialogue always keep listeners in mind when speaking. In so doing, they may discover more about themselves as well.

Temporal flow. Dialogue unfolds over time—drawing from the past, filling the present, and leading to the future. It is a process that can't be cut into segments and analyzed.

Genuineness and authenticity. Participants in dialogue give each other the benefit of the doubt, assuming that the other person is being honest and sharing from personal experience. While speakers don't share all their thoughts, they don't deliberately hide ideas and feelings that are relevant to the topic and to the relationship.

We have to make several ethical commitments if we hope to engage in the kind of conversation described by Cissna and Anderson.[5] First, we must be committed to the good of others in order to treat them as unique beings. Second, we need to value relationships and the common good, recognizing that organizations are made up not of autonomous individuals but of people living in relation to one another. Third, we have to be open to influence and be willing to take criticism. Fourth, we ought to allow others to hold and express opinions different from ours. Fifth, we have to commit ourselves to honesty, not just during dialogue but also when we engage in monologue and technical dialogue. We often need to get others to follow our directions or to change their opinions. However, let's not disguise our motives by pretending to engage in dialogue when we really only want to get our way. Sixth, we need to invest ourselves in the hard work of dialogue. Focusing on the needs and positions of others takes a good deal of time and energy, as does mastering the necessary communication competencies to make dialogue successful.

Ethical Communication Competencies

While dialogue can't be forced, it is much more likely to take place when we have the necessary competencies. Productive communication behaviors that foster I-Thou relationships include mindfulness, effective listening, confirmation, emotional intelligence, trust building, and moral argument. These strategies can also help us make better choices. When used in conjunction with the principles and practices of sound moral reasoning introduced in the last chapter, they further increase our likelihood of coming up with a well-reasoned ethical conclusion.

Mindfulness

Dialogue demands our complete attention. Not only is it unscripted, unrehearsed, and unpredictable, but this type of interaction also requires that we simultaneously focus on our own thoughts as well as on the positions of our conversational partners. Psychologists use the term *mindfulness* to describe the process of devoting full attention to the task at hand, to being fully present in the moment. They report that mindfulness produces a number of positive effects. Mindful individuals are more likely to experience positive moods and are less likely to suffer from depression and anxiety. At the same time, they recover more quickly from negative events. Mindful people are better able to control their behavior in order to complete their tasks and reach their goals. Such individuals also enjoy better physical health because they deal more effectively with pain and stress.[6]

Mindfulness stands in sharp contrast with *mindlessness,* which is inflexible, thoughtless activity. Individuals acting mindlessly don't take in useful information, or they misinterpret the data they do receive.[7] As a result, they behave inflexibly, overlook alternative choices, and become locked into a single course of action. Mindlessness can be costly. We get stuck in our current roles and self-perceptions, stop developing intellectually, engage in unintended cruelty by rationalizing our immoral behaviors, lose control of our choices to advertisers and other outsiders, give into helplessness when we can control the situation, and limit our potential.

The benefits of mindfulness carry over into interpersonal relationships both on and off the job. Researchers report that mindfulness promotes relational connection and closeness because (1) communicators are more receptive to the messages being sent by their relational partners, and (2) they are more aware of, and thus in more control of, their own responses. In addition, mindful individuals aren't as concerned about their egos, so they feel less threatened by rejection and more compassionate toward others.[8]

Ellen Langer identifies three psychological processes of a mindful state of being that help us reap the benefits of mindfulness while sidestepping the dangers of mindless behavior in our interpersonal relationships.[9] (See Case Study 4.2 for a historical example of these characteristics in action.) The first psychological process is the *creation of new categories*. Being mindful breaks us out of our old rigid categories and makes us more sensitive to differences. These distinctions enhance our thinking and relationships. We become better problem solvers when we realize that moral reasoning can be broken down into smaller stages, as we saw in Chapter 3. We're much less likely to stereotype individuals and act in a prejudiced manner if we refuse to lump people into broad categories based on age, race, gender, or role.

The second psychological process involves *welcoming new information*. In mindful communication, we seek new information as we closely monitor our behavior along with the behavior of others. These data allow us to revise our conclusions and adjust our responses. Mindless communication, on the other hand, closes us off to new information. As a result, we make costly mistakes and fail to adjust to changes in our environments. We assume that others hold our ethical values when they don't, settle on the first solution when a better one might be available, fail to meet the changing expectations of our audiences, and so on.

The third psychological process is *openness to different points of view*. Any event or behavior can be viewed from more than one perspective. What seems like thoughtless, hurtful behavior on the part of a coworker may have been intended as playful or harmless. Exploring multiple perspectives gives us more options, reduces the probability that we will get locked into an extreme position, and equips us to change our behavior. For instance, we are more likely to change the way we act when we realize that others take offence at what we're currently doing.

Langer and others argue that mindfulness is a mode of thinking, not a personality trait. As a consequence, we can consciously shift to this frame of mind when needed. It's easy to identify situations that clearly demand a mindful state: dealing with strangers and people of other cultural backgrounds, public presentations, brainstorming sessions, interviews, performance reviews, strategy meetings, change efforts. However, even routine interactions like casual conversations with coworkers can be enhanced with mindful awareness. You can practice shifting your thinking modes by deliberately paying more attention during common communication events. For example, approach a classroom lecture with a mindful attitude, noting elements of delivery, audience response, and other factors you usually overlook. Or you might analyze a film from more than one point of view (see Application Project 2).

Effective Listening

Listening is key to coming to mutual understanding through dialogue. We can't come up with a joint, shared solution or speak to the needs of the other party unless we comprehend the other party's perspective. Skillful listening is also essential to process-ing the informational messages that make up technical dialogue. According to Judi Brownell of Cornell University, communication is best understood as listening cen-tered, not speaking centered.[10] She offers the multistage HURIER model to describe her listener-focused approach to communication. This model consists of the following six components:

Component 1: Hearing. The environment is filled with all kinds of stimuli. Listening begins when we focus on one or more of these elements—music, a radio announcer, the voice of a friend, a supervisor's phone call. What we choose to hear is dependent on our perceptual filters, which are made up of our cultural background, beliefs and values, past experiences, interests, family history, and other factors. Consider how you and a friend respond to the same stimuli, for example. If you are an avid skiboarder, you'll listen carefully to the morning radio report on mountain snow conditions. Your conversational partner (who is not interested in heading for the slopes) may change stations when this segment comes on.

Component 2: Understanding. Once the message is received, it must be processed. Like reading comprehension, listening comprehension is based on the literal meanings of the words and signals received. Shared language and vocabulary greatly increase the likelihood of understanding.

Component 3: Remembering. Memory allows an individual to retrieve information in order to come up with an appropriate response. Memory, like hearing, is especially influenced by our perceptual filters. Information we're interested in is retained; other messages are quickly forgotten.

Component 4: Interpreting. During this stage, meaning is assigned to the message based on words and nonverbal cues like context (location, previous events, partici-pants), vocal qualities, and body language.

Component 5: Evaluating. At this stage, the receiver makes a judgment about the accuracy and truthfulness of the message by evaluating evidence and reasoning, source credibility, the situation, emotional appeals, and other factors.

Component 6: Responding. We can only respond appropriately if we've successfully completed the first five steps of the model. Since listening is continuous, we must also adjust our messages even as we're speaking. If a coworker gives us a puzzled look while we're explaining a new technical process, for instance, we need to pause to ask if he or she understands our directions.

Listening can fail at any stage of the HURIER model. We might tune out impor-tant messages or fail to comprehend their meanings, forget essential data, come up with an inaccurate interpretation, misjudge the message, or formulate the wrong response. However, listening effectiveness increases when we approach conversations with a mindful attitude and incorporate the skills outlined in Ethics in Action 4.1.

ETHICS IN ACTION 4.1 LISTENING SKILLS

Hear Messages: Focus Attention and Concentrate

- Take a sincere interest in other people and ideas.
- Listen to new and difficult information.
- Stay active by taking notes, paraphrasing, etc.
- Manipulate the physical environment to make listening easier.
- Use the thought-speech differential (extra time generated by the ability to process speech faster than it is delivered) wisely.

Understand What You Hear

- Listen to the entire message.
- Distinguish main ideas from details.
- Recognize your personal assumptions and meanings.
- Increase your vocabulary.
- Check your perceptions.

Remember Messages

- Improve your short-term memory.
- Learn long-term memory techniques and use them regularly.
- Create associations.
- Use visual imagery.

Interpret Messages

- Develop empathy.
- Increase awareness of and sensitivity to nonverbal cues.
- Take into account the speaker's background attitudes and other variables.
- Take into account the communication context.
- Strive to be a high self-monitor (monitor the impact your behavior has on the other person).

Evaluate What You Hear

- Consider the speaker's credibility.
- Recognize personal bias.
- Understand persuasive strategies.
- Analyze logic and reasoning to identify logical fallacies.
- Recognize emotional appeals.

SOURCE: Brownell, J. (2003, November 22). *The skills of listening-centered communication.* Paper presented at the National Communication Association Convention, Miami, FL. Reprinted with permission of Dr. Judi Brownell.

Understanding how we prefer to listen can also improve our performance as listeners. Listening consultants Larry Barker and Kittie Watson identify four listening preferences.[11] Each has its own unique combination of strengths and weaknesses. Knowing the downside of our listening profiles can help us avoid listening errors.

People-oriented listeners put a priority on maintaining relationships. They are concerned, caring, and nonjudgmental and provide clear feedback. However, these communicators can get overly involved with others and may overlook their faults.

Action-oriented listeners concentrate on the task and are good at keeping meetings on topic while encouraging speakers to organize their thoughts. Unfortunately, they often come across as impatient, quick to jump to conclusions, and disinterested in relationships.

Content-oriented listeners (often those in technical fields) evaluate messages carefully, even highly complex ones, and explore all sides of an issue. Their weaknesses include getting bogged down in details and taking forever to come to a decision.

Time-oriented listeners value effectiveness and efficiency. They are good at saving time (theirs and others') but tend to interrupt, look at clocks and watches, and limit creativity by setting time limits.

While most people have one or two preferred styles, effective listeners know how to match their preferences or habits to the communication context. The action-oriented style works well in processing business proposals, for example, but is not so effective in the break room, where messages are not likely to be clearly structured. Time-oriented executives often get in trouble when they take this style home to conversations with their spouses and children. In these cases, effective listeners would adopt a people-centered approach. Conversely, a content-oriented style works better than a people-focused preference when the listener is engaged in technical processes like debugging software and creating engineering designs. (See this chapter's "Ethics and Technology" box for more information on how technology can interfere with effective listening.)

Confirmation

Treating the other person as a unique human being is at the heart of dialogue. Buber used the term *confirmation* to describe the process of recognizing and acknowledging the presence and value of others. He made this recognition of personhood the defining characteristic of human society:

> The basis of man's life with man is twofold, and it is one—the wish of every man to be confirmed as what he is, even as what he can become by men; and the innate capacity in man to confirm his fellow men in this way. . . . Actual humanity exists only where this capacity unfolds.[12]

Confirmation occurs when we value ourselves more after interacting with another person; disconfirmation takes place if we value ourselves less. Confirming behaviors (1) express recognition of the other person's existence, (2) acknowledge a relationship or affiliation, (3) express awareness of the significance or value of the other, and (4) accept or "endorse" the other person's experience or way of seeing the world. Disconfirming behaviors send the opposite message.[13]

Examples of disconfirming and confirming responses are outlined below. Ethical communicators try to avoid the first category of remarks and engage in the second set of behaviors.

Disconfirming Responses

Impervious: Failing to acknowledge the messages of the other person; ignoring; shunning

Interrupting: Cutting the other speaker short; beginning before he or she is finished

Irrelevant: Responding in a way that seems unrelated to what the other person has just said

Tangential: Acknowledging the previous message but immediately taking the conversation in a new direction

Impersonal: Conducting a monologue, speaking in an overly intellectual or impersonal way

Ambiguous; Responding with messages containing multiple or unclear meanings

Incongruous: Engaging in nonverbal behavior that is inconsistent with the verbal content of the message, as when a speaker denies being angry even as his voice rises and his face turns red

Confirming Responses

Recognition: Responding to the presence of the other person; treating the other person with respect

Acknowledgment: Providing a direct, relevant response to the message of the other person; asking questions, disagreeing, paraphrasing

Endorsement: Accepting the feelings of the other party as legitimate; letting the other person "be" without trying to analyze, blame, or change him or her

Researchers initially studied confirmation in the family setting. They discovered that confirming communication increases marital satisfaction and intimacy, helps build positive father-son relationships, and encourages children to have higher perceptions of their self-worth, appearance, intellectual capacity, and physical appearance.[14] More recently, investigators have begun to explore the effects of confirmation in the organizational context, focusing on the relationship between teachers and students. They point out that teaching has a relational component.[15] Professors want students to learn course content and have fulfilling interactions with them. For their part, college students want to learn and earn good grades. However, students have other goals as well, like feeling good about themselves and believing they have significant ideas to contribute.

According to confirmation researcher Kathleen Ellis, teacher confirmation is critical to helping students establish their identities. She discovered that teachers communicate confirmation through four behavioral patterns.[16] First, they are supportive of students' questions and comments by, for example, expressing appreciation for student input and listening attentively. Second, confirming instructors demonstrate interest in students and their learning both inside and outside of class. They make themselves available to answer questions before and after class sessions and make an effort to get to know students. Third, confirming professors use an interactive teaching style, which employs a variety of strategies and exercises to improve learning. Fourth, they avoid such disconfirming behaviors as embarrassing students in class or refusing to listen to those who disagree with them.

Instructor confirmation has a strong positive influence on the student-teacher relationship.[17] Students with confirming instructors learn more and develop a positive attitude toward the subject matter and the teacher. They also participate more frequently in class and are more likely to talk one on one with the instructor. Professors who engage in confirmation behaviors receive higher teaching evaluations.

ETHICS AND TECHNOLOGY

Waging War on Laptops in the Classroom

Laptops are a fixture in the typical college classroom. Universities encourage students to purchase these devices and, in some cases, provide them for incoming freshmen. Laptops can be used for note taking, accessing course materials from websites, linking to library databases, gathering information from the Internet, forwarding notes to those who miss class, and communicating with instructors. However, professors and institutions are discovering that laptops can interfere with learning as well as support it. The problem occurs when students bring their computers to class and use them to instant message their friends, visit websites, watch television shows and movies, check game scores, send e-mails to their families, and play Solitaire, Mindsweeper, and other games. Georgetown law professor David Cole sums up the temptations of the computer this way:

This is like putting on every student's desk, when you walk into class, five different magazines, several television shows, some shopping opportunities and a phone, and saying, "Look if your mind wanders, feel free to pick any of these up and go with it."[1]

Students sitting next to the computer user may find their attention diverted as well, creating what one instructor at the University of Colorado at Boulder calls the "cone of distraction." Even class members who take notes on their machines may see their performance suffer because they turn into stenographers who try to record every word a professor says. Several professors have compared the performance of their students who bring laptops to class with that of students who don't. Students who leave their computers at home generally do better; those who stop bringing their laptops to class see their grades improve.

A growing number of instructors and universities have begun to "wage war" on laptops in the classroom. Law schools at the University of Michigan and the University of Virginia have blocked wireless Internet in class. Instructors at Harvard Law School, Georgetown University, American University, the College of William and Mary, and other institutions have banned the use of laptops in their classrooms. In a vivid warning about bringing laptops to class, a University of Oklahoma physics professor poured liquid nitrogen onto a laptop and shattered it on the floor.

Not every instructor supports attempts to ban classroom laptops and Internet access. Some professors encourage students to bring their machines for classroom activities. The UCLA Anderson School of Management gave up on attempts to block Internet access, noting that students would still be able to text and send e-mails by hooking up their cell phones to their computers. As an alternative to outright bans, other schools provide lists of classroom technology etiquette guidelines. These standards cover both laptop and cell phone use. For instance, professors at the University of Wisconsin at Madison can download a set of technology guidelines from an online site to use in their syllabi.

The war on laptops in the classroom raises questions about the ethical responsibilities of students and instructors. Do students have an ethical duty to listen to their professors no matter how boring they are? Or do professors have an ethical duty to keep the attention of their students?

Note

1. De Vise, D. (2010, March 9). Web of diversions evicts laptops from lecture halls. *Washington Post,* p. A01.

Sources

Bugeja, M. (2007, January 26). Distractions in the wireless classroom. *Chronicle of Higher Education,* Careers, p. 1.

Mortkowitz, L. (2010, April 25). Laptops and other devices in class? For more colleges, it doesn't compute. *The Washington Post,* p. G03.

Ridberg, M. (2006, May 4). Professors want their classes 'unwired.'" *Christian Science Monitor,* Currents, p. 16.

Emotional Intelligence

Understanding and responding to emotions plays a critical role in building relationships. Emotionally sensitive individuals get along better with people in general, experience few negative interactions with friends, and are more supportive team members. In addition, they make better choices because they recognize how their moods influence their thinking, and they manage their feelings instead of falling victim to them. Researchers use the term *emotional intelligence (EI)* to describe the capacity to identify and influence emotions in others and in the self. However, they disagree as to what this competence entails. Many writers define EI as a collection of traits. For example, Daniel Goleman, who is credited with introducing EI to popular audiences, identifies 20 EI abilities, including such traits as empathy, self-confidence, achievement drive, trustworthiness, communication, conflict management, and organizational awareness.[18] He claims that EI is more important than traditional IQ in determining who emerges as "star" organizational performers.[19]

A number of critics point out that the trait approach to emotional intelligence has serious weaknesses. It is not clear why some competencies are considered part of emotional intelligence while others are left out. Including so many traits makes EI less useful as a teaching, training, and research tool. Then, too, EI traits, like those identified by Goleman, seem to include everything from self-perceptions, attitudes, and behaviors to motivations and moral virtues. Further, proponents of the traits approach often overstate the importance of EI in the workplace. There is little evidence to support claims that emotional sensitivity is the single most important factor in job performance or success.[20]

Psychologists Peter Salovey, John Mayer, and David Caruso offer a much narrower definition of emotional intelligence that avoids the pitfalls described above. They tie emotional intelligence to how individuals process information, describing EI as "the ability to engage in sophisticated information processing about one's own and others' emotions and the ability to use this information as a guide to thinking and behavior."[21] This intelligence is made up of the following four skill sets.[22] Each skill set is increasingly difficult and builds on the levels that come before.

1. *Identifying Emotions.* Emotions provide important data about what's happening to us, to others, and in the environment. Effective communication depends on accurately reading these signals and on accurately conveying how we feel. Unfortunately, research suggests that when it comes to interpreting emotional expressions, we are not as skilled as we think.[23] Most people can pick out intense emotional expressions but are less adept at identifying slight or partial displays of the same feelings. Accurate decoding is further complicated by the fact that facial displays of emotion during conversation last only a short time (generally from ½ to 2½ seconds). Skillful communicators have mastered these challenges and can do the following:

- Recognize their internal emotional states
- Talk about their feelings
- Communicate internal emotional states so that their feelings are understood as intended
- Accurately read people even when people try to disguise or repress their emotions
- Pick up on the emotional meaning of messages sent through body language, vocal cues, and facial expressions

2. *Using Emotions.* Emotions play an important role in reasoning and can enhance our thinking. Positive moods promote new ideas and risk taking; negative moods focus attention on details and possible errors.[24] Our chances of coming up with a good solution are greatest when we employ both modes of reasoning. For that reason, we might put ourselves in a positive frame of mind for a brainstorming session but wait until the next day to evaluate our ideas when we're not so optimistic and can do a better job of catching potential

problems. (Turn to Chapter 3 for more information on the link between emotions and ethical decision making.) Those with high emotional intelligence can do the following:

- Demonstrate creative thinking and imagination
- Inspire and motivate others
- Closely monitor events that generate strong emotions
- Match their emotions to the task and select tasks based on their mood

3. *Understanding Emotions.* Emotions aren't chaotic but have underlying causes and follow progressions. Annoyance leads to anger and then to rage, for example, but not the other way around. If we understand these patterns, we can better forecast how others will respond to events and plan accordingly. Emotionally sensitive individuals can do these things:

- Make correct assumptions about how others will behave
- Have an extensive emotional vocabulary that enables them to accurately communicate what they are experiencing
- Appreciate emotional complexity—the fact that communicators can experience contradictory emotions at the same time
- Accurately predict how others will respond and choose the right message

4. *Managing Emotions.* Emotions (even the unwelcome ones) need to be factored into reasoning, evaluation, and behavior. However, we need to manage our feelings instead of being controlled by them. Emotions can generate more productive outcomes if they are integrated into our thinking. Emotionally intelligent people can do these things:

- Resist unhealthy impulses
- Know when to follow their feelings and when to set them aside temporarily
- Are open to their own feelings and the emotions of those around them
- Let emotions activate productive behavior, like fighting against injustice when angry and avoiding risks when afraid
- Regulate their moods to achieve their goals; for example, getting "pumped up" before a class presentation or consciously shifting attention from a source of irritation to preparing for an upcoming meeting
- Establish genuine interpersonal connections
- Manage the feelings of coworkers in appropriate ways (cheer them up, calm them down)

Salovey, Mayer, and Caruso developed the Mayer-Caruso-Salovey Emotional Intelligence Test (MCSEIT) to measure these abilities.[25] The instrument asks respondents to complete a variety of tasks, including labeling facial displays of emotion, comparing emotions to physical sensations, and responding to emotional scenarios. Follow-up studies reveal that those who score higher on this test have more productive work relationships.[26] For example, in one study employees with high EI scores were rated by their colleagues as easier to work with and were credited with helping to create a positive work environment. Their leaders rated them as more interpersonally sensitive and sociable. In another project, managers who scored high on the MCSEIT were seen as engaging in more effective behaviors like communicating clearly and mentoring. Employees also noted that these supervisors supported the overall goals of the organization. In a third study, researchers found that customers were more satisfied when working with claims adjusters with high emotional intelligence.

The four skill sets of emotional intelligence, taken together, provide an "emotional blueprint" for dealing with organizational relationships of all kinds. This blueprint can be used to analyze past encounters or to prepare for important or difficult situations (client presentations, performance evaluations, termination interviews). One way to raise your emotional intelligence quotient is by evaluating a past conversation from the vantage point of emotion using the set of questions found in the Self-Assessment below. You can also use these same queries to analyze an upcoming event.

SELF-ASSESSMENT

Emotional Analysis Questions

Think of a recent communication encounter, and apply the following questions both to yourself and to the other person involved. Respond to each query. Then, apply the same questions to an upcoming conversation. Summarize your conclusions.

1. **Questions to Help You Identify Emotions**

   - How aware are you (was the other party) of your (his or her) emotions?
   - Were you aware of how you felt during this situation?
   - How do you feel right now?
   - How did you feel during this interaction?
   - How emotional were you?
   - Did you express your feelings to others? Appropriately so?
   - Were you expressing your true feelings or trying to cover them up?
   - Were you focused only on your feelings, or were you aware of the other person's feelings?

2. **Questions to Help You Use Emotions**

   - Did it help (will it help) you (the other party) to feel this way?
   - Did your mood focus you on the issue or away from it?
   - Did you find yourself feeling negative or positive about things?
   - Did your mood help you see the other person's point of view?
   - Were you able to feel what the other person was feeling?
   - How much did you pay attention to the problem?
   - Did you try to feel the emotions or block them out?

3. **Questions to Help You Understand Emotions**

   - Why did (do) you (does the other party) feel this way?
   - What caused you to feel the way you feel?

- Describe the intensity of your feelings.
- How will you feel next?

4. **Questions to Help You Manage Emotions**

- What did (do) you (does the other party) want to happen?
- What did happen?
- What did you do?
- How did it work out?
- Was there a better way to have handled it?
- Why didn't you handle it better?
- How satisfied were you with the outcome?
- How satisfied do you think the other person was with the outcome?
- What could you have done differently?
- What did you learn from this situation?

SOURCE: From Caruso, D. R., & Salovey, P., *The emotionally intelligent manager: How to develop and use the four key emotional skills of leadership.* Copyright © 2004. Reprinted with permission of Jossey-Bass, an imprint of John Wiley & Sons, Inc.

Trust Building

Interpersonal trust is often the "glue" that binds organizational members together. Those in trusting relationships feel a greater sense of interdependence, help one another, and are more willing to learn and to take risks, including the risk of engaging in dialogue. A group whose members trust each other makes higher-quality decisions, is more productive, and operates more efficiently.[27]

Trust is defined as "a psychological state comprising the intention to accept vulnerability based upon positive expectations of the intentions or behavior of another."[28] A cluster of attitudes and behaviors defines trusting relationships. First, trust involves optimistic expectations. Trusting individuals believe that the other party will carry through on promises and commitments. Second, those who trust put themselves in a vulnerable position. They depend on the behavior of others and have much to lose if these individuals break their commitments. Third, trust is willingly offered. Participants entering into trust relationships hope to increase cooperation and generate benefits, not only for themselves, but also for the group as a whole. All organizational stakeholders gain from such partnerships. Fourth, trust is hard to enforce. Organizations try to ensure cooperation through contracts, legal requirements, and other means. However, formal enforcement mechanisms don't have much impact on informal relationships between group members and can't, by themselves, create a trusting climate. Fifth, trust imposes an obligation or duty to protect the rights and interests of others. The target of trust is expected (a) not to harm the other party, and (b) to act in a way that benefits both individuals.

Interpersonal trust, because it involves obligation or duty, has a moral dimension.[29] More than just a strategy for ensuring cooperation and better results, trust also imposes ethical demands. We have a moral responsibility to protect and promote the interests of those who rely on us (put themselves in a vulnerable position). Breaking trust can be considered unethical because interpersonal trust serves the greater organizational good.

Earning the trust of others starts by demonstrating the character virtues described in Chapter 2. We need to express concern; to act in a consistent manner; and to be honest, open, and loyal. In addition, we need to demonstrate our competence. Others are more likely to trust us when we display knowledge and expertise by turning out high-quality work, responding to questions, completing assignments on time, and so on.

As a leader, you can take steps to help create organizations that encourage the development of trusting interpersonal relationships. Foster an atmosphere that encourages openness and sharing, be consistent in your behavior, and focus attention on the organizational mission by communicating vision and values.[30] These steps are described in more detail in Ethics in Action 4.2.

ETHICS IN ACTION 4.2 BUILDING BLOCKS OF ORGANIZATIONAL TRUST

Dialogue of Openness and Sharing

- Honesty with self and others (sharing humanness).
- No hidden agendas.
- No need to worry that what you say will be used against you.
- People feel valued for their contribution.
- People feel safe in expressing honest opinions.
- People do not withhold information for power.
- Basic belief that all people have good potential.
- Willingness to listen.
- Willingness to be vulnerable.

Consistency in Behavior

- Say it and do it.
- Do the right thing.
- Consistency in how decisions are made.
- Keep promises and commitments.

Everyone Committed to the Mission

- Know where the organization is headed.
- People know and believe in organizational goals.
- Teamwork.
- Sharing similar values.

SOURCE: Bruhn, J. G. (2001). *Trust and the health of organizations.* New York: Kluwer/Plenum, p. 82. Used by permission.

Despite our best efforts, we are likely to betray the trust of others and to be betrayed ourselves. Betrayal can be classified as major or minor, intentional or unintentional.[31] Major betrayals generate intense feelings of distress and disappointment; minor betrayals are less disruptive but can seriously undermine trust if they accumulate over time. Intentional betrayal is deliberate, consciously aimed at harming others. Unintentional betrayal is a byproduct of other actions and activities. Major intentional betrayals include deliberately withholding information, sharing corporate secrets, and sabotaging equipment. Major unintentional betrayals include layoffs resulting from restructuring and pay freezes produced by slumping sales. Minor intentional betrayals include gossiping, backbiting, and accepting credit for another person's work (see Case Study 4.1). Minor unintentional betrayals include consistently showing up late for work and regularly missing scheduled appointments.

When we experience betrayal, we need to work through our painful feelings and move forward. Consultants Dennis and Michelle Reina offer seven steps for healing.[32] First, observe and acknowledge what has happened. In this initial step, take note of what happened and how you are feeling as a result (i.e. e. depressed, angry, betrayed). Second, allow these feelings to surface—work through the pain, but refuse to wallow in worry and guilt. Third, get support by reaching out to family, friends, and coworkers who can act as "trusted advisors." Fourth, reframe the experience. Try to figure out why this event happened and what you learn from it. Fifth, take responsibility by considering if you played a role through your actions and choices. Think about what you could do differently next time. Sixth, forgive yourself and others. Forgiveness promotes our healing and provides insight into the motivations of the betrayer. Seventh, let go and move on. Make a choice to take what you have learned, and use those insights to improve your future work relationships.

In addition to managing our personal response to betrayal, we also need to work with the other party to rebuild the relationship. Organizational behavior scholars Roy Lewicki and Barbara Bunker argue that restoring trust requires the involvement of both parties—the violator and the violated.[33] Violators must take ownership of having destroyed trust, and the violated must commit themselves to the restoration process. The investigators outline five steps to restoring work relationships:

Step 1: Recognize and acknowledge that a violation has occurred. The violation has to be acknowledged if restoration is to take place. A violator may come to the realization that trust has been broken, or the victim may have to bring the offending acts to the offender's attention.

Step 2: Determine the nature of the violation—its causes and the offender's responsibility. Violators must recognize that they have caused harm (broken promises, failure to carry through, shared confidences) and assume responsibility for their actions. They may resist, however, by denying that they caused the problem or that the problem is important enough to warrant correction.

Step 3: Admit that the event damaged trust. Rebuilding trust requires discussion of what happened and the ensuing consequences. The violator needs to understand the victim's reactions and how the relationship has been undermined.

Step 4: Be willing to accept responsibility for the violation. Offenders need to be accountable for the relational damage, even if their actions were well intentioned and they were unaware of the consequences of what they had done. What's important is the perception of the trustor. If he or she perceives that trust has been broken, then it has been. Failing to acknowledge that fact will intensify the victim's anger and cause further relational deterioration.

Step 5: Repair trust. In this stage, balance is restored to the relationship. The violator tries to atone for the transgression, following the direction of the victim, who sets the conditions for the repair effort. Trust reconstruction can follow any of four paths. In the first sequence, the victim initially refuses any attempts to reestablish the relationship. He or she may feel too angry or injured or may believe that the relationship is not worth saving and/or can't be repaired. The violator then unilaterally takes action to change the victim's perspective by apologizing, asking forgiveness, sending letters, and demonstrating kindness. Both parties move on to trust repair if the offender changes the perspective of the victim.

In the second path, the victim sets unreasonable expectations for the violator out of the desire for revenge. When the violator resists these demands, the relationship is once again put at risk. The parties must come to a common agreement about the conditions for restoration if repair is to continue.

In the third path, the victim offers forgiveness without requiring any further acts of reparation. Both parties try to put the breach of trust behind them and move on. Nonetheless, there will probably be lingering relational tension as the offender feels embarrassed and the offended party remains suspicious.

In the fourth sequence, the victim offers forgiveness and spells out reasonable acts of reparation and restoration. These acts are designed to test the violator's sincerity and investment in the relationship to the victim's satisfaction. At the same time, the offender works through any guilt or remorse.

CASE STUDY 4.1

Taking Credit When Credit's Not Due

Monique Myerson works for the human resources department of a regional bank in the southeastern United States. This is her first job after college. Monique's performance reviews are outstanding. After handling the paperwork for benefits packages her first 2 years, she is now in charge of the department's minority hiring initiative. In just 12 months, she developed an internship program called Minority Advance in conjunction with her alma mater and other area universities. Under the program, students of color receive a stipend for interning with the bank their senior year. If their performance is satisfactory, they are offered permanent positions after graduation. Initial results are very encouraging. The percentage of minority hires is steadily increasing.

The success of Minority Advance attracted the attention of the local newspaper, which was doing a feature on diversity initiatives in business. That's when the trouble began. A reporter came to the bank and interviewed Monique's manager (the human resources director) when Monique was on vacation. The director described Minority Advance as her own brainchild and took credit for the program's success. When the article came out, it spoke in glowing terms of the program, citing it as a model workplace diversity effort. Monique Myerson was not mentioned once in the article.

Furious at seeing her ideas and hard work "stolen" by the director, Monique has arranged an appointment to meet with her tomorrow morning.

Discussion Probes

1. Why do you think the Human Relations director claimed credit for this program?

2. What should Monique say during her appointment to address this breach of trust?

3. How should the human resources director respond?

4. How can Monique and her manager restore their relationship based on the five steps of relational repair outlined in the chapter? Or can they?

5. Can you think of times when your trust was betrayed on the job? How did you respond? What would you do differently the next time a similar event occurs?

Moral Argument

Disagreement puts dialogue to the test. Buber encouraged disputants to walk the narrow ridge between opposing points of view. However, when we disagree, we tend to set up camp on one side of the ridge or the other. Remaining in dialogue during such encounters is never easy, but we are more likely to succeed if we follow guidelines for moral argument. The German philosopher Jürgen Habermas provides one set of ground rules, called *discourse ethics,* for engaging in argument.[34] Habermas believes that communities (towns, societies, organizations) develop their policies and moral norms through making and refuting claims and assertions. For community standards to be valid, Habermas argues that everyone affected by the decision must be allowed to freely participate in the discussion without fear of coercion. Every idea presented must be open to challenge, and all participants must have roughly the same power to influence one another. Individuals engaged in these discussions should be prepared to justify the claims they make during the argument. They must demonstrate that their statements are logically true, morally right, and sincerely offered.

Communication professor Rebecca Meisenbach offers a set of five steps for "enacting" discourse ethics in the organizational context.[35] The first step is to make a statement about actions or decisions that will have an impact on others. Not every decision needs to be guided by the rules of moral argument, only those that affect other organizational members, the local community, and the larger society. A proposal to reduce company contributions to an employee retirement plan would meet these criteria, for example.

The second step is to identify those who may be affected by the decision. In the case of modifying a retirement plan, this might include board members, stockholders, government regulators, and financial institutions, in addition to current and past employees.

The third step is to communicate to the parties identified in the second step. Interpersonal conversations, employee meetings, and Internet conferences could be used as channels for discussing the retirement plan changes.

The fourth step is to fully debate the consequences of the proposal (in this case, reduction of the current retirement plan) and decide if they are acceptable. Ensuring that all parties have an equal opportunity to be heard is critical in this stage.

The fifth and final step is to make a judgment about the claim and its consequences, determining if it is acceptable to all groups and therefore ethical. If the parties can reach a consensus that the retirement plan should be restructured, then the decision to make the changes is a moral one. (For another example of how moral argument can be applied in the organizational setting, turn to Case Study 4.3, "The Stem Cell Account.")

Discourse ethics sets a high standard for argument that is difficult to reach. For example, the hierarchical nature of organizations makes it difficult for all participants to have an equal voice; coercion is all too common. Nevertheless, you can take steps to improve your ability to promote and engage in moral argument. Practice perspective taking by imagining how others will be impacted by decisions. Make an effort to locate and involve everyone who has a stake in the decision, and involve these individuals in the decision process. (I'll have more to say about stakeholders in Chapter 12.) Engage in active listening to better understand the claims of others. Try to ensure that all groups and individuals have a roughly equal voice in the decision process. Most importantly, develop your ability to make valid claims and to evaluate the claims of others. Valid arguments are based on sound evidence and reasoning. Evidence consists of the information (facts, conditions, opinions, beliefs) used to support a position. For example, if you are arguing that more of your company's manufacturing process should be outsourced, then you might point to the fact that the firm has been losing money the last two years as evidence that your employer needs to cut costs. The strongest evidence has these characteristics:[36]

Reliability: Comes from a trusted source that has been accurate in the past, like a respected industry analyst.

High in expertise: Comes from sources knowledgeable about the topic at hand.

Objectivity: Draws from unbiased sources that don't have distorted judgment or prejudice related to the topic.

Consistency: Does not conflict with other sources of information or with other information provided by the same source.

Recentness: Reflects the latest developments.

Relevance: Directly relates to the claim being made.

Accessibility: Reflects the source's firsthand knowledge of, or access to, the topic being discussed.

Like evidence, reason or logic can be used to support your position and to dispute the arguments of others. (See Chapter 3 for more information on moral reasoning.) Common patterns of reasoning include (1) analogical (making comparisons between two objects or cases); (2) inductive (generalizing from one or a few cases to many cases); (3) deductive (moving from a larger category to a smaller one); and (4) causal (arguing that one situation or event causes another). Be alert to the potential weaknesses in each form of reasoning when constructing your argument or when analyzing the arguments of others.

Analogies hold only if the similarities between the two items being compared outweigh their differences. Take the case of comparisons between two schools, for example. You might be able to draw valid analogies between two neighboring small colleges, but it will be harder do so when comparing a small college and a major research university.

Generalizations must be made with care because a particular example may not hold for others in the same class or category. For instance, one graduate from a particular university may be a poor worker, but that doesn't mean that others from the same school will be poor performers, too.

Deductive arguments falter when communicators falsely assume that qualities from the larger group apply to every case within that category. Just because some neighbors object to a new plant doesn't mean that everyone in the area feels the same way, for instance.

Finally, causal relationships are often hard to establish. A sales decline is generally the product of several forces (new competition, an economic downturn, poor marketing), not just one. Be wary of inferring that chronological order means that the first event caused the second. A case in point: The university where I work has tripled in size since I was hired. However, it would be a mistake to say that my presence on campus accounts for the school's growth!

CHAPTER TAKEAWAYS

- Our attitudes set the moral tone for organizational conversations. Treat others as unique human beings (I-Thou) rather than as objects (I-It).
- Technical dialogue (information-centered speech) makes up the majority of communication in organizational settings. However, open a space for dialogue to occur by developing your communication skills and taking advantage of opportunities for I-Thou interaction.
- To engage in dialogue, you will need to commit yourself to (1) seeking the good of others, (2) valuing relationships and the common good, (3) openness to influence, (4) allowing others to hold differing opinions, (5) honesty, and (6) the willingness to invest time and energy in the process.

- Learn to be mindful; give your full attention to an encounter. Create additional categories in order to make greater distinctions, to welcome novel information, and to be open to new points of view.
- Understand communication as listening centered, not speaking centered. Keep in mind that listening is a multistage process made up of hearing, understanding, remembering, interpreting, evaluating, and responding (HURIER). This process can break down at any step along the way. Master listening skills and avoid listening errors by understanding the weaknesses of your listening profile.
- Confirmation is the process of recognizing and acknowledging the presence and value of others. You can affirm others by recognizing the other person, by acknowledging your relationship with that individual, by signaling your awareness of the other's significance, and by accepting the other person's experience and perspective.
- Master the four skill sets of emotional intelligence in order to get along better with others, to become a more effective manager, and to make wiser choices. These skills include (1) accurately identifying emotions, (2) using emotions to enhance reasoning, (3) understanding the causes and progressions of emotions to predict events, and (4) managing emotions to generate productive outcomes.
- Trust means putting ourselves in a vulnerable position, expecting that the other party will carry through on promises and commitments. We have a moral obligation to protect others who are relying on us, and we can build our trustworthiness by demonstrating moral virtues and competence.
- When someone violates your trust, you'll need to work through your painful feelings and learn from the incident. If you violate trust, you will need to accept responsibility for what has occurred and engage in trust repair with the other party.
- Moral argument involves everyone who would be affected by a decision, and each organizational member freely participates without fear of coercion. As a participant in a moral discussion, speak from the conviction that your arguments are right, and be consistent with your other statements and actions.
- Develop your ability to make valid claims and to evaluate the claims of others. Employ strong evidence, and be alert to potential weaknesses in analogical, inductive, deductive, and causal reasoning.

APPLICATION PROJECTS

1. Describe a time when you engaged in dialogue. When did it occur and with whom? What did each party say and do? What was the outcome of your encounter? How did both parties feel when it ended? What did you learn from the experience?

2. As a group, select a film, and assign each member to view it from a different point of view. Then, discuss the film based on each perspective. What insights do you gain from this perspective? What does this project reveal about the value of being open to many different points of view?

3. Based on the HURIER listening model, what are your strengths and weaknesses as a listener? What skills do you need to develop to become more effective?

4. As a small or large group, discuss Buber's assertion that confirmation (recognizing one another's personhood) is the defining characteristic of humankind.

5. Write up your responses from the Self-Assessment. Compare your current perspective to your thinking before you completed this exercise. How has your understanding of the past conversation changed? How might you prepare differently for the upcoming encounter?

6. Describe a time when trust was broken and then restored in one of your work relationships. Outline the effects of the breach of trust, how you worked through the painful feelings (if you were the victim), and how trust was restored.

7. Employ Habermas's moral argument guidelines in an ongoing disagreement. Report on the success (or the lack of success) of your efforts.

CASE STUDY 4.2

Mindlessness Meets Mindfulness: Napoleon Versus the Russian Bear

When Napoleon invaded Russia, he appeared to the world as a brilliant conquering hero, yet again proving his military genius by daring to march against a giant. But behind the proud banners and eagles, he carried a dangerous mind-set, the determination to have Russia no matter what the cost in human life. As Tolstoy describes him in *War and Peace,* Napoleon had no use for alternatives; his determination was absolute.

Opposite Napoleon stood the old Russian bear of a general, Kutuzov, a mellowed veteran who liked his vodka and had a habit of falling asleep at state occasions. An uneven match, or so it would appear.

As Napoleon's army advanced, Kutuzov let his army fall back and then fall back some more. Napoleon kept coming, deeper into Russia, farther from his supply lines. Finally, as Kutuzov knew it would, a powerful ally intervened: the Russian winter. The French army found itself fighting the cold, the wind, the snow, and the ice.

When Napoleon at last achieved his single, obsessive goal—Moscow—there was no one there for him to conquer. The Russians had set their holy city on fire to greet the invader. Once more, Kutuzov played the seeming loser.

At that moment, when Napoleon had no choice but to retreat—from the burned city, from the winter—the mindful old general attacked. He appealed to Mother Russia, an appeal that Stalin was to use with similar success years later. He appealed to the people to save their land, and that appeal revived all of Russia. The French had everything against them, including the Cossacks, who rode down off the winter steppes. Mother Russia prevailed, just as she would when Hitler was to repeat Napoleon's mistake.

Discussion Probes

1. How did the Russian Bear demonstrate each of the characteristics of mindfulness?

2. How did Napoleon demonstrate mindless behavior?

3. Can you think of other battles that have been won or lost because one army or the other engaged in mindful or mindless behavior?

4. How would your rate the level of mindfulness in your organization?

5. How can organizations encourage mindful behavior on the part of their members?

6. How can you become more mindful in your work communication and relationships?

SOURCE: From Langer, E., *Mindfulness,* copyright © 1989 by Ellen J. Langer. Reprinted by permission of Da Capo Press, a member of Perseus Books, L.L.C.

CASE STUDY 4.3

The Stem Cell Account

Tim O'Shannon is the owner of a small public relations agency located in the capital city of a midwestern state. Much of his firm's business comes from representing builders, solid waste haulers, and other groups to state agencies and lobbying on their behalf when the legislature is in session. Recently, he was approached by the local branch of the Stem Cell Research Alliance to lobby on behalf of a bill that would fund stem cell research in the state.

Tim knows that stem cell research is highly controversial and anticipates that he will have employees on both sides of the issue. Supporters want to use human embryos to generate tissue that can be used to fight Parkinson's disease, Lou Gehrig's disease, diabetes, and other illnesses. Opponents of stem cell research argue that embryos are humans and that using them for research is murder.

As the owner of the agency, O'Shannon knows that he alone could make the decision to accept or reject the stem cell account. Nonetheless, he worries that an arbitrary decision on his part could seriously damage morale and split the agency into warring factions. (Tim himself doesn't have a strong opinion on the issue but does have a brother who suffers from diabetes.) Further, he has always been committed to empowering employees and giving them a voice in the operation of the firm.

After letting the account proposal sit on his desk for several days, O'Shannon decides to involve his employees in the decision process. He will abide by the group's conclusion. He wants to set some ground rules, though, to ensure that the discussion, which could get very heated, is conducted fairly. He is open to bringing people from outside the agency into the discussion as well.

Discussion Probes

1. What groups are affected by this decision?

2. Who should be involved in the discussion?

3. How should the discussion take place? What communication channels should be used?

4. How can O'Shannon make sure that all participants are heard?

5. What instructions should Tim give the participants?

6. What kinds of claims could be made for or against accepting the account?

7. What types of evidence and reasoning could be used to support these claims?

Notes

For more information on the stem-cell research controversy, see:

Gardner, H. (2010, September 10). Stem cell financing ban ends, for now. *The New York Times*, p. 14.
Herper, M., & Langreth, R. (2006, September 4). Anti-ban billionaires. *Forbes*, pp. 124–130.
Munrol, N. (2002). Patient-lobbyists divided over cloning. *National Journal, 34*, pp. 1490–1491.
Vogel, G. (2001, March 3). Nobel laureates lobby for stem cells. *Science*, pp. 1683–1684.

ENDNOTES

1. Buber, M. (1970). *I and thou.* (R. G. Smith, Trans.). New York: Scribner's; Arnett, R. C., & Arneson, P. (1999). *Dialogic civility in a cynical age: Community, hope, and interpersonal relationships.* Albany: State University of New York Press; Johannesen, R. L. (2002). *Ethics in human communication* (5th ed.). Prospect Heights, IL: Waveland Press, Chap. 4; Biemann, A. D. (Ed.). (2002). *The Martin Buber reader: Essential writings.* New York: Palgrave Macmillan; Mayhall, C. W., & Mayhall, T. B. (2004). *On Buber.* Belmont, CA: Wadsworth-Thomson Learning.

2. Stewart, J. (2008). Cosmopolitan communication ethics understanding and action: Religion and dialogue. In K. Glenister Roberts & R. C. Arnett (Eds.), *Communication ethics: Between cosmopolitanism and provinciality* (pp. 105–119). New York: Peter Lang.

3. Arnett, R. C. (1986). *Communication and community: Implications of Martin Buber's dialogue.* Carbondale: Southern Illinois University Press; Czubaroff, J. (2000). Dialogic rhetoric: An application of Martin Buber's philosophy of dialogue. *Quarterly Journal of Speech, 2,* 168–189.

4. Cissna, K. N., & Anderson, R. (1994). Communication and the ground of dialogue. In R. Anderson, K. N. Cissna, & R. C. Arnett (Eds.), *The reach of dialogue: Confirmation, voice, and community* (pp. 9–30). Cresskill, NJ: Hampton Press.

5. Brown, C. T., & Keller, P. W. (1994). Ethics. In R. Anderson, K. N. Cissna, & R. C. Arnett (Eds.), *The reach of dialogue: Confirmation, voice, and community* (pp. 284–290). Cresskill, NJ: Hampton Press.

6. Brown, K. W. (2007). Mindfulness: Theoretical foundations and evidence for its salutary effects. *Psychological Inquiry, 18*(4), 211–237; Brown, K. W., & Ryan, R. M. (2003). The benefits of being present: Mindfulness and its role in psychological well-being. *Journal of Personality and Social Psychology, 84*(4), 822–848.

7. Langer, E. J., & Burgoon, J. K. (1995). Language, fallacies, and mindlessness-mindfulness in social interaction. In B. Burleson (Ed.), *Communication yearbook 18* (pp. 83–104). Thousand Oaks, CA: Sage.

8. Brown (2007); Brown & Ryan (2003); Burgoon, J. K., Berger, C. R., & Waldron, V. R. (2000). Mindfulness and interpersonal communication. *Journal of Social Issues, 56*(1), 105–127.

9. Langer, E. J. (1989). *Mindfulness.* Reading, MA: Addison-Wesley; Langer, E. J. (1997). *The power of mindful learning.* Reading, MA: Addison-Wesley; Langer, E. J., (1989) Minding matters: The consequences of mindlessness-mindfulness. *Advances in Experimental Social Psychology, 22,* 137–173; Sternberg, R. J. (2000). Images of mindfulness. *Journal of Social Issues, 56*(1), 11–26.

10. Brownell, J. (2003, November 22). *The skills of listening-centered communication.* Paper presented at the National Communication Association convention, Miami, FL; Brownell, J. (2002). *Listening: Attitudes, principles, and skills* (2nd ed.). Boston: Allyn & Bacon.

11. Barker, L., & Watson, K. (2000). *Listen up: How to improve relationships, reduce stress, and be more productive by using the power of listening.* New York: St. Martin's Press; Watson, K. W., Barker, L. L., & Weaver, J. B., III. (1995). The Listening Styles Profile (LSP-16): Development and validation of an instrument to assess four listening styles. *International Journal of Listening, 9,* 1–13; Chesebro, J. L. (1999). The relationship between listening styles and conversational sensitivity. *Communication Research Reports, 16*(3), 233–238; Villaume, W. A., & Bodie, G. D. (2007). Discovering the listener within us: The impact of trait-like personality variables and communicator styles on preferences for listening style. *The International Journal of Listening, 21*(2), 102–123.

12. Buber, M. (1965). *The knowledge of man: Selected essays* (M. Friedman, Ed.). New York: Harper & Row, pp. 67–68.

13. Cissna, K. N., & Sieburg, E. (1990). Patterns of interactional confirmation and disconfirmation. In J. Stewart (Ed.), *Bridges not walls: A book about interpersonal communication* (5th ed., pp. 237–246). New York: McGraw-Hill; Laing, R. D. (1994). Confirmation and disconfirmation. In R. Anderson, K. N. Cissna, &

R. C. Arnett (Eds.), *The reach of dialogue: Confirmation, voice, and community* (pp. 73–78). Cresskill, NJ: Hampton Press.

14. Ellis, K. (2004). Perceived parental confirmation: Development and validation of an instrument. *Southern Communication Journal, 67,* 319–334; Ellis, K. (2000). Perceived teacher confirmation: The development and validation of an instrument and two studies of the relationship to cognitive and affective learning. *Human Communication Research, 26*(2), 264–291.

15. Frymier, A. B., & Houser, M. L. (2000). The teacher-student relationship as an interpersonal relationship. *Communication Education, 49*(3), 207–219.

16. Ellis, K. (2004). The impact of perceived teacher confirmation on receiver apprehension, motivation, and learning. *Communication Education, 53,* 1–20.

17. Ellis, K. (2000; 2004); Goodboy, A. K., & Myers, S. A. (2008). The effect of teacher confirmation on student communication and learning outcomes. *Communication Education, 57*(2), 153–179; Schrodt, P., Turman, P. D., & Soliz, J. (2006). Perceived understanding as a mediator of perceived teacher confirmation and students' rating of instruction. *Communication Education, 55*(4), 370–388; Turman, P. D., & Schrodt, P. (2006). Student perceptions of teacher power as a function of perceived teacher confirmation. *Communication Education, 55*(3), 265–279.

18. Goleman, D. (2001). An EI-based theory of performance. In C. Cherniss & D. Goleman (Eds.), *The emotionally intelligent workplace: How to select for, measure, and improve emotional intelligence in individuals, groups, and organizations* (pp. 27–44). San Francisco: Jossey-Bass.

19. Goleman, D. (1998). *Working with emotional intelligence.* New York: Bantam Books.

20. Mayer, J. D., Salovey, P., & Caruso, D. R. (2008). Emotional intelligence: New ability or eclectic traits? *American Psychologist, 63*(6), 503–517.

21. Mayer, Salovey, & Caruso (2008), p. 503.

22. Caruso, D. R., & Salovey, P. (2004). *The emotionally intelligent manager: How to develop and use the four key emotional skills of leadership.* San Francisco: Jossey-Bass. See also: Mayer, J. D., & Salovey, P. (1993). The intelligence of emotional intelligence. *Intelligence, 17,* 433–442; Mayer, J. D., & Salovey, P. (1995). Emotional intelligence and the construction and regulation of feelings. *Applied and Preventive Psychology, 4,* 197–208; Mayer, J. D., & Salovey, P. (1997). What is emotional intelligence? In P. Salovey & D. J. Sluyter (Eds.), *Emotional development and emotional intelligence: Educational implications* (pp. 3–31). New York: Basic Books; Mayer, J. D., Caruso, D. R., & Salovey, P. (2000). Emotional intelligence meets traditional standards for an intelligence. *Intelligence, 27,* 267–298; Mayer, J. D., Salovey, P., & Caruso, D. R. (2004). Emotional intelligence: Theory, findings, and implications. *Psychological Inquiry, 15*(3), 197–215.

23. Ekman, P. (2003). *Emotions revealed: Recognizing faces and feelings to improve communication and emotional life.* New York: Times Books.

24. Gaudine, A., & Thorne, L. (2001). Emotion and ethical decision-making in organizations. *Journal of Business Ethics, 31,* 175–187.

25. Mayer, Salovey, & Caruso (2004); Salovey, P., & Grewal, D. (2005). The science of emotional intelligence. *Current Directions in Psychological Science 14*(6), 281–285; Caruso, D. R., Bien, B., & Kornacki, S. A. (2006). Emotional intelligence in the workplace. In *Emotional intelligence in everyday life* (2nd ed., pp. 187–205). New York: Psychology Press.

26. Lopes, P. N., Cote, S., & Salovey, P. (2006). An ability model of emotional intelligence: Implications for assessment and training. In V. J. Druskat, F. Sala, & G. Mount (Eds.), *Linking emotional intelligence and performance at work: Current research evidence with individuals and groups* (pp. 53–80). Mahwah, NJ: Lawrence Erlbaum; Mayer, Salovey, & Caruso (2004); Mayer, Salovey, & Caruso (2008).

27. Examples of the effects of trust and its qualities are drawn from the following sources: Brockner, J., Siegel, P. A., Daly, J. P., Tyler, T., & Martin, C. (1997). When trust matters: The moderating effect of outcome favorability. *Administrative Science Quarterly, 42,* 558–583; Dirks, K. T. (1999). The effects of interpersonal trust on work group performance. *Journal of Applied Psychology, 84,* 445–455; Dirks, K. T., & Ferrin, D. L. (2002). Trust

in leadership: Meta-analytic findings and implications for research and practice. *Journal of Applied Psychology,* *87,* 611–628; Mayer, R. C., & Davis, J. H. (1995). An integrative model of organizational trust. *Academy of* *Management Review, 29,* 709–734; McAllister, D. J. (1995). Affect- and cognition-based trust as foundations for interpersonal cooperation in organizations. *Academy of Management Journal, 38,* 24–61; Mishra, A. K. (1996). Organizational responses to crisis: The centrality of trust. In R. M. Kramer & T. R. Tyler (Eds.), *Trust in organiza-* *tions: Frontiers of theory and research* (pp. 261–287). Thousand Oaks, CA: Sage; Shaw, R. B. (1997). *Trust in the* *balance: Building successful organizations on results, integrity and concern.* San Francisco: Jossey-Bass; Zand, D. E. (1972). Trust and managerial problem solving. *Administrative Science Quarterly, 17,* 229–239.

28.   Rousseau, D. M., Sitkin, S. B., Burt, R. S., & Camerer, C. (1998). Not so different after all: A cross-discipline view of trust. *Academy of Management Review, 23,* 393–404.

29.   Hosmer, L. T. (1995). Trust: The connecting link between organizational theory and philosophical ethics. *Academy of Management Review, 20,* 279–403. See also: Michalos, A. C. (1995). *A pragmatic approach* *to business ethics.* Thousand Oaks, CA: Sage, Chap. 6.

30.   Bruhn, J. G. (2001). *Trust and the health of organizations.* New York: Kluwer/Plenum, p. 82.

31.   Reina, D. S., & Reina, M. L. (20006). *Trust and betrayal in the workplace.* San Francisco: Berrett-Koehler.

32.   Reina & Reina.

33.   Lewicki, R. J., & Bunker, B. B. (1996). Developing and maintaining trust in work relationships. In R. M. Kramer & T. R. Tyler (Eds.), *Trust in organizations: Frontiers of theory and research* (pp. 114–139). Thousand Oaks, CA: Sage.

34.   Habermas, J. (1970). Towards a theory of communicative competence. *Inquiry, 13,* 360–375. Habermas, J. (1990). *Moral consciousness and communicative action* (C. Lenhardt & S. Weber Nicholsen, Trans.) Cambridge, MA: MIT Press; Finlayson, J. G. (2000). Modernity and morality in Habermas's discourse ethics. *Inquiry, 43,* 319–340; Finlayson, J. G. (2005). *Habermas: A very short introduction.* Oxford, UK: Oxford University Press.

35.   Meisenbach, R. J. (2006). Habermas's discourse ethics and principle of universalization as a moral framework for organizational communication. *Management Communication Quarterly, 20*(1), 39–62.

36.   Inch, E. S., & Warnick, B. (2002). *Critical thinking and communication: The use of reason in argu-* *ment* (4th ed.). Boston: Allyn & Bacon; Infante, D. A. (1988). *Arguing constructively.* Long Grove, IL: Waveland Press.

5

Exercising Ethical Influence

O n the job, you can expect to devote much of your time to influencing others. Over the course of a day, you may find yourself urging the mail room to ship your package first, asking a subordinate to complete a project on time, convincing a customer to place another order, and persuading your boss to increase the budget for your department. The exercise of influence is not an option in the workplace. We must influence others if we are to fulfill our roles. If we don't, our work groups and organizations (not to mention our careers) will suffer.

While we don't have much choice as to whether or not we exert influence, we do have control over *how* we go about modifying the behaviors of others. These choices will go a long way toward determining the ethical health of our organizations. In this chapter, we'll address ethical questions that arise when influencing others. We'll begin with a look at power and then address moral issues related to impression management, deception, emotional labor, and the communication of expectations.

Questions of Power

The exercise of ethical influence is founded on an understanding of power, the capacity to control the behavior of others. Power is the foundation for influence. The greater the power we have, the more likely that others will comply with our wishes no matter what particular strategy we employ. However, to wield power ethically, we need to answer some important questions.

"But how do you know for sure you've got power unless you abuse it?"

SOURCE: © Robert Makoff 11/16/1992, The New Yorker Collection, www.cartoonbank.com

Question 1: Are Some Forms of Power More Ethical Than Others?

Power comes from a variety of sources. The most popular power classification system identifies five power bases:[1]

1. *Coercive power* is based on penalties or punishments; for example, verbal warnings, wage cuts, staffing reductions, and student suspensions.

2. *Reward power* depends on being able to deliver something of value to others, whether tangible (bonuses, health insurance, grades) or intangible (praise, recognition, cooperation).

3. *Legitimate power* resides in the position. Supervisors, judges, police officers, and instructors have the right to control our behavior within certain limits. A professor sets the requirements in her course, for example, but has no influence over what we do in our other classes.

4. *Expert power*, in contrast to legitimate power, is based on the characteristics of the individual regardless of his or her official position. Knowledge, skills, education, and certification all build expert power. As a result, those who are not in positions of authority can be very influential because they possess valued information.

5. *Referent (role model) power* rests on the admiration one individual has for another. We're more likely to do favors for a peer we admire or to agree to work over the weekend for a supervisor we respect.

No form of power is inherently immoral. In fact, we need to draw from a variety of power sources. The manager who is appointed to lead a task force is granted legitimate power that enables her to reward or punish. In order to succeed, she'll also have to demonstrate her knowledge of the topic, skillfully direct the group process, and earn the respect of task force members through hard work and commitment to the group. The effective use of one form of power can increase other power bases.[2] A widely admired employee who demonstrates expertise is more likely to be promoted. Conversely, the boss who has more access to information is better equipped to solve problems and thus will appear more expert. (Complete the Personal Power Profile in the Self-Assessment to determine how you prefer to influence others.)

SELF-ASSESSMENT

Personal Power Profile

Instructions

Below is a list of statements that describe possible behaviors of leaders in work organizations toward their followers. Carefully read each statement, thinking about *how you prefer to influence others*. Mark the number that most closely represents how you feel.

	Strongly Disagree	Disagree	Neither Agree nor Disagree	Agree	Strongly Agree
I prefer to influence others by					
1. Increasing their pay level	1	2	3	4	5
2. Making them feel valued	1	2	3	4	5
3. Giving undesirable job assignments	1	2	3	4	5
4. Making them feel like I approve of them	1	2	3	4	5
5. Making them feel that they have commitments to meet	1	2	3	4	5
6. Making them feel personally accepted	1	2	3	4	5
7. Making them feel important	1	2	3	4	5
8. Giving them good technical suggestions	1	2	3	4	5
9. Making the work difficult for them	1	2	3	4	5
10. Sharing my experience and/or training	1	2	3	4	5
11. Making things unpleasant here	1	2	3	4	5
12. Making work distasteful	1	2	3	4	5
13. Helping them get a pay increase	1	2	3	4	5
14. Giving them the feeling that they have responsibilities to fulfill	1	2	3	4	5
15. Providing them with job-related advice	1	2	3	4	5
16. Providing them with special benefits	1	2	3	4	5
17. Helping them get a promotion	1	2	3	4	5
18. Giving them the feeling that they have responsibilities to fulfill	1	2	3	4	5
19. Providing them with needed technical knowledge	1	2	3	4	5
20. Making them recognize that they have tasks to accomplish	1	2	3	4	5

Scoring

Record your responses to the 20 questions in the corresponding numbered blanks below. Total each column, then divide the result by 4 for each of the five types of influence.

	Reward	Coercive	Legitimate	Referent	Expert
	1	3	5	2	8
	13	9	14	4	10
	16	11	18	6	15
	17	12	20	7	19
Total					
Divide by 4					

Interpretation

A score of 4 or 5 on any of the five dimensions of power indicates that you prefer to influence others by using that particular form of power. A score of 2 or less indicates that you prefer not to employ this particular type of power to influence others. Your power profile is not a simple addition of each of the five sources. Some combinations are more synergistic than the simple sum of their parts. For example, referent power magnifies the impact of other power sources because these other influence attempts are coming from a "respected" person. Reward power often increases the impact of referent power because people generally tend to like those who can give them things. Some power combinations tend to produce the opposite of synergistic effects. Coercive power, for example, often negates the effects of other types of influence.

SOURCE: Modified version of Hinken, T. R., & Schreisheim, C. A. (1989). Development and application of new scales to measure the French and Raven (1959) Bases of Social Power. *Journal of Applied Psychology, 74,* 561–567.

Ultimately, the morality of a particular power source depends on the ends or goals that it serves. We need to ask if our exercise of power serves worthy objectives. However, arguing that no form of power is unethical in and of itself should not obscure the fact that some types of power are more likely to be abused. *Hard* power linked to organizational position (coercive, reward, and legitimate) is more dangerous than *soft* power linked to the person (expert, referent). Positional power gets immediate results, securing compliance and boosting short-term performance—but at a high cost. The use of legitimate, reward, and coercive power reduces trust and lowers task satisfaction and performance over the long term.[3] Of the three forms of positional power, coercive tactics pose the greatest risk. Extreme coercion can be devastating to individuals, attacking their dignity and value while threatening their mental and physical health.

To sum up, select your power bases carefully. Positional power should be used with caution. Reduce your reliance on authority, reward, and coercion by developing your skills and knowledge while modeling the behaviors you want to see in others. Coercion should only be employed as a last resort. It is best used for preventing and punishing incivility, dishonesty, aggression, discrimination, criminal activity, sexual harassment, and other destructive behaviors.

Question 2: Is It Possible to Have Too Much Power?

Concentration of power produces a wide range of unethical behavior, as Britain's Lord Acton noted in the 1800s. "Power corrupts," asserted Acton, "and absolute power corrupts absolutely." Lord Acton could have been commenting on the organizational scandals of our day. In case after case, powerful individuals abused their positions and put their organizations at risk. Enron CEOs Kenneth Lay and Jeffrey Skilling intimidated employees, making it harder for them to object to the unethical schemes that drove the company into bankruptcy.[4] John Bolton, former U.S. ambassador to the United Nations, was accused of treating his bosses with respect while bullying subordinates.[5] Richard Scrushy, disgraced former CEO of HealthSouth, berated his management team during weekly staff meetings.[6]

Positional power is most susceptible to abuse. Lord Acton probably had this type of control in mind when he noted power's corrosive effects. History's most infamous leaders—Nero, Stalin, Hitler, Pol Pot, Milosevic, Amin—used their lofty positions to darken the lives of followers through purges, torture, murder, and other means. However, many of these same leaders also misused their personal power. Followers believed that these leaders were endowed with special gifts and looked to them as role models.

There are a number of possible explanations for why unfettered power is so susceptible to misuse. The first ties in with our discussion of the shadow side of the personality in Chapter 2. Powerful individuals who fail to master their inner monsters are free to project their inner darkness on others. Without checks and balances, they cast deeper and deeper shadows on larger and larger audiences. Second, powerful people are more susceptible to judgment biases.[7] They typically devote little attention to finding out how others think and feel. As a consequence, they are more likely to hold and act on harmful stereotypes, which justify their lofty positions. In addition, they believe they deserve their high status because those who are powerless aren't as capable as they are. Third, powerful people protect their positions by attacking those they perceive as threats. Fourth, those in power often ignore the needs of others. They see subordinates as a means to achieving their ends. (Turn to Case Study 5.3, "The Two Faces of Steve," at the end of the chapter for an example of someone who has been known to intimidate followers.) Fifth, powerful individuals are tempted to rely upon positional power. Rather than building personal power bases, they employ coercion. Power holders are more likely to order subordinates to complete a task when a softer tactic (making a request, offering a reason) would achieve the same result at less emotional and relational cost.[8]

If you have considerable power, be open to influence. Influence needs to be reciprocal; leaders exert power but, at the same time, respond to the influence attempts of followers. Enact formal mechanisms like appeals procedures, subordinate feedback, recalls, and elections to encourage yourself to be responsive to your less powerful colleagues.[9]

Having too little power also poses ethical dilemmas.[10] Powerless members can't achieve worthy objectives and feel like they have no control over their environments. They focus on maintaining the little power they have instead of on achieving collective goals. Along with taking out their frustrations on other employees, they harm the organization through work slowdowns, breaking equipment, calling in sick, and other aggressive behaviors. Powerlessness also impairs cognitive functioning, making errors more likely.

Question 3: Should I Play Politics?

In organizational politics, members accumulate and use informal power to achieve personal and/or organizational objectives. Political behavior is not officially sanctioned by the organization and operates outside the formal power structure.[11] Examples of engaging in organizational politics include lobbying for a higher salary, forming a coalition with other managers to push through a project, or doing a favor for someone in another department in hopes that this individual will reciprocate in the future.

Most of us associate "playing politics" with hidden agendas, selfishness, backroom deals, manipulation, and deceit. More often than not, those who engage in politics get what they want while more deserving, nonpolitical individuals do not. Members who perceive that they work in highly political organizational climates are less satisfied with their jobs and less committed to their organizations. At the same time, they report higher stress levels and are more likely to leave the group.[12] (Turn to the Ethics and Technology feature for more information on how negative politics is conducted online.)

Given its poor reputation, it would appear that engaging in organizational politics is unethical. But that is not always the case. Sometimes going outside formal channels is the only way to achieve worthy objectives like getting top management to deal with safety problems, or to introduce innovative new products, or to keep the organization going when formal authority breaks down.[13] Then, too, informal power is an inescapable fact of organizational life. It is most frequently used in lateral or peer relationships to promote projects, to allocate resources like people and equipment, and to coordinate work flow. Dwight Eisenhower used his political skill to organize the successful invasion of Europe in World War II. Earlier in his career, he developed a network of friendships with George Patton, George Marshall, and Omar Bradley, generals who were to play a critical role in the assault. From a young age, Eisenhower was skilled at settling disputes and getting classmates to focus on a shared goal, abilities that were to serve him well as he planned the Normandy landing.[14]

Ensuring that our political behavior generates positive outcomes begins with a shift in our mindset. Organizational behavior experts Ronnie Kurchner-Hawkins and Rina Miller argue that we need to abandon our negative image of organizational politics and begin to think of the use of informal power as an opportunity to foster cooperation and collective achievements.[15] In Figure 5.1, they contrast the "dark side" of political power on the left side of the continuum with the bright, or positive, mindset on the right side.

Negative politics is self-centered, focused on achieving individual goals like promoting one's job or career; positive political action supports the vision and values of the group. In positive politics, power is no longer used to control others but is used to serve them instead. While negative politics relies on controlling through intimidation and manipulation, positive politics focuses on achieving a shared vision and living out shared values. Negative political behavior focuses on winning at all costs; positive politics stresses collaboration and working together (win-win). Negative organizational politics often ignores ethical standards and focuses only on efficiency ("doing things right."). Positive political strategies, on the other hand, recognize the importance of considering the ethical implications of actions and following moral standard ("doing the right things").

Kurchner-Hawkins and Miller go on to suggest that we need to develop strategies for achieving our goals through positive political means. When developing a political strategy for, say, promoting an organizational redesign, consider the following:

1. Identify and name the political behavior you want to engage in.

2. Identify your purpose and what you want to achieve; keep your focus on the organizational vision.

3. Consider the context of the group, its history and culture, and past interactions.

4. Identify who is involved and must influence or be influenced.

5. Anticipate the possible reactions to your plan and what's at stake.

6. Take responsibility for your behavior, considering what you are contributing and the effect of your actions on others in the organization both now and in the future.

7. Consider whether your actions will be consistent with personal and organizational values.

8. Consider how you might most effectively leverage change—how you can employ your influence, communication/information, alliances/relationships, and networks.

Question 4: What Factors
Contribute to Empowerment?

There are both ethical and practical reasons for giving power away. Distributing power to others supports such important ethical values as individual autonomy, fairness (equality), and concern for others. At the same time, empowering followers

Figure 5.1 Political Mindset Shift Continuum

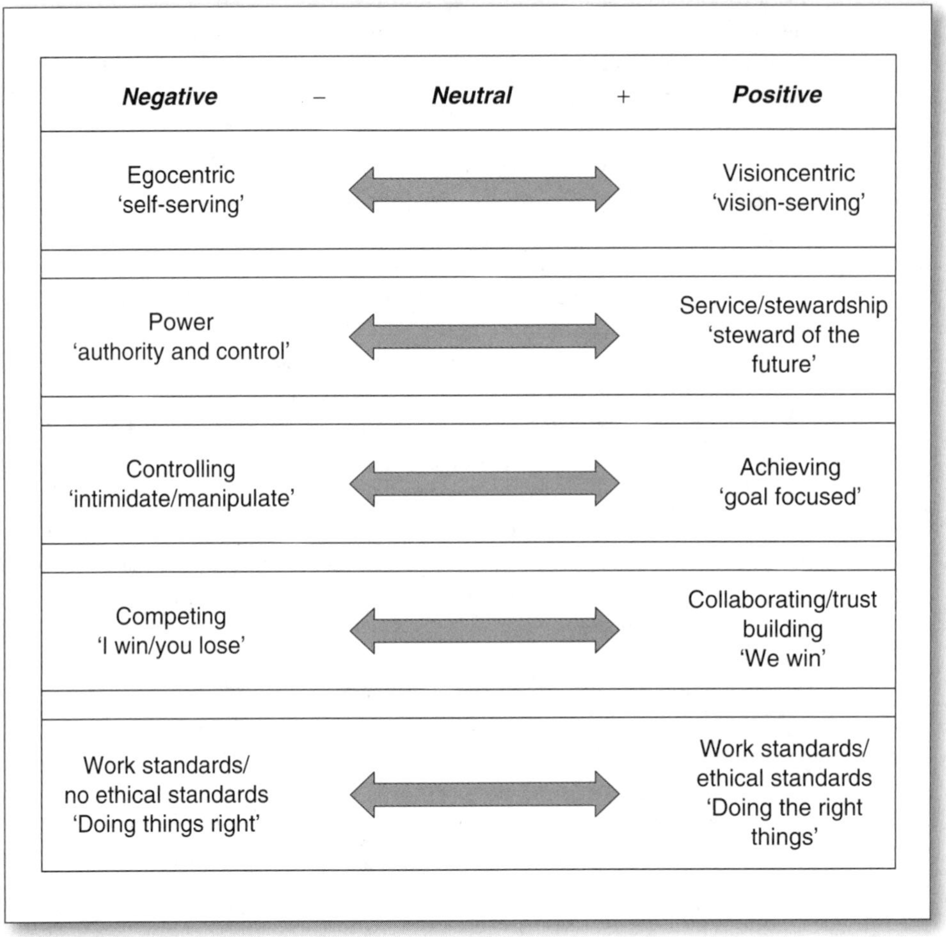

Negative	–	Neutral	+	Positive
Egocentric 'self-serving'				Visioncentric 'vision-serving'
Power 'authority and control'				Service/stewardship 'steward of the future'
Controlling 'intimidate/manipulate'				Achieving 'goal focused'
Competing 'I win/you lose'				Collaborating/trust building 'We win'
Work standards/ no ethical standards 'Doing things right'				Work standards/ ethical standards 'Doing the right things'

SOURCE: Kurchner-Hawkins, R., & Miller, R. (2006). Organizational politics: Building positive strategies in turbulent times. In E. Vigoda-Gadot & A. Drory (Eds.), *Handbook of organizational politics* (Figure 19.1, p. 332). Cheltenham, UK and Northampton, MA: Edward Elgar. Used by permission.

boosts the bottom line. Researchers report that empowered individuals and groups perform better. People like their jobs more, work harder, take more responsibility, and are more committed to their organizations when they feel that they have a significant voice in shaping decisions.[16] They're more likely to cooperate as well. Paradoxically, you gain more power by distributing it to others.[17] The performance of the group increases as a result (as do perceptions of your power). Empowerment also fosters the personal growth of followers. Sharing power can help them learn new skills, tackle new challenges, and find greater fulfillment.

Psychological empowerment refers to increased motivation to carry out tasks associated with work roles. According to organizational scholars Kenneth Thomas and Betty Velthouse, this heightened motivation is the product of four factors:[18]

Meaning: Meaning is the value placed on a task, goal, or purpose based on personal standards. The better the fit between the purpose of the task and our standards, the greater our motivation to do the job.

Competence: Competence is the belief that we can do the job required. It is part of a broader sense of personal power or self-efficacy. Self-efficacy is the conviction that we can deal with the events, people, and situations at work and in other environments.[19]

Self-Determination: Self-determination is the sense that we have a choice in how we carry out our jobs—when to start, how fast to work, how to prioritize tasks.

Impact: Impact is the extent to which we can influence the larger organizational environment. Those with a high sense of impact believe that they make a difference in the work group's operating procedures, plans, and goals.

All four of the cognitive components of empowerment are shaped by elements of the work group environment. As a consequence, we can boost perceptions of empowerment as managers by modifying the setting where work occurs, including reward systems, job duties, organizational structure and work flow, rules, and physical layout. Elimination of situational factors that create feelings of powerlessness is an excellent place to start. Get rid of petty regulations, authoritarian supervision, and strict routines. Next, shift more decision-making authority to followers. Allow those assigned to do the task a great deal of leeway in how the task gets done. Invite employees into organizational decision-making processes. At the same time, supply resources. Completing a task depends on having adequate funds and supplies, sufficient time to devote to the job, and a place to work. The support of leaders is essential for major projects. The introduction of new products, accounting systems, and software programs requires the endorsement of important individuals who also encourage other leaders to buy into initiatives.[20]

Information may be the most important resource for empowerment. Data about the competition, consumers, and strategy help members see the "big picture." They gain a better understanding of their roles in the organization and how their efforts help achieve collective goals. Access to information builds self-efficacy and enables individuals to make better decisions while exerting influence over the direction of their work units. Newly empowered followers, in particular, need information in order to carry out more demanding assignments. At one pet supply manufacturer, managers gave employee teams the power to shut down the production line and set production schedules. To prepare workers for this added responsibility, they provided employees with production schedules and information on customer requirements. The company developed a set of criteria for shutdowns, trained teams to diagnose line malfunctions, and told them how much it cost to shut down and restart production. Workers discussed case studies involving line shutdown decisions. They then exercised their new powers for three months with review by managers. At the end of that period, they controlled the production process entirely on their own.[21]

ETHICS AND TECHNOLOGY

Negative E-Politics

In e-politics, organizational members engage in negative political behaviors online. Several features of e-mail facilitate the creation and dissemination of self-serving messages. First, electronic distribution lists make it easier to influence large numbers of people without having to be physically present. Second, attachments (letters, video clips, and photos) can be used to support the e-mailer's position. (Attaching lots of documents can also confuse receivers and obscure issues.) Third, the impersonal nature of e-mail reduces the stress and risk of confronting others in person. Aggressive people can attack others simply by hitting the "send" button. Fourth, e-mail systems allow communicators to secretly forward messages without the sender's knowledge.

A group of University of Louisville professors surveyed 244 employees from a variety of businesses to determine how employees utilize e-mail and other communication channels to send selfish political messages. They discovered that e-mail is most frequently used to send work-related messages. Negative political messages are more likely to be communicated face to face, though e-mail was the second most popular political communication channel, rating ahead of the phone and memo or letter. Ingratiation was the most popular online impression management strategy, followed by developing a base of support and forming coalitions.

The investigators offer these guidelines for reducing the frequency of negative e-politics:

1. Send attachments only when they help the receiver ("Seek to express, not impress.")
2. Even if an attachment is necessary, don't overload the receiver with information.
3. When you consider forwarding e-mail without the permission of the sender, think carefully about the possible impact on the message source.
4. Before forwarding copies, make sure your goal is to help the team and the organization.
5. Just because you can e-mail the entire organization doesn't mean that you ought to do so. Create smaller recipient groups instead.

Sources

Kuzmits, F., Sussman, L., Adams, A., & Raho, L. (2002, October). Using information and e-mail for political gain. *The Information Management Journal*, pp. 76–80.

Sussman, L., Adams, A. J., Kuzmits, F. E., & Raho, L. E. (2002). Organizational politics: Tactics, channels, and hierarchical roles. *Journal of Business Ethics, 40,* 313–329.

Question 5: How Do I Overcome Barriers to Empowerment?

Empowerment efforts face significant obstacles. Keeping, not sharing, authority is rewarded in traditional, top-down organizations. Managers in these systems are afraid to let go of their power for fear of failure. Adopting any new approach is risky, particularly when it comes to empowerment. Managers lose control and have to rely on the efforts of team members. They may be punished if their subordinates fail to produce. Success in a more equalitarian system also requires a different skill set. Empowering managers must provide resources instead of direction, share information, and facilitate the group process. Newly empowered followers are anxious, too. They're used to having one person make the final decision and must take on greater responsibilities. Some are not eager to learn new skills and are afraid of making mistakes.

Management professor and consultant Alan Randolph admits that empowerment is hard to put into practice but notes it has been successfully implemented at such companies as the Marriott Corporation, General Electric, AES, Springfield Remanufacturing, and Pacific Gas and Electric. Companies who want to take "the long journey to empowerment" must pass through three stages.[22]

Stage 1: Starting and orienting the process of change. Any major empowerment initiative must begin not with a grand vision but with practical answers to personal concerns. People want to know why the change is needed and what's wrong with the way things operate now. Further, they want to understand how the change will impact them and how they stand to gain (or lose). Providing information—financial statements and projections, data on market changes—motivates members to do a better job. At the same time, managers need to set boundaries so members don't feel overwhelmed. Boundaries can be established through setting goals and by providing training that equips employees to reach those objectives. Most successful empowerment efforts replace hierarchy with self-directed work teams.

Stage 2: Making changes and dealing with discouragement. In this stage, the focus shifts to concerns about implementation and impact. Workers wonder what they need to do to be empowered, where to go for help, and why the process is so difficult. They also question whether the effort is worth it and doubt that any progress is being made. Once again, members desire data, this time about how to proceed. They need to know where to get help, what to do if things go wrong, and whether the initiative is producing results. Instead of backing off empowerment efforts, leaders need to expand boundaries further. Work teams ought to be given even more responsibility for work flow, not less. The good news is that once results begin to appear, members will promote the advantages of empowerment to their colleagues. One key during this step is to change performance appraisal systems to reward collaboration instead of individual efforts.

Stage 3: Adopting and refining empowerment to fit the organization. At this stage, a culture of empowerment emerges. Concerns turn to collaboration and refinement. Individuals in this final step want help getting everyone involved in the process because they know empowerment works. They also want to learn how to perform even better. Managers and teams share data with each other about how to make improvements. Employees internalize commitment to the values and goals of the organization.

Organizational empowerment has its share of critics.[23] Some complain that empowerment is just a management fad and that far too many organizations give it lip service only, resisting any meaningful change efforts. Employees then become disillusioned and resentful as trust breaks down. Others complain that managers and employees understand the term *empowerment* differently. Empowered employees may expect to be treated equally, while managers view empowerment as a means for better getting the work done. The most cynical observers believe that empowerment is a form of exploitation. In participative systems, workers contribute more ideas and energy but don't get rewarded for their additional efforts.

These criticisms are valid. Empowerment can be faddish and exploitive. Yet it doesn't have to be. Truly empowering organizations back up their talk with their walk, following through on their commitment to change. These groups recognize that genuine empowerment benefits both workers and management. They boost compensation for those who accept more responsibility.

Ethical Issues in Influence

Selecting the appropriate tactic is one of the most important choices we make when exerting influence. Ethical considerations should always play a central role in this determination. In the remainder of this chapter we'll look at the ethical issues raised by four widely used organizational influence strategies: impression management, deception, emotional labor, and the communication of expectations.

Impression Management

In the organizational setting, you'll have little chance of getting what you want unless you create the desired image. Want a raise? Then you must convince your supervisor that you are hardworking and productive. Want to be assigned to be a project leader? Then you must be seen as competent and able to manage others. Want to make a sale? Then customers must perceive that you are honest and trustworthy. Want more staff for your work group? Then you'll have to convince the management team that your group is critical to the organization's success.

Scholars use the term *impression management* to describe how people try to control the images others have of them through their behaviors.[24] Impression management is a part of all human interaction, but it is particularly evident in the organizational setting. In a very real sense, organizations act as stages. On the organizational stage, members perform a variety of roles for different audiences. Consider the average professor, for example. Faculty members are typically evaluated on their teaching, scholarship (research), and service. To succeed, our instructor will have to perform well in the classroom, write for scholarly publications and present papers to academic peers, and demonstrate leadership at the university and in the local community. Each of these audiences requires a different performance. The highly technical jargon of the academic journal or presentation won't work well, for instance, with community audiences. The ability to accurately evaluate student work is essential to a successful teaching performance but has little relevance to research and service.

There are a variety of ways to manage the image that others have of us in the organizational setting, ranging from what we say and wear to the layout of our dorm rooms and offices. These tactics can be divided into two major categories: *acquisitive impression management* and *protective impression management.*[25] Acquisitive tactics are attempts to be seen in a positive light; protective tactics are attempts to avoid looking bad. Both sets of tactics, in turn, can be directly or indirectly applied. Parties use direct tactics during interactions, while indirect tactics involve the process of association. If Dan wants to convince Mary that he deserves a raise, he might point out how hard he works. Or he might take a more indirect approach, counting on her to remember that he was part of the team that launched the company's hottest new product. A catalog of organizational impression management tactics is provided in Ethics in Action 5.1.

ETHICS IN ACTION 5.1 IMPRESSION MANAGEMENT TACTICS

Acquisitive/Direct Tactics

1. *Ingratiation*

   Goal: To appear more likeable and attractive

   Examples: Expressing similar attitudes, doing favors, flattering, complimenting, publicizing one's desirable qualities

2. *Self-Promotion*

   Goal: To appear competent.

   Examples: Claiming relevant work experience on a résumé, mentioning a high grade point average in a job interview

3. *Intimidation*

   Goal: To gain social power and influence by appearing dangerous

   Examples: Using coercive power to ensure follower compliance, using counterpower (lawsuits, a tough image) to intimidate superiors

4. *Exemplification*

   Goal: To generate impressions of integrity and morality

   Examples: Publicizing self-sacrifice (working over the weekend or while sick), going beyond the call of duty

5. *Supplication*

   Goal: To secure help by appearing incompetent

   Examples: Asking for help with a new computer program, claiming poor speaking skills to get someone else to make the class presentation

(Continued)

(Continued)

Acquisitive/Indirect Tactics

1. *Acclaiming*

   Goal: To highlight a relationship or association with a successful occurrence

   Examples: Claiming to be responsible for success (softball team victory, higher sales), maximizing the value of a positive event (noting that not only did you graduate from college, you graduated from one of the country's top-rated universities)

2. *Nonverbal Impression Management*

   Goal: To encourage liking through nonverbal behaviors

   Examples: Smiling and leaning forward during a job interview, renting expensive office furniture to create an image of financial stability

Protective/Direct Tactics

1. *Accounts*

   Goal: To lessen or repair the damage after a failure has occurred

   Examples: Making excuses—admitting that an action is wrong but denying responsibility for it ("It wasn't my fault"); offering justifications—accepting responsibility but claiming that the event wasn't as bad as it seemed or that the behavior was justified

2. *Disclaimers*

   Goal: To lessen the potential damage that might be caused by an upcoming failure event

   Examples: Claiming credentials to make racist comments ("some of my best friends are . . ."), claiming an exception to the rules, asking for a suspension of judgment

3. *Self-Handicapping*

   Goal: To put self-imposed barriers in place when outcomes are uncertain, in order to maximize the value of success and minimize the penalties for failure

   Examples: Claiming to be coming back from an injury prior to a racquetball game with a coworker, mentioning an illness that prevented you from doing as much research as you wanted

4. *Apologies*

   Goal: To obtain pardon by admitting responsibility and blame

   Examples: Expressions of remorse, offers of restitution, requests for forgiveness

Protective/Indirect Tactics

1. *Blaring*

   Goal: To disassociate from a negative event or person

   Examples: Publicizing a lack of connection with the occurrence or individual ("I had nothing to do with that project"; "I was always suspicious of him")

2. *Blasting*

   Goal: To exaggerate the bad qualities of a person to whom we are connected but don't want to be

   Examples: Pointing out the poor work habits of another team member, claiming that a supervisor is abusive

SOURCE: Excerpt from *Impression Management in Organizations: Theory, Measurement, Practice* by Rosenfeld, P., Giacalone, R. A., & Riordan, C.A. (1995). Permission granted by Cengage Learning EMEA Ltd.

Some observers equate impression management with manipulation. To them, impression managers are phonies who try to deceive others by projecting a false image when they should strive to reflect their "true" selves instead. They note that competent performers get passed over in favor of employees who ingratiate themselves with the boss.

It is easy to see why impression management would be viewed with suspicion. We probably have all encountered individuals who are "all style and no substance." These coworkers are all too ready to change their behaviors and standards to conform to the wishes of others. They get ahead by projecting a good image instead of through hard work. Our academic and work careers may have languished because professors and supervisors played favorites.

Research confirms that we are right to be concerned about the ethics of impression management. Skilled impression managers are more likely to be hired and promoted regardless of ability. This puts women, who are more likely to rely on their performance to get ahead, at a disadvantage. Careerists who care little about coworkers and organizational goals use self-promotion to advance themselves at the expense of others.[26] Deceit can quickly turn impression management into manipulation, as in the case of job applicants who overstate their skills and background (see Case Study 5.1, "To Pad or Not to Pad?"). One study reported that 95% of college students were willing to make at least one false statement in order to get a job. More than 40% of the respondents in the same study had already done so. This happens despite the fact that falsifying credentials and past accomplishments can serve as grounds for dismissal. Padded résumés cost George O'Leary the opportunity to coach at Notre Dame and Kenneth Lonchar his job as Veritas Software's chief financial officer.[27] We'll take a closer look at the ethics of deception in the next section.

CASE STUDY 5.1

To Pad or Not to Pad

Johann Schultz is graduating in the spring from Midwestern University with a degree in computer science. He knows that landing a job out right out of college will be tough in a tight economy. Employers have their pick of applicants to choose from. He will have to stand out in order to be noticed.

Recently, a local consulting firm announced it would open a division to provide computer security advice and systems to large corporations. Some of the positions in the division will require extensive work experience, but others will be open to college graduates. In addition to a degree in computer science, requirements for the entry-level openings include oral and written communication skills, a working knowledge of the SpyEye X security program, a 3.5 grade point average, and the ability to lead project teams.

Meeting the communication criteria is no problem for Schultz, who always found writing papers and making presentations easier than taking tests. Fulfilling the other requirements will be more of a problem, however. Johann is familiar with the other leading security programs but not SpyEye X. He knows someone who works with the program, though, and could practice with it before he is interviewed and hired. His cumulative GPA is 3.3, not 3.5. Further, while he was a member of several successful project groups in school, Johann's work schedule prevented him from taking a leadership role in any of these teams.

Johann believes that some of the criteria (like the GPA) were arbitrarily selected to weed out applicants and aren't a true reflection of ability. He is convinced that, if he can land this job, he can succeed and help this employer.

Discussion Probes

1. Should Johann alter any details on his résumé in order to land this job? Why or why not? If you answered yes, which information should he change?

2. Are slight exaggerations more justified than outright lies on résumés?

3. Why is lying on résumés and in job interviews so widespread?

4. What are the potential long-term consequences to an applicant for lying or withholding part of the truth on a résumé? What are the consequences to the employer?

5. What responsibility do organizations have to check up on the claims that applicants make on their résumés? What actions should they take when they discover deceit?

Recognition that impression management is prone to abuse does not mean we should abandon this form of influence. In fact, it would be impossible to do so. Impression management is found in every culture. Whatever the particular setting, humans want to achieve their goals and to be seen in a favorable light. Impression management is also hard to eliminate because it can occur at the unconscious or semiconscious level. For example, you may not have given much thought to why you brushed your teeth this morning or chose a particular shirt or top to wear. Yet both of these activities help shape the impressions you make on others throughout the rest of the day.

Other organizational members are forming impressions of us, whether we are intentional about our behaviors or not. Even our attempts to avoid impression management tactics influence the impressions of others. Take the example of the job applicant who thinks that dressing up for an interview is "fake." His sloppy appearance manages the impressions of the employer, only in a negative manner. The interviewer may think that the applicant doesn't understand what the business world is like, that he didn't care enough about this job to make an effort to look good, or that his work habits may match his appearance.

Impression management serves many useful purposes (see Case Study 5.2, "Taking Charge at the Assisted Living Facility" at the end of the chapter). More often than not, individuals use IM to project an image that is congruent with who they think they are. Rather than deceiving or manipulating others, they want to accurately reflect their identities. Impression management is also essential to accomplishing moral objectives. Convincing management that a department legitimately needs more resources benefits both the work unit and the total organization. Department members will feel fairly treated and produce more. Organizational performance will likely increase because budget and personnel will be strategically allocated.

Organizational impression management experts Paul Rosenfeld, Robert Giacalone, and Catherine Riordan offer the following standards for determining if impression management is beneficial or detrimental to an organization.[28] Beneficial impression management (1) facilitates positive interpersonal relationships both inside and outside the organization; (2) accurately portrays positive people, products, and events to insiders and outsiders; and (3) facilitates effective decisions. Dysfunctional impression management (1) inhibits or obstructs internal and external relationships; (2) inaccurately casts persons, events, and products in a bad light; and (3) distorts information, which leads to erroneous conclusions and decisions.

These standards place ethical demands on impression managers as well as on their audiences. We have a responsibility to generate accurate images. In particular, we need to resist the temptation to exaggerate, for example, by claiming more than our fair share of the credit for a class group project or overstating how much we like the boss's ideas. Self-interest should always take a back seat to the interests of others, which means that impression management ought to be a tool for carrying out our roles in a way that benefits both the organization and its constituencies. One way to ensure that our performances are honest and effective is through pursuing our vocations (see Chapter 2). Finding the right job fit will put us in roles that we are passionate about and well suited to fill.

Targets of impression management tactics have an ethical responsibility to ensure that agents aren't unduly or unfairly shaping decisions and outcomes. Job interviewers and human resources personnel need to use objective criteria in hiring decisions. Managers need to be aware that they are susceptible to ingratiation and beware of playing favorites. They, too, need to base personnel decisions on objective criteria, knowing that women in particular may not trumpet their accomplishments as much as men do. Careerists should be confronted. Their success should be tied to how well they cooperate in a group, not on how well they promote themselves.

Deception

Deceit, as noted above, is often used when influencing others. Deception is defined as knowingly trying to mislead others. While deception can occur when parties keep secrets or reveal only part of the truth, lies are the most obvious example of messages designed to convince others of something we ourselves don't believe. Liars are (a) aware that the information is false, and (b) knowingly deliver a message, with (c) the intent to mislead someone else.

Explanations for the causes of organizational lying generally fall into two categories: self-interest and role conflict.[29] Members lie for personal benefit—to cover up a mistake, save money, further a career, or avoid conflict with the boss. They also lie in order to relieve tension between the various roles they play. For example, a contractor who is unable to complete two remodeling projects at the same time may falsely claim to be waiting for materials in order to placate one homeowner while working at the other job site.

The combination of role conflict and self-interest is more likely to result in deceit than is either factor on its own. Role conflict acts as a stimulus, providing the reason to lie; rewards then provide the motivation or encouragement to engage in lying. The contractor in our example feels caught between two sets of role obligations, and his lie pays off by buying him more time to complete (and to get paid for) both tasks.

Most moral thinkers concur that lying is wrong.[30] Deontological theorists (and some theologians) generally prohibit lying on the basis that such behavior violates moral law or duty. If everyone lied, we would lose our confidence in verbal commitments and in the value of speech itself. Many utilitarians point out that lies typically cause more harm than good. Even if the benefits of a particular lie outweigh the harm (telling "white" lies to protect the feelings of a coworker, for example), the practice of lying generates more costs than benefits. Virtue ethicists note the damage done to the character of the person who lies. Habitual lying becomes second nature, driving out such virtues as honesty, consistency, and integrity.

Researchers who study lying in the organizational context also take a dim view of the practice. They note that lying is costly to organizational performance. Lies not only undermine trust, they corrupt the flow of information essential to organizational decisions and coordination. Deception damages the reputation of the organization, lowers job satisfaction, drives out ethical employees, and encourages further dishonesty.[31]

While the preponderance of evidence suggests that lying and related forms of deception are unethical, there are a number of exceptions to this general rule. The law allows police officers to lie to suspects in order to obtain confessions, for instance, and we applaud investigators who go undercover to uncover fraud and corruption. Organizations maintain trade secrets, and nations attempt to dupe each other during war.

Ethicist Sissela Bok offers the *principle of veracity* as a way to affirm our commitment to the truth while acknowledging that deceit may be justified in special circumstances.[32] She contends that truth should function as the moral standard. Liars must assume the burden of proof if they want to violate this standard, establishing that deceit is justified. In particular, they need to look at the lie from the target's point of view. Deception might be justified from the liar's vantage point, but it's much more difficult to defend lying when taking the other person's perspective. Targets of deception typically feel victimized even by well-intentioned lies.

What special circumstances might permit lying? Bok doesn't offer a definitive list but suggests that deception might be justified when (1) there is significant threat to life and safety; (2) society has publicly agreed that certain forms of deceit can be used, like unmarked patrol cars, surprise audits, and random drug tests; and (3) both parties acknowledge that the situation calls for mutual deceit (a poker game, bargaining at a foreign bazaar).

The principle of veracity would outlaw many common lies and other forms of deception, like overstating a company's income, offering an unrealistically optimistic status report on a project, or padding résumés and expense accounts. Salespeople would have a duty to tell the entire truth about their products (including possible hazards) and to refuse to steer customers toward purchases that might harm them.[33]

You may think Bok's guideline is too restrictive. Or you may hold a deontological position that outlaws any exceptions to total honesty. Nevertheless, the principle of veracity does address the need for truth telling while acknowledging that lying can pose complex ethical dilemmas. It also encourages us to take a closer look at how we might promote truthfulness in organizational relationships.

As a leader, you can reduce the frequency of deception in your organization because you determine both the roles that employees play and the rewards they receive. Reduce the pressure of role conflicts through clarifying expectations and chains of command, opening up lines of communication to resolve role issues, and making sure that you don't set unreasonably high expectations that tempt workers to lie. "Teach" employees that honesty pays by rewarding integrity while punishing offenders. Further, make honesty a core value, highlighting it in mission statements while promoting truthful interactions with all constituencies.

Emotional Labor

Emotional labor is a special form of impression management that is increasingly common in the modern economy, in which an estimated 8 out of every 10 workers are employed in service industries.[34] In emotional labor, frontline workers (baristas, restaurant servers, sales representatives, counter staff, receptionists, retail clerks) manage their feelings so that they can present the desired bodily and facial displays to the public. Service personnel may have to hold back their anger at obnoxious clients, project enthusiasm to everyone entering the store, or answer the same questions with "smiles in their voices" time after time after time. Emotional labor is different from other forms of impression management because (a) control of feelings is done for pay; (b) emotional laborers interact with outsiders, not with other organizational members; and (c) this form of influence raises its own special set of ethical issues.

Sociologist Arlene Hochschild, who coined the term *emotional labor,* studied the emotional performances of Delta flight attendants who had to project a warm, helpful persona to passengers, even rude ones. Subsequent researchers examined the emotional labor of frontline service workers in a wide variety of settings, including, for example, convenience stores, schools, hospitals, fast-food restaurants, a cruise ship, Disneyland, door-to-door insurance sales, and a 911 call center.[35] Investigators discovered that emotions can be managed for neutral or negative displays as well as for "nice" ones. For example, psychiatric workers try to remain calm in the face of abuse, and police officers and bill collectors express irritation and anger to intimidate suspects and to collect delinquent accounts.[36]

Emotional labor works. Employees who express positive moods through greeting, smiling, and eye contact encourage customers to develop positive feelings about the organization and its products and services. These feelings, in turn, prompt customers to buy.[37] Emotional contagion helps account for much of the relationship between positive emotional displays, sales, and satisfaction. In service encounters, the happy affect of employees often spreads to customers, who return greetings, smile, and make eye contact. Emotional influence is particularly powerful because it often operates below the level of consciousness. We are often unaware that our emotions (in this case, positive moods) have been aroused and that they are influencing our behavior. Since we don't realize that our emotions are being managed, we can't counteract their effects by, say, reminding ourselves to think more carefully about the possible disadvantages of a product or service.

Because emotional labor is so effective, organizations go to great lengths to control the emotional behavior of their frontline workers. Managers ("emotional supervisors") may only hire individuals deemed to have "friendly, outgoing" personalities. Once hired, new employees go through orientation and training sessions that introduce them to the corporation's guidelines and formulas for customer service. Emotional routines or scripts tell workers both what to say and how to act. They are given lines like "Welcome to McDonald's" "How are you today?" and "Have a great day!" These lines are packaged with uniforms (smocks, aprons, name tags, blazers), smiles, eye contact, attentive posture, and vocal enthusiasm.

The practice of emotional labor raises a number of important ethical issues. To begin, all these programmed emotional displays can be costly to employees. (To reflect upon your experiences as an emotional laborer, turn to Application Project 4 at the end of this chapter.) Emotions, traditionally considered the worker's private concern, are now "owned" by the organization.[38] As service providers, we feel the tension between wanting to maintain our ideal or authentic selves and following organizational rules. Being forced to display emotions that aren't felt (or that contradict feelings) can produce dissonance. This dissonance may lead to stress, cynicism, burnout, low self-esteem, illness, job turnover, and difficulties in work relationships. For example, one JetBlue flight attendant, unable any longer to cope with the emotional demands of the job, became a hero to many service workers. After dealing with a rude customer during a flight, he took dramatic action when the plane landed. He got on the intercom to berate passengers, grabbed a couple of beers, and then exited the plane on an inflatable emergency chute. Intrusive emotional scripts threaten the dignity of the individual and can reinforce gender stereotypes. Women programmed to be flirtatious, outgoing, and friendly (such as waitresses at Hooters restaurants) run a higher risk of becoming the targets of sexual harassment.

Not everyone is convinced that emotional labor is harmful.[39] Some researchers defend these performances. They point out that service providers aren't robots. Frontline employees sometimes fight the organization's attempts to control their feelings and can adjust their performances when needed. Convenience-store clerks are friendlier during slow periods, for instance. When lines develop, they adopt a more efficient manner. Emotional labor can also be enjoyable. One group of 911 dispatchers reported that emotional work was the highlight of their jobs, providing comic relief and excitement. Those who embrace their roles experience little dissonance and often find their moods shifting to fit their performances. There is some evidence that acting cheerful, even when we are not feeling particularly cheerful, reduces levels of stress hormones and increases resistance to disease. Further, in some roles, like nursing, positive affect is a form of altruistic behavior. We expect nurses to express optimism and concern for patients in order to alleviate their suffering and promote healing.[40]

As we can see, emotional labor can have both negative and positive effects on employees. Research continues to explore the reasons for these contradictory effects. So far, investigators have discovered that emotional labor is most damaging when employees (a) experience a great deal of dissonance between their felt and expressed emotions, (b) are not suited for service roles, (c) must suppress negative emotions, (d) become emotionally exhausted from high levels of customer interaction, (e) must deal with aggressive clients, and (f) receive little emotional support from coworkers and the organization.

Organizations can reduce the damage done by emotional labor by recognizing their moral obligation to members. This might mean doing the following:

- Providing potential employees with a realistic preview of the emotional demands of the job
- Hiring applicants who are emotionally sensitive and expressive
- Relying less on scripts
- Providing more opportunity for workers to develop personal performance styles
- Protecting employees from rude and aggressive customers
- Providing opportunities to discuss the emotional demands of the job
- Limiting the amount of acting required during a work shift
- Encouraging supervisors to be supportive of emotional laborers
- Encouraging peer support networks
- Providing adequate compensation for emotional laborers
- Allowing for expression of negative emotions when appropriate

Organizations also have a moral obligation to consider the impact of emotional labor on outsiders as well as on employees. As noted earlier, positive moods created through emotional work unconsciously influence buying decisions. The emotional labor provided by frontline employees should therefore benefit the consumer as well as the organization. In addition, customers, like employees, can experience emotional dissonance.[41] Consider the tensions inherent in the pleasant service encounter, for instance. All displays of positive emotion in this setting, no matter how authentic they appear, are suspect because they are designed to sell products and services. These emotional routines are logically and ethically inconsistent because they attempt to standardize "personal" service. In addition, service recipients who are offered pleasant performances might not want to respond in kind if they suspect they are being manipulated or are in a foul mood. Most of us play along, acting the role of the "good customer," even when we don't feel very friendly or are having a bad day. But a few consumers resist. When dining out, for instance, they complain to management when the waitstaff is too attentive and friendly. They may use put-down lines like "What's the worst thing on the menu?" or "Hi, my name's Dave, and I'll be your customer tonight."[42] Those who play along run the risk of lying about how they really feel (unhappy, tense, angry). Those who resist may maintain their integrity but little else. They come across as mean spirited and have little impact on organizational policy. Instead, resisters make the job of the emotional laborer (who is generally underpaid and overworked) all the harder. As an alternative, we could strive for personal consistency and authenticity in the consumer role by responding tactfully but honestly to emotional displays. For instance: "I'm not doing too well today, but thanks for asking"; "I appreciate your friendliness, but it is a little overwhelming this early in the morning."

Communication of Expectations

The communication of expectations is a powerful organizational influence tool. That's because we have a tendency to live up to the expectations others place on us. Researchers refer to this phenomenon as self-fulfilling prophecy, or the Pygmalion effect, after the sculptor of Greek mythology. Pygmalion created a statue of a beautiful woman, whom he named Galatea. After the figure was complete, he fell in love with his creation. The goddess Aphrodite took pity on the dejected prince and brought Galatea to life.

Evidence of the Pygmalion effect has been discovered in a variety of organizational settings. For example:[43]

- Nursing home residents are less depressed and less likely to be admitted to hospitals when staff members believe that these clients will respond more favorably to rehabilitation.
- Industrial trainees designated as "high-aptitude personnel" learn more quickly and are less likely to drop out.
- Patients in medical experiments improve when they receive placebos because they believe they will get better.
- The high expectations of teachers lead to higher student test and IQ scores as well as better performance on cognitive tasks.
- Subordinates can improve the performance of their supervisors by expressing high upward expectations (the reverse Pygmalion).
- Military personnel labeled as having high potential perform up to the expectations of their superiors. Those told that they can succeed are more likely to volunteer for dangerous special duty.
- In international relief agencies, the positive expectations of headquarters aid workers can improve the performance of local staff members.

The Pygmalion effect is more pronounced with some individuals than others. Disadvantaged groups (those stereotyped as low achievers) tend to benefit most from positive expectations, as do those who lack a clear sense of their abilities or find themselves in a novel situation. Men seem to be more influenced by the expectancies of their managers than are women.[44] Negative expectations also have an impact on performance. This is sometimes referred to as the Golem effect (*golem* means "dumbbell" in Yiddish). Unless counteracted, these reduced expectancies lower performance.[45]

Verbal persuasion is the straightforward way to communicate expectations—for example, offering compliments, assuring others that they have the necessary ability, and stating that you expect great things from them. However, self-fulfilling prophecies are most often communicated indirectly through these four channels:[46]

1. *Climate.* Climate describes the social and emotional atmosphere individuals create for others. Communicators act in a friendly, supportive, accepting, and encouraging manner with people they like. This is done through using nonverbal behaviors that portray respect and warmth while avoiding behaviors that communicate disrespect, coolness, and superiority. Supervisors, for example, signal positive expectations by giving adequate time to employees, holding appointments in pleasant surroundings, sitting or standing close to workers, nodding and smiling, making frequent eye contact, and using a warm tone of voice.

2. *Input.* Positive expectations are also communicated through the number and type of assignments and projects given to workers. High expectations create a positive performance spiral. As employees receive and successfully complete more tasks, they gain self-confidence and the confidence of superiors. These outstanding performers are then given further duties, which they are more likely to complete as well.

3. *Output.* Those tagged as high performers are given more opportunities to speak, to offer their opinions, and to disagree. Superiors pay more attention to these employees when they speak and offer more assistance to them when they're solving problems. In the classroom, teachers call on "high achievers" more than "low achievers," wait less time for low achievers to answer questions, and provide fewer clues and follow-up questions to low achievers.[47]

4. *Feedback.* Supervisors give more frequent positive feedback when they have high expectations of employees, both praising them more often for success and criticizing them less often for failure. In addition, managers provide more detailed performance feedback to high-expectation employees. Just the opposite occurs with those labeled as poor performers. Supervisors praise their minimal performance more, reinforcing the impression that they expect less from these employees.

Pygmalion investigators wrestle with the ethical implications of this influence strategy, beginning with the use of deception. Experimenters typically deceive leaders by informing them that groups differ in abilities, even though they have been randomly assigned. Such tactics could be used in the organizational setting by telling managers that selected subordinates have more potential when, in reality, there are no data to support that assertion. Some researchers argue that this deceit would be justified because the organization would benefit from the superior performance of those described as high performers. However, to carry off this deception, managers would have to be misled by their supervisors or staff personnel, which would undermine trust. Deliberately privileging one group of people is unjust and might result in lawsuits.

Even when deception isn't involved, the separation of groups into different ability groupings is problematical. Organizations routinely label some individuals as exceptional employees according to some set of criteria. These members are then given extra training, assigned to mentors, placed into more challenging assignments, and so on. These measures generate the Pygmalion effect for the chosen few and the Golem effect for everyone else. Those labeled as average or low performers receive fewer benefits and may live down to reduced expectations.

Communicating high expectations to everyone in the organization is an ethical alternative to deception and ability grouping.[48] Such an approach not only maintains integrity, it encourages everyone to function at his or her best. Strategies for improving organizationwide performance include (a) building follower self-efficacy (a sense of personal power) through breaking down tasks into manageable segments, role modeling, and verbal persuasion; (b) encouraging a learning orientation that emphasizes improvement over perfection; (c) creating a friendly atmosphere; (d) raising consciousness of the impact of negative expectations; (e) creating opportunities for employees to start anew in different departments and assignments; (f) fostering a culture that demands high productivity.

Even if our organization doesn't adopt a high-expectations orientation, we can do so as individuals. The power of self-fulfilling prophecy places a moral burden upon us. If others are to reach their full potential, we need to communicate positive expectations to them, not negative ones. We should carefully monitor our behavior to reduce inequities, particularly subtle ones, in our treatment of others. The strategies outlined above for communicating high expectations can be employed in our peer relationships and organizational units. Also, we can use the Galatea effect to insulate ourselves from the negative expectations of our leaders. The Galatea effect (named after the statue in the Greek myth) refers to the tendency for high self-expectation to produce high performance. High self-expectancies can keep us from lowering our standards when others expect little of us. We can encourage leaders to raise their expectations of us by meeting and exceeding standards.

CHAPTER TAKEAWAYS

- While the exercise of influence is not an option in the workplace, you do have control over how you go about modifying the behaviors of others.
- Understand that no form of power is inherently immoral, but positional power (legitimate, coercive, reward) is more likely to be abused than person-centered power (expert, referent).
- Use a variety of power sources when pursuing worthy objectives.
- Recognize that concentration of positional power (in yourself or others) is dangerous, that it can produce a wide range of unethical behavior.
- Adopt a positive mind-set toward organizational politics—the use of informal or unofficial power. Positive political behavior supports the organization's vision and values, serves others, focuses on achieving shared goals, fosters collaboration, and meets widely accepted ethical standards.

- Increase psychological empowerment—the motivation of others to carry out tasks, based on meaning, competence, self-determination, and impact—by modifying the work setting and supplying adequate resources.

- Overcome barriers to empowerment by managing the journey through the three stages of the empowerment process: (1) starting and orienting the process of change, (2) making changes and dealing with discouragement, and (3) adopting and refining empowerment to fit the organization.

- You'll have little chance of getting what you want unless you project the desired image. However, you have a moral responsibility to ensure that you use impression management tactics to build positive relationships, to accurately portray your personal image and that of your organization, and to facilitate effective decisions. You also have a duty to ensure that others don't manipulate you through their use of impression management strategies.

- Truth telling should be your moral standard. If you decide to lie, the burden of proof is on you. Reduce the frequency of lying and other forms of deception in your organization by limiting role conflicts and rewarding truth telling.

- Emotional labor, the management of feelings by frontline workers that leads to facial and bodily displays, can pose significant dilemmas for employees and customers. Take steps to reduce the emotional dissonance that workers experience and provide them with organizational support. As a customer, respond tactfully and honestly to emotional displays.

- Communication of expectations can be one of your most powerful influence tools. Your individual moral responsibility is to encourage those around you to live up to their full potential. Generate positive self-fulfilling prophecies (the Pygmalion effect) through creating a warm emotional climate, providing valuable assignments, giving opportunities for others to express their opinions, and offering frequent positive feedback. Have high expectations of your own behavior (employ the Galatea effect) even if others don't.

APPLICATION PROJECTS

1. Analyze a leader's use of power. Determine whether this leader acted ethically or unethically. Explain why. Write up your findings.

2. Debate the following propositions:

   Empowerment takes advantage of workers.

   Empowerment should not be practiced in some organizations.

   Impression management is unethical.

   Nothing good can come from playing organizational politics.

   The costs of emotional labor are overstated.

   Communicating positive expectations to everyone in a work group is impossible.

   Communicating high expectations to people you don't like is unethical.

3. Create a case study based on an organization's attempts to empower its employees. What went right? What went wrong? What conclusions can you draw from this organization's experience?

4. In a small group, discuss your experiences as emotional laborers. What characteristics did you have to demonstrate to land your jobs? What training did you receive, and what scripts did you have to follow? What did it take to be successful? What were the costs of your performances? What were the benefits of engaging in emotional labor? What do you conclude about the ethics of emotional labor? Report to the rest of the class. As an alternative, discuss your experiences with positive and negative organizational politics.

5. Under what circumstances is lying justified? See if you can reach a consensus in a small group and report your conclusions to the rest of the class.

6. Have you ever been the victim of low expectations (the Golem effect)? How did you respond? What happened as a result? Share your story orally or in writing.

7. Create an organizational politics case study. Describe how political skill was exercised in this situation and what happened as a result. Determine whether this is an example of negative or positive politics, and highlight the lessons you take from this situation.

CASE STUDY 5.2

Taking Charge at the Assisted Living Facility

Cynthia Peng has been the associate director at a large assisted living facility for the elderly over the past three years. This facility is one of several in the region owned by a for-profit elder-care company. The corporation is expanding its operations and has acquired a new location in a small town, far from the firm's city headquarters. Peng has been selected to be the director of this new residence, which has 25 employees, including caregivers, nursing and office staff, cooks, servers, and maintenance personnel. Residents live in their own apartments but eat their meals together and participate in group recreational activities. Several clients need assistance getting in and out of bed and with medications. The quality of care had suffered under the previous owners, who were cited by the state for safety violations and client mistreatment. Those responsible for the problems were let go, but the rest of the staff was retained. However, employee morale is extremely low, and the facility is only half full due to its poor reputation.

Cynthia knows that she faces a variety of challenges in her new position. She must convince her employees, most of whom are much older than she and skeptical of female managers, that she is a competent leader. Peng must help them improve their performance so that there are no more violations. At the same time, she has to reassure headquarters that she is doing a good job. Cynthia also needs to persuade the community that conditions have improved and attract more residents in order to make the facility profitable. As if that weren't enough, locals are likely to view her with suspicion as a big city newcomer who doesn't understand how things work in a small community.

Discussion Probes

1. What sources of power are available to Cynthia? Which ones should she use, and how should she employ each?

2. Identify the groups that Peng must influence. What image does she need to create for each audience?

3. What impression management strategies should Cynthia use with each group? Are there any strategies she should avoid because they are unethical?

4. How can the new director ethically communicate positive expectations to her employees?

5. What are the emotional demands faced by caregivers working at the facility? How can Cynthia help her employees deal with these stresses?

6. How can Cynthia's supervisors at corporate headquarters help her succeed through the communication of positive expectations?

CASE STUDY 5.3

The Two Faces of Steve

Customers of Apple Computer often act like members of a religious cult. Thousands of them flock to the annual MacWorld convention to hear about Apple Computer's newest gadgets. They form long lines outside Apple retail outlets to purchase the latest iPhone or iPad. Millions pay more than they would for competing products to own iBook and iMac computers. Apple believers helped revolutionize the music industry by purchasing iPods and buying songs from the iTunes store.

If Apple is a cult, then cofounder and CEO Steven Jobs serves as the group's leader and chief evangelist. Jobs and Steve Wozniak started Apple Computer in 1976, working at first out of a garage. Jobs's vision was to make the world a better place through technology, by designing electronic tools for the average person. However, he was forced out of the company during a power struggle with CEO John Sculley in 1985. He then founded NeXT, Inc., and purchased most of Pixar Animation Studios. Pixar produced a series of successful computer-animated features, including *Toy Story* and *Finding Nemo,* making it one of the most profitable studios in the history of Hollywood. Jobs eventually sold the production company to Disney, pocketing billions. NeXT was much less successful, though the firm developed an operating system that was adopted by Apple in 1996. As part of the operating system purchase agreement, Jobs rejoined Apple, first as a consultant and then as CEO. When Jobs came back in 1996, the firm's computer market share had shrunk to 8%, and it seemed that it would take a miracle for the company to turn its fortunes around.

Apple's rebound under Jobs could indeed be considered miraculous. A flow of new products, ranging from stylish new computers to music devices and phones, has generated record sales and profits. The company's market capitalization jumped from $2 billion to $16 billion in the first two and a half years after his return. Apple stock, at $4 a share when Jobs returned to Apple, soared to over $170 a share in 2009.

Steven Jobs is now synonymous with Apple. He oversees every stage of product development, constantly pushing for designs that are stylish as well as functional. (Jobs even insists that the circuit boards of Apple devices be attractively designed.) The CEO refuses to rely on consumer research, arguing, "A lot of times, people don't know what they want until you show it to them."[1] A charismatic leader, Jobs is able to command allegiance through the force of his will, personality, and persuasive abilities. His persuasive power is showcased during his 90- to 120-minute new-product presentations before the Apple faithful and FOS (Friends of Steve) at MacWorld. Biographers Jeffrey Young and William Simon describe a Jobs performance this way:

> Steve Jobs has the same uncanny instinct for achieving dramatic flair that will produce maximum audience impact as the legendary moguls of Hollywood's early days.
>
> Working with the technical crew is often as far as he goes to prepare. He knows the product, he knows the details, and he knows which features will make the eyes of the Macintosh faithful light up. While his public relations people stand in the wings, panicked because they have no idea what to expect, Steve takes the stage with the aura of Mick Jagger. He is a sensational speaker, gripping, magnetic. To know that he does this without notes, without a TelePrompTer, without rehearsal, is to know you are witnessing a magic act. Steve Jobs, magician extraordinaire, pulls the rabbit out of the hat every time. (p. 273)

Jobs's impressive achievements have come at a significant cost to his followers. Employees describe the "good Steve" and the "bad Steve." The good Steve is a creative visionary able to bring out the best in his followers, helping them achieve more than they ever imagined possible. Observers note that he has matured since his initial removal from Apple. He is much more willing to give credit to others and, at times, can be lavish in his praise of them. The "bad Steve" is an obsessive bully. Not only does the CEO constantly intervene in the design process and routinely shut down projects, he has a reputation for mistreating others. When an executive at Pixar went too far in challenging his authority, Jobs not only fired him but also removed any mention of his name from the company's history. At NeXT, he would routinely challenge employees he met in the hall by asking, "What do you do here and why are you worth what I am paying you?"[2] Apple employees would take the stairs rather than risk being stuck with him on an elevator and losing their jobs before the doors opened. They continue to endure his routine temper tantrums and fear "being Steved" (becoming the target of his wrath).

CEO Jobs routinely clashes with outsiders. In one case, he told a reporter to "f**k off," for asking the "stupidest, lamest question" he had ever heard."[3] He called another reporter to say, "I think you're a slime bucket who gets most of his facts wrong."[4] He is a notoriously hard bargainer, continually renegotiating or nullifying contracts made with suppliers and business partners like Disney.

Since his return to Apple, Jobs has created a culture of secrecy. Earlier in the firm's history, employees would routinely leak information to the press to undermine corporate executives. Now, talking to the press is grounds for instant dismissal, and executives deliberately release misinformation in one part of the company in order to trace leaks back to the source. New products are literally kept under wraps. Developers are monitored by cameras and are required to cover up their work when leaving their stations. The initial iPod prototypes were kept in sealed boxes; wires and controls were randomly placed so no one could determine how they were placed on the actual unit.

Secrecy has also surrounded the CEO's health. In 2003, Jobs was diagnosed with a rare, treatable form of pancreatic cancer and underwent successful surgery, facts that were not released until months later. In 2008, cancer appeared again, on his liver. The Apple faithful and the press noted that he was losing weight, but Jobs claimed at first that he was suffering from a bug or a hormone imbalance. In reality, his cancer required a life-saving liver transplant. Only when news of the operation leaked out did Jobs acknowledge he had received a new liver. During this period, Apple's board refused to reveal any information on Jobs's medical condition. Although federal law doesn't require the release of CEO health information, governance experts believe that in the case of Apple, such data are critical to shareholders because the success of Apple is directly tied to Steve. In fact, when Jobs took six months off to deal with his health issues, Apple's stock price plummeted. The SEC is investigating to determine if Apple gained any financial advantage from keeping news about Jobs's health from the public.

Jobs returned to his full-time position as CEO after his liver transplant and continued to wow Apple cult members. However, in 2010 he again took a leave of absence, though he did appear at the unveiling of the newest iPad in March 2011. Though he mellowed, those who dealt with him could expect to encounter the two faces of Steve, described by one reporter as "fearless leader, savvy pitchman, inscrutable guru, notorious nitpicker, obsessive perfectionist, ruthless man-child, ultimate death-defying comeback kid—and top CEO of the first decade of the second millennium."[5]

Discussion Probes

1. Do Apple products and Steven Jobs have a cultlike following? If so, what accounts for this extreme loyalty?

2. Do you own any Apple products? Have you stood in line to buy any Apple devices? Why or why not?

3. Would Jobs be as effective if he didn't periodically intimidate employees?

4. Why do you think employees continue to work for Jobs even when they have experienced the "bad Steve"?

5. Would you want to work for Steve Jobs? Why or why not?

6. Was Jobs justified in lying about his health? Why or why not?

7. Should companies be required to release medical information about their CEOs to investors and the public?

Notes

1. Rodriguez, J. (2010, April 3). Inside the cult of Apple. *The Star Phoenix,* p. E1.
2. Young, J. S., & Simon, W. L. (2005*). Icon: Steve Jobs, the greatest second act in the history of business.* Hoboken, NJ: John Wiley, p. 218.
3. Pontin, J. (2000, July 3). Foul-mouthed genius—What did you expect Apple's Steve Jobs to be like? *The Scotsman,* p. 18.
4. Nocera, J. (2008, July 26). Apple's culture of secrecy. *The New York Times,* p. C1.
5. Rodriguez.

Sources

Abate, T. (2009, January 6). High tech icon breaks silence of his health. *San Francisco Chronicle,* p. A1.
Apple CEO's prognosis 'excellent' surgeon says. *The Toronto Star,* p. B01.
Appleyard, B. (2009, August 16). The god of cool things. *The Sunday Times,* Magazine, pp. 40ff.
Guglielmo, C. (2009, June 23). When Steve Job returns to his CEO job, experts disagree on whether Apple should reveal if he had a liver transplant. *The Houston Chronicle,* p. B7.
Guglielmo, C. (2010, May 12). A year after surgery, "he's the Jobs of old." *Edmonton Journal,* p. F9.
Kim, R. (2009, January 22). SEC reportedly looks at Jobs' health. *San Francisco Chronicle,* p. C1.
Pilkington, E. (2009, June 23). What's driving Steve Jobs? *The Guardian,* Features, p. 4.

ENDNOTES

1. French, R. P., & Raven, B. (1959). The bases of social power. In D. Cartwright (Ed.), *Studies in social power* (pp. 150–167). Ann Arbor: University of Michigan, Institute for Social Research.
2. Yukl, G. (2006). *Leadership in organizations* (6th ed.). Upper Saddle River, NJ: Prentice Hall.
3. Hackman, M. Z., & Johnson, C. E. (2009). *Leadership: A communication perspective* (5th ed.). Prospect Heights, IL: Waveland Press, Chap. 5; Yukl (2006).
4. Cruver, B. (2002). *Anatomy of greed: The unshredded truth from an Enron insider.* New York: Carroll & Graf.
5. Carney, J. (2005, May 2). Temper, temper, temper. *Time,* pp. 55–57.
6. Jennings, M. M. (2006). *The seven signs of ethical collapse: How to spot moral meltdowns in companies . . . before it's too late.* New York: St. Martin's Press.

7. Fiske, S. T. (1993). Controlling other people: The impact of power on stereotyping. *American Psychologist, 48,* 621–628; Goodwin, S. A. (2003). Power and prejudice: A social-cognitive perspective on power and leadership. In D. van Knippenberg & M. A. Hogg, *Leadership and power: Identity processes in groups and organizations* (pp. 138–152). London: Sage.

8. Kipnis, D., Schmidt, S. M., Swaffin-Smith, C., & Wilkinson, I. (1984). Patterns of managerial influence: Shotgun managers, tacticians, and bystanders. *Organizational Dynamics, 12,* 58–76.

9. Yukl (2006).

10. Kanter, R. M. (1977). *Men and women of the corporation.* New York: Basic Books, Chap. 7; Bennett, R. J. (1998). Perceived powerlessness as a cause of employee deviance. In R. W. Griffin, A. O'Leary-Kelly, & J. M. Collins (Eds.), *Dysfunctional behavior in organizations: Violent and deviant behavior* (pp. 221–239). Stamford, CT: JAI; Smith, P. K., Jostmann, N. B., Galinsky, A. D., & van Dijk, W. W. (2008). Lacking power impairs executive function. *Psychological Science, 19,* 441–447.

11. Drory, A., & Romm, T. (1990). The definition of organizational politics: A review. *Human Relations, 43*(11), 1133–1154; Champoux, J. E. (2003). *Organizational behavior: Essential tenets* (2nd ed.). Mason, OH: South-Western.

12. Miller, B. K., Rutherford, M. A., & Kolodinsky, R. W. (2008). Perceptions of organizational politics: A meta-analysis. *Journal of Business Psychology, 22,* 209–222.

13. Fedor, D., Maslyn, J., Farmer, S., & Bettenhausen, K. (2008). The contribution of positive politics to the prediction of employee reactions. *Journal of Applied Social Psychology, 38,* 76–96; Perrewe, P. L., Ferris, G. R., Stoner, J. S., & Brouer, R. L. (2007). The positive role of political skill in organizations. In D. Nelson & C. L. Cooper (Eds.), *Positive organizational behavior* (pp. 117–128). London: Sage.

14. Valle, M. (2006, May/June). The power of politics: Why leaders need to learn the art of influence. *Leadership in Action,* pp. 8–12.

15. Kurchner-Hawkins, R., & Miller, R. (2006). Organizational politics: Building positive political strategies in turbulent times. In E. Vigoda-Gadot & A. Drory (Eds.), *Handbook of organizational politics* (pp. 328–351). Cheltenham, UK: Edward Elgar.

16. See, for example: Spreitzer, G. M., Kizilos, M. A., & Nason, S. W. (1997). A dimensional analysis of the relationship between psychological empowerment and effectiveness, satisfaction, and strain. *Journal of Management, 23,* 679–705; Tuuli, M. M., & Rowlinson, S. (2009). Empowerment in project teams: A multi-level examination of the job performance implications. *Construction Management and Economics, 27,* 473–498; Seibert, S. E., Silver, S. R., & Randolph, W. A. (2004). Taking empowerment to the next level: A multiple-level model of empowerment, performance, and satisfaction. *Academy of Management Journal, 47,* 332–349; Kirkman, B. L., & Rosen, B. (1999). Beyond self-management: Antecedents and consequences of team empowerment. *Academy of Management Journal, 42,* 58–74; Ugboro, I. O., & Obeng, K. (2000). Top management leadership, employee empowerment, job satisfaction, and customer satisfaction in TQM organizations: An empirical study. *Journal of Quality Management, 5,* 247–272.

17. Bass, B. M. (1990). *Bass and Stogdill's handbook of leadership* (3rd ed.). New York: Free Press; Hackman & Johnson (2004).

18. Thomas, K. W., & Velthouse, B. A. (1990). Cognitive elements of empowerment: An "interpretive" model of intrinsic task motivation. *Academy of Management Review, 15,* 666–681; Spreitzer, G. M. (1996). Social structural characteristics of psychological empowerment. *Academy of Management Journal, 39,* 483–504; Spreitzer, G. M. (1995). Psychological empowerment in the workplace: Dimensions, measurement, and validation. *Academy of Management Journal, 38,* 1442–1485; Spreitzer, G. M., Kizilos, M. A., & Nason, S. W. (1997). A dimensional analysis of the relationship between psychological empowerment and effectiveness, satisfaction, and strain. *Journal of Management, 23,* 679–705.

19. Bandura, A. (1977). Self-efficacy: Toward a unifying theory of behavioral change. *Psychological Review, 84,* 191–215.

20. Kanter, R. M. (1979, July-August). Power failure in management circuits. *Harvard Business Review,* pp. 65–75.

21. Example taken from: Forrester, R. (2000). Empowerment: Rejuvenating a potent idea. *Academy of Management Executive, 14*, 67–80.

22. Randolph, W. A. (2000). Re-thinking empowerment: Why is it so hard to achieve? *Organizational Dynamics, 29*, 94–107.

23. Lincoln, N. D., Travers, C., Ackers, P., & Wilkinson, A. (2002). The meaning of empowerment: The interdisciplinary etymology of a new management concept. *International Journal of Management Reviews, 4*, 271–290.

24. Goffman, E. (1959). *The presentation of self in everyday life.* Garden City, NY: Doubleday; Schlenker, B. R. (1980). *Impression management: The self-concept, social identity, and interpersonal relations.* Monterey, CA: Brooks/Cole; Leary, M. R., & Kowalski, R. M. (1990). Impression management: A literature review and two-component model. *Psychological Bulletin, 107*, 34–47.

25. Rosenfeld, P., Giacalone, R. A., & Riordan, C. A. (1995). *Impression management in organizations: Theory, measurement, practice.* London: Routledge.

26. Gardner, W. L. (1992). Lessons in organizational dramaturgy: The art of impression management. *Organizational Dynamics, 21*, 33–47; Stevens, C. K., & Kristof, A. L. (1995). Making the right impression: A field study of applicant impression management during job interviews. *Journal of Applied Psychology, 80*, 587–606; Singh, V., Kumra, S., & Vinnicombe, S. (2002). Gender and impression management: Playing the promotion game. *Journal of Business Ethics, 37*, 77–89; Bratton, V. K., & Kacmar, K. M. (2004). Extreme careerism: The dark side of impression management. In W. Griffin and K. O'Reilly (Eds.), *The dark side of organizational behavior* (pp. 291–308). San Francisco: Jossey-Bass.

27. Seabright, M. A., & Moberg, D. J. (1998). Interpersonal manipulation: Its nature and moral limits. In M. Schminke (Ed.), *Managerial ethics: Moral management of people and processes* (pp. 153–175). Mahwah, NJ: Lawrence Erlbaum; Kidwell, R. E. (2004). "Small" lies, big trouble: The unfortunate consequences of résumé padding, from Janet Cooke to George O'Leary. *Journal of Business Ethics, 51*, 175–184; Padded résumés: Fake laurels that went unnoticed for years. (2003, January 13). *BusinessWeek,* p. 1C.

28. Rosenfeld, Giacalone, & Riordan (1995).

29. Grover, S. (1993). Lying, deceit, and subterfuge: A model of dishonesty in the workplace. *Organization Science, 4*, 478–494; Grover (1997); Ross, W. T., & Robertson, D. C. (2000). Lying: The impact of decision context. *Business Ethics Quarterly, 10*, 409–440; Sims, R. L. (2000). The relationship between employee attitudes and conflicting expectations for lying behavior. *Journal of Psychology, 134*, 619–633; Aquino, K. (1998). The effects of ethical climate and the availability of alternatives on the use of deception during negotiation. *International Journal of Conflict Management, 9*, 195–217.

30. Solomon, R. C. (1993). What a tangled web: Deception and self-deception in philosophy. In M. Lewis & C. Sarni (Eds.), *Lying and deception in everyday life* (pp. 30–58). New York: Guilford Press.

31. Grover, S. L. (1997). Lying in organizations: Theory, research, and future directions. In R. A. Giacalone & J. Greenberg (Eds.), *Antisocial behavior in organizations* (pp. 68–84). Thousand Oaks, CA: Sage; Cialdini, R. B., Petrova, P. K., & Goldstein, N. J. (2004, Spring). The hidden costs of organizational dishonesty. *MIT Sloan Management Review,* pp. 67–73.

32. Bok, S. (1978). *Lying: Moral choice in public and private life.* New York: Pantheon Books; Bok, S. (1989). *Secrets: On the ethics of concealment and revelation.* New York: Random House.

33. Carson, T. (2001). Deception and withholding information in sales. *Business Ethics Quarterly, 11*, 275–306.

34. Duke, A. B., Goodman, J. M., Treadway, D. C., & Breland, J. W. (2009). Perceived organizational support as a moderator of emotional labor/outcomes relationships. *Journal of Applied Social Psychology, 39*(5), 1013–1034.

35. Hochschild, A. R. (1983). *The managed heart: Commercialization of human feeling.* Berkeley: University of California Press; Leidner, R. (1991). Selling hamburgers and selling insurance: Gender, work, and identity in interactive service jobs. *Gender & Society, 5*, 154–177. Leidner, R. (1993). *Fast food, fast talk: Service work and the routinization of everyday life.* Berkeley: University of California Press; Tracy, S. J. (2000).

Becoming a character for commerce: Emotion labor, self-subordination, and discursive construction of identity in a total institution. *Management Communication Quarterly, 14,* 90–128; Tracy, S. J., & Tracy, K. (1998). Emotional labor at 911. *Journal of Applied Communication Research, 26,* 390–411; Van Maanen, J. (1991). The smile factory: Work at Disneyland. In P. J. Frost, L. F. Moore, M. R. Louis, C. C. Lundberg, & J. Martin (Eds.), *Reframing organizational culture* (pp. 58–76). Newbury Park, CA: Sage.

36. Yanay, N., & Sharar, G. (1998). Professional feelings as emotional labor. *Journal of Contemporary Ethnography, 27,* 345–373; Sutton, R. I. (1991). Maintaining norms about expressed emotions: The case of bill collectors. *Administrative Science Quarterly, 36,* 245–268.

37. Fulmer, I. S., & Barry, B. (2009). Managed hearts and wallets: Ethical issues in emotional influence by and within organizations. *Business Ethics Quarterly, 12,* 155–191.

38. Fineman, S. (1995). Stress, emotion and intervention. In T. Newton (Ed.), *Managing stress: Emotion and power at work* (pp. 120–136). London: Sage.

39. Waldron, V. R. (1994). Once more, with feeling: Reconsidering the role of emotion at work. In S. A. Deetz (Ed.), *Communication yearbook 17* (pp. 388–428). Thousand Oaks, CA: Sage; Sutton, R. I., & Rafaeli, A. (1988). Untangling the relationship between displayed emotions and organizational sales: The case of convenience stores. *Academy of Management Journal, 31,* 461–487; Zapf, D., & Holz, M. (2006). On the positive and negative effects of emotion work in organizations. *European Journal of Work and Organizational Psychology, 15*(1), 1–28.

40. Smith, P., & Lorentzon, M. (2005). Is emotional labour ethical? *Nursing Ethics, 12,* 638–642.

41. Steinberg, R. J., & Figart, D. M. (1999). Emotional labor since The Managed Heart. *Annals of the American Academy of Political and Social Sciences, 561,* 10–26.

42. Rafaeli, A., & Sutton, R. I. (1989). The expression of emotion in organizational life. In L. L. Cummings & B. M. Staw (Eds.), *Research in organizational behavior* (Vol. 2, pp. 1–42). Greenwich, CT: JAI.

43. See, for example: Eden, D., & Shami, A. B. (1982). Pygmalion goes to boot camp: Expectancy, leadership, and trainee performance. *Journal of Applied Psychology, 67,* 194–199; Eden, D. (1984). Self-fulfilling prophecy as a management tool: Harnessing Pygmalion. *Academy of Management Review, 9,* 64–73; Eden, D. (1990). *Pygmalion in management.* Lexington, MA: Lexington Books/D.C. Heath; Eden, D. (1993). Interpersonal expectations in organizations. In P. D. Blanck (Ed.), *Interpersonal expectations: Theory, research, and applications* (pp. 154–178). Cambridge, UK: University of Cambridge Press; Rosenthal, R., & Jacobson, L. (1968). *Pygmalion in the classroom.* New York: Holt, Rinehart & Winston; Collins, M. H., Hari, J. F., & Rocco, T. S. (2009). The older-worker-younger-supervisor dyad. A test of the reverse Pygmalion effect. *Human Resource Development Quarterly, 20*(1), 21–41; Inamori, T., & Analoui, F. (2010). Beyond Pygmalion effect: The role of managerial perception. *Journal of Management Development, 29*(4), 306–321; Reynolds, D. (2007). Restraining Golem and harnessing Pygmalion in the classroom: A laboratory study of managerial expectations and task design. *Academy of Management Learning & Education, 6*(4), 475–483.

44. White, S. S., & Locke, E. A. (2000). Problems with the Pygmalion effect and some proposed solutions. *The Leadership Quarterly, 11,* 389–415; McNatt, D. B. (2000). Ancient Pygmalion joins contemporary management: A meta-analysis of the result. *Journal of Applied Psychology, 85,* 314–322; Divir, T., Eden, D., & Banjo, M. L. (1995). Self-fulfilling prophecy and gender: Can women be Pygmalion and Galatea? *Journal of Applied Psychology, 80,* 253–270.

45. Oz, S., & Eden, D. (1994). Restraining the golem: Boosting performance by changing the interpretation of low scores. *Journal of Applied Psychology, 79,* 744–754.

46. Rosenthal, R. (1993). Interpersonal expectations: Some antecedents and some consequences. In P. D. Blanck (Ed.), *Interpersonal expectations: Theory, research, and applications* (pp. 3–24). Cambridge, UK: Cambridge University Press.

47. Good, T., & Brophy, J. (1980). *Educational psychology: A realistic approach.* New York: Holt, Rinehart & Winston.

48. White & Locke (2000).

6

Ethical Conflict Management and Negotiation

CHAPTER PREVIEW

Conflict in Organizational Life

Conflict is a daily occurrence in every organization. Managers estimate that they spend between 20 and 40% of their time dealing with disagreements. Common sources of organizational conflict include these:[1]

Interests: Benefits, budgets, organizational policies, office location, and other wants and needs

Data: The best sources of information; the reliability or the interpretation of data

Procedures: How to solve problems; how to make decisions; how to solve conflicts

Values: How to prioritize interests and options; determining organizational direction

Dysfunctional relationships: Those marked by distrust, disrespect, lack of integrity, and lack of mutual concern

Roles: Expectations related to organizational roles; power imbalances between roles

Communication: How something was said; emotions triggered by words; withholding information

Some observers believe that we can expect even more conflicts in the years to come.[2] They note that there is growing pressure on organizations to innovate, change, and adapt. These pressures increase workloads and generate job insecurity. In a global society, the workforce is increasingly diverse, which produces more conflicts between those of different cultural backgrounds. Organizational members now work in different geographical locations and communicate over the Internet rather than face to face. These developments mean that miscommunication is more likely. As organizations empower groups to carry out projects, team members must manage the conflicts that come from working collaboratively.

Conflict experts William Wilmot and Joyce Hocker define conflict as "an expressed struggle between at least two interdependent parties who perceive incompatible goals, scarce resources, and interference from others in achieving their goals."[3] Conflict begins when the parties express their thoughts and feelings to each other through their behaviors. They engage in conflict because they depend to some degree on one another. The choices of one party affect the options of others, as when one employee's choice of vacation time interferes with the vacation plans of a fellow worker. Wilmot and Hocker believe that the sources of conflict identified earlier can be condensed into two general categories. Conflict can be over perceived incompatible goals (if I get promoted, then you don't) or over scarce resources like office space, staffing, or funding for new projects. Interference sets the stage for conflict. Goals may be incompatible and resources scarce, but conflict develops only if we perceive that the other party is interfering with our efforts to achieve our goals and get the resources we want.

Many of us fear and avoid conflict because of our past experiences. Early struggles cost us relationships and left us feeling bruised and battered. Chances are, one or both parties behaved unethically by making threats, engaging in ridicule and sarcasm, losing their tempers, and so on. Aversion to conflict is counterproductive, however. To begin with, organizational conflict is inevitable. Trying to avoid conflict means that we are not equipped to deal with it when it arises. Further, conflicts can promote personal and relational growth. Resolving a conflict successfully builds our skills and generates a sense of accomplishment. Often, conflict over an idea or a proposal produces a higher-quality solution.

The objective of this chapter is to help you become a more ethical, competent conflict manager. We'll identify important steps you need to take to achieve this goal and help you recognize the ethical issues you'll face if you decide to use negotiation to resolve differences. Then we will shift our focus to aggression, which deserves special attention because it is the most destructive type of organizational conflict. We will examine ways to reduce aggression and to prevent sexual harassment, which is a form of aggression generally usually engaged in by men toward women.

Becoming an Ethical Conflict Manager

Investigators have identified five steps you can take to increase the odds that you will behave ethically when engaged in conflict. Your ability to ethically manage conflict will depend on recognizing the difference between productive and unproductive conflicts; identifying your personal conflict style; managing your emotions; setting up guidelines for conflict resolution; and using collaborative communication tactics.

Step 1: Recognize the Differences
Between Functional and Dysfunctional Conflicts

Several factors distinguish between productive and unproductive conflicts.[4] Functional conflicts focus on the content of messages—ideas, values, beliefs, proposals, procedures, budgets, and so on. Participants in these kinds of conflicts are out to solve the problem, not to damage the other party. They make supportive comments, engage in effective listening, signal that they want to collaborate to come up with a solution, and avoid verbal abuse. Dysfunctional conflicts often center on the personalities of those involved. Strong negative emotions as well as verbal attacks (e.g., threats, sarcasm, name calling) characterize these encounters. Discussants locked in unproductive conflicts engage in fight-or-flight responses. They either escalate the conflict or try to avoid it. Conflict spirals when each party retaliates at successively higher levels. An employee who feels unjustly treated may retaliate by trying to undermine the authority of her supervisor, who, in turn, may retaliate against the subordinate by reducing her work hours. Avoidance, as we noted earlier, is the other common destructive pattern. Participants may reduce their dependence on one another, refuse to cooperate, withdraw, harbor resentment, and complain to third parties. In doing so, they leave conflicts unresolved and poison the relationship.

While task-oriented conflicts are to be preferred over relational ones, it would be a mistake to assume that constructive conflict always produces positive outcomes.[5]

Even productive disagreements about ideas can frustrate members if they drag on too long, and conflicts can divert energy from other priorities. Healthy conflicts can quickly turn nasty when strong emotions are sparked by a poor choice of words or doubts about the other party's motivations. Our task, then, is not only to avoid relational conflicts but to prevent task conflicts from deteriorating into dysfunctional exchanges.

Step 2: Manage Your Emotions

Chapter 4 introduced the components of emotional intelligence that are critical to maintaining positive interpersonal relationships. These skill sets are particularly important in conflict settings, where the potential for misunderstanding is high and we need to predict how the other party will react. Since conflict can spark intense feelings of anger and frustration that, as noted above, can derail even healthy disputes, managing our emotions takes on added importance.

Eckerd College conflict experts Craig Runde and Tim Flanagan offer a three- phrase model specifically designed to help us keep our negative emotions from getting out of control.[6] This approach can keep us from turning task conflict into relational conflict or help us convert a dysfunctional dispute into a collaborative problem-solving effort.

Phase 1: Cooling down. Determine what makes you angry. Hot buttons (behaviors that upset us) vary from person to person. For you, it might be coworkers who don't put in a full day's work. For me, it might be supervisors who micromanage. Just reflecting on your hot buttons reduces their power over you. In addition, determine how you can better respond when these buttons are pushed. You might concentrate on not clenching your fists or not raising your voice when someone irritates you, for example.

Phase 2: Slowing down. Have a backup strategy (Plan B) if you can't keep your cool and you find yourself getting mad and defensive. If you can, withdraw from the encounter to give your negative emotions time to dissipate. Deep breathing and thinking about more pleasant topics and places can help you relax. When you begin to slow down, determine why you feel so strongly, and consider that the other party may have logical reasons for his or her behavior, instead of assuming that the other person is out to hurt or upset you.

Phase 3: Engaging constructively. Once you have your emotions under control, you are ready to actively resolve the conflict. Consider the other person's perspective—both their reasoning and their emotional responses. Listen carefully to determine the other party's point of view (this also defuses the tension). Disclose how the conflict is making you feel. If the conversation has stalled, reach out to restart the communication. Approach the other party, point out the impasse, and encourage the resumption of talks. Once re-engaged, you and the other person can create win-win solutions that meet the needs of both of you. Solutions are more likely to emerge because you have controlled your negative emotions, defused the tension, and you and the other person have a clearer understanding of each other's logic and feelings.

Step 3: Identify Your Personal Conflict Style

Conflict styles describe the ways that individuals typically approach conflict situations. Researchers report that there are five approaches to conflicts.[7] (Complete the Self-Assessment on the next page to determine which style you prefer.) Conflict styles are based on two dimensions: (a) concern for one's own needs, and (b) concern for the needs of others:

• The *avoiding* style is low on both concern for self and concern for others. Avoiders steer clear of conflict by keeping their distance from other disputants, changing topics, withdrawing, and so on.

• The *accommodating* style reflects low concern for self and high concern for others. Accommodators give in while helping other parties reach their goals.

• The *compromising style* demonstrates moderate concern for self and others. Compromisers call for concessions from everyone in order to reach an agreement.

• The *competing style* puts the needs of self first with little concern for the other side. Competitors are aggressive and focused on meeting their own needs, often at the expense of other parties.

• The *collaborative style* reflects a high degree of concern for both the self and others. Collaborators listen actively, stay focused on the issues, and hope to reach solutions that meet the needs of both sides.

Avoiding, competing, compromising, and accommodating can be effective and ethical in certain situations.[8] Avoiding works best when there is danger of physical violence. It is ethically appropriate when an organization is temporarily dealing with more significant moral issues. Accommodation can maintain relationships and may be the morally right choice for a follower when a leader is more knowledgeable about an issue. Compromising can generate quick solutions and is ethically justified when both parties have valid interests and want to avoid a stalemate. Competing also produces rapid results and may be an ethical approach when implementing unpopular decisions.

In contrast to the other conflict styles, collaboration appears to be the most successful and ethical option across a variety of contexts. Collaboration has the greatest chance of producing agreements, improves decisions, and leads to greater satisfaction with outcomes.[9] It is the only approach that incorporates high regard for both the self and the other party. There also appears to be a direct link between an individual's level of moral development and his or her choice of conflict style.[10] Those in the lowest stage of moral development (see Chapter 3) tend to use the dominating and avoiding approaches. Those who display a moderate level of moral reasoning rely heavily on compromise. Those who engage in the highest level of moral reasoning are more likely to take an integrative or collaborative approach.

Since collaboration is more effective and ethical, seek to meet the needs of both sides whenever possible. Look to collaborate first, but adopt another style if the situation warrants.

SELF-ASSESSMENT

Conflict Style Inventory

Think of an organizational setting (school, work, nonprofit) where you have conflicts or disagreements with others. With this setting in mind, complete the following scale. Rate each item on the following scale:

1 = never   2 = seldom   3 = sometimes   4 = often   5 = always

1. I avoid being "put on the spot"; I try to keep conflicts to myself.
2. I use my influence to get my ideas accepted.
3. I usually try to "split the difference" in order to resolve an issue.
4. I generally try to satisfy the other's needs.
5. I try to investigate an issue to find a solution acceptable to both of us.
6. I usually avoid open discussion of my differences with the other.
7. I use my authority to make a decision in my favor.
8. I try to find a middle course to resolve an impasse.
9. I usually accommodate the other's wishes.
10. I try to integrate my ideas with those of others to come up with a joint decision.
11. I try to stay away from disagreement with others.
12. I use my expertise to make decisions that favor me.
13. I propose a middle ground for breaking deadlocks.
14. I give in to the wishes of others.
15. I try to work with others to find solutions that satisfy both our expectations.
16. I try to keep my disagreement to myself in order to avoid hard feelings.
17. I generally pursue my side of an issue.
18. I negotiate with others in order to reach a compromise.
19. I often go with others' suggestions.
20. I exchange accurate information with others so we can solve a problem together.
21. I try to avoid unpleasant exchanges with others.
22. I sometimes use my power to win.
23. I use "give-and-take" so that a compromise can be reached.
24. I try to satisfy others' expectations.
25. I try to bring all our concerns out in the open so that the issues can be resolved.

Scoring:

Add up your scores on the following questions:

	Avoidance	Competition	Compromise	Accommodation	Collaboration
	1. _____	2. _____	3. _____	4. _____	5. _____
	6. _____	7. _____	8. _____	9. _____	10. _____
	11. _____	12. _____	13. _____	14. _____	15. _____
	16. _____	17. _____	18. _____	19. _____	20. _____
	21. _____	22. _____	23. _____	24. _____	25. _____
Total					

SOURCE: From Wilmot, W., & Hocker, J. L. (2001). *Interpersonal conflict* (6th ed., pp. 131–132). McGraw-Hilll. Adapted from M. A. Rabim & N. R. Mager (1995). Confirmatory factor analysis of the styles of handling interpersonal conflict: First-order factor model and its invariance across groups, *Journal of Applied Psychology, 80*(1), 122–132.

Step 4: Develop Conflict Guidelines

Guidelines can help both sides engage in collaborative conflict management and generate better outcomes. Organizational communication expert Pamela Shockley-Zalabak offers one set of conflict strategies. When it comes to your participation in conflict, she recommends the following:[11]

Monitor your personal behavior and the behavior of the other party for signs of destructive conflict. Be alert to behaviors that indicate that you or the other party is contributing to escalation or avoidance cycles.

Identify common goals and interests. Think about what both parties have in common and want to achieve. Consider overlapping needs, concerns, goals, and fears.

Develop norms to work on problems. Rules of behavior can be developed for both individual- and group-level conflicts. Relational partners may want to agree to take "time-outs" when discussions get too heated (see our earlier discussion of emotion management), meet in a neutral location, and avoid personal attacks. Groups may want to encourage dissent, seek consensus rather than vote on a solution, and resist speedy outcomes that fail to take advantage of productive conflict over ideas.

Focus on mutual gain. Identify and state what everyone can gain from working through the conflict. Think win-win rather than win-lose. One party does not have to win at the expense of another. Try to expand the resource "pie" instead so that both parties can get what they want.

Create a process for productive conflict. Set up procedures that encourage parties to constructively engage with one another to resolve the issues. There are seven steps in a productive conflict process: (1) engage in self-analysis to identify the issues, the parties involved, and possible solutions; (2) set up a meeting to work on the problem; (3) define the problem to the satisfaction of both sides; (4) develop a wide range of solutions; (5) narrow the choices based on the definition of the problem; (6) commit to the solution along with an implementation and evaluation plan; and (7) monitor the implementation of the solution.

Step 5: Employ Collaborative Conflict Management Tactics

Conflict guidelines set the stage for collaboration, but it is what we say during a conflict episode that generates mutual gains. Collaborative messages reflect a high level of concern for the interests of both parties as well as for the health of the relationship. Collaborative tactics are either analytic or conciliatory. Analytic remarks include the following:[12]

• *Descriptive statements:* Nonevaluative comments that report on observable events surrounding the conflict. ("I was short with you yesterday when you turned in that report.")

• *Disclosing statements:* Nonevaluative statements about conflict events that the partner can't observe—thoughts, feelings, intentions, past history, motivations. ("I didn't intend to criticize you in front of the rest of the staff.")

• *Qualifying statements:* Remarks that qualify the nature and the boundaries of the conflict. ("Tensions between our departments are greatest near the end of the fiscal year, when both groups are swamped with work.")

• *Solicitation of disclosure:* Nonhostile queries that seek information from the other party that can't be observed, like thoughts, feelings, intentions, past history, and motivation. ("What was your goal in raising this issue at this time?")

• *Solicitation of criticism:* Nonhostile questions aimed at soliciting criticism of the self. ("Does it frustrate you that I don't get the sales figures in every Monday?")

Conciliatory verbal messages include:

• *Supportive remarks:* Statements that reflect positive affect, understanding, and acceptance for the partner along with shared interest and goals. ("I appreciate the stress you must be under in your new job.")

• *Concessions:* Comments that signal flexibility, a willingness to change, a conciliatory attitude, and concern for reaching mutually acceptable solutions. ("I would be willing to extend the due date for the project an additional month.")

• *Acceptance of responsibility:* Remarks that attribute responsibility to one or both partners. ("I'll admit that I overreacted at first.")

Resolving Conflict Through Ethical Negotiation

Negotiation is one common method of resolving organizational conflicts. For example, employees negotiate with supervisors for higher salaries and promotions; workers bargain with each other when they need to switch work schedules; corporate purchasing agents and outside suppliers settle on the price of goods and services; members of production and marketing departments haggle over product features and delivery dates; and store owners bargain with property companies over lease agreements.

In negotiation, parties settle their disputes by generating a joint agreement or solution.[13] The negotiation process highlights the interdependent nature of conflicts. Bargainers must have some common goal, or they wouldn't negotiate. On the other hand, at least one issue must divide them, or they wouldn't need to negotiate to reach an agreement. Consider management and union relationships. Both sides share a common interest in seeing the company survive and prosper. However, management wants to keep labor costs as low as possible, while union workers want wage and benefit increases and job security. Management and union representatives will have to successfully negotiate their differences to keep the company in business. Similar disagreements can be found in project teams. Everyone in the group wants the project to succeed, but members will have to negotiate assignments, timelines, and a host of other details.

Because negotiation is so widely used, it is important to recognize the moral dilemmas inherent in this form of conflict resolution and to highlight the ethical benefits of taking an integrative approach to bargaining.

Ethical Issues in Negotiation

Ethical issues in negotiation typically fall into one of three categories: the choice of tactics, the distribution of benefits, and the impact of the settlement on those who are not at the bargaining table.[14]

When approaching a negotiation, bargainers have decisions to make about which tactics they will use when interacting with the other party. Most of these tactical dilemmas involve deceit. Do I share what I am really willing to settle for, or do I argue for a higher price? Do I lie when asked if I have other offers when I don't? Do I reveal problems (e.g., upcoming lawsuits, hidden debts) when negotiating with someone who wants to buy my company? Is it okay to bluff by threatening to walk out of the auto dealership when I don't really intend to?

Some argue that deception is okay because both parties know that deceit is to be expected in negotiation settings. They treat bargaining like a poker game. Just as we expect players to hide their cards and bluff, those who enter negotiations know to expect deceit. They agree with the British statesman Henry Taylor, who claimed, "Falsehood ceases to be falsehood when it is understood on all sides that the truth is not expected to be spoken."[15] Bargaining thus meets one of the standards of the principle of veracity described in Chapter 4, which is that lying is permissible in situations where parties know that deception is the norm.[16] However, it is not clear that everyone understand the "rules" of negotiation. A cooperative negotiator operates by a different set of assumptions than a competitive one. Those from other cultures play by different sets of rules, which are unclear to visitors. (For example, should a foreign visitor haggle with every street vendor in Kenya?) By its very nature, deceit shows disrespect for the worth of the other party and thus violates Kant's imperative to treat people as ends and not as the means to our ends.[17] (See Ethics in Action 6.1 for one list of deceptive tactics or "dirty tricks" frequently used by negotiators.)

David Lax and James Sebenius suggest that we ask ourselves the following questions when determining whether or not to use deceit as a bargaining tactic.[18] Responding to these queries can help us determine if we should tell the truth. (Turn to Ethics in Action 6.2 for a description of concrete ways to avoid lying during a bargaining session.)

- Will you be comfortable with yourself the next morning? Would you want friends and family to know what you have done? The public?
- Does this tactic conform to the norm of reciprocity—that we treat others like we would like to be treated? How would you feel if the roles were reversed?
- Would you be comfortable counseling someone else to use this strategy?
- If you were to design a negotiation system from scratch, would you allow this strategy? How would you rule on this tactic if you were an outside arbitrator?
- What if everyone used the same method? Would this tactic create a desirable society?
- Are there alternative tactics you can use to avoid lying and deception?
- How can you create value instead of claiming what you think is rightfully yours?
- Does using this tactic further poison the ethical atmosphere for this type of negotiation or in this industry?

The next set of ethical issues in negotiation stems from the distribution of outcomes. Unequal settlements raise questions of fairness. For example, most of us feel uneasy if one party appears to take advantage of the other, as in the case of a buyer who convinces an elderly widow to sell her house at well below market value, or a giant food processing firm that squeezes the absolutely lowest price out of a small farmer. (Case Study 6.2, "The $2.3 Million Handshake," provides another example of a disproportionate settlement.) Determining exactly what is fair can be difficult, but making sure that both sides benefit is a good starting point.[19] Also, some of the questions outlined above can be applied to determining fairness as well. Does the settlement violate norms of reciprocity? Would you counsel others to follow the same approach? What if everyone claimed a disproportionate amount of the benefits; what kind of society would that create?

The third set of ethical concerns shifts the focus beyond the parties directly involved in the negotiation process. Decisions made by bargainers can have a negative impact on outside groups. For instance, when a public utilities commission negotiates higher power rates with power companies, members of the community have to pay larger utility bills. Then, too, settlements can adversely effect the environment and future generations. Take the case of landowners who negotiate mineral rights with mining companies. The property owners get generous settlements, and the firms gain access to the materials they need to generate significant profits. However, extracting the minerals can cause environmental damage that will scar the landscape for decades to come. One way to minimize the potential damage is to keep the interests of outside stakeholders (current and future) in mind. Weigh the benefits generated at the negotiation table against the harms that will be caused to outsiders. Consider the legacy you want to leave behind. (Do you want to be known and remembered for the terms of this settlement?)[20]

ETHICS IN ACTION 6.1 RESPONDING TO DIRTY TRICKS

Distributive negotiators who view negotiations as a battle or test of wills commonly use "dirty tricks" (unethical behaviors) to get their way. Responding effectively to these tactics is key to maintaining an ethical negotiation climate and reaching an integrative solution without being taken advantage of. When confronted with any of the following dirty tricks (which are all designed to deceive or manipulate), label the behavior to let the other party know that you recognize what is going on. Point out that these strategies can delay or prevent agreement. Warn the other side that you will only participate in the discussions as long as you are convinced that they are being honest and want to reach a fair conclusion.

Here are some common dirty tricks:

Good guy/bad guy. This is a variation of the good cop/bad cop routine portrayed in crime dramas. One negotiator (the good cop) is friendly and cooperative, while the other (the bad cop) is aggressive and demanding. Just as criminal suspects are more willing to offer information and concessions to good cops than to bad cops, negotiators are more cooperative with the pleasant party. In another version of this trick, the good guy asks for concessions in order to please the bad guy negotiator.

Bad-faith negotiating. The negotiator claims to want to reach a win-win agreement but is really stalling for time or probing for information to use later. Or the unethical negotiator agrees to a settlement, only to reopen it later in hopes of getting more concessions. The temptation is to give in since so much time and energy have already been invested in the agreement.

Lack of authority. The other person lacks decision-making power. This tactic is frequently used in car showrooms, where the salesperson must "talk to the sales manager" before agreeing to a deal. The use of a third party keeps negotiators off balance and, as many car buyers have found out, makes it more likely that they will take any agreement just to finish the negotiation process and get out of the dealership.

Inaccurate data. One side presents inaccurate, false, or misinterpreted information. Since data are critical to reaching equitable solutions, false information or misrepresentation can put one side at a significant disadvantage.

Many for one. Early in the negotiations, one party makes small, unimportant concessions. Later, this negotiator asks for a major concession as payback for his or her earlier concessions.

Information overload. One negotiator overwhelms the other with massive amounts of data and information. The recipient of all this information may not question its validity or may give too much power to the provider who seems so knowledgeable. The mass of information may contain errors and biases that can be used to undermine or delay negotiations.

SOURCE: Isenhart, M. W., & Spangle, M. L. (2000). *Collaborative approaches to resolving conflict.* Thousand Oaks, CA: Sage, pp. 57–58. Tactic descriptions used by permission.

Conflicts of interest arise in negotiations when bargainers act as agents for outside parties. Lawyers negotiate on behalf of clients, real estate agents on behalf of sellers, union representatives on behalf of the union membership. Negotiation agents often face conflicting interests. On the one hand, they are being paid to get the best deal possible for their clients. On the other hand, there may be an incentive to settle for an outcome that benefits them rather than their employers. A lawyer may urge her clients to accept a smaller settlement so she can collect the fee that she might lose if the plaintiffs continue their lawsuit. By the same token, a real estate agent may encourage buyers to purchase a less desirable property so that he can collect his commission. Lessen potential conflicts of interest by aligning your incentives with those of your employer (e.g., a bonus if you generate a better settlement for your client). Avoid even the appearance of a conflict of interest. For instance, don't accept trips and golf outings from suppliers lest you be tempted to make a deal that is not advantageous for your firm.

ETHICS IN ACTION 6.2 FIVE WAYS TO AVOID LYING DURING A NEGOTIATION

Harvard business professor Deepak Malhotra believes that we tell the truth at the bargaining table without suffering significant losses. He offers the following five "ethical superior alternatives" to lying.

1. *Don't succumb to time pressures.* Many lies come when negotiators are caught off guard and resort to deception when responding to unanticipated questions. Pretend that you are selling a business, for instance. You can expect to be asked, "Do you have any other offers for your company?" Prepare your answer for this question before the talks start. You might point out that you haven't advertised your business for sale yet or that the market for your kind of company is strong.

2. *Refuse to answer certain questions.* Despite preparation, you may still be taken by surprise by a tough question. You may need to tell the other party that you are not authorized to answer or need to gather more information. There may also be certain questions that you will never feel comfortable answering (nor would other parties if they were in your shoes). For instance, you may not want to reveal to a purchasing agent the production cost of an item you are selling. Instead, you might offer to share other information, such as the details of the manufacturing process and the quality control systems you have in place.

3. *Adopt the logic of exchange.* When you exchange important information, you should receive similar privileged information in return. If you reveal your timeline for completing a deal, you should expect to learn the time constraints of the other party, for example.

4. *Eliminate the lie by making it true.* Reduce the temptation to lie by reshaping reality prior to bargaining. For instance, a lawyer might ask her client to limit the concessions

she, the lawyer, can make during a mediation session, or a department head may ask for more time to gather information instead of submitting an inflated budget request.

5. *Observe the shadow of the future.* Focus on building long-term, trusting relationships through truth telling. You are less likely to lie if you and the other negotiator have a truthful relationship. Further, if you both have been truthful in the past, this pattern will generally continue into the future.

SOURCE: Malhotra, D. (2004, May). Smart alternatives to lying in negotiation. *Negotiation, 7*(5), 3–5.

Adopt an Integrative Approach to Negotiation

Bargainers typically adopt either a distributive or integrative approach to negotiation. Distributive negotiators adopt the win-lose conflict management style described earlier. Their basic assumption is that they are engaged in a battle over a fixed "pie," or value. As a result, whatever one party gains is at the expense of the other. Integrative negotiators take a win-win approach. They are convinced that the pie can be expanded and that both parties can benefit. They view the negotiation as a joint problem-solving session. Here is a summary of the behaviors that come from adopting each perspective:

Integrative Negotiation	*Distributive Negotiation*
Open sharing of information	Hidden information
Trade of valued interests	Demand of interests
Interest-based discussion	Positional discussion
Mutual goals	Self-goals
Problem solving	Forcing
Explanation	Argument
Relationship building	Relationship sacrificing
Hard on problem	Hard on people

SOURCE: Spangle, M. L., & Isenhart, M. W. (2003). *Negotiation: Communication for diverse settings.* Thousand Oaks, CA: Sage, p. 15. Used by permission.

In comparing the two approaches, it is clear that distributive bargainers are more likely to engage in unethical negotiation behavior. They are tempted to deceive, generate unfair settlements, fall victim to conflicts of interests, and generate solutions that benefit them at the expense of outsiders. As a result, we should adopt an integrative perspective whenever possible. However, there do appear to be times when the rules call for a win-lose approach, such as when buying a motorcycle. We also risk being taken advantage of if we come to the table with an integrative approach and the other party is out to get as much as he or she can.

Harvard negotiation experts Roger Fisher and William Ury outline one widely used integrative approach that enables negotiators to take a win-win approach while protecting themselves from being victimized. They call their problem-solving approach the *principled negotiation model.*[21] Here are the four steps of principled negotiation:

1. *Separate the people from the problem.* Make sure that you address the human dimension of negotiation. Set the stage for productive discussions by building a working relationship. Think of yourself as working side by side to reach an agreement that is good for both of you. Once in the negotiation, address three types of people problems: perception, emotion, and communication. Don't blame the other party, but try to understand her or his perspective. Recognize and address the emotions both sides feel; don't react to emotional outbursts, but reach out to build positive emotional connections. Address the other party directly (not third parties), actively listen, and use "I" language ("I was disappointed in your response") rather than "you" language ("You lied to me.").

2. *Focus on interests, not positions.* A bargaining position is the negotiator's public stance (i.e., "I want to hire two new employees for my project."). An interest, on the other hand, is the reason why the negotiator takes that position ("I need additional help so that my team can finish the project on time."). Focusing on positions can blind participants to the reality that there may be several ways to meet an underlying need or interest. The company in the example above might decide not to hire additional staff yet meet the project leader's need for help by reassigning current employees to his team.

The Camp David peace treaty between Egypt and Israel demonstrates how separating interests from positions can generate productive settlements. When the two nations began negotiating with the help of President Jimmy Carter in 1978, they argued over ownership of the Sinai Peninsula, which Israel seized from Egypt during the Six-Day War in 1967. Egypt took the position that all occupied lands should be returned immediately. Israel took the position that only some of the Sinai should be returned to Egyptian control, fearing that Egyptian tanks would be stationed on its border. As a result, the talks went nowhere. However, once the parties realized that Israel's real interest was national security and that Egypt's interest lay in regaining sovereignty over her land, an agreement was reached. Israel gave back the occupied territory in return for pledges that Egypt would not use the Sinai for military purposes. Tensions in the region continue, but the two nations have remained at peace.

3. *Invent options for mutual gain.* Spend time expanding the pie before trying to divide it. In other words, generate solutions that can meet the needs of both negotiators. Brainstorm a variety of possible ideas (either on your own or with the other party) that you can draw from later on, look for shared and complementary interests that can lead to creative outcomes, and develop options that will be attractive to the other side. Fisher and Ury offer the following example of a creative solution that met the interests of both parties.

Consider the story of two men quarreling in a library. One wants the window open, and the other wants it closed. They bicker back and forth about how much to leave it open: a crack, halfway, three quarters of the way. No solution satisfies them both. Enter the librarian. She asks one why he wants the window open: "To get some fresh air." She asks the other why he wants it closed: "To avoid the draft." After thinking a minute, she opens wide a window in the next room, bringing in fresh air without a draft.[22]

4. *Insist on objective criteria.* Avoid a test of wills when reaching the final agreement. If you pit your will against theirs, one of you will have to back down. One party may force the other into accepting an unsatisfactory solution as a result. Instead, agree on a set of criteria when determining a settlement. Employ fair standards (market value, industry standards, replacement costs, scientific findings) and fair procedures (taking turns, letting another party decide). Negotiators typically accept agreements that are in line with widely accepted principles.

Combating Aggression and Sexual Harassment

Types and Sources of Aggression

Aggressive behavior is the most destructive form of conflict at work. Interpersonal aggression consists of conscious actions that hurt or injure. Such behavior can take a variety of forms, from refusing to return phone calls to screaming at employees to murder. One widely used typology categorizes aggression along three dimensions: (1) physical-verbal (destructive words or deeds); (2) active-passive (doing harm by acting or by failing to act); and (3) direct-indirect (doing harm directly to the individual or indirectly through an intermediary and by attacking something the individual values).[23] Examples of behaviors that fit into each of these categories can be found in Ethics in Action 6.3.

ETHICS IN ACTION 6.3 FORMS OF AGGRESSIVE BEHAVIOR

Type of Aggression	Examples
Physical-active-direct	Punching, kicking, stabbing, shooting another person
Physical-active-indirect	Sabotaging a piece of equipment so that another person will be hurt; removing tools and supplies
Physical-passive-direct	Physically preventing another person from obtaining a desired goal or performing a desired act (e.g., by failing to move out of the person's way when asked to do so)
Physical-passive-indirect	Refusing to perform necessary tasks (e.g., refusing to provide information or help needed by a coworker)

(Continued)

(Continued)

Verbal-active-direct	Insulting or derogating another person in some manner
Verbal-active-indirect	Spreading malicious rumors or gossip about another person
Verbal-passive-direct	Refusing to speak to another person or refusing to answer questions posed by this person
Verbal-passive-indirect	Failing to speak up in another person's defense when he or she is unfairly criticized

SOURCE: Adapted from Baron, R. A. (2004). Workplace aggression and violence: Insights from basic research. In R. W. Griffin & A. M. O'Leary-Kelly (Eds.), *The dark side of organizational behavior,* p. 29. San Francisco: Jossey-Bass. Reprinted by permission of John Wiley & Sons, Inc.

Interpersonal workplace aggression is all too prevalent.[24] An estimated 2 million U.S. workers are physically assaulted yearly; 16 million are threatened with violence; 6 million experience physical assault; and homicide is one of the leading causes of death on the job. In Canada, assault rates are higher than in the United States. While violence attracts the most media attention, milder forms of workplace aggression are far more common. Studies conducted in Europe and the United States indicate that for every physical assault, there are several instances of less serious aggression, like being shouted at, insulted, and receiving threatening gestures. In Europe, 30% of men and 55% of women surveyed said that they had been victims of these milder aggressive behaviors during the last year. Approximately 41% of U.S. wage and salary workers experienced psychological aggression during a 12-month period.

Not surprisingly, aggression can do extensive damage to both individuals and the organization as a whole.[25] Victims may be injured, experience higher stress levels leading to poor health, become fearful or angry or depressed, lose the ability to concentrate, and feel less committed to their jobs. Observers who witness aggressive incidents may suffer some of the same negative outcomes. They, too, experience more anxiety and a lowered sense of well-being and commitment. At the organizational level, performance drops as a result of aggressive actions. Workplace aggression is correlated with lower productivity, higher absenteeism and turnover rates, lawsuits, and negative publicity.

Aggressive behavior is the product of a number of factors—personal, social, and situational—outlined below.[26]

Personal Causes of Aggression

Type A personality. Type A behavior-pattern people are extremely competitive, generally in a hurry, and highly irritable. Such individuals are more likely to engage in hostile actions both on and off the job (child and spousal abuse, for instance).

Hostile attributional bias. Those with this perceptual bias tend to assume the worst in others. They believe that peers and subordinates are out to hurt them, and then they respond accordingly. For example, an employee with a hostile perspective who doesn't get notice of an important meeting will assume that his boss deliberately snubbed him, even if this omission was a harmless oversight. He may refuse to answer questions from his supervisor the next time they meet. (Another example of an employee with a hostile attributional bias can be found in Case Study 6.1.)

Inflated (or deflated) self-esteem. Those who hold extremely high views of themselves are particularly sensitive to negative feedback, which threatens their self-image. They are more likely to respond with anger and nurse grudges. Individuals with low self-esteem are more prone to seeking revenge.

Low self-monitoring. High self-monitors pay close attention to situational cues and then modify their behavior to act appropriately. Low self-monitors, on the other hand, pay more attention to their inner attitudes and feelings. As a result, they are more likely to escalate conflict and misinterpret motives.

Social Causes of Aggression

Frustration. Interference with the pursuit of goals produces anger and hostility. Frustration is most likely to cause aggression when the interference is seen as illegitimate. An employee turned down for a promotion, for instance, will be more upset if he thinks that the job went to a much less-qualified candidate.

Direct provocation. Aggression begets further aggression. Most people respond to verbal and physical assaults by retaliating with more extreme measures of their own.

Displaced aggression. If it's too dangerous or costly for a member to retaliate against someone who provokes her (the boss, for example), she may then take frustrations out on someone else (subordinates, friends, family members).

Triggered displaced aggression. Sometimes a weak provocation will trigger a strong aggressive response. This may occur because the individual recently experienced a much stronger provocation. For instance, an employee may lash out at a peer who suggests minor modifications to a project after being subjected to severe criticism about the same project from her supervisor.

Aggressive models. Aggressive individuals act as role models for other organizational members. Observers learn new ways to aggress that are often more subtle, like stalling initiatives or quietly sabotaging the work of another department. Seeing aggression also "primes" hostile thoughts. Coworkers begin to think about the wrongs they have suffered at the hands of others. Finally, role models demonstrate that aggression is a legitimate means for dealing with frustration or provocation. Soon an organizational culture of aggression emerges.

Contextual Causes of Aggression

Oppressive supervision. Employees are more likely to strike out against their supervisors when they (a) sense that they have little influence over the workload and work pace, (b) are the victims of bullying bosses, and (c) feel overly controlled (given little power, monitored extremely closely).

Job stressors. Layoffs, demanding performance standards, role ambiguity, conflicts, increasing competition, and other job factors produce stress that can sow the seeds of aggression.

Use of alcohol. Alcohol weakens resistance to anger and aggression. Intoxicated people can still restrain themselves but are more likely to go along with suggestions to harm others and to attack helpless victims.

Perceived unfairness. Individuals are more likely to retaliate when they perceive that they have been treated unjustly. They may take issue with how resources are distributed (distributive injustice) and how decisions are reached (procedural injustice). However, being treated with disrespect (interactional or informational injustice) appears to be the strongest determinant of aggression. (For more information on organizational justice, see Chapter 10.)

Unpleasant working conditions. Extremely high or low temperatures, crowding, noise, and other uncomfortable environmental factors generate negative emotions and increase aggressive behavior. As a result, attempts to save money by cutting back on the quality of the work environment (shutting down the air conditioning, lowering the thermostat in the winter, removing carpet) often backfire, lowering productivity while producing more aggression.

CASE STUDY 6.1

Sparks of Aggression

Pedro, a clerk at a credit union, became angry with one of his fellow employees, a college student working there as a summer fill-in. Pedro informed the student that he knew the student was out to get him, was spreading false rumors about him, and was trying to sabotage his career. When the student strongly denied these charges, Pedro became verbally abusive, cursing him loudly in front of other employees and accusing him of receiving special treatment because he was related to a high official at the credit union. A supervisor stepped in and ended this episode, but the next day Pedro loudly accused the student and a female employee, who had previously rebuffed Pedro's romantic overtures, of "making fun of him" as they conversed. They vigorously denied this accusation, stating that they were talking about a totally unrelated topic, but Pedro refused to believe them and threatened to "make them pay" for their actions. The situation reached a climax about a week later, on a suffocatingly hot day when the credit union's air conditioning failed. During that steamy afternoon, Pedro informed the student that this was the day on which he would get his revenge and teach him that he could not treat people from his country this way. That evening, Pedro followed the student home on public transportation, muttering curses and grimacing all the way. He kept fingering his pocket, and the student was certain that Pedro was carrying a weapon. Fortunately, the student had arranged for several friends to meet him, and they were standing on the train station platform when he got off. When Pedro saw them, he shook his fist but retreated. That night, he was arrested for assaulting and seriously wounding a neighbor. He never returned to the credit union.

What factors contributed to Pedro's aggressive behavior?

SOURCE: Folger, R., & Baron, R. A. (1996). Violence and hostility at work: A model of reactions to perceived injustice. In G. VandenBos & E. Q. Bulato (Eds.), *Violence on the job: Identifying risks and developing solutions* (pp. 51–85). Washington, DC: American Psychological Association, p. 56. Used by permission.

Reducing Aggression

Strategies for reducing aggression must address its personal, social, and contextual origins.[27] Careful screening of potential employees is a good place to start. Try to weed out individuals with aggressive tendencies and strong Type A personalities through interviews, testing, and reference checks. Ask applicants how they responded when unfairly treated or what they would do in a difficult job-related situation. Careful reference checks can identify individuals who should not be hired because of their patterns of abusive behavior. For current employees, provide training in social skills. Some workers get caught up in aggressive interactions because they unwittingly provoke others. They may not understand that their behavior irritates their peers and generates negative feelings.

Next, address social factors. To reduce frustration, establish legitimacy for decisions and actions by providing background information and rationale to your employees. Short-circuit the development of a climate of aggression by eliminating aggressive role models and punishing offenders. Effective punishment is prompt, highly certain, strong, and justified.

Finally, reduce negative contextual factors. Cut back on tight supervision, eliminate unnecessary rules, and avoid intrusive monitoring practices. Give your employees more control over how they complete their tasks, and outlaw drinking on the job (even at lunch). Reduce the impact of stressors by lowering work demands, by providing physical and emotional outlets (recreation areas, nap rooms, office celebrations), and by supplying stress management training. Create pleasant working environments with adequate space, comfortable temperatures, soundproofing, attractive furnishings, and so on. Prevent perceptions of injustice by treating others with respect, using the communication skills described in Chapter 4. (See Ethics in Action 6.4 for ways to control one common form of workplace aggression.)

ETHICS IN ACTION 6.4 PROMOTING A MORE CIVIL WORKPLACE

Incivility consists of rude, discourteous actions that disregard others and violate norms of respect. Examples of workplace incivility include leaving a mess for custodians to clean up, sending a "flaming" e-mail, making a sarcastic comment about a peer in front of coworkers, and claiming credit for someone else's work. While incivility is a mild form of aggression, it nonetheless appears to be rampant in the workplace. A series of studies involving employees in the United States and Canada found that 10 to 25% of their sample witnessed incivility daily, and 20 to 50% were the targets of uncivil messages every week.

Like other forms of aggression, incivility has both direct and indirect negative effects. Direct effects include lower job satisfaction; reduced motivation, performance, organizational loyalty, and creativity; and more resistance to helping others. Indirect effects include the erosion of shared values and cooperation as well as the escalation of conflict spirals. Incivility sets the stage for more aggressive, damaging behaviors.

Incivility may be on the rise because of increasing job demands; downsizing and outsourcing, which reduce organizational loyalty; and the spread of the "casual" workplace that deemphasizes rules of conduct. To curtail incivility and reduce its costly effects, adopt the following strategies:

1. *Set a zero-tolerance policy.*

   Communicate that employee-to-employee incivility will not be tolerated, and repeat this message on a regular basis both verbally and in writing. Such statements set a baseline for evaluating and correcting behavior. For example, Boeing requires that workers "treat each other with respect." Southwest Airlines states that employees will be treated with the "same concern, respect, and caring attitude" that they are expected to display to customers.

2. *Take an honest look in the mirror.*

   Managers and executives must live by the civility standard they set. Employees follow the example set by their leaders. If mid- and upper-level managers behave uncivilly, their subordinates are much more likely to do the same.

3. *Weed out trouble before it enters your organization.*

   Some individuals are repeat offenders, leaving a trail of disrespectful behaviors in their wake. Often, they are shuttled from department to department, organization to organization. Try to screen out these offenders through thorough reference checks that go beyond the contacts provided by the candidate.

4. *Teach civility.*

   Introduce training designed to improve listening, confirmation, and conflict management skills. Tie performance evaluations and career advancement to the use of these competencies. Reduce the stress that may drive people to act poorly, and emphasize that there is always enough time to be "nice."

5. *Put your ear to the ground and listen carefully.*

Collect feedback to identify repeat offenders and to keep them from poisoning their colleagues. Anonymous feedback from employees can help reveal if managers are being uncivil to subordinates while presenting a positive image to superiors. Provide channels (human relations departments, open-door policies) for employees who want to report disrespectful behavior.

6. *When incivility occurs, hammer it.*

Since incivility breeds further incivility, such behavior needs to be curtailed immediately, even at the lowest level of the organization. Failure to punish incivility signals that such behavior is sanctioned and enables perpetrators to advance their careers.

7. *Heed warning signals.*

Managers must take action when informed of abuse and protect those who report problems. Employees will keep silent if leaders fail to investigate and correct uncivil patterns or if they fear retaliation.

8. *Don't make excuses for powerful instigators.*

All violators, no matter how powerful or talented, must be confronted. Managers must be required to discipline instigators who report to them, despite the temptation to rationalize their behavior. They must also refuse to transfer troublemakers, because violators will continue to cause problems in their new locations.

9. *Invest in post-departure interviews.*

Incivility can be hard to track because victims don't leave immediately but often remain in their current positions until they can land new jobs in other organizations. Targets are often reluctant to give the true reason for their departure, believing that the organization doesn't really care or because they fear that they will appear weak if they do speak up. Conduct post-departure interviews with former employees who have been gone for some time to determine if incivility was a factor in their decision to leave.

Sources

Andersson, L. M., & Pearson, C. M. (1999). Tit for tat? The spiraling effect of incivility in the workplace. *Academy of Management Review, 24*, 452–471.

Pearson, C. M., Andersson, L. M., & Porath, C. L. (2000). Assessing and attacking workplace incivility. *Organizational Dynamics, 29*, 123–137.

Pearson, C. M., & Porath, C. L. (2004). On incivility, its impact, and directions for future research. In R. W. Griffin & A. M. O'Leary-Kelly (Eds.), *The dark side of organizational behavior* (pp. 23–61). San Francisco: Jossey-Bass.

Pearson, C. M., & Porath, C. L. (2005). On the nature, consequences and remedies of workplace incivility: No time for "nice"? Think again. *Academy of Management Executive, 19*, 7–18.

Preventing Sexual Harassment

Sexual harassment is a distinctive form of aggression that is overwhelmingly directed at women. There are three types of sexual harassment behaviors.[28] The first is *gender harassment,* which consists of gender-based (nonsexual) comments and behaviors designed to demean women. For example, a supervisor may claim that a woman can't do a job defined as "men's work." The second form of harassment consists of *unwanted sexual attention.* This category includes both verbal (repeated requests for dates) and nonverbal behaviors (gestures, touching, kissing). The third is *sexual coercion,* which is forcing employees into sexual activity through promises or threats. A boss might promise a promotion to a subordinate who sleeps with him or threaten to fire her if she does not.

There are also legal definitions of sexual harassment, which is prohibited by law. Title VII of the Civil Rights Act of 1964 forbids discrimination in employment based on "race, color, religion, sex, or national origin." The Equal Employment Opportunity Commission (EEOC) enforces this statute, as do the Americans with Disabilities Act and the Equal Pay Act. State laws also apply to harassment cases.

According to the EEOC and a number of court decisions, there are two forms of sexual harassment under the law.[29] The first is called *quid pro quo,* which is a legal term roughly meaning "something for something." Plaintiffs in quid pro quo cases claim that they were coerced into providing sexual favors to their supervisors in return for keeping their jobs or getting promotions and raises. This constitutes discriminatory behavior because victims were required to submit to conditions not placed on other workers. The second type of harassment involves the creation of a "hostile work environment." Plaintiffs in hostile work environment cases claim that working conditions interfered with their job performance. The following have been identified as components of a hostile work environment:

• *Harassment aimed at one gender.* For example, comments or slurs directed at only one gender, not the other.

• *Severe and sustained negative behavior.* Generally, a pattern of behavior must be established, like a series of lewd comments and offensive gestures, not just one isolated remark.

• *Negative effects of behavior on the receiver.* Behavior is considered harassing when it offends the recipient, regardless of the expressed intent of the perpetrator. A male worker may put up a sexual poster "for fun," for instance, but this display is illegal because it makes his female coworkers uncomfortable.

• *Violation of the "reasonable woman" standard.* The behavior must violate what the typical woman would see as appropriate. A business lunch between a male and female colleague would not be seen as harassment under this standard. Harassment would occur, however, if a supervisor kept asking a subordinate for a date despite her repeated refusals.

- *Significant damages.* Claimants must establish that the behavior had a significant negative impact (caused discomfort, lowered work performance).

- *Unwelcome behavior.* Consensual behavior is not illegal, but unwanted behavior is. Researchers have discovered that men and women often interpret the same behavior differently. Males often see "friendly" behavior on the part of women as sexual in nature. They are more likely to be flattered by sexual attention, whereas females find it offensive. Conversely, men are less likely than women to define teasing sexual remarks, jokes, and suggestive looks and gestures as harassing behavior.

Sexual harassment, while unique, does have elements in common with other forms of workplace aggression. (Turn to the Ethics and Technology feature for more information on how technology is increasing the damage done by sexual harassment and other forms of aggression.) Like other aggressive behavior, it occurs with distressing frequency. An analysis of 55 surveys involving more than 86,000 women found that 58% had experienced potentially harassing behaviors at work.[30] Harassment is most frequent in male-dominated, blue-collar jobs (construction worker, machinist), but female doctors, lawyers, and other professionals are not immune from such behavior. Neither are women students. The rate of harassment among female college students is roughly that of female workers; approximately 50% report being targeted for such harassing actions as insulting remarks, propositions, bribes, threats, and sexual assault.[31]

The costs of sexual harassment mirror those of other aggressive behaviors. The work performance of targets suffers due to stress, decreased morale, damaged relationships, withdrawal, and career changes. Many victims quit their jobs or are fired for filing complaints. Targets experience headaches, sleep loss, weight loss or gain, nausea, sexual dysfunction, and eating and gastrointestinal disorders. Negative psychological effects include depression, a sense of helplessness and loss of control, fear, detachment, and decreased motivation.[32]

Many of the same personal, social, and contextual factors that promote other forms of aggression also contribute to harassment. Offenders are more likely to harbor hostility and to be low self-monitors. Men may be frustrated because they believe that women as a group are taking away their privileges, and they retaliate. Perpetrators also take their cue from others who model harassing behavior.

In addition to these general factors, there are unique determinants of harassment:[33] First, male sexual aggressors hold more traditional (less egalitarian) views of females. They expect women to function in nurturing roles and believe that some professions should be closed to females. Harassment punishes those who violate these prescriptions and victimizes women while reinforcing the masculine image of the perpetrator. Second, violators hope to win sexual favors and other payoffs, like reduced competition for jobs. Third, rates of sexual harassment are substantially higher in organizations that don't take complaints seriously, fail to investigate charges or punish offenders, and retaliate against whistle-blowers. Fourth, harassment preserves male-dominated organizational systems that give men power over women.

You can take a number of steps to prevent sexual harassment, beginning with creating a zero-tolerance organizational climate. Adopt a written policy that condemns such actions, spells out what types of behavior qualify as harassing, encourages victims to come forward, identifies penalties, and prohibits retaliation. Then, back up the policy with an effective investigation procedure using an impartial third party who interviews all participants. Attack gender stereotypes through training, which also encourages men to understand how women perceive behavior that men interpret as harmless. Increase the proportion of women in the organization to reduce the likelihood of harassment.

ETHICS AND TECHNOLOGY

Cyberaggression

Researchers use the term *cyberaggression* to describe aggressive or hostile workplace behaviors that employ information and communication (ICT) technologies. Such behaviors include these:

Verbal abuse (e.g., flaming e-mails; discriminatory, racist, abusive messages posted on message boards)

Harassment (e.g., offensive jokes, sexual images sent as attachments)

Sexual harassment (e.g., flirting via e-mail, cyberstalking, sexual bragging)

Hacking users (e.g., damaging personal systems; gathering information for purposes of revenge or retaliation; threatening to place pornographic material on a computer or work system; planting computer viruses)

Identity theft (unauthorized use of personal accounts and names)

The effects of cyberaggression can be far reaching. Abusive messages can be sent to the entire company, as in the case of the fired Intel worker who sent disparaging remarks about the company's leaders to 3,500 other employees. Or workers can reach broader audiences by posting derogatory information to websites or releasing internal e-mails to news outlets. For example, the stock of Cerner Corporation dropped dramatically when an e-mail from the firm's president criticizing the work habits of employees was forwarded to a public Yahoo message board. Not only does technology increase the number of victims beyond the individual or immediate work group, but it also multiplies the number of observers who suffer negative effects from witnessing the behavior. Strategies for combating cyberaggression fall into three categories:

- *Technical interventions* prevent or reduce misuse through changing the technology itself. Systems can be designed, for instance, to prevent the forwarding or transmitting of personal or confidential information. Software can monitor and scan e-mails for key words or phrases to prevent employees from sending messages containing vulgar or racist language or pornographic materials.

- *Managerial interventions* involve the development and enforcement of policies that outline the appropriate and inappropriate use of ICTs.
- *Social interventions* focus on establishing organizational norms that discourage online aggression. Employees can be trained to craft better messages (to avoid flaming messages, for example) or to use corporate e-mail ethically. It is particularly important to screen out aggressive job applicants, since technology enables such individuals to do greater damage than ever before.

The most effective cyberaggression prevention programs utilize all three types of strategies, moving beyond technical and managerial solutions to address the organization's ethical culture.

Source

Weatherbee, T., & Kelloway, E. K. (2005). A case of cyberdeviancy: Cyberaggression in the workplace. In E. K. Kelloway, J. Barling, & J. J. Hurrell, Jr. (Eds.), *Handbook of workplace violence* (pp. 445–487). Thousand Oaks, CA: Sage.

University of Arkansas business professor Anne O'Leary-Kelly and her colleagues suggest that paying more attention to the moral dimension of sexual harassment would also reduce its frequency.[34] Clearly, such behavior, which is harmful, selfish, and unfair, is unethical as well as illegal. The stronger the employees' sense that harassment has a moral component (the higher its degree of *moral intensity*—see Chapter 3), the more likely it is that those workers will avoid sexually aggressive actions and intervene when they observe harassment. Professor O'Leary-Kelly suggests that you can increase the moral intensity of sexual harassment through the following actions:

1. *Make aggressors aware of the effects of their actions.* Some individuals, as noted earlier, aren't aware that their actions are harmful. Others may think they are only hurting the target of their sexual advances or remarks. Perpetrators need to learn that their actions are destructive not only to the target but to other women, the work team, and the entire organization. This is particularly important in light of the fact that the majority of victims do not file complaints for fear of retaliation. Offenders therefore get the mistaken notion that their behavior is not destructive.

2. *Encourage consensus about the definition and immorality of sexual harassment.* Create a shared understanding of what harassment might be in your particular organization, and develop clear standards of behavior that highlight the unethical nature of harassing actions. Promote discussion about situations that make participants uncomfortable.

3. *Shorten the time between conduct and consequences.* Moral intensity drops when there is a substantial delay between a behavior and its consequences. Immediate response is difficult in hostile-environment harassment cases, since a pattern of behavior

must be established. Offenders feel distanced from their harmful actions as a result. Try to shorten this psychological distance by investigating and responding promptly. Begin investigations immediately after complaints surface, and come to a quick resolution.

4. *Emphasize similarities.* Our sense of moral obligation is highest when we perceive similarities between others and ourselves. Even though harassment is based on the differences between agents and targets, build a sense of similarity by emphasizing shared organizational goals and values. Provide opportunities for men and women to discuss their similar personal values, goals, and dreams.

5. *Promote individual responsibility.* Moral intensity is heightened by acknowledgment of personal accountability. Harassers will more likely desist if they stop trying to diffuse responsibility by blaming the work environment or the behavior of their colleagues. Highlight the fact that sexual harassment damages the character of the perpetrator and is inconsistent with such personal values as equality, respect, and concern for others.

CHAPTER TAKEAWAYS

- Conflict is an inevitable and increasingly common fact of organizational life. Conflict arises when interdependent parties perceive incompatible goals and scarce resources and believe that others are keeping them from reaching their objectives.
- Don't try to avoid conflict; instead, learn how to ethically manage disagreements.
- Functional or productive conflicts focus on the content of messages and are designed to solve problems. Dysfunctional or unproductive conflicts center on personalities and generate strong negative emotions, which produce escalation or avoidance behaviors.
- Managing your emotions can help keep constructive conflicts from becoming destructive. Take steps to cool down your emotions and let them dissipate; reengage constructively with the other person.
- Adopt a collaborative personal conflict style as your first option; employ other conflict styles when the situation calls for it.
- Put conflict guidelines in place that foster problem solving and mutual gains.
- Negotiation resolves conflict by generating joint agreements or solutions. When negotiating, you will encounter three types of ethical issues: choice of tactics, distribution of benefits, and the impact of the settlement on outsiders.
- Distributive bargainers take a win-lose approach to negotiation, which encourages unethical behavior; integrative bargainers view negotiation as a process of joint problem solving.
- Take an integrative approach to negotiation by following the steps of principled negotiation. Separate the people from the problem, focus on interests and not positions, invent options for mutual gains, and insist on the use of objective criteria.
- Aggression, which is aimed at hurting others, is the most destructive form of conflict. Reduce aggression by addressing its personal, social, and contextual origins: (1) Screen out potential offenders. (2) Provide interpersonal skills training for employees. (3) Share your rationale for decisions. (4) Punish offenders and eliminate aggressive role models. (5) Cut back on intrusive management practices. (6) Reduce stressors. (7) Empower workers. (8) Create pleasant working conditions.
- Sexual harassment is a special form of aggression that targets women. You can prevent quid pro quo and hostile-environment sexual harassment by creating a zero-tolerance climate, by training, by hiring more women, and by raising awareness that this type of behavior is immoral.

APPLICATION PROJECTS

1. Reflect on the results of the Self-Assessment. Record your responses to the following questions: What is your conflict style? Why do you think you take this approach to conflict? How has this style been effective? Ineffective? What are the ethical strengths and weaknesses of this approach? What steps can you take to develop a more collaborative conflict style?

2. Create a set of conflict guidelines (a conflict covenant) for your small group. These guidelines should outline the procedures you will follow in conflict situations, what type of comments members may and may not make, and so on.

3. Try to employ collaborative guidelines and tactics in an ongoing conflict. Report on the success (or lack of success) of your efforts.

4. Evaluate your ethical performance in a recent negotiation. Based on material from the chapter, identify the ethical issues you faced. Describe how you responded to these dilemmas. What, if anything, would you do differently next time? Write up your analysis and reflections.

5. Prepare for an upcoming negotiation using the steps of principled negotiation. Determine how you will deal with people issues, focus on interests, invent a variety of solutions, and identify objective criteria you can use when reaching an agreement.

6. Create a case study dealing with workplace aggression. What factors contributed to this incident, and how could they be reduced or eliminated?

7. Have you ever been the victim of aggression or sexually harassing behaviors? How did you feel and respond? What suggestions would you make to others who might be victims? Write up your conclusions.

CASE STUDY 6.2

The $2.3 Million Handshake

Former University of Oregon football coach Mike Bellotti has been called a state icon. Bellotti earned the admiration of Oregonians by turning the university's lackluster football program into a national power-house. In 2008, Bellotti left his coaching position to become athletic director. He served in that position for nine months before resigning to become a football commentator for the ESPN television network.

Controversy erupted after it was revealed that the University of Oregon had agreed to pay the ex-coach a $2.3 million severance package. Not only was the payout extremely generous given the short time that Bellotti spent as athletic director, but the terms of the negotiations were never written down. Both sides reached a handshake agreement, and the athletic director worked without a contract. Bellotti claimed that he had agreed to a $4 million package, but the new university president, Richard Lariviere, who came into office after the initial agreement was reached, decided to pay $2.3 million to the former coach. (This amount could increase to $3 million after interest and taxes.) The money for the settlement came from specific athletic donors, not from public funds or student fees.

The Oregon state attorney general's office investigated the settlement and found no criminal wrongdoing. However, that office criticized the Athletic Department and the university's general counsel for their lax procedures and secrecy (the terms of the agreement weren't revealed to the public until Bellotti resigned). The general counsel was replaced, and President Lariviere vowed to change way the Athletic Department operates: "This institution did not follow acceptable business practices in the past," Lariviere declared; "That will not be repeated under my administration."[1] Changes began almost immediately. When a new men's basketball coach was hired, the Athletic Department immediately released terms of his deal.

For his part, Coach Bellotti is unapologetic about his severance package, asserting, "I'm not taking anything that wasn't owed."[2] He notes that it is hard to put a dollar value on the creation of a successful football program.

Discussion Probes

1. Did Bellotti deserve his generous buyout package?

2. Was the decision to pay the $2.3 million settlement fair to the parties involved?

3. What is the possible impact of this agreement on students, taxpayers, donors, and others outside the immediate negotiations?

4. Would your perspective on this settlement be different if it were paid out of public funds or student fees? Why or why not?

5. What steps should the University of Oregon and other schools take to make sure that their athletic and other negotiations are conducted in a more professional, ethical manner?

Notes

1. Manning, J. (2010, April 21). Melinda Grier, attorney at center of Mike Bellotti scandal, on the way out. *The Oregonian.* Retrieved from Oregonlive.com.
2. Hunt, J. (April 6, 2010). The 2.3$ million question: How Mike Bellotti's buyout sets with Oregon donors. *The Oregonian.* Retrieved from Oregonlive.com.

Source

Goe, K. (2010, April 29). Dual report on Mike Bellotti's Oregon settlement find no criminal wrongdoing or public expense. *The Oregonian.* Copyright by Oregonian Publishing Company.

CASE STUDY 6.3

The Top 10 Reasons NOT to Sleep With the Boss

The office has become a hotbed of romance. In one survey, 40 to 60% of workers surveyed reported that they had dated a coworker sometime during their careers. And the percentage of workplace romances is likely to climb as younger workers (ages 25 to 34) put in more hours at work. According to one pollster, "The office has become the 21st-century singles bar. Water is the next gin and tonic, and Muzak the new club beat."[1]

Many office romances, like that of Barack and Michelle Obama, end in happy marriages. However, serious problems can arise when superiors and subordinates date and then break up. The subordinate (often a young female assistant) may claim that she was sexually harassed because she was pressured into having sex to keep her job or that her supervisor (often an older male executive) retaliated when the relationship ended.

The nation was reminded of the dangers of superior–subordinate romances when late-night talk show host David Letterman admitted that he had engaged in a series of sexual relationships with female writers and staffers at his production company. Letterman went public with his affairs after a CBS producer who had dated Letterman's long-term girlfriend Stephanie Birkitt tried to extort money from the entertainer in return for keeping quiet about his affairs. Letterman's relationships appeared to be consensual. In fact, one disappointed staffer wanted to marry the comic. Nonetheless, the women dating Letterman received special benefits. For example, Birkitt was featured in broadcast segments even though she did not appear to be particularly talented.

Given the popularity of office romances, it is unrealistic to try to ban them altogether. Instead, human resource and legal experts advise firms to establish policies and procedures to reduce their liability while not meddling in the personal affairs of employees. Such policies should prohibit personal relationships that generate a conflict of interest, such as in a direct reporting relationship. If such a relationship develops, one of the parties may need to be transferred or leave the company. The relationship should be conducted in a way that doesn't cause discomfort for other workers, and any mistreatment needs to be reported immediately. Dating policies need to be applied to everyone, even top performers. Firms may even want to consider having employees sign "love contracts." Consultants at Workforce Management developed once such agreement. On the form, employees acknowledge that the relationship is "voluntary, consensual, and welcome."[2]

Letterman's career survived his sex scandal, though his marriage may not. (His ratings went up the week he made his on-air confession.) Nevertheless, Letterman's self-described "creepy" behavior demonstrates the dangers of superior–subordinate romances. Here are the top 10 reasons to never, ever sleep with the boss:

10. Jealousy from coworkers.

9. Complaints of favoritism.

8. Company liability (charges of sexual harassment).

7. Creation of an uncomfortable work environment.

6. Loss of integrity—those who cheat on their spouses may also break workplace rules and policies.

5. The female subordinate usually ends up suffering the most after the breakup.

4. Public humiliation if the affair is discovered.

3. Job loss.

2. Divorce, if the relationship is an extramarital affair.

1. "Your career should never be in the hands of someone who you are regularly naked with."[3]

Discussion Probes

1. What is your experience with office romance, either as an observer or as a participant?

2. Do you agree that it would be impossible to outlaw personal relationships in the workplace?

3. What policies does your current or past organization have about relationships between coworkers? Superiors and subordinates? Can these policies be improved?

4. Do you think it is ethical to require employees to sign "love agreements" when entering into relationships?

5. What items would you add to the top 10 reasons not to sleep with the boss?

Notes

1. Baird, J. (2009, October 19). We are all getting lucky: But we are not all the boss. *Newsweek,* p. 26.

2. Baird.

3. Baird.

Sources

Carter, B., & Stelter, B. (2009, October 3). Extortion case raises questions for Letterman and his network. *The New York Times,* p. A1.

Dowd, M. (2009, October 7). Men behaving madly. *The New York Times,* p. A29.

Greenwald, J. (2009, November 2). Scandals put spotlight on workplace romance: Task for employers is finding balance of protection, privacy. *Business Insurance,* News, p. 3.

Kinz, H. (2010, March 10). Ex-producer pleads guilty in Letterman extortion case. *The Washington Post,* p. C01.

Top 10 reasons why David Letterman's sex saga is not funny. (2009, October 9). *The Christian Science Monitor,* Editorial, p. 8.

Trumbull, M. (2009, October 8). Letterman didn't violate his company's harassment policy. *The Christian Science Monitor,* USA, p. 2.

ENDNOTES

1. Isenhart, M. W., & Spangle, M. (2000). *Collaborative approaches to resolving conflict.* Thousand Oaks, CA: Sage, Ch. 2; Runde, C. E., & Flanagan, T. A. (2007). *Becoming a conflict competent leader.* San Francisco: Jossey-Bass.

2. De Dreu, C. K. W., & Gelfand, J. J. (2008). Conflict in the workplace: Sources, functions, and dynamics across multiple levels of analysis. In C. K. W. De Dreu & M. J. Gelfand (Eds.), *The psychology of conflict and conflict management in organizations* (pp. 3–54). New York: Lawrence Erlbaum.

3. Wilmot, W. W., & Hocker, J. L. (2001). *Interpersonal conflict* (6th ed.). New York: McGraw-Hill.

4. Amason, A. C. (1996). Distinguishing the effects of functional and dysfunctional conflict on strategic decision-making: Resolving a paradox for top management teams. *Academy of Management Journal, 39*(1), 123–148; Scileppi, P. A. (2005). *Values for interpersonal communication; How then shall we live?* Belmont, CA: Star, Chap. 10; Folger, J., Poole, M., & Stutman, R. (1993). *Working through conflict.* New York: HarperCollins.

5. See, for example: De Dreu, C. K. W., & Weingart, L. R. (2003). Task versus relationship conflict, team performance, and team member satisfaction: A meta-analysis. *Journal of Applied Psychology, 88*(4), 741–749; Jehn, K. A. (1995). A multimethod examination of the benefits and detriments of intragroup conflict. *Administrative Science Quarterly, 40,* 256–282; Robins, S. P., & Judge, T. A. (2011). *Organizational behavior* (14th ed.). Boston: Prentice Hall.

6. Runde, C. E., & Flanagan, T. A. (2008, Winter). Conflict competent leadership. *Leader to Leader,* pp. 46–51.

7. Rahim, M. A. (1983). A measure of styles of handling interpersonal conflict. *Academy of Management Journal, 26,* 368–376; Thomas, K. W., & Kilmann, R. (1977). Developing a forced-choice measure of conflict-handling behavior: The MODE instrument. *Educational and Psychological Measurement, 37,* 390–395.

8. Rahim, M. A., Garrett, J. E., & Buntzman, G. F. (1992). Ethics of managing interpersonal conflict in organizations. *Journal of Business Ethics 11,* 423–432.

9. Isenhart & Spangle.

10. Rahim, M. A. & Buntzman, G. F., & White, D. (1999). An empirical study of the stages of moral development and conflict management styles. *The International Journal of Conflict Management, 10,* 154–171.

11. Shockley-Zalabak, P. S. (2006). *Fundamentals of organizational communication: Knowledge, sensitivity, skills, values* (6th ed.). Boston: Pearson.

12. Wilmot & Hocker; Sillars, A. L. (1986). *Procedures for coding interpersonal conflict* (Rev.). University of Montana: Department of Communication Studies.

13. Spangle, M. L., & Isenhart, M. W. (2003). *Negotiation: Communication for diverse settings.* Thousand Oaks, CA: Sage; Sims, R. R. (2002). *Managing organizational behavior.* Westport, CT: Quorum Books.

14. Lax, D. A., & Sebenius, J. K. (2004). Three ethical issues in negotiation. In C. Menkel-Meadow & M. Wheeler (Eds.), *What's fair: Ethics for negotiators* (pp. 5–14). San Francisco: Jossey-Bass.

15. Lax & Sebenius, p. 7.

16. Bok, S. (1978). *Lying: Moral choice in public and private life.* New York: Pantheon Books.

17. Cohen, J. R. (2004). The ethics of respect in negotiation. In C. Menkel-Meadow & M. Wheeler (Eds.), *What's fair: Ethics for negotiators* (pp. 257–263). San Francisco: Jossey-Bass.

18. Lax & Sebenius.

19. Wheeler, M. (2004, March). Fair enough: An ethical fitness quiz for negotiators. *Negotiation,* pp. 3–5.

20. Why your negotiating behavior may be ethically challenged—and how to fix it. (2008, April). *Negotiation, 11*(4), pp. 1–5.

21. Fisher, R., Ury, W., & Patton, B. (1991). *Getting to yes: Negotiating agreement without giving in* (2nd ed.). New York: Bantam Books.

22. Fisher & Ury, p. 40.

23. Buss, A. H. (1961). *The psychology of aggression.* New York: John Wiley.

24. Information on the prevalence of workplace violence and aggression taken from Glomb, T. M., & Hui, L. (2003). Interpersonal aggression in work groups: Social influence, reciprocal, and individual effects. *Academy of Management Journal, 46,* 486–496; O'Leary-Kelly, A. M., Griffin, R. W., & Glew, D. J. (1996). Organization-motivated aggression: A research framework. *Academy of Management Review, 21,* 225–253; Depre, K. E., & Barling, J. (2003). Workplace aggression. In A. Sagie, S. Stashevsky, & M. Koslowsky (Eds.), *Misbehaviour and dysfunctional attitudes in organizations* (pp. 13–32). Hampshire, UK: Palgrave Macmillan; Neuman, J. H. (2004). Injustice, stress, and aggression in organizations. In R. W. Griffin & A. M. O'Leary-Kelly (Eds.), *The dark side of organizational behavior* (pp. 62–102). San Francisco: Jossey-Bass; Schat, A. C. H., Frone, M. R., & Kelloway, E. K. (2006). Prevalence of workplace aggression in the U.S. workforce: Findings from a national study. In E. K. Kelloway, J. Barling, & J. J. Hurrell (Eds.). *Handbook of workplace violence* (pp. 47–89). Thousand Oaks, CA: Sage.

25. Glomb, T. M., Steel, P. D. G., & Arvey, R. D. (2002). Office sneers, snipes, and stab wounds: Antecedents, consequences, and implications of workplace violence and aggression. In R. G. Lord, R. J. Klimoski,

& R. Kanfer (Eds.), *Emotions in the workplace* (pp. 227–259). San Francisco: Jossey-Bass; Barling, J. (1996). The prediction, experience, and consequences of workplace violence. In G. R. VandenBos & E. Q. Bulato (Eds.), *Violence on the job: Identifying risks and developing solutions* (pp. 29–49). Washington, DC: American Psychological Association.

26. Baron, R. A. (2004). Workplace aggression and violence: Insights from basic research. In R. W. Griffin & A. M. O'Leary-Kelly (Eds.), *The dark side of organizational behavior* (pp. 23–61). San Francisco: Jossey-Bass; Neuman, J. H., & Baron, R. A. (1997). Aggression in the workplace. In R. A. Giacalone & J. Greenberg (Eds.), *Antisocial behavior in organizations* (pp. 37–67). Thousand Oaks, CA: Sage; O'Leary-Kelly, Griffin, & Glew (1996); Douglas, S. C., & Martinko, M. J. (2001). Exploring the role of individual differences in the prediction of workplace aggression. *Journal of Applied Psychology, 86,* 547–559; Barling; Folger, R., & Baron, R. A. (1996). Violence and hostility at work: A model of reactions to perceived injustice. In G. R. VandenBos & E. Q. Bulato (Eds.), *Violence on the job: Identifying risks and developing solutions* (pp. 51–85). Washington, DC: American Psychological Association; Hershcovis, M. S., Turner, N., Barling, J., Arnold, K. A., Dupre, K. E., Inness, M., . . . Sivanathan, N. (2007). Predicting workplace aggression: A meta-analysis. *Journal of Applied Psychology, 92,* 228–238.

27. Hershcovis, M. S., & Barling, J. (2008). Preventing insider-initiated workplace violence. In E. K. Kelloway, J. Barling, & J. J. Hurrell (Eds.), *Handbook of workplace violence* (pp. 607–632). Thousand Oaks, CA: Sage.

28. Woods, K. C., & Buchanan, N. T. (2008). Sexual harassment in the workplace. In M. Paludi (Ed.), *The psychology of women at work: Challenges and solutions for our female workforce* (Vol. 1, pp. 119–132). Westport, CT: Praeger.

29. Levy, A. C., & Paludi, M. A. (2002). *Workplace sexual harassment* (2nd ed.). Upper Saddle River, NJ: Prentice Hall; Arens Bates, C., Bowes-Sperry, L., & O'Leary-Kelly, A. M. (2008). Sexual harassment in the workplace: A look back and a look ahead. In E. K. Kelloway, J. Barling, & J. J. Hurrell (Eds.), *Handbook of workplace violence* (pp. 381–415). Thousand Oaks, CA: Sage.

30. Ilies, R., Hauserman, N., Schwochau, S., & Stibal, J. (2003). Reported incidence rates of work-related sexual harassment in the United States: Using meta-analysis to explain reported rate disparities. *Personnel Psychology, 56,* 607–651.

31. Fitzgerald, L. F. (1993). Sexual harassment: Violence against women in the workplace. *American Psychologist, 48,* 1070–1076.

32. Levy & Paludi (2002); Fitzgerald (1993).

33. See, for example: Fitzgerald, L. F., Drasgow, F., Hulin, C. L., Gelfand, M. J., & Magley, V. (1997). Antecedents and consequences of sexual harassment in organizations: A test of an integrated model. *Journal of Applied Psychology, 82,* 578–589; Offermann, L. R., & Malamut, A. B. (2002). When leaders harass: The impact of target perceptions of organizational leadership and climate on harassment reporting and outcomes. *Journal of Applied Psychology, 87,* 885–893; O'Leary-Kelly, A. M., Paetzold, R. L., & Griffin, L. W. (2000). Sexual harassment as aggressive behavior: An actor-based perspective. *Academy of Management Review, 25,* 372–388; Wiener, R. L., & Gutek, B. A. (1999). Advances in sexual harassment research, theory, and policy. *Psychology, Public Policy and Law, 5,* 597–518; Wilson, F., & Thompson, P. (2001). Sexual harassment as an exercise of power. *Gender, Work and Organization, 8,* 61–83.

34. O'Leary-Kelly, A. M. (2001). Sexual harassment as unethical behavior: The role of moral intensity. *Human Resource Management Review, 11,* 73–92; Bowes-Sperry, L., & O'Leary-Kelly, A. M. (2005). To act or not to act: The dilemma faced by sexual harassment observers. *Academy of Management Review, 30,* 288–306; Bowes-Sperry, L., & Powell, G. N. (1996). Sexual harassment as a moral issue: An ethical decision-making perspective. In M. S. Stockdale (Ed.), *Sexual harassment in the workplace: Perspectives, frontiers, and response strategies* (Vol. 5, pp. 105–124). Thousand Oaks, CA: Sage.

PART IV

Practicing Group, Leadership, and Followership Ethics

7

Improving Group Ethical Performance

Groups play a larger role than ever in the workplace. Most significant projects—creating a video game or film, building an apartment complex, opening a new market, raising money for a nonprofit—require the efforts of teams of people. Self-directed work groups are now charged with everything from organizing the assembly line to hiring and firing. Teams, not individuals, generally make important organizational decisions.

Groups tend to bring out the moral best and worst in us. If you're like me, some of your proudest moments are associated with small groups. Your team may have completed a service project for your local community or determined how to fairly distribute student fees to campus organizations. (See Case Study 7.1 for an example of extraordinary group moral performance.) At the same time, some of your most regrettable moments (like mine) may also relate to group experiences. Your team may have made poor moral choices and convinced you to engage in unethical activities.

CASE STUDY 7.1

A Miracle of Cooperation

More than 35,000 Sri Lankans died when a tsunami, triggered by an earthquake off the Indonesian island of Sumatra, struck on the morning of December 26, 2004. A thousand of these victims were passengers and railroad workers on a commuter train traveling from the country's capital city of Colombo to the coastal town of Matara. Two giant waves toppled 8 rail carriages and destroyed 80 miles of track.

At first, it appeared as if the 77,000 passengers who rode the train daily would have to wait many months, if not years, for service to be restored. Government officials believed that it would take foreign experts and tens of millions of dollars of foreign aid to get the trains running again in a minimum of 6 months. Priyal de Silva, the general manager of the railways, thought differently. He argued that the line could be rebuilt in 3 months. However, to accomplish the task would take the cooperation of the railroad's union. Union officials routinely clashed with management; they had led a 14-day strike in January 2004. Plans were underway for another walkout when the tsunami struck.

Fortunately for general manager de Silva and the Sri Lankan public, union leaders decided that they had a duty to the nation as well as a chance to improve the railway workers' public image as "an inefficient, lazy lot." They mobilized 1,000 volunteers to clear the tracks and within 3 days had removed fallen trees, bodies, and other debris. Engineers then surveyed the damage and the reconstruction began. Crews worked on four different sections of the track simultaneously so that restoration continued even when progress slowed on one portion of the project. April 13, the traditional Sri Lankan New Year, was set as the completion date.

Repairing the track was a massive effort requiring the cooperative efforts of union members and management alike. Workers toiled 12 hours a day or more, sleeping in makeshift camps or on the job site. Managers worked alongside their employees. According to one laborer: "Even the officials didn't pull rank. Usually the higher officers don't do as much work, [but] they stayed by our sides without eating or drinking."[1] Crews dug through 2 feet of muck to salvage rail ties and other parts. At one point, they replaced a bridge embankment by hand, stone by stone.

The rebuilding effort was completed in only 57 days (February 27), well ahead of schedule. One advisor to the project called it a "marvelous achievement." However, in light of the obstacles faced by de Silva and his team, this accolade seems like an understatement. "Miraculous" may better describe this accomplishment. Not only did two previously warring groups have to join forces, but they had to contend with shortages of supplies, materials, and money; the opposition of government officials who wanted to turn the project over to outsiders even as it neared completion; and the fact that many laborers were recovering from injuries suffered in the tidal wave at the same time that they were grieving for dead family members. The success of the project was even more remarkable given the failure of efforts to rebuild the rest of Sri Lanka. Over a year after the disaster, tens of thousands of residents remained in temporary wooden shelters.

Discussion Probes

1. What would likely have happened if the repair project had been turned over to foreigners?

2. What factors fostered cooperation in this situation? Can any of these factors be used to encourage a cooperative orientation in other settings?

3. Do you think this collaborative effort will permanently change union–management relations in Sri Lanka?

4. Have you ever been in a group that was highly successful due to the collaborative efforts of members? Did you exceed expectations?

Note

1. Wiseman, P. (2005), p. 16A.

Source

Wiseman, P. (2005, December 9). On the train tracks in Sri Lanka, life does move on. *USA Today,* pp. 15A–16A. From USA TODAY, a division of Gannett Co., Inc. Reprinted with permission http://www.usatoday.com

---

Transforming our teams so that they spur us to higher, not lower, moral performance is the goal of this chapter. Achieving that end requires that we act as morally responsible group members and help our teams steer clear of ethical dangers.

Acting as a Morally Responsible Team Member

Group membership does not excuse us from our individual ethical responsibilities. Quite the contrary; in small groups, our behaviors can have a significant impact on the team's ethical success or failure.[1] We have a duty to apply the concepts and skills discussed in earlier chapters (ethical theories, character, moral reasoning, and ethical communication competencies) to the team setting. In addition, we need to adopt a cooperative orientation, do our fair share of the work, be open and supportive, and offer dissent.

Adopting a Cooperative Orientation

In Chapter 4, we noted that the outcome of interpersonal communication is dependent on the attitude we bring to our conversations. The same is true for our group interactions. Groups committed to cooperation can accomplish great things, as Case Study 7.1 demonstrates. Conversely, if we lack this commitment to working together, our performance, as well as that of the team as a whole, is likely to suffer.

A cooperative orientation is based on the realization that an individual's success is dependent on the success of other team members.[2] To reach shared goals, everyone must do her or his part. This perspective stands in sharp contrast to individualistic and competitive points of view. Individualistic members rely on their own efforts to achieve their private agendas. For example, an individualist assigned to a class project group puts personal goals (developing a romantic relationship with someone else on the team, earning an A in another class) ahead of the collective goal of producing an excellent presentation. Competitive group members achieve their objectives at the expense of others. They want to earn the highest grade in the class, for instance, or get promoted ahead of other employees. In order to succeed, they may withhold information or claim too much credit for the group's success.

Individualism and competition are celebrated in Western culture but are counterproductive in small groups. In an analysis of the results of over 100 studies, brothers David and Roger Johnson and their colleagues found that in the vast majority of cases, cooperative groups had higher levels of achievement and productivity.[3] No matter what the subject matter (math, psychology, physical education), task (problem solving, retention and memory, categorization), and age group (elementary school through adult), cooperative groups are more successful. That's because cooperative team members are more likely to do these things:[4]

- Help one another
- Put forth more effort and invest more time in completing the task
- Support (reinforce) the identities of other group members
- Be open to influence from others
- Detect and correct errors in reasoning
- Generate more new ideas, strategies, and solutions
- Think clearly because they feel relaxed
- Engage in healthy conflict that refines solutions
- Develop positive relationships with other group members
- Understand the perspectives of other team members
- Share accurate messages and accurately interpret messages from others
- Provide positive feedback to other members, which builds self-esteem
- Value and accept differences
- Demonstrate a positive attitude towards the task
- Act in trustworthy ways
- Enjoy better psychological health
- Share resources

In light of this evidence, we have an ethical duty to behave in a cooperative manner while encouraging others to do the same. We need to ask ourselves if we are committed to the success of the group and can put aside our desire to pursue personal agendas and to best others. If we can't answer in the affirmative, a change in attitude or withdrawal from the group is in order. We can foster cooperation through such communication behaviors as proposing compromises or concessions, carrying through on promises, pointing out the need to cooperate, asking for help, and accurately paraphrasing others' points of view.[5] The group as a whole needs to make sure that the team pursues a joint product, which fosters interdependence, and not a series of individual products, which encourages individualistic or competitive behavior. Collectively, members should divide the work fairly, reward the group as whole (not individual members), involve everyone in decision making, and emphasize shared values, like a commitment to service or quality.

Fostering cooperation is key to project management. Project managers direct teams that build bridges, develop new products, manage software installations, and carry out other major initiatives. We can adopt the strategies they use to encourage collaboration in our class project teams and other groups. Successful project managers engage in collaborative decision making, helping team members define their goals, logistics, schedules, subtasks, and deliverables as the group launches. They require documentation of individual and collective work through traditional (memos, project logs, reports) and electronic means (blogs, online discussion). Such documentation keeps members informed about the activities of others and can help the team work together more effectively. Project leaders also encourage ongoing assessment and reflection. This allows members to adjust roles and assignments as needed to better coordinate their efforts.[6]

Doing Your Fair Share (Not Loafing)

Many attempts to create a cooperative climate falter because participants fail to do their fair share of the work. Scholars use the term *social loafing* to describe the tendency of individuals to reduce their efforts when working in a group. Interest in this phenomenon can be traced back to the 1880s. In one of the first experimental studies in social psychology, a researcher asked male volunteers to pull on a rope.[7] He discovered that as the size of the group increased, each man exerted less force. Modern investigators have determined that social loafing is common on all kinds of teams, though individuals differ in their tendency to slack off. Women and people from Eastern cultures are less likely to reduce their efforts, for example. Those who enjoy thinking maintain their efforts when engaged in intellectually demanding group activities. Conscientious individuals and those motivated by a high need for achievement continue to work as hard in a group as they do on their own.[8] (Complete the Self-Assessment to determine how much social loafing goes on in your group.)

SELF-ASSESSMENT

The Social Loafing Scale

Instructions

This scale is written for the retail sales setting but can easily be adapted to other work contexts. Indicate how characteristic each of the items is of the person you are rating: 1—Not at all characteristic; 2—Slightly characteristic; 3—Somewhat characteristic; 4—Characteristic; 5—Very characteristic.

Sum up the responses to the 10 items to come up with a score for each person (Range: 10–50). To come up with an overall score for the group, rate all the members (including yourself), add up the scores, and divide by the number of group members.

1. Defers responsibilities he or she should assume to other salespeople.

2. Puts forth less effort on the job when other salespeople are around to do the work.

3. Does not do his or her share of the work.

4. Spends less time helping customers if other salespeople are present to serve customers.

5. Puts forth less effort than other members of his or her work group.

6. Avoids performing housekeeping tasks as much as possible.

7. Leaves work for the next shift that he or she should really complete.

8. Is less likely to approach a customer if another salesperson is available to do this.

9. Takes it easy if other salespeople are around to do the work.

10. Defers customer service activities to other salespeople if they are present.

SOURCE: From George, J. M. (1995). Asymmetrical effects of rewards and punishments: The case of social loafing. *Journal of Occupational and Organizational Psychology, 68,* 327–338. Reproduced with permission of John Wiley & Sons Ltd.

Social psychologists Steven Karau and Kipling Williams developed the collective effort model (CEM) to identify the causes of social loafing.[9] They theorize that the motivation of group members depends on three factors: (1) *expectancy:* how much an individual expects that his or her effort will lead to high group performance; (2) *instrumentality:* the strength of the perceived relationship between personal and group effort and group achievement; and (3) *valence:* how desirable the outcome is for individual group members. (The Ethics and Technology box describes how these factors also operate in the online environment.)

Motivation drops when any of these factors is low. Individuals are more likely to slack off in collectives because the group can still succeed even if they do less (low expectancy). Participants may also believe that the group won't succeed (win a majority of its games, secure a contract), no matter how hard they and their fellow group members try (low instrumentality). Or participants may not value the group's goal or outcome (low valence). Karau, Williams, and other investigators treat social loafing as undesirable, unethical behavior that undermines cooperation, encourages others to slack off for fear of being seen as "suckers," and diminishes the productivity of the group as a whole. They've identified ways to reduce or eliminate this phenomenon through the strategies outlined below. Each set of tactics is designed to address one of the three elements of motivation.[10]

Strategies for Increasing Expectancy

Take these steps to reinforce the tie between individual efforts and successful group performance:

- Select members carefully and match them to tasks.
- Provide training in needed skills.
- Set challenging yet realistic goals.

- Supply needed resources and support.
- Build feelings of self-efficacy.
- Raise the visibility of individual tasks.
- Monitor individual efforts.

Strategies for Increasing Instrumentality

Use the following to link individual performance to group performance:

- Make sure tasks are not too demanding.
- Reduce the size of the group so that members don't feel that their efforts are redundant.
- Point out that each member is making a unique, valuable contribution.
- Clarify how individual efforts relate to the team's final product.

Link group performance and outcomes this way;

- Recognizing group work.
- Evaluating team products.
- Creating norms that emphasize high performance standards.

Outcomes

Use these methods to increase the positive value of the group's collective product to members:

- Offer meaningful, interesting work that becomes intrinsically motivating.
- Provide tangible incentives like raises and bonuses.
- Encourage members to identify with the group.
- Strengthen the social bonds between members.
- Create norms that foster a sense of group pride and mutual obligation.

ETHICS AND TECHNOLOGY

Social Loafing in Virtual Teams

Virtual teams are geographically scattered groups that collaborate primarily though technology. Such teams can draw upon the expertise of individuals from different locations around the world. They have low operating costs, since members don't have to travel to a central location. Instead, they communicate through e-mail, videoconferencing, bulletin boards, and other electronic means. Large corporations—like Hewlett-Packard, IBM, Intel, NCR, and Microsoft—rely on virtual teams to carry out a variety of functions, including project engineering, customer service, consulting, and marketing.

Initial indications are that social loafing is more common in virtual teams than in face-to-face groups. Two factors apparently account for the prevalence of social loafing in technology-supported

(Continued)

(Continued)

groups. One, virtual teams are often large. In bigger groups, members feel as though their contributions aren't as important to the team's success, and therefore they are less motivated to contribute. It is harder to identify who contributes and who doesn't. Two, members of virtual teams are widely dispersed. In face-to-face groups, members know instantly what others are doing, a fact that can encourage them to keep working. Feedback in virtual teams, on the other hand, can be delayed for hours or days. Virtual team members also have less contact with each other, which can reduce cohesion.

Researchers Omar Alnuaimi, Lionel Robert, and Likoebe Maruping tested the effects of team size and dispersion in an experiment using 32 groups of students. They assigned approximately half of the groups to work on a brainstorming task with their teammates in the same room, while members of the rest of the teams worked in separate locations and interacted online. Group size ranged from 3 to 10 members. The investigators recorded the number of ideas produced by each group and surveyed the attitudes of team members. Dispersed and larger teams generated fewer ideas. Members of these groups felt less responsible for the group's final product and less connected to other members. At the same time, they were more likely to blame others for the fact they were loafing. They saw themselves as victims who were justified in reducing their efforts.

Based on their findings, Alnuaimi and his colleagues urge managers to change how they structure and coordinate virtual teams. Keep teams as small as possible. Emphasize that each team member has responsibility for accomplishing the group's task. Implement an evaluation system that identifies each individual's contribution (or lack of contribution). Remind participants that they are dealing with other people, not computers. Use richer communication channels (like videoconferencing, for example) that are better at fostering personal connections.

Sources

Alnuaimi, O. A., Robert, L. P., & Maruping, L. M. (2010). Team size, dispersion, and social loafing in technology-supported teams: A perspective on the theory of moral disengagement. *Journal of Management Information Systems, 27*(10), 203–230.

Blaskovich, J. L. (2008). Exploring the effect of distance: An experimental investigation of virtual collaboration, social loafing, and group decisions. *Journal of Information Systems, 22*(1), 27–46.

Bryant, S. M., Albring, S. M., & Murthy, U. (2009). The effects of reward structure, media richness and gender on virtual teams. *International Journal of Accounting Information Systems, 10,* 190–213.

Chidambaram, L., & Tung, L. L. (2005). Is out of sight, out of mind? An empirical study of social loafing in technology-supported groups. *Information Systems Research, 16*(2), 149–168.

Displaying Openness and Supportiveness

Ethical team members are both open and supportive.[11] *Openness* refers to an individual's willingness to surface issues and talk about problems while, at the same time, enabling others to do the same. *Supportiveness* denotes the desire to help others succeed. Supportive group members encourage and defend others, help teammates overcome obstacles, and put the goals of the group first. These two characteristics work together. Openness by itself could pave the way for brutal honesty, insults, and sarcasm, so ethical issues must be discussed in a supportive manner. Otherwise, participants feel threatened and divert their attention from understanding and problem solving to defending themselves. Poorer ethical choices result.

Psychologist Jack Gibb identified six pairs of behaviors that promote either a defensive or a supportive group climate.[12] Our moral duty as group members is to engage in supportive communication that contributes to a positive emotional climate and accurate understanding. At the same time, we need to draw attention to the comments of others that spark defensive reactions.

Evaluation versus description. Evaluative messages are judgmental. They can be sent through statements ("What a jerk!") or through such nonverbal cues as using a sarcastic tone of voice or rolling one's eyes. Those being evaluated put up their guard. Insecure group members are likely to respond by assigning blame ("You messed up"), by making judgments of their own ("At least my proposal didn't go over budget"), and by questioning the motives of the speaker. Descriptive messages, such as asking for information and reporting data and feelings, create a more positive environment.

Control versus problem orientation. Controlling messages imply that the recipient is inadequate (uninformed, immature, stubborn, overly emotional) and needs to change. Control, like evaluation, can be communicated through both verbal (issuing orders, threats) and nonverbal (stares, threatening body posture) means. Problem-centered messages ("What will be your next step?") reflect a willingness to collaborate in defining and solving problems. They demonstrate that the sender has no predetermined solution and give the receiver permission to set his or her own direction.

Strategy versus spontaneity. Strategic communicators are seen as manipulators who try to hide their true motivations. They appear to be playing games, withholding data, or developing special sources of information. Worse yet, strategic communicators engage in "false spontaneity" by using gimmicks to disguise their intentions. Some supervisors solicit the input of employees in order to appear open minded, for instance, when they have already made the decision. In contrast, behavior that is truly spontaneous (unplanned) and honest reduces defensiveness.

Neutrality versus empathy. Neutral messages, like "Don't worry" and "Don't take it personally," communicate little warmth or caring. These low-affect messages may be meant as supportive, but listeners come away feeling disconfirmed. Empathetic statements, such as "I can see why you would be worried" and "No wonder you were offended by the boss's comment," communicate reassurance and acceptance.

Superiority versus equality. Attempts at "one-upmanship," like claiming to be smarter or more knowledgeable, generally provoke such defensive responses as ignoring the message, competition, and jealousy. Those claiming superiority communicate that they don't want help or need feedback and may try to reduce the social standing of receivers. Status and power differences are less disruptive if participants indicate that they want to work with others on an equal basis. Supportive communicators treat others as partners worthy of respect and trust.

Certainty versus provisionalism. Dogmatic, inflexible individuals claim to have all the answers and are unwilling to change or to consider other points of view. They have little patience with those they consider "wrong." As a consequence, they appear more interested in being right than in solving the problem and maintaining group relationships. Gibb found that listeners often perceive the certainty of dogmatic individuals as a mask hiding their feelings of inferiority. Conversely, provisional individuals are willing to experiment and explore. They want to investigate issues instead of taking sides or controlling outcomes. These communicators gladly accept help from others as they seek information and answers.

Psychological safety is an important byproduct of open, supportive communication. Psychological safety refers to the shared belief that individuals can speak up without fear of being embarrassed or rejected. Members trust and respect each other and know that they can challenge the leader's decisions if necessary.[13] Lack of psychological safety played an important role in the 1996 climbing disaster on Mt. Everest.[14] That year, the leaders of two climbing groups and several of their clients died after getting caught in a storm. The climbers perished because they continued to the summit long after they should have turned back. Both clients and guides were reluctant to challenge the decision to continue on because they didn't feel safe doing so. Clients were strangers who didn't trust one another and feared being embarrassed if they expressed an unpopular opinion. Group leaders also made it clear that they weren't open to discussing issues or problems. One told his group that his word was "absolute law" and that he would tolerate no dissension during the climb.

Being Willing to Stand Alone

This final responsibility may be the toughest to assume. Being in the minority is never easy, because it runs contrary to our strong desire to be liked and accepted by others. Nevertheless, the difficulty of standing alone should not be an excuse for keeping quiet instead of speaking up. As we'll see in the second half of the chapter, team members' willingness to take issue with the prevailing group opinion is essential if the team is to avoid moral failure. Further, minority dissent can significantly improve group performance. Teams with minority members generally come up with better solutions even if the group doesn't change its collective mind.[15] Group members focus on one solution when there is no minority. They have little incentive to explore the problem in depth. As a result, they disregard novel solutions and converge on one position. Minorities cast doubt on group consensus, stimulating more thought about the dilemma. Members exert more effort because they must resolve the clash between the majority and minority solutions. They pay closer attention to all aspects of the issue, consider more viewpoints, and use a wider variety of problem-solving strategies. Such divergent thinking leads to more creative, higher-quality solutions. Responding to the dissenting views of minorities also encourages team members to resist conformity in other settings.[16]

In some cases, minorities are successful in persuading the rest of the group to their point of view. Often, this influence is slow and indirect. Majorities initially reject dissenters and their ideas but, over time, forget the source of the arguments and focus instead on the merits of their proposals. This can gradually convert them to the minority viewpoint.[17] However, minorities can have an immediate, powerful impact on group opinion under certain conditions.[18] Minorities are more likely to convince the rest of the group when members are still formulating their attitudes about an issue. Well-respected dissenters who consistently advocate for their positions are generally more persuasive.

Recognizing the importance of minority opinion should increase our motivation to play this role. We'll also need to exercise courage in order to accept the consequences for doing so. Teams can do their part to spark dissent by (a) making sure that members come from significantly different backgrounds and perspectives, and by (b) protecting rather than attacking those who disagree.

Responding to Ethical Danger Signs

Accepting our moral responsibilities is a good start to improving group ethical performance. However, we also need to be alert to moral pitfalls that arise during team interaction. These traps account for the ethical failure of a great many groups and their members. In this section, I'll identify five signs that indicate that a team is in ethical danger—groupthink, mismanaged agreement, escalating commitment, excessive control, and moral exclusion—and provide some suggestions for responding to the risks posed by each.

Groupthink

Earlier, I noted that adopting a cooperative orientation is critical to group success. However, there is significant danger in making team unity the group's primary goal. Social psychologist Irving Janis popularized the term *groupthink,* which describes teams that put unanimous agreement ahead of reasoned problem solving.[19] Janis first noted faulty thinking in small groups of ordinary citizens. For example, he observed one group of heavy smokers meeting to kick the habit who decided that quitting was impossible. One member had stopped, but the rest of the group pressured him back into smoking two packs a day.

The term *groupthink* became part of the national vocabulary largely based on Janis's analysis of major U.S. policy disasters, like the failure to anticipate the attack on Pearl Harbor, the invasion of North Korea, the Bay of Pigs fiasco, and the escalation of the Vietnam War. In each of these incidents, some of the brightest (and presumably most ethically minded) political and military leaders in our nation's history made terrible choices. More recent examples of groupthink include the *Challenger* and *Columbia* space shuttle disasters, the decision to storm the Branch Davidian compound in Waco, Texas, the accounting fraud at WorldCom, and the Iraq War.[20] (Case Study 7.2, "Groupthink in the Sweat Lodge," describes another instance of the powerful impact of group conformity.)

Groups are more likely to fall victim to this syndrome when they (a) are highly cohesive; (b) find themselves insulated or isolated from other groups; (c) lack decision-making formats like those described in Chapter 3; (d) have highly directive leaders and members who push for a particular solution; (e) close themselves off from outside information or use such information to reinforce their biases; and (f) are under stress with little hope of coming up with alternatives to the ideas offered by their leaders. These forces exert pressure on members to agree and produce the following symptoms, which I'll illustrate through examples taken from Janis's analysis of major policy disasters. The greater the number of these characteristics displayed by a group, the greater the likelihood that members have made cohesiveness their top priority.[21]

Signs of Overconfidence

1. *The illusion of invulnerability.* Members think they can do no wrong. They are overly optimistic and prone to take extraordinary risks. President Lyndon Johnson and his advisors kept escalating the war in Vietnam because they thought the North Vietnamese would back down. One policy maker later remarked, "We thought we had the golden touch."

2. *Belief in the inherent morality of the group.* Participants do not question the inherent morality of the group and therefore ignore the ethical consequences of their actions and decisions. In discussions of the Cuban Bay of Pigs operation (which resulted in the death or capture of all the invading troops), President Kennedy's policy group barely noted the ethical implications of attacking a small neighboring country or of lying to the American public about the invasion. Later, during the deliberations that safely ended the Cuban missile crisis, many of the same group members debated at length the morality of a surprise air attack. The team decided that this option was not in the best, moral American tradition.

Signs of Closed-Mindedness

1. *Collective rationalization.* Group members invent rationalizations to protect themselves from any feedback that would challenge their operating assumptions. In 1941, U.S. naval officers rationalized that any enemy carriers headed for Hawaii would be detected before attack. Warships anchored in Pearl Harbor would be safe from torpedo bombs because the water was too shallow.

2. *Stereotypes of outside groups.* Decision makers underestimate the capabilities of other groups (armies, citizens, teams), thinking that people in these groups are weak or stupid. President Truman and his advisors fell victim to the belief that the Chinese wouldn't be able to respond to an invasion of North Korea by the United States. As a result of this miscalculation, China entered the Korean conflict, and the war ended in a stalemate.

Signs of Group Pressure

1. *Pressure on dissenters.* Majority members coerce dissenters to go along with the prevailing opinion in the group. Former presidential advisor Bill Moyers felt the power

of this pressure after taking issue with the escalation of the Vietnam War. When he arrived at one strategy discussion, President Johnson greeted him by saying, "Well, here comes Mr. Stop-the-Bombing."

2. *Self-censorship.* Individuals keep their doubts about group decisions to themselves. Perhaps because of being labeled as "Mr. Stop-the-Bombing," Moyers became a "domesticated dissenter" who expressed reservations only about a few details of the plan to ratchet up the war in Vietnam.

3. *The illusion of unanimity.* Since members keep quiet, the group mistakenly assumes that everyone agrees on a course of action. Historian Arthur Schlesinger, a participant in the Bay of Pigs planning sessions, had serious doubts about the project, but he and others remained silent because they assumed the group had consensus.

4. *Self-appointed mind-guards.* Certain members take it upon themselves to protect the leader and others from dissenting opinions that might disrupt the group's consensus. President Kennedy's brother Robert took this role during the Bay of Pigs decision. He told Schlesinger, "You may be right or you may be wrong, but the President has made his mind up. Don't push it any further. Now is the time for everyone to help him all they can."[22]

The symptoms of groupthink seriously disrupt the decision-making process. Members fail to consider all the alternatives, outline objectives, or gather additional information. They follow preconceived notions, are less likely to reexamine a course of action when it's not working, don't carefully weigh risks or work out contingency plans. While groupthink undermines all types of decisions, it is particularly destructive to ethical reasoning. This helps explain why, in the 1980s, Beech-Nut employees decided to sell adulterated apple juice, and E. F. Hutton officials defrauded financial institutions by writing checks before they had deposited the funds to cover them. Nearly everyone (including employees of these two firms) would agree that selling "phony" apple juice and bouncing checks are wrong. However, groupthink banished any moral considerations.[23]

Interest in the causes and prevention of groupthink remains high decades after Janis first offered his theory.[24] Contemporary researchers have discovered that social cohesion is dangerous, while task cohesion (agreement about how to complete the group's work) is not. A group is in greatest danger when the leader actively promotes his or her agenda and when it doesn't have any procedures in place for solving problems. Investigators note that self-directed teams, which incorporate an estimated 40% of the workforce, are particularly vulnerable to groupthink. Members work under strict time limits and are often isolated and undertrained. They may fail at first, and the need to function as a cohesive unit may blind them to ethical dilemmas.[25]

Janis and his successors offer the following suggestions for preventing groupthink:

- As a leader, don't express a preference for a particular solution; solicit ideas instead.
- Utilize a decision-making format.
- Divide the group regularly into subgroups, and then bring the entire group back together to negotiate differences.

- Construct and then debate counterproposals.
- Bring in outsiders—experts or colleagues—to challenge the group's ideas.
- Appoint individuals to act as devil's advocates at each session to air doubts and objections.
- Realistically assess dangers and anticipate possible setbacks.
- Train members to speak up.
- Encourage dissenting points of view.
- Think through the ethical implications of options.
- Adopt an optimistic frame of mind, viewing obstacles as opportunities and envisioning success.
- Develop group norms that encourage critical thinking about reasoning, assumptions, and alternatives.
- Avoid isolation; keep the group in contact with other groups.
- Initiate role-play of the reactions of other groups and organizations to reduce the effects of stereotyping and rationalization.
- Once a decision has been made, give group members one last chance to express any remaining doubts about the decision.

Mismanaged Agreement

Groups frequently run into trouble when members publicly express their support for decisions that they oppose in private. Teams continue to pour time and money into new products that no one believes will succeed, for example, or engage in illegal activities that everyone in the group is uneasy about. George Washington University management professor Jerry Harvey refers to this phenomenon as *mismanaged agreement*, or the Abilene paradox.[26] He describes a time when his family decided to drive (without air conditioning) 100 miles across the Texas desert, one hot July afternoon, from their home in Coleman to Abilene so they could eat a bad meal at a rundown cafeteria. After returning home, family members discovered that no one had really wanted to make the trip. Each had agreed to go to Abilene on the assumption that everyone else in the group was enthusiastic about eating out.

Harvey believes that failure to manage agreement, not failure to manage conflict, is the biggest problem facing organizations. Like his family, teams also take needless "trips":

> I now call the tendency for groups to embark on excursions that no group member wants "the Abilene Paradox." Stated simply, when organizations blunder into the Abilene Paradox, they take actions in contradiction to what they really want to do and therefore defeat the very purposes they are trying to achieve.[27]

Members of groups caught in the Abilene paradox agree in private about the nature of the problem and what ought to be done about it. However, they fail to communicate their desires and beliefs, misleading others into believing that consensus exists. Based on faulty assumptions, members act in counterproductive ways that undermine their purposes. These actions generate lots of anger and irritation, and participants blame each other for the group's failures. The cycle of miscommunication and misunderstanding continues unless confronted.

Why do members publicly support decisions they privately oppose? Harvey offers the following five psychological factors to account for the paradox:

1. *Action anxiety.* Group members know what should be done but are too anxious to follow through on their beliefs. They choose to endure the negative consequences of going along (professional and economic failure) instead of speaking up.

2. *Negative fantasies.* Action anxiety is driven in part by the negative fantasies members have about what will happen if they voice their opinions. These fantasies ("I'll be shunned or branded as disloyal") serve as an excuse for not attacking the problem, absolving the individual (in his or her own eyes) of any responsibility.

3. *Real risk.* There are risks to expressing dissent: getting fired, lost income, damaged relationships. However, most of the time the danger is not as great as we think.

4. *Fear of separation.* Separation, alienation, and loneliness constitute the most powerful force behind the paradox. Ostracism is strong punishment. Group members fear being cut off or separated from others. To escape this fate, they cheat, lie, take bribes, use accounting tricks to boost earnings, and so forth.

5. *Psychological reversal of risk and certainty.* In the Abilene paradox, participants let their negative fantasies drive them into real dangers. Fearing that something bad may happen, decision makers act in a way that fulfills the fantasy. For instance, group members may support a project with no chance of success because they are afraid they will be fired or demoted if they don't. Ironically, they are likely to be fired or demoted anyway when the flawed project fails.

Harvey takes issue with proponents of groupthink who blame moral failure on group pressure. He contends that as long as we can blame our peers, we don't have to accept personal responsibility. In reality, we always have a choice as to how we respond. He uses the Gunsmoke myth to drive home this point. In this myth, the lone Western sheriff (Matt Dillon in the radio and television series *Gunsmoke*) stands down a mob of armed townsfolk out to lynch his prisoner. If group tyranny is really at work, Harvey argues, Dillon stands no chance. After all, he is outnumbered 500 to 1 and could be felled with a single bullet from one rioter. The mob disbands because its members really didn't want to lynch the prisoner in the first place.

Breaking out of the paradox begins with diagnosing its symptoms in your group or organization. Important indicators of mismanaged agreement include frustration and blaming, contradictions between privately and publicly expressed opinions, and the inability to solve problems. If you believe that the group is on its way to its own Abilene, call a meeting where you own up to your true feelings and invite feedback. The team may immediately come up with a better approach, or it may engage in extended conflict that generates a more creative solution. You might suffer for your honesty, but you could be rewarded for saying what everyone else was thinking. In any case, you'll feel better about yourself for speaking up.

Escalating Commitment

As we've seen, one of the products of mismanaged agreement is continuation along a failed course of action. Social psychologists refer to this phenomenon as the *escalation of commitment*.[28] Instead of cutting their losses, groups redouble their efforts, pouring in more resources. Costs continue to multiply, until the moment when the team finally admits defeat. Escalating commitment helps explain why bankers continue to loan money to problem borrowers, why managers maintain support for failing employees, and why investors put more money into declining stocks. Well-publicized cases of this phenomenon include creation of the automated baggage system at the Denver International Airport (which delayed the opening of the airport and never worked), the decision to introduce the New Coke, and the failed Shoreham Nuclear Power Plant. Costs for the Shoreham project on New York's Long Island ballooned from $75 million to over $5 billion over a 23-year period. The installation failed to produce a single kilowatt of electric power. Escalation of commitment also played a role in the Everest tragedy described earlier. Clients paid $60,000 to $70,000 each to summit the mountain. Once they were near the top, it was very difficult to convince some of them to turn around after they had invested so much time, money, and effort.

Teams may stay the course to justify their earlier choices, to remain consistent, and to retain their credibility. (In some cases, the larger organization pressures them to continue.) Group members may have a personal stake in continuing the project because their jobs and reputations are at stake. They often hope to recoup their "sunk costs" (previous investments). Setbacks are viewed as temporary; success is seen as just around the corner. Groups have a tendency to take more risks than individuals (a phenomenon referred to as *risky shift*), which can encourage members to contribute more resources than they would on their own. Teams also fall victim to cognitive biases that encourage escalation. They may (1) ignore negative feedback or interpret evidence so it supports their point of view (selective perception); (2) believe that they have more control outcomes than they actually do (illusion of control); (3) blame those who bring bad news; and (4) become overconfident based on past successes.[29]

Group members have a moral obligation to avoid escalation of commitment. Continuing to invest in doomed projects wastes resources that could go to better uses and puts the organization at risk. Often, maintaining a failing course of action involves unethical behaviors, like overstating potential benefits or hiding safety problems. We can take a number of steps to de-escalate commitment to destructive courses of action.[30] First, don't ignore negative feedback or external pressure. Combat the tendency to be overly optimistic by being alert to red flags like missed deadlines, cost overruns, and pressure from outsiders who take issue with the project. Second, bring new group members or leaders into the group who are less invested in the program. Third, hire an outside auditor to provide a "fresh set of eyes" to assess the severity of the problem and to suggest alternative courses of action. Fourth, don't be afraid to withhold further funding until more information can be gathered. Fifth, look for opportunities to deinstitutionalize the project by separating it from the key goals of the organization or by isolating it physically. Corporations frequently spin off troubled units, for example, and risky projects can be redefined as "experiments."

Excessive Control

Members of newly formed self-directed work teams frequently find that the group exerts more control over their behavior than their former managers ever did. One team member at a small manufacturing company complained, for example, that his group had stricter rules about tardiness than his old boss and that he was more closely observed than before:

> [Now] I don't have to sit there and look for the boss to be around; [before] if the boss is not around, I can sit there and talk to my neighbor or do what I want. Now the whole team is around me and the whole team is observing what I'm doing.[31]

The experience of this employee illustrates the power of *concertive control.* Concertive control has replaced the traditional rules-based bureaucracy in many organizations.[32] Groups empowered to direct their own behaviors exert control by agreeing on a common set of values, engaging in high levels of coordination, and creating their own enforcement mechanisms. Concertive control (sometimes referred to as *unobtrusive control*) is subtler than its bureaucratic predecessor and often goes unrecognized. This combination of high power and low visibility makes concertive influence particularly dangerous. Members can unwittingly exert excessive, unhealthy influence over one another.

Organizational communication expert James Barker describes how self-directed work teams transition from freeing to imprisoning their members.[33] In the first phase, newly formed groups develop their vision and values statements. These values then become the basis for making ethical decisions in the group. Members commit themselves to reaching shared goals and develop norms for putting their values into action. A group might implement its concern for customer service, for instance, by adopting the norm that it will do whatever it takes to ship products on time.

In the second phase, members turn their norms into specific behavioral rules, like "You must stay late in order to meet shipping schedules." These rules are then used to regulate the behavior of new members. In the third phase, the rules are formalized. They are written down and used for evaluation. A member may be removed from the team if he or she doesn't work overtime to help ship products, for example. These rules can be stricter than those operating in a bureaucracy. Group members are thus imprisoned in an "iron cage" of regulations of their own making.

Barker is concerned that "concertive control is the next step on our long march toward totally organized lives."[34] Members pay a high price for remaining in good standing with the team, including burnout and the sacrifice of family and personal time. Teams can make sure that concertive control is put to constructive use by continually criticizing their own actions, according to Barker. They need to set aside regular times (perhaps an hour a month) to talk about their moral reasoning and the positive and negative effects of their practices. Some values and rules will be reaffirmed, while others will be modified. In such discussions, it is critical that everyone be heard and that members engage in dialogue, working through their differences. This ongoing group analysis is the best way to ensure that a team creates a fair and reasonable system of norms and regulations to guide its members.

Moral Exclusion

The worst examples of group behavior arise out of the process of moral exclusion. In moral exclusion, group and societal members set a psychological boundary around justice.[35] Those inside the boundary treat each other fairly, are willing to sacrifice for one another, and share collective resources. However, insiders treat outsiders much differently. Fairness is no longer a consideration. Those beyond the scope of justice (often members of low-status groups) are seen as unimportant and expendable. Insiders don't feel remorse when outsiders are harmed but believe that the mistreatment is morally justified.

Mild forms of exclusion are part of everyday life and include, for example, acting in a patronizing manner, applying double standards to judge the behavior of different groups, and making unflattering comparisons to appear superior to others. An example of ordinary exclusion would be a work team that mocks other groups while excusing its own failings. Milder forms of exclusion are common in conflicts over environmental issues, where opposing sides claim the moral high ground and are quick to label their opponents as "ecofreaks," or "foot-dragging big businesses."[36] Extreme forms of exclusion produce human rights violations, torture, genocide, and other atrocities. For instance, Japanese soldiers in World War II viewed the Chinese with contempt. Murdering them was no more troubling than "squashing a bug or butchering a hog."[37] Driven by this belief, they were willing to rape, torture, and slaughter civilians in the Chinese city of Nanking, killing approximately 300,000 residents. Similar exclusionary reasoning has been to justify genocide in Serbia and Guatemala, attacks on villages in the Darfur region of Sudan, and the abuse of prisoners at Iraq's Abu Ghraib prison (see Case Study 7.3). A list of the symptoms of moral exclusion is given in Ethics in Action 7.1.

Dispute resolution expert Susan Opotow believes that moral exclusion progresses through five stages or elements, which can reinforce one another. The presence of one or more of these elements serves as a warning that this danger is present.[38]

1. *Conflicts of interest are salient.* Moral exclusion is more likely to occur during conflicts where one group wins at the expense of the other. As tensions increase, members separate themselves from their opponents, focusing on differences based on religion, education, ethnic background, social status, skin color, job functions, and other factors.

2. *Group categorizations are salient.* The characteristics of members of the opposing group are given negative labels, dividing the world into those who deserve empathy and help and those who don't. These derogatory labels excuse unfair treatment and negative outcomes. Romanians and Hungarians, for example, reinforce negative stereotypes of Gypsies or Romanies by describing them as "dirty," "thieves," and "lazy."[39]

3. *Moral justifications are prominent.* Damaging behavior is justified and even celebrated as a way to strike a blow against a corrupt foe. Such exclusionary moral claims are self-serving, excuse wrongdoing, and set boundaries by denigrating outsiders. For instance, Hutu leaders in Rwanda whipped their followers into a murderous rage by playing on their resentments toward their higher status Tutsi neighbors.

4. *Unjust procedures are described as expedient.* Harm is often disguised through policies and procedures, what some observers label "administrative evil."[40] In administrative evil, ordinary people commit heinous crimes while carrying out their daily tasks. The Holocaust demonstrates administrative evil in action. Extermination camps would not have been possible without the cooperation of thousands of civil servants who identified undesirables and seized their assets, managed the ghettos, built concentration camp latrines, and shipped prisoners to their deaths.

Procedures can be identified as unjust when they fail to serve the interests of those they are supposed to benefit. For example, government bureaucrats in the United States and Australia claimed to be helping Native peoples even as they stole their lands and tried to eradicate their cultures. Military officials in Japan believed that committing atrocities would ultimately benefit the Chinese because, once subjugated, they would prosper under Japanese rule.

5. *Harmful outcomes occur.* The negative products of exclusion are both physical and psychological. Members of excluded groups may suffer physical harm and, at the same time, suffer from a loss of self-esteem and identity as they internalize the negative judgments of the dominant group. Perpetrators also pay a high price. They have to expend significant energy and resources to deal with conflicts, excuse their conduct, and maintain exclusionary systems. The harm they cause overshadows any good that they do.

Opotow argues that adopting a pluralistic perspective—one that acknowledges the legitimacy of a variety of groups—can help us deter moral exclusion at each stage of its development.[41] This approach sees conflicts as opportunities to integrate the interests of all parties, not as win-lose battles. Members of pluralistic groups enlarge the definition of moral community by including people of all categories and try to understand their perspectives. Participants engage in critical analysis of moral justifications, calling into question suspect claims at the same time they develop equitable procedures for distributing resources. They also support dissenters.

ETHICS IN ACTION 7.1 SYMPTOMS OF MORAL EXCLUSION

Symptom	Description
Double standards	Having different norms for different groups
Concealing effects of harmful outcomes	Disregarding, ignoring, distorting, or minimizing injurious outcomes that others experience
Reducing moral standards	Asserting that one's harmful behavior is proper while denying one's lesser concern for others
Utilizing euphemisms	Making and sanitizing harmful behavior and outcomes

(Continued)

(Continued)

Symptom	Description
Biased evaluation of groups comparisons	Making unflattering between-group comparisons that bolster one's own group at the expense of others
Condescension and derogation	Regarding others with disdain
Dehumanization	Denying others' rights, entitlements, humanity, and dignity
Fear of contamination	Perceiving contact or alliances with other stakeholders as posing a threat to oneself
Normalization and glorification of violence	Glorifying and normalizing violence; viewing violence as an effective, legitimate, or even sublime form of human behavior while denying the potential of violence to damage people, the environment, relationships, and constructive conflict resolution processes
Victim blaming	Placing blame on those who are hated
Deindividuation	Believing one's contribution to social problems is undetectable
Diffusing responsibility	Denying personal responsibility for harms by seeing them as the result of collective rather than individual decisions and actions
Displacing responsibility	Identifying others, such as subordinates or supervisors, as responsible for harms inflicted on victims

SOURCE: Opotow, S., Gerson, J., & Woodside, S. (2005). From moral exclusion to moral inclusion: Theory for teaching peace. *Theory into Practice 44*(4), 303–318, p. 307.

CHAPTER TAKEAWAYS

- Your behavior will have a significant impact on your team's ethical success or failure.
- Recognize that your success in a group is dependent on the efforts of others. Adopt a cooperative orientation, not an individualistic or competitive perspective, and encourage others to do the same.
- Do your fair share. Combat the tendency to engage in social loafing by strengthening connections between individual effort and group performance as well as between group performance and group success. Increase the positive value of the team's collective product to members.
- Be open and supportive. Talk about issues and help others to succeed. Promote a supportive climate by engaging in communication that is descriptive, problem oriented, spontaneous, empathetic, egalitarian, and provisional. Create an atmosphere in which members feel safe to discuss problems and challenge leaders.
- Have the courage to stand alone. Expressing a minority opinion is key to avoiding moral failure and increases group decision-making effectiveness even when the majority does not adopt the dissenters' point of view. In some cases, you might convert the rest of the group to your way of thinking.

- Signs of groupthink—putting unanimity ahead of careful problem solving—include overconfidence (the illusion of invulnerability and belief in the inherent morality of the group), closed-mindedness (collective rationalization and stereotypes of outside groups), and group pressure (pressure on dissenters, self-censorship, the illusion of unanimity, and self-appointed mind-guards).
- Reduce the likelihood of groupthink by (a) withholding your initial opinion, (b) dividing the group into subgroups, (c) bringing in outsiders, (d) keeping the group in contact with other groups, (e) role-playing the reactions of other teams, and (f) revisiting the decision.
- Mismanaged agreement—Abilene paradox—occurs when members publicly express support for decisions that they oppose in private. The group then acts in counterproductive ways that undermine its goals. Owning up to your doubts can stop the team from taking unwanted "trips."
- Groups trapped in escalating commitment pursue failed courses of action, continuing to pour in additional resources when they should go in another direction instead. They may want to justify their earlier choices, hope to recoup their previous investments, or fall victim to cognitive biases that encourage escalation. You can de-escalate the situation by noting warning signs, bringing in new members or outside auditors, withholding funding, and deinstitutionalizing the project (making it less central to group goals and physically isolating it).
- Be aware of the power of concertive control, in which teams manage the behavior of members by agreeing on a common set of values, engaging in high levels of coordination, and creating their own enforcement mechanisms. Such control is often more intrusive than traditional bureaucracy. However, you can put this form of group influence to constructive use by encouraging your team to regularly examine, criticize, and modify its values and rules.
- Resist the temptation to engage in moral exclusion—placing members of other groups outside the scope of justice where the rules of fairness do not apply. The five stages or elements of moral exclusion are these: (1) Conflicts of interest are salient. (2) Group categorizations are salient. (3) Moral justifications are prominent. (4) Unjust procedures are described as expedient. (5) Harmful outcomes occur. Deter moral exclusion by adopting a pluralistic perspective that respects the rights of all groups.

APPLICATION PROJECTS

1. What was your best small-group experience? Your worst? What accounts for the differences between these two experiences? How would your rate the moral behavior of each group?

2. Interview a project manager. What strategies does this individual use to foster collaboration and individual and team accountability? Report your findings to the rest of the class.

3. Record a group discussion, and then identify and categorize the defensive and supportive comments made by team members. What do you conclude about the communication climate of the group? Report your conclusions to the team you observe.

4. Rate your performance as a morally responsible group member. What behaviors do you demonstrate? Need to develop? What steps can you take to improve?

5. If you are part of an ongoing group, meet together to discuss members' tendencies to loaf and how the team exercises control over its members. Develop an action plan to address these issues.

6. Create a case study based on a group that fell victim to escalation of commitment. Why did the group stay the course? Was it able to deescalate? What was the end result? What do you learn from the case?

7. Examine a significant conflict between groups that produced negative outcomes. Analyze the role played by moral exclusion in this situation. Provide examples of the five elements of exclusion in action. Write up your findings.

8. Which of the dangers described in the chapter does the most damage to the ethical performance of groups? Defend your choice.

CASE STUDY 7.2

Groupthink in the Sweat Lodge

In October 2009, a group of spiritual seekers paid from $9,000 to $10,000 each to attend a five-day Spiritual Warrior Retreat near Sedona, Arizona, led by self-help expert and New Age guru James Arthur Ray. Ray is the author of the best-selling book *Harmonic Wealth: The Secret of Attracting the Life You Want* and is featured in the video *The Secret.* His company, James Ray International, took in over $9 million in 2008.

The Spiritual Warrior Retreat, which participants were told "will push you beyond your perceived limits," included seminars, spiritual cleansing exercises, and other activities.[1] The week culminated in a 36-hour vision quest without food or water in the desert, followed by a meal and a closing sweat lodge ceremony. The ceremony was designed as an intense "rebirthing" experience to help participants make significant life changes. Held in a 415-square-foot enclosure built of blankets and plastic sheeting surrounding a fire pit, the lodge could comfortably handle 20 to 25 people but was packed with more than 60 seekers that day. Heated rocks were periodically brought in, placed in the fire pit, and doused with water. Sandalwood (believed to be toxic when burned) was added to produce incense. Participants sat in darkness, while Ray, standing near the tent door, exhorted them to continue despite their extreme discomfort. He reportedly told the group, "Play full on, you have to go through this barrier."[2]

The sweat lodge soon became what one reporter called "a human cooking pot," searing the lungs of retreat-goers and baking their internal organs.[3] Not only was the sweat lodge overcrowded, but the plastic sheeting also didn't let the steam escape, further increasing the temperature in the enclosure. Three people died, and 20 more received emergency medical treatment for dehydration, burns, breathing problems, organ failure, and elevated body temperature. Those in the lodge report that Ray ignored signs that something was terribly amiss. When people started vomiting, he declared that vomiting "was good for you, that you are purging what your body doesn't want, what it doesn't need."[4] When told that a woman had fainted just after he closed the enclosure door between rounds of the ceremony, Ray continued on, noting, "We will deal with that after the next round."[5]

Police and other observers wonder why participants didn't leave the tent even when they literally began to cook to death. (It should be noted that some might have been overcome before they could save themselves.) Escalation of commitment might be partially to blame. Retreat-goers spent thousands of dollars and invested several days in the event and wanted to continue to the end, hoping for a final spiritual breakthrough. However, groupthink appears to be a more significant contributing factor. The retreat experience put a good deal of pressure on participants to conform. They were isolated, under the direction of a powerful authority figure, and subjected to significant physical stress even before entering the sweat lodge. Thus, it is not surprising that followers displayed symptoms of groupthink. Ray allegedly pressured possible dissenters. He discouraged members from leaving the tent by his presence at the door and by telling those tempted to exit, "You can do better than this."[6]

Individuals apparently engaged in self-censorship, keeping their doubts about the safety of the lodge to themselves. One client, for example, was troubled about a game played earlier in the week in which Ray (dressed in white robes) played God and ordered some participants to commit mock suicide. However, she didn't leave then because she didn't want to ruin the experience for others. There was also the illusion of unanimity. Some members of the group may have concluded that if the rest of the participants thought conditions in the lodge were tolerable, then it must be safe to stay. The darkness may have hidden the fact that others were in serious trouble.

Ray was convicted of three counts of negligent homicide and could spend up to 30 years in prison. Ray claims that what happened in the lodge was a tragic accident, not a crime. He and his attorneys and supporters point out that the participants were warned of the dangers of the experience (they signed waivers indicating that death could result). A nurse was on duty outside the lodge, and drinks were available. People were free to leave the lodge when they wished. However, events that day suggest that while participants may have been physically free to exit, the power of groupthink kept them trapped in the tent as the temperature soared.

Discussion Probes

1. What other symptoms of groupthink (if any) do you see in this case?

2. Is groupthink a greater danger for spiritual groups than other types of groups? Why or why not?

3. What other ethical danger signs do you see in the sweat lodge tragedy?

4. What steps could retreat participants have taken to protect themselves and others?

5. Were the deaths and injuries the product of a crime or an unfortunate accident?

6. What do you learn from this case that you can apply as a group member?

Notes

1. Archibold, R. C., & Berger, J. (2010, February 5). Sweat lodge leader is indicted in deaths. *The New York Times on the Web.*

2. Dougherty, J. (2009, October 23). New Age vibes strike tragic chord. *The International Herald Tribune,* p. 2.

3. Gumbel, A. (2009, October 22). Death in Arizona. *The Guardian,* Features, p. 5.

4. Dougherty, J. (2009, October 22). A witness recalls a grim end to a quest for spiritual rebirth. *The New York Times,* p. A1.

5. Dougherty (2009, October 23).

6. Dougherty (2009, October 22).

Sources

Archibold, R. C. (2010, January 14). Sweat lodge deaths not criminal, Guru's lawyer says. *The New York Times,* p. A22.

Dougherty, J. (2009, October 12). Sweat lodge deaths: Bring soul-searching to area deep in seekers. *The New York Times,* p. A13.

Lacey, M. (2011, June 23). New age guru guilty in sweat lodge deaths. *The New York Times,* p. 16.

Lirbyson, F. (2009, October 24). Police probe deaths at 'sweat lodge.' *National Post,* p. A7.

CASE STUDY 7.3

Moral Exclusion at Abu Ghraib

Images of prisoner abuse at Iraq's Abu Ghraib prison sickened viewers around the world when they were released in the spring of 2004 and again in 2005. The photos record soldiers of the 372nd Military Police Company unit subjecting detainees to physical and psychological abuse as well as sexual humiliation. Naked male prisoners cower before police dogs, pose in simulated sex acts, and form human pyramids. Smiling soldiers of both sexes stand by, flashing the thumbs-up sign, mocking the plight and the genitals of their victims. In the image that has come to symbolize Abu Ghraib, a hooded prisoner stands with his arms outstretched on a box, with electric wires attached to his hands, feet, and private parts.

Abu Ghraib demonstrates a failure of both individual and shared moral responsibility. Soldiers involved in the abuse were unwilling to stand alone. Specialist Jeremy Spivits admitted that all of the incidents of abuse were wrong, but he went along because "I try to be friends with everyone."[1] Pfc. Lynndie England (seen leading a naked prisoner around on a leash in one picture) told a judge that she had a choice not to participate but caved in to peer pressure.

Moral exclusion played a critical role in the scandal at Abu Ghraib. Following the events of 9/11, a small group of lawyers at the Justice Department's Office of Legal Counsel drafted a new set of policies dealing with the treatment of terrorists. They believed that saving Americans from further attacks justified extreme measures. White House counsel Alberto Gonzalez, who was later to become attorney general, advised the president that the Geneva Convention didn't apply to terrorists. According to Gonzalez, "The war on terrorism is a new kind of war . . . a new paradigm [that] renders obsolete Geneva's strict limitations on questioning of enemy prisoners and renders quaint some of its principles."[2]

Under the Geneva accord, prisoners of war (a category that includes members of the armed forces, militias, and resistance groups) can refuse to answer questions beyond name, rank, and serial number and are guaranteed humane treatment. No "physical or moral coercion" should be used to obtain information from civilians. Noncombatants are also protected from "outrages upon personal dignity, in particular, humiliating and degrading treatment." If there is any doubt as to who should be covered under the treaty, belligerents are protected by its provisions until a "competent tribunal" determines otherwise.[3]

President Bush followed the advice of the Legal Counsel lawyers and declared that terrorist suspects were "unlawful combatants" excluded from provisions that apply to prisoners of war. Suspects were then taken to Guantanamo Bay, where they were held without trial. Administration officials also narrowed the definition of torture to acts involving serious mental or physical damage (organ failure, for example). Under this new definition, interrogators were free to engage in variety of aggressive tactics, such as sleep deprivation, isolation, the use of dogs, stress positions, yelling, loud music, and light control. The revised interrogation guidelines were exported from Guantanamo to Abu Ghraib in the summer of 2003 after the Department of Defense grew frustrated by the lack of intelligence coming out of Iraq.

Guards at Abu Ghraib went far beyond anything sanctioned by the less restrictive interrogation guidelines. However, excluding terror suspects from the rule of international law made it easier to justify their mistreatment. Conflicts of interest and group categories were particularly salient at Abu Ghraib, where interrogators and guards were pitted against insurgents and detainees. Soldiers might have also shared a broader dislike for Iraqis, whom some military personnel describe as "rag heads," "turbans," and "haji" (a derogatory term used like *gook* and *Charlie* during the Vietnam War). Tougher measures appeared justified in the face of a rising insurgency.

Members of the 372nd company appearing in the photos were tried and sentenced to jail. However, no high-level officials were court-martialed for what happened. A later check of prison records revealed that military police at Abu Ghraib tortured innocent people. Many prisoners were criminals, not terrorists, and others were released without being charged.

Abu Ghraib highlights the dangers of moral exclusion, even when engaged in a cause as important as the War on Terror. Severe interrogation methods did elicit valuable information, such as details about the 9/11 plot and future Al Qaeda operations. This intelligence may have helped prevent future attacks like the one on the World Trade Center. However, tales of the abuse further fanned anti-American sentiment, making it easier to recruit new terrorists. The moral authority of the nation was undermined. Arab observers referred to the hooded detainee on the box as "the statue of liberty" and wondered how the United States could claim to model democracy even as it engaged in acts that are typically practiced in dictatorships. American military officers warned that violating the Geneva Convention put U.S. soldiers at risk. Future captured Americans may receive the same treatment that the United States dished out. Other governments may now use the terrorist label to excuse all kinds of injustice.

Discussion Probes

1. Is torture justified if it saves innocent lives from terrorist attacks? How do you reach this conclusion?

2. Should terrorists be treated like other prisoners of war, according to the provisions of the Geneva Convention?

3. Are the revised interrogation tactics used by the United States (sleep deprivation, loud music, dogs, light control) forms of torture? Why or why not?

4. What factors do you think contributed to the abuse at Abu Ghraib? How far up the chain of command does the responsibility extend?

5. What can be done to prevent abuses of military prisoners in the future?

Notes

1. McGeary (2004), p. 44.
2. Danner (2004), p. 42.
3. Barry, Hirsh, & Isikoff (2004), p. 29.

Sources

Badger, T. A. (2005, May 3). Soldier says peers pressed for abuse. *The Oregonian,* pp. A1, A3.

Barry, J., Hirsh, M., & Isikoff, M. (2004, May 24). The roots of torture. *Newsweek,* pp. 26–34.

Danner, M. (2004). *Torture and truth: America, Abu Ghraib, and the War on Terror.* New York: New York Review Books.

Herbert, B. (2005, May 2). From "gook" to "raghead." *The New York Times,* p. A21.

McGeary, J. (2004, May 24). Pointing fingers. *Time,* pp. 43–47, 50.

Murphy, D. (2004, June 4). Abu Ghraib holds mirror to Arabs. *The Christian Science Monitor*, p. 1c.

Ripley, A. (2004, June 21). Redefining torture. *Time*, pp. 49–50.

Risen, J. (2004, May 3). The struggle for Iraq: Prisoners. *The New York Times*, p. A1.

Scelfo, J., & Nordland, R. (2004, July 19). Beneath the hoods. *Newsweek*, pp. 40–42.

Zernike, K. (2004, June 27). Defining torture: Russian roulette, yes. Mind-altering drugs, maybe. *The New York Times*, p. 7.

ENDNOTES

1. Locke, E. A., Tirnauer, D., Roberson, Q., Goldman, B., Lathan, M. E., & Weldon, E. (2001). The importance of the individual in an age of groupism. In M. E. Turner (Ed.), *Groups at work: Theory and research* (pp. 501–528). Mahwah, NJ: Lawrence Erlbaum.

2. Rothwell, J. D. (1998). *In mixed company: Small group communication* (3rd ed.). Fort Worth, TX: Harcourt Brace.

3. Johnson, D. W., Maruyama, G., Johnson, R., Nelson, D., & Skon, L. (1981). Effects of cooperative, competitive, and individualistic goal structures on achievement: A meta-analysis. *Psychological Bulletin, 82,* 47–62.

4. Tjosvold, D. (1984). Cooperation theory and organizations. *Human Relations, 37,* 743–767; Tjosvold, D. (1986). The dynamics of interdependence in organizations. *Human Relations, 39,* 517–540; Johnson, D. W., & Johnson, R. T. (1974). Instructional goal structure: Cooperative, competitive, or individualistic. *Review of Educational Research, 44,* 212–239; Milton, L. P., & Westphal, J. D. (2005). Identity confirmation networks and cooperation in work groups. *Academy of Management Journal, 48,* 191–212; Johnson, D. W., & Johnson, F. P. (2006). *Joining together: Group theory and group skills* (9th ed.). Boston: Pearson.

5. Johnson, D. W. (1974). Communication and the inducement of cooperative behavior in conflicts: A critical review. *Speech Monographs, 41,* 64–78; Rubin, J. Z., & Brown, B. R. (1975). *The social psychology of bargaining and negotiation.* New York: Academic Press.

6. Ding, H., & Ding, X. (2008). Project management, critical praxis, and process-oriented approach to teamwork. *Business Communication Quarterly, 71*(4), 456–471.

7. Williams, K. D., Harkins, S. G., & Karau, S. J. (2003). Social performance. In M. A. Hogg & J. Cooper (Eds.), *The Sage handbook of social psychology* (pp. 333–346). London: Sage.

8. Amichai-Hamburger, Y. (2003). Understanding social loafing. In A. Sagie, S. Stashevsky, & M. Koslowsky (Eds.), *Misbehaviour and dysfunctional attitudes in organizations* (pp. 79–102). New York: Palgrave Macmillan; Smith, B. N., Kerr, N. A., Markus, M. J., & Stasson, M. F. (2001). Individual differences in social loafing: Need for cognition as a motivator in collective performance. *Group Dynamics: Theory, Research, and Practice, 5*(2), 150–158.

9. Karau, S. J., & Williams, K. D. (2001). Understanding individual motivation in groups: The collective effort model. In M. E. Turner (Ed.), *Groups at work: Theory and research* (pp. 113–141). Mahwah, NJ: Lawrence Erlbaum; Karau, S. J., & Williams, K. D. (1993). Social loafing: A meta-analytic review and theoretical integration. *Journal of Personality and Social Psychology, 65,* 681–706.

10. Karau & Williams (2001); Sheppard, J. A. (2001). Social loafing and expectancy-value theory. In S. G. Harkins (Ed.), *Multiple perspectives on the effects of evaluation on performance: Toward an integration* (pp. 1–24). Boston: Kluwer; Sheppard, J. A. (1993). Productivity loss in performance groups: A motivation analysis. *Psychological Bulletin, 113,* 67–81.

11. LaFasto, F., & Larson, C. (2001). *When teams work best.* Thousand Oaks, CA: Sage.

12. Gibb, J. R. (1961). Defensive communication. *Journal of Communication, 11–12,* 141–148.

13. Edmundson, A. (1999). Psychological safety and learning behavior in work teams. *Administrative Science Quarterly, 44,* 350–383, p. 354.

14. Roberto, M. A. (2002). Lessons from Everest: The interaction of cognitive bias, psychological safety, and system complexity. *California Management Review, 45*(1), 136–158.

15. For summaries of research on minority influence process, see: Moscovici, S., Mugny, G., & Van Avermaet, D. (Eds.). (1985). *Perspectives on minority influence.* Cambridge, UK: Cambridge University Press; Mass, A., & Clark, R. D. (1984). Hidden impact of minorities: Fifteen years of minority influence research. *Psychological Bulletin, 95,* 428–450; Wood, W., Lundgren, S., Ouellette, J. A., Busceme, S., & Blackstone, T. (1994). Minority influence: A meta-analytic review of social influence processes. *Psychological Bulletin, 115,* 323–345; Moscovici, S., Mucchi-Faina, A., & Mass, A. (1994). *Minority influence.* Chicago: Nelson-Hall; Crano, W. D., & Seyranian, V. (2009). How minorities prevail: The context/comparison-lenience contract model. *Journal of Social Issues, 65*(2), 335–363.

16. Nemeth, C. (1985). Dissent, group process and creativity: The contribution of minority influence research. In E. Lawler (Ed.), *Advances in group processes* (Vol. 2, pp. 57–75). Greenwich, CT: JAI; Nemeth, C., & Chiles, C. (1986). Modeling courage: The role of dissent in fostering independence. *European Journal of Social Psychology, 18,* 275–280.

17. Mugny, G., & Perez, J. A. (1991). *The social psychology of minority influence* (V. W. Lamongie, Trans.). Cambridge, UK: Cambridge University Press.

18. Crano & Seyranian; De Dreu, C. K. W., & Beersma, B. (2001). Minority influence in organizations: Its origins and implications for learning and group performance. In C. K. W. De Dreu & N. K. DeVries (Eds.), *Group consensus and minority influence: Implications for innovation* (pp. 258–283). Oxford: Blackwell.

19. Janis, I. (1971, November). Groupthink: The problems of conformity. *Psychology Today,* pp. 271–279; Janis, I. (1982). *Groupthink* (2nd ed.). Boston: Houghton Mifflin; Janis, I. (1989). *Crucial decisions: Leadership in policymaking and crisis management.* New York: Free Press.

20. For additional examples of groupthink in action, see: Schafer, M., & Crichlow, S. (2010). *Groupthink versus high-quality decision making in international relations.* New York: Columbia University Press; 't Hart, P. (1990*). Groupthink in government.* Amsterdam: Swets & Zeitlinger.

21. Portions of this material were adapted from: Johnson, C. E., & Hackman, M. Z. (1995). *Creative communication: Principles and applications.* Prospect Heights, IL: Waveland Press, Chap. 5.

22. Janis (1982), p. 40.

23. Sims, R. R. (1992). Linking groupthink to unethical behavior in organizations. *Journal of Business Ethics, 11,* 651–662.

24. See, for example: Bernthal, P. R., & Insko, C. A. (1993). Cohesiveness without groupthink: The interactive effects of social and task cohesion. *Group & Organizational Management, 18,* 66–87; Chen, A., Lawson, R. B., Gordon, L. R., & McIntosh, B. (1996). Groupthink: Deciding with the leader and the devil. *Psychological Record, 46,* 581–590; Esser, J. K. (1998). Alive and well after 25 years: A review of groupthink research. *Organizational Behavior and Human Decision Processes, 73,* 116–141; Flippen, A. R. (1999). Understanding groupthink from a self-regulatory perspective. *Small Group Research, 30,* 139–165; Postmes, T., Spears, R., & Cihangir, S. (2001). Quality of decision-making and group norms. *Journal of Personality and Social Psychology, 80,* 918–930; Street, M. D. (1997). Groupthink: An examination of theoretical issues, implications, and future research suggestions. *Small Group Research, 28,* 72–93; 't Hart, P. (1990). *Groupthink in government: A study of small groups and policy failure.* Baltimore, MD: Johns Hopkins University Press; Packer, D. J. (2009). Avoiding groupthink. *Psychological Science, 20*(5), 546–548; Park, W-W. (2000). A comprehensive empirical investigation of the relationships among variables of the groupthink model. *Journal of Organizational Behavior, 21,* 873–887.

25. Moorhead, G., Neck, C. P., & West, M. S. (1998). The tendency toward defective decision making within self-managing teams: The relevance of groupthink for the 21st century. *Organizational Behavior and Human Decision Processes, 73,* 327–351; Manz, C. C., & Neck, C. P. (1995). Teamthink: Beyond the groupthink syndrome in self-managing work teams. *Journal of Managerial Psychology, 10,* 7–15.

26. Harvey, J. (1988). *The Abilene Paradox and other meditations on management.* Lexington, MA: Lexington Books; Harvey, J. (2001). The Abilene Paradox: The management of agreement. *Organizational Dynamics, 33,* 17–34; Kanter, R. M. (2001). An Abilene defense: Commentary one. *Organizational Dynamics, 33,* 37–40.

27. Harvey (2001), p. 15.

28. See, for example: Staw, B. M. (1981). The escalation of commitment to a course of action. *Academy of Management Review, 6,* 577–587; Ross, J., & Staw, B. M. (1993). Organizational escalation and exit: Lessons from the Shoreham Nuclear Plant. *Academy of Management Journal, 36,* 701–732; Bobocel, D. R., & Meyer, J. P. (1994). Escalating commitment to a failing course of action: Separating the roles of choice and justification. *Journal of Applied Psychology, 79,* 360–363; McNamara, G., Moon, H., & Bromiley, P. (2002). Banking on commitment: Intended and unintended consequences of an organization's attempt to attenuate escalation of commitment. *Academy of Management Journal, 45,* 443–452.

29. Whyte, G. (1991). Diffusion of responsibility: Effects on the escalation tendency. *Journal of Applied Psychology, 76,* 408–415; Jones, P. E., & Roelofsma, P. H. M. P. (2000). The potential for social contextual and group biases in team decision-making: Biases, conditions and psychological mechanisms. *Ergonomics, 43,* 1129–1152; Drummond, H. (1996). *Escalation in decision-making: The tragedy of Taurus.* New York: Oxford University Press; Drummond, H. (2001). *The art of decision-making: Mirrors of imagination, masks of fate.* Chichester, UK: John Wiley.

30. Keil, M., & Montealegre, R. (2000, Spring). Cutting your losses: Extricating your organization when a big project goes awry. *Sloan Management Review,* pp. 55–58; Ross & Staw (1993); Drummond, H. (2001); Huan, C-L., & Chang, B-G. (2010). The effects of manager's moral philosophy on project decision under agency problem conditions. *Journal of Business Ethics, 94,* 595–611; Keil, M., Depledge, G., & Rai, A. (2007). Escalation: The role of problem recognition and cognitive bias. *Decision Science, 38*(3), 391–417.

31. Barker, J. R. (1993). Tightening the iron cage: Concertive control in self-managing teams. *Administrative Science Quarterly, 38,* 408–437.

32. Tompkins, P. K., & Cheney, G. (1985). Communication and unobtrusive control in contemporary organizations. In R. D. McPhee & P. K. Tompkins (Eds.), *Organizational communication: Traditional themes and new directions* (pp. 179–210). Newbury Park, CA: Sage; Bullis, C. (1991). Communication practices as unobtrusive control: An observational study. *Communication Studies, 42*(3), 254–271.

33. Barker, J. R. (1999). *The discipline of teamwork: Participation and concertive control.* Thousand Oaks, CA: Sage; Barker (1993).

34. Barker (1999), p. 177.

35. Opotow, S. (1990). Moral exclusion and injustice: An introduction. *Journal of Social Issues, 46,* 1–20; Opotow, S., & Weiss, L. (2000). Denial and the process of moral exclusion in environmental conflict. *Journal of Social Issues, 56*(3), 475–490.

36. Opotow, S. (2005). Hate, conflict, and moral exclusion. In R. J. Sternberg (Ed.), *The psychology of hate* (pp. 121–154). Washington, DC: American Psychological Association.

37. Chang, I. (1997). *The rape of Nanking: The forgotten holocaust of World War II.* New York: Basic Books, p. 218.

38. Opotow (1990).

39. Tileaga, C. (2006). Representing the 'other': A discursive analysis of prejudice and moral exclusion in talk about Romanies. *Journal of Community & Applied Social Psychology, 16,* 19–41.

40. Adams, G. B., & Balfour, D. L. (1998). *Unmasking administrative evil.* Thousand Oaks, CA: Sage.

41. Opotow, S. (1990). Deterring moral exclusion. *Journal of Social Issues, 46,* 173–182; Opotow, S. (1995). Drawing the line: Social categorization, moral exclusion, and the scope of justice. In B. B. Bunker & J. Z. Rubin (Eds.), *Conflict, cooperation, and justice: Essays inspired by the work of Morton Deutsch* (pp. 347–369). San Francisco: Jossey-Bass.

8

Leadership Ethics

Leaders are critical to the ethical performance of any organization. They are largely responsible for determining mission and values, developing structure, and creating ethical climates. As a consequence, leaders deserve a good deal of credit for ethical success and a good deal of the blame when groups fall short. That's why names of prominent leaders are linked to well-publicized ethical successes (Starbucks CEO Howard Schultz, Southwest Airlines president emeritus Colleen Barrett, Special Olympics founder Eunice Shriver) and failures (Martha Stewart, Enron's Ken Lay, Countrywide Mortgage's Anthony Mozilo, Tony Hayward of BP).

Social learning theory helps explain why and how organizational leaders exert so much influence over the ethical behavior of followers and the organization as a whole.[1] Social learning theory is based on the premise that people learn by observing and then emulating the values, attitudes, and behavior of people they find legitimate, attractive, and credible. When it comes to ethics, organizational members look to their leaders as role models and follow their example. Leaders who occupy positions of authority with status and power are typically seen as legitimate, credible, and attractive. According to researchers Michael Brown and Linda Trevino, ethical leaders build on this foundation. They raise their legitimacy by treating employees fairly and boost their attractiveness by expressing care and concern for followers. They enhance their credibility (particularly perceptions of trustworthiness) by living up to the values they espouse. Such leaders are honest and open and set clear, high standards that they themselves follow.

Behaving morally and serving as a role model (the *moral person* dimension of ethical leadership) is not enough to create ethical organizational cultures. Brown and Trevino argue that leaders must act as *moral managers* as well. Moral leaders keep ethics in the forefront of organizational life. They make sure ethics messages aren't drowned out by messages about tasks and profits. They maintain a constant focus on ethics by communicating frequently about mission, values, codes of conduct, and the significance of moral behavior. They reinforce follower learning by using punishments and rewards to regulate behavior, making it clear which actions are acceptable and which are not.

Unethical leaders fail as moral persons and/or as moral managers. Some are hypocritical, talking a lot about moral values but not living up to their rhetoric. Other leaders may not engage in unethical behavior themselves but leave followers unsure about where they stand on moral issues because they don't send out strong messages about ethics. The worst leaders engage in unethical behaviors (lying, cheating, stealing, bullying subordinates), setting a poor example for followers. They communicate that ethics don't matter, just results, and reward the wrong behaviors.

In this chapter, we'll pay particular attention to the moral person dimension of ethical leadership. (I'll have more to say about the role of leaders in creating ethical organizational climates in Chapter 10.) The first section, "The Ethical Challenges of Leadership," introduces the special ethical demands that come with serving in a leadership role. The second section, "The Shadow Side of Leadership," examines the dark side of leadership that results when we or other leaders fail to meet these ethical challenges. The final section of the chapter surveys normative leadership theories that can equip us to live up to our moral responsibilities as leaders and to avoid casting shadows.

The Ethical Challenges of Leadership

Leadership is the exercise of influence in a group context.[2] Leaders engage in furthering the needs, wants, and objectives shared by leaders and followers alike. Because leadership is exercised in the group context in pursuit of common goals, leaders and followers function collaboratively. They are relational partners who play complementary roles. Leaders take more responsibility for the overall direction of the group; followers are more involved in implementing plans and doing the work itself. While leaders and followers work together, they face different sets of ethical demands based on the roles they play.

Leaders, by virtue of the fact that they exert greater influence and have broader responsibility for organizational outcomes, face six principal ethical challenges: power, privilege, responsibility, information management, consistency, and loyalty. These challenges are described below. (We'll take a closer look at the ethical responsibilities of followers in the next chapter.)

The Challenge of Power

I talked at length about power and influence in Chapter 5. However, it is worth noting that power is of greater concern to leaders because (a) they generally have more of it, and (b) power is the tool or currency that leaders use to exercise influence over the direction of the group. Abuse of power appears to be common in organizations; 90% of those who responded to one survey reported that they had experienced disrespect from a boss at some point in their careers.[3] Bully bosses feel the strong urge to put others down in order to feel good about themselves. Angry and bitter, they frequently threaten and lash out at others, particularly when they feel threatened (which is much of the time). Engaging in hostile, denigrating, verbal personal attacks is one of their favorite tactics.[4]

Concentration of power, which tends to corrupt power holders as we saw in Chapter 5, is also an issue. Media giant Viacom's CEO Sumner Redstone knows first-hand the seductive nature of power. He reportedly advised Disney CEO Michael Eisner (who was later removed from his post) to hang onto his job despite the efforts of stockholders who opposed him. Redstone told Eisner, "Once you've had this kind of power, Michael, let's face it, nobody wants to give it up."[5] Top leaders like Redstone and Eisner are particularly likely to think themselves godlike, believing that they are omniscient (all knowing), omnipotent (all powerful), and invulnerable (safe from all harm).[6] They mistakenly conclude that they know everything they need to know because they have access to many different sources of information and are used to having followers look to them for answers. They are convinced they can do whatever they want because they have so much power. Surrounded by subservient followers, they believe that they will be protected from the consequences of their actions. Disgraced former New York governor Eliot Spitzer may have fallen victim to these delusions. At the same time that he was waging war on Wall Street corruption as perhaps the most famous state attorney general in U.S. history, he was frequenting a prostitution ring and lying to hide his activities.

The Challenge of Privilege

Power and privilege generally operate in tandem. The more power a leader has, generally the greater the privileges he or she enjoys. Evidence of this fact can be found in the wide gulf between the nation's highest and lowest paid workers. The gap between the compensation packages of top executives and those of average workers in the United States is wider than ever. The average CEO in the United States makes $301 for every $1 paid to the typical employee, up from a $42 to $1 ratio in 1982.[7]

The appetites of some CEOs are insatiable. Ken Lay wasn't satisfied with being wealthy. He declared, "I don't want to be rich, I want to be world-class rich."[8] Martha Stewart was sentenced to jail and house arrest for lying about a stock sale, which saved her $52,000, a tiny percentage of her billion-dollar net worth.[9] The enormous chasm between the haves and the have-nots extends well beyond organizational boundaries. According to the Economic Policy Institute, the top 1% of Americans own 34% of the country's wealth; 10% of the population controls more than 70% of the nation's total net worth. The gap between the richest and the poorest Americans is much larger than it was a few decades ago. Economic inequality in the United States is now greater than in Europe and in a number of Latin American countries.[10]

Leaders probably deserve higher salaries and more benefits because they shoulder greater responsibility for the success or failure of the organization as a whole. At the same time, it is clear that far too many leaders get more than they deserve. We must answer such questions as these: How much should top managers be paid? How many additional privileges should they enjoy? What should be the relative difference in pay and benefits between employees and supervisors? What can be done to narrow the current gap in wages and benefits between the top and bottom organizational layers?

The Challenge of Responsibility

Leaders are accountable for the entire group (a sports franchise, a nonprofit, a public relations agency), while followers are largely responsible for their own actions. Determining the extent of a leader's responsibility is difficult, however. That becomes evident when ethical standards are violated. Should Wal-Mart be held responsible for the actions of subcontractors who clean their stores using undocumented workers making subminimum wages? Can we hold the editor of a newspaper responsible for reporters who plagiarize stories? What should be the penalty for military officers if they sanctioned prisoner abuse in Iraq and Afghanistan? Should they receive the same sentences as the soldiers who followed their orders, or harsher ones? How do we respond to managers who fail to follow the codes of ethics they write for their employees? (Turn to Case Study 8.1 for examples of leaders who have failed to take their responsibilities seriously in the past but are taking steps to improve.)

Answers to these questions can vary depending on the particular situation. Nevertheless, there are some general expectations of leaders. If we hope to be considered as responsible leaders, we must take the following steps:

- Admit our duties to followers
- Take reasonable steps to prevent crimes and other follower abuses
- Acknowledge and try to correct ethical problems
- Take responsibility for the consequences of our orders and actions
- Hold ourselves to the same standards as our followers

CASE STUDY 8.1

Ethical Progress in the Boardroom?

Prominent executives get most of the press when organizations misbehave, but boards of directors share much of the blame. Boards are charged with hiring and firing chief operating officers, shaping policies, monitoring financial performance, and representing the interests of shareholders and donors. Board members can prevent criminal activities if they take their duties seriously. Unfortunately, at the beginning of this century, a great many directors did not. Directors at Enron, for example, failed to exercise proper oversight. Many members of the energy giant's board didn't seem to understand the company's operations or its numbers. They rarely challenged management decisions. In fact, the Enron directors helped doom the company by approving exceptions to Enron's code of ethics. These waivers allowed chief financial officer Andrew Fastow to create illegal, off-the-books partnerships that ultimately led to bankruptcy. Directors at WorldCom, like those at Enron, had no inkling of the company's imminent collapse until it was too late. The board of the New York Stock Exchange approved an outrageous pay and benefits package ($140 million as well as a car and driver, private club memberships, and private jet privileges) for former CEO Richard Grasso. However, some NYSE directors later claimed they had no knowledge of the details of the agreement.

A number of factors account for the irresponsible behavior of business and nonprofit boards. In theory, boards are supposed to be independent, but many are beholden to the organization's CEO. They are stacked with friends and relatives of the chief executive who generally rubber-stamp his or her proposals and approve generous raises. For instance, NYSE's Grasso handpicked his compensation committee, which was chaired by Home Depot cofounder Ken Langone, a close friend. Far too many board members have financial ties to the organizations they are supposed to oversee, serving as consultants or suppliers. They don't want to endanger their lucrative arrangements by "rocking the boat," or they may use their board positions to enrich themselves further. A lack of both time and expertise also weakens board oversight. Those who serve on several boards don't have the time and energy to carry out their duties. Individuals who lack financial training sometimes staff board compensation and accounting committees.

The Enron and WorldCom scandals sparked board reform efforts. The SEC now requires companies to disclose whether they have any financial experts on their audit committees. Firms listed on the New York Stock Exchange must have a majority of independent directors who have no connection to the firm. These directors must meet regularly without management present. A smaller, more independent board now governs the NYSE itself. The IRS took a closer look at the generous pay packages given a number of nonprofit CEOs (see the case study "Nonprofit Executive Compensation" in the Introduction). State attorney generals also investigated nonprofit boards that misappropriated donations.

Evidence suggests that boards are making ethical progress. A survey by the Business Roundtable, an association made up of 160 CEOs of the largest companies in the United States, found a significant increase in the number of firms that tie executive pay to long-term performance. Nearly all of the companies surveyed have formal qualifications for directors, and the percentage of companies conducting director evaluations is up sharply. More independent directors serve on boards and boards meet more often in executive session without management present. One half of the Business Roundtable respondents also reported a significant increase in the number and length of audit and compensation committee meetings.

Ethical progress will be limited unless those who serve as directors take their responsibilities seriously. They need to study the company's operations carefully, challenge management proposals, engage in vigorous debate, and act immediately when ethics are violated. The board at Apria Healthcare Group models this kind of activism. Less than a day after learning that the wife of CEO Philip Carter had been hired for a company position, they demanded his resignation and rescinded her job offer.

Discussion Probes

1. Why do we often overlook the role of the board of directors in ethical scandals or, conversely, in ethical organizational successes?

2. Can you think of other factors that might encourage boards to act irresponsibly?

3. Which of the reforms is most important to board performance? Why?

4. What other steps could be taken to make boards of directors more effective?

5. How would you rate the board of your college or university? Why?

6. Have you ever served on a board? Was the group irresponsible or active and informed? What elements contributed to its high or poor performance?

Sources

Borrus, A., McNames, M., Symonds, W., Byrnes, N., & Park, A. (2003, February 2). Reform: Business gets religion. *BusinessWeek,* pp. 40–41.

Brooker, K. (2002, June 24). Fire the chairman of the bored. *Fortune,* pp. 72–73.

Elkind, P. (2004, June 14). The trials of Eliot Spitzer. *Fortune,* pp. 33–35.

Greed is bad. (2004, May 29). *The Economist,* pp. 72–73.

Hempel, J., & Borrus, A. (2004, June 21). Now the nonprofits need cleaning up. *BusinessWeek,* pp. 107–108.

Lavelle, L. (2002, June 17). When directors join CEOs at the trough. *BusinessWeek,* p. 57.

Lavelle, L. (2002, October 7). The best and worst boards. *BusinessWeek,* pp. 104–114.

Marshall, J., & Heffes, E. M. (2006, June). Roundtable survey finds clear trends, *Financial Executive,* p. 10.

The Challenge of Information Management

Leaders generally have access to more information than do followers. They network with other managers, participate in task forces, keep personnel files, receive financial data, get advance notice of new programs, and so forth. Being "in the know" is a mixed blessing. Leaders need lots of data to carry out their tasks. Yet, possessing knowledge raises some sticky ethical dilemmas. The most obvious is deciding whether to tell the truth or to conceal it. Leaders must also determine whether to reveal that they have important information, when to release that information, and to whom. Consider the case of the manager who gets early notice of increases in employee health insurance costs. He is asked to keep this knowledge to himself until the official announcement is made. In the meantime, his subordinates are angered by rumors that health coverage is going to be cut altogether. Does he let it slip that he knows what will happen? Does he immediately try to squelch the rumors, or does he maintain his silence? Finally, how information is gathered is yet another concern. For example, leaders of virtual teams must be careful about how they monitor the online behavior of group members (see the Ethics and Technology feature).

You can use the following behaviors as signs that you or your leaders are failing to meet the ethical challenge of information management:

- Lying, particularly for selfish ends
- Using information solely for personal benefit
- Denying having knowledge that is in one's possession
- Gathering data in a way that violates privacy rights
- Withholding information that followers legitimately need
- Sharing information with the wrong people
- Releasing information at the wrong time (too early or too late)
- Putting followers in moral binds by insisting that they withhold information that others have a right to know

ETHICS AND TECHNOLOGY

E-ethical Leadership in Virtual Project Teams

While all project managers are responsible for seeing that their groups carry out their work in an ethical manner, leaders in virtual project teams face a special set of ethical dilemmas. Project management expert Margaret Lee identifies the following as E-ethical leadership issues. She also outlines responses to help team leaders resolve these ethical dilemmas.

1. *Unethical use of sensitive material.* Computers provide team members with access to confidential information. At the same time, team leaders have access to software that enables them to secretly monitor the computer use of group members.

   Ethical response: Model ethical behavior, and reinforce standards for the collection and use of information. Don't "spy" on team members, but hold private discussions about violations of confidentiality.

2. *Aggressive and disrespectful communication.* Destructive communication is more likely in virtual teams because team members are separated by distance and interact online instead of face to face. Aggressive communication often provokes aggressive responses from other team members.

   Ethical response: Model ethical behavior, and reinforce group standards against disrespectful behavior. Intervene to stop destructive behavior.

(Continued)

(Continued)

3. *Superficial codes of conduct.* Ethical codes are essential for virtual teams because members are physically separated and need clearly stated rules to guide their behavior. Well-constructed codes can also create a sense of community. However, many codes have a minimal impact on behavior. They are easily ignored and hard to enforce in the online environment.

   Ethical response: Develop a code or list of roles and responsibilities during the project planning stage (be sure to address computer policies). Carefully monitor code compliance during the project completion stage. Bring the group together to review the code when significant problems surface.

4. *Social isolation.* Members of virtual teams face physical and social isolation, which may lower self-esteem and undermine their sense of organizational identity.

   Ethical response: Demonstrate concern and care. Fulfill members' need for recognition and inclusion by meeting personally with each individual to discuss personal growth and goals. Require periodic live interpersonal interactions, and provide space at the home office for members to use if they need. Encourage ongoing communication between members about personal interests in addition to project work.

5. *Stakeholder management.* Virtual team members have little personal interaction with outsiders who have an interest in the project. As a result, group members may be less sensitive to the needs and concerns of stakeholders, and the reputation of the team may suffer.

   Ethical response: Engage stakeholders, and build the positive reputation of the project group. Value outsiders as well as team members. Ask for feedback, consult subject-matter experts, update stakeholders on progress, and seek needed organizational resources.

SOURCE: Lee, M. R. (2008). E-ethical leadership for virtual project teams. *International Journal of Project Management, 27,* 456–463.

The Challenge of Consistency

In an ideal world, leaders would treat all followers equally, and all followers would respond in an identical fashion. This is not the case, of course. All too often, leaders act inconsistently, giving more favorable treatment (extra pay and time off, special attention, longer deadlines) to their friends and their favorite subordinates. Followers react to leaders in a variety of ways because of diverse backgrounds, skill levels, and personalities. Those from individualistic cultures respond well to personal rewards, while members of collectivist groups (where group unity is prized) do not. Some followers are better at their tasks than others. In addition, tactics that motivate certain individuals will backfire on their colleagues. Wise coaches, for example, know that there are some players who work harder when yelled at in practice and others who get discouraged. The latter group responds better when quietly taken aside for private instruction.

Obviously, a one-size-fits-all approach to managing followers doesn't work. Throw in the fact that rules may have to bend to fit changing circumstances like weather emergencies and flu epidemics, and you can see why consistency puts ethical demands on leaders. They have to determine (a) how to adapt to individual needs while acting justly; (b) when to bend the rules and for whom; (c) how to adjust to the reality that some followers are going to be more competent than others; and (d) how to be fair to those who aren't as close to them.

Some degree of inconsistency appears inevitable, but leaders generate resentments when they seem to act arbitrarily and unfairly. To be a consistent leader, respond to the individual preferences of each constituent while supporting the principle that all followers deserve the same level of respect and attention. Go out of your way to treat "fringe" subordinates (those who are less skilled, less committed, and less connected to you) justly and compassionately, providing equal access to promotions and other benefits. Also try to be evenhanded in your dealings with outsiders; treat your opponents as well as your friends with respect.

The Challenge of Loyalty

Leaders have to balance a variety of loyalties, weighing their commitments to employees, suppliers, families, investors, their professions, the larger society, and the environment. To be a model leader, put the needs of the larger community ahead of selfish interests (see Chapter 12). Reject decisions that benefit you and your organization at the expense of such outside constituencies as consumers, neighborhoods, local governments, and fellow professionals. You will also face the challenge of honoring the loyalty that followers and others place in you. Followers trust leaders to act in their best interests, and the public trusts leaders to act as responsible members of the community. Many organizational leaders fail to live up to this challenge. Managers at the Imperial Food Products chicken-processing plant, for example, betrayed the trust of workers by padlocking exit doors and failing to install a sprinkler system. When fire broke out in 1991, 25 employees died and 56 were injured. Severely damaged, the plant closed down, and the town of Hamlet, North Carolina, lost its largest employer.[11]

The Shadow Side of Leadership

As we've seen, failure to meet the ethical challenges of the leadership role can lead to a variety of misbehaviors—abuse of power and privilege, irresponsibility, deception, invasion of privacy, injustice, and misplaced and broken loyalties. Recognizing the dark or "shadow" side of leadership can help us become more ethical leaders.[12] By understanding the nature and origins of destructive leadership, we are less likely to cast shadows ourselves (see Chapter 2). In this section, we'll examine four perspectives on the negative face of leadership.

Bad Leadership

Harvard political scientist Barbara Kellerman is critical of the positive bias of most leadership research and training. To scholars and laypeople alike, leadership has a positive connotation. After all, we wouldn't take leadership classes and attend leadership workshops if we thought that to be a leader was undesirable! Kellerman believes that limiting leadership solely to good leadership ignores the reality that a great many leaders engage in destructive behaviors.[13] Until we acknowledge that reality, our attempts to become better leaders are likely to fall short. "I take it as a given that we promote good leadership not by ignoring bad leadership," Kellerman says, "nor by presuming that it is immutable, but rather by attacking it as we would a disease that is always pernicious and sometimes deadly."[14]

According to Kellerman, bad leaders can be ineffective, unethical, or both ineffective and unethical. She identifies seven types of bad leaders:

Incompetent Leaders. These leaders don't have the motivation or ability to sustain effective action. They may lack emotional or academic intelligence, for example, or may be careless, distracted, or sloppy. Some can't function under stress, and their communication and decisions suffer as a result. Former International Olympic Committee president Juan Antonio Samaranch (1961–2000) is one example of an incompetent leader. Toward the end of his tenure, he turned a blind eye to commercialism, drug scandals, and corruption in the Olympic movement. Federal Emergency Management Agency (FEMA) director Michael Brown was widely considered to be an incompetent leader following Hurricane Katrina. Under his leadership, FEMA's slow, inadequate response led to unnecessary deaths and widespread lawlessness.

Rigid Leaders. Rigid leaders may be competent, but they are unyielding and cannot accept new ideas, new information, or changing conditions. Thabo Mbeki is one such leader. After becoming president of South Africa in 1999, he insisted that HIV did not cause AIDS and withheld antiretroviral dugs from HIV-positive women. These medications would have dramatically cut the transmission of the disease to their babies. Leaders in the U.S. banking industry proved inflexible prior to the mortgage crisis. They believed that home prices would continue to rise despite evidence that the housing market was overpriced and overbuilt.

Intemperate Leaders. Intemperate leaders lack self-control and are enabled by followers who don't want to intervene or can't. Marion Barry, Jr.'s political career demonstrates intemperate leadership in action. Barry served as mayor of Washington, D.C., from 1979 to 1991. He ignored widespread corruption in his administration, perhaps in part because he was busy cheating on his wife and doing drugs. Barry was convicted of possessing crack cocaine and served 6 months in jail. After being released from prison, he was elected to the city council in 1992 and was reelected as mayor in 1994. During his administrations, the district's schools and public services deteriorated while the murder rate soared. More recently, a number of prominent state and national politicians have demonstrated a lack of sexual self-control. Senator John Ensign of Nevada, South Carolina Governor Mark Sanford, and former vice-presidential candidate John Edwards, among others, all admitted to having extramarital affairs.

Callous Leaders. The callous leader is uncaring or unkind, ignoring or downplaying the needs, wants, and wishes of followers. Former hotel magnate Leona Helmsley personified the callous leader. She earned the epithet "The Queen of Mean" by screaming at employees and firing them for minor infractions like dirty fingernails. Helmsley later served time for tax evasion. (She once quipped, "Only the little people pay taxes.") BP oil executive Tony Hayward appeared callous during the Gulf oil spill. Several weeks into the crisis, he complained that he "wanted his life back," a comment that came across as extremely insensitive to the families of the victims who had died in the oil rig explosion that triggered the spill. Later, he took time off to participate in a yacht race with his son.

Corrupt Leaders. These leaders and at least some of their followers lie, cheat, and steal. They put self-interest ahead of public interest. Former United Way of America chief William Aramony was an exemplar of this type of leader. Aramony used United Way funds to buy and furnish an apartment for his girlfriend and to pay for vacations. His top financial officers helped him hide his illegal actions. Aramony and his colleagues were convicted on fraud-related charges. Financier Bernie Madoff bilked billions from investors, spending a portion of the money on maintaining his lavish lifestyle (he owned a penthouse in Manhattan, a mansion in Florida, and a villa in France).

Insular Leaders. The insular leader draws a clear boundary between the welfare of his or her immediate group or organization and that of outsiders. Former President Bill Clinton behaved in an insular manner when he didn't intervene in the Rwandan genocide that took the lives of 800,000 to 1,000,000 people in 1994. He later traveled to Africa to apologize for failing to act even though he had reliable information describing how thousands of Tutsis were being hacked to death by their Hutu neighbors.

Evil Leaders. Evil leaders commit atrocities, using their power to inflict severe physical or psychological harm. Foday Sankoh is one example of an evil leader. He started a civil war in Sierra Leone in 1991. His army, which included many boy soldiers, carried out a campaign of rape and murder. The rebels were also known for chopping off the legs, hands, and arms of innocent civilians. Former Iraqi leader Saddam Hussein is another example of evil leadership in action. He executed his enemies and used poison gas to kill thousands of his citizens.

Kellerman makes several suggestions to leaders who want to be both effective and ethical:

1. *Limit your tenure.* If we stay in power too long, we are more likely to become complacent, overreach, lose touch with reality, and lose touch with our moral foundation.

2. *Share power.* Centralized power is more likely to be abused. Delegate and collaborate instead.

3. *Don't believe your own hype.* Far too many leaders begin to believe press accounts of their greatness. They forget that they are fallible human beings.

4. *Get real and stay real.* Bad leaders block out reality, ignoring corruption in their organizations as well as their addictions, self-destructive behaviors, and crimes.

5. *Compensate for your weaknesses.* Recognize your limitations, and surround yourself with followers and other leaders who can help you compensate for these deficiencies.

6. *Stay balanced.* Avoid becoming a workaholic. Spend time with family and friends.

7. *Remember the mission.* Put the mission of the organization (particularly if it is focused on serving others) above your own desires.

8. *Stay healthy.* Take care of your physical and mental health, and seek professional counsel when needed.

9. *Develop a personal support system.* Don't drive off friends, family, and associates who will always tell you the truth.

10. *Be creative.* Don't get stuck in the past, but think of new options for solving problems.

11. *Know and control your appetites.* Don't let your hunger for power, money, success, or sex take over your life.

12. *Be reflective.* Take time for self-refection. Get to know yourself, and develop self-control and good habits.

Toxic Leadership

Claremont Graduate University professor Jean Lipman-Blumen introduces the term *toxic* when addressing the shadow side of leadership.[15] Toxic leaders engage in the destructive behaviors and demonstrate the dysfunctional characteristics described in Table 8.1. These behaviors and qualities cause significant harm to leaders, groups, organizations, and societies. Toxic leaders appear in every segment of society and in every region of the globe. Examples of toxic corporate leaders include "Chainsaw" Al Dunlap, former CEO of Sunbeam, who ruthlessly eliminated costs and personnel; "junk bond king" Michael Milken, whose illegal financial activities ruined the firm

Table 8.1 The Behaviors and Personal Characteristics of Toxic Leaders

Destructive Behaviors	Toxic Qualities
Leaving followers worse off	Lack of integrity
Violating human rights	Insatiable ambition
Feeding followers' illusions; creating dependence	Enormous egos
Playing to the basest fears and needs of followers	Arrogance
Stifling criticism; enforcing compliance	Amorality (unable to discern right from wrong)
Misleading followers	Avarice (greed)
Subverting ethical organizational structures and processes	Reckless disregard for the costs of their actions

Destructive Behaviors	Toxic Qualities
Engaging in unethical, illegal, and criminal acts	Cowardice (won't make tough choices)
Building totalitarian regimes	Failure to understand problems
Failing to nurture followers, including successors	Incompetent in key leadership situations
Setting constituents against one another	
Encouraging followers to hate or destroy others	
Identifying scapegoats	
Making themselves indispensable	
Ignoring or promoting incompetence, cronyism, and corruption	

SOURCE: Adapted from Lipman-Blumen, J. (2005). *The allure of toxic leaders: Why we follow destructive bosses and corrupt politicians—And how we can survive them.* Oxford, UK: Oxford University Press, pp. 19–23.

Drexel Burnham Lambert; and A. Alfred Taubman, chairman of the auction house Sotheby's, who engaged in price fixing. Toxic nonprofit leaders include TV evangelist Jim Bakker (who served prison time for fraud) as well as priests who abused children and the bishops who protected them. Toxic political figures include former FBI chief J. Edgar Hoover and former House of Representatives majority leader Tom DeLay, who was convicted of money laundering.

Lipman-Blumen is most concerned with how followers can keep themselves from being taken in by toxic leaders (see the discussion of toxic followership in the next chapter). However, she does make suggestions that can help us recognize the early signs of toxicity in ourselves. Ask yourself these questions:

Do I inflict harm on my enemies or competitors first and then on others in the organization?

Do I demonstrate disdain for others?

Have I changed my lifestyle and circle of friends, avoiding my old acquaintances and colleagues?

Do I keep my own counsel or take advice from just a few others in my inner circle?

Do I use others to do my dirty work and then get rid of them?

Have I begun to mistreat the lowest or weakest members of the group?

Have I begun to engage in excess (lavish spending and lifestyle)?

Have I become evasive, denying accountability for results?

Do I blame others for my decisions and actions?

Am I acting in my self-interest instead of the organization's interest?

Do I attempt to disguise unethical behavior as noble and altruistic?

Destructive Leadership

Norwegian researcher Ståle Einarsen and his colleagues offer a typology of destructive leadership behaviors specifically focused on the organizational context.[16] They emphasize that most leaders are not completely good or bad, toxic or nontoxic, but engage in a mix of constructive and destructive behaviors. Destructive leadership is directed primarily at subordinates, the organization, or both. Based on these dimensions, Einarsen's group identifies five types of leadership behaviors.

Constructive leadership behavior serves the legitimate interests of the organization while supporting followers through consideration, inspiration, and empowerment. Constructive actions are designed to motivate subordinates to make the best use of organizational resources in order to achieve ethical, shared goals.

Tyrannical leadership behavior achieves organizational objectives at the expense of subordinates. Tyrannical leaders may have excellent technical skills, may be highly efficient, and may successfully complete assignments. Nonetheless, they manipulate, humiliate, deceive, bully, and otherwise abuse followers as they help the organization carry out its mission.

Derailed leadership behavior is both antiorganization and antisubordinate. Such activities simultaneously undermine the organization and followers. Derailed leaders engage in such antiorganizational behaviors as taking unauthorized time off, committing fraud, and stealing, while at the same time attacking followers.

Supportive-disloyal leadership behavior consists of activities that benefit subordinates at the cost of the organization. Supportive-disloyal leaders are very supportive of their followers but deprive the organization of resources. For example, a supervisor may grant too much time off to employees or may look the other way when workers loaf or steal. Supportive-disloyal leaders may also have a different vision or strategy from the organization's and may encourage workers to pursue those objectives instead of the organization's official mission. In other cases, these leaders are well liked by followers at the same time that they engage in theft, fraud, and embezzlement.

Laissez-faire leadership behaviors are more passive than active. Laissez-faire leaders avoid interaction with followers, delay decisions, and make little attempt to motivate followers or to reach organizational objectives. Their inaction reduces employee satisfaction and commitment and undermines collective performance.

Using their category system, Einarsen and his colleagues tried to determine the relative frequency of constructive and destructive behaviors. They discovered that constructive behaviors are far more common ("Most leaders behave constructively most of the time"), but the majority of the respondents they surveyed noted at least one type of negative behavior in their immediate supervisors.[17] This means that as leaders, we have the potential to be a force for both good and bad. We should identify those factors (stress, lack of skills, organizational pressure) that encourage us to engage in counterproductive behaviors and take steps to limit their effects on us.

Selfish Leadership

Concern for others is essential for ethical leadership, since leaders exercise influence on behalf of others. Unfortunately, leadership roles, which call for selfless behavior—like understanding and meeting the needs of followers, taking personal risks, and self-sacrifice—are also highly attractive to selfish individuals who focus on their own needs instead.[18] Using their positions for personal gain, they steal, lie, bully, and dominate followers, break promises, and so on. Selfish leaders can be classified as impulsive, narcissistic, or Machiavellian.

Impulsive, selfish people are more likely to seek powerful positions and to be identified as leaders by others. They are often extraverts who come across as charismatic and energetic. Once in power, impulsive individuals are free to fill their selfish desires. They consume more of the group's resources, are more likely to engage in sexual aggression, and frequently violate social norms. Selfish leaders justify their actions by narrowly defining morality. They put more emphasis on individual rights and freedoms than on obligations and duties to others. They want to allocate resources based on contributions (which favors them) rather than according to needs (which favors less powerful individuals), and typically fail to take into consideration other points of view when deciding on ethical issues. Sadly, organizational environments can reinforce the selfish tendencies of leaders. Powerful leaders often silence the criticisms of followers. Unchallenged, they are able to exert even more control over subordinates. Over time, low-power individuals adjust their emotions and attitudes to match those of powerful people.

Narcissism, like impulsiveness, is common among leaders.[19] The word *narcissism* has its origins in an ancient Greek fable. In this tale, Narcissus falls in love with the image of himself he sees reflected in a pond. Like their ancient namesake, modern-day narcissists are self-absorbed and think highly of themselves. They are attracted to leadership roles because they like to be the center of attention. They are often named to leadership positions because they are socially skilled; they make a positive first impression because they come across as bold and self-confident. Once in power, they are effective at holding on to their authority (which they believe they deserve). Narcissistic leaders engage in a wide range of unethical behaviors. They claim special privileges, demand admiration and obedience, dismiss negative feedback, respond defensively and aggressively if their egos are threatened, abuse power for their personal ends, ignore the welfare of others, and exercise an autocratic leadership style. Their unrealistic visions and expectations put the organization at risk. For example, some retiring CEOs want to "go out with a bang," so they involve their firms in mergers and acquisitions that may undermine the long-term health of their firms.[20]

Machiavellianism is a third manifestation of self-centered leadership. Psychologists Richard Christie and Florence Geis first identified Machiavellianism as a personality factor in 1970. Christie and Geis named this trait after the Italian philosopher Niccolò Machiavelli, who argued in *The Prince* that political leaders should maintain a virtuous public image but use whatever means necessary (ethical or unethical) to achieve their ends.[21] Highly Machiavellian individuals are skilled at manipulating others for their own ends. As a result, they are more likely to end up in leadership roles. They have a better grasp of their abilities and of reality than narcissists but, like their narcissistic colleagues, they engage in lots of self-promotion and are emotionally cold and prone to aggressive behavior. Machiavellian leaders often engage in deception because they want to generate positive impressions while they get their way. They may pretend to be concerned for others, for example, or assist in a project solely because they want to get in good with the boss. Machiavellians often enjoy a good deal of personal success (organizational advancement, higher salaries) because they are so skilled at manipulation and at disguising their true intentions. Nonetheless, Machiavellian leaders put their groups in danger. They may be less qualified to lead than others who are not as skilled as they in impression management. They are more likely to engage in unethical practices that put the organization at risk because they want to succeed at any cost. If followers suspect that their supervisors are manipulating them, they are less trusting and cooperative, which can make the organization less productive.[22]

Combating selfishness is an important ethical responsibility. To start, we need to look for selfish tendencies in ourselves, asking why we want to take leadership roles and exercise power. We need to determine if we are overestimating our abilities, demanding admiration and obedience, dismissing negative feedback, manipulating followers for our own purposes, and so on. We also need to keep selfish individuals from assuming leadership roles.[23] Impulsive individuals, narcissists, and Machiavellians all have excellent self-presentation skills, so we need to be careful not to be taken in by initial impressions. Employ objective criteria when making hiring and promotion decisions (see our discussion of impression management in Chapter 5). Look for predictors of failure in previous positions, like changing jobs frequently; ask questions that may reveal selfish tendencies, such as blaming others for previous failures and claiming all the credit for success. Use personality instruments to identify narcissistic and Machiavellian personality traits. (You may also want to complete these instruments yourself to determine if you have these characteristics.)

We can curb the selfish tendencies of current leaders (in others or in ourselves) by building in checks and balances on the use of power and by making leaders accountable for their actions. Performance reviews should be designed to reveal potential trouble spots like employee mistreatment and defensiveness. Those working for selfish leaders should carefully document abuses and form coalitions with others to confront them. Encourage employee development and succession planning. (Self-centered leaders are not likely to want to develop or promote others, because they are threatened by competent coworkers and fear the loss of power.) Create a culture that emphasizes honesty and collaboration over competition and self-promotion.

Normative Leadership Theories

Normative leadership theories tell leaders how to act. They are designed to help us manage our ethical duties when we take on leadership roles and can help us avoid the shadow side of leadership. Each encourages selfless behavior, urging leaders to focus on the needs of followers, raise the moral performance of the group, address community needs, avoid manipulative behaviors, and so on. While specifically focused on the leader–follower relationship, these approaches draw heavily from general ethical perspectives, character ethics, and other material presented in earlier chapters.

Transformational Leadership

Since the late 1970s, the transformational approach has emerged as the dominant perspective in leadership studies. Former presidential advisor, political scientist, and historian James MacGregor Burns laid the groundwork for this approach in his book *Leadership*.[24] Burns identified two forms of leadership, which he labeled transactional and transformational. *Transactional leadership* is based on leader-member exchange. Leaders trade money, benefits, and recognition for the labor and obedience of followers. They emphasize values that make routine transactions go smoothly—responsibility, fairness, and honesty—and take a utilitarian approach to ethical decision making, judging the morality of choices based on their outcomes. The underlying system remains unchanged. *Transformational leadership* is more powerful and inspiring. Transformational leaders speak to higher-level needs—the need to belong, to feel good about oneself, and to reach one's full potential. They spotlight values that are more likely to mobilize and energize followers, like equality, liberty, justice, and freedom. In the process, these leaders change the very nature of the group, the organization, or the society.

Burns sketched the broad outline of transformational leadership; it was up to other researchers to fill in the details. Bernard Bass, Bruce Avolio, and their colleagues identified seven dimensions of transactional and transformational leadership.[25] Transactional leaders rely on *contingent reward* and *management-by-exception*. They provide rewards and recognition for acceptable performance while disciplining followers who fall below performance standards. The poorest transactional leaders are *passive-avoidant* or *laissez-faire*. They are inactive, failing to provide goals or standards or to clarify expectations.

Transformational leaders engage in the following:

1. *Idealized Influence.* Transformational leaders serve as admired role models for followers. They put the needs of others first, engage in self-sacrifice, share risks with followers, and act in a way that is consistent with the group's values and principles. Such leaders set high standards and look for the good in followers.

2. *Individualized Consideration.* Transformational leaders act as coaches and mentors, continually encouraging follower development. They provide learning opportunities along with a supportive climate. Their coaching, mentoring, and teaching efforts are tailored to the personal concerns of each follower.

3. *Inspirational Motivation.* Transforming leaders motivate and inspire through providing meaning and challenge to the work of followers. They are enthusiastic and optimistic, arousing team spirit and focusing follower attention on desirable organizational visions. They have the courage to take risks and keep their focus (and that of the group) on a common purpose.

4. *Intellectual Stimulation.* Transformational leaders foster creativity and innovation in followers by questioning assumptions, reframing situations, and tackling old problems in new ways. They don't criticize mistakes or new approaches. At the same time, they are open to creative ideas that may challenge their opinions.

Burns believed that leaders were either transactional or transformational, but later investigators found that highly effective leaders use *both* transactional and transformational tactics. Transformational leaders may inspire, but they aren't afraid to set standards and monitor performance as well as issue rewards and punishments.

Transforming leadership has attracted so much attention largely because it generates outstanding results. Transformational leaders are more successful than their transactional counterparts in a variety of settings—sales organizations, military units, schools, large corporations.[26] However, Burns left no doubt that transforming leadership rests on an ethical foundation. "Such leadership," stated Burns, "occurs when one or more persons engage with others in such a way that leaders and followers raise one another to higher levels of motivation and morality."[27] There is a growing body of evidence that demonstrates that Burns was right: transforming leaders are moral leaders. Studies have found that transformational leaders exhibit the following characteristics:[28]

- Display higher levels of moral reasoning
- Are more altruistic
- Receive high integrity ratings
- Model ethical behaviors and actions
- Are rated as more ethical by followers
- Establish organizational practices (e.g., performance and reward systems) that reinforce moral behavior
- Create positive ethical climates
- Help to improve the moral reasoning of followers
- Are effective at leading ethical organizational turnarounds

One caution is in order. Individuals can use transformational tactics to reach immoral ends. When it comes to idealized influence, some leaders appear to be honest and supportive of their people, but privately they are unreliable and all too willing to sacrifice their followers for their own goals. They engage in inspirational motivation by appealing to the worst in people—their fears, anger, and insecurities. Their approach to intellectual stimulation relies on false assumptions and appeals to their own authority instead of on reason and dialogue. Instead of coaching and mentoring followers into leaders, the individualized attention they give followers encourages dependency and blind obedience.

Bernard Bass adopted the terms *authentic* and *pseudo-transformational* to distinguish between ethical and unethical transformational leaders.[29] Authentic transformational leaders are altruistic, genuinely concerned for others and the purposes of the organization as a whole. They channel their energies in constructive ways to serve the greater good. They permit their followers free choice in the hope that the followers will voluntarily commit themselves to worthy moral principles. Pseudo-transformational leaders provide a sharp contrast. They are ultimately self-centered. Instead of caring for others, they may secretly despise them. They use power to manipulate others for personal ends instead of on behalf of shared objectives.

Debate over whether or not there is a distinction between ethical and unethical transformational leaders continues. (Application Project 4 gives you the opportunity to discuss this issue with classmates.) Nevertheless, if you want to become a more ethical, effective leader, transformational leadership has a lot to offer. The goal of this approach is to raise the level of morality of the group or organization, encouraging those in both leadership and followership roles to set and meet higher ethical standards. In the process of pursuing this objective, employees engage in higher-level moral reasoning, and the moral climate and culture of the entire organization improves. At the same time, workers achieve better results. The fact that transforming leadership consists of a set of behaviors means that anyone can act as a transformational leader by adopting these practices. You can employ transformational behaviors in a variety of contexts (work, sports, the family, volunteer activities) as well as in virtual groups.[30] In addition, transforming leadership appears to have universal appeal. A study conducted in 62 countries found that effective leaders in all of these cultures exhibit transformational behaviors. They have high integrity, demonstrate foresight, and inspire others by being positive, dynamic, encouraging and by building their confidence.[31]

Servant Leadership

The servant leadership model is based on the premise that leaders should put the needs of followers before their own needs. This approach has its roots in both Eastern and Western thought. Taoist philosophers encouraged leaders to act like children and humble valleys instead of mountains.[32] Jesus told his disciples, "Whoever wants to become great among you must be your servant, and whoever wants to be first must be slave of all."[33]

Current interest in leaders as servants can be traced back to management expert Robert Greenleaf. He coined the term *servant leader* in 1970 to describe those whose primary concern is the growth and development of their followers.[34] Greenleaf later founded a nonprofit organization to promote servant leadership. A number of businesses (Toro Company, TD Industries, The Container Store, Synovus), nonprofit groups, and community leadership programs have adopted this approach. Other notable advocates of servant leadership include James Autry, Margaret Wheatley, Max DePree, and Peter Block.

Much of the early support for the theory of servant leadership was anecdotal, consisting of examples of servant-leaders and lists of servant characteristics. For example, Larry Spears, director of the Greenleaf Center for Servant Leadership, identified the following ten characteristics of the servant leader drawn from Greenleaf's writings:[35]

1. *Listening.* Servant leaders put a high priority on listening. They listen intently to others to identify and clarify the needs of the group. They listen to themselves by hearing their inner voices and analyzing what their bodies, minds, and spirits are communicating. Listening to the self, combined with periods of reflection, promotes personal growth.

2. *Empathy.* Servant leaders seek both to understand and to empathize with followers. They accept coworkers as unique human beings and assume that others act out of good intentions. However, at the same time, servant-leaders refuse to accept destructive behavior or poor performance.

3. *Healing.* Servant leaders bring followers to wholeness, helping them recover from emotional injury and to experience the personal ethical development described in Chapter 2.

4. *Awareness.* Servant leaders are attuned to elements of a situation as well as to their own thoughts and emotions. Such awareness heightens their sensitivity to the ethical dimension of situations.

5. *Persuasion.* Servant leaders rely on persuasion rather than on positional power when making decisions in the organizational setting. While authoritarian leadership relies on coercion, servant leadership builds group consensus.

6. *Conceptualization.* Servant leaders master the day-to-day operations but also engage in big-picture, long-range thinking. They create an attractive long-term vision for the organization.

7. *Foresight.* Servant leaders can foresee or anticipate the likely outcome of a situation, such as the possible negative consequences of an ethical choice or marketing plan. This ability also enables them to understand the lessons of the past and the realities of the present.

8. *Stewardship.* Servant leaders act as stewards who "hold something in trust for another." Greenleaf believed that CEOs, executive staffs, and boards of directors are particularly responsible for holding their institutions in trust for the greater good of society as a whole. Stewardship is a key element of servant leadership because it focuses on serving the needs of others.

9. *Commitment to the Growth of People.* Servant leaders believe in the intrinsic value of people that extends beyond their roles as workers. They seek to promote the personal, professional, and spiritual growth of all employees through, for instance, providing development funds, soliciting suggestions from everyone, and involving workers in the decision-making process.

10. *Building Community.* Servant leaders recognize that the influence of organizations has supplanted that of local communities. As a result, they seek to build communities of employees. In this way, a sense of community is rebuilt in society as a whole, one organization at a time.

More recently, scholars have begun to subject servant leadership to empirical testing. They have developed servant leadership questionnaires like the one in the following Self-Assessment and then have used these tools to determine how servant leadership influences followers, organizational culture, and organizational performance. While the specific attributes of servant leaders vary between studies, there are some common themes. First, servant leadership is person centered or altruistic. Servant leaders are genuinely concerned about their followers as well as their organizations and communities (reflecting an ethic of care). They measure their success based on what happens in the lives of their followers, not on what they themselves have accomplished. Concern for followers, organizational stakeholders, and society comes before concern for self. Putting the needs of others first discourages shadowy behavior. Other-centered leaders are less likely to accumulate power and privilege for themselves, to lie to followers, to take advantage of them, or to act inconsistently or irresponsibly.

Second, servant leadership promotes equity or justice. Servant leaders distribute power by delegating authority to carry out important tasks, by sharing information, by engaging in collaborative decision making, and by encouraging constituents to develop and exercise their talents. (See Chapter 5 for more information on empowerment.) Servant leaders are also concerned with distributing rewards fairly. When the company as a whole does well, for example, both employees and executives receive bonuses.

Third, servant leadership rests on ethical character. Servant-leaders possess such virtues as empathy, integrity, honesty, and wisdom. They set a high moral example for the rest of the organization through their consistent ethical behavior.

Four, servant leadership incorporates stewardship. Servant leaders work on behalf of others—employees, shareholders, communities. They recognize that their positions and organizations are entrusted to them. (Turn to the case study, "The Looting of Bell, California," at the end of the chapter to see what happens when leaders fail to act as responsible stewards.)

Practicing servant leadership has a positive influence on followers as well as on collective performance.[36] Subordinates working under servant leaders are more likely to engage in organizational citizenship behaviors, to have a greater sense of self-efficacy, to believe their needs are being met, to report higher job satisfaction, and to say they will stay with their organizations. They also spend more time building relationships with customers and responding to consumer needs. Employees who work for servant leaders believe that they are being treated fairly, which encourages them to work hard. In sum, servant leadership, like transformational leadership, can help us become more ethical and effective leaders. Putting others first helps us meet the ethical challenges of leadership while avoiding destructive leadership behaviors. At the same time, our organizations benefit.

SELF-ASSESSMENT

Servant Leadership Questionnaire

Respond to each of the following items on a scale of 1 to 5 (1 = strongly disagree, 5 = strongly agree). The scale asks you to evaluate a department manager, but you can substitute another type of leader instead (CEO, instructor, team leader). Total scores can range from 14 to 70. The higher the score, the more this leader demonstrates servant leader behaviors and attributes.

1. My department manager spends the time to form quality relationships with department employees.
2. My department manager creates a sense of community among department employees.
3. My department manager's decisions are influenced by department employees' input.
4. My department manager tries to reach consensus among department employees on important decisions.
5. My department manager is sensitive to department employees' responsibilities outside the workplace.
6. My department manager makes the personal development of department employees a priority.
7. My department manager holds department employees to high ethical standards.
8. My department manager does what she or he promises to do.
9. My department manager balances concern for day-to-day details with projections for the future.
10. My department manager displays wide-ranging knowledge and interests in finding solutions to work problems.
11. My department manager makes me feel like I work with him/her, not for him/her.
12. My department manager works hard at finding ways to help others be the best they can be.
13. My department manager encourages department employees to be involved in community service and volunteer activities outside of work.
14. My department manager emphasizes the importance of giving back to the community.

SOURCE: Ehrhart, M. G. (2004). Leadership and procedural justice climate as antecedents of unit-level organizational citizenship behavior. *Personnel Psychology, 57*(1), p. 93. Used by permission.

Authentic Leadership

Authentic leadership theory (ALT) is an offshoot of positive psychology and positive organizational scholarship. Positive psychologists, as we saw in Chapter 2, believe in developing people's strengths instead of trying to fix their weaknesses; positive organizational scholars try to bring out the collective best in organizations. Fred Luthans, Bruce Avolio, and their colleagues assert that this positive approach is also a more productive way to develop leaders.[37] Traditional development programs address deficiencies in a leader's skills, knowledge, and motivations. Failure and other negative events are seen as critical to leader development. ALT proponents argue, instead, that we ought to build on the strengths of individuals and look for positive moments that foster their growth as leaders.

To Luthans, Avolio, and others, authenticity is the "root construct," or principle, underlying all forms of positive leadership. Authentic leaders know themselves well, and they behave in ways that are consistent with their beliefs. (In other words, they "walk their talk.") Self-awareness, balanced processing, internalized moral perspective, and relational transparency all play an important role in authentic leadership.[38] *Self-awareness* means being conscious of, and trusting in, motives, desires, feelings, and self-concept. Self-aware people know their strengths and weaknesses, personal traits, and emotional patterns, and they are able to use this knowledge when interacting with others and their environments. *Balanced processing* denotes remaining objective when receiving information. Inauthentic responses involve denying, distorting, or ignoring negative feedback. Authentic leaders accept their blind spots and failings and try to address them. *Internalized moral perspective* refers to regulating behavior according to internal standards and values, not according to what others say. Authentic leaders act in harmony with what they believe and do not change their behavior to please others or to earn rewards or avoid punishment. *Relational transparency* is presenting the authentic self to others, openly expressing true thoughts and feelings appropriate for the situation. (See Ethics in Action 8.1 for sample questionnaire items designed to measure each of these dimensions.)

Authentic leadership has a strong moral component.[39] Not only has authenticity been seen as a virtue since ancient Greece and Rome, but ALT theorists define authentic leaders as "those who are deeply aware of how they think and behave and are perceived by others as being aware of their own and others' values/moral perspectives, knowledge, and strengths; aware of the context in which they operate; and who are confident, hopeful, optimistic, resilient, and of high moral character."[40] Such leaders acknowledge the ethical responsibilities of their roles, can recognize and evaluate ethical issues, and take moral actions that are thoroughly grounded in their beliefs and values. Proponents of authentic leadership argue that it is impossible to achieve a high level of authenticity without reaching an advanced level of moral development and holding to high ethical standards.[41]

Critical incidents called *trigger events* play an important role in the development of moral component of authentic leadership.[42] These events can be positive or negative and promote introspection and reflection. Trigger experiences are often dramatic (facing racial hatred, visiting a third-world village). However, authentic leadership theorists posit that, more often than not, these experiences are more mundane—for example, reading an important book, seeing a powerful film, serving under an authentic leader. Sometimes a series of small events, such as several minor successes or failures, can have a cumulative effect, triggering significant thought. Leaders develop a clearer sense of who they are, including their standards of right and wrong, through these experiences. They build a store of moral knowledge that they can draw on to make better choices when facing future ethical dilemmas.

Authentic leadership produces a number of positive effects in followers.[43] Followers are likely to emulate the example of authentic leaders who set a high ethical standard. They feel empowered to make ethical choices on their own without the input of the leader. They align themselves with the values of the organization and become authentic moral agents themselves. (I'll have more to say about authentic followership in the next chapter.) Leader authenticity fosters feelings of self-efficacy (competence), hope, optimism, and resilience in followers, what positive psychologists refer to as *psychological capital*.[44] Followers who believe in their abilities are more likely to take initiative and to achieve more, even in the face of difficult circumstances. Feelings of hope and optimism foster their will power. Resiliency enables followers to recover more quickly from setbacks.

Authenticity also pays dividends for leaders. Followers provide feedback that increases the leaders' self-knowledge. They reward authentic leaders by giving them more latitude to make difficult, unpopular choices and by getting more done. (Followers are also more productive because they have to waste less time and energy figuring out what their leaders will do next.) In addition, authentic leaders engender more trust; and trust, in turn, has been linked to higher organizational productivity and performance. Those who work in a trusting environment are more productive because they have high job satisfaction, enjoy better relationships, stay focused on their tasks, feel committed to the group, sacrifice for the greater organizational good, and are willing to go beyond their job descriptions to help out fellow employees.[45]

The benefits of authenticity demonstrate the truth of the familiar adages "Know thyself" and "To thine own self be true." Avolio and Luthans encourage you to look to the past, present, and future in order to build your self-awareness, which, in turn, will promote your development as an authentic leader.[46] First, reflect on your past experiences (both good and bad) to see what you can learn from them, and then develop ways to improve. For example, if you successfully managed a conflict with a roommate, consider what that experience can teach you about handling a conflict at work, and put those insights into practice. Next, actively monitor how you currently think and feel and how your actions influence others. Build your self-confidence or self-efficacy through visualization and by observing positive role models; hold high positive expectations for yourself (employ the Galatea effect; see Chapter 5). Finally, focus on the future, identifying emerging trends that may impact you and your organizations. You are more likely to spot such developments if you read outside of your field of study, attend seminars, and develop social networks.

ETHICS IN ACTION 8.1 AUTHENTIC LEADERSHIP QUESTIONNAIRE SAMPLE ITEMS

Self-Awareness

1. Seeks feedback to improve interactions with others.

2. Accurately describes how others view his or her capabilities.

Relational Transparency

3. Says exactly what he or she means.

4. Is willing to admit mistakes when they are made.

Internalized Moral Perspective

5. Demonstrates beliefs that are consistent with actions.

6. Makes decisions based on his/her core beliefs.

Balanced Processing

7. Solicits views that challenge his or her deeply held positions.

8. Listens carefully to different points of view before coming to conclusions.

SOURCE: Walumbwa, F. O., Avolio, B. J., Gardner, W. L., Wernsing, T. S., & Peterson, S. J. (2008). Authentic leadership: Development and validation of a theory-based measure. *Journal of Management, 34*(1), 89–126. Used by permission.

Postindustrial and Relational Leadership

In 1991, University of San Diego professor Joseph Rost published an influential critique of the field of leadership studies.[47] Rost complained that popular leadership theories are too person centered. Success in the transformational approach, for example, depends almost entirely upon the skill of a leader who sets direction, exercises influence, encourages commitment, helps the group adapt to change, and so on. Rost argued that leader-centered approaches are ill suited to an increasingly complex, interconnected, global society. Successful leadership in the postindustrial 21st century will be based on collaboration, consensus, diversity, dealing with ambiguity, and participation. These characteristics emerge not from the qualities or behaviors of individual leaders but out of the relationships between leaders and followers that enable them to get things done.

Rost offers what he calls a postindustrial definition of leadership as an alternative to traditional leadership models. *Postindustrial leadership* highlights the partnership between leaders and followers. Leadership, according to Rost, "is an influence relationship among leaders and followers who intend real changes that reflect their mutual purposes."[48] Influence in the leadership relationship is noncoercive and flows in many different directions (leaders to followers, followers to leaders, followers to followers, and leaders to leaders). Followers are active partners with leaders. Even though leaders have more power to influence, they work together with constituents. The parties in the relationship work to bring about substantial changes and come to a common agreement about what they hold to be important.

Ethics in postindustrial leadership is process focused. Professor Rost argues that leaders need to generate ethical *products* or content (decisions, policies, programs) as they follow ethical *processes*. Influence in the leader-follower relationship should be based on persuasion, not coercion (physical force, psychological intimidation, obedience to authority), and followers must be free to choose whether or not to participate. Goals ought to be jointly created through discussion and argument. Rost concludes by offering the following ethical standard: "The leadership process is ethical if the people in the relationship (the leaders and followers) *freely* agree that the intended changes *fairly* reflect their mutual purposes."[49]

Rost objects to utilitarianism, the Ten Commandments, and other well-established ethical perspectives and standards on the grounds that they are designed to help individuals solve ethical problems and don't help large groups of people solve complex societal dilemmas like genetic engineering or disposing of nuclear waste. He advocates a more communitarian approach, shifting the focus from individual choices to those made by the community, and argues that leaders and followers should pursue the common good.[50] He also suggests that leaders ought to be concerned about how to create virtuous organizations and communities, not just about how to become more virtuous individuals.

Relational leadership has much in common with postindustrial leadership. Wilfred (Bill) Drath of the Center for Creative Leadership uses the term *relational leadership* to describe how people with very different but equally valid worldviews (beliefs, attitudes, values) must accomplish leadership tasks together in the postmodern world.[51] Drath rejects the idea that there is one objective truth or reality. He acknowledges that some worldviews are unworthy because they destroy life and try to dominate other perspectives. However, the ultimate moral value is shared understanding, which is reached through relational dialogue—talk aimed at the goal of people understanding each other's experience. (Turn to Chapter 4 for an in-depth look at dialogue.) Together, members of groups and organizations open conversations that make sense of new subjects. Organizational and community members meet to develop a common language to identify and to describe problems before attempting to solve them.

To summarize, both postindustrial and relational leadership highlight the fact that *how* we interact with followers should be ethical. We need to pay close attention to leadership processes along with the final product. Ethical processes are inclusive, respect the dignity of others, are noncoercive, allow for mutual influence, and permit freedom of choice. To lead these processes, we will have to put a high value on mutual understanding. Both theories also encourage us to broaden our focus, to consider how our decisions and actions can help create a more virtuous society.

CHAPTER TAKEAWAYS

- Leaders are critical to the ethical performance of any organization. They serve as moral persons and as moral managers. As moral persons, they act as role models for followers. As moral managers, they keep the organization focused on the importance of ethical behavior.
- The ethical challenges of leaders and followers are a product of their complementary roles. As a leader, you will have power, broader authority, and more responsibility for the overall direction of the group. As a follower, you are accountable for implementing plans and carrying out the work.
- The six moral demands you'll face as a leader include (1) the challenge of power, (2) the challenge of privilege, (3) the challenge of information management, (4) the challenge of consistency, (5) the challenge of loyalty, and (6) the challenge of responsibility.
- Failure to meet the ethical challenges of the leadership role leads to a variety of misbehaviors that comprise the dark, or shadow, side of leadership. Understanding this side of leadership can keep you from casting shadows.
- Shadow leaders have been described as bad (ineffective and/or unethical), toxic (engaging in antisocial behaviors and demonstrating dysfunctional characteristics), destructive (acting in ways that damage subordinates, the organization, or both), and selfish (impulsive, narcissistic, Machiavellian).

- We can keep from casting shadows by sharing power, remaining accountable, and being alert to signs of toxicity and selfishness in ourselves.
- To be a transformational leader means speaking to the higher-level needs of followers and raising the ethical standards of the organization. This requires practicing idealized influence, individualized consideration, inspirational motivation, and intellectual stimulation. Such behaviors can help you become a more ethical leader as well as a more effective one.
- Servant leaders avoid the ethical pitfalls of the leadership role by putting the needs of followers first. They are person centered (altruistic), promote justice, demonstrate ethical character, and practice stewardship.
- Authentic leaders reflect a high level of self-understanding, and their actions are consistent with their core values. They demonstrate self-awareness, balanced processing (they can remain objective when receiving information), and an internalized moral perspective based on internal standards and relational transparency. You can develop authenticity by developing your ethical skills and knowledge and by increasing your level of self-awareness. You can become more self-aware by drawing lessons from past events, building your current level of self-efficacy, and identifying emerging trends that will shape you and your organization in the future.
- Postindustrial and relational leadership both emphasize that leaders need to be concerned about ethical processes as well as ethical products. Keep in mind that you accomplish shared goals together with followers. Your goal is to generate ethical outcomes (decisions, policies, procedures) through ethical processes that encourage free choice and participation.

APPLICATION PROJECTS

1. In a group, identify additional ethical demands on leaders that you would add to those in the chapter.

2. Create a case study that illustrates how a leader responded to one of the ethical challenges.

3. Which ethical challenge is the most difficult to resolve? Write up your conclusions.

4. Debate the following propositions.

    Studying the dark side of leadership can help us become more ethical leaders.

    Authenticity is the most important characteristic a leader can have.

    Incompetent leaders can't be ethical leaders.

    It is possible to use transformational leadership strategies to reach unethical objectives.

    No action or decision is ethical unless a leader reaches it using ethical processes.

    Traditional leadership theories and moral standards are not adequate to help citizens solve complex social issues.

5. Share your score from the Servant Leadership Questionnaire in Ethics in Action 8.1 with a partner. Explain why you rated this individual the way did and how she/he might improve. How do you think you would rate if others evaluated you?

6. If you serve in a leadership role, spend a week trying to function as a servant leader. Summarize your experience, paying particular attention to how acting as a servant may have changed your attitudes and behaviors.

7. Apply the characteristics of transformational leadership to a leader of your choice. Determine if this person is transactional or transformational. Defend your conclusion.

8. Identify the strengths and weaknesses of each of the normative leadership theories presented in the chapter. Which one do you find most useful and helpful?

CASE STUDY 8.2

The Looting of Bell, California

Bell, California, is a small, largely Hispanic, working-class community located just outside of Los Angeles. The median household income is $40,000, and many citizens live below the poverty line. No wonder residents were shocked to learn from a report in the *Los Angeles Times* that their city leaders were some of the highest-paid municipal officials in the United States. City Manager Robert Rizzo, along with the assistant city manager and the police chief, took home $1.6 million a year. At the same time, Bell homeowners paid the second-highest property tax rate in Los Angles County, at least 50% higher than the rate paid by wealthier homeowners in Bel Air.

Investigations by the Los Angeles County district attorney's office, state auditors, and federal officials revealed what Los Angeles County attorney Steve Cooley called "corruption on steroids."[1] City manager Rizzo was accused of illegally writing his own employment contracts, giving himself huge raises without permission from the city council, keeping his salary arrangements secret, steering city contracts to friends, and making $1.9 million in unauthorized loans to himself and other city officials. Part-time city council members were charged with receiving $8,000 a month ($100,000 a year) for attending meetings that lasted only a few seconds or were not held at all. To support this excess, city leaders not only imposed high property taxes but also illegally raised taxes on businesses and assessed improper sewer, trash, and recycling fees.

Several factors made Bell, California, ripe for looting by unscrupulous officials. One, electoral participation was extremely low, in part because many residents cannot vote due to their immigrant status. Second, city officials falsified documents to hide their salaries. Third, Rizzo was granted nearly unlimited control of the city's finances. Fourth, there was little media scrutiny of area city governments because cutbacks reduced the number of investigative reporters available to uncover fraud and corruption.

New city officials in Bell were quick to cut their salaries by 90%; businesses and homeowners can expect refunds on their utility bills. Residents rejoiced when the mayor, current and former city council members, former city manager Rizzo, and the former assistant city manager were taken away in handcuffs in an early-morning raid on their houses. Nevertheless, the outrage continues. Rizzo is in line to receive the highest pension of any official in California—$600,000 a year, an estimated $30 million over the course of his lifetime.

Discussion Probes

1. What signs of bad leadership do you note in this case? How much blame should Bell residents receive for the misbehavior of their leaders?

2. What ethical challenges of leadership did Bell city officials fail to meet?

3. If you were a newly elected or newly appointed city official in Bell, what would you do to restore the public's trust?

4. What steps can be taken to prevent similar fraud and corruption from taking root in other cities?

5. What is a reasonable salary for city managers, city councilors, and other city officials? How should city salaries compare to those in business?

6. How can government officials act as servant leaders?

Note

1. Gottlieb, J., Vives, R., & Leonard, J. (2010, September 22). Crisis in Bell. *Los Angeles Times,* p. A1.

Sources

Anderson, J. (2010, August 2). Californians wonder how city officials got high pay. *The Washington Times,* p. A1.

Gottlieb, J., Yoshino, K., & Vives, R. (2010, September 23). Fee hikes flowed to Rizzo's pay. *Los Angeles Times,* p. A1.

Nagourney, A., & Cathcart, R. (2010, September 22). Well-paid officials arrested to cheers. *The New York Times,* p. A14.

Saillant, C., & Gottlieb, J. (2010, July 22). Huge pensions await Bell leaders. *Los Angeles Times,* p. AA1.

CASE STUDY 8.3

Leading in the Darkness and the Light

The rescue of 33 Chilean miners in October 2010 was cause for worldwide celebration. After being trapped more than 2,000 feet below ground for 69 days, the rescued men emerged one by one from a capsule, to the cheers of the crowd gathered at the site as well as to the cheers of television viewers around the world.

The happy ending to the Chilean mining crisis was largely due to inspirational leadership both below and above ground. When 700,000 tons of rock collapsed on August 5, the miners were trapped near an underground rescue hut. Under the direction of mine foreman Luis Urzúa, they organized themselves, dividing into work groups to look for escape routes, to police the living area and to monitor the shaft for evidence of rescue attempts. Together, the men decided to divide their food supply, which consisted of a few cans of tuna, into equal shares and to eat only a few bites every day. They also tried to maintain a routine by setting up a regular sleep schedule.

Conditions in the pit were brutal. The polluted air burned the lungs of the miners, and the temperature averaged 92 degrees with nearly 100% humidity. According to one survivor, "It was like being in a filthy sauna where the air is full of dirt."[1] The men were forced to sleep on the wet, muddy floor of the mine or on the floors and hoods of vehicles trapped below. They used their light sparingly, for work and to keep up their morale, and took sips of contaminated water from metal drums. Fortunately, the group had an adequate air supply, discovered a waterfall that acted as a shower, and had access to adjoining tunnels. Nonetheless, the men were in desperate shape by the time rescuers located them, dehydrated and malnourished. Determined to die as a group, they had written good-bye letters to their families before they were located.

On the surface, key leaders included Chilean president Sebastián Piñera, mining minister Laurence Golborne, and mining engineer Andre Sougarret. Piñera ordered Golborne to spare no expense in launching a rescue despite estimates that there was only a 10% chance of finding anyone alive. "We made a commitment to look for the miners as if they were our sons," said Piñera.[2] The president remained committed to the effort, even as the days passed and he learned that the chances of anyone surviving had shrunk to less than 2%. The president told his advisors, "Even if there's less than one tenth of one per cent chance, it's our duty to keep searching."[3]

Mining minister Golborne organized the rescue effort, dividing rescuers into three teams. One group was assigned to locate the miners, one group focused on how to keep them alive if they were found, and the third group determined how to bring them safely to the surface. The minister spent most of time on site, supervising every aspect of the operation and providing regular reports to the media. Engineer Sougarret was in charge of the drilling project. For 17 days, he and his team tried to make contact with the miners through a series of boreholes. On August 22, the drill broke through near the miners' refuge. Rescuers thought they heard banging on the drill head. When they pulled it up, they found a plastic bag pressed into the drill thread that said, "*Estamos bien en el refugio, los 33*—We're all OK in the refuge, the 33."[4]

Once the men were located, the rescue effort kicked into high gear. Additional boreholes were drilled and used to send down food, medicine, messages, and a phone line. Chilean officials weren't shy about asking for help. They consulted NASA about how best to keep the miners healthy and used the agency's expertise when designing the escape capsule. Chilean leaders brought in contractors from the United States and Canada to simultaneously drill three rescue shafts in the hopes of speeding the recovery.

The trapped miners were actively involved in their rescue. They provided ideas and maps to Sougarret and his team. At the same time, a variety of group members emerged as leaders, doing their part to keep the group healthy and in good spirits. A miner trained as a paramedic conducted medical tests. Based on information he gathered, the survivors were advised to double their intake of water and to slowly build up their intake of calories. Another miner kept up the group's morale through humor (when he got to the top of the shaft, he presented Piñera with souvenir rocks from below). Yet another was named the group's official "pastor," helping his colleagues keep up their hopes of rescue.

The trip up the rescue shaft in an escape capsule painted in Chile's national colors was as carefully planned as the rest of the operation. Healthier miners went first, in case there were any unanticipated problems early on. Engineers periodically lubricated the capsule's wheels to keep them running smoothly and to prevent them from overheating. Much like the captain of a sinking ship, shift foreman Urzúa was the last to leave the mine. Each man emerged from the hole wearing Oakley sunglasses (donated by the company) to help their eyes adjust to the brightness of the surface. The survivors were treated for any medical conditions on the spot or, in the case of more serious illness, taken to a nearby hospital.

Observers wonder if the triumphal rescue, which featured images of humble miners embracing their billionaire president, will help to bridge the sharp economic divide between the country's haves and have-nots. A growing number of Chileans are falling into poverty. Chilean American playwright Ariel Dorfman hopes that that the rescue operation will prompt leaders to address this issue as well. He asks, "Is it too much to hope that the ordeal these men have gone through will trouble the conscience of Chile? Now that would be a real miracle."[5]

Discussion Probes

1. What risks did President Piñera face in launching a rescue despite the low chances of success?

2. How did the miners demonstrate transformational leadership? Servant leadership? Authentic leadership?

3. How did the Chilean president, mining minister, and drilling supervisor act as transformational leaders? As servant leaders? As authentic leaders?

4. Compare how Chilean leaders managed this crisis to how leaders in the United States responded to Hurricane Katrina and the BP oil spill. What are the key differences between the management of the Chilean mining disaster and the less successful responses to these earlier disasters?

5. How can Chilean leaders build on the goodwill generated by the rescue to create a more just society?

6. What did you learn from this case that you can apply as a manager or supervisor?

Notes

1. Graham, C. (2010, October 17). For 14 days we were all in pitch darkness. There was no night and no day. We begged God to help us. *London Mail.*

2. Fletcher, M. (2010, October 16). 'We decided to look for the miners as if they were our sons.' *The Times* (London), News, pp. 4, 5.

3. Fletcher.

4. Sequera, V. (2010, October 16). Calm engineer led rescue of miners. *The Register-Guard,* p. A6.

5. Carroll, R. (October 17, 2010). When the miners' leader met the president, two sides of Chile embraced. *The Observer,* p. 18.

Sources

Carroll, R., & Franklin, J. (2010, October 14). Chile's triumph. *The Guardian,* Home p. 1.
Carroll, R., & Franklin, J. (2010, October 16). Chilean miners: Tales from the tomb. *The Guardian,* International, p. 30.
Fountain, H. (2010, October 13). Plan B turns out to be fastest path for rescue in Chile. *The New York Times,* p. A8.
Hampson, R., & Dorell, O. (2010, October 14). Thrilling rescue made for TV. *USA Today,* pp. 1A, 5A.
McNeil, Jr., D. G. (2010, October 14). Welcome to life. *The Oregonian,* pp. A1, A7.
Vanderklippe, N. (2010, October 16). Chile's CEO moment. *The Globe and Mail,* p. F1.

ENDNOTES

1. Brown, M. E., & Trevino, L. K. (2006). Ethical leadership: A review and future directions. *The Leadership Quarterly, 17,* 595–616; Brown, M. E., Trevino, L. K., & Harrison, D. (2005). Ethical leadership: A social learning perspective for construct development and testing. *Organizational Behavior and Human Decision Processes, 97,* 117–134.

2. Yukl, G. (2002). *Leadership in organizations* (5th ed.). Upper Saddle River, NJ: Prentice Hall, Chap. 1.

3. Hornstein, H. (1996). *Brutal bosses and their prey.* New York: Riverhead.

4. Whicker, M. L. (1996). *Toxic leaders: When organizations go bad.* Westport, CT: Quorum Books.

5. Sellers, P. (2005, August 22). Retire? No way! *Fortune,* p. 18.

6. Sternberg, R. J. (2002). Smart people are not stupid, but they sure can be foolish: The imbalance theory of foolishness. In R. J. Sternberg (Ed.), *Why smart people can be so stupid* (pp. 232–242). New Haven, CT: Yale University Press.

7. Fonda, D., & Kadlec, D. (2004, May 31). The rumble over executive pay. *Time*, pp. 62–64.

8. Cruver, B. (2002). *Anatomy of greed: The unshredded truth from an Enron insider.* New York: Carroll & Graf, p. 23.

9. Naughton, K., & Gimbel, B. (2004, March 14). Martha's fall. *Newsweek*, pp. 28–36.

10. Kristof, N. (2010, November 19). Becoming our own version of a banana republic. *The Oregonian*, p. B7.

11. Wright, J. P., Cullen, F. T., & Blankenship, M. B. (2002). Chained factory fire exits: Media coverage of a corporate crime that killed 25 workers. In M. D. Ermann & R. J. Lundman (Eds.), *Corporate and governmental deviance* (6th ed., pp. 262–276). New York: Oxford University Press.

12. Portions of this chapter are adapted from: Johnson, C. E. (2012). *Meeting the ethical challenges of leadership: Casting light or shadow* (4th ed.). Thousand Oaks, CA: Sage.

13. Kellerman, B. (2004). *Bad leadership: What it is, how it happens, why it matters.* Boston: Harvard Business School Press.

14. Kellerman, p. xvi.

15. Lipman-Blumen, J. (2005). *The allure of toxic leaders: Why we follow destructive bosses and corrupt politicians—and how we can survive them.* Oxford, UK: Oxford University Press.

16. Einarsen, S., Skogstad, A., & Aasland, M. S. (2010). The nature, prevalence, and outcomes of destructive leadership: A behavior and conglomerate approach. In B. Schyns & T. Hansbrough (Eds.), *When leadership goes wrong: Destructive leadership, mistakes, and ethical failures* (pp. 145–171). Charlotte, NC: Information Age; Einarsen, S., Aasland, M. S., & Skogstad, A. (2007). Destructive leadership behavior: A definition and conceptual model. *The Leadership Quarterly, 18*, 207–216.

17. Einarsen, Skogstad, & Aasland, p. 156.

18. Keltner, D., Langner, C. A., & Allison, M. L. (2006). Power and moral leadership. In D. L. Rohde (Ed.), *Moral leadership: The theory and practice of power, judgment, and policy* (pp.177–194). San Francisco: Jossey-Bass.

19. McFarlin, D. B., & Sweeney, P. D. (2010). The corporate reflecting pool: Antecedents and consequences of narcissism in executives. In B. Schyns & T. Hansbrough (Eds.), *When leadership goes wrong: Destructive leadership, mistakes, and ethical failures* (pp. 247–283). Charlotte, NC: Information Age; Higgs, M. (2009). The good, the bad and the ugly: Leadership and narcissism. *Journal of Change Management, 9*, 165–178; Lubit, R. (2002). The long-term organizational impact of destructively narcissistic managers. *Academy of Management Executive, 18*, 127–183; Padilla, A., Hogan, R., & Kaiser, R. B. (2007). The toxic triangle: Destructive leaders, susceptible followers, and conducive environments. *The Leadership Quarterly, 18*, 176–194.

20. McFarlin, D. B., & Sweeney, P. D. (2000). *Where egos dare.* London, UK: Kogan Page.

21. Christie, R., & Geis, F. L. (1970). *Studies in Machiavellianism.* New York: Academic Press.

22. Becker, J. A. H., & O'Hair, H. D. (2007). Machiavellians' motives in organizational citizenship behavior. *Journal of Applied Communication Research, 35*, 246–267; Paulus, D. L., & Williams, K. M. (2002). The dark triad of personality: Narcissism, Machiavellianism, and psychopathy. *Journal of Research in Personality, 36*, 556–563.

23. Keltner, Langner, & Alison; McFarlin & Sweeney.

24. Burns, J. M. (1978). *Leadership.* New York: Harper & Row; Burns, J. M. (2003). *Transforming leadership: A new pursuit of happiness.* New York: Atlantic Monthly Press.

25. Avolio, B. J. (1999). *Full leadership development: Building vital forces in organizations.* Thousand Oaks, CA: Sage; Bass, B. M., Avolio, B. J., Jung, D. I., & Berson, Y. (2003). Predicting unit performance by

assessing transformational and transactional leadership. *Journal of Applied Psychology, 88,* 207–218; Bass, B. M. (1996). *A new paradigm of leadership: An inquiry into transformational leadership.* Alexandria, VA: Army Research Institute for the Behavioral and Social Sciences.

26. Lowe, K. B., & Kroeck, K. G. (1996). Effectiveness correlates of transformational and transactional leadership: A meta-analytic review. *The Leadership Quarterly, 7,* 385–425.

27. Burns (1978), p. 20.

28. See: Turner, N., Barling, J., Epitropaki, O., Butcher, V., & Milner, C. (2002). Transformational leadership and moral reasoning. *Journal of Applied Psychology, 87,* 304–311; Graham, J. (1995). Leadership, moral development, and citizenship behavior. *Business Ethics Quarterly, 5,* 43–54; Van Aswegen, A. S., & Engelbrecht, A. S. (2009). The relationship between transformational leadership, integrity, and an ethical climate in organizations. *South Africa Journal of Human Resource Management, 7*(1), pp. 221–279; Schwepker, C. H., & Good, D. J. (2010). Transformational leadership and its impact on sales force moral judgment. *Journal of Personal Selling & Sales Management, 30*(4), 299–317; Engelbrecht, A. S., van Aswegen, A. S., & Theron, C. C. (2005). The effect of ethical values on transformational leadership and ethical climate in organizations. *South Africa Journal of Business Management, 36*(2), 19–26; Puffer, S. M., & McCarthy, D. J. (2008). Ethical turnarounds and transformational leadership: A global imperative for corporate social responsibility. *Thunderbird International Business Review, 50,* 303–313. Toor, S., & Ofori, G. (2009). Ethical leadership: Examining the relationships with full range leadership model, employee outcomes, and organizational cultures. *Journal of Business Ethics, 90,* 533–547.

29. Bass, B. M. (1995). The ethics of transformational leadership. In J. Ciulla (Ed.), *Ethics: The heart of leadership* (pp. 169–192). Westport, CT: Praeger; Bass, B. M., & Steidlmeier, P. (1999). Ethics, character, and authentic transformational leadership behavior. *The Leadership Quarterly, 10,* 181–227.

30. Ruggieri, S. (2009). Leadership in virtual teams: A comparison of transformational and transactional leaders. *Social Behavior and Personality, 36*(8), 1017–1022; Hoyt, C. L., & Blascovich, J. (2003). Transformational and transactional leadership in virtual and physical environments. *Small Group Research, 34,* 678–715.

31. House, R. J., Hanges, P. J., Javidan, M., Dorfman, P. W., & Gupta, V. (2004). *Culture, leadership, and organizations: The GLOBE study of 62 societies.* Thousand Oaks, CA: Sage.

32. Johnson, C. E. (2000). Taoist leadership ethics. *Journal of Leadership Studies, 7,* 82–91.

33. Matthew 20:26 in *The Holy Bible: New International Version* (1973). Grand Rapids, MI: Zondervan.

34. Greenleaf, R. K. (1977). *Servant leadership.* New York: Paulist Press; Ruschman, N. L. (2002). Servant-leadership and the best companies to work for in America. In L. C. Spears & M. Lawrence (Eds.), *Focus on leadership: Servant-leadership for the twenty-first century* (pp. 123–139). New York: John Wiley.

35. Spears, L. C. (2002). Introduction: Tracing the past, present and future of servant leadership. In L. C. Spears & M. Lawrence (Eds.), *Focus on leadership: Servant-leadership for the twenty-first century* (pp. 1–18). New York: John Wiley.

36. See: McCuddy, M. K., & Cavin, M. C. (2008). Fundamental moral orientations, servant leadership, and leadership effectiveness: An empirical test. *Review of Business Research, 8*(4), 107–117; Jaramillo, F., Grisaffe, D. B., Chonko, L. B., & Roberts, J. H. A. (2009a). Examining the impact of servant leadership on sales force performance. *Journal of Personal Selling & Sales Management, 29,* 257–275; Walumbwa, F. O., Hartnell, C. A., & Oke, A. (2010). Servant leadership, procedural justice climate, service climate, and organizational citizenship behavior: A cross-level investigation. *Journal of Applied Psychology, 95,* 517–529; Mayer, D. M., Bardes, M., & Piccolo, R. F. (2008). Do servant-leaders help satisfy follower needs? An organizational justice perspective. *European Journal of Work and Organizational Psychology, 17*(2), 180–197; Jaramillo, F., Grisaffe, D. B., Chonko, L. B., & Roberts, J. A. (2009b). Examining the impact of servant leadership on salesperson's turnover intention. *Journal of Personal Selling & Sales Management, 29,* 351–365: 22.

37. Luthans, F., & Avolio, B. J. (2009). The "point" of positive organizational behavior. *Journal of Organizational Behavior, 30,* 291–307.

38. Avolio, B. J., & Gardner, W. L. (2005). Authentic leadership development: Getting to the root of positive forms of leadership. *The Leadership Quarterly, 16,* 315–340; Chan, A., Hannah, S. T., & Gardner, W. L. (2005). Veritable authentic leadership: Emergence, functioning, and impacts. In W. L. Gardner, B. J. Avolio, & F. O. Walumbwa (Eds.), *Authentic leadership theory and practice: Origins, effects and development* (pp. 3–41). Amsterdam: Elsevier; Kernis, M. H. (2003). Toward a conceptualization of optimal self-esteem. *Psychological Inquiry, 14,* 1–26; Walumbwa, F. O., Avolio, B. J., Gardner, W. L., Wernsing, T. S., & Peterson, S. J. (2008). Authentic leadership: Development and validation of a theory-based measure. *Journal of Management, 34*(1), 89–126.

39. May, D. R., Chan, A. Y. L., Hodges, T. D., & Avolio, B. J. (2003). Developing the moral component of authentic leadership. *Organizational Dynamics, 32,* 247–260; Hanna, S. T., Lester, P. B., & Vogelgesang, G. R. (2005). Moral leadership: Explicating the moral component of authentic leadership. In W. L. Gardner, B. J. Avolio, & F. O. Walumbwa (Eds.), *Authentic leadership theory and practice: Origins, effects and development* (pp. 43–81). Amsterdam: Elsevier.

40. Avolio & Gardner, p. 321.

41. Chan, Hannah, & Gardner.

42. Gardner, W. J., Avolio, B. J., & Walumbwa, F. O. (2005). Authentic leadership development: Emergent themes and future directions. In W. L. Gardner, B. J. Avolio, & F. O. Walumbwa (Eds.), *Authentic leadership theory and practice: Origins, effects and development* (pp. 387–406). Amsterdam: Elsevier. Gardner, W. L., Avolio, B. J., Luthans, F., May, D. R., & Walumbwa, F. O. (2005). "Can you see the real me?" A self-based model of authentic leader and follower development. *Leadership Quarterly, 16,* 343–372; May et al.

43. Ilies, R., Morgeson, F. P., & Nahrgang, J. D. (2005). Authentic leadership and eudemonic well-being: Understanding leader–follower outcomes. *The Leadership Quarterly, 16,* 373–394; Gardner et al. (2005); Harvey, P., Martinko, M. J., & Gardner, W. L. (2006). Promoting authentic behavior in organizations: An attributional perspective. *Journal of Leadership and Organizational Studies, 12,* 1–11; Zhu, W., May, D. R., & Avolio, B. J. (2004). The impact of ethical leadership behavior on employee outcomes: The roles of psychological empowerment and authenticity. *Journal of Leadership and Organizational Studies, 11,* 16–26; Avolio, B. J., Gardner, W. L., Walumbwa, F. O., Luthans, F., & May, D. R. (2004). Unlocking the mask: A look at the process by which authentic leaders impact follower attitudes and behaviors. *The Leadership Quarterly, 15,* 801–823; Clapp-Smith, R., Vogelgesang, G. R., & Avey, J. B. (2009). Authentic leadership and positive psychological capital: The mediating role of trust at the group level of analysis. *Journal of Leadership & Organizational Studies, 15*(3), 227–240.

44. Clapp-Smith, Vogelgesang, & Avey.

45. See, for example: Bruhn, J. G. (2001). *Trust and the health of organizations.* New York: Kluwer/Plenum, p. 82; Shockley-Zalabak, P., Ellis, K., & Winograd, G. (2000). Organizational trust: What it means, why it matters. *Organizational Development Journal, 18,* 35–47.

46. Avolio, B. J., & Luthans, F. (2006). *The high impact leader: Moments matter in accelerating authentic leadership development.* New York: McGraw-Hill.

47. Rost, J. C. (1991). *Leadership for the twenty-first century.* New York: Praeger. See also: Rost, J. (1993). Leadership in the new millennium. *Journal of Leadership Studies, 1,* 92–110; Rost, J. C. (2008). Followership: An outmoded concept. In R. E. Riggio, I. Chaleff, & J. Lipman-Blumen (Eds.), *The art of followership* (pp. 53–64). San Francisco: Jossey-Bass.

48. Rost (1991), p. 102.

49. Rost (1991), p. 109.

50. Rost, J. C. (1995). Leadership: A discussion about ethics. *Business Ethics Quarterly, 5*(1), 129–142.

51. Drath, W. (2001). *The deep blue sea: Rethinking the source of leadership.* San Francisco: Jossey-Bass.

9

Followership Ethics

The Growing Power of Followers

Followers have long functioned as the silent partners in the leader-follower relationship. Most press reports focus on the actions of executives, politicians, and other leaders, not on their subordinates.[1] Billions are spent every year on training leaders; very little is spent on training followers. There are thousands of academic books and articles on leadership but only a handful on followership.

Ignoring followers is shortsighted. Followers do most of the work and therefore deserve the lion's share of credit for a group's success. And the old adage is true: There can be no leaders without followers. Leaders can retain their positions only if they have the support of subordinates. While leaders largely determine the ethical direction of organizations, this does not excuse followers from their moral responsibilities. Followers have a choice whether or not to follow a particular leader, to maintain the status quo or to work for change, to obey commands or to object, to draw attention to wrongdoing or to keep silent.

Fortunately, there are signs that the voices of followers are increasingly being heard. Recently an entire conference was devoted to followership and a new follower interest group formed as part of the International Leadership Association. Books and articles about followers and followership are becoming more common. Harvard University professor Barbara Kellerman points to several global developments that suggest that the power and influence of followers is increasing at the same time the power and influence of leaders is shrinking.[2] She notes that the 1960s changed attitudes toward authority. Widespread protests on college campuses, as well as the civil rights and antiwar movements, ushered in a new era of equalitarianism and skepticism about hierarchy and institutions. The information revolution has converted employees into knowledge workers who generally know more than their bosses. Consumers can now attack companies online; governments are finding it increasingly difficult to censor information. Kellerman provides a number of examples of follower power in action, including political revolutions in the Ukraine, Nepal, and Lebanon; the removal of Paul Wolfowitz as president of the World Bank; and the ouster of shock jock Don Imus from the NBC radio network.

With the growing influence of followers in mind, this chapter examines the particular ethical moral responsibilities associated with the follower role and discusses principles and strategies we can use to meet the ethical challenges of followership.

The Ethical Challenges of Followership

Followers, like leaders, face a special set of demands or challenges based on the nature of the role they play. Followers are charged with carrying out the work and implementing the directives of leaders. They have less power and status than leaders do. In light of these realities, here are important moral challenges confronted by followers.

The Challenge of Obligation

All followers have obligations to their leaders as well as to the institutions that provide them with paychecks, retirement plans, friendships, prestige, training, fulfilling work, and other benefits. Obligations don't end at the organizational door, however. Followers must frequently fulfill duties to external stakeholders. For instance, government employees "owe" it to taxpayers to use their money wisely by working hard and spending carefully. Members of a law firm owe their clients the best possible representation as well as accurate billing.

Determining minimal responsibilities is easier than deciding how far follower obligations should extend. At the very least, employees shouldn't rip off their employers by showing up late (or not at all), doing nothing, and stealing property. Yet, some workers are asked to sacrifice too much for their organizations. Consider the case of technology and consulting firms that demand that employees travel constantly, work nights and weekends, and attend meetings instead of their kids' school events. Giving into the excessive demands of workaholic organizations generates stress and burnout, endangering mental health, marriages, and relationships with children. Volunteers must also determine what they owe their leaders and groups. Religious cults are criticized for demanding that followers devote long hours to the cause, turn over their paychecks to leaders, and cut off their connections to families and friends.

Every situation is different, so followers have to determine if they are meeting their ethical obligations or giving too little or too much. However, the questions below can serve as a guide to sorting out the obligations we owe as followers.

- Am I doing all I reasonably can to carry out my tasks and further the mission of my organization? What more could I do?
- Am I earning the salary and benefits I receive?
- Can I fulfill my organizational obligations and, at the same time, maintain a healthy personal life and productive relationships?
- If not, what can I do to bring my work and personal life into balance?

The Challenge of Obedience

Followers must routinely obey orders and directives, even the ones they don't like. Deciding when to disobey is the challenge. There's no doubt that following authority can drive followers to engage in illegal and immoral activities in which they would never participate on their own. This point was driven home in experiments carried out by Stanley Milgram in the 1970s.[3] Students playing the role of teacher were asked to administer shocks to a learner, hidden behind a partition, when the learner answered incorrectly. Subjects continued to ramp up the voltage of the shocks at the request of the experimenter, even though the learner (really an actor who received no shock at all) expressed more and more discomfort. Two thirds of the students obeyed the experimenter despite the pleas and screams of the learner.

Milgram's findings only confirm what has been repeated time and again in real life. Serbian soldiers charged with war crimes, members of Rwandan death squads, and Saddam Hussein's torturers committed atrocities because they were "following orders." However, following orders is no excuse. This is called the Nuremberg principle.[4] At the Nuremberg war crime trials following World War II, the tribunal rejected claims that atrocities were justified because German defendants were obeying authority. Based on this principle, the U.S. Army punishes those who follow illegal orders.

Every follower has to consider such factors as these: (a) Does this order appear to call for unethical behavior? (b) Would I engage in this course of action if I weren't ordered to? (c) What are the potential consequences for others if these directions are followed? For myself? (d) Does obedience threaten the mission and health of the organization as a whole? (e) What steps should I take if I decide to disobey?

The Challenge of Cynicism

It's easy for followers to become cynical. They don't have much power, and they are often left out of the information loop and important decisions. Often, the choices and actions of their leaders appear arbitrary if not stupid.

Cynicism can be justified (just look at what happened to thousands of loyal, hard-working employees at Enron, WorldCom, Countrywide, Washington Mutual Savings and Loan, and elsewhere). Nevertheless, cynicism acts like acid, reducing commitment levels, destroying trust, cutting off communication, and lowering organizational performance. Few of us give our best effort when we are skeptical about the organizations we've committed ourselves to. The more cynical we become, the more energy we put into critiquing and complaining and the less we devote to the task at hand. Followers must walk a fine line between healthy skepticism, which prevents them from being exploited, and unhealthy cynicism, which undermines their efforts and those of the group as a whole.

The Challenge of Dissent

Followers frequently take issue with policies, procedures, orders, working conditions, pay, benefits, values, and other factors. They can't make the changes themselves, so they must express their disagreement to those who can. At this point, followers must make a number of strategic decisions. To begin with, they have to determine when to speak up and when to keep silent. There may be several points of contention, but generally followers have to "pick their battles." Raising too many issues may turn leaders off and can label the follower as a whiner. On the other hand, silence can be immoral, as in the case of the engineer who discovers his company is shipping defective airplane parts but decides to keep this information to himself. (See Case Study 9.2, "Helping Harvard Medical School Make the Grade," to learn more about how one group of followers successfully challenged the system.)

Once the decision to protest has been made, followers must then determine the following:

- How to express dissent (when, what to say, through what channels)
- Whom to contact with their concerns (immediate supervisor, professional supervisor, etc.)
- How to respond if their opinions are rejected
- When to go outside the organization with concerns and complaints

The Challenge of Bad News

Few of us have a problem with telling our superiors what they want to hear. For example, we've reached our goals, sales are up, the project is under budget, and the software implementation will be done on time. Delivering bad news is much riskier. Telling our bosses what they don't want to hear can incur their wrath, bring penalties, and seriously damage our standing in the organization. The risk is highest when we are directly at fault. No wonder that researchers report that subordinates routinely keep negative information from their superiors, including feedback about leader behaviors that could be undermining the group's success.[5]

Organizations can pay a high price when followers hide or cover up bad news, deny responsibility, or shift blame. Leaders can't take corrective steps if they don't know a problem exists. Their failure to address serious deficiencies, like safety hazards and accounting fraud, can destroy an organization. Further, leaders who don't get feedback about their ineffective habits can't change these patterns. Teachers who use lots of "ums" and "ahs" in their lectures, for example, need feedback about their speech behaviors from students if they are to eliminate these language features. Finally, denying accountability and shifting blame undermines trust and focuses people on defending themselves instead of on solving the problem.

Declaring that ethical followers should faithfully deliver bad news and accept responsibility for their actions is easier than doing so ourselves. Being the bearer of bad tidings takes courage, as we'll see later in the chapter. The challenge is not so much in determining what to do but in following through. As in delivering all messages, selecting the right time, place, and channel is critical. Significant problems should be brought to light as soon as possible, when the receiver is most receptive, and delivered face to face, not through e-mail or other less personal channels.

William J. LeMessurier is an excellent example of someone who didn't hesitate to deliver bad news that revealed his errors. LeMessurier was the lead structural engineer for the Citicorp tower in New York City, which was completed in 1979. After the building was finished, he discovered that the structure's design and braces made it susceptible to wind damage. The building would likely collapse in a violent storm, which might occur every 16 years. LeMessurier could have kept silent. Instead, he put his professional reputation on the line and admitted his mistakes to the architect and to top Citicorp officers. Working together, LeMessurier and company officials developed a plan to fix the brace problem. In 3 months, the mistake was fixed. The project manager for the project described the incident and LeMessurier this way: "It started with a guy who stood up and said, 'I got a problem, I made the problem, let's fix the problem.'"[6]

Meeting the Moral Demands of Followership: Principles and Strategies

This section of the chapter introduces key concepts and tactics designed to help you master the ethical duties of the followership role. To be an ethical, effective follower, you will need to overcome unhealthy motivations, act in an exemplary manner, engage with leaders, demonstrate courage and support, learn how to manage and lead up, and determine when to bring organizational misconduct to the attention of outsiders.

Overcoming Unhealthy Motivations

All too often, followers seek leaders for the wrong reasons. These unhealthy motivations encourage subordinates to tolerate and support the bad leaders described in the last chapter. Toxic followership makes toxic leadership possible. Meeting the ethical challenges of followership, then, begins with avoiding these motivational traps. Claremont Graduate University professor Jean Lipman-Blumen argues that there are a number of factors that "seduce" us into toxic followership:[7]

- Our need for authority (parentlike) figures
- Our need for security and certainty, which prompts us to abandon our freedom
- Our need to feel chosen or special, which we meet by following a leader apparently engaged in a greater cause
- Our need to be part of a community

- Our fear of being ostracized and isolated from the group
- Our fear that we are powerless to challenge a bad leader
- Our anxiety about life and death, which makes us vulnerable to the illusion that heroic, godlike leaders can protect us
- Our need to be at the center of the action in order to feel alive, meaningful, and in control
- Our desire to identify with a noble vision (which may turn out to be toxic)
- Our feelings of anxiety, caused by uncertainty, change, and crisis, that drive us to leaders for protection
- Our worship of achievement, which makes us admire gifted individuals who may have serious flaws
- Our need for self-esteem, which we meet by aligning ourselves with successful leaders (even when they have toxic qualities)

Lipman-Blumen offers five strategies that can keep us from becoming dependent on toxic leaders while helping us become self-reliant instead. One, recognize that anxiety is a fact of life. Any serious change sparks fear and uncertainty, but we need to step out and take risks despite our fears. Two, learn to act independently—develop the leader within. Become proactive rather than reactive. Work with others to develop democratic organizations where many individuals share leadership responsibilities. Three, demand leaders who tell the truth, no matter how unpleasant that truth might be. Such leaders disillusion us and force us to take our follower duties seriously. Four, beware of leaders with grandiose visions who divide the world into us versus them (see the discussion of moral exclusion in Chapter 7). Five, don't let a few individuals self-select for top positions. View leadership as responsibility to be shared by a variety of group members. Draft worthy candidates for leadership roles based on their character, and limit their terms of service; rotate individuals in and out of leadership positions.

Servant (Exemplary) Followership

Business professor, consultant, and author Robert Kelley believes that servant followership is more important than servant leadership. He points out that most people spend most of their time in follower roles and that (as we noted earlier) followers contribute the most to organizational success. From an ethical perspective, seeking to be a follower rather than a leader reduces the destructive competition and conflict that occur when individuals compete against each other for leadership positions. Servant followers are more likely to build trust and keep the focus on organizational goals. They avoid the temptation to adopt authoritarian, self-centered styles when they do land in leadership roles.[8]

Kelley uses the term *exemplary* to describe ideal servant followers. The best followers score high in two dimensions: independent, critical thinking and active engagement. They think for themselves and, at the same time, take initiative. Outstanding followers contribute innovative ideas and go beyond what is required. Leaders can count on them to take on new challenges, to follow through on projects without much supervision, to disagree constructively, and to think through the implications of their actions.

Kelley contrasts exemplary followers with their less effective counterparts based on the independent thinking and engagement dimensions described below in the Self-Assessment:

Passive followers demonstrate little original thought or commitment. They rely heavily on leaders for directions and meet only minimal expectations. Kelley compares them to sheep because they follow herd instincts: "They can be trained to perform necessary simple tasks and then wander around while awaiting further directions."[9]

Conformist followers are more enthusiastic than their passive coworkers but still depend on leaders to tell them what to do. They follow exactly what the leader says and only tell the leader what he or she wants to hear. Not surprisingly, insecure leaders prefer this type of subordinate.

SELF-ASSESSMENT

Followership Styles

Followership Questionnaire

For each statement, think of a followership situation and how you acted. Choose a number from 0 to 6 to indicate the extent to which the statement describes you, with 0 indicating "rarely applies" and 6 indicating "almost always."

_____ 1. Does your work help you fulfill some societal goal or personal dream that is important to you?

_____ 2. Are your personal work goals aligned with the organization's priority goals?

_____ 3. Are you highly committed to and energized by your work and organization, giving them your best ideas and performance?

_____ 4. Does your enthusiasm also spread to and energize your coworkers?

_____ 5. Instead of waiting for or merely accepting what the leader tells you, do you personally identify which organizational activities are most critical for achieving the organization's priority goals?

_____ 6. Do you actively develop a distinctive competence in those critical activities so that you become more valuable to the leader and the organization?

_____ 7. When starting a new job or assignment, do you promptly build a record of successes in tasks that are important to the leader?

_____ 8. Can the leader give you a difficult assignment without the benefit of much supervision, knowing that you will meet your deadline with highest-quality work and that you will "fill in the cracks" if need be?

_____ 9. Do you take the initiative to seek out and successfully complete assignments that go above and beyond your job?

_____ 10. When you are not the leader of a group project, do you still contribute at a high level, often doing more than your share?

_____ 11. Do you independently think up and champion new ideas that will contribute significantly to the leader's or the organization's goals?

_____ 12. Do you try to solve the tough problems (technical or organizational), rather than look to the leader to do it for you?

_____ 13. Do you help out coworkers, making them look good, even when you don't get any credit?

_____ 14. Do you help the leader or group see both the upside potential and downside risks of ideas or plans, playing the devil's advocate if need be?

_____ 15. Do you understand the leader's needs, goals, and constraints and work hard to help meet them?

_____ 16. Do you actively and honestly own up to your strengths and weaknesses rather than put off evaluation?

_____ 17. Do you make a habit of internally questioning the wisdom of the leader's decision rather than just doing what you are told?

_____ 18. When the leader asks you to do something that runs contrary to your professional or personal preferences, do you say "no" rather than "yes"?

_____ 19. Do you act on your own ethical standards rather than the leader's or the group's standards?

_____ 20. Do you assert your views on important issues, even though it might mean conflict with your group or reprisals from the leader?

Finding Your Followership Style

Use the scoring key below to score your answers to the questions.

Independent Thinking Items	Active Engagement Items
Question	Question
1. _____	2. _____
5. _____	3. _____
11. _____	4. _____
12. _____	6. _____
14. _____	7. _____

Independent Thinking Items	Active Engagement Items
16. _____	8. _____
17. _____	9. _____
18. _____	10. _____
19. _____	13. _____
20. _____	15. _____
Total Score _____	Total Score _____

Add up your scores on the Independent Thinking items. Record the total on a vertical axis, as in the graph below. Repeat the procedure for the Active Engagement items, and mark the total on a horizontal axis. Now, plot your scores on the graph by drawing perpendicular lines connecting your two scores.

The juxtaposition of these two dimensions forms the basis upon which people classify followership styles.

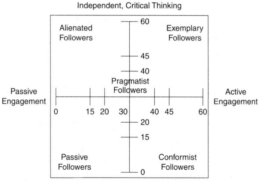

Independent Followership Style	Active	
	Thinking Score	**Engagement Score**
EXEMPLARY	High	High
ALIENATED	High	Low
CONFORMIST	Low	High
PRAGMATIST	Middling	Middling
PASSIVE	Low	Low

Alienated followers are highly independent thinkers who are only minimally committed to their roles and organizations. They put their energies into fighting the leader or the organization instead of into reaching shared goals. Alienated followers are highly cynical. They may have started out as exemplary followers but become disillusioned with the leader and/or the group as a whole.

Pragmatic followers fall in the middle of the independent thinking and engagement continua. Pragmatists often have been victimized by frequent layoffs, restructurings, and leadership changes. They are more interested in surviving than in serving.

Kelley outlines five behavior patterns that you need to adopt if you hope to become an exemplary follower.

1. *Leading yourself.* Excellent followers know how to lead themselves. They step up to their responsibilities and view their work as equal in importance to that of leaders because they recognize that implementation is critical to success.

2. *Commit and focus.* Exemplary followers are committed to ideas and causes bigger than themselves. They look beyond their personal careers and needs to serve an elevating purpose like fighting illness or protecting the environment. Because they're committed to a broad principle, exemplary followers feel less need for status or titles. They consider leaders part of the team and will take steps to keep the leader's ego from getting in the way of achieving the goal.

3. *Develop competence and credibility.* Enthusiastic commitment is not enough. Or, as Kelley tells his students and clients, "Highly committed and motivated incompetence is still incompetence."[10] Exemplary followers set high personal standards that are more strenuous than those set by the leader or the organization as a whole. They are proactive, taking advantage of continuing education and performance development opportunities. Outstanding followers also know their weaknesses and take steps to compensate either by acquiring the necessary skills or by stepping aside to let others complete the task.

4. *Use your courageous conscience.* Exemplary followers are very concerned about the ethics of their actions even if their leaders are not. Such followers serve as ethical watchdogs. They refuse to abandon personal principles but challenge immoral directives instead (see the discussion of courageous followership in the next section).

5. *Disagree agreeably.* Exemplary followers recognize that their job is to make the job of the leader easier, not harder. They work cooperatively with the leader. However, when conflicts arise and decisions must be challenged, outstanding followers disagree using the following strategies:

- Be proactive. Assume that the leader wants the best and operate from that assumption. Sometimes leaders slip because they lack information or are out of touch with followers.
- Gather the facts. Gathering solid evidence makes it easier to disagree and to object in good conscience.
- Seek wise counsel. Find others, most often outsiders, who can provide good advice, and test the strength of your position.
- Play by the rules. Exemplary followers want to be seen as part of the community and do so by working within established guidelines whenever possible.

- Persuade by speaking the language of the organization. Proactive followers draw upon the purpose and values of the organization to make their case.
- Prepare your courage to go over heads when absolutely necessary. Exemplary followers don't just go along but test their courage regularly by challenging small ethical breaches.
- Take collective action or plan well to stand alone. Chances of success are greater if you work with others, but prepare to step out on your own. Develop contingency plans (other job prospects, savings accounts) when acting individually.

Engaged Followership

Like Robert Kelley, Barbara Kellerman uses engagement with leaders as a criterion for distinguishing between good and bad followers. Kellerman believes that some level of follower engagement is always superior to not being engaged at all. Based on this premise, she places followers into these categories:[11]

1. *Isolates.* Isolates can barely be categorized as followers, because they are detached and alienated. By doing and saying nothing, isolates increase the power of leaders who already occupy positions of authority. The millions of Americans who don't vote are isolates. Their lack of engagement means that they exert minimal influence over the direction of the country.

2. *Bystanders.* Bystanders have a low level of engagement with their leaders. They observe but make a conscious choice to stand aside. Their decision to remain neutral serves as a form of tacit support for the status quo. Ordinary Germans who stood by during Hitler's regime can be classified as bystanders. By remaining silent, they enabled Hitler to wage world war and carry out the Holocaust.

3. *Participants.* Participants have a moderate level of engagement. They actively support or oppose their leaders by investing their time, loyalty, and money in order to exert influence. Middle managers and research scientists at Merck Pharmaceuticals served as participants during the development of the now-discredited pain drug Vioxx. They actively promoted the painkiller in spite of evidence linking it to a greatly increased risk of heart attack.

4. *Activists.* Activists are highly engaged with their leaders. They have a heavy investment in the group or organization and its leadership. Activists work hard on behalf of their leaders or work just as hard to undermine and remove them when they fall short. Under Hitler, Nazi Party members served as supportive activist followers. They helped keep Hitler in power, carried out Nazi programs, and so on. Recently, members of Voice of the Faithful, a group of American Catholic laypeople, served as activist opponents. They helped oust Boston bishop Bernard Law for his handling of the priest sex abuse scandal.

5. *Diehards.* Diehards are the most engaged group of followers. They are willing to risk all, including death, for their causes and leaders (or against leaders they oppose). Totally dedicated, they are defined by their commitment to their leaders and groups. According to Kellerman, "Being a Diehard is all-consuming. It is who you are. It determines what you do."[12] Hitler's inner circle could be classified as diehards. The same can be said for members of many elite military groups.

Kellerman acknowledges that engagement alone does not make someone a good follower. Obviously, Germans who engaged with Hitler should be classified as toxic, not good. She notes, "The question is, Willingness to engage to what end, for what purpose?"[13] She introduces motivation as a second criterion for distinguishing between bad and good followership. Good followers pursue the public interest, not selfish interest.

Kellerman urges us to take advantage of the growing power of followership, to oppose bad leadership as soon as it appears. The longer we wait to speak up, the harder it is to stop unethical leaders. Resistance is more effective if we prepare ourselves by gathering facts, collecting resources, seeking counsel, and developing a careful strategy. If at all possible, we should join forces with other followers when we oppose unethical leaders.

Courageous Followership

Government and business consultant Ira Chaleff believes that followership requires courage.[14] He defines courage as accepting a higher level of risk. It's risky for a camp counselor to confront a camp director who is demeaning children, for a shift supervisor to oppose new work rules developed by the plant manager, or for a member of the cabinet to challenge the decision of the President of the United States. (For an outstanding example of follower courage, turn to Case Study 9.3, "Courage Under Fire.") Acting courageously is easier if followers recognize that their ultimate allegiance is to the purpose and values of the organization and not to the leader. Chaleff identifies five types of follower courage.

1. *The courage to assume responsibility.* The first dimension of courageous followership specifically addresses the challenge of obligation. Courageous followers assume responsibility for themselves and the organization as a whole. They assess their own performance, elicit feedback from others, seek opportunities for personal growth, manage their tasks, and maintain a healthy personal life. At the same time, they are passionate about the work of the organization as a whole, taking initiative to challenge the status quo by modifying the culture, challenging rules and mind-sets, and improving processes.

2. *The courage to serve.* Courageous followers actively support their leaders, often by working behind the scenes. This service takes the following forms:

- Helping leaders conserve their energies by focusing their attention on the most important tasks
- Organizing communication flow from and to the leader
- Controlling and allowing access to the leader
- Screening out unsubstantiated criticism of the leader and defending the leader from unjust criticism
- Relaying a leader's messages in an accurate, effective manner
- Acting on behalf of the leader when appropriate
- Shaping a leader's public image
- Focusing the creative leader on the most fruitful ideas
- Presenting options during decision making
- Encouraging the leader to develop healthy peer relationships
- Preparing for and preventing crises
- Helping the leader and the group cope with the leader's illness
- Mediating conflicts between leaders
- Promoting performance reviews for leaders

3. *The courage to challenge.* Inappropriate behavior threatens the leader-follower relationship and the entire organization. Leaders may engage in petty theft, scream at or use demeaning language with employees, display an arrogant attitude, and engage in sexual harassment. Such behavior needs to be confronted immediately, before it becomes a habit. In some instances, a gentle, indirect approach will do, as in questioning the wisdom of a policy or focusing attention on the idea or program rather than on the personal shortcomings of the leader. In more extreme cases, followers will need to directly challenge or disobey orders.

4. *The courage to participate in transformation.* Left unchecked, negative behavior patterns can lead to a leader's destruction. But changing ingrained habits is a long, difficult process. Leaders often deny the need to change or justify their behavior. They may claim that anger is an effective management tool or that misleading investors boosts company profits. To modify their behavior, leaders must admit they have a problem, accept responsibility, and desire to change. They are more likely to persist in the change process if they can visualize positive outcomes, like more productive employees, better health, restored relationships, and higher self-esteem. Followers play a critical role in the transformation process by (a) drawing attention to what needs to be changed (and not reinforcing dysfunctional behavior), (b) providing honest feedback, (c) suggesting resources and outside facilitators, (d) creating a supportive climate, (e) modeling openness to change and empathy, (f) helping contain abusive behavior, and (g) providing positive reinforcement when the leader adapts effective new patterns.

5. *The courage to leave.* There are lots of reasons to leave an organization. A new setting may offer more opportunities for personal growth, leaving may help the group as a whole, and followers may be experiencing exhaustion and burnout. However, leaving for principled reasons takes the most courage because it may mean the loss of a job, career, or reputation. Followers should resign when they have failed to fulfill the organization's purpose or have violated an important trust. They may also withdraw their support when those in authority continue their abuse, violate their professed values, serve their own agendas, and ask followers to engage in unethical and illegal behavior.

Chaleff is quick to point out that courageous followership involves more than challenge; it also involves support for the leader. The best followers serve as *partners* with leaders, providing high challenge and high support. Other types of followers fall short on one or both of these dimensions. *Individualistic* followers will speak up when others don't but are seen as unsupportive and thus may be ignored. *Resource* followers don't provide much support or challenge, doing just enough to get by. *Implementer* followers are very supportive but rarely challenge their leaders. Leaders often like followers who use this style. Nevertheless, implementers put their leaders at risk because they don't warn them about problems.

According to Chaleff, identifying your follower style is the first step in developing your courage.[15] Determine whether you function as a partner with your leaders or as an individualist, resource, or implementer instead. Be willing to support your leader, and practice the skills you need to act courageously by role-playing confrontation scenarios like the ones in Application Project 7. When preparing to challenge a leader, try to identify any misperceptions or blind spots you might have as a follower by asking yourself the following questions:

Does what I want from the leader seem reasonable?

Do I need to build or repair trust by giving my leader more or better support?

Is a better strategy needed for raising the issue with the leader?

Do I need to conduct more research or gather more documentation to present my case effectively?

What options should I develop for the leader to consider?

Do I need to change anything about my behavior if I want the leader to transform her or his behavior?

Do I need to do something to reinforce changes already agreed to in earlier conversations?

Are there any other observations or suggestions that I should keep in mind?

Authentic Followership

Proponents of Authentic Leadership Theory (ALT) believe that authenticity is the key to ethical followership, just as it is for ethical leadership. As we saw in the last chapter, authentic leaders promote authentic followership by modeling authentic behaviors and by helping constituents develop feelings of competence, hope, and optimism. Followers can also take steps to become more authentic on their own. In particular, they need to develop psychological ownership, foster trust, and practice transparency.[16]

Psychological ownership. Authentic followers "feel as though they own their process, product and performance."[17] This feeling of ownership is founded on a sense of belonging ("This is *my* place"), a sense of self-identity ("I am a ____ employee"), a sense of accountability ("*I* am responsible for what happens"), and a sense of efficacy ("I know I *can* do it.") Ownership encourages such ethical behaviors as (1) meeting the needs of customers when they first come into contact with a company, (2) taking responsibility for making decisions at lower organizational levels, (3) going beyond what the job requires, and (4) doing whatever it takes to solve problems. The staff members at one Veterans Administration hospital demonstrate the positive power of ownership. They see themselves as serving soldiers who "sacrifice their tomorrows for our todays." As a result, these medical personnel are dedicated to providing the highest level of care and challenge their leaders to do the same.

Trust. Authentic followers own up to their shortcomings at the same time they encourage their leaders to follow their example. For example, when nurses admit making mistakes that could cost lives, this prompts doctors to report potential missteps as well. Authentic followers take the risk to share their failures with leaders. At the same time, they don't take advantage of leaders who admit their mistakes.

Transparency. Authentic followers say what they mean. Their willingness to honestly share their thoughts, values, and feelings builds transparent relationships that are marked by honesty, feedback, and effective communication. Authentic followers also contribute to the formation of transparent organizational climates focused on shared goals. In such climates, members can predict how others will act and are more willing to welcome creative ideas and to acknowledge potential weaknesses. Because they feel safe, employees reveal problems rather than creating the impression that everything is okay.

Authentic followership equips us to meet several of the ethical challenges of followership: obligation, cynicism, delivering bad news, expressing dissent. As we engage in authentic behavior as followers, we reinforce the authentic behaviors of our leaders. We are more likely to develop a sense of ownership if we realize that we serve a greater purpose and are accountable for actions. We should be willing to address problems whatever our role and status in the organization. At the same time, we can establish trusting relationships with our leaders by becoming vulnerable and by not taking advantage of their vulnerability. Owning up to our errors encourages our leaders and peers to do the same.

Managing Up/Leading Up

Knowing how to work effectively with leaders is key to ethical followership. Harvard Business professors John Gabarro and John Kotter use the phrase *managing your boss* to describe "the process of consciously working with your superior to obtain the best possible results for you, your boss, and the company."[18] They emphasize that it is the responsibility of followers to establish good working relationships with their leaders. Bosses depend on their subordinates. When followers misbehave, they can do serious damage to their leaders and to others in the organization.

Managing the boss begins with understanding the boss. As followers, we need to recognize the pressures our superiors face, their strengths and weaknesses, and their preferred working styles. Some leaders seek detailed background information, whereas others want only the basic facts. Some leaders are readers who like information in report form, whereas others are listeners who prefer information presented in person so that they can ask questions. High-involvement bosses want to be consulted every step of the way; low-involvement managers delegate instead.

We also need to understand our own strengths and weaknesses and preferred working styles. In particular, we need to determine if we are counterdependent or overdependent. Counterdependent followers resent the fact that they have to depend more on the boss than the boss has to depend on them. They view the leader as the enemy, rebelling and escalating conflict. Overdependent followers hold back their anger and refuse to disagree even when the manager makes a bad decision. Gabarro and Kotter point out that both of these orientations overlook the fact that leaders are imperfect and struggle with their own pressures and concerns that may put them at odds with the wishes of their subordinates. Knowing if we tend to rebel or submit can help us take steps to correct our attitudes and behaviors. We may have to make a conscious effort not to view our leaders as enemies, checking our tendency to engage in needless conflict. Or we may need to disagree with our leaders more often.

In order to develop and maintain a good relationship with your boss, you will need to learn how to blend your working styles together. You may have to shorten your reports, provide information in advance, and get your manager involved from the start of the project. Make sure you clarify what your manager expects from you and what you expect from your manager (e.g., how much data each party needs, when projects should be completed). Never overestimate what your leader already knows, and determine the best way to communicate bad news as well as good. Be dependable and consistent—don't underplay problems or overpromise results. Make good use of your boss's time and energy. Every request you make is a drain on your leader's resources, so plan your withdrawals carefully.

Wharton Business School professor Michael Useem distinguishes between managing up and leading up. While *managing up* is working well with bosses to get daily tasks done, *leading up* is about exceeding expectations and bringing added value—what Useem describes as "the effective exercise of power for the greater good."[19] Those who lead up have a bias for action. They are willing to take charge of a situation even when they aren't the officially designated leader. Useem provides a number of examples of individuals who were significant leaders in their own right but still had to influence their superiors, often in crisis situations. Some, like the Civil War general Robert E. Lee and Charles Schwab's president David Pottruck (who convinced the brokerage's namesake to move to online trading), succeeded as upward leaders. Others, like the commander of the UN forces during the Rwandan genocide and former CBS CEO Thomas Wyman (who tried to sell the company without his board's permission), did not. (See Case Study 9.1 for examples of ordinary people engaged in leading up.)

Useem draws a number of leading up lessons from these examples. Among the most important: (1) keep your superiors well informed, and don't surprise them; (2) make a compelling case for policies and initiatives, using facts and evidence; (3) press your leader for more information if instructions are unclear; (4) step up to make a difference, even if your superiors don't recognize the need or the opportunity; (5) communicate the interests of your superiors to your subordinates and the interests of your subordinates to your superiors in order to meet the needs of both groups.

CASE STUDY 9.1

Leading Up at Every Level of the Organization: Tempered Radicals

Harvard professor Debra Myerson demonstrates that ordinary organizational members, not just those near the top of the hierarchy, can successfully lead up. She conducted more than 200 interviews with change agents she calls *tempered radicals*. Tempered radicals are people who want to stay and succeed in their organizations, even if their identities and values are different from the dominant cultures of their groups. Their goal is to remain true to themselves while changing their organizations slowly over time. According to Myerson, "They want to rock the boat, and they want to stay in it" (p. xi). Examples of tempered radicals include gays who hope to make their organizations more sexually inclusive, employees of color out to foster diversity, parents who want to set aside family time while working in demanding high-tech companies, and those who promote social responsibility in profit-making corporations.

To succeed, tempered radicals use a variety of strategies, which range from resisting quietly and operating behind the scenes to enlisting others and making a public attempt to change the entire organization. One set of influence strategies—leveraging small wins—is particularly useful to those engaged in leading up. Small wins are limited, manageable projects that produce concrete, visible results. Those engaged in small wins have a plan for change and actively promote their agendas. Small wins are low risk. They demonstrate that change is possible while building hope. Over time, a series of small wins can lead to significant cultural change. One African American manager at a large financial institution, for example, worked to identify and recruit minority candidates. He asked the individuals he hired to pledge that they would also actively recruit other people of color. Over 30 years, he was directly or indirectly responsible for hiring more than 3,500 minority employees.

Being a tempered radical is far from easy. These individuals always feel somewhat out of sync with the dominant culture and run the risk of giving up their values. At the same time, outsiders may accuse them of selling out. To keep going, tempered radicals (1) know who they are and what is most important to their sense of self, remaining true to their core values while being flexible about how to fulfill them; (2) favor taking action; (3) recognize that they have a choice in how they respond; (4) see choices in mundane organizational activities and interactions; (5) act on opportunities that present themselves; (6) connect small wins and events to generate greater change and encourage others to learn from their victories; and (7) remain tied to others, drawing upon their support to maintain their identities and to collectively work for change.

Not all tempered radicals are successful, of course. Nevertheless, they deserve our respect for trying to make a difference every day, whatever their organizational status or position.

Discussion Probes

1. Do you consider yourself a tempered radical? Why? Have you ever played this role in the past? How did you differ from the dominant culture of your organization?

2. Do you work with individuals you would consider to be tempered radicals? How successful have they been in bringing about change?

3. How do you decide when you can no longer stay loyal to an organization and remain true to your core values?

4. What would be examples of small wins in your organization? Have these small victories led to major changes?

5. What examples of leading up have you seen in your workplace? At your college or university?

Source

Myerson, D. E. (2001). *Tempered radicals: How people use difference to inspire change at work.* Boston, MA: Harvard Business School Press.

Whistle-Blowing

Whistle-blowers are organizational members who decide to remain in the organization but take their concerns about abuses (for example, bid rigging, bribery, unsafe products, substandard working conditions) to outsiders in the hope of correcting the problem.[20] They often begin by expressing their dissent through organizational channels but end up making problems public when their concerns are ignored. Prominent whistle-blowers have become national heroes in recent years. The film *The Insider* profiled scientist Jeffrey Wigand's decision to turn over tobacco company documents to *60 Minutes*. These records and his courtroom testimony revealed that tobacco executives knew about the health risks of cigarettes despite sworn testimony to the contrary. Three whistle-blowers—FBI agent Colleen Rowley, WorldCom auditor Cynthia Cooper, and Enron vice-president Sherron Watkins—were named *Time* magazine's Persons of the Year in 2002.[21] (The Ethics and Technology box demonstrates how technology is taking whistle-blowing to a whole new level.)

ETHICS AND TECHNOLOGY

WikiLeaks: Whistle-Blowing on a Global Scale

WikiLeaks is a powerful new tool for would-be whistle blowers. The global website, which declares that it wants to be the "intelligence service of the people," uses secure servers to publish documents and video supplied by those who want to remain anonymous.[1] Notable posts on the site include information on Scientology, the membership list of a racist British political party, the content of U.S. airport security manuals, scientists' e-mails questioning the existence of global warming, and evidence of illegal banking activities in Iceland and Switzerland. However, WikiLeaks gained the most notoriety for publishing U.S. military secrets, including video of a helicopter crew killing a group of unarmed Iraqis, more than 400,000 documents from the Iraq War, and thousands more documents from the war in Afghanistan. These written materials revealed extensive prisoner abuse and widespread (and previously underreported) civilian casualties.

WikiLeaks and other, similar sites have the potential to greatly increase transparency in business and government. Journalism expert Jay Rosen notes that WikiLeaks is the first stateless news organization. According to Rosen,

> In media history up to now, the press is free to report on what the powerful wish to keep secret because the laws of a given nation protect it. But WikiLeaks is able to report on what the powerful wish to keep secret because the logic of the Internet permits it. This is new.[2]

The volunteers who run WikiLeaks have discovered that revealing secrets is risky business. Governments in Australia, China, Russia, Thailand, North Korea, and Zimbabwe have all tried to block the site, and the U.S. military launched a campaign to undermine its credibility. Local police raided the home of the owner of the German WikiLeaks domain. WikiLeaks founder Julian Assange was detained on rape charges that he claimed were politically motivated.

Opponents of WikiLeaks, both inside and outside of government, argue that the site publishes stolen materials that violate privacy and intellectual property rights. They warn that the group has no qualms about posting confidential records of religious and social organizations and note that the site published an entire book online without the permission of the author. An even greater concern is that WikiLeaks puts lives at risk. U.S. Army officials believe that insurgents will kill Afghan intelligence sources identified in leaked documents and use information in this material in their battles against American troops. One critic sums up the case against WikiLeaks this way: "Their [WikiLeaks'] response to indiscriminate secrecy has been to adopt a policy of indiscriminate disclosure. They tend to disregard considerations of personal privacy, intellectual property, as well as security."[3]

Notes

1. McGreal, C. (2010, April 10). Who watches WikiLeaks? *The Guardian,* Comment, p. 32.
2. Wente, M. (2010, July 27). When nothing is secret any more. *The Globe and Mail,* p. A13.
3. McGreal.

Sources

Beckford, M. (2010, December 6). Arrest warrant for website's founder 'a political stunt.' *The Daily Telegraph,* News, p. 18.

Burns, J. F., & Somaiya, R. (2010, October 25). Amid disclosures, a quest for secrecy. *The International Herald Tribune,* p. 4.

Cloud, D. S., & Parker, N. (2010, October 23). Leaks focus on U.S. role in Iraq. *Los Angeles Times,* p. AA1.

Cohen, M. (2010, August 2). A renegade site, now working with the news media. *The New York Times,* p. B3.

O'Dwyer, D. (2010, April 3). Why online whistleblowers need protection from the powerful. *The Irish Times,* Weekend, p. 2.

All the favorable publicity given to famous whistle-blowers could give the impression that going public with concerns is easy and rewarding. Nothing could be further from the truth. Even successful whistle-blowers pay a steep price for speaking up. Wigand lost his high-paying job and his marriage at the same time that his character was attacked in the press. Fellow officers criticized Agent Rowley for being disloyal and threatened her with criminal charges for publicizing the FBI's failure to monitor some of the 9/11 hijackers. Cooper was screamed at and shunned by some of her fellow employees. Not one senior WorldCom executive has ever thanked her or her internal audit team that brought the company's accounting scandal to light. Watkins was demoted and given little to do after warning Enron CEO Kenneth Lay about the company's shaky finances.

After conducting a national survey of past whistle-blowers, Terrence Miethe concludes, "Most whistleblowers discover that exposing organizational misconduct is a low-reward and high-risk activity."[22] Dissenters can expect to be attacked instead of supported, despite federal and state laws designed to protect those who come forward and support groups for those who do. They will likely be abandoned by coworkers, criticized or humiliated by superiors, denied promotions, relegated to meaningless positions, cut off from neighbors, and on and on. As a consequence, of employees who witness unethical conduct, only half (52%) report the misconduct to the proper authorities.[23]

The experience of Mike Quint illustrates the negative consequences of whistle-blowing. Quint was an engineer assigned to inspect construction of the Los Angeles Metro Rail Project between 1987 and 1991.[24] Quint noted a number of problems on the project that could pose safety hazards to riders, including missing reinforcement bars, poor inspection procedures, and violations of structural codes. After his concerns were ignored, Quint notified a variety of government officials and the local press. Later the Army Corps of Engineers confirmed his allegations, and the problems were corrected. Nonetheless, Quint was transferred and terminated, blacklisted from getting another inspection job. He reports feeling depressed, isolated, and distrustful and in poorer physical health.

In light of the risks, blowing the whistle on organizational wrongdoing takes a great deal of courage. Yet courage by itself is not enough. Whistle-blowers must also engage in careful ethical reasoning. They have to determine where their ultimate loyalty should rest and whether the disruption they will cause is justified. When the whistle blows, everyone in the organization suffers. Workers lose their jobs, the credibility of the organization is damaged, stock prices decline, and so forth.

Ethicist Sissela Bok divides the act of whistle-blowing into three parts to help ethical decision makers weigh the moral implications of exposing misbehavior to outsiders.[25] Each element of the process raises ethical questions, which are summarized by R. A. Johnson in Ethics in Action 9.1. *Dissent* addresses the relative benefits of going public. Most whistle-blowers believe that their actions will benefit society as a whole. Before going forward, they need to determine if this is indeed the case. Whistle-blowers break their *loyalty* to fellow members and to the group as a whole. Therefore, whistle-blowing should only be used as a last resort, when time is limited and internal channels aren't an option. Whistle-blowers bring serious charges against individuals in public. *Accusation* highlights the fact that dissenters are ethically obligated to consider such issues as fairness, the public's right to know, anonymity, and their personal motives.

ETHICS IN ACTION 9.1 THE WHISTLE-BLOWER CHECKLIST

Dissent: When whistle-blowers claim their dissent will achieve a public good, they must ask:

✓ What is the nature of the promised benefit?

✓ How accurate are the facts?

✓ How serious is the impropriety?

✓ How imminent is the threat?

✓ How closely linked to the wrongdoing are those accused?

Loyalty: When whistle-blowers breach loyalty to their organization, they must ask:

✓ Is whistle-blowing the last and only alternative?

✓ Is there no time to use routine channels?

✓ Are internal channels corrupted?

✓ Are there no internal channels?

Accusation: When whistle-blowers are publicly accusing others, they must ask:

✓ Are the accusations fair?

✓ Does the public have a right to know?

✓ Is the whistle-blower *not* anonymous?

✓ Are the motives *not* self-serving?

SOURCE: Johnson, R. A. (2003). *Whistle-blowing: When it works—and why.* Boulder, CO: Lynne Rienner, p. 30. Used by permission.

As managers, we can take steps to encourage employees to blow the whistle internally so corrective actions can be taken without incurring the costs of going public.[26] Create tough antiretaliation policies, and disseminate those policies throughout the organization. Identify types of unethical behavior, and spell out what employees should do if they observe such actions. When an employee makes a complaint, concentrate on the wrongdoing and not on the whistleblower. Thoroughly investigate all reports, and take quick action when justified. Publicize corrective actions, and monitor to make sure retaliation doesn't occur.

CHAPTER TAKEAWAYS

- The power and influence of followers is growing, making ethical followership more important than ever before.
- The moral demands you'll face as a follower are the challenge of obligation, the challenge of obedience, the challenge of cynicism, the challenge of dissent, and the challenge of delivering bad news.
- Beware of fear, anxiety, the need to belong, and other forces that can make you dependent on toxic leaders. Learn to live with anxiety, and don't be afraid to act independently. Demand leaders who tell the truth; avoid those with grandiose visions. Don't let a few selfish individuals select themselves as leaders, but draft a large number of organizational members to take on leadership responsibilities.
- In order to act as an exemplary follower, you'll need to practice service to your leaders and organizations by exercising independent, critical thought and by becoming actively engaged in organizational affairs. You can become an exemplary follower by leading yourself, committing yourself to ideas and

causes, developing your competence and credibility, using your courageous conscience, and learning to disagree agreeably.

- Good followers are engaged with their leaders and serve the public good, not selfish interests. Don't wait to resist bad leadership, but respond as soon as possible, joining forces with other followers if you can.

- You will need to demonstrate courage if you are to fulfill your ethical duties as a follower. Dimensions of courage include (a) the courage to assume responsibility, (b) the courage to serve, (c) the courage to challenge, (d) the courage to participate in transformation, and (e) the courage to leave. Develop your courage by seeking to serve as a partner with your leader, practicing the skills you need to act courageously, and identifying possible misperceptions or blind spots you have as a follower.

- Become an authentic follower by developing psychological ownership, fostering trusting relationships with leaders, and practicing transparency—being honest and willing to admit problems.

- Managing up is taking the ethical responsibility for establishing a good working relationship with your supervisor and learning how to work together effectively.

- Leading up is taking initiative to improve the organization and the group without being given formal authority. To effectively lead up, keep superiors informed, and build support for your policies and initiatives by using facts and evidence. You may need to step up even when your superiors don't recognize the need or the opportunity.

- Whistleblowing is bringing wrongdoing to the attention of outsiders. Not only will you need courage to be a whistle-blower, but you'll also have to engage in careful moral reasoning, weighing the relative benefits of going public, breaking loyalties, and publicly accusing others. Take steps to encourage others to blow the whistle by setting tough antiretaliation policies and by taking quick corrective action when complaints surface.

APPLICATION PROJECTS

1. In a group, identify additional ethical demands on followers that you would add to those in the chapter.

2. Create a case study that illustrates how a follower responded to one of the ethical challenges.

3. Which ethical challenge of followership is the most difficult to resolve? Write up your conclusions.

4. Develop a definition of toxic followership. Explain how toxic followership and toxic leadership are related.

5. Determine your follower style using the questionnaire in Ethics in Action 9.1. Explain what your scores mean to you. Describe how you might become a more exemplary follower based on the five behavior patterns described on page 282.

6. Have you had to display any of the dimensions of courageous followership? Share your story in a small group.

7. Confrontation role-plays:

   You are the vice president for product development at a large manufacturing firm. Your division is ready to begin work on a major new product line. Due to the investment required to develop the new products, the board of directors has to give its approval. Your boss, the company CEO, has enthusiastically supported the project. That's why his behavior at last night's board meeting was so disappointing. When several board members began to express opposition to your plans after your presentation, the CEO agreed with them and stated that the new product line was "not well thought out." You are scheduled to meet with the CEO this morning to debrief the board session.

You are the director of an MBA program at a private university. On more than one occasion, the president of your school has exaggerated the number of students in your program when making presentations to donors. He continues to overstate enrollments, even though you have provided him with the correct figures. You have an appointment with him to discuss other items but want to address this issue as well.

You are a junior accountant at a small accounting firm. You notice that your supervisor, who generates the most income for your business, appears to be advising clients to claim unauthorized deductions on their tax forms. She denies that she is doing anything illegal and claims that she is trying to save money for her hardworking clients. You, however, are unconvinced by her arguments and set up a meeting to confront her about the deductions.

8. Do you feel like an owner of your organization? Why or why not? What can you do as a follower to increase the sense that you have an ownership stake in your company, nonprofit, or government agency? What can your leaders do to foster your feeling of ownership?

9. Develop a strategy for managing up and/or leading up with one of your supervisors.

10. Analyze the actions of a whistle-blower using Bok's checklist. Was this person justified in coming forward?

CASE STUDY 9.2

Helping Harvard Medical School Make the Grade

In 2008, Harvard Medical School received an F grade from the American Medical Student Association for how it tracked and controlled money from the drug industry. Some Harvard Medical School faculty received hundreds of thousands of dollars a year from pharmaceutical firms for consulting and speaking. The school's former dean, for example, sat on the board of Baxter International, a medical supply company, where he received up to $197,000 a year in addition to his salary from the college. Companies like Merck and Pfizer also gave trips, meals, and tickets to faculty and their families while underwriting endowed chairs, faculty prizes, and research programs. Disclosure rules were lax, and professors didn't have to reveal their industry ties in class.

A few Harvard students became concerned that the flow of pharmaceutical money was biasing material presented in the classroom. First-year medical student Mark Zerden became suspicious when his pharmacology professor promoted the benefits of cholesterol drugs while belittling a student who asked whether the drugs had side effects. Zerden did online research and discovered that the instructor was a paid consultant to 10 drug companies, including 5 that made cholesterol medications. Another student noted, "Before coming here, I had no idea how much influence companies had on medical education. And it's something that's purposely meant to be under the table, providing information under the guise of education when that information is also presented for marketing purposes."[1]

The concerns of a few students soon sparked a movement to limit the influence of pharmaceutical money at the university and its related teaching hospitals. Along with sympathetic faculty, 200 Harvard medical students convinced administrators to adopt a requirement that all professors and lecturers must disclose any industry ties in class. (One professor had 47 such company affiliations.) The school dean formed a committee made up of faculty, students, and administrators to look at conflict of interest policies. The task force adopted new guidelines that (1) limited industry advertising and exhibitions on campus, (2) called for review of faculty members' participation on for-profit biomedical boards, (3) prohibited faculty participation in industry speakers bureaus, (4) banned industry gifts, meals, and travel, and (5) placed stricter limits on the amount of money professors and lecturers can earn from outside sources.

At the same time that Harvard students were lobbying for changes, the Massachusetts legislature passed limits on gifts to physicians, and U.S. Senator Charles Grassley held hearings into corporate funding for three Harvard psychiatrists who advocated for the use of antipsychotic drugs with children. These researchers failed to report at least $4.2 million in industry payments. One promoted the use of the medicine Risperdal while working for a subsidiary of Johnson & Johnson, the drug's maker. He signed off on a scientific abstract he hadn't authored and provided advice to Johnson & Johnson on how to deal with the fact that children given placebos did just as well as those given the medication.

Harvard student efforts to eliminate conflicts of interest involving medical companies encountered significant resistance. A smaller, rival group signed a petition calling for continuing the school's strong ties to the biomedical industry. Said the leader of this group, "To say that because these industry sources are inherently biased, physicians should never listen to them, is wrong."[2] One professor argued that Harvard should be even more aggressive in seeking private industry funds. "You see industry interaction has produced far more good than harm," he argued. "Harvard absolutely could get more from industry but I think they're very skittish. There's a huge opportunity we ought to mine."[3]

Harvard administrators tried to muzzle the conflict of interest movement. After students talked with *The New York Times*, the school adopted a policy requiring that every interaction between students and the media be coordinated through the Office of the Dean of Students and the Office of Public Affairs. (It later dropped the new policy after criticism from both inside and outside the university.) A Merck employee admitted taking pictures of students protesting the influence of drug companies at Harvard, though he claimed it was for "personal" reasons and not to intimidate protestors.

Harvard Medical School's new policy helped raise its grade from the American Medical School Student Association from an F to a B. The grade likely would have been higher, but Harvard still allows faculty to consult and work with businesses and permits pharmaceutical companies to fund postgraduate medical courses.

Discussion Probes

1. Do you think drug company money produces more good than harm for medical schools?

2. What limits, if any, should be placed on what medical faculty and researchers receive from pharmaceutical firms?

3. What risks did students take by protesting Harvard's conflict of interest policies?

4. Do you think that Harvard students would have been successful in changing the school's conflict of interest policy if the state legislature and U.S. Senate had not also been concerned about the issue?

5. Have you ever been in a class where you thought that the professor was presenting biased information because of his or her work outside the university? Did you express your opinion to the instructor, fellow students, and/or administrators? Why or why not?

6. What did you learn about expressing dissent from this case?

Notes

1. Wilson, D. (2009, March 3). Patching a wound. *The New York Times*, p. B1.
2. Wilson (2009, March 3).
3. Wilson (2009, March 3).

Sources

Expert or shill? (2008, November 30). *The New York Times*, p. WK7.
Harvard Medical School conflict of interest policy receives approval from American Medical Student Association. Retrieved from http://www.amsa.org?AMSA/Homepage/About/News/072110.aspx
Wilson, D. (2009, March 3). Pfizer worker photographed student protest at Harvard. *The New York Times*, p. B6.
Wilson, D. (2009, March 4). Senator asks Pfizer to detail pay to Harvard. *The New York Times*, p. B3.
Wilson, D. (2009, September 2). Harvard backs off media policy. *The New York Times*, p. B4.
Wilson, D. (2010, July 22). A tougher conflict policy at Harvard Medical School. *The New York Times*, p. B4.

CASE STUDY 9.3

Courage Under Fire: Hugh Thompson at My Lai

The massacre of 500 unarmed civilians at the Vietnamese village of My Lai is one of the darkest moments in U.S. military history. On the morning of March 16, 1968, troops from Task Force Barker entered the village of My Lai in South Vietnam. American soldiers expected stiff resistance from a large contingent of Vietcong reportedly in the area. Task force members were in a vengeful mood, bitter at local residents who had failed to warn them about booby traps and minefields. When they encountered no Vietcong, soldiers turned on innocent villagers—women, elderly men, children, and babies—instead. For several hours, members of Charlie Company, under the direction of Lieutenant William Calley, went on a murderous rampage. They threw fragmentation grenades into houses, gunned down villagers who were trying to surrender, slit the throats of some of their victims, and raped others.

In the midst of this evil, one small group of men acted with courage. Army helicopter pilot Hugh Thomson and crew members Lawrence Colburn and Glenn Andreotta were assigned to fly over the village to draw enemy fire. When they came back from refueling, what they saw didn't make sense. The ground was littered with the bodies of civilians and water buffalo. They saw a teenage girl, seriously injured, lying on her back in a rice field. They marked her location with a smoke flare and radioed for help. An American soldier walked up, nudged her with his foot, and then shot her.

After confirming that the Americans were killing unarmed villagers, Thompson landed his helicopter between a band of soldiers and a group of Vietnamese huddled in a bunker. Thompson told Colburn to shoot if they began to fire at the civilians. He warned the commanding officer, "You see my guns? If you open up, they open up."[1] The pilot was able to get 10 people out of the bunker and safely to a bigger chopper for evacuation.

Andreotta noticed movement on their last pass over an irrigation ditch containing many of the victims. Thompson set the helicopter down and, covered by the weapons of his fellow crew members, Andreotta rescued a 4-year-old boy. The child was covered with blood but otherwise unhurt. Thompson then flew back to base and confronted his superiors. However, the story of My Lai didn't become public until 18 months later, when Ron Ridenhour, a GI who had heard about My Lai from buddies in Task Force Barker, brought the story to the attention of *New York Times* writer Seymour Hirsch and government officials.

Nearly 80 soldiers participated in the killing and subsequent cover-up. Of the 25 who stood trial, only William Calley was convicted. Calley was seen as a scapegoat by both supporters and opponents of the war and eventually served only 3 years of house arrest. For his part, Thompson received death threats for testifying about the crime. It took 30 years for Thompson and Colburn to be officially acknowledged for their heroics. In 1998, they were given the highest noncombat military honor—the Soldiers Medal—despite resistance from some at the Pentagon. (Andreotta died during the war.) That same year, the former pilot and his crew member returned to My Lai to be reunited with the little boy they had rescued from the killing fields.

Thompson labels what happened at My Lai "premeditated murder." He told a My Lai symposium, "It did not take a rocket scientist to realize it was wrong."[2] The chief prosecutor for the My Lai courts-martial sums up Thompson's courage this way: "When you have evil, sometimes, in the midst of it, you will have incredible, selfless good. And that's Hugh Thompson."[3]

Discussion Probes

1. How do you account for Thompson's courage and that of his crew?

2. Can you think of other examples of followers who risked their lives in the face of evil?

3. What parallels do you see between the massacre at My Lai and prisoner abuse in Iraq and Afghanistan?

4. Why do you think so few were punished for their actions at My Lai?

5. Why is it so difficult for organizations to admit their guilt?

6. How can the military and other organizations encourage followers to act with moral courage?

Notes

1. Thompson (1999).
2. Berry (1995), p. 11.
3. Boyce (2001), p. 33.

Sources

Belknap, M. R. (2002). *The Viet Nam War on trial: The My Lai Massacre and the court-martial of Lieutenant Calley.* Lawrence: University of Kansas Press.

Berry, J. (1995, February 24). My Lai Massacre was an American tragedy. *National Catholic Reporter,* pp. 10–11.

Boyce, N. (2001, August 20). Hugh Thompson. *U.S. News and World Report,* pp. 33–34.

Hitchens, C. (2001, May 28). Leave no child behind? *The Nation,* pp. 9–10.

Thompson, H. (1999, March 8). The massacre at My Lai. *Newsweek,* p. 64.

Vistica, G. L. (1997, November 24). A quiet war over the past. *Newsweek,* p. 41.

ENDNOTES

1. Johnson, C. E. (2009). Book review: Followership and the Art of Followership. *International Leadership Journal, 1,* 107–109.

2. Kellerman, B. (2008). *Followership: How followers are creating change and changing leaders.* Boston: Harvard Business School Press.

3. Milgram, S. (1974). *Obedience to authority.* New York: Harper & Row.

4. Chaleff, I. (2003). *The courageous follower: Standing up to and for our leaders* (2nd ed.). San Francisco: Berrett-Koehler.

5. Roloff, M. E., & Paulson, G. D. (2001). Confronting organizational transgressions. In J. M. Darley, D. M. Messick, & T. R. Tyler (Eds.), *Social influences on ethical behavior in organizations* (pp. 53–68). Mahwah, NJ: Lawrence Erlbaum.

6. Susskind, L., & Field, P. (1996). *Dealing with an angry public: The mutual gains approach to resolving disputes.* New York: Free Press, p. 223.

7. Lipman-Blumen, J. (2005). *The allure of toxic leaders: Why we follow destructive bosses and corrupt politicians—and how we can survive them.* Oxford, UK: Oxford University Press; Lipman-Blumen, J. (2008). Following toxic leaders: In search of posthumous praise. In R. E. Riggio, I. Chaleff, & J. Lipman-Blumen (Eds.), *The art of followership: How great followers create great leaders and organizations* (pp. 181–194). San Francisco: Jossey-Bass.

8. Kelley, R. E. (1998). Followership in a leadership world. In L. C. Spears (Ed.), *Insights on leadership* (pp. 170–184). New York: John Wiley. See also: Kelley, R. E. (1992). *The power of followership: How to create leaders people want to follow and followers who lead themselves.* New York: Doubleday/Currency.

9. Kelley (1998), p. 175.

10. Kelley (1998), p. 178.

11. Kellerman (2008).

12. Kellerman, p. 179.

13. Kellerman, p. 229.

14. Chaleff (2003).

15. Chaleff, I. (2008). Creating new ways of following. In R. E. Riggio, I. Chaleff, & J. Lipman-Blumen (Eds.), *The art of followership: How great followers create great leaders and organizations* (pp. 67–92). San Francisco: Jossey-Bass.

16. Avolio, B. J., & Reichard, R. J. (2008). The rise of authentic followership. In R. E. Riggio, I. Chaleff, & J. Lipman-Blumen (Eds.), *The art of followership: How great followers create great leaders and organizations* (pp. 325–338). San Francisco: Jossey Bass. See also: Luthans, F., Norman, S., & Hughes, L. (2006). Authentic

leadership: A new approach for a new time. In R. J. Burke & C. L. Cooper (Eds.), *Inspiring leaders* (pp. 84–194). London: Routledge.

17. Avolio & Reichard, p. 328.

18. Gabarro, J. J., & Kotter, J. P. (2005, January). Managing your boss. *Harvard Business Review,* pp. 92–99.

19. Useem, M. (2001). *Leading up: How to lead your boss so you both win.* New York: Crown Business, p. 3.

20. Johnson, R. A. (2003). *Whistle-blowing: When it works—and why.* Boulder, CO: Lynne Rienner.

21. Lacoay, R., & Ripley, A. (2003, January 6). Persons of the year. *Time,* pp. 30–60.

22. Miethe, T. D. (1999). *Whistleblowing at work: Tough choices in exposing fraud, waste, and abuse on the job.* Boulder, CO: Westview Press, p. 209.

23. Hudson Employment Index. (2005). *One in three workers witness ethical misconduct despite clearly communicated guidelines.* Washington, DC: Hudson. Retrieved from http://us.hudson.com/node.asp?kwd= survey-2005-archive

24. Miethe (1999).

25. Bok, S. (1980). Whistleblowing and professional responsibilities. In D. Callahan & S. Bok (Eds.), *Ethics teaching in higher education* (pp. 277–295). New York: Plenum Press.

26. Miceli, M. P., Near, J. P., & Dworkin, T. M. (2009). A word to the wise: How managers and policy- makers can encourage employees to report wrongdoing. *Journal of Business Ethics, 86,* 379–396; Miceli, M. P., Near, J. P., & Dworkin, T. M. (2008). *Whistle-blowing in organizations.* New York: Routledge.

PART V

Practicing Ethics in Organizational Systems

10

Building an Ethical Organization

Making Ethics Matter

As we've seen throughout this text, fallen organizations pay a high price for their moral shortcomings in the form of damaged reputations; declining revenues, earnings, donations, and stock prices; downsizing and bankruptcy; increased regulation; and civil lawsuits and criminal charges. Unfortunately, managers and employees looking to integrate moral values into their work structures and processes often settle for superficial measures that have little influence on day-to-day operations. They focus on complying with legal requirements through official policies; ethical issues are rarely discussed, and decisions are typically made without reference to core values or moral standards. In other words, their ethical efforts are easily disconnected or "decoupled" from the most important organizational activities.[1]

The poor track record of contemporary organizations is proof that the decoupled approach to ethics doesn't work. Our task, then, is to make sure that ethics matter,

(a) by ensuring that members recognize the moral dimension of every aspect of organizational life, and (b) by encouraging improvement in collective ethical performance. Investigators use a variety of terms to describe such an ethics-based approach, including *integrated, integrity focused, purpose driven,* and *values centered.*[2] However, *transformational* is a more inclusive descriptor. This broader label incorporates integration, integrity, purpose, and values. To transform something means to alter its very nature or essence for the better, producing fundamental, long-lasting, positive change.[3] When applied to ethics, transformation goes beyond lip service to moral values or grudging compliance with legal requirements. Transformation places ethics at the center of the workplace, significantly altering attitudes, thinking, communication, behavior, culture, and systems. Key values drive individual decisions, interpersonal relationships, group interaction, and organizational goals.

Ethics in Action 10.1 contrasts the qualities of ethically decoupled and ethically transformed organizations. The objective of this chapter is to help you move your organization from the disconnected column to the transformed column or to help it maintain its transformed status. To reach this goal, you will need to understand the components of ethical culture and engage in successful cultural change efforts.

ETHICS IN ACTION 10.1 CHARACTERISTICS OF ETHICALLY DECOUPLED AND ETHICALLY TRANSFORMED ORGANIZATIONS

Ethically Decoupled Organizations	Ethically Transformed Organizations
See ethics as a means to an end (profit, better public image)	See ethics as an end in itself
Comply with legal requirements	Exceed legal requirements
Exhibit organizational behavior inconsistent with stated values	Take actions that reflect collective values; the transformed organization "walks its talk"
Are insensitive to potential moral issues	Are highly sensitive to moral dilemmas
Emphasize rules and penalties	Emphasize adherence to shared values
Have a low awareness of ethical duties Dysfunctional conflict Tolerate misbehavior	Have a high awareness of individual and collective ethical responsibilities Functional conflict Swiftly punish misbehavior
Rarely discuss ethics; rarely use moral vocabulary	Routinely discuss ethics using moral vocabulary
Omit ethics from daily decisions and operations	Make ethics part of every decision and operation
Are driven by practical or pragmatic considerations (the bottom line)	Are driven by mission and values

Ethically Decoupled Organizations	Ethically Transformed Organizations
React to destructive behaviors	Prevent destructive behaviors
Have ethically inconsistent reward structures	Have reward systems that promote moral behavior
Show a high concern for self	Show a high concern for others
Sacrifice individual rights for organizational good	Honor and protect individual rights
Engage in self-centered communication (monologue)	Engage in other-centered communication (dialogue)
Have low to moderate trust and commitment levels	Have high trust and commitment levels
Have teams that routinely fall victim to unethical group processes	Have teams that are rarely victimized by unethical group processes
Show high concern for the organization	Show high concern for stakeholders, society, and the global environment
Hold and build power bases	Give power away
Exhibit low-level moral reasoning	Base reasoning on universal ethical principles
Prevent members from making moral choices	Equip members to make moral choices
Respond to changes in the ethical environment	Anticipate changes in the ethical environment
Invest little in building a positive ethical climate	Invest significantly in creating and maintaining an ethical workplace (i.e., training, socialization, leader involvement)
Are at significant risk of ethical misbehavior and scandal	Are at low risk of ethical misbehavior and scandal

Components of Ethical Culture

Scholars from a variety of fields borrow the concept of culture from the field of anthropology to describe how organizations create shared meanings. As members meet and interact, they develop common beliefs, values, and assumptions, which are expressed through architecture, ceremonies, rituals, dress, and other visible artifacts. Culture binds the organization together and, at the same time, greatly influences the behavior of individuals. What members wear and drive to work, the way they carry out their tasks and organize their time, and with whom they socialize at lunch are all products of shared culture. Ethicists are particularly interested in how cultural elements, both formal and informal, promote or discourage moral action. Formal cultural components include core values, mission statements, codes of ethics, structure, reward and evaluation systems, reporting and communication systems, and ethics officers. Informal components include language, norms, rituals, and stories.[4] In this section, I'll describe each of these elements and its relationship to ethical behavior. I will also outline ways you can use each component to contribute to the formation of an ethical environment.

Formal Elements

1. Core Values

Core values serve as enduring, guiding principles. Most organizations have between three and five such values, which are central to their collective identities.[5] Leaders at the Sealed Air Corporation (the makers of bubble wrap) consider their "bedrock values" to be personal accountability, respect for the individual, truth, and fair dealing. They take these values seriously. Concern for truth and fair dealing, for example, prevent company salespeople from slamming the competition. Independent energy producer AES incorporated the following values in the prospectus for its initial public offering: (1) integrity (wholeness, honoring commitments, adhering to the truth, consistency); (2) fairness to all stakeholders and just rewards; (3) fun (creating an enjoyable work atmosphere); and (4) social responsibility (doing a good job of fulfilling the company's purpose and doing something extra for society).[6]

Organizations run into trouble when they either fail to identify and communicate their core values or fail to live up to them. Some groups have never taken the time and effort to isolate those principles that set them apart; others have clearly defined values but don't put enough effort into publicizing them. To shape behavior, values must be continually reinforced through training, public meetings, annual reports, corporate videos, brochures, and other means. In addition, leaders must "walk the talk," living out the values through their performance.

Implementation Guidelines. There is no universal set of correct organizational core values. Instead, the key is to determine what members find intrinsically valuable in your work group, regardless of what outsiders think. Bring members from around the organization together to consider such questions as these: "If we were penalized for holding this core value, would we still hold on to it?" "Would we want to keep this value no matter how the world around us changes in the next 10 years?" "What are the very best attributes of our organization?"[7] Once they have been selected, incorporate these values into decision-making processes and evaluation systems; continually communicate them. Hold your leaders as well as followers to these standards.

2. Mission (Purpose) Statements

A mission statement identifies an organization's reason for being, which reflects the ideals of its members. This statement combines with core values to form what management experts James Collins and Jerry Porras refer to as *core ideology.*[8] Core ideology is the central identity or character of an organization. Collins and Porras found that the character of the outstanding companies they studied remained constant, even as those firms continued to learn and adapt. Some examples of purpose statements are found in Ethics in Action 10.2.

ETHICS IN ACTION 10.2 SAMPLE MISSION STATEMENTS

To make a positive difference in the lives of children and youth. (Big Brothers/Big Sisters)

A human relations organization dedicated to fighting bias, bigotry, and racism in America. (National Conference of Christians and Jews)

To solve unsolved problems innovatively. (3M)

To nourish and delight everyone we serve. (Darden Restaurants)

To bring inspiration and innovation to every athlete in the world. (Nike)

To build shareholder value by delivering healthcare products, services, and solutions in innovative and cost-effective ways. (AmerisourceBergen)

To serve the needs of investors. (Charles Schwab)

Dedication to the highest quality of Customer Service delivered with a sense of warmth, friendliness, individual pride, and Company Spirit. (Southwest Airlines)

To be the best by offering the most innovative, highest quality products to advance the health and well-being of people around the world. (Warner-Lambert)

To collect the proper amount of tax revenue at the least cost; serve the public by continually improving the quality of our products and services; and perform in a manner warranting the highest degree of public confidence in our integrity, efficiency, and fairness. (Internal Revenue Service)

To earn money for shareholders and increase the value of their investment. (Cooper Tire & Rubber)

To become the leading premium ice cream company in America. (Dreyer's Grand Ice Cream)

To provide products and services which increase the efficiency and profitability of the world's farmers. (Pioneer Hi-Bred International)

We fulfill dreams through the experience of motorcycles . . . (Harley Davidson)

To be the world standard for quality and performance in general aviation, related products, and services. (Beechcraft)

To produce, distribute, and market a variety of high-quality beers in a manner that meets or exceeds the expectations of our customers. (Stroh Brewery)

To be the information partner of choice in each market we serve—helping people gain the knowledge they need to work, live and govern themselves. (Times Mirror)

To constantly improve what is essential to human progress by mastering science and technology. (Dow Chemical)

(Continued)

(Continued)

Sources

Abrahams, J. (1999). *The mission statement book: 301 corporate mission statements from America's top companies.* Berkeley, CA: Ten Speed Press.

Collins, J. C., & Porras, J. I. (1996, September-October). Building your company's vision. *Harvard Business Review,* pp. 65–77.

MissionStatements.com (2010). Retrieved from http://www.missionstatement.com/fortune_500_mission_statements.html

Radtke, J. M. (1998). *Strategic communications for nonprofit organizations: Seven steps to creating a successful plan.* New York: John Wiley.

Many mission statements fail to guide and inspire or promote moral conduct. "Maximize shareholder wealth" is a purpose that provides minimal guidance or inspiration to members. Not only does it fail to distinguish a company from its competitors, but few people get excited about increasing earnings per share. Pursuing this objective may promote such unethical activities as overstating revenue, hiding expenses, lying to investors, and shipping shoddy products. In contrast, pursuing such goals as "to bring inspiration and innovation to every athlete in the world" (Nike) and "helping people gain the knowledge they need to work, live and govern themselves" (Times Mirror) is likely to inspire employees and encourage them to produce quality goods and services that benefit others.

Like core values, mission statements must be continually communicated and reinforced. They, too, can be undermined by inconsistent behavior. Lofty official goals do little to promote morality when leaders and followers ignore them in order to pursue their personal agendas.

Implementation Guidelines. To create your organizational mission statement, try to identify what members of your organization are passionate about, and capture this passion in your document. In the case of a business, ask what purpose would keep employees working for the group even if they had enough money to retire. Evaluate the mission statement on how well it guides, inspires, and promotes moral behavior.

3. Codes of Ethics

Codes of ethics are among the most common ethics tools. Nearly all major corporations have them, along with a great many government departments, professional associations, social service agencies, and schools.[9] Under Securities and Exchange Commission guidelines designed to enforce the Sarbanes-Oxley Act, all publicly traded companies must have codes and enforcement procedures that apply to top-level financial and other managers. The New York Stock Exchange (NYSE), the American Stock Exchange (AMEX), and the NASDAQ Stock Market all require listed companies to adopt ethics codes and disclose their content to the public.[10] Codes must include provisions that describe how the code will be enforced and how the company will respond to violations.

Codes typically address these six areas:[11]

- *Conflicts of interest.* Conflict provisions deal with cases in which employees benefit at the expense of the organization or in which an individual's judgment might be compromised. Cases of conflict of interest include accepting gifts from suppliers or diverting contracts to relatives. Former Enron CFO Andrew Fastow provides one blatant example of conflict of interest. While working for Enron, he set up partnerships that generated millions in fees for himself at the company's expense. Now, federal guidelines dictate that any waiver of conflict of interest provisions must be promptly reported to shareholders. (We'll take a closer look at financial conflicts of interest in the next chapter.)

- *Records, funds, and assets.* All chartered and tax-exempt organizations must keep accurate financial records. Under the Sarbanes-Oxley accounting act, large corporations now submit more extensive documentation than ever before. Publicly traded firms must follow SEC (Security and Exchange Commission) regulations as well as state and local laws and their own bylaws.

- *Information.* For-profit organizations try to keep information from competitors. Revealing such data (even to family members) can result in legal action. Public-sector organizations, on the other hand, may have codes that encourage compliance with "sunshine laws" that require the release of information.

- *Outside relationships.* Relationships with suppliers, competitors, government agencies, and others have legal and ethical ramifications. Members must avoid behaviors ranging from collusion, price-fixing, and insider trading to gossiping about the competition.

- *Employment practices.* Employment provisions deal with discrimination, drug use, sexual harassment, aggression, and related issues.

- *Other practices.* This category incorporates statements about employee health and safety, the use of technology, treatment of the environment, political activities, overseas conduct, and other topics. One provision found in many codes forbids the use of organizational assets for personal benefit. According to Coca-Cola's code of ethics, such assets include work time, work products, equipment, vehicles, computers, and software, as well as the company's information, trademarks, and name.[12] (See the Ethics and Technology feature on p. 311 for a closer look at the ways employees use organizational technology for personal use.)

Despite their popularity, formal ethics statements are controversial. Skeptics argue that they are vague public relations documents designed to improve an organization's image. Few employees know what the codes say, and their provisions are rarely enforced. Worse yet, critics say, codes are ineffectual. These documents do nothing to improve ethical behavior.

Defenders of ethical codes point out that such documents describe an organization's ethical position to insiders and as well as outsiders. They are particularly important to newcomers who are learning about the work group's ethical standards and potential moral problems they may face. Referring to a code can encourage members both new and old to resist unethical group and organizational pressures. In the case of wrongdoing, an organization can point to the code as evidence that the immoral behavior is not official policy. Most important, ethics codes can have a direct, positive influence on ethical behavior.[13] Students who sign honor codes, for example, are significantly less likely to plagiarize and cheat on tests.[14] Codes influence ethical perceptions even when organizational members don't remember exactly what is in them. Those in organizations with codes judge themselves and their coworkers as more ethical than those in organizations without codes. They believe that their organizations are more supportive of ethical behavior, and they are more satisfied with their group's moral decisions. These employees feel freer to act ethically and are more committed to their organizations.[15]

Researcher Mark Schwartz identified eight metaphors that can help explain how codes influence ethical behavior. These metaphors and their impact on the actions of organizational members are described below.[16]

Rule Book: The code clarifies what behavior is expected of employees. Outcome: Members read the code and follow its provisions.

Signpost: The code encourages members to consult with others or organizational policies to determine if an action is ethical. Outcome: Members speak with a manager or an ethics officer and follow the advice they receive.

Mirror: The code confirms whether or not a behavior is acceptable. Outcome: Greater compliance with required behaviors.

Magnifying Glass: The code cautions members to exercise care before moving forward. Outcome: Reduces the likelihood of unintentional violation of rules.

Shield: The code equips members to challenge unethical behavior and helps them resist the pressure to engage in unethical activities. Outcome: Increased resistance to unethical requests.

Smoke Detector: The code empowers individuals to warn others about inappropriate activities and to convince them to stop. Outcome: Members are more likely to end their unethical behavior.

Fire alarm: The code causes members to contact the appropriate people or offices to report violations. Outcome: The organization intervenes to stop unethical behavior; members are deterred from engaging in immoral activities.

Club: The code is used to force members to comply with its provisions. Outcome: Members modify their behavior due to the threat of discipline.

Implementation Guidelines. While adopting a code doesn't guarantee moral improvement, the evidence cited above demonstrates that codes can play an important role in fostering an ethical environment. You need to encourage your organization to develop a formal set of ethical guidelines, using the input of a variety of organizational members. Standards will have most impact when senior executives make them a priority and follow their provisions while at the same time rewarding followers who do the same. Back your code up with enforcement. Create procedures for interpreting the code and applying sanctions. Set up systems for reporting problems, investigating charges, and reaching conclusions.[17] Listen carefully to determine which metaphors are used to describe the code of ethics in your organization, and adjust these perceptions if necessary. For example, if employees at your firm see the code as a club used to punish unethical behavior, you may want to encourage them to take a more positive perspective, viewing the code as a signpost instead.

ETHICS AND TECHNOLOGY

Cyberloafing

Internet access has created a new way to procrastinate at work called *cyberloafing* or *cyberslacking*. In cyberloafing, employees use organizational computers for nonproductive activities like surfing the Web for personal information or shopping and chatting online. Computer-mediated slacking is widespread. In one survey, 88% of respondents reported surfing the Internet for information irrelevant to their jobs while at the office, with 66% spending between 10 minutes and an hour on such activity every workday.

Many observers consider cyberloafing unethical because it diverts time and attention from organizational tasks and lowers productivity. However, some researchers suggest that cyberslacking can have positive effects. Non–job-related Internet use reduces stress, can stimulate creativity, enhances employees' sense of well-being, and helps workers manage their lives so that they can spend more time at work. For example, instead of leaving the office to meet with their children or to run errands, employees can e-mail their kids and conduct banking and other tasks online.

Rather than trying to outlaw cyberloafing, organizations can regulate and monitor it instead. Companies should create "e-charters" that spell out organizational policies and guidelines for Internet use. Such charters might limit the amount of time spent on non–work-related business or specify times when such activity is forbidden. Organizations can also provide forums for addressing communication technology issues, including cyberloafing. At the same time, they need to reduce stress levels caused by high workloads and other factors. Employees who are less stressed will turn less often to the Internet for stress relief.

Sources

D'Abate, C. P. (2005). Working hard or hardly working: A study of individuals engaging in personal business on the job. *Human Relations, 58,* 1009–1032.

Garrett, R. K., & Danziger, J. N. (2008). On cyberslacking: Workplace status and personal Internet use at work. *CyberPsychology & Behavior, 11,* 287–292.

Henle, C. A., & Blanchard, A. L. (2008). The interaction of work stressors and organizational sanctions on cyberloafing. *Journal of Managerial Issues 20,* 383–400.

Lavoie, J. A. A., & Pychyl, T. A (2001). Cyberslacking and the procrastination superhighway: A web-based survey of online procrastination, attitudes, and emotion. *Social Science Computer Review, 12,* 431–444.

4. Structure

Structure influences moral behavior through the creation of authority relationships, delineation of lines of accountability, and allocation of decision-making rights.[18] As we saw in Chapter 8, leaders are granted a great deal of power over the lives of followers. Their power is enhanced by the fact that people appear "programmed" to obey authority.[19] The greater the demand for obedience, the higher the likelihood that employees will engage in unethical activities and keep silent about the ethical violations they observe.[20]

Lines of accountability are blurred in many large, complex organizations, diffusing responsibility for choices and actions. The result can be an increase in immoral behavior. Managers may deliberately keep themselves in the dark about illegal activities so that they can maintain "plausible deniability" if this wrongdoing ever comes to light. Division of labor and compartmentalization can distance employees from the consequences of their choices.[21] One department can develop a drug, for example, and expect that another department will test it for side effects. At the same time, another unit will market the drug, assuming that the medication is safe. However, the testing group may fail to communicate that there is no way to accurately determine side effects. A harmful drug (like thalidomide, which caused serious birth defects) is released as a result.[22] Individuals may also shift ethical responsibilities from themselves to their roles. They use their jobs as cover by claiming that (a) they had no choice but to engage in unethical behavior, or that (b) there was little that they could do to stop immoral and/or illegal activities.

Allocation of decision-making rights is another important structural determinant of moral behavior. Empowered employees are more likely to make better ethical choices (see Chapter 5). Those closest to the problem are best equipped to solve it and are more likely to be sensitive to ethical issues. Denying decision-making authority to such knowledgeable workers can be costly. This was vividly illustrated in the *Challenger* and *Columbia* space shuttle disasters. In both cases, managers overruled lower-level engineers who had safety concerns.

Implementation Guidelines. Try to modify structural defects that contribute to immoral behavior. As a leader, encourage others to challenge orders and at times disobey them. Help your employees to recognize how their activities relate to the organization's overall direction and to consider how their actions affect others. Ensure that those closest to the ethical dilemma have significant input into how it is resolved.

5. Reward and Performance Evaluation Systems

Organizational members determine what actions are measured and rewarded. They then engage in those activities, moral or otherwise. That fact makes reward systems a powerful determinant of ethical or unethical behavior. Unfortunately, ethical behavior often goes unnoticed and unrewarded. (Who gets praised for NOT padding expense accounts or NOT inflating earnings?)[23] Organizations often reward immoral behavior instead, as in the case of Washington Mutual Savings. Loan officers approved unsuitable and fraudulent mortgages because they were rewarded for doing so. The bank collapsed when losses from these bad loans mounted.[24]

Focus on ends to the exclusion of means is another problem with many reward and performance appraisal systems. Consumed with the bottom line, leaders set demanding performance goals but intentionally or unintentionally ignore how these objectives are to be reached. They pressure employees to produce sales and profits by whatever means possible. Followers then feel powerless and alienated, becoming estranged from the rest of the group. Sociologists use the term *anomie* to refer to this sense of normlessness and unease that results when rules lose their force.[25] Anomie increases the likelihood that group members will engage in illegal activities, and reduces their resistance to demands from authority figures who want them to break the law. Loss of confidence in the organization encourages alienated employees to retaliate against coworkers and the group as a whole.

Implementation Guidelines. Use the following strategies to help ensure that reward and performance systems in your organization reinforce rather than undermine ethical behavior:

• *Catch people doing good (reward moral behavior that might otherwise go unappreciated).* Publicly acknowledge workers who offer outstanding customer service, government departments that spend taxpayer money wisely, and so on.

• *Evaluate current and proposed reward and performance systems to ensure that they are not reinforcing undesirable behavior.* In particular, take note of possible unintended consequences. Consider the case of teacher performance standards based on student test scores. Such standards are supposed to improve learning but can encourage teachers to cheat (provide too much assistance to pupils) in order to boost test results.

• *Avoid a bottom-line mentality.*[26] Financial returns (profits, donations) are critical to business and nonprofits alike. Yet, focusing solely on the bottom line blinds decision makers to other important responsibilities, like supporting workers and the community. Develop other measures of performance, such as civic involvement and work-family balance. (We'll take an in-depth look at alternative performance scorecards in Chapter 12.)

• *Evaluate based on processes as well as on results.* Measuring how individuals achieve their goals should be part of any performance review process. Provide incentives for moral behavior and disincentives for unethical actions. Punish salespeople who lie about delivery times or exaggerate the features of products, for instance. Resist the temptation to forgive organizational "stars" who generate great results while bending the rules. To reinforce the importance of ethical process, the army's chief recruiting officer held a daylong "values stand-down." He took this action after recruiters were accused of making their enlistment quotas by helping unqualified applicants cheat (pass drug tests, hide criminal records). During the stand-down, recruiters viewed a video on army values, reviewed their oaths of office and correct procedures, and discussed current recruiting challenges.[27]

6. Reporting and Communication Systems

As noted earlier, SEC guidelines require publically held companies to have systems in place for reporting ethical violations. Ethics hotlines (telephone, Web based, or e-mail) are the most common reporting tool. Employees use the hotlines to ask for advice and to report ethical problems. Northrop Corporation, for example, estimates that approximately 5% of its 32,000 employees used its hotline in one year. NYNEX's hotline also receives thousands of calls annually (10% of the callers report possible violations, while 50% seek information or clarification about the provisions of the corporate code).[28] Members should also be able to contact ethics staff in person for advice and to report problems. To be effective, a reporting system must have the support of top management, protect whistleblowers, and promptly follow up on allegations of wrongdoing.

Organizations also need systems for communicating ethics messages. Managers should use a wide variety of channels (e.g., e-mail, newsletters, bulletin boards, video, speeches, meetings) to send messages about corporate values, the provisions of ethics codes, disciplinary actions, and so on. Constant communication is essential to reinforce the importance or salience of ethics. However, ethics communication systems need to allow for reflection and feedback. Managers and employees ought to have regular opportunities to discuss ethical issues and values, to analyze past mistakes, and to admit and rectify errors.[29]

Implementation guidelines. Get the buy-in of top leaders for any reporting system. Provide adequate funding to staff the ethics office and hotlines. Ensure that all reports are confidential and that whistle-blowers are shielded from retribution. If most of your hotline users seek information, take that as a good sign that the system is working. Employees seeking advice are likely trying to prevent problems before they develop. Use every channel possible to continually communicate ethics messages. Create an atmosphere where members feel free to discuss ethical issues. Set aside time for ethical reflection and feedback; engage in active listening.

7. Ethics Officers

Ethics officers are charged with making sure that their organizations comply with the law and engage in ethical conduct. They "provide strategic and operational leadership to the ethics and compliance program."[30] The number of ethics officers at large corporations has skyrocketed in recent years. According to one survey, the percentage of companies with a chief ethics and compliance officer soared from 10% to 75% between 2005 and 2010.[31] Much of this increase is undoubtedly due to the fact that having a chief ethics officer signals to regulators that the company is serious about compliance. When firms with ethics officers violate the law, they generally receive lower fines. However, organizations are increasingly recognizing the importance of the position. In the past, ethics officers used to hold other titles, like general counsel or human resource director. Now, more chief ethics officers focus exclusively on their ethics and compliance duties.

Two factors are key to the success of chief ethics officers. First, they must have sufficient power and status to command the respect of organizational members and enforce ethical standards.[32] In ethical turnaround situations like the ones at Computer Associates and KPMG, for example, former judges and prosecutors were given wide-ranging power to root out unethical behavior. (An ethics officer also plays an important role in Case Study 10.2, "Transforming Tyco," at the end of the chapter.) Second, EOs must have the necessary independence to function effectively. Some experts argue that the EO should report directly to the board of directors, not to senior management. Those who report to the CEO may be hesitant to challenge his or her behavior for fear of being fired. That was the case at Strong Capital Management. Tom Hooker, the chief compliance officer, knew that company chairman Richard Strong was engaged in irregular trading practices that favored some shareholders (including Strong himself) while hurting others. However, Hooker didn't try to stop Strong. The Securities and Exchange Commission not only punished Strong but also fined Hooker $50,000 and banished him from the investment industry for aiding and abetting the former CEO.

Common duties of ethics officers include these:

- Advising top management and the board of directors
- Ensuring that the company makes the necessary regulatory filings
- Resolving discrimination and sexual harassment cases
- Creating ethics training
- Instituting ethics reforms
- Developing and revising ethics codes
- Monitoring ethical performance
- Ensuring continual ethical improvement
- Overseeing complaint systems
- Chairing ethics committees
- Creating ethics policies
- Communicating ethics concerns and policies to employees
- Enforcing the discipline process
- Representing the interests of shareholders and stakeholders

Implementation Guidelines. Make the ethics officer role a full-time position, and have the board of directors make a strong statement of support for the position. Give the EO the power to interview, challenge, and discipline anyone in the organization. Be sure the office gets adequate funding and that the CEO consults regularly with this person. Have the EO report directly to the board of directors.

Informal Elements

1. Language

Informal language is the type of talk used in daily organizational conversations. Such talk often inhibits ethical behavior. Ethics officers report that the word *ethical* is "charged" and "emotional" for some workers.[33] These employees become defensive if their decisions are challenged. They're more comfortable using words like *shared values, mission,* and *integrity* instead. The fact that many employees are uneasy with ethical terminology, coupled with the fact that many managers are morally mute (see Chapter 3), makes it less likely that members will identify the ethical implications of their choices. They decide based on efficiency, profitability, convenience, or other criteria instead of on moral principles. Unethical choices are more likely to result.

Not only do organizational members avoid ethical terminology, they sometimes invent euphemisms to avoid thinking about the true ethical implications of their choices.

It is easier to send troops on a military "mission" than into a full-fledged war, for example, or to "counsel someone out of an organization" instead of firing this individual.

Implementation Guidelines. You and your colleagues need to become comfortable with moral terminology to encourage ethical behavior. Employ such vocabulary when discussing routine decisions and behaviors. Further, you need to be alert to euphemisms and reject terms that hide the moral dimension of activities.

2. Norms

Norms are widely accepted standards of behavior that reveal how an organization "really works."[34] Some norms ("Deal honestly with suppliers"; "Pitch in to help team members") support ethical conduct. Others ("Do whatever it takes to get the lowest price"; "Do as little as you can") encourage immoral behavior instead. Norms generally exert more influence over individual behavior than formal rules and policies do, which helps explain why some codes of ethics are ineffectual. Members will generally do what is expected and accepted even if it is officially forbidden.

Implementation Guidelines. Your organization's norms should be aligned with its ethical codes and policies. Identify important informal standards, and then determine if these norms support your organization's stated rules, mission, and values. If they don't, consider how they might be modified (see Application Project 5 at the end of the chapter).

3. Rituals

Rituals are organizational dramas that are repeated at regular intervals. Actors follow carefully planned scripts in front of selected audiences; costumes and props may be involved. At one metal foam manufacturer, for instance, managers and employees gathered daily for "pour time." At this critical juncture in the manufacturing process, they don white smocks, safety glasses, and asbestos mitts to pour molten metal into a large cylinder. Flames shoot out of the cylindrical vessel and are doused. The container is then sealed for cooling. Pour time is a particularly dramatic ritual because any mistake will cause an expensive failure, and participants could be injured by molten metal and fire.[35]

Rituals serve many functions, some more obvious than others. The manifest or stated function of the pour time ritual is to complete the manufacturing process and demonstrate just how difficult it is. Latent or hidden functions of this rite might include reinforcing the importance of teamwork, boosting the importance of employees (the top manager steps aside during the process), and building commitment to the organization.

Harrison Trice and Janice Beyer provide the most popular typology of organizational rites based on their functions. These six rituals include the following:[36]

- *Rites of passage.* These dramas mark important changes in roles and statuses. One of the most dramatic rites of passage is military boot camp. New recruits are stripped of their civilian identities and converted into soldiers, with new haircuts, uniforms, and prescribed ways of speaking, standing, and walking. Rites of passage impart important values and enforce behaviors. In military boot camps, recruits learn the importance of obeying authority. In company boot camps in Japan, new employees develop loyalty to their firms.

- *Rites of degradation.* Degradation rituals lower the status of organizational members, as when an officer is stripped of rank or when a player is kicked off the team. These routines identify punishable behaviors and signal the organization's willingness to stand behind its values (see Case Study 10.1).

CASE STUDY 10.1

Sending Mixed Signals at Boeing

The board of directors at Boeing Company faced a series of difficult choices in March 2005. Upon arriving for a semiannual meeting, members learned of written allegations that married CEO Harry Stonecipher was carrying on a consensual affair with a vice president in the firm's Washington office. Stonecipher was accused of helping his lover's career and using company resources (including the corporate jet) to pursue the relationship.

The board initially responded by confronting Stonecipher, who admitted to the affair, and by confronting the vice president. It hired an outside investigator to determine if the CEO had abused his power or company funds. The outside counsel determined that he had not. However, a series of potentially embarrassing, sexually explicit e-mails came to light during the investigation.

The board then had to determine whether or not to fire Stonecipher who, like Boeing's other 160,000 workers, had signed a pledge that stated, "Employees will not engage in conduct or activity that may raise questions as to the company's honesty, impartiality, reputation or otherwise cause embarrassment to the company."[1] The company's strict code of ethics was instituted after the firm was caught stealing secrets from competitor Lockheed Martin and offering an Air Force procurement official a job in return for federal contracts. Boeing was banned from bidding on Air Force rocket launching contracts as punishment.

CEO Stonecipher was brought out of retirement to help clean up the company's image and restore the firm's stock price. His efforts were largely successful. By the time of the board meeting, the Department of Defense was leaning toward lifting the bidding ban, airplane orders were up, and the firm's stock price was recovering.

Consensual affairs are not specifically banned in the Boeing code of ethics. Nonetheless, board members were disappointed that the CEO had engaged in such behavior while the firm was under intense ethical scrutiny. They determined that they had to protect Boeing's image. In explaining the board's decision to fire Stonecipher, board chair Lewis Platt said, "The CEO must set a standard for unimpeachable professional and personal behavior."[2] He noted that the board's investigation had revealed "some things that we thought reflected poorly on Harry's judgment and would impair his ability to lead the company going forward."[3] Public relations experts praised Boeing's directors for fully disclosing the reasons behind their decision to dismiss the CEO.

Boeing's board offered Stonecipher a generous severance package. They decided to pay him a $2.1 million bonus for 2004, provide him with financial counseling, pay an additional six weeks' salary, and allow him to use the company car. He was prevented from using the company jet without the permission of the board chair, however, and was declared ineligible for any future bonuses and employee benefits. The woman involved in the affair resigned and forfeited all employment benefits.

If the board of directors at Boeing hoped to send a clear signal about the importance of ethics, it failed. Observers cheered the company for firing Stonecipher but noted that his compensation package undercut the board's attempts to punish misbehavior. According to a military analyst at Taxpayers for Common Sense, "At the beginning of the week, it looked like the Boeing board was getting tough on unethical behavior. By the end of the week, they were giving Harry Stonecipher millions of dollars. This lush compensation package hurts any efforts of the board to make Boeing look better."[4] Employees wondered if Stonecipher had been fired for having sex or for writing about it in his e-mails. After all, other Boeing executives (including past CEOs) had engaged in affairs and remained on the job. They doubted that Stonecipher would have been fired if Boeing had not been under the "ethical microscope."

Discussion Probes

1. Evaluate the decisions made by Boeing's board of directors. What did members do right? Wrong?

2. What course of action would you have recommended if you were a member of the Boeing board?

3. Why do you think the board decided both to fire Stonecipher and to give him a generous severance package?

4. The female executive involved in the affair did not receive a severance package. Was that fair?

5. What messages did the board send through its handling of this incident? Do you agree that board members sent mixed signals?

6. Do you think the board would have acted differently if the company had not been under ethical scrutiny because of previous ethical and legal problems?

Notes

1. Holt (2005).
2. Holt (2005).
3. Wayne (2005, March 8).
4. Wayne, (2005, March 11).

Sources

Gates, D. (2005, March 8). Boeing faces CEO dilemma. *The Seattle Times*, p. A1.
Holt, S. (2005, March 8). Personal lives of executives under scrutiny. *The Seattle Times*, p. C1.
McGuire, C. (2006, November 27). Managing a graceful bon voyage. *PR Week*, p. 18.
Mundy, A. (2005, March 8). The board took 8 days to decide CEO had to go. *The Seattle Times*, p. A1.
Norris, F. (2005, March 8). Moving from scandal to scandal, Boeing finds its road to redemption paved with affairs great and small. *The New York Times*, p. C5.
Wayne, L. (2005, March 8). Boeing chief is ousted after admitting affair. *The New York Times*, p. A1.
Wayne, L. (2005, March 11). Ousted chief of Boeing gets $2.1 million bonus for 2004. *The New York Times*, p. C6.
Wayne, L. (2005, March 19). Executive involved with chief has resigned, Boeing says. *The New York Times*, p. C10.
Westneat, D. (2005, March 11). Boeing's message puzzling. *The Seattle Times*, p. B1.

- *Rites of enhancement.* In contrast to rites of degradation, rites of enhancement raise the standing of organizational members. Giving vacation trips to top salespeople, announcing the university's teacher of the year, and identifying the team's most valuable player are examples of this type of ritual. Recipients become positive role models, illustrating how members can get ahead in the organization.

- *Rites of renewal.* These rituals strengthen and improve the current system. Examples include team-building exercises, Six Sigma quality processes, and organizational development (OD) programs. The manifest function of such rituals is to bring about improvement. However, they also have hidden consequences, like reassuring members that the organization is dealing with problems and focusing attention toward some issues and away from others.

- *Rites of conflict reduction.* Organizations develop rituals for releasing tension and managing conflicts. Common conflict resolution rituals are collective bargaining sessions and committee meetings. In collective bargaining, union and management representatives engage in such ritualistic behavior as presenting demands and proposals, talking long hours, and threatening to walk out. In committees, members try to resolve differences between competing interests and cooperate to solve problems. The formation of a task force or committee signals that organizational leaders are serious about addressing issues.

- *Rites of integration.* Integration dramas tie members into larger systems, reinforcing feelings of commitment and belonging. The pour time ritual described earlier brings members of different departments of the metal manufacturer together for an important shared activity. Other companies hold Christmas parties and picnics where members of all ranks mix informally. Integration ceremonies also bind individuals to regional, national, and international associations. Annual conventions and conferences connect professors, lawyers, and doctors to larger professional communities.

Rites of passage, degradation, and enhancement have manifest ethical functions. They reinforce important values, provide role models, and identify desirable and undesirable behaviors. In contrast, rites of renewal, conflict reduction, and integration have latent moral effects. One of the latent ethical effects of renewal rites is the highlighting of important organizational priorities. For example, a company may focus on cost cutting while ignoring diversity issues. Rites of conflict reduction send indirect yet important messages about how an organization values its people. Most airlines are locked into hostile relationships with their unions, for instance. Not so at Southwest Airlines. It treats unions as partners, thus reinforcing the firm's emphasis on building high-quality relationships.[37] Integration rituals, which are designed to increase feelings of belonging, also have the latent effect of tying members to the values and codes of conduct of larger groups.

Implementation Guidelines. Since every ritual has an impact on ethical behavior, direct or indirect, you will need to carefully analyze each one. Some questions to consider include these: What values and behaviors are being reinforced? What priorities are being communicated? Are these values, behaviors, and priorities desirable and ethical? Are important ethical issues being ignored? What might be the unintended ethical consequences of this ritual?

Trice and Beyer suggest modifying rituals rather than eliminating them. Discontinuing rituals can be risky, since they are important events in the life of the organization. Instead, change current rites and add new ones. Open your firm's books to union personnel during negotiations instead of shutting them out, for example. Introduce an ethics award to your company's annual gathering, or reward teams of salespeople rather than individuals.

4. Stories

One way to determine an organization's ethical stance is to examine its stories. Narratives, as noted in Chapter 2, provide meaning, impart values, and promote desired behavior. A tale qualifies as an organizational story when (1) many people know it, not just a few individuals, (2) the narrative focuses on one sequence of events rather than an extended history of a person or organization, (3) central characters are organization members, and (4) the story is supposedly true.

Joanne Martin of Stanford University divides organizational stories into two parts: the narrative itself and the interpretations or morals of the story that follow.[38] Both the narrative and its meaning vary depending on the storyteller, audience, and organizational context. Martin provides three examples of a common story that illustrate how the same basic narrative pattern can send different ethical messages. In the first version of the story, a security guard refused to let IBM chair Thomas Watson enter a restricted area without the proper badge. Instead of firing her, Watson sent someone off to get his badge. In the second version, an assembly-line worker ordered the president of another company to leave the work area and return with his safety glasses. He apologized and obeyed, impressed with the fact that she was not intimidated by his organizational rank.

These two accounts demonstrate the importance of upholding the rules regardless of status. In both cases, the high-ranking official complied, thus reinforcing the behavior of the employee. The third variation of the story is quite different and paints a much more negative picture of corporate values. At the Revlon Company, everyone was to sign in when they arrived in the morning. One morning, company founder Charles Revson arrived and picked up the sign-in sheet. The receptionist, who was new, refused to let him take the sheet because she was under "strict orders that no one is to remove the list." Revson then asked her, "Do you know who I am?" She replied that she did not. "Well," Revson said, "when you pick up your final paycheck this afternoon, ask 'em to tell ya."[39]

Heroes play a particularly important role in organizational narratives. They embody organizational values while modeling desirable behaviors. IBM's Thomas Watson was one such figure. Watson's response to the lowly security guard demonstrated how important it was to obey the rules and to treat others with respect. Stories about Watson are still told at IBM and continue to guide behavior. Another enduring corporate legend is that of the 1950s-era Motorola senior executive who negotiated a large sale that would have increased company profits by 25% for that year. However, he walked away from negotiations when the other party demanded a $1 million bribe. Motorola CEO Robert Galvin publicly backed the executive's action and made him an example by telling and retelling his story. Of course, heroes aren't always executives. Wal-Mart's website told the story of a local employee, Norman Price, who returned $11,000 he discovered in a shopping cart.

Not all those cast as heroes truly deserve that label. Enron's Jeffrey Skilling and top trader Lou Pai created a fictional trading floor to impress financial analysts during a 1998 meeting. Visitors were escorted into what was called the Enron Energy Services war room. During their 10-minute tour, they "beheld the very picture of a sophisticated, booming business: a big open room bustling with people, all busily working the telephones and hunched over computer terminals, seemingly cutting deals and trading energy."[40] In reality, it was all a ruse. The room was filled with secretaries and other employees who were brought in for the demonstration and coached to look busy. One administrative assistant reports that she was told to bring her personal pictures to make it look like she worked at the desk where she sat. The analysts (who were charged with evaluating the financial health of the firm) were completely fooled. Skilling and his accomplices were seen as heroes, which helped foster the climate of deception that led to the firm's collapse.

Implementation Guidelines. Strive to find heroes who embody worthy values and provide positive role models; tell their stories at every opportunity. However, your most pressing task may be to reduce the damage done by stories currently being told in your work or volunteer group. Take the case of a tale of an abusive executive, for instance. This narrative, which illustrates how poorly the company treats its employees, can be reframed. If you fire the abuser, the tale serves as an example of how the organization has changed. Lay the groundwork for more positive stories by modeling moral behavior, which can become the basis for future tales.

Cultural Change Efforts

Every component of culture contributes to the formation of an ethical organizational environment. However, by focusing on each element, it is easy to lose sight of the reality that cultures function as interrelated systems. If you want to change an organization's ethical culture, you must simultaneously address all the components described in the previous section. In fact, introducing piecemeal changes can backfire. Members can become more entrenched in their current behavior patterns when, for example, managers create a new values statement without also changing the way employees are rewarded and evaluated. Disillusioned workers conclude that management isn't really serious about moral behavior. They greet future ethics initiatives with skepticism.

Highly ethical organizations make sure that cultural components align or support one another.[41] Ethical codes are backed by norms, stories reflect core values, structure supports individual initiative, and so forth. These collectives also demonstrate ethical consistency. All units and organizational levels share a commitment to high moral standards. Ethical values are factored into every organizational activity, be it planning and goal setting, spending, gathering and sharing of information, or marketing. Further, constituents are encouraged and equipped to make ethical choices following core principles.

Ethical Drivers

Ethical drivers are factors that play a particularly significant role in promoting or driving systematic ethical change. Without them, any change effort is likely to fail. These drivers include ethical diagnosis, engaged leadership, targeted socialization processes, ethics training, and continuous ethical improvement.

Driver #1: Ethical Diagnosis

Determining the organization's current ethical condition should be the first step in any systematic change initiative. Diagnosis surfaces moral strengths and weaknesses, areas of misalignment, the criteria for making ethical choices, and shared perceptions of the organization's moral health. These data should then drive the rest of the change effort. For example, the American Hospital Association (AHA) created a six-part organizational assessment tool that focuses on ethics documents, ethics training, organizational structure, organizational character, specific ethical challenges facing the organization, and employee assessment of the organization's ethical performance. Follow-up to the AHA assessment includes developing detailed plans to address problem areas, establishing new policies, redesigning orientation and training programs, and creating a casebook on ethical dilemmas.[42]

Auditing the cultural components described earlier is one way to diagnose your workplace's current ethical condition. The ethical culture audit probes both formal and informal systems, using the questions listed in the Self-Assessment. When conducting the audit, use surveys, interviews, observation, and analysis to gather information. You could also ask these questions when you apply for jobs, to assess the ethical status of prospective employers.

SELF-ASSESSMENT

Ethics Audit Questions

Use the following set of questions to evaluate the ethical culture of your current organization or one that you would like to join.

Selected Questions for Auditing the Formal System

1. How are organizational leaders perceived in terms of their integrity? Is ethics part of the leadership agenda?

2. How are ethics-related behaviors modeled by organizational leaders?

3. Are workers at all levels encouraged to take responsibility for the consequences of their behavior? To question authority when they are asked to do something that they consider to be wrong? How?

4. Does a formal code of ethics and/or values exist? Is it distributed? How widely? Is it used? Is it reinforced in other formal systems, such as reward and decision-making systems?

5. Are whistle-blowers encouraged, and are formal channels available for them to make their concerns known confidentially?

6. Is misconduct disciplined swiftly and justly in the organization, no matter what the organizational level?

7. Are people of integrity promoted? Are means as well as ends important?

8. Is integrity emphasized to recruits and new employees?

9. Are managers oriented to the values of the organization in orientation programs? Are they trained in ethical decision making?

10. Are ethical considerations a routine part of planning and policy meetings, new venture reports? Is the language of ethics taught and used? Does a formal committee exist high in the organization for considering ethical issues?

Selected Questions for Auditing the Informal System

1. Identify informal organizational norms. Are they consistent with formal rules and policies?

2. Identify the organization's heroes. What values do they represent? Given an ambiguous ethical dilemma, what decision would they make, and why?

3. What are some important organizational rituals? How do they encourage or discourage ethical behavior? Who gets the awards, people of integrity who are successful or individuals who use unethical methods to attain success?

4. What ethical messages are sent to new entrants into the organization—must they obey authority at all costs, or is questioning authority acceptable or even desirable?

5. Does analysis of organizational stories and myths reveal individuals who stand up for what's right despite pressure, or is conformity the valued characteristic? Do people get fired or promoted in these stories?

6. Does acceptable language exist for discussing ethical concerns? Is this language routinely incorporated and encouraged in business (organizational) decision making?

7. What informal socialization processes exist, and what norms for ethical or unethical behavior do they promote? Are these different for different organizational subgroups?

Conclusion

What is your overall evaluation of this organization's ethical culture? What are its areas of strength and weakness?

SOURCE: Trevino, L. K., & Nelson, K. A. (2004). *Managing business ethics: Straight talk about how to do it right* (3rd ed.). Hoboken, NJ: John Wiley, p. 259. Reprinted by permission of John Wiley & Sons, Inc.

Climate analysis is another way to measure moral performance. Ethical climate refers to the "shared perceptions of what is ethically correct behavior and how ethical issues should be handled in the organization."[43] Management ethicists Bart Victor and John Cullen developed the Ethical Climate Questionnaire (ECQ) to measure these perceptions. The ECQ classifies moral climates according to (a) the ethical principles that members use to make moral choices, and (b) the groups that members refer to when making ethical determinations. Members out to maximize their self-interest are guided by egoism. Individuals may also seek to benefit others (benevolence) or act according to universal standards (principle). To determine what is ethically correct, they may rely on their own judgments, refer to local organizational standards, or look to outside groups for help.

Victor and Cullen identify five climate types. *Instrumental* climates encourage self-serving (egoistic) behavior, which is often economically driven. *Caring* climates emphasize concern for others and the organization as a whole, even at the cost of meeting individual needs. *Rules* climates are governed by the policies, rules, and procedures (principles) developed within the organization. *Law and code* climates turn to external criteria or principles, like professional codes of conduct or state laws, for guidance. *Independence* climates are also principled but encourage individuals to make choices based on their personal values and ethics.

Victor and Cullen suggest that an organization's ethical orientation might make it more susceptible to some forms of unethical behavior and shape its response to change efforts. For instance, members of caring organizations may break laws in order to help others. A written code of ethics is likely to receive a better reception in a rules or law and code climate than in a caring or independence environment.

When it comes to the relationship between climate types and ethical behavior, researchers have discovered the following:[44]

- Ethical climates often vary between departments and locations within an organization.
- Rates of immoral behavior are highest in instrumental climates.
- Organizational commitment and positive feelings toward the organization are greatest in caring climates and lowest in instrumental climates.
- For-profit climates are more likely to be driven by self-interest, while nonprofit climates are more likely to be founded on benevolence.
- An emphasis on obeying the law and adhering to professional codes reduces unethical behavior, particularly when internalized within the organization.
- Employees are more satisfied when they work for organizations with ethical climates that reflect their personal preferences.
- Professionals prefer to work for organizations with rule or law and code climates.

According to these findings, self-interest poses the greatest threat to ethical performance, and you need to confront this attitude, whether at the unit level or organization wide. Creating a more caring environment in your work group can pay off in higher trust and commitment levels; referring to rules and codes can decrease immoral behavior. Finally, match the person (yourself or potential hires) with the climate. Employees are more satisfied and are less likely to leave if their personal ethical preferences match those of the organization.

Driver #2: Engaged Leadership

Significant cultural change is extremely difficult without the buy-in of top leadership.[45] We've already noted how leaders are largely responsible for shaping organizations, play a key role in curbing or promoting destructive behaviors, reinforce or undermine values and standards, and so on.

Organizational psychologist Edgar Schein outlines six primary mechanisms that you can use in a leadership role to establish, maintain, and change ethical culture.[46] (Case Study 10.3, "Creating an Unethical Workplace at Salomon," illustrates how these mechanisms can be misused to create an unethical culture.)

1. *Attention.* Followers will pick up on your priorities through what you pay attention to, measure, and control. Ethics won't be taken seriously unless you consistently talk about the importance of ethical behavior, act ethically, measure moral performance, and punish those who fall short of standards. Systematically and persistently emphasize core values and mission.

2. *Reactions to critical incidents.* The way you respond to stressful events sends important messages about underlying organizational values. Some firms that value efficiency, for example, handle financial setbacks through layoffs. Others, valuing cooperation, cut costs by asking everyone to work fewer hours. Major crises quickly reveal the true ethical character of a leader and his or her organization. Johnson & Johnson CEO James Burke is a case in point. He earned widespread praise for his response to the Tylenol product-tampering crisis. Under his leadership, the company cooperated with authorities, voluntarily recalled the product, admitted when it released faulty information, and developed new packaging. In contrast, the leaders of Toyota waited months after learning of sudden acceleration problems before issuing a recall in the United States; the delay put the lives of thousands of drivers at risk. Executives at BP grossly understated the amount of oil gushing into the Gulf of Mexico following an oil rig explosion.[47]

3. *Resource allocation.* How an organization spends its money is a key indicator of its values and priorities. What types of projects get supported? How much money is devoted to ethics programs and training? Does the organization invest in the health and well-being of its employees? Does it support their personal development? The process of budgeting also reveals underlying moral assumptions. The greater the organization's commitment to empowering its members, the more likely it is to involve people from all levels of the organization in setting financial targets. Because resource allocation and budgeting send strong cultural signals, think carefully about what you want to communicate when deciding how to create the departmental or organizational spending plan.

4. *Role modeling.* Acting as a role model is more than setting an example; it also means developing others. Become a coach and teacher to others, particularly to those who report directly to you. Help them identify and manage ethical issues and develop their ethical problem-solving skills.

5. *Rewards.* Rewards, discussed earlier in the chapter as an element of performance and evaluation systems, also go hand in hand with attention mechanisms. Use them to draw attention to important goals, shared values, and desirable and undesirable behaviors.

6. *Selection.* Organizations tend to perpetuate current cultural components by hiring people who fit into the current system. If you want to reform the culture, recruit members who share the new ethical standards rather than the old ones. Include ethics in the recruiting process by highlighting corporate values and looking closely at the character of the candidate. Ask applicants such questions as "What ethics coursework did you take in college?" and "Would you accept a free gift from a supplier?"[48] One outstanding candidate for a pharmaceutical position was asked if he had ever been asked to do anything illegal in business. The candidate was happy to report that he had falsified billing records so that he and a previous supervisor could make their revenue goals. (He didn't get the job.) When selecting individuals for promotion, advance those who support the group's mission values and, if necessary, remove those who don't.

Driver #3: Targeted Socialization Processes

Socialization describes the process of becoming a group member. To make this transition, individuals have to learn how to perform their individual roles and, at the same time, absorb information about the organization's culture.[49] There are several reasons why socialization can play a key role in driving ethical change. First, new members are most susceptible to influence and open to instruction about ethical behavior. Their values and perceptions are being formed, and they are anxious to learn how to behave in a new environment. Second, discussion of ethics can be incorporated into existing socialization programs. Third, the values learned during the socialization process will shape an employee's behavior throughout her or his career with the organization. Fourth, when newcomers become ethical veterans, they then communicate and model important values to new generations of members.

Socialization begins even before a member joins a new organization or organizational unit. Job applicants typically have expectations about the prospective organization gathered from recruitment brochures, websites, and other channels. The employment interview plays a particularly significant role in shaping these expectations. Applicants come away with an image of what the organization is like, which may be unrealistic. This can lead to dissatisfaction and a quick exit after they join.

Formal socialization mechanisms kick in when newcomers begin their membership. As they "learn the ropes," rookies participate in training and orientation sessions designed to integrate them into the organization. They also come under the influence of socializing agents. Important socializing agents include: (a) veteran coworkers who serve as day-to-day guides and sounding boards; (b) respected senior peers who guide by example and impart organizational standards and values; (c) supervisors who act as official guides to policies and procedures; and (d) mentors and/or advisors who model core organizational values and philosophy. Mentoring relationships can play a particularly critical role in ethical socialization.[50] Mentors and mentees are accountable to one another and can discuss how to live out organizational values. They establish trusting relationships in which parties can reveal what they believe and why they hold those convictions. Close contact gives the mentor the opportunity to observe the character and behavior of the mentee in both normal and stressful situations.

Socialization concludes when newcomers become accepted members of the group. It should be noted that new members aren't merely sponges that soak up cultural information. They also help to shape the culture by introducing new values and practices.

Unfortunately, socialization processes may contribute to immoral behavior. New members can be corrupted through co-optation, incrementalism, and compromise.[51] In *co-optation,* the organization uses rewards to reduce newcomers' discomfort with unethical behaviors. Targets may not realize that these incentives are skewing their judgment, making it easier to rationalize poor behavior. For example, brokers who are rewarded for pushing certain stocks may convince themselves that these picks are outstanding investments. *Incrementalism* gradually introduces new members to unethical practices, leading them up the "ladder of corruption." Newcomers are first persuaded to engage in a practice that is only mildly unethical. They turn to the rationalizations offered by their peers ("Everybody does it"; "Nobody was really hurt"; "They deserved it") to relieve the cognitive dissonance produced by this act. After the first practice becomes normal, acceptable behavior, individuals are then encouraged to move on to increasingly more corrupt activities. In the end, they find themselves participating in acts that they would have rejected when they first joined the organization. *Compromise* "backs" members into corruption as they strive to solve dilemmas and conflicts. Politicians, for instance, enter into lots of compromises in order to keep and expand their power. Cutting deals and forming networks makes it harder for them to take ethical stands.

The danger of dysfunctional socialization is greatest when newcomers join a social cocoon. A *social cocoon* is a strong culture in which norms and values are very different from those in the rest of the organization or society. In cocoons, members highly prize their membership in the group and tend to compartmentalize their lives, holding one set of values outside work and another on the job. At a prestigious law firm, a cocoon may develop as new attorneys strive to become partners. Veterans of the firm (whom newcomers admire) may encourage rookies to overbill for services and to neglect their families by working extremely long hours. The recent law school graduates put aside their misgivings about these patterns, blaming themselves for their doubts rather than blaming the firm for encouraging unhealthy practices.

As a change agent, target the socialization process in your work group to promote positive ethical change rather than reinforce corrupt behavior. Start with clearly describing your organization's values and ethical climate in the employment interview. Paint a truthful picture of conditions in your organization. Ask applicants about their ethical experiences and standards. Ensure that ethics is a top priority in orientation and training sessions. Communicate core values and mission statements, present the code of ethics, highlight potential ethical dilemmas, introduce ethics officers and procedures, and engage in ethics discussions. Then, place newcomers with socializing agents, particularly mentors, who reinforce rather than undermine values and standards. Provide channels for new hires to express their concerns about ongoing practices. Puncture the social cocoon by training employees to think about the perspectives of outsiders and by bringing in external change agents (new leaders, consultants, speakers).

Driver #4: Ethics Training

Formal ethics training, as we've seen, should be part of the socialization process. However, the need for ethics education doesn't end when members are assimilated into the group. Ongoing training can play an important role in creating and maintaining ethical environments. Training sessions can increase moral sensitivity and moral judgment, make it easier to use moral vocabulary, reduce destructive behaviors, prevent scandals, reinforce mission and values, and integrate ethical considerations into the fabric of organizational life.

Of course, offering ethics training is not a panacea. There is no guarantee that those who attend will make better decisions or change their behaviors; poorly designed training programs can actually increase resistance to change. Nonetheless, effective ethics training can make a positive difference in your organization. Effective training does the following:[52]

1. *Focuses on your organization's unique ethical problems.* The most useful training addresses the dilemmas encountered by group members. Issues that professors face (grading, academic freedom, tenure decisions) will be different from those encountered by physicians (managed care, patient privacy, malpractice), for example. Help your organization's employees identify potential ethical issues that may be hidden at first. Introduce examples drawn directly from the organization, industry, and profession. Equip trainees with the tools they need to solve these dilemmas.

2. *Allows plenty of time for discussion and interaction.* Key concepts can be presented in lectures and handouts, but spend most of your class time in dyadic, small-group, and large-group discussion. Introduce case studies, raise questions, and debate issues. Trainees can also interact about ethical issues outside of class via the Internet.

3. *Taps into the experiences of participants.* Ask your trainees to provide dilemmas and insights drawn from their own experiences. Participants then become the instructors, "teaching" one another. They also receive feedback that enables them to better handle their dilemmas.

4. *Is integrated into the entire curriculum.* The stand-alone ethics workshop or class promotes moral reasoning but is easily disconnected from the rest of the organization's activities. Whenever possible, you should integrate ethics discussion into other subjects, like sales skills, leadership development, conflict management, and supervision.

CHAPTER TAKEAWAYS

- Strive to create organizations that are ethically transformed rather than ethically decoupled. Transformed organizations are ethics driven; values and standards shape behaviors, decisions, and relationships.
- Both the formal and informal components of your organization's culture will influence the ethical behavior of employees. You need to address all of these elements to foster an ethical workplace.
- Core values serve as enduring, guiding principles that reflect what organizational members find intrinsically valuable. However, to have a positive influence on behavior, your group's collective values must be clearly identified, continually reinforced, and modeled by leaders.
- Create a powerful mission or purpose statement that reflects the ideals of your members while inspiring and promoting ethical behavior.
- Codes of ethics can play a vital role in improving an ethical climate. Your organization's ethical guidelines need to address the specific ethical dilemmas faced by members and have the backing of senior managers who consistently enforce them.
- Structure shapes behavior through the creation of authority relationships, delineation of lines of accountability, and the allocation of decision-making rights. Encourage employees to challenge orders when necessary, help them understand how their actions impact others, and empower them to resolve the dilemmas they face.
- To promote moral behavior, acknowledge ethical performance, reward desirable (not undesirable) activities, and make sure goals are reached through ethical means.
- Create reporting channels that members can use to report misbehavior and ask for information. Use a variety of communication channels to send ethics messages and encourage ethical reflection and feedback.
- Appoint ethics officers to oversee compliance and ethics programs. Ensure that they have the power and independence to carry out their duties.
- Use moral vocabulary even when making routine decisions, and avoid euphemisms, which hide the ethical implications of your choices.
- Create norms (widely accepted standards of behavior) that support, not undermine, your formal codes and policies.
- Analyze rituals to determine the behaviors, values, and priorities they promote. Modify those rites that poison the ethical climate.
- Tell and retell organizational stories that model desired behaviors, and identify worthy heroes. Reframe negative stories so they deliver a more positive moral message.
- Your attempts to change the ethical culture must be systematic, simultaneously addressing multiple components. Cultural elements should align (support) one another and consistently demonstrate ethical values.
- Diagnosis should be the first step in any ethical change initiative. Use an ethics audit to measure the relationship of cultural components and ethical behavior.
- Conduct an ethical climate analysis to determine how members perceive what is ethically correct behavior and how they believe the organization deals with ethical issues.
- As a leader, be actively engaged in creating, maintaining, and changing ethical culture through (1) attention, (2) your reaction to critical incidents, (3) resource allocation, (4) role modeling, (5) rewards, and (6) selection.
- Communicate positive moral values and standards to newcomers through employment interviews, formal orientation programs, and socializing agents.
- Focus your ongoing ethics training on your organization's unique ethical problems, allow plenty of time for trainees to discuss issues, tap into the experiences of participants, and integrate discussion of ethics into the entire curriculum.

APPLICATION PROJECTS

1. Brainstorm a list of ethically decoupled organizations and a list of ethically transformed organizations. How do these organizations differ?

2. List the core values of your organization. How well are they publicized? How well are they supported by the behavior of organizational leaders?

3. Evaluate the effectiveness of the mission statements in Ethics in Action 10.2, or, as an alternative, collect and evaluate your own examples. How well do these statements guide, inspire, and promote ethical behavior? What characteristics separate the effective statements from their ineffective counterparts?

4. Partner with an organization to develop a code of ethics for its members. Determine the common ethical issues faced by the group. Follow the guidelines presented in the chapter to create the code provisions. Get feedback from the organization on the usefulness and effectiveness of your document.

5. With your fellow employees, volunteers, or students, identify a list of norms in your organization. Compare these norms with the group's formal code of ethics, core values, and mission statement. Do the norms support the formal cultural components? Brainstorm strategies for bringing them into alignment. Report your findings to a significant organizational decision maker.

6. Do an in-depth analysis of an important organizational ritual. Identify its manifest and latent ethical functions. Write up your findings.

7. Complete the Self-Assessment to analyze your organization's ethical culture. Record your answers to each question. Conclude with an overall evaluation of the group's moral condition and suggestions for improvement. If you can, distribute the ethics audit questions to others, and discuss your findings as a group.

8. Analyze your socialization experience from an ethical vantage point. How well did the organization communicate its values and standards? Was ethics incorporated into the job interview? What could be done to improve the socialization process?

9. Attend an ethical training program, and evaluate its effectiveness using the guidelines in the chapter.

10. Interview an organizational ethics officer, basing your questions on material presented in the chapter. Report the results of your conversation to the rest of the class.

11. Create a case study based on an organization's attempt to change its ethical culture. Outline what can be learned from this group's experience.

CASE STUDY 10.2

Transforming Tyco

At the turn of the new century, the name Tyco was synonymous with corporate excess and scandal. Ousted CEO Dennis Kozlowski (serving an 8- to 25-year prison sentence) looted the construction-manufacturing conglomerate to buy such luxuries as an expensive New York City apartment, a $15,000 umbrella stand, and a $6,000 shower rod, as well as to throw a million-dollar birthday party for his wife. (He was fond of declaring, "Money is the only way to keep score.")[1] Kozlowski also went on a massive merger spree, making some 600 deals—some of them illegally hidden from stockholders—that produced a tangle of unrelated businesses. *Business Week* called what happened at Tyco "one of the most spectacular governance failures in history."[2] Leadership expert Michael Useem, hired to help repair the damage, declared, "Tyco really needs to go from worst to first. It really does need to transform itself."[3]

In 2002, Ed Breen, former president and COO of Motorola, was hired as the new CEO to oversee the transformation. Breen started by firing 290 out of 300 senior executives and replacing the board of directors, some of whom had financial ties to the company. One of his key hires was Eric Pillmore, Vice President of Corporate Governance, who reported directly to the board. Breen then launched a review of Tyco's 15 largest acquisitions to determine if there had been fraud during these transactions and to ensure that effective financial procedures and controls were in place. Finance teams from each business segment then conducted reviews of 2,154 separate balance sheets, and internal audit teams made on-site visits, asking specific questions about how managers arrived at their estimates of reserves.

Breen separated financial management from operations management, encouraging financial managers to provide a check against inappropriate expenditures. Members of the finance group were no longer evaluated based on doing deals and acquisitions but on financial basics, like reconciling accounts and doing physical inventories. Doubling its staff strengthened the internal audit team. The audit function began to report directly to the board instead of to the chief financial officer, to guarantee greater independence. The firm shed many acquisitions to focus on security, fire, and industrial valves.

A number of Tyco's reforms were aimed at ensuring that future corporate executives would not engage in the same excesses as past leaders. Bonuses and stock options were capped; directors' stock options were converted to stock units to be vested when they retired from the board. Senior officials now have to retain a minimum percentage of their company shares, and cash severance payments are limited to 2.99 times base salary and bonuses.

Reform efforts didn't end with the executives. For the entire workforce, Pillmore created a guide to ethical conduct (translated into 14 languages) as well as a website containing vignettes and videos on problem situations. Managers were issued a "Passport to Ethical Leadership," which included an ethical self-assessment instrument. Performance evaluations are now based partially on adherence to the values of integrity, excellence, accountability, and teamwork. Pillmore and other managers visited sites around the world to roll out the corporate governance effort.

Transformation efforts were a success. The firm, which was 100 days from bankruptcy, is now on solid financial ground.

Tyco was named as the most improved U.S. company in governance for the period 2002–2005.

Discussion Probes

1. Was it necessary to fire nearly all of Tyco's senior managers and remove all board members?

2. What formal elements of ethical culture do you see instituted at Tyco?

3. Do you think that the company has made enough changes to prevent a future Kozlowski?

4. Can you think of any other examples of organizations that have undergone ethical transformations? What elements do they have in common with what happened at Tyco?

5. What are the signs that an organization has succeeded in becoming ethically transformed?

Notes

1. Pillmore, E. M. (2003, December). How we're fixing up Tyco. *Harvard Business Review,* pp. 96–97.
2. Eisenberg, D., Fonda, D., & Zagorin, A. (2002, June 17). Dennis the menace. *Time,* pp. 46–49.
3. Lavelle, L. (2002, November 11). Rebuilding trust in Tyco. *BusinessWeek,* pp. 94–96.

Sources

Hindo, B. (2008, February 16). Solving Tyco's identity crisis. *BusinessWeek,* pp. 62–66.

Puffer, S. M., & McCarthy, D. J. (2008). Ethical turnarounds and transformational leadership: A global imperative for corporate social responsibility. *Thunderbird International Business Review, 50,* 303–313.

Staczek, J. J. (2008). An interview with Eric M. Pillmore: Hitting the CSR bull's-eye in a shifting corporate environment. *Thunderbird International Business Review, 50,* 295–301.

CASE STUDY 10.3

Creating an Unethical Workplace at Salomon

In the 1980s, the giant brokerage house Salomon Inc. was one of the most influential players in the financial world. *BusinessWeek* magazine proclaimed CEO John Gutfreund "The King of Wall Street." However, in 1991 the firm faced an ethical crisis that threatened its very existence. The trouble began in the firm's government securities division. When the U.S. government issues treasury bonds to finance the national debt, it relies on a select group of dealers to acquire and then resell the bonds to other dealers and private individuals. This arrangement worked well for many years until one of Salomon's government securities traders, Paul Mozer, began to corner a large share of the market. He secretly violated Treasury Department rules limiting how much any one brokerage and its customers could bid at any given auction. Gutfreund took no action against the rogue trader when he discovered the illegal bids and waited months before notifying Treasury. Treasury then threatened to suspend Salomon's trading privileges. Soon Gutfreund resigned, and investor Warren Buffett assumed his role on a temporary basis. Buffett appointed himself chief legal compliance officer, ordered all Salomon officers to report every legal and moral violation (except parking tickets) directly to him, and spent hours answering the questions of federal investigators and the press.

Warren Buffett's single-minded devotion to restoring the firm's ethical image kept it from collapse; but the fallout, nevertheless, was severe. In addition to paying millions of dollars in fines, the company lost three quarters of its stock underwriting business, was prevented from making $4 billion in bond trades, and saw its stock value plummet. Trader Mozer spent four months in jail, Gutfreund lost his pension and stock options, and several executives received limited or lifetime bans from the securities market. Salomon largely regained its financial health but was acquired by the Travelers Group insurance company in 1997. A year later, Travelers merged with Citicorp, and Salomon Smith Barney began to operate as the investment banking/brokerage arm of the new conglomerate.

Gutfreund gets much of the blame for what happened at Salomon. He helped create an unhealthy ethical culture using the following cultural transmission mechanisms:

What leaders pay attention to. Gutfreund paid "absolute attention to a short-term business focus and what was happening that day or that week."[1] He never created a long-term strategy but focused on immediate profits, which encouraged Mozer to ignore the law.

How leaders react to critical incidents. When Gutfreund learned that Mozer had exceeded legal bid limits, he tried to cover it up. The CEO waited months before firing the trader, and tried to save his own job. He kept information from federal authorities. The actions of Gutfreund and Mozer were particularly troubling, since bond traders depend on verbal commitments. A promise can have the same weight or importance as a legal contract.

How leaders behave (role modeling). Stock and bond trading is a high-stakes, high-risk business. Gutfreund sanctioned this "bet the company" atmosphere. His formula for success was to wake up every day "ready to bite the ass off a bear." Gutfreund once challenged another executive to a million-dollar game of liar's poker. The executive responded by raising the stakes to $10 million. In liar's poker, two or more players hold a dollar bill against their chests. They make statements, some true and some false, about the serial numbers on the bills. The winner is the person who correctly challenges the false claims of the other players. Gutfreund and the executive never played their winner-take-all game. However, their reckless example helped create a go-for-broke atmosphere that was to cost the company dearly. Gutfreund also modeled how to take advantage of others by selling Salomon to another company without consulting Billy Salomon, whose name was on the company door.

How leaders allocate awards. Salomon paid extremely high bonuses for short-term performance. In 1990, for example, 106 employees earned $1 million each, and one arbitrage trader pocketed a $23 million bonus. News of these high bonuses probably prompted a jealous Mozer to defraud the government and his firm.

How leaders hire and fire individuals (selection). Gutfreund hired ambitious young people and turned them loose. They could reap high rewards if they succeeded but were quickly let go if they didn't generated significant profits. Further, performance guidelines and criteria for dismissal were unclear; the CEO seemed to dismiss employees based on such subjective measures as his own feelings. Those who wanted to be promoted had to follow Gutfreund's example by dedicating their lives to the company and getting deals done by any means possible.

Though decades have passed, the financial industry continues to be plagued by many of the same cultural failings as Salomon. Wall Street bankers who focused on short-term profits helped trigger the recent Great Recession. They made risky investments in order to qualify for generous bonuses. In some cases, they received bonuses even though their investments later failed, and their employers had to be bailed out by the federal government. Bonus payments totaling $1.6 billion went to executives at 17 firms receiving government funds, including CITI Group, Goldman Sachs, and AIG.

Discussion Questions

1. Which cultural transmission mechanism did the most to create an unhealthy ethical culture at Salomon?

2. Can you think of other organizations that have ethical cultures similar to that found at Salomon?

3. Can you think of leaders who have been positive role models for you? What impact have they had on your attitudes and behavior?

4. Can you think of leaders who have been negative role models? What did you learn from their bad examples?

5. What will it take to change the ethical culture on Wall Street?

Note

1. Sims, R. R., & Brinkmann, J. (2002). Leaders as moral role models: The case of John Gutfreund at Salomon Brothers. *Journal of Business Ethics, 35,* 327–339, p. 331.

Sources

Associated Press. (2010, July 23). Pay czar will not fight banks over $1.6 billion in executive pay. *The Oregonian.* Retrieved November 10, 2010, from OregonLive.com.

Etzel, B. (2002, July 1). WorldCom's wrong number. *Investment Dealers' Digest,* pp. 9–12.

Guyon, J. (2002, October 14). The king and I. *Fortune* (Europe), p. 38.

Lewis, M. (1989). *Liar's poker.* New York: Norton.

Loomis, C. J., & Kahn, J. (1999, January 11). Citigroup: Scenes from a merger. *Fortune,* pp. 76–83.

Timmons, H., Cohn, L., McNamee, M., & Rossant, J. (2002, August 5). CITI's sleepless nights. *BusinessWeek,* pp. 42–43.

Useem, M. (1998). *The leadership moment.* New York: Times Business, Ch. 7.

ENDNOTES

1. Weaver, G. R., Trevino, L. K., & Cochran, P. L. (1999). Integrated and decoupled corporate social performance: Management commitments, external pressures, and corporate ethics practices. *Academy of Management Journal, 42,* 539–552; Weaver, G. R., Trevino, L. K., & Cochran, P. L. (1999). Corporate ethics practices in the mid-1990s: An empirical study of the Fortune 1000. *Journal of Business Ethics, 18,* 283–294.

2. See, for example: Pearson, G. (1995). *Integrity in organizations: An alternative business ethic.* London: McGraw-Hill; Schminke, M. (Ed.). (1998). *Managerial ethics: Moral management of people and processes.* Mahwah, NJ: Lawrence Erlbaum; Paine, L. S. (1996, March-April). Managing for organizational integrity. *Harvard Business Review,* pp. 106–117; Paine, L. S. (2003). *Value shift: Why companies must merge social and financial imperatives to achieve superior performance.* New York: McGraw-Hill.

3. Burns, J. M. (2003). *Transforming leadership: A new pursuit of happiness.* New York: Atlantic Monthly Press, p. 24.

4. Trevino, L. K. (1990). A cultural perspective on changing and developing organizational ethics. In W. A. Pasmore & R. W. Woodman (Eds.), *Research in organizational change and development* (Vol. 4). Greenwich, CT: JAI; Trevino, L. K., & Nelson, K. A. (2004). *Managing business ethics: Straight talk about how to do it right* (3rd ed.). Hoboken, NJ: John Wiley.

5. Collins, J. C., & Porras, J. I. (1996, September-October). Building your company's vision. *Harvard Business Review,* pp. 65–77.

6. Paine (2003).

7. Collins & Porras (1996).

8. Collins, J. C., & Porras, J. I. (1994). *Built to last: Successful habits of visionary companies.* New York: HarperBusiness.

9. Adams, J. S., Tashchian, A., & Shore, T. H. (2001). Codes of ethics as signals for ethical behavior. *Journal of Business Ethics, 29,* 199–211.

10. Brasswell, M. K., Foster, C. M., & Poe, S. L. (2009, Summer). A new generation of corporate codes of ethics. *Southern Business Review,* pp. 1–10.

11. Hoppen, D. (2002, Winter). Guiding corporate behavior: A leadership obligation, not a choice. *Journal for Quality & Participation, 25,* 15–19; Boudreaux, G., & Steiner, T. (2005, Spring). Developing a code of ethics. *Management Quarterly,* pp. 2–19.

12. Barth, S. R. (2003). *Corporate ethics: The business code of conduct for ethical employees.* Boston: Aspatore Books.

13. Stevens, B. (2007). Corporate ethical codes: Effective instruments for influencing behavior. *Journal of Business Ethics, 78,* 601–609.

14. McCabe, D., & Trevino, L. K. (1993). Academic dishonesty: Honor codes and other contextual influences. *Journal of Higher Education, 64,* 522–569.

15. Adams, Tashchian, & Shore (2001); Valentine, S., & Barnett, T. (2003). Ethics code awareness, perceived ethical values, and organizational commitment. *Journal of Personal Selling & Sales Management, 23,* 359–367.

16. Schwartz, M. (2001). The nature of the relationship between corporate codes of ethics and behaviour. *Journal of Business Ethics, 32,* 247–262.

17. Brandl, P., & Maguire, M. (2002, Winter). Codes of ethics: A primer on their purpose, development and use. *Journal for Quality & Participation, 25,* 9–12; Johannesen, R. L. (2002). *Ethics in human communication* (5th ed.). Prospect Heights, IL: Waveland Press, Chap. 10.

18. Harvey, S. J., Jr. (2000). Reinforcing ethical decision making through organizational structure. *Journal of Business Ethics, 28,* 43–58.

19. Cialdini, R. B. (2001). *Influence: Science and practice* (4th ed.). Boston: Allyn & Bacon.

20. Trevino, L. K., Weaver, G. R., Gibson, D. G., & Toffler, B. L. (1999). Managing ethics and legal compliance: What works and what hurts. *California Management Review, 41,* 131–151.

21. Zyglidopoulos, S. C., & Fleming, P. J. (2007). Ethical distance in corrupt firms: How do innocent bystanders become guilty perpetrators? *Journal of Business Ethics, 78,* 265–274.

22. Darley, J. M. (1996). How organizations socialize individuals into evildoing. In D. M. Messick & A. E. Tenbrunsel (Eds.), *Codes of conduct: Behavioral research into business* ethics (pp. 13–43). New York: Russell Sage Foundation.

23. Trevino (1990).

24. Goodman, P. S., & Morgenson, G. (2008, December 28). Saying yes to anyone, WaMu built empire on shaky loans. *The New York Times,* p. A1.

25. Cohen, D. V. (1993). Creating and maintaining ethical work climates: Anomie in the workplace and implications for managing change. *Business Ethics Quarterly, 3,* 343–358.

26. Estes, R. (1996). *Tyranny of the bottom line.* San Francisco: Berrett-Koehler.

27. Lumpkin, J. L. (2005, May 11). One-day halt called in Army recruiting. *Associated Press.*

28. Carroll, A. B., & Buchholtz, A. K. (2009). *Business and society: Ethics and stakeholder management* (7th ed.). Mason, OH: South-Western.

29. Stevens (2007).

30. Hoffman, W. M., & Rowe, M. (2007). The ethics officer as agent of the board: Leveraging ethical governance capability in the post-Enron corporation. *Business & Society Review, 112*(4), 553–572, p. 556.

31. Klein Aguilar, M. (2010, February). CCO role is now a full-time job. *Compliance Week,* pp. 29–31.

32. Weber, J. (2008, February 13). The new ethics enforcers. *BusinessWeek*, pp. 76–77; Liopis, J., Gonzalez, M. R., & Gasco, J. L. (2007). Corporate governance and organizational culture: The role of ethics officers. *International Journal of Disclosure and Governance, 4*(2), 96–105. Hoffman, W. M., Neill, J. D., & Stovall, O. S. (2007). An investigation of ethics officer independence. *Journal of Business Ethics, 78*, 87–95; Hoffman & Rowe (2007).

33. Trevino & Nelson (2004).

34. Trevino & Nelson (2004).

35. Martin, J. (2002). *Organizational culture: Mapping the terrain.* Thousand Oaks, CA: Sage.

36. Beyer, J. M., & Trice, H. M. (1987). How an organization's rites reveal its culture. *Organizational Dynamics, 15*, 5–24; Trice, H. M., & Beyer, J. M. (1984). Studying organizational cultures through rites and ceremonials. *Academy of Management Review, 9*, 653–699.

37. Gittell, J. H. (2003). *The Southwest Airlines way.* New York: McGraw-Hill.

38. Martin (2002).

39. Tobias, A. (1976). *Fire and ice.* New York: William Morrow, pp. 98–99.

40. McLean, B., & Elkind, P. (2003). *The smartest guys in the room: The amazing rise and fall of Enron.* New York: Portfolio.

41. Unruh, G. (2008). Should you manage ethics or corruption? *Thunderbird International Business Review, 50*, 287–293; Trevino & Nelson (2004); Paine, L. S. (1996, March-April). Managing for organizational integrity. *Harvard Business Review*, pp. 106–117; Tenbrunsel, A. E., Smith-Crowe, K., & Umphress, E. E. (2003). Building houses on rocks: The role of ethical infrastructure in organizations. *Social Justice Research, 16*, 285–307.

42. Hofmann, P. B. (2006, March/April). The value of an ethics audit. *Healthcare Executive*, pp. 44–45.

43. Victor, B., & Cullen, J. B. (1988). The organizational bases of ethical work climates. *Administrative Science Quarterly, 33*, 101–125; Victor, B., & Cullen, J. B. (1990). A theory and measure of ethical climate in organizations. In W. C. Frederic & L. E. Preston (Eds.), *Business ethics: Research issues and empirical studies* (pp. 77–97). Greenwich, CT: JAI.

44. See, for example: Brower, H. H., & Shrader, C. B. (2000). Moral reasoning and ethical climate: Not-for-profit vs. for-profit boards of directors. *Journal of Business Ethics, 26*, 147–167; Sims, R. L., & Keon, T. L. (1997). Ethical work climate as a factor in the development of person-organization fit. *Journal of Business Ethics, 16*, 1095–1105; Peterson, D. K. (2002). The relationship between unethical behavior and the dimensions of the Ethical Climate Questionnaire. *Journal of Business Ethics, 41*, 313–326; Fritzche, D. J. (2000). Ethical climates and the ethical dimension of decision making. *Journal of Business Ethics, 24*, 125–140; Trevino, L. K., Butterfield, K. D., & McCabe, D. L. (1998). The ethical context in organizations: Influences on employee attitudes and behaviors. *Business Ethics Quarterly, 8*, 447–476; Wimbush, J. C., Shepard, J. M., & Markham, S. E. (1997). An empirical examination of the relationship between ethical climate and ethical behavior from multiple levels of analysis. *Journal of Business Ethics, 16*, 1705–1716; Cullen, J. B., Parboteeah, K. P., & Victor, B. (2003). The effects of ethical climates on organizational commitment: A two-study analysis. *Journal of Business Ethics, 46*, 127–141; Victor, B., Cullen, J. B., & Boynton, A. (1993). Toward a general framework of organizational meaning systems. In C. Conrad (Ed.), *Ethical nexus* (pp. 193–216). Norwood, NJ: Ablex; Martin, K. D., & Cullen, J. B. (2006). Continuities and extensions of ethical climate theory: A meta-analytic review. *Journal of Business Ethics, 69*, 175–194.

45. Gellerman, S. W. (1989, Winter). Managing ethics from the top down. *Sloan Management Review*, pp. 73–79; Longnecker, J. G. (1985). Management priorities and management ethics. *Journal of Business Ethics, 4*, 65–70; Trevino, L. K., Hartman, L. P., & Brown, M. (2000). Moral person and moral manager: How executives develop a reputation for ethical leadership. *California Management Review, 42*, 128–142; Weaver, G. R., Trevino, L. K., & Cochran, P. L. (1999). Corporate ethics programs as control systems: Influence of executive commitment and environmental factors. *Academy of Management Journal, 42*, 41–57; Andreoli, N.,

& Lefkowitz, J. (2008). Individual and organizational antecedents of misconduct in organizations. *Journal of Business Ethics, 85,* 309–332.

46. Schein, E. H. (1992). *Organizational culture and leadership* (2nd ed.). San Francisco: Jossey-Bass.

47. Bunkley, N., & Maynard, M. (2010, April 19). Toyota is expected to pay $16.4 million fine sought by U.S. over recall of sticking pedals. *The New York Times,* p. B3; Gillis, J., & Fountain, H. (2010, June 7). Rate of oil leak, still not clear, puts doubt on BP. *The New York Times,* p. A1.

48. Unruh (2008).

49. Albrecht, T. L, & Bach, B. W. (1997). *Communication in complex organizations: A relational approach.* Fort Worth, TX: Harcourt Brace.

50. Staczek, J. J. (2008). An interview with Eric M. Pillmore: Hitting the CSR bull's-eye in a shifting corporate environment. *Thunderbird International Business Review, 50,* 295–301.

51. Anand, V., Ashforth, B. E., & Joshi, M. (2004). Business as usual: The acceptance and perpetuation of corruption in organizations. *Academy of Management Executive, 18,* 39–53.

52. Heames, J. T., & Service, R. W. (2003). Dichotomies in teaching, application, and ethics. *Journal of Education for Business, 79,* 118–122; Rice, D., & Dreilinger, C. (1990, May). Rights and wrongs of ethics training. *Training and Development Journal,* pp. 103–108; Piper, T. R., Gentile, M. C., & Parks, S. D. (1993). *Can ethics be taught? Perspectives, challenges, and approaches at Harvard Business School.* Boston: Harvard Business School Press; Hartog, M., & Frame, P. (2004). Business ethics in the curriculum: Integrating ethics through work experience. *Journal of Business Ethics, 54,* 399–409; Mintzberg, H. (2004). *Managers, not MBAs.* San Francisco: Berrett-Koehler; Rest, J. R. (1994). Background: Theory and research. In J. R. Rest & D. Narvaez (Eds.), *Moral development in the professions: Psychology and applied ethics* (pp. 1–25). Hillsdale, NJ: Lawrence Erlbaum; Swanson, D. L., & Fisher, D. G. (Eds.). (2008). *Advancing business ethics education.* Charlotte, NC: Information Age.

11

Managing Ethical Hot Spots in the Organization

F orest fire fighting crews provide summer employment for college students, particularly for those studying in the western United States. An important part of the forest fire fighter's job is managing hot spots so they don't flare up and become major blazes. Hotshot crews parachute in to put out small fires caused by lightning strikes, and when a major fire is contained, fire fighters are careful not to leave areas that could reignite.

While forest fire crews have to be alert for physical hot spots, organizational leaders and followers have to recognize ethical "hot spots." These are organizational activities or functions that frequently put the group at risk. Three common ethical hot spots are marketing, finance/accounting, and human resources. Failure to manage these moral danger zones is behind many of the organizational scandals described in previous chapters, including, for example, Johnson & Johnson; Countrywide; Bell, California; the U.S. Army; AIG; Salomon; BP; NASA; and Imperial Food Processing. Not only do marketing, financial, and human relations practices offer lots of opportunity to engage in unethical behavior, they are essential to all types of organizations. Every organization must deal with customers, must track and invest financial resources, and must meet the needs of its members.

In this chapter, I'll introduce principles and strategies specifically designed to help you and your organization manage the ethical dangers posed by marketing, financial operations, and human resource management. We can never completely eliminate these hot spots, but we can help prevent them from exploding into ethical fires. In this chapter, I'll describe some of the ethical issues that arise in the practice of each function and then introduce guidelines for responding to these challenges.

Ethical Marketing

Ethical Issues in Marketing

All types of organizations have to manage relationships with customers, including businesses selling products and services, government agencies encouraging citizens to take advantage of their programs, and nonprofits soliciting donors. However, marketing involves far more than the transaction between buyer and seller. Instead, this function "involves all aspects of creating a product or service and bringing it to market where an exchange can take place."[1] These aspects include product, price, promotion, and place. Product describes *what* is being marketed. Price refers to the cost, which is determined by the parties in an exchange. Promotion deals with *how* products and services are marketed. Placement is concerned with *where* a product or service gets placed in the marketplace.

Ethical dilemmas arise throughout the marketing process. Important ethical issues are identified in Ethics in Action 11.1

ETHICS IN ACTION 11.1 ETHICAL ISSUES IN MARKETING

1. *Ethical issues related to product:* Product safety, product quality, product design, packaging, labeling, and ethical products.

2. *Ethical issues related to price:* Price fairness, price fixing, price discrimination, price gouging, and misleading pricing.

3. *Ethical issues related to place:* Exclusive distribution rights, channel control, and slotting allowances.

(Continued)

(Continued)

4. *Ethical issues related to promotion:* Advertising, ethics, product placement, direct marketing, and sales promotion.

5. *Ethical issues related to sales:* Ethical conflicts of salespeople, ethical values and behavior of salespeople.

6. *Corporate ethical decision making:* Corporate ethical decision making, ethical values and ethical behavior of managers, corporate social responsibility (CSR), and marketing.

7. *Codes and norms:* Marketing ethics theory, ethical norms, and codes of ethics.

8. *Ethical issues related to consumers:* Consumer ethical decision making, ethical values and ethical perceptions of consumers.

9. *Ethical issues related to vulnerable consumers:* Ethical aspects of marketing decisions regarding children, the elderly, and poor people.

10. *International/Cross-cultural marketing ethics:* Unethical conduct of multinational corporations, cross-national comparisons of various topics, such as corporate ethical decision making and consumer ethical decision making.

11. *Ethical issues related to marketing research:* Ethical responsibility and conduct of marketing research enterprises and their customers, such as embellishing results, privacy issues, etc.

12. *Ethical issues related to marketing education:* Integration of ethical questions in marketing education.

13. *Ethical issues related to social marketing:* Concept and definition of social marketing, ethical dimensions of social marketing, social responsibility of marketing managers, and cause-related marketing.

14. *Ethical issues related to green marketing:* Social responsibility and costs of green marketing.

15. *Ethical issues related to law:* Relationship between law and ethics within the marketing field.

16. *Ethical issues related to the Internet:* Web privacy, identity theft, phishing, and online auctions.

17. *Ethical issues related to religion:* Impact of religion and religious values on marketing ethics.

SOURCE: Schlegelmilch, B. B., & Oberseder, M. (2010). Half a century of marketing ethics: Shifting perspectives and emerging trends. *Journal of Business Ethics, 93,* pp. 2–3. Used with kind permission from Springer Science & Business Media.

Ethical Principles and Strategies

As you can see from Ethics in Action 11.1, ethical issues in marketing vary greatly. Fortunately, researchers and practitioners offer guidelines that can help us deal with these issues no matter what form they take. Two such sets of ethical marketing guidelines are the marketing ethics continuum and the seven basic marketing perspectives.

The Marketing Ethics Continuum

Determining how much importance to place on the producer or on the consumer is one way to sort through the ethical issues involved in marketing. Ethics professor N. Craig Smith offers the marketing ethics continuum as a tool for measuring an organization's commitment to the seller or to the buyer.[2] At one end of the continuum are marketers who put the interests of producers first. This is sometimes referred to as the *caveat emptor,* or "buyer beware," school. Caveat emptor firms operate within the law while maximizing profits. They look for loopholes in the law in order to gain a competitive advantage and believe that if a strategy is legal, then it is ethical. Interviews with ad agency executives suggest that this view might be widely held by advertising professionals. Researchers found widespread "moral myopia" and moral muteness among respondents.[3] Many ad executives didn't see that ethical issues posed a major problem. If they did notice an ethical dilemma, they kept their doubts to themselves. These professionals believed the following:

Consumers are too smart to be fooled.

The family, the media, regulators, and other groups are to blame for the negative effects of advertising; advertising only reflects what society wants.

What is legal is also moral.

If a product is legal, then it deserves to be promoted.

Any attempt to impose ethical standards is a form of illegal censorship.

Agency representatives should identify with their clients, not with consumers.

Ignorance of ethical issues is bliss.

Personal standards should be separated from agency and client standards.

The client is always right.

Ethics is bad for business.

Acknowledging ethical issues reduces the effectiveness of ad executives and may prompt them to leave the industry.

Caveat venditor, or "seller beware," is at the other extreme of the marketing ethics continuum from the caveat emptor stance. According to this position, customer satisfaction is the primary ethical standard. The seller takes special care to make sure that consumers are not harmed. Steps to achieve this goal may include product testing, eliminating defects, providing clear use instructions, and making sure that buyers are capable of using what they purchase. Some advocates of this position go so far as to argue that manufacturers should be liable for unforeseen risks associated with their goods.

There are three positions in between the extremes of caveat emptor and caveat venditor. The *industry practice* position is a step beyond buyer beware. Marketers who take this position follow general industry standards, such as refusing to make "commission payments," which are widely viewed as a form of bribery. The *ethics codes* stance is a step closer to the seller beware position and formalizes industry standards. Codes help employees determine appropriate actions and contribute to building an ethical organizational culture.

Consumer sovereignty comes closest to the caveat venditor position but places some responsibility on the consumer to, say, follow safety guidelines when using a product. (Putting all the responsibility for product safety on manufacturers appears to be unjust.) Smith argues that this is the ethical position we should typically adopt. Consumer sovereignty is essential to capitalism and honors individual autonomy and freedom of choice. To be considered ethical, marketing activities must pass the consumer sovereignty test. This test consists of adequately addressing three criteria: the capability of the consumer, adequacy of information, and freedom of choice. When audiences are vulnerable and therefore less capable, special care must be taken not to take advantage of them. Marketers must also determine if consumers have adequate information. They need to satisfactorily answer this question: Has the organization provided enough information to consumers so that they can determine whether their expectations about a purchase will be fulfilled? A sales representative who oversells the features of his product would violate this standard. Consumers must also have freedom of choice—the option to go elsewhere to make their purchases. Organizations that monopolize a market fall short on this principle, as do manufacturers who lock customers into additional purchases. For example, some printer manufacturers force consumers to buy their ink products by making it impossible to use other brands.

The Seven Basic Ethical Marketing Perspectives

Marketing professors Gene Laczniak and Patrick Murphy provide a comprehensive set of ethical marketing guidelines that incorporate both moral principles as well as ethical problem-solving strategies. They call each guideline a basic perspective, or BP. The seven basic perspectives (BPs) are as follows:[4]

BP1—Societal benefit: Ethical marketing puts people first. This principle acts as the foundation for all the others. Marketing should always serve people. Further, "People should never be treated merely as cogs in the marketing system, whether they are customers, employees, suppliers, distributors, or some other stakeholder."[5] Selling tactics that treat people as means to an end include the high-pressure sales techniques used by some car dealers, big-box stores' demand for price concessions based on their economic power, extreme fear appeals, sexual exploitation of women in advertising, and price gouging. Putting people first means more than satisfying customers, however. Aggressively marketing credit to college populations may satisfy some students, but it can put others seriously in debt even before they graduate. The most ethical marketing strategies benefit society as a whole. On the other hand, socially irresponsible marketing practices can bring sanctions. No-call lists were created, for example, to curb phone solicitations by telemarketers and others.

BP2—Two realms: Ethical expectations for marketing must exceed legal requirements. Ethical marketers go beyond what is required by the law, which sets the baseline expectations of society. Many marketing techniques, while not illegal, still raise ethical concerns. Take the case of "ambush marketing." Creating an ad campaign similar to a competitor's special event promotion is not forbidden by law, but it is widely perceived as unfair. This second perspective urges marketing managers to follow societal and professional standards. They should look beyond maximizing shareholder return to serving other groups as well—employees, suppliers, and distributors. (We'll examine stakeholder groups in detail in the next chapter.)

BP3—Intent, means, and end: Three essential components of ethical analysis. Any ethical analysis of a particular marketing tactic must keep in mind what the marketers want to happen (intention), how they carry out the action (means), and the outcome (consequences). Intention is hardest to judge, though it is sometimes apparent. For example, deception seems to be the *intent* when marketers use colors and logos similar to those of competitors. The *means* of a marketing strategy is suspect when, for instance, it makes it extremely hard for consumers to cash in rebates, or when women are portrayed as sex symbols in beer ads. The outcome of a marketing campaign also needs to be considered. Ad campaigns for all-terrain vehicles have boosted sales but at a significant cost in deaths and injuries, particularly to children. Advertisers have an ethical duty to communicate safety messages that reduce the risk to riders.

BP4—Marketing managers differ in moral imagination and development: Four types. Organizations that want to improve their ethical marketing performance should hire executives who demonstrate the ability to come up with creative ethical decisions (moral imagination) as well as a high level of moral reasoning (see Chapter 3). Laczniak and Murphy offer a typology of marketing managers based on their level of moral development that can be used to evaluate prospective and current employees. *Egoistic marketing managers* are at the lowest level of moral development. Interested only in meeting their personal needs, they should be screened out of the organization. If unwittingly hired, they should be given little chance to earn improper rewards through unethical behavior. *Legalist marketing managers* fail to fulfill Basic Principle 2 because they are interested only in following the law, not in bettering society. *Moral strivers,* typically the largest group in most organizations, can balance the needs of a variety of groups when making ethical choices. They have a high degree of empathy for others. However, moral strivers still rely heavily on company rules and policies for ethical direction and sometimes revert to following the law or their own egos. Their performance can be improved through training and by providing organizational rules and values to help them in decision making. *Principled marketing managers* can apply ethical norms and relevant laws to specific situations. They have the imagination to foresee the impact of their choices on outside groups. They are the most desirable employees, who can serve as ethical role models for the rest of the organization.

BP5—Five essential ethical precepts for enlightened marketing. When marketing, we should embrace five ethical principles. The first is the *principle of nonmalfeasance.*

Do not consciously do harm by promoting health supplements that carry the risk of possible harmful side effects, or weight-loss programs that have no basis in scientific fact, for example. The second moral precept is the *principle of nondeception.* Never intentionally mislead or manipulate consumers. Misleading activities include making false claims, selling suspect extended warranties, exaggerating product features, and "channel stuffing"—selling unneeded products to meet quarterly sales projections. The third precept is *protecting vulnerable market segments,* such as children, the elderly, the mentally ill, and the poor. Special care must be taken to preserve the human dignity of members of these groups. Fast-food chains, for instance, should acknowledge that their advertising campaigns targeted at children may contribute to childhood obesity. (See Case Study 11.2, "Should Ronald McDonald Retire?" at the end of the chapter for a closer look at the issues raised by marketing fast food to kids.)

The fourth essential principle is *the principle of distributive justice.* In keeping with the difference principle of John Rawls (see Chapter 1), marketing practices are unethical if they further disadvantage already disadvantaged groups, like those described in the previous paragraph. One example of taking advantage of marginalized groups would be the supermarket chain that puts better-quality products in stores in affluent neighborhoods while charging consumers in poor neighborhoods more for inferior goods.

The fifth and final moral precept is *the principle of stewardship.* Try to minimize the costs of operations on society and the physical environment while promoting responsible consumption.

BP6—Six basic stakeholders: Embracing the stakeholder concept. Basic Principle 6 builds on Basic Principle 2 by asserting that organizations operate on behalf of society and must consider the interests of outside groups. Six key groups are (1) primary—consumers, employees, and others who have the most significance to the organization, (2) secondary—suppliers/distributors and others who have a contractual relationship with the marketing organization, (3) host communities, (4) the general public, (5), the media, and (6) legal and political institutions. Failure to look beyond the needs of stakeholders can put organizations in danger. Firestone lost much of its market share when it ignored customer safety and was slow to recall faulty tires; Toyota sales plummeted when it delayed vehicle recalls.

BP7—The seven steps of moral reasoning for marketing managers. Laczniak and Murphy offer an ethical analysis format, similar to those presented in Chapter 3, which is designed specifically for marketing decisions. The first two steps are to become aware of an ethical problem, and then to frame that problem as an ethical issue. The third step is to determine the stakeholders affected by the marketing action. Are they employees? Shareholders? Community groups? The fourth step is to select the ethical standards or perspectives (utilitarianism, justice as fairness) that could be applied to this situation. The fifth step is to engage in the ethical analysis. Steps six and seven are to make the decision and to implement it.

Ethical Finance and Accounting

Ethical Issues in Finance and Accounting

Finance and accounting are closely related functions that support the ongoing operations of the organization.[6] *Finance* is concerned with "the generation, allocation, and management of monetary resources for any purpose."[7] The field of finance includes personal finance (how individuals invest and spend); corporate finance (raising and spending capital); public finance (government taxation, borrowing, and spending); financial markets where stocks, bonds, and other financial instruments are traded; and financial intermediaries, such as banks and other lenders that make financial transactions. Ethical issues in finance generally coalesce around these themes:[8]

Financial markets. Fairness is the key to ethical behavior in financial markets. Securities must be priced fairly, and buyers must be able to determine the true value of a stock or bond. Unfair trading practices include making false statements about the true value of the company, omitting important information from financial reports (e.g., the company is facing a major lawsuit, the CEO is retiring), or bidding up a stock price in hopes of selling at a peak price to other, unwary investors. Unfair trading conditions exist when some people have access to more information. Unfair financial contracts (home mortgages and futures options, for example) are vague and deceptive.

Financial services. The financial services industry includes banks, investment firms, insurance companies, financial planners, and mutual fund and pension firms that generally act as intermediaries between buyers and financial providers. (In some cases, they may market their own financial products directly to consumers.) Acting as an intermediary or as an agent on behalf of someone else brings fiduciary duties or responsibilities. Conflicts of interest—where the interests of the agent interfere with acting in the best interest of the client—are common ethical problems for those in fiduciary roles. (See the discussion of conflicts of interest in negotiation in Chapter 6.) Brokers may sell inferior in-house mutual funds to clients because they generate higher commissions. Or they may use confidential information from clients to enrich themselves by copying or "piggybacking" on the moves of successful investors. Financial sales practices also raise ethical concerns. Agents may peddle investment products that are unsuitable for clients, or they may encourage homeowners to continually refinance their homes in order to generate fees and bonuses. Pushing unsuitable home loans helped cause the collapse of Washington Mutual Savings, the largest bank failure in the history of the United States.[9] Those who manage portfolios for mutual funds, pension funds, and endowments must determine where to put their money. Should they invest in mining companies with operations in war-torn Congo? Buy stock in tobacco makers?

Financial management. Financial managers make decisions about how to allocate organizational resources. They, too, have fiduciary duties, in this case to their employers. Financial managers are obligated to use organizational assets wisely and not for personal gain. Insider trading violates these duties, as do excessive compensation and benefits. Balancing competing interests raises additional ethical concerns. Financial managers make decisions that impact a variety of stakeholders both inside and outside the organization. They have an obligation to consider the claims of competing groups. Closing a plant may reduce costs, producing higher returns for company investors. However, this determination should not be made without considering the impact on laid-off employees, suppliers, and the local community.

Financial people. Financial employees must make a variety of individual ethical choices that typically challenge their integrity. They may be pressured to overstate earnings or the likely financial return on a project. Or they might be encouraged to make an underserved stock "buy" recommendation for a company that is a client of the firm. Or they must decide whether or not to accept underwriting business that was secured through a bribe. Employees at giant insurance broker Marsh USA failed to act with integrity when they accepted undisclosed payments from insurance companies for recommending them to clients.

Accounting, as the name suggests, tracks or accounts for the operations of the organization. Accountants provide a picture or report of the organization's health or status. Ethical issues arise in each of the four major functions of accounting:[10]

1. *Auditing.* Maintaining independence is a constant challenge for those who audit organizations. Auditors worry that they will lose valuable clients if they point out financial irregularities. Before the Sarbanes-Oxley Act of 2002, many major accounting firms earned much more from consulting than from auditing. Auditors and their supervisors signed off on many questionable accounting practices for fear of losing lucrative consulting contracts with the same firms they were monitoring.

2. *Management accounting.* Managerial accountants prepare financial statements for managers and, in some cases, for those outside the organization. Their obligation is to create a truthful picture of the firm's financial situation, even if it hurts the company or organization. There are plenty of pressures to be less than candid. Executive bonuses may depend on painting a rosy picture of 4th-quarter earnings; banks are more willing to lend funds if they believe that the organization is in good financial condition. Then, too, accountants have a good deal of discretion in interpreting rules. They may decide to use "aggressive" accounting procedures that, while legal, may disguise the true state of the company.

3. *Tax accounting.* Tax accountants determine what their clients owe the government. They have a responsibility both to the client and to the public through the government. After all, without revenue the government cannot operate, and society suffers. Tax returns should be truthful, and by signing a tax form the preparer is attesting to its accuracy. Common unethical practices include promoting dubious tax shelters, taking advantage of unintended tax loopholes, and signing off on fraudulent returns.

4. *Consulting.* Those who work in accounting firms offer their accounting and consulting (training, financial) services to organizations. As noted above, this has made it difficult for accountants to maintain their objectivity, leading to a number of audit failures. Focusing strictly on profit tempts accountants to ignore the needs of society and to engage in dishonest, deceptive practices.

Ethical Principles and Strategies

The past two decades have not been kind to the accounting and finance professions. Between 1997 and 2000, 700 firms were forced by the Securities and Exchange Commission to restate their earnings.[11] Then came massive accounting scandals at WorldCom, Enron, Freddie Mac, Global Crossing, K-Mart, and Parmalat. Fraud and mismanagement in the financial services industry led to the near collapse of the U.S. and world economies near the end of the first decade of the millennium. All too often, financial experts violated ethical standards and lost the trust of their fellow citizens, prompting some to describe accounting as "a profession in crisis."[12] To add insult to injury, researchers have discovered that the moral reasoning level of accounting students is lower than that of students in other majors. There is also evidence to suggest that the moral judgment of accounting graduates declines still further after they enter the workforce and later become supervisors and partners in accounting firms![13]

All this bad news has sparked a good deal of soul searching among financial educators and practitioners. What is it, they wonder, about accounting and finance that makes students and professionals susceptible to moral failure? What can be done to encourage the ethical practice of finance and accounting? I will highlight three responses to these questions: (1) recognize the ethical foundations of these fields, (2) follow widely held professional principles, and (3) become a questioning professional.

Recognize the Ethical Foundations of Accounting and Finance

Many financial experts consider their work to be value neutral. They view people as rational decision makers driven solely by economic values.[14] These professionals have lost sight of the fact that economic values are not always most important. Financial considerations need to be balanced against concern for others, care for the environment, and other priorities. Focusing only on the bottom line has also made financial experts susceptible to the pressure to "make the numbers" by any means possible. Trained to believe that they serve only their immediate client or organization, they deny their responsibility to other groups, the environment, and their professions. They are reluctant to blow the whistle when they see financial wrongdoing. On the other hand, accountants and other financial workers find it all too easy to view people as numbers or assets, which makes it easier to treat them cruelly.[15] During the Holocaust, for example, accountants tracked the costs of building the concentration camps and gas chambers as well as the expense of shipping Jews to their deaths in rail cars.

Any attempt to improve the ethical performance of financial professionals, then, needs to address the mind-set of practitioners. Recognizing the ethical implications of accounting and finance is a good place to start. These are not ethically neutral activities. In reality, "Virtually all aspects of their [accountants'] work have an ethical dimension."[16] The origins of financial reporting demonstrate that fact. In Jewish tradition, the earliest financial records were kept to ensure that precious metals donated to the tabernacle weren't stolen or misused.[17] In the Middle Ages, double-entry bookkeeping was created to keep track of what was owed to individuals and organizations.[18] In modern times, the work of accountants has a significant impact both inside and outside the organization. As we've seen, corporate leaders use financial reports to make budgets and allocate resources. Investors also depend on the financial description of firms.

Boston University professor Sandra Waddock summarizes the ethical core of accounting this way:

> The accounting profession seems to have failed to acknowledge that accounting is fundamentally an ethical, rather than a technical, discourse. Accountability inescapably assumes the fulfilling of some dutiful requirements. . . . Accountants have positions that are inherently value-laden and imbued with ethical responsibilities. Their decisions affect other people, organizations, communities and the natural environment.[19]

Waddock goes on to suggest that as an accountant you are more likely to take your ethical duties seriously and to better serve society if you take a more holistic approach to your preparation. First, develop a sense of balance. The marketplace is NOT all important. Acknowledge the significance of other values, like love, community, spirituality, the desire for meaning, and nature. The needs of business have to be balanced against these other priorities. Second, strive for the integration of body, mind, and heart. Study a variety of disciplines to develop a unified perspective on the organization and its role in society. Look beyond corporate stakeholders to consider how auditing and accounting practices influence the community and the environment.

Third, seek holistic understanding. Recognize the fact that we live in a world of limited resources and that technology has made the world more interdependent. Economic choices have a significant impact on the environment, on societies, and on individuals. Fourth, respect diversity. Honor other cultures, and recognize that accounting is done differently in other countries. Develop the ability to synthesize these differences when making decisions. Fifth, develop a grasp of complex change. Technology, the spread of HIV/AIDS, food shortages, the rise of Islam, and other forces are reshaping the world. Financial professionals will need to develop conflict resolution and collaboration skills at the same time they are transparent and accountable.

Accounting professors Michael Shaub and Dann Fisher also believe that the ethical performance of the accounting profession will improve if graduates take a different set of values with them into the workforce. They urge accounting students to adopt the following three guiding values:[20]

1. *Don't be stupid.* This principle takes aim at the self-interest or egocentrism that lies at the heart of many accounting scandals. Those who fall victim to moral failure are generally interested only in serving themselves. Shaub and Fisher apply the selfish leadership fallacies introduced in Chapter 8 to the reasoning of financial professionals.[21]

Enron's CFO Andy Fastow fell victim to the *fallacy of omnipotence*, convinced that he was all powerful and could pretty much do whatever he wanted. He believed that he was so skilled at creating ways to hide company debt that he could divert profits to himself and a few others without being discovered. Fastow and CEO Jeffrey Skilling thought they were smarter than anyone else and could keep the special accounting schemes from failing while, at the same time, propping up Enron's stock price (the *fallacy of omniscience*). Former AIG CEO Hank Greenberg, at one time one of the most important leaders in the insurance industry, fell victim to the *fallacy of invulnerability*, believing that he could survive as CEO despite a series of accounting misstatements. (He was wrong.) Ordinary auditors can become convinced of their invulnerability as well, tending to be overconfident about their knowledge and that of their subordinates. As a result, they may rely on outdated procedures and assign tasks to employees that the followers cannot handle. Executives at the KPMG Personal Financial Planning division fell victim to the *fallacy of unrealistic optimism* when they advised clients that the aggressive tax strategies they recommended would survive any challenge from the IRS. Instead, the company had to pay a $456 million fine to avoid prosecution for advocating these tactics.

2. *Tell the truth.* There are three duties to truth telling: integrity, objectivity, and transparency. *Integrity* refers to being honest and candid with other financial experts as well as with the public. Client confidentiality should not keep you, as an auditor, from revealing that a firm has violated widely held accounting or auditing standards. *Objectivity* refers to being impartial and avoiding conflicts of interest. *Transparency* is the duty to make sure that generally accepted accounting principles are carefully applied and that information is openly shared with the public.

3. *Find fraud and expose liars.* Auditors need to be sensitive to the possibility of fraud and to develop creative new ways of uncovering wrongdoing. For example, some colleges and universities are introducing forensic accounting and fraud examination coursework into their curricula. Unfortunately, many accounting programs promote conformity instead of creativity, turning out graduates who are good fits for existing accounting firms. They are ill prepared to dissent when the situation calls for it. These newly minted accountants lack the skepticism they need to question assumptions and claims.

Follow Professional Principles

Codes of ethics have long played an important role in regulating ethics in the financial field. Of course, as all the accounting and financial scandals demonstrate, these codes have not always been effective. Professional codes of ethics suffer from all the shortcomings of organizational codes described in the last chapter, including a lack of specifics and enforcement.[22] They do not solve all the ethical dilemmas that arise in accounting and finance. Nevertheless, the principles outlined in these codes are useful. If you are a financial professional, they identify your ethical duties and set a high standard for your behavior. Those of us who are not involved in financial operations can use these guidelines to evaluate the behavior of those who are. (Test the usefulness of these standards by applying them to the scenarios in Case Study 11.1.)

The Chartered Financial Analyst (CFA) Code of Ethics and Standards of Professional Conduct is an important ethical statement for the finance profession. The CFA code was drafted by the CFA Institute, which is made up of over 100,000 licensed financial analysts and professionals. The CFA code begins by identifying a set of important ethical standards, which are described in Ethics in Action 11.2.

ETHICS IN ACTION 11.2 THE CERTIFIED FINANCIAL ANALYST ETHICAL STANDARDS

- Act with integrity, competence, diligence, respect, and in an ethical manner with the public, clients, prospective clients, employers, employees, colleagues in the investment profession, and other participants in the global capital markets.
- Place the integrity of the investment profession and the interests of clients above [one's] own personal interests.
- Use reasonable care and exercise independent professional judgment when conducting investment analysis, making investment recommendations, taking investment actions, and engaging in other professional activities.
- Practice and encourage others to practice in a professional and ethical manner that will reflect credit on themselves and the profession.
- Promote the integrity of and uphold the rules governing capital markets.
- Maintain and improve [one's] professional competence and strive to maintain and improve the competence of other investment professionals.

SOURCE: From Codes, Standards, and Position Papers. June 2010, Vol. 2010, No. 14, CFA Institute, http://www.cfainstitute.org/learning/products/publications/ccb/Pages/ccb.v2010.n14.1.aspx

---

The Association of Independent Certified Public Accountants (AICPA) Code of Professional Conduct is based on the premise that accounting professionals share a set of moral standards. Here are the six principles or professional standards:[23]

Principle I. Responsibilities: In carrying out their responsibilities to professionals, members should exercise sensitive professional and moral judgments in all their activities. This principle highlights the moral dimension of accounting. Professional behavior is ethical behavior. Sensitive moral judgment involves consideration of possible harm and benefit, fairness, respect for persons and concern for others.

Principle II. Serve the public interest: Members should accept the obligation to act in a way that will serve the public interest, honor the public trust, and demonstrate commitment to professionalism. Accounting serves a social purpose, which is to facilitate commerce. Public interest is defined as the "collective well-being of the community of people and institutions the profession serves." Serving the public also best serves the interests of clients and employers.

Principle III. Integrity: To maintain and broaden public confidence, members should perform all professional responsibilities with the highest sense of integrity. Integrity means being honest and candid and putting service above personal interests. When specific rules and standards are not available, the financial professional should ask, "Am I doing what a person of integrity would do?" This principle also requires practitioners to follow "the spirit of technical and ethical standards." Hiding liabilities in off-the-books accounts violates this principle, as does trying to circumvent the intent of tax legislation.

Principle IV. Objectivity and independence: A member should maintain objectivity and be free of conflicts of interest in discharging professional responsibilities. A member in public practice should be independent in fact and appearance when providing auditing and other attestation services. Accountants are to be impartial (removing personal feelings and interests from judgments or recommendations), intellectually honest, and free of conflicts of interest. Members of the profession should avoid even the appearance of a conflict of interest.

Principle V. Due care: A member should observe the profession's technical and ethical standards, strive continually to improve competence and the quality of services, and discharge professional responsibility to the best of the member's ability. Due care means the accountant should strive for excellence, and continually improve his or her knowledge and skills. The accountant should never accept duties that he or she is not competent to fulfill. Due care also means doing prompt, careful work.

Principle VI. Scope and nature of services: A member in public practice should observe the Principles of the Code of Professional Conduct in determining the scope and nature of services to be provided. Professional accountants are obligated to follow the AICPA principles in all activities. This means practicing in firms with good quality control systems, avoiding situations where providing consulting services would conflict with auditing functions, and determining whether an activity would be inconsistent with what a true professional would do.

CASE STUDY 11.1

Accounting/Finance Ethics Scenarios

Scenario 1

Tom Waterman is a young management accountant at a large, diversified company. After some experience in accounting at headquarters, he has been transferred to one of the company's recently acquired divisions run by its previous owner and president, Howard Heller. Howard has been retained as vice-president of the new division, and Tom is his accountant. With a marketing background and a practice of calling his own shots, Howard seems to play by a different set of rules than those to which Tom is accustomed. So far, it is working; earnings are up, and sales projections are high.

The main area of concern to Tom is Howard's expense reports. Howard's boss, the division president, approves the expense reports without review and expects Tom to check the details and work out any discrepancies with Howard. After a series of large and questionable expense reports, Tom challenges Howard directly about charges to the company for word processing that Howard's wife did at home. Although company policy prohibits such charges, Howard's boss again signed off on the expense. Tom feels uncomfortable with this and tells Howard that he is considering taking the matter to the Board Audit Committee for review. Howard reacts sharply, reminding Tom that "the Board will back me anyway" and that Tom's position would be in jeopardy.

ACTION: Tom decides not to report the expense charge to the Board Audit Committee.

Evaluate Tom's action based on the AICPA and CFA codes of conduct.

Scenario 2

Anne Devereaux, company controller, is told by the chief financial officer that, in an executive committee meeting, the CEO told them that the company "has to meet its earning forecast, is in need of working capital, and that's final." Unfortunately, Anne does not see how additional working capital can be raised even through increased borrowing, since income is well below the forecast sent to the bank. The CFO suggests that Anne review bad debt expense for possible reduction and holding sales open longer at the end of the month.

At home on the weekend, Anne discusses the situation with her husband, Larry, senior manager of another company in town. "They're asking me to manipulate the books," she says. "On the one hand," she complains, "I'm supposed to be the conscience of the company, and on the other, I am supposed to be absolutely loyal." Larry tells her that companies do this all the time, and when business picks up, then she will be covered. He reminds her how important her salary is to maintaining their comfortable lifestyle and that she should not do anything drastic that might cause her to lose her job.

ACTION: Anne decides to go along with the suggestions proposed by her boss.

Evaluate Anne's decision based on the AICPA and CFA codes of conduct.

Scenario 3

Drew Isler, the plant's chief accountant, is having a friendly conversation with Leo Sullivan, operations manager and old college buddy, and Fred LaPlante, the sales manager. Leo tells Drew that the plant needs a computer system to increase operating efficiency. Fred adds that with the increased efficiency and decreased late deliveries, their plant will be the top plant next year.

However, Leo wants to bypass the company policy that requires the purchase of items costing more than $20,000 to receive prior board approval and to be capitalized. Leo would prefer to generate orders for each component part of the system, each of which is under the $20,000 limit, and thereby avoid the approval "hassle." Drew knows that this is clearly wrong from a company standpoint as well as an accounting and financial standpoint, and he says so. Nevertheless, he eventually says that he will go along.

Six months later, the new computer system has not lived up to its expectations. Drew indicates to Fred that he is really worried about the problems with the computer system and that the auditors will discover how the purchase was handled in their upcoming visit. Fred acknowledges the situation by saying that production and sales are down, and his sales representatives are also upset.

Leo wants to correct the problems by upgrading the system (and increasing the expenses) and urges Drew to "hang in there."

ACTION: Feeling certain that the system will fail without the upgrade, Drew agrees to approve the additional expense.

Evaluate Drew's decision to invest the additional funds based on the AICPA and CFA codes of conduct.

SOURCE: Sweeney, B., & Costello, F. (2009). Moral intensity and ethical decision-making: An empirical examination of undergraduate accounting and business students. *Accounting Education: An International Journal, 18*(1), 75–97, pp. 92–94. Reprinted by permission of the publisher (Taylor & Francis Group, http://www.informaworld.com).

Become a Questioning Professional

Systematic inquiry is fundamental to the practice of law and medicine. For example, a competent doctor doesn't make a diagnosis without asking questions of the patient and perhaps of fellow physicians. Like doctors, accountants need to pose queries in order to accurately diagnose the financial health of organizations and to find fraud and expose liars.[24] Australian business professors Jack Flanagan and Kenneth Clarke draw upon the insights of philosopher Bernard Lonergan to outline a four-tiered process of inquiry for financial professionals.[25] The first level is *to be attentive.* In this stage, determine what is really going on by asking, Who? What? When? and Where? Answering such questions takes research that, in turn, generates data. Good data are impartial and objective; flawed data lead to faulty conclusions.

The second level is *to be intelligent,* which means applying insight and experience to interpret the data and to develop explanations, which makes the information intelligible. This stage produces assertions that can be contested by colleagues. For example, the company has a cash-flow problem, or its assets are overvalued.

The third level is *to be reasonable.* Reason is applied at this stage to determine if the explanations generated in the previous step are correct. When assertions hold up to questioning, they are judged as factual or true. Protect against personal bias, and seek expert opinion when determining what is fact and what is not.

The fourth level is *to be responsible.* In this final stage, come to a defensible conclusion, and take responsibility for your decisions and actions. Determine what good or value will be produced by this decision. Instrumental goods include those elements that have immediate benefit to the organization, like positive cash flow and efficient, high-quality financial work. Higher-order goods serve the profession and society. For instance, an accurate, well-done financial report benefits the reputation of accountants and contributes to public trust.

Flanagan and Clarke note several barriers to ethical inquiry. You will need to overcome the following if you want to become a questioning professional:

- The fear of embarrassment or conflict that may arise from asking questions
- The pressure to minimize the expression of negative feelings in meetings
- Single-minded focus on shareholders at the expense of other stakeholders
- Fixation on profit and loss that does not consider the effects of decisions on human beings

Ethical Human Resource Management

Ethical Issues in Human Resource Management

Human resource management (HRM) addresses the human, or "people," side of the organization. It has been defined as "the process of acquiring, training, appraising, and compensating employees, and of attending to their labor relations, health and safety, and fairness concerns."[26] All managers carry out some human relations functions, like determining personnel needs and conducting performance reviews, but HR managers focus exclusively on these duties.[27] Important human resource management activities include the following:

Conducting job analyses

Determining staffing needs

Hiring

Conducting new employee orientation

Designing compensation systems

Providing benefits

Holding performance reviews

Enforcing disciplinary procedures

Training and development

Implementing workforce reductions

Each of these activities, in turn, is an ethical hot spot that can flare up, generating lawsuits and unfavorable publicity while undermining morale and productivity. Ethical issues in human resource management include:[28]

Bogus job requirements

Employment discrimination

Lack of workforce diversity

Favoritism in hiring and promotion

Invalid job placement tests

Inconsistent interviewing procedures

Overselling the benefits of working for an organization

Invasion of applicant and employee privacy

Intrusive monitoring of employee activities

Unfair compensation systems

Excessive executive compensation

Biased performance appraisal systems

Conflicts of interest in selecting HR consultants

Indoctrinating employees in a particular religion

Morally objectionable training

Inadequate safety training

Unsafe working conditions

Pressuring employees for charitable contributions or forcing them to engage in volunteer activities

Requiring employees to work long hours

Failure to discipline unethical or illegal behavior

Treating dismissed employees disrespectfully

Contract negotiation disputes

Violations of employee rights

Providing inadequate notification of layoffs

In a market economy, there are three moral hazards or dangers that frequently lead to unethical human resource management behaviors. The first is "regarding employees as mere commodities."[29] Commodifying people means treating them like inanimate objects or impersonal goods. Even the term "human resources" is problematic because it suggests that people are just another resource or commodity like raw materials, money, or land. When people are seen as commodities, it is easy to lose sight of their humanness and to use them to get what we want. Corporations then see their workforces as tools to generate profits, tools that can be downsized or jettisoned altogether if the economy sours. Any notion that people are intrinsically valuable is lost. By the same token, employees can view their employers solely as a means to a paycheck.

The doctrine of employment at will (EAW) encourages managers to treat people as tools.[30] In the United States, employers are generally allowed to fire individuals without providing specific reasons, unless there are employment contracts spelling out grounds for dismissal. This stands in contrast to Europe, where employees can be let go only with justification—the just cause doctrine. While employment at will provides a lot of freedom to employees, who can also leave for any reason, this approach clearly favors employers. As long as they don't violate laws against discrimination or certain state statues, organizations can fire workers as they see fit. As the Ethics and Technology feature illustrates, online activities are now serving as grounds for dismissal.

Exploitation is the second moral hazard of human resources. Organizations focused solely on profits or reducing expenses are tempted to exploit their members by cutting their wages, forcing them to work more hours, reducing their benefits, and so on. Layoffs become an exercise in cost cutting; human costs are overlooked. Profit is a legitimate goal, but other objectives are also important, like meeting the needs of employees and serving stakeholders.

Defining people in economic terms is the third moral hazard. Like their colleagues in finance, HR managers are tempted to view people only in economic terms. (See Case Study 11.3, "'Dead Peasant' Insurance Policies," for example.) Taking a utilitarian approach, one that bases personnel decisions solely on financial grounds, ignores the human component of human resources. People have intrinsic value and should be able to develop their competencies at work. In addition, they have the right to engage in significant labor.[31]

ETHICS AND TECHNOLOGY

Caution: Cyberspace Can Be Hazardous to Your Career Health

The Internet is the newest legal and ethical testing ground for employee rights. Workers have been fired for posting derogatory comments about coworkers and bosses or for revealing too much information about their employers in their blogs (online journals) or on Facebook and other social media sites. A reporter at a North Carolina newspaper was sacked after the editors discovered that she was the anonymous source of a blog criticizing her fellow workers. A Delta flight attendant lost her job after she posted sexy pictures of herself in her uniform on Facebook. A British supermarket employee was fired after attacking the chain's owners on his Facebook page. Though he limited access to his site, a colleague printed off the remarks and gave them to his boss.

Laws guarding free speech were designed to protect citizens from their governments, not to protect employees who express their opinions about their workplaces. However, the National Labor Relations Board recently ruled that employees have the right to discuss working conditions online just as they would around the water cooler. The NLRB determined that an ambulance company had illegally dismissed a worker for complaining about her supervisor on Facebook, although the precedent set by the suit may only apply to unionized workplaces.

Employee blogs and social media postings raise important ethical questions as well as legal ones. How much freedom should employers give their workers to blog, for example? Is it right to fire employees for what they say online on their own time? Are employees ever justified in attacking their employers and coworkers in cyberspace? Is it ethical to blog anonymously? Should employers monitor the blogs and social media sites of job applicants?

Human relations professionals, managers, and employees will need to address these questions in the years to come. In the meantime, bloggers and Facebook friends would do well to remember that the Internet can be a dangerous place for workers.

Sources

Armour, S. (2005, June 15). Warning: Your clever little blog could get you fired. *USA Today*, p. 1B.

Burling, S. (2005, August 21). Your blog could get you recruited—or fired. *The Philadelphia Inquirer*, p. A01.

Company settles case in firing tied to Facebook. *The New York Times*, p. B7.

Dotinga, R. (2005, February 7). Office memo: 'Blogging' can get you bounced. *The Christian Science Monitor*, p. 13.

Greenhouse, S. (2010, November 9). Labor board says rights apply on net. *The New York Times*, p. B1.

Joyce, A. (2005, February 11). Free expression can be costly when bloggers bad-mouth jobs. *The Washington Post*, p. A01.

Ethical Principles and Strategies

All three of the ethical approaches in this final portion of the chapter address the moral hazards described above. Taking a Kantian approach, acting justly, and recognizing the potential harm caused by human resource decisions will help us to recognize the dignity of employees, keep us from exploiting them, and encourage us to treat others as people, not as economic resources.

A Kantian Approach to Human Resource Management

Kant, as noted in Chapter 1, urges us to "treat the humanity in a person as an end and never as a means merely." In other words, we need to recognize that persons have inherent dignity. University of Minnesota professor Norman Bowie argues that applying Kantian principles would encourage managers to look beyond shareholders and profit when making human resource decisions.[32] For example, downsizing might reduce costs, but that doesn't mean it should be put into effect. Work hours for all employees could be reduced instead. Retirees and pension holders would also continue to receive their promised benefits despite economic downturns. In addition, companies would no longer coerce or deceive their employees, as Enron did, but would be transparent by opening their financial books to employees. Further, everyone coming into with the organization (customers, vendors, neighbors) would be treated with respect.

A Kantian perspective on human resources treats businesses and other organizations as moral communities in which members have a significant voice in the rules and policies that govern them. Kantian organizations operate more like democracies, and members are organizational citizens with both rights and duties.[33] These organizational citizens enjoy free speech and privacy rights and receive information on the future of the group. Leaders persuade rather than impose, helping groups make well-reasoned choices.

Providing meaningful work is another way to treat people as ends and to promote their autonomy. From a Kantian perspective, meaningful work supports the right of workers to make decisions, provides a living wage, enables employees to develop their reasoning abilities, does not interfere with moral decision making and reasoning, and lets workers decide what makes them happy. This approach differs sharply from the scientific management tradition that emphasizes division of labor and requires workers to carry out specialized—and often repetitive and boring—tasks in the name of efficiency.

Current human resource practices at a number of corporations clearly violate Kantian principles. A number of companies, Wal-Mart among them, do not appear to be paying a living wage, leading to a growing number of "working poor" who are forced to go on welfare. At the same time that these corporations claim they can't pay workers better, they reward top executives with lucrative pay packages. Other organizations deny the autonomy of employees by acting paternalistically, trying to regulate what employees do on their own time.

Acting Justly

Many of the ethical issues in human resource management described earlier—employment discrimination, favoritism in hiring and promotion, biased performance and appraisal systems—involve violations of fairness or justice. Researchers report that there are three types of organizational justice.[34] *Distributive justice* refers to how resources and benefits are allocated. Perceptions of injustice arise, for example, when applicants and employees perceive that jobs and promotions go to less-qualified candidates. As we saw in Chapter 1, John Rawls specifically addresses this type of justice, advocating that we protect the rights of individuals but also encourage the more equal distribution of benefits. That means providing a minimum level of benefits, such as health insurance and a living wage, while lowering the difference in compensation between the bottom and top layers of an organization. At the same time, employees are rewarded based on their contributions.

Procedural justice describes how allocation decisions are made. We may not like the outcome of a decision, but we are generally more willing to accept the determination if it was made using fair procedures. Judgments of procedural justice are based on (1) consistency—everyone is treated the same; (2), lack of bias—no person or group receives unfair treatment; (3) accuracy—determinations are based on accurate information; (4) representation—all relevant stakeholders have input into the decision; (5) correction—there is a process for fixing mistakes; and (6) ethics—professional standards of conduct are not violated.[35]

Interactional justice describes how individuals perceive their treatment by authority figures. Managers are seen as more just if they treat members with dignity and share relevant information with them. (To determine the level of justice in your organization, complete the Organizational Justice Scale in the Self-Assessment.)

Employees care a great deal about organizational justice. They want to be assured that they will be treated well over the long term; fair treatment signals that they have status and worth in the group. Further, people see fairness as a virtue in and of itself. Treating others fairly is the right thing to do because it protects their value as humans.[36] It's not surprising, then, that investigators have found a strong link between justice perceptions and organizational behavior. If employees believe their organizations are fair, they perform better, are more likely to help one another out, are more satisfied with their jobs, and are more committed to their organizations. At the same time, they are less likely to engage in unethical behavior. Conversely, when organizational members feel unjustly treated, they are more apt to be absent, withdraw, quit, and engage in destructive behavior.[37]

There are a number of ways to foster perceptions of justice when carrying out human resource functions.[38] When it comes to selecting candidates, procedural justice is key. Make sure that questions and criteria are related to the job, and give candidates enough opportunity to make a case for themselves. For example, set aside adequate interview time, and allow for retaking standardized tests. Interactional justice also plays a role in the selection process. Be considerate of applicants, and provide timely feedback. When it comes to rewards, distributive justice is important, but procedural justice is also a consideration. Being denied a raise is less damaging if the system for making salary determinations is perceived as fair. When it comes to performance appraisal, due process is important. Provide adequate notice of the review—when it will occur and the criteria to be used. Also, involve workers in setting performance standards. Provide a just hearing setting that focuses on the "evidence" of worker performance (not on personal attack); allow employees to provide their own interpretations and to disagree. When it comes to downsizing, procedural and interactional justice are significant factors in how employees respond to these negative events. You can reduce feelings of anger and betrayal (and reduce the risk of lawsuits) by apologizing when appropriate, explaining the reasons why the workforce reduction was necessary, and treating those laid off with dignity and respect.

SELF-ASSESSMENT

The Organizational Justice Scale

Evaluate your employer or another organization of your choice on the following items. Respond to each of the statements on a scale of 1 (strongly disagree) to 5 (strongly agree).

1. In general, this company (organization) treats its employees (members) fairly.

   1   2   3   4   5

   Strongly disagree   Strongly agree

2. Generally employees (members) think of this company (organization) as fair.

   1   2   3   4   5

   Strongly disagree   Strongly agree

3. Rewards are allocated fairly in this firm (organization).

   1   2   3   4   5

   Strongly disagree   Strongly agree

4. Employees (members) in this firm (organization) are rewarded fairly.

   1   2   3   4   5

   Strongly disagree   Strongly agree

5. In this firm (organization), people get the reward or punishment they deserve.

   1   2   3   4   5

   Strongly disagree   Strongly agree

6. Supervisors (leaders) in this company (organization) treat employees (members) with dignity and respect.

   1   2   3   4   5

   Strongly disagree   Strongly agree

7. Employees (members) can count on being treated with courtesy and respect in this firm (organization).

1   2   3   4   5
Strongly disagree   Strongly agree

Scoring

Scores can range from 7 to 35. The higher the score, the more just you believe your organization to be. You may want to give this instrument to other organizational members to determine if their perceptions are similar to your own.

SOURCE: Adapted from Trevino, L. K., & Weaver, G. R. (2001). Organizational justice and ethics program "follow through": Influences on employees' harmful and helpful behavior. *Business Ethics Quarterly 11*(4), 651–671. Used by permission.

Three Ethical Standards for Dealing With Harm

Many human resource management decisions cause harm to at least some organizational members. Some applicants are hired, but the vast majority of job-seekers are turned away. When one employee receives a salary increase, others may not. Achieving organizational objectives also comes at a cost to people working in the organization. Layoffs, for example, are often justified as serving the greater good (saving the organization, keeping the majority of members employed) but are extremely costly to those dismissed. This final set of ethical principles is specifically designed to address the reality that many human resource decisions hurt human beings.[39]

Standard #1: Advance the Organization's Objective. All HR activities need to be aligned with particular goals they are supposed to advance. As a manager, you need to make sure that the practice really does serve the objective. For example, forced-ranking appraisals (also known as "rank and yank" systems) inflect harm on those who rate lowest, even if their performance has been good. Perhaps there is another, less painful way to accomplish the same objective, which is to improve the performance of the work unit. Having a sense of direction makes it easier to carry through on difficult duties and to see that these activities serve a larger purpose. Remember that advancing the organization's objectives does serve employees, owners, suppliers, and clients despite any unpleasant outcomes.

Standard #2: Enhance the Dignity of Those Harmed by the Action. Fair procedures, as noted previously, must be followed when making harmful choices. In addition, you must help those who are hurt function effectively *after* the damage has been done. Significant numbers of people undergo suffering as profits and nonprofits alike participate in "cycles of destruction" involving restructuring and downsizing. Others are victimized when they lose out on promotions and pay raises. In these cases, as a human resource specialist, you need to see yourself as more than a messenger bringing bad news; you need to view yourself as a helper who can assist victims as they deal with the consequences of decisions. The goal is to help members recover from the blow and move forward.

Standard #3: Sustain the Moral Sensibility of Those Executing Morally Ambiguous Tasks. This standard focuses on those doing the work of human resource management. As a manager or human resource professional, you must live with the reality that a bonus may go to the wrong person, the layoff was not needed to save the company, or that an individual suffered greatly from a poor performance review that benefited his or her work team. This dissonance can tempt you to ignore unpleasant tasks or to rationalize your behaviors. If you can't deal with the negative emotions that come with making harmful decisions, then you will not consider the dignity of those negatively impacted by those choices. Instead of reducing your dissonance or being overcome with guilt, learn to live with these feelings. Doing so will make you more sensitive to the needs of others, encourage you to address inequities, and help you carry out your responsibilities.

CHAPTER TAKEAWAYS

- Marketing, finance/accounting, and human resources are three important organizational activities or functions that put organizations at risk. You need to manage these ethical hot spots in order to reduce the likelihood that they will damage your group.
- Marketing includes every aspect of generating a product or service and then bringing it to market for an exchange with buyers, including product, price, placement, and performance. Each of these elements, in turn, raises significant ethical issues.
- When engaging in marketing activities, make sure that consumers are capable, have adequate information, and are free to go elsewhere to purchase similar products and services.
- Ethical marketing puts people first and serves the needs of society. Five key ethical marketing principles are (1) the principle of nonmalfeasance (do no conscious harm); (2) the principle of nondeception (never intentionally mislead or manipulate consumers); (3) the principle of protecting vulnerable market segments (e.g., children, the elderly); (4) the principle of distributive justice (provide benefits to the disadvantaged); and (5) the principle of stewardship (minimize costs to society and the physical environment).
- Finance is concerned with the generation and use of funds; accounting tracks the operations of an organization. Remember that both activities have an ethical dimension. Financial priorities need to be balanced with other significant values like the community and the environment. Be careful not to overestimate your abilities, tell the truth, and be alert to fraud and deception in others.
- Accounting and finance codes of ethics outline the moral obligations of finance professionals. While not the final word on financial ethics, they can be a useful reminder of the importance of serving the public and maintaining high moral standards.
- Systematic inquiry helps generate an accurate picture of the financial health of an organization while revealing possible fraud. To become a questioning professional, you will need to be attentive (generate data), be intelligent (develop explanations), be reasonable (test explanations through logic), and be responsible (take responsibility for your decisions and actions).
- Human resource management is concerned with the "people," or human, side of the organization and involves such functions as hiring, training, compensation and benefits, performance appraisal, discipline, and downsizing. The moral hazards you will face as a manager or as a HRM specialist include treating members as commodities, exploitation, and viewing people in economic terms.

- One way to avoid the moral hazards of human resource management is by adopting Kantian principles. This means treating people with dignity and respect while creating moral communities where members have a significant voice.
- Many ethical issues in human resources come from perceptions of unfairness and injustice. Organizational justice is distributive, procedural, and interactional. Distribute benefits as equitably as possible. At the same time, make sure that the procedures for allocating goods are fair, and treat members with courtesy and respect.
- Human resource management decisions often cause harm to some organizational members. You can mitigate such harm by making sure that (1) actions advance organizational objectives, (2) you enhance the dignity of those harmed by an action, and (3) you grapple with the moral tensions that come from making decisions that have negative impacts.

APPLICATION PROJECTS

1. Analyze a contemporary marketing campaign using the ethical marketing guidelines presented in the chapter. How ethical is the campaign based on your analysis?

2. Debate the following:

   Certain products should never be marketed.

   Advertising should never target young children.

   Credit card companies should not be allowed to advertise on college campuses.

   Accounting majors are not as ethical as other majors.

   Finance and accounting are fundamentally ethical activities.

   Employees should only be terminated for just cause.

   Employees should be treated as organizational citizens.

3. Apply the AICPA and CFA code principles to a case study involving finance and accounting that was presented in an earlier chapter of this text. What conclusions do you draw and why?

4. Do a research project on what it means to be a professional. What are the hallmarks of a profession? What is the relationship between professionalism and ethics? Write up your findings.

5. Identify other professional codes of ethics, and compare them to the codes described in the chapter. What similarities do you note? Differences? How useful are such codes in promoting ethical behavior?

6. Organizational Justice Analysis: Analyze your response to the Self-Assessment. What factors contributed to your perceptions or justice or injustice? Based on material from the chapter, what can the organization do to be perceived as more just? Expand your analysis by having others in the organization take the instrument. Interview them to find out why they responded as they did and what they think needs to be done to make the organization more just. Write up your findings.

7. Profession Ethical Analysis: Determine the ethical challenges you are likely to face if you enter the professions of marketing, finance, accounting, or human resource management. Collect information online and through press reports and written materials. Interview a professional and a professor who teaches in that field. Identify the ethical issues you are likely to face and what your interviews and research reveal about how to best prepare for these ethical challenges.

CASE STUDY 11.2

Should Ronald McDonald Retire?

Ronald McDonald is a marketing legend. He first appeared in the 1960s, dressed up in a food-tray hat and hamburger-shaped shoes. Since then, the red-headed clown has become the face of McDonald's, the world's largest restaurant chain. He appears in every McDonald's market in the world and speaks 25 languages. The company claims that he is as recognizable as Santa Claus.

Ronald's success in marketing fast food to children has drawn fire from health experts and food activists. After the movie *Super Size Me* appeared (which tracked the physical problems of a man who ate only McDonald's food for a month), Ronald slimmed down and gave up his clown suit for a track-suit. He then began promoting fitness in schools. Corporate officials claimed that Ronald's popularity would encourage kids to become more active; critics claimed that his appearances would only encourage kids to consume more hamburger Happy Meals, which have 600 calories and 20 grams of fat.

More recently, the watchdog group Corporate Accountability International, which helped to ban the cigarette advertising icon Joe Camel, launched a campaign to retire Ronald McDonald, blaming him for contributing to the country's growing children's obesity epidemic. One out of every three American kids is overweight or obese, leading to Type II diabetes and other health problems. Said a spokesperson, "This clown is no friend to our children or their health."[1] The group also blames McDonald's for helping to create an industrial food system that mass produces unhealthy food at significant cost to the environment.

Corporate Accountability International (CAI) conducted a poll in which nearly half of the respondents said it was time for Ronald to quit. CAI representatives and supporters presented petitions calling for the clown's retirement at McDonald's locations around the nation. Patrons at a Chicago outlet were invited to sign retirement cards. The campaign, which has the support of many parents and health professionals, calls for McDonald's (1) to end its use of cartoons and licensed characters that appeal to children, (2) to eliminate gifts and toys from kids' meals, and (3) to remove all advertising and promotional materials from school playgrounds and other areas frequented by children.

In response to its critics, McDonald's added healthier items, like fruits and salads, to its menu, and Happy Meal options now include low-fat milk, apple juice, and apple dippers. Ronald McDonald may already be in semiretirement, as he is no longer featured in television commercials. However, company officials reject any attempt to completely retire Ronald, calling him "a beloved brand ambassador for McDonald's."[2] In its response to the protestors at its stores, the company noted, "He [Ronald] is the heart and soul of Ronald McDonald House Charities, which lends a helping hand to families in their time of need, particularly when families need to be near their critically-ill children in hospitals."[3]

Discussion Probes

1. How much blame do you place on McDonald's and other fast-food outlets for the nation's children's obesity epidemic? What other factors are to blame for this health problem?

2. Has McDonald's done enough to make its menus healthier?

3. Is it ethical for McDonald's to tie its advertising symbol to its charitable efforts?

4. Should fast-food chains be prevented from advertising to children? Why or why not?

5. Should there be bans on marketing other unhealthy food products to children, like soft drinks and sugared cereals?

6. Should Ronald McDonald be retired?

Notes

1. Lucadamo, L, (2010, April 1). Poll's got beef with Ronald. *Daily News,* News, p. 13.
2. Lucadamo.
3. Smith, E. E. (2010, February 3). National campaign against McDonald's mascot kicks off in Cedar Mill. *The Oregonian,* pp. B1 & B3.

Sources

Corporate Accountability International. (2011). Clowning with kids' health: The case for Ronald McDonald's retirement. Retrieved from http://www.RetireRonald.org

Mayer, C. E. (2005, January 28). McDonald's makes Ronald a health ambassador. *The Washington Post,* p. E1.

Teather, D. (2005, June 9). Fatboy Ronald McDonald downsizes to head off critics. *The Guardian,* City, p. 19.

CASE STUDY 11.3

"Dead Peasant" Insurance Policies

Insuring the lives of top executives is common practice in corporate America. The death of a CEO or CFO can put the future of the company at risk; replacing these individuals can be costly. Large companies often take out life insurance policies, called corporate-owned life insurance (COLI) polices, on their leaders to help offset these expenses.

Some firms extend their COLI policies to cover low-level employees. These policies, sometimes referred to as "dead peasant" or "dead janitor" insurance, are taken out on rank-and-file workers like convenience store clerks, electrical linemen, and cake decorators. The company pays the premiums and receives the death benefits when the employee dies. Often, workers and their surviving family members do not know that these policies exist, prompting one attorney to call these policies corporate America's "dirty little secret."[1] In a case featured in the film *Capitalism: A Love Story,* the widow of an Amegy bank project manager discovered that the bank had received a $3.8 million payout after her husband's death. Her husband's salary, before the bank fired him, was $70,000. (She later sued Amegy and settled for an undisclosed sum.) In another instance, Wal-Mart collected $381,000 after the death of an employee but didn't reveal that fact to his spouse.

Dead peasant policies can be profitable. The lump sum paid to the company is tax free, and in the past, the cost of the premiums could also be written off. Press reports name Proctor & Gamble, AT&T, Walt Disney, Portland General Electric, and Nestlé as corporations carrying COLI policies on low-level workers. At one time, as many as one quarter of the Fortune 500 purchased such policies, covering as many as 5–6 million workers. However, fewer companies took out such insurance after the tax laws were tightened. Wal-Mart says it discontinued its program when the tax law changed and after it lost several lawsuits. Nonetheless, policies purchased earlier may still be in place at a number of firms. Rules on dead peasant policies vary between states. Some jurisdictions outlaw this type of insurance, requiring that companies demonstrate that they have an "insurable interest" (would suffer significant loss of income) in the individual covered by the policy. Others require that employees give their consent before such insurance can be put in force.

Corporations defend their use of dead peasant policies by claiming that the insurance helps defray the expenses of providing benefits for executives and of providing health insurance for employees and retirees. Critics scoff at this explanation, noting that insurance payout monies are generally mingled with general revenue. They point out that taking out such policies without the knowledge or consent of employees is disrespectful and treats workers as resources, not as human beings. Such insurance also sets up a potentially deadly conflict of interest. Employers, who are in charge of safety, now have a financial stake in the early death of employees. As one surviving spouse asked, "What incentive is there for a safe work environment if companies can do·this?"[2]

Discussion Probes

1. Do you think it is ethical to insure top corporate leaders? What criteria should be used in determining who should be covered?

2. Would you agree to a company-owned insurance policy on your life if it was required for employment?

3. What would Immanuel Kant say about dead peasant policies?

4. Are dead peasant policies unjust?

5. Do you think that employers have a conflict of interest if they hold life insurance policies on their employees? Why or why not?

6. Are dead peasant policies ethical if workers are notified of their existence? If the proceeds go towards supporting employee benefits?

7. Would you support a total ban on dead peasant policies? Why or why not?

Notes

1. Mason, J. (2002, October 2). Time runs out for bill to limit companies' secret life insurance policies. *The Houston Chronicle.*
2. Roesler, R. (2003, March 3). Lawmakers may tighten up "dead peasant" laws. *Spokesman Review*, p. A6.

Sources

Duin, S. (2002, April 28). Dead peasants may return to haunt PGE. *The Oregonian,* p. B01.
Reddan, F. (2010, March 8). Taking a morbid approach to investment in workers. *The Irish Times,* Finance, p. 19.
Sixel, L. M. (2010, January 7). "Dead peasant" policies. *The Houston Chronicle,* Business, p. 1.
Sixel, L. M. (2010, January 9). Widow settles life insurance case. *The Houston Chronicle,* Business, p. 1.

ENDNOTES

1. DesJardins, J. (2011). *An introduction to business ethics* (4th ed.). New York: McGraw-Hill.

2. Smith, N. C. (1993). Ethics and the marketing manager. In N. C. Smith & J. A. Quelch (Eds.). *Ethics in marketing* (pp.1–34). Burr Ridge, IL: Irwin.

3. Drumwright, M. E., & Murphy, P. E. (2004). How advertising practitioners view ethics: Moral muteness, moral myopia, and moral imagination. *Journal of Advertising, 33*(2), 7–24.

4. Laczniak, G. R., & Murphy, P. E. (2006). Normative perspectives for ethical and socially responsible marketing. *Journal of Macromarketing, 26,* 154–177. Many of the examples used in this section come from this source.

5. Laczniak & Murphy, p. 157.

6. Wicks, A. C., Freeman, R. E., Werhane, P. H., & Martin, K. E. (2010). *Business ethics: A managerial approach.* Boston: Prentice-Hall.

7. Boatright, J. R. (2008). *Ethics in finance* (2nd ed.). Malden, MA: Blackwell, p. 5.

8. Boatright, J. R. (1999). Finance ethics. In R. E. Frederick (Ed.), *A companion to business ethics* (pp. 153–163). Malden, MA: Blackwell; Boatright, J. R. (2010). Ethics in finance. In J. R. Boatright (Ed.), *Finance ethics: Critical issues in theory and practice* (pp. 3–19). Hoboken, NJ: John Wiley.

9. Dash, E., & Sorkin, A. R. (2008, September 26). In largest bank failure, U.S. seizes, then sells. *The New York Times,* p. A1.

10. Duska, R. F., & Duska, B. S. (2003). *Accounting ethics.* Malden, MA: Blackwell.

11. Flanagan, J., & Clarke, K. (2007). Beyond a code of professional ethics: A holistic model of ethical decision-making for accountants. *ABACUS, 43,* 488–518.

12. Duska & Duska, p. 186.

13. See, for example: Trevino, L. K., & Weaver, G. R. (2003). *Managing ethics in business organizations: Social scientific perspectives.* Stanford, CA: Stanford University Press; Ponemon, L. A. (1990). Ethical judgments in accounting: A cognitive-developmental perspective. *Critical Perspectives on Accounting, 1,* 191–215; Ponemon, L. A. (1992). Ethical reasoning and selection-socialization in accounting. *Accounting, Organizations and Society, 17*(3/4), 239–258; Abdolmohammadi, M. J., Read, W. J., & Scarbrough, D. P. (2003). Does selection-socialization help to explain accountants' weak ethical reasoning? *Business Ethics, 42,* 71–81.

14. Ryan, L. V., Buchholtz, A. K., & Kolb, R. W. (2010). New directions in corporate governance and finance: Implications for business ethics research. *Business Ethics Quarterly, 20*(4), 673–694; Kolb, R. W. (2010). Ethical implications of finance. In J. R. Boatright (Ed.), *Finance ethics: Critical issues in theory and practice* (pp. 23–43). Hoboken, NJ: John Wiley.

15. McPhail, K. (2001). The other objective of ethics education: Re-humanising the accounting profession—a study of ethics education in law, engineering, medicine and accountancy. *Journal of Business Ethics, 34,* 279–298.

16. Flanagan & Clarke (2007), p. 488.

17. Gellis, H., Giladi, K., & Friedman, H. H. (2002). Biblical and Talmudic basis of accounting ethics. *CPA Journal, 72*(9), 11–13.

18. Dolfsma, W. (2006). Accounting as applied ethics: Teaching a discipline. *Journal of Business Ethics 63,* 209–215.

19. Waddock, S. (2005). Hollow men and women at the helm . . . Hollow accounting ethics? *Issues in Accounting Education, 20*(2), 145–150, p. 147.

20. Shaub, M. K., & Fisher, D. G. (2008). Beyond agency theory: Common values for accounting. In D. L. Swanson & D. G. Fisher (Eds.), *Advancing business ethics education* (pp. 305–328). Charlotte, NC: Information Age.

21. Sternberg, R. J. (2002). Smart people are not stupid, but they sure can be foolish: The imbalance theory of foolishness. In R. J. Sternberg (Ed.), *Why smart people can be so stupid* (pp. 232–242). New Haven, CT: Yale University Press.

22. Beets, S. D. (2006). The vanishing AICPA code: Past, present, and future significance. In J. E. Ketz (Ed.), *Accounting ethics: Critical perspectives on business and management* (Vol. 1, pp. 270–306). London: Routledge.

23. The provisions of the AICPA code and material on code provisions come from Duska & Duska.

24. Flanagan & Clarke.

25. Lonergan, B. (1957). *Insight: A study of human understanding.* Longmans, Green. See also: Melchin, K. R. (1998). *Living with other people: An introduction to Christian ethics based on Bernard Lonergan.* Collegeville, MN: The Liturgical Press.

26. Dessler, G. (2008). *Human resource management.* Upper Saddle River, NJ: Pearson, p. 2.

27. Scarpello, V. G. (2008). Parallel approaches to development of the HRM field and HRM education. In V. G. Scarpello (Ed.), *The handbook of human resource management education: Promoting an effective and efficient curriculum* (pp. 3–37). Thousand Oaks, CA: Sage.

28. Scott, E. D. (2005). The ethics of human resource management. In J. W. Budd & J. G. Scoville (Eds.), *The ethics of human resources and industrial relations* (pp. 173–201). Champaign, IL: Labor Relations and Employment Association; Shaw, W. H. (2011). *Business ethics: A textbook with cases* (7th ed.). Boston, MA: Wadsworth.

29. Walsh, A. J. (2007). HRM and the ethics of commodified work in a market economy. In A. H. Pinnington, R. Macklin, & T. Campbell (Eds.), *Human resource management: Ethics and employment* (pp. 102–116). Oxford, UK: Oxford University Press, p. 103.

30. McCall, J. J. (2003). A defense of just cause dismissal rules. *Business Ethics Quarterly, 13*(2), 151–175; Radin, T. J., & Werhane, P. H. (2003). Employment-at-will, employee rights, and future directions for employment. *Business Ethics Quarterly, 13*(2), 113–130.

31. Radin & Werhane. See also: Ciulla, J. (2000). *The working life.* New York: Times Books; Pfeffer, J. (1998). *The human equation: Building profits by putting people first.* Boston, MA: Harvard Business School Press.

32. Bowie, N. E. (2005). Kantian ethical thought. In J. W. Budd & J. G. Scoville (Eds.), *The ethics of human resources and industrial relations* (pp. 61–87). Champaign, IL: Labor Relations and Employment Association.

33. Radin & Werhane.

34. Fortin, M. (2008). Perspectives on organizational justice: Concept clarification, social context, integration, time and links with morality. *International Journal of Management Reviews, 10*(2), 93–126.

35. Cropanzano, R., Bowen, D. E., & Gilliland, S. W. (2007). The management of organizational justice. *Journal of Management Perspectives, 21*(4), 34–48.

36. Cropanzano, R., & Stein, J. H. (2009). Organizational justice and behavioral ethics: Promises and prospects. *Business Ethics Quarterly, 19*(2), 193–233.

37. Trevino, L. K., & Weaver, G. R. (2001). Organizational justice and ethics program "follow-through": Influences on employees' harmful and helpful behavior. *Business Ethics Quarterly, 11*(4), 651–671; Viswesvaran, C., & Ones, D. S. (2002). Examining the construct of organizational justice: A meta-analytic evaluation of relations with work attitudes and behaviors. *Journal of Business Ethics, 38,* 193–203; Cohen-Charash, Y., & Spector, P. E. (2001). The role of justice in organizations: A meta-analysis. *Organizational Behavior and Human Decision Processes, 86*(2), 278–321.

38. Cropanzano, Bowen, & Gilliland.

39. Margolis, J. D., Grant, A. M., & Molinsky, A. L. (2007). Expanding the ethical standards of HRM: Necessary evils and the multiple dimensions of impact. In A. H. Pinnington, R. Macklin, & T. Campbell (Eds.), *Human resource management: Ethics and employment.* Oxford, UK: Oxford Press.

12

Promoting Organizational Citizenship in a Global Society

In this final chapter, we'll look beyond the borders of our organizations to focus on the role that they should play in local, national, and international communities. Our individual responsibility is to equip our groups to act as socially responsible citizens in a world marked by rapid globalization. The first two sections outline what it means for an organization to act as a citizen and how we can encourage our organizations to play this role. The third section describes the demands of global citizenship and introduces strategies for meeting these challenges.

The Organization as Citizen

"From those to whom much has been given, much will be required." That saying encapsulates the relationship between organizations and Western society over the past several decades. Organizations wield more power than ever before. The decline of the extended family, urbanization, industrialization, and other factors have increased our reliance on corporations, governments, schools, nonprofit agencies, and other institutions. At the same time, societal expectations of organizations have greatly expanded. We now demand that organizations, even for-profit entities, be socially responsible. As evidence of the importance of *corporate social responsibility (CSR),* consider the following:[1]

- Seventy-nine percent of Americans believe that businesses should support social causes; three quarters of business leaders say that the public should expect good citizenship from companies.
- Eighty-nine percent of U.S. respondents reported they would switch brands to one associated with a worthy cause if price and quality were similar.
- Sales of organic foods and green packaged products increased even during a major global recession.
- A survey of citizens in 23 countries found that 90% of respondents wanted firms to focus on more than profits.
- Over $2 trillion is invested in socially conscious mutual funds that screen out "sin stocks" like tobacco companies, distillers, and weapons manufacturers.
- America's Most Admired Companies earn that label in part because they are concerned about the community and the environment.
- Watchdog groups regularly monitor the financial status and effectiveness of charities.
- AIDS activists, disability advocates, environmentalists, and other groups are quick to bring suit against governments and businesses that don't fulfill their social duties.

The term *organizational citizenship* best describes what society expects from businesses, governments, and nonprofits. Good citizens acknowledge their obligations to their communities. These responsibilities are economic, legal, ethical, and philanthropic.[2] A corporation, for example, should seek to be profitable, obey the law, do what is right and just, and contribute to the community. Organizational citizens also develop ongoing processes for anticipating and responding to societal pressures. They continually scan the environment for emerging issues and actively engage their critics in dialogue. Finally, they back up their convictions with concrete actions—treating workers fairly, sending volunteers to local schools, promoting cancer awareness, and so on.

Organizational citizenship also means meeting environmental responsibilities. Corporate citizens reduce greenhouse gases and waste, develop environmentally friendly products, and so on. In fact, sustainability serves as the primary standard or guideline for corporate citizenship in Europe and other parts of the world. Sustainability means preserving the natural environment while at the same time creating long-lasting economic and social value. Sustainable organizations want to meet their current needs, but they want to do so in a way that doesn't reduce the ability of future generations to meet their needs.[3] They adopt a long-term perspective, hoping to create conditions that foster decades of economic health and social responsibility and assure the well-being of future generations. Sustainability is a high standard that demands constant improvement. For instance, manufacturers seeking to boost their environmental records generally begin by transitioning from pollution control to pollution prevention.[4] Instead of cleaning up messes after they occur, they try to prevent them from happening in the first place by reducing smokestack emissions and waste. Such tactics can greatly reduce the costs of disposing of toxic substances. However, if manufacturers want to continue to improve, they shift their focus from minimizing pollution to considering all the possible environmental impacts over the life cycle of a product. They create goods that are easier to recover, recycle, or reuse. Xerox took this approach by taking parts from leased copiers and reconditioning them for use in new machines. If environmentally conscious organizations want to progress still further, they must invest in clean technology that is environmentally sustainable. Hybrid gas and electric cars are a step in this direction. So are BMW automobiles, which are built to be easier to disassemble when they leave the road for good.

According to scholars at Boston College Center for Corporate Leadership, organizational citizenship follows a developmental path.[5] Knowing your company's stage of development can help you identify the challenges the group faces and set goals for going forward.

Stage 1: Elementary. This is the lowest developmental stage. Companies at this stage don't understand corporate citizenship. They are interested only in complying with laws and industry standards. Department heads make sure the company obeys the law to prevent harm to the group's reputation. Nike was in this phase when it was first accused of abusive labor practices (see Case Study 12.2, "Nike Becomes a Global Citizen"). Elementary-level firms are particularly vulnerable to crises that threaten their credibility.

Stage 2: Engaged. These organizations have "awakened" to the need for social responsibility. DuPont's leaders, for example, determined that the company would move from complying with environmental regulations to actively seeking to win the public's trust. Engaged companies adopt policies to lower the risk of lawsuits and reputational damage. These policies generally call for exceeding legal requirements for safety, environmental health, and employment. Corporate units begin to participate in CSR efforts. Developing capacity is the biggest challenge in this phase. The group must develop its ability to address a variety of needs.

Stage 3: Innovative. Such organizations develop creative ways to improve and measure social performance. In this stage, leaders become even more involved in CSR, engage in dialog with a greater variety of stakeholders, and develop new citizenship initiatives. In 2000, for example, Ford Motor Company developed a set of CSR principles after hosting a forum with company executives and citizenship experts, followed by discussions with employees. As an outcome of these conversations, the firm converted one of its aging plants into a highly efficient, environmentally friendly facility. Data collection is another important component of this phase. Innovative organizations monitor their social and environmental activities and may report the results to the public. (Turn to Ethics in Action 12.1 for more information on conducting social audits.) Creating coherence is the primary challenge for Stage 3 organizations. Managers typically work independently on citizenship initiatives, and these efforts are not tied to corporate strategy and culture.

Stage 4: Integrated. In this stage, organizations take a more unified approach to citizenship than their counterparts in Stage 3. They try to incorporate citizenship concerns throughout every level and unit of the firm, making CSR part of the business plan. Leaders set citizenship goals, create performance indicators, and then monitor how well they do. They report the findings of all social and environmental audits, even when they are not favorable. Integrated organizations (Henkel, Groupe Danone) often have committees made up of senior executives or board members to oversee these efforts. Deepening commitment is the primary challenge in Stage 4. Maintaining and strengthening commitment to citizenship is difficult when tackling significant problems like sustainability and poverty.

Stage 5: Transformative. Companies like Ben & Jerry's, The Body Shop, and Patagonia make citizenship central to their mission and reputation. Consumers buy their products in part because of their citizenship activities. Transformative organizations hope to create new markets by merging their social commitment with their business strategies. They are willing to lose money in the short term if there is the possibility of a significant social and economic payoff in the long term. Stage 5 organizations often have visionary leaders who, troubled by the world's problems, are out to make it a better place. Firms in the transformative stage often partner with nonprofits, other businesses, and community groups to address these problems. Hewlett-Packard demonstrates how organizations can simultaneously meet both social and financial goals. HP worked with other groups and organizations in India, South Africa, and São Paulo, Brazil, to provide communication technology infrastructure that enables underserved residents to access the Web. This effort not only improved the lives of poor citizens in these areas but also gave HP an advantage in these markets. (Case Study 12.1 describes another a firm that reached out to the poorest of the poor.)

ETHICS IN ACTION 12.1 SOCIAL AUDITS

Social audits are standardized procedures for evaluating social and environmental impact. For example, Charity Navigator rates the performance of nonprofits based on these categories: (1) program expenses, (2) administration expenses, (3) fund-raising expenses, (4) fund-raising efficiency (the percentage of the budget spent on raising money), (5) primary revenue growth (the ability to sustain income over time), (6) program expenses growth (the ability to expand programs), (7) working capital (the ability to survive a short downturn in revenue), (8) accountability (willingness to explain actions to the public), and (9) transparency (willingness to share critical data with outsiders).

A number of companies sponsor their self-audits, which are conducted by outside auditors. Starbucks' annual "Living Our Values" report is one such example. This instrument measures whether the company's partners believe that the company is fulfilling the company's guiding

(Continued)

(Continued)

principles, which include embracing diversity, sustaining coffee communities, and making a positive contribution to local communities and the environment. Organizations can also sponsor standardized audits like Social Accountability 8000, which was designed to measure labor practices at overseas suppliers. A firm must meet measurable, verifiable performance standards in nine areas to be certified. These standards forbid child labor, forced labor, coercion, discrimination, unlimited overtime, and substandard wages.

The Global Reporting Initiative, which has been adopted by such organizations as Baxter International, Canon, Deutsche Bank, and Ford Motor Company, is a popular standardized measure of sustainability. This instrument examines three sets of performance indicators. Economic indicators look at an organization's direct and indirect impacts on stakeholders and on local, national, and global economic systems. These include such elements as wages, pensions and benefits, payments to suppliers, taxes, and subsidies received. Environmental indicators reveal an organization's impacts on natural systems. They cover energy, material and water use, greenhouse gases and waste generation, hazardous materials, recycling, pollution, and fines and penalties for environmental violations. Social indicators concern an organization's influence on social systems and cluster around labor practices (diversity, health and safety), human rights (child labor, for example), and other social issues (bribery and corruption, community relations).

Social auditing is gaining popularity but still is plagued with a number of problems. Standardized social performance instruments are relatively new, and they aren't as universally accepted as financial audits. There are questions about who is qualified to conduct social audits, what they should cover, how data should be collected, who should have access to the results, and how to draw comparisons between organizations. Self-audits are particularly prone to abuse. Firms may use them as public relations tools, limiting the analysis to just a few areas of strength or reporting only favorable findings. However, despite these concerns, the use of social audits is likely to continue to increase in the years to come.

Sources

Adams, C. A., & Evans, R. (2004). Accountability, completeness, credibility and the audit expectations gap. *Journal of Corporate Citizenship, 14,* 97–115.

Boele, R., & Kemp, D. (2005, Spring). Social auditors: Illegitimate offspring of the audit family? Finding legitimacy through a hybrid approach. *Journal of Corporate Citizenship,* 109–119.

Charity navigator (www.charitynavigator.org).

Global Reporting Initiative. (2002). *The 2002 sustainability reporting guidelines.* Retrieved from http://www.globalreporting.org

Johnson, H. H. (2001). Corporate social audits—this time around. *Business Horizons, 44,* 29–36.

Martin, R. L. (2003). The virtue matrix: Calculating the return of corporate responsibility. *Harvard Business Review on Corporate Responsibility* (pp. 83–104). Boston: Harvard Business School Press.

Norman, W., & MacDonald, C. (2004). Getting to the bottom of "triple bottom line." *Business Ethics Quarterly, 14,* 243–262.

Sethi, S. P. (1975). Dimensions of corporate social performance: An analytical framework. *California Management Review, 17,* 58–64.

Social Accountability International. (2010). *Overview of SA8000.* Retrieved from http://www.sa-intl.org

Promoting Organizational Citizenship

Many of the drivers of ethical organizational cultural change described in Chapter 10 can be applied to promoting organizational citizenship as well. Promoting organizational citizenship takes ethical diagnosis, engaged leadership, targeted socialization processes, training, and continuous improvement. However, when it comes to moving our organizations to a higher stage or level of citizenship development, two additional factors are critical: (1) taking on a stewardship mentality, and (2) actively engaging with all types of stakeholders. Let's take a closer look at each of these elements.

Adopting a Stewardship Mind-Set

Organizational citizenship is founded in large part on a commitment to stewardship. Stewardship, as we noted in our discussion of servant leadership in Chapter 8, means acting on behalf of others. Stewards seek to serve the interests of the organization and followers rather than pursuing selfish concerns. On an organizational level, stewardship theory operates on the premise that virtuous managers will meet the needs of internal and external groups and society as a whole.[6] By pursuing long-term organizational benefits or goals instead of short-term gain, stewards are better able to serve the needs of all stakeholders and the common good.

Several characteristics set organizational stewards apart from their organizational colleagues. First, they are intrinsically motivated. They seek such intangible rewards as personal growth, affiliation, achievement, and self-actualization rather than tangible rewards like bonuses and company cars. Second, stewards identify themselves with the goals, mission, and vision of their organizations. They take credit for the group's success and shoulder the blame for its failure when it falls short. Third, stewards rely on personal power instead of on positional forms of power (see Chapter 5) to achieve their goals. Fourth, stewards demonstrate a high level of concern not only for the performance of the organization but also for employees, customers, and the disadvantaged.

Covenantal relationships are critical to organizational stewardship.[7] Unlike traditional transactional contracts, which are based on exchanges between parties (labor for money, money for products), covenantal relationships are based on the commitment of parties to each other and on loyalty to shared values. The relational partners realize that they may not benefit from every decision but remain committed to the relationship. Covenants are directly tied to social responsibility. Covenantal relationships between workers and employers are more likely to develop in organizations that invest in social welfare. Employees are more likely to buy into the ideology of groups that promote community interests. Of course, establishing covenantal relationships can be difficult, particularly with those outside the organization. Nonetheless, if you place collective interests over selfish concerns, you are less tempted to engage in such ethical abuses as excessive executive compensation and lying to boost short-term profits. By acting as a steward, you are more likely to be a committed, productive organizational member who reaches out to help your colleagues and outsiders.

CASE STUDY 12.1

SC Johnson and the Base of the Economic Pyramid

SC Johnson is a U.S.-based, family-owned and -led company that manufactures such popular home cleaning and pest control products as Windex, Glad, Pledge, and Raid. Citizenship appears to be part of the company's corporate DNA. In 1935, for example, company leader H. F. Johnson headed an expedition to Brazil to locate a sustainable source of wax for the firm's floor wax product. Under current CEO Fisk Johnson, the company is committed to the philosophy "Do what's right." Sustainability is part of the SC Johnson strategic plan, and the company invests time and resources in four areas or global platforms: (1) using earth-responsible raw materials, (2) advancing social progress and health, (3) preventing insect-borne diseases, and (4) reducing energy consumption and greenhouse gas emissions. The firm sponsors projects to reduce mosquito-borne illnesses, including a Dengue fever program in the Philippines, a mosquito trap project in Ghana, and a malaria prevention education program in South Africa.

SC Johnson has also been involved in efforts to address the "base of the pyramid" (BoP for short). The base of the pyramid refers to the more than four billion people, 65% of the world's population, who make up the lowest economic level. Members of this group earn less than $1,500 a year (one billion people earn less than a dollar a day). This economic segment has been largely ignored by big business and, as a result, the poor often have limited access to goods and services and pay higher prices than their wealthier neighbors. Scholars at Cornell University, the University of Michigan, and elsewhere contend that products and services developed for this audience can be profitable because, though individual incomes are low, collectively this group has significant buying power. Targeting the poorest of the poor could also substantially reduce poverty, destruction of the environment, political instability, and other social ills. To address the bottom of the pyramid, SC Johnson began by underwriting development of the Base of the Pyramid Protocol. The first step of the protocol is opening up—an immersion into the culture designed to identify needs and business opportunities with the help of local residents. The second step is building the ecosystem—developing partnerships to develop a business plan. The third step is enterprise creation, which involves pilot testing and evaluating and modifying business ventures to meet economic, social, and environmental needs.

Once the protocol was developed, SC Johnson sent a team of university student interns to field-test the guidelines in Kibera, the largest slum in Nairobi, Kenya. Like other slums, Kibera is without clean water, sanitation, and decent roads. Residents live in mud, brick, and tin houses. The interns identified business opportunities with residents, and two years later, SC Johnson launched Community Cleaning Services (CCS) in conjunction with a local community-based youth organization. Instead of buying SC Johnson air care, cleaning, and pest control products (the company's typical business model), customers instead hire young entrepreneurs to come and apply the chemicals. Company officials thought residents would want only pest control, but customers also ordered Windex glass cleaner service for hard surfaces and Pledge furniture polish service to treat the one piece of wooden furniture many families owned.

According to Scott Johnson, SC Johnson's vice-president for global environmental and safety actions, the Kibera BoP project did not reach its initial financial objectives. The company encountered gang violence, political unrest, high turnover, and natural disasters. As time went on, the local partners added a number of other services, like painting and repair, that didn't use SC Johnson products. The entrepreneurs earned more from these activities, but the company did not.

While the Kibera venture wasn't as profitable as hoped, the company is satisfied with the results. Scott Johnson notes that the project empowered the youth group partners, who developed their business skills. Some of them have gone on to start their own businesses. The environmental vice president concludes,

> Doing the right thing is not always easy. That's the nature of responsible leadership. It's having the courage to make brave decisions and try something new. We also know that we must be patient. Sustainable change takes time, and we are committed to taking the long view in hopes of making a better future for the next generation.[1]

Discussion Probes

1. Is SC Johnson at the transformative stage of citizenship development? Why or why not?

2. Is it easier to engage in social responsibility (and to remain patient in the face of setbacks) if you are family owned and led like SC Johnson?

3. Do you think that BoP business ventures can be profitable? How do they benefit communities?

4. What long-term benefits might come to SC Johnson from participating in the Kibera slum project?

5. Can you think of other companies that are addressing the base of the pyramid?

6. Would you like to be involved in a BoP project? Why or why not?

Note

1. Johnson, S. (2007, September/October). SC Johnson builds business at the base of the pyramid. *Global Business and Organizational Excellence,* pp. 6–17, p. 16.

Sources

Gordon, M. D. (2008). Management education and the base of the pyramid. *Journal of Management Education, 32*(6), 767–781.

London, T., Anupindi, R., & Sheth, S. (2010). Creating mutual value: Lessons learned from ventures serving base of the pyramid producers. *Journal of Business Research, 63,* 582–594.

Prahalad, C. K., & Hammond, A. (2002, September). Serving the world's poor, profitably. *Harvard Business Review,* pp. 48–57.

Engaging With Stakeholders

The stakeholder framework first developed as an alternative way to define the relationship between large businesses and society but since has been extended to organizations of all types—partnerships, small businesses, governments, and nonprofits.[8] Traditionally, corporate executives were viewed as agents who acted on behalf of the company's owners. According to this perspective (called *agency theory*), the manager's primary ethical obligation is to promote the interests of stockholders. Companies that operate efficiently and profitably benefit the community through the creation of jobs and wealth as well as through higher tax revenues.

Stakeholder theorists challenge the notion that a manager's sole moral duty is to company owners.[9] They note that the pursuit of corporate wealth doesn't benefit everyone. When a major retailer forces its suppliers to cut costs, for example, lots of groups suffer. Employees manufacturing the goods see their wages and benefits cut, and jobs are lost; local businesses and economies decline. Also, shareholders aren't the only groups with an interest or stake in what the company does. Governments charter corporations based in part on the expectation that they will provide benefits to society. Governments invest in businesses by supplying them with cheap land, building access roads, and offering tax breaks.

Advocates of stakeholder theory argue that organizations of all kinds have an ethical obligation to "heed the needs, interests, and influence of those affected by their policies and operations."[10] (See Ethics in Action 12.2 for a list of the possible stakeholders of one organization.) Drawing from Kant's categorical imperative, some proponents believe that all stakeholders have intrinsic value.[11] It is wrong to use any group of people as a means to organizational ends. The interests of diverse stakeholder groups are valid and worthy of respect. Other supporters of this approach draw upon justice-as-fairness theory to emphasize that outside groups and individuals need to be treated fairly by the organization.[12] Still others believe that the stakeholder framework best reflects the feminist commitment to relationships. Feminists see corporations as webs of relationships with stakeholders, not as independent entities.[13] One final group adopts a communitarian perspective to point out that serving stakeholders, not just stockholders, is more likely to promote cooperation and the development of networks that contribute to the common good of society.[14]

ETHICS IN ACTION 12.2 ORGANIZATIONAL STAKEHOLDERS

Stakeholder	*Nature of the Stakeholder Claim*
Shareholders	Participation in distribution of profits, additional stock offerings, assets on liquidation; vote of stock; inspection of company books; transfer of stock; election of board of directors; and such additional rights as have been established in the contract with the corporation.
Employees	Economic, social, and psychological satisfaction in the place of employment. Freedom from arbitrary and capricious behavior on the part of company officials.
	Share in fringe benefits, freedom to join union and participate in collective bargaining, individual freedom in offering up their services through an employment contract. Adequate working conditions.
Customers	Service provided with the product; technical data to use the product; suitable warranties; spare parts to support the product during use; R&D leading to product improvement; facilitation of credit.

Creditors	Legal proportion of interest payments due and return of principal from the investment. Security of pledged assets; relative priority in event of liquidation. Management and owner prerogatives if certain conditions exist with the company (such as default of interest payments).
Suppliers	Continuing source of business; timely consummation of trade credit obligations; professional relationship in contracting for, purchasing, and receiving goods and services.
Unions	Recognition as the negotiating agent for employees. Opportunity to perpetuate the union as a participant in the business organization.
Competitors	Observation of the norms of competitive conduct established by society and the industry. Business statesmanship on the part of peers.
Governments	Taxes (income, property, and so on); adherence to the letter and intent of public policy dealing with the requirements of fair and free competition; discharge of legal obligations of businesspeople (and business organizations); adherence to antitrust laws.
Local communities	Place of productive and healthful environment in the community. Participation of company officials in community affairs, provision of regular employment, fair play, reasonable portion of purchases made in the local community, interest in and support of local government, support of cultural and charitable projects.
The general public	Participation in and contribution to society as a whole; creative communications between governmental and business units designed for reciprocal understanding; assumption of fair proportion of the burden of government and society. Fair price for products and advancement of the state-of-the-art technology that the product line involves.

SOURCE: From Sims, R. R., *Ethics and corporate social responsibility: Why giants fall,* copyright © 2003. Reproduced with permission of ABC-Clio, Inc.

Recognizing the concerns of multiple stakeholders has strategic as well as ethical implications. Identifying the needs of stakeholders should be part of any major decision, like entering additional markets, establishing a new social service program, or changing an investment strategy. You will want to engage in stakeholder management in order to improve organizational performance at the same time that you respond to your moral responsibilities. According to business ethicists Archie Carroll and Ann Buchholtz, stakeholder management means answering five key questions:[15]

1. *Who are our stakeholders?* Categorizing stakeholders can make it easier to answer this question. Those with an interest in the organization can be classified as primary or secondary stakeholders. Primary stakeholders (customers, investors, employees, suppliers) have a direct stake in the organization's success or failure and thus exert

significant influence. Their interests generally are given priority. Secondary stakeholders (social pressure groups, media, trade bodies) have an indirect stake in the organization. Accountability to these groups is therefore less.

2. *What are our stakeholders' stakes?* As Ethics in Action 12.2 illustrates, stakeholder groups have different interests, concerns, and demands. Some of these stakes are more legitimate than others. Owners, for example, have a legal interest in a corporation, while suppliers do not. Further, some groups have more power than others. The board of trustees of a university system typically wields more power than the faculty or students.

3. *What opportunities and challenges do our stakeholders present?* Opportunities allow organizations to build cooperative, productive relationships with stakeholder groups. An inner-city church, for instance, might view other religious groups, local merchants, civic associations, and government agencies as potential allies in combating neighborhood blight. Challenges take the form of demands from groups who believe that the organization is at fault. These must be handled carefully, or they may result in significant damage. Home Depot faced such a challenge from the Rainforest Action Network.[16] The retailer pulled old-growth lumber from the shelves after the environmental group threatened to picket if it did not.

4. *What responsibilities does the firm have to its stakeholders?* These include the economic, legal, ethical, and environmental factors described earlier.

5. *What strategies or actions should management take to best handle stakeholder challenges and opportunities?* Organizations can take the offensive or go on the defensive when dealing with stakeholders, decide to accommodate or negotiate, use one strategy or a combination of several, and so on. One consideration is the potential for cooperation or threat posed by a particular group. Typically, the best strategy is to become involved with groups that are currently supportive or could be cooperative in the future and to defend against those who pose a significant threat.

University of Virginia business professor Edward Freeman and his colleagues urge organizations to focus on creating value for all stakeholders.[17] Freeman believes that it is possible to simultaneously meet the needs of a variety of groups. For example, companies are more likely to survive over the long term if they generate profits for owners and at the same time treat employees well, deal fairly with suppliers, and serve the community. Trade-offs—meeting the needs of one group at the expense of another—are inevitable but should not become standard operating procedure. Freeman is also convinced that businesses should take the initiative to engage all stakeholders in dialogue, including those who could be seen as a threat. It is not always possible to satisfy every critic, but opponents provide an alternative point of view. Understanding their concerns can open up new opportunities to generate value (e.g., enter new markets, meet unmet needs, reduce costs). Engaging with both primary and secondary stakeholders also provides information that can be used to better meet their needs. Corporations like McDonald's and 3M, for instance, have radically altered their production processes in response to stakeholder concerns, reducing their waste while enhancing their environmental reputations.

In addition to managing ongoing relationships with stakeholders, organizations also need to identify and respond to changing social and ethical conditions. This process is called *issues management.* Ethical sensitivities and moral customs continually evolve. Smoking, which once was allowed nearly everywhere in this country, is now banned from many indoor public spaces, for instance. Fast-food outlets now have to contend with charges that they contribute to the nation's obesity epidemic.

Issues management is a function of public relations departments at major corporations. SC Johnson credits its issues management program for the firm's decision to eliminate fluorocarbons from aerosol sprays three years before federal regulations took effect. Sears noted the potential dangers of flammable nightwear early on and quickly removed these products before federal regulations were passed.[18] Despite these successes, it would be wrong to make issues management solely a public relations function. All employees have a responsibility to be on the lookout for future trends through scanning and monitoring. In this context, *scanning* refers to surveying the environment to identify potential issues that might impact your organization. Surf the Web, and read a wide variety of issues-oriented publications (*The Nation, Mother Jones, The Standard,* for example), monitor news sources and talk shows, and interact with stakeholder groups. Once an issue is identified, actively monitor it. Track its progress, and work with others to develop a response.[19]

One model of the stages of issue development is shown in the Self-Assessment. You can monitor the progress of any issue using this format. Take the issue of global warming, for example. At first, only a few environmental groups were aware of this problem, and evidence of its existence was scarce. Next, the issue began to grab political and media attention, and some businesses began to take note. Currently, this concern appears to be moving from the consolidating to the institutionalized stage with increasing recognition of the ethical dimension of the problem. A number of nations have passed measures aimed at reducing greenhouse emissions, and businesses around the world have joined in the effort.

SELF-ASSESSMENT

The Four Stages of Issue Maturity Scale

Pharmaceutical company Novo Nordisk created a scale to measure the maturity of societal issues and the public's expectations surrounding the issues. An adaptation of the scale appears here.

Stage	Characteristics
Latent	Activist communities and NGOs (nongovernment organizations) are aware of the societal issue.
	There is weak scientific or other hard evidence.
	The issue is largely ignored or dismissed by the business community.

Emerging	There is political and media awareness of the societal issue.
	There is an emerging body of research, but data are still weak.
	Leading businesses experiment with approaches to dealing with the issue.
Consolidating	There is an emerging body of business practices around the societal issue.
	Sectorwide and issue-based voluntary initiatives are established.
	There is litigation and an increasing view of the need for legislation.
	Voluntary standards are developed, and collective action occurs.
Institutionalized	Legislation or business norms are established.
	The embedded practices become a normal part of a business-excellence model.

Brainstorm three or four ethical issues that could pose a challenge to your college or university or your employer. Track each issue's stage of development using the issue maturity scale. Determine how your school or employer should respond to each issue.

SOURCE: Zadek, S. (2004, December). The path to corporate responsibility, *Harvard Business Review*, p. 128. Used by permission.

Ethical Global Citizenship

Globalization is having a dramatic impact on life in the 21st century. We inhabit a global society knit together by free trade, international travel, immigration, satellite communication systems, and the Internet. In this interconnected world, ethical responsibilities extend beyond national boundaries. Decisions about raw materials, manufacturing, outsourcing, farm subsidies, investments, marketing strategies, suppliers, safety standards, and energy use made in one country have ramifications for residents of other parts of the world (see the Ethics and Technology feature). Organizational citizenship is now played out on a global stage.

To act as ethical global citizens, organizations must confront and master the dangers of globalization and the dilemmas of ethical diversity. In this section, I'll describe these obstacles and offer tactics for overcoming them.

The Dangers of Globalization and the Challenges of Ethical Diversity

The benefits of living in a global economy are obvious: lower labor costs, higher sales and profits, cheaper goods and services, instant communication to anywhere on Earth, increased information flow, and cross-cultural contact. What's often hidden is the downside of globalization. Of particular concern is the growing divide between the haves and the have-nots. The richest 20% of the global population controls over 85% of the world's assets and income. Governments of wealthy nations appear more interested in promoting the sale of their goods (including agricultural products) than in opening up their markets to poor countries.[20] Lumber, minerals, and oil are extracted from poor regions and consumed in privileged areas, leaving environmental damage behind. At the same time, the United States sends solid and toxic waste to the developing world.

Critics also note that global capitalism frequently promotes greed rather than concern for others. Ethical and spiritual values have been shunted aside in favor of the profit motive. Few industrialized countries give even the suggested minimum of .07 of gross national product (70 cents of every $100 produced by the economy) to alleviate global poverty.[21] Local cultural traditions are being destroyed in the name of economic progress. As McDonalds, KFC, Taco Bell, and other popular American foods replace local fare, people around the world can expect to suffer the same kinds of chronic health problems as U.S. residents do—Type II diabetes, obesity, and heart failure.

The big winners in globalization are multinational corporations. Fueled by international trade, the hundred biggest companies combined have annual revenue greater than the gross domestic product of half of the world's nations.[22] If Wal-Mart were a country, for instance, its economy would rank 15th among free market democracies.[23] So far, many multinationals have pursued free trade at the cost of human rights and the environment. They have employed sweatshop and slave labor, stood by as repressive regimes tortured their citizens, and plundered local resources.

Along with the potential moral pitfalls of globalization, organizations also face the challenges of ethical diversity.[24] Nations, tribes, ethnic groups, and religions approach moral dilemmas differently. What members of one group accept as right may raise serious ethical concerns for another. For example, in Germany contracts are highly detailed and strictly enforced. In Egypt, contracts spell out guidelines for business deals rather than specific requirements. Egyptians expect to renegotiate and revise contracts, and there is no moral stigma attached to violating a signed agreement. In Mexico, honoring a contract is based on the signer's personal ethics. There is little legal recourse if a contract is violated.

Bribery offers another instance of conflicting moral standards. In South American countries, it is nearly impossible to move goods through customs without making small payments to cut through red tape. At the other extreme, Malaysia executes corporate officials who offer and accept bribes. U.S. corporations are prevented from exchanging money or goods for favors or services under the Foreign Corrupt Practices Act of 1977. However, in recognition of the fact that petty bribery is common in some parts of the world, small payments to facilitate travel and business are permitted under the statute. Cultures also clash over intellectual property rights (which are strictly enforced in the West but not protected in parts of Southeast Asia) and deception (Americans lie to protect their privacy, whereas Mexicans are more likely to lie to protect the group or family).

The challenges posed by globalization and ethical diversity can undermine ethical decision making. For some organizations, it is business as usual. Interested only in making a profit or expanding their influence, they fail to weigh the possible negative consequences of their choices in the global environment. Leaders faced with ethical diversity sometimes behave as ethical imperialists by imposing their personal moral standards on members of other cultures. Or they may opt for cultural relativism by always following local customs ("When in Rome, do as the Romans do"). Nevertheless, being in a new culture or working with a diverse group of followers doesn't excuse managers from careful ethical deliberation. Standards from one culture can't be blindly forced upon another; conversely, just because a culture has adopted a practice doesn't make it right. For example, trafficking in humans takes place in some parts of the world, but most societies condemn this practice.

Fortunately, you can develop your cross-cultural ethical competence and help your organizations to do the same. To achieve this goal, you must first wrestle with ethnocentrism. Next, you have to recognize the value orientations of cultural groups and how these patterns influence ethical decision making. Then, you need to adopt universal moral principles that should govern behavior in every cultural setting and employ guidelines for sorting through conflicts between competing ethical norms.

Coming to Grips With Ethnocentrism

Overcoming the challenges of globalization and ethical diversity is impossible if we fall victim to ethnocentrism. *Ethnocentrism* is viewing the world from our cultural group's point of view, which makes our customs and values the standard by which the rest of the world is judged. Our ways are "right," while their ways fall short. A certain degree of ethnocentrism is probably inevitable; it can help a group band together and survive in the face of outside threats. Nevertheless, high levels of ethnocentrism can lead to reduced contact with outsiders, racial slurs, insensitivity to strangers, pressure on other groups to conform, justification for violence and war, and other negative outcomes.[25]

A number of the ethical communication competencies introduced earlier in the text can be used to confront ethnocentrism. Pursue dialogue in cross-cultural conversations by treating members of other cultures as equal partners and by trying to understand their point of view (Chapter 4). Mindfulness is particularly important in diverse cultural settings because the scripts we follow in our own groups don't work when we find ourselves in other cultures. Adopt a pluralistic perspective that acknowledges the legitimacy of other groups and customs in order to avoid moral exclusion (Chapter 7).

Personal virtues (Chapter 2) can help undermine ethnocentric attitudes and at the same time lay the groundwork for meeting the challenges of globalization and ethical diversity. Philosopher and theologian Michael Novak identifies four cardinal or hinge virtues essential to encouraging global cooperation: cultural humility, truth, dignity, and solidarity.[26] Cultural humility means acknowledging the shortcomings of our own cultures as well as our personal biases. A commitment to truth allows for reasoned argument based on evidence and logic. Recognition of human dignity forbids using others as a means to an end. Solidarity is being aware that each individual lives in communion with others and has responsibility for their welfare.

ETHICS AND TECHNOLOGY

Blood Cell Phones

Few who wait in line to buy the latest iPhone or electronic gaming system realize that their purchases may be underwriting the deadliest conflict since World War II. The Congo is a major source of the titanium, tantalum, tungsten, and gold used in the manufacture of cell phones, computers, portable music players, gaming consoles, and other electronic devices. Profits from the sale of these minerals support warlords and rebel groups in Eastern Congo who use mass rape, murder, and forced labor as tools of war. The Congo death toll as of 2007 was 5.4 million; an additional 45,000 soldiers and civilians have died each month since.

To reduce funding for the slaughter in the Congo, the human rights group called the Enough Project started a campaign to pressure Apple, Intel, and Research in Motion (the makers of BlackBerry) to eliminate the use of "conflict minerals" in their products. Activists created a YouTube video, protested at an Intel production facility in Oregon, and posted messages on the company's Facebook site. These efforts generated media reports that linked the horrors in the Congo to upscale U.S. consumers who want the latest electronics gadgets.

The conflict mineral movement scored its first major victory with the passage of congressional legislation requiring electronics manufacturers to disclose whether they use minerals mined in the Congo. (The additional cost of tracing supplies is estimated at a penny per phone). Activists hope to shame companies into changing suppliers and then to create a mineral certification program similar to the diamond certification program. International pressure led to the end of the sale of "blood diamonds" from war-torn Sierra Leone and Liberia. Once funding was cut off, peace and economic prosperity followed in these countries. Those pushing to end the sale of conflict metals believe that the same can happen in the Congo.

Intel, Apple, and other electronics companies can expect even more pressure to force them to cut off mineral purchases from the Congo. Consumers, once they realize how their latest gadgets are made, are likely to be as resistant to "blood phones" as they were earlier to blood diamonds.

Sources

Kristof, N. D. (2010, June 27). Death by gadget. *The New York Times*, p. WK11.

Congo-Kinshasa: Peace campaigners turn up heat on Apple, Intel over conflict minerals. (2009, September 18). *Africa News.*

ICT and Telecom: How technology is fueling conflict in the country. (2009, December 7). *The East African.*

Mieszkowski, K. (2020, June 13). Stanford considers guideline for 'conflict minerals.' *The New York Times*, p. A31.

Polgreen, L. (2008, November 16). Congo's riches, looted by renegade troops. *The New York Times*, p. A1.

Rogoway, M. (2010, June 25). Conflict minerals rule will affect Oregon's high-tech sector. *The Oregonian*, pp. B4, B5.

Understanding Ethical Diversity

Ethical decisions and practices are shaped by widely held cultural values. Every culture has its own set of ethical priorities; however, researchers have discovered that ethnic groups and nations hold values in common. As a result, cultures can be grouped according to their value orientations. Understanding these orientations helps explain ethical differences and enables us to better predict how members of other societies will respond to moral dilemmas. Three widely used cultural classification systems include Hofstede's programmed value patterns, the GLOBE studies, and Moral Foundations Theory.

1. Programmed Value Patterns

Gert Hofstede of the Netherlands argues that important values are "programmed" into members of every culture. To uncover these value dimensions, he conducted the first extensive international investigation of cultural value patterns, surveying more than 100,000 IBM employees in 50 countries and 3 multicountry regions.[27] He then checked his findings against those of other researchers who studied the same countries. Four value orientations emerged:

Power distance. The first category concerns how societies deal with human inequality. While status and power differences are universal, cultures treat them differently. In high–power distance cultures (Malaysia, Guatemala), inequality is accepted as part of the natural order. Leaders are set apart and enjoy special privileges and make no attempt to reduce power differentials. Low–power distance cultures (Israel, Austria), on the other hand, are uneasy with large gaps in wealth, power, privilege, and status. Superiors tend to downplay status and power differentials, and such societies stress equal rights.

Individualism versus collectivism. This category divides cultures according to their preference for either the individual or the group. Individualistic cultures (the United States, Australia, Great Britain) put the needs and goals of the person and her or his immediate family first. Members of these cultures see themselves as independent actors and believe that everyone should take care of themselves and their immediate family. In contrast, collectivistic cultures give top priority to the desires of the larger group—extended family, tribe, community. Members of these societies (Guatemala, Ecuador, Panama) think in terms of "we," not "I." They want to fit into the collective, not stand out.

Masculinity versus femininity. The third dimension reflects attitudes toward the roles of men and women. Highly masculine cultures (Japan, Austria, Saudi Arabia) maintain clearly defined sex roles. Men are expected to be tough and focus on performance; women are to be tender and focus on relationships. Men should be ambitious and assertive, while women are expected to care for the weak. Feminine cultures (Sweden, Norway, Netherlands) blur the differences between the sexes. Both men and women can be competitive and caring, assertive and nurturing. These cultures are more likely to stress cooperation, quality of life, and concern for others.

Uncertainty avoidance. This dimension describes the way in which cultures respond to uncertainty about the future. Members of high–uncertainty avoidance societies (Greece, Portugal, Uruguay) feel anxious about uncertainty and view it as a threat. They are less likely to break the rules; they value loyalty to the company, accept directives from those in authority, and view outsiders and change as threats. In addition, they are reluctant to change jobs or to express dissatisfaction with their current employers. People who live in low–uncertainty avoidance cultures (Sweden, Denmark, Jamaica) are more comfortable with uncertainty, viewing ambiguity as a fact of life. They experience lower stress and are more likely to pursue their ambitions by, for example, starting a new company or accepting a new job in another part of the country. These people are more likely to trust their own judgments instead of obeying authority figures. As a result, they are more likely to break rules and regulations.

Hofstede argues that the value patterns he identifies have a significant influence on ethical behavior.[28] For instance, masculine/high power distance/high uncertainty avoidance countries are generally more corrupt. Masculine European countries give little to international development programs but invest heavily in weapons. Feminine European nations do just the opposite. High–uncertainty avoidance cultures are prone to ethnocentrism and prejudice because they follow the credo "What is different is dangerous." Low–uncertainty avoidance cultures follow the credo "What is different is curious" and are more tolerant of strangers and new ideas.

Other researchers have also linked Hofstede's value patterns to ethical attitudes and behavior.[29] They have discovered that members of feminine cultures are more sensitive to the presence of moral issues. Consumers from societies characterized by short-term orientation, low power distance, and low uncertainty avoidance generally punish socially irresponsible firms. Individualistic countries prefer universal ethical standards, such as Kant's categorical imperative.[30] Collectivistic societies take a more utilitarian approach, seeking to generate the greatest good for in-group members. Citizens of these nations are more sensitive to elements of the situation. Examples of how individualism and collectivism affect ethical decisions are presented in Table 12.1.

Table 12.1

Issue	Individualistic	Collectivistic
Bribery	Seen as a form of corruption	A way to meet community obligations, more common
False Information	Lie to protect privacy	Lie to protect the group or family
Expressing Disagreement	Direct	Indirect; save face

(Continued)

Table 12.1 (Continued)

Issue	Individualistic	Collectivistic
Intellectual Property	Protected by copyright laws	Knowledge is to be shared
Gender Equality	Promote equal opportunity	Women seen as an out-group; need to protect status quo
Nepotism	Hire based on qualifications	Hire based on connections (family and friends)
Privacy	Right to privacy	Public interests take priority over privacy
Wealth	Wealth distributed more equally	Large differences in wealth
Human Rights	High human rights ratings	Low human rights ratings
Laws	The same for all	Vary according to tradition and status

SOURCE: Carroll, S. J., & Gannon, M. J. (1997). *Ethical dimensions of international management.* Thousand Oaks, CA: Sage. Copyright © 1996, SAGE Publications, Inc. Used by permission.

2. Project GLOBE

Project GLOBE (Global Leadership and Organizational Behavior Effectiveness) is an ongoing international effort. To date, 200 researchers from around the world have gathered data from more than 17,000 managers in 62 countries. The goal of the project is to identify the relationship between cultural values and effective leadership behaviors. This information can help managers become more successful in cross-cultural settings. The GLOBE researchers incorporate into their study Hofstede's dimensions of power distance, uncertainty avoidance, gender differentiation (masculinity and femininity), and individualism versus collectivism. However, they also extend Hofstede's list by identifying four additional values patterns:[31]

Performance orientation. This is the "extent to which a community encourages and rewards innovation, high standards, and performance improvement."[32] Places such as Hong Kong, Singapore, and the United States are results focused. Citizens value competition and materialism and want to be rewarded for individual achievement. In countries such as Russia, Italy, and Argentina, people put loyalty and belonging ahead of performance. They are uncomfortable with competition and merit pay and put more weight on someone's seniority, and family and background than on his or her performance.

Future orientation. This is the extent to which a society fosters and reinforces such future-oriented activities as planning and investing (Singapore, Switzerland, the Netherlands) rather than immediate rewards (Russia, Argentina, Poland).

Assertiveness. Assertiveness is defined as the extent to which a culture encourages individuals to be tough, confrontational, and competitive, as opposed to modest and tender. Spain and the United States rate high on this dimension; Sweden and New Zealand rate low. Those in highly assertive societies have a take-charge, can-do attitude and value competition. They admire the strong and assertive and are not particularly sympathetic to the weak and less fortunate. Members of less assertive cultures place more value on empathy, loyalty, and solidarity. They have empathy for the weak and want to live in harmony with the environment rather than control it.

Humane orientation. Humane orientation refers to the extent to which a culture encourages and honors people for being altruistic, caring, kind, fair, and generous. Support for the weak and vulnerable is particularly high in such countries as Malaysia, Ireland, and the Philippines. Members of society care for one another and rely much less on the government. In contrast, power and material possessions are more likely to motivate people in the former West Germany, Spain, and France; self-enhancement takes precedence. Individuals are to solve their own problems, and the state provides more support for the less fortunate.

The GLOBE values dimensions have also been linked to ethical diversity. People oriented toward the future will save and invest. They will condemn those who live in the moment and spend all they earn. Future-oriented organizations are also more likely to engage in practices that benefit society. Competition, direct communication, power, and personal advancement are applauded in assertive, performance-oriented, less humane groups. These elements are undesirable to people who put more value on harmony, cooperation, family, and concern for others. Those living in assertive, performance-oriented cultures are tempted to engage in unethical activities in order to succeed. The businesses they create are more likely to be focused on shareholders, profits, and results instead of on stakeholders and social responsibility (including care for the environment).[33]

3. Moral Foundations Theory

Hofstede and the GLOBE researchers treat ethical diversity as just one of the outcomes of cultural diversity. In contrast, moral foundations theory was developed specifically to account for the ethical differences between cultures. University of Virginia moral psychologist Jonathan Haidt and others believe that to understand ethical diversity we first need to understand the psychological systems or foundations of morality. These mental foundations, which are part of our genetic makeup, enable humans to successfully live together in groups. Cultures shape how these systems are used, emphasizing one or more values over the others. Haidt compares these moral systems to taste buds. Nearly everyone is born with the same set of taste receptors, but each culture develops its own cuisine, which highlights different tastes.

Haidt identifies five foundations for our moral intuitions.[34] They include the following:

Harm/care. All species are sensitive to suffering in their own offspring, but for primates and humans sensitivity to suffering extends beyond the family. We can also feel compassion for outsiders. Attuned to cruelty and harm, we generally approve of those who prevent or alleviate suffering. Kindness and compassion are therefore important human virtues. However, the other moral foundations described below temper the amount of compassion that individuals in different cultures display.

Fairness/reciprocity. Reciprocity (paying back others) is essential for the formation of alliances between individuals who are not related to each other. As a result, all cultures have virtues related to justice and fairness. Individual rights and equality are highly prized in the West. However, many traditional societies put little value on personal autonomy or equal treatment.

In-group/loyalty. Trust and cooperation have been critical to human survival. Individuals need to work effectively with others in their group while being wary of outsiders. As a result, they value those who sacrifice on behalf of the in-group while despising members who don't come to their aid in times of conflict. They are disturbed when fellow citizens challenge symbols of group unity, like the pledge of the allegiance to the national flag.

Authority/respect. Hierarchy is fact of life in primate as well as human groups. Dominant individuals get special perks but are expected to provide services (e.g., protection, food) in return. Primates rely on brute strength to assert their authority; people use such factors as prestige and deference. Followers in many cultures feel respect, awe, and admiration for leaders and expect them to act like wise parents. Many of these same societies make virtues out of duty, obedience, respect, and other subordinate behaviors.

Purity/sanctity. Only humans appear to feel disgust, which helps to protect the body against the transmission of disease through corpses, feces, vomit, and other possible contaminants. Disgust has a social dimension as well, becoming associated with those who are diseased or deformed or with certain occupations (grave diggers and those who dispose of excrement, for example). Members of most cultural groups admire those who are spiritually minded or pure and disapprove of individuals who seem to be ruled by lust, gluttony, greed, and uncontrolled anger. For example, in the United States, one of the most materialistic societies in the world, most citizens still look down on those who regularly "shop until they drop."

The United States and many other Western nations largely focus on reducing harm and promoting autonomy. But as Haidt points out, that is not the case in much of the rest of the world. In Brazil, morality is based on loyalty, family, respect, and purity, in addition to care. Confucian and Hindu value systems emphasize authority and stability. Muslim societies place a high priority on purity, which is reflected in the segregation of men and women and separation from infidels. Haidt urges us to keep all five moral systems in mind when dealing with diverse groups. Purity and authority may not be important to us, but they are to a great proportion of the world's population. Our ethical appeals will be most effective if they speak to loyalty, authority, and purity in addition to care and fairness.

Professor Haidt developed his theory to explain moral differences between cultures, but he soon discovered that moral foundations explain the differences between liberals and conservatives in the United States.[35] Contrasts between these political philosophies further demonstrate how the moral foundations shape ethical attitudes. Haidt believes that the purity/sanctity dimension is the best predictor of positions on abortion, for example. American liberals who value autonomy want to preserve the woman's right to choose, and conservatives want to preserve the sanctity of the fetus. Authority predicts competing attitudes toward gay marriage. Liberals believe that individuals have a right to do as they choose if they don't hurt anyone else. In their minds, opposition to gay marriage is homophobic. Conservatives, on the other hand, see gay marriage as a threat to the family, which serves as the foundation of society. Those on the political left and right are also divided by their attitudes toward loyalty. Liberals believe that citizens can protest against a war while at the same time supporting the soldiers fighting in the conflict. This argument offends conservatives, who believe it is unpatriotic to protest when the country is at war.

Finding Moral Common Ground

Some organizations and their members respond to ethical diversity by practicing ethical relativism, which is conformity to local customs. Ethical relativism avoids the problem of ethnocentrism while simplifying the decision-making process. We never have to pass judgment and can concentrate on fitting in with the prevailing culture. However, this approach is fraught with difficulties. Without shared standards, there is little hope that people of the world can come together to tackle global problems. There is no basis upon which to condemn the actions of governments (like Sudan, for example) that are engaged in genocide and torture, or to criticize businesses that exploit their employees and the environment. Cultural relativism obligates us to follow (or as least not to protest against) abhorrent local practices like female circumcision. Without universal rights and wrongs, we have no grounds for contesting such practices.

There appears to be a growing consensus that ethical common ground can be found. In fact, the existence of common moral standards has enabled the world community to punish crimes against humanity in Germany, Serbia, and Rwanda. Responsible multinational corporations like Starbucks, The Body Shop, and Proctor & Gamble adhere to widely held moral principles as they do business in a variety of cultural settings. Activist groups use these same guidelines to condemn irresponsible firms.

One group of researchers used the "trolley problem" to determine if there are similarities in cross-cultural reasoning.[36] In the trolley problem, an out-of-control trolley threatens to kill five people unless immediate action is taken. In one case, the trolley operator is incapacitated, and a passenger has to decide whether or not to throw a switch that will divert the vehicle to safety on a side track (and save the five passengers) but will kill a pedestrian who happens to be standing on the rails. In the other case, someone standing by the tracks must decide whether or not to directly intervene by throwing another bystander into the path of the trolley to slow it down and save the five passengers.

Responses to the trolley problem from 30,000 subjects in 120 countries revealed widespread agreement across all groups, regardless of nationality, educational level, or religion. By a significant margin, participants said it was justified to throw the switch to save the trolley passengers but not to throw someone onto the tracks to accomplish the same goal. Respondents reported that throwing a switch is an impersonal act, and they saw the death of the pedestrian as an unfortunate consequence. On the other hand, throwing a bystander onto the track is a deliberate, highly personal act that makes the victim a means to an end.

The hypothetical trolley problem has parallels in real life. For example, most of us would allow terminally ill patients to refuse treatment and thus die sooner than they would have with the additional care. (This approach is similar to throwing the trolley switch). However, it is illegal in most states to give a drug overdose to hasten a terminally ill patient's death (which raises the same concerns as throwing a bystander onto the trolley track).

Universal standards provide additional evidence that members of diverse societies can find moral common ground. Such global standards have enabled members of the world community to punish crimes against humanity and to create the United Nations and its Universal Declaration of Human Rights. I'll describe four different approaches to universal ethics, any one of which could serve as a worldwide standard. You'll note a number of similarities between the lists. Decide for yourself which approach or combination of approaches best captures the foundational values of humankind (see Application Project 6 at the end of the chapter).

The United Nations Universal Declaration of Human Rights

Human rights are granted to individuals based solely on their status as persons. Such rights protect the inherent dignity of every individual regardless of background. Rights violations are unethical because they deny human value and potential.[37]

The most influential list of basic human rights was adopted by the United Nations immediately following World War II, a conflict fought in large part to protect human freedoms. Among the key rights spelled out in the universal declaration are the following:[38]

> *Article 4.* No one shall be held in slavery or servitude; slavery and the slave trade shall be prohibited in all their forms.
>
> *Article 5.* No one shall be subjected to torture or to cruel, inhuman, or degrading treatment or punishment.
>
> *Article 9.* No one shall be subjected to arbitrary arrest, detention, or exile.
>
> *Article 13.* Everyone has the right to freedom of movement and residence.
>
> *Article 17.* Everyone has the right to own property alone as well in association with others.
>
> *Article 19.* Everyone has the right to freedom of thought, conscience, and religion.

Article 25. Everyone has the right to a standard of living adequate for the health and well-being of himself [or herself] and of his [or her] family.

Article 26. Everyone has the right to education.

In 2000, the United Nations launched a program called the Global Compact to encourage multinational corporations to honor human rights, labor rights, and the environment. Members agree to the principles outlined in Ethics in Action 12.3 and specify how they are complying with these guidelines. Nonprofit watchdog groups meet regularly with corporate representatives to talk about their firms' performance. Membership in the Global Compact has grown rapidly. It is now the largest voluntary corporate citizen group in the world.

ETHICS IN ACTION 12.3 UNITED NATIONS: THE GLOBAL COMPACT

The Ten Principles

Human Rights

Principle 1: Businesses should support and respect the protection of international human rights within their sphere of influence; and

Principle 2: make sure that they are not complicit in human rights abuses.

Labour

Principle 3: Businesses should uphold the freedom of association and the effective recognition of the right to collective bargaining;

Principle 4: the elimination of all forms of forced and compulsory labour;

Principle 5: the effective abolition of child labour; and

Principle 6: the elimination of discrimination in respect of employment and occupation.

Environment

Principle 7: Businesses should support a precautionary approach to environmental challenges;

Principle 8: undertake initiatives to promote greater environmental responsibility; and

Principle 9: encourage the development and diffusion of environmentally friendly technologies.

Anti-Corruption

Principle 10: Businesses should work against corruption in all its forms, including extortion and bribery.

SOURCE: United Nations Global Compact: The ten principles. Retrieved from http://unglobalcompact.org

Eight Global Values

Rushworth Kidder and his colleagues at the Institute for Global Ethics identify eight core values that appear to be shared the world over. They isolated these values after conducting interviews with 24 international "ethical thought leaders."[40] Kidder's sample included former heads of state, professors, activists, business executives, writers, and religious figures drawn from such nations as Vietnam, Mozambique, New Zealand, Bangladesh, Britain, the United States, China, Japan, Sri Lanka, Costa Rica, and Lebanon. Each interview ran from 1 to 3 hours and began with this question: "If you could help create a global code of ethics, what would be on it?" These global standards emerged:[41]

1. *Love.* Spontaneous concern for others; compassion that transcends political and ethnic differences.

2. *Truthfulness.* Achieving goals through honest means; keeping promises; being worthy of the trust of others.

3. *Fairness (justice).* Fair play, evenhandedness, equality.

4. *Freedom.* The pursuit of liberty; right of individual conscience, free expression and action.

5. *Unity.* Seeking the common good; cooperation, community, solidarity.

6. *Tolerance.* Respect for others and their ideas; empathy; appreciation for variety.

7. *Responsibility.* Care for self and others, the community, and future generations; responsible use of force.

8. *Respect for life.* Reluctance to kill through war and other means.

Kidder admits that there are few surprises on this list. Yet, the commonsense nature of these values is good news, signaling that these standards are widely shared:

> This is not . . . an off-the-wall, unique, bizarre list. It may even strike us as familiar, ordinary, and unsurprising. That's a comforting fact. Codes of ethics, to be practicable, need to have behind them a broad consensus. The originality of the list matters less than its consistency and universality.[42]

The Global Business Standards Codex

Harvard business professor Lynn Paine and her colleagues argue that outstanding ("world-class") corporations base their codes of ethics on a set of eight universal, overarching moral principles.[43] Paine's group came to this conclusion after surveying a variety of global and corporate codes of conduct and government regulations. They offer the following Global Business Standards Codex as a benchmark for those who want to conform to universal standards of corporate conduct.

I. *Fiduciary principle.* Act on behalf of the company and its investors. Be diligent and loyal in carrying out the firm's business. As a trustee, be candid (open and honest).

II. *Property principle.* Respect and protect property and the rights of its owners. Don't steal or misuse company assets, including information, funds, and equipment. Avoid waste and take care of property entrusted to you.

III. *Reliability principle.* Honor all commitments. Keep promises and follow through on agreements even when they are not in the form of legally binding contracts.

IV. *Transparency principle.* Do business in a truthful manner. Avoid deceptive acts and practices and keep accurate records. Release information that should be shared in a timely fashion but maintain confidentiality and privacy as necessary.

V. *Dignity principle.* Respect the dignity of all who come in contact with the corporation, including employees, suppliers, customers, and the public. Protect their health, privacy, and rights. Avoid coercion. Promote human development instead by providing learning and development opportunities.

VI. *Fairness principle.* Deal fairly with everyone. Engage in fair competition, provide just compensation to employees, and be evenhanded in dealings with suppliers and corporate partners. Practice nondiscrimination in both employment and contracting.

VII. *Citizenship principle.* Act as a responsible member of the community by (a) obeying the law, (b) protecting the public good (not engaging in corruption, protecting the environment), (c) cooperating with public authorities, (d) avoiding improper involvement in politics, and (e) contributing to the community (e.g., economic and social development, giving to charitable causes).

VIII. *Responsiveness principle.* Engage with groups (neighborhood groups, activists, customers) that may have concerns about the company's activities. Work with other groups to better society while not usurping the government's role in protecting the public interest.

The Caux Principles

The Caux Round Table is made up of corporate executives from the United States, Japan, and Europe who meet every year in Caux, Switzerland. Round Table members believe that businesses should improve economic, social, and environmental conditions and hope to set a world standard by which to judge business behavior. Their principles are based on twin ethical ideals. The first is the Japanese concept of *kyosei*, which refers to living and working together for the common good. The second is the Western notion of human dignity, the sacredness and value of each person as an end rather than as a means to someone else's end.[44] The Caux Principles for Business, perhaps because they were written by corporate executives from around the world, have gained widespread support. Business schools in Latin America, Asia, Europe, and the United States have endorsed them, and a number of international firms have used them as a guide when developing their own mission statements and ethics codes.

Principle 1. Respect stakeholders beyond shareholders.[45] Businesses should have goals that extend beyond economic survival. Corporations have a responsibility to improve the lives of everyone they come in contact with, starting with employees, customers, shareholders, and suppliers, and then reaching out to local, national, regional, and global communities.

Principle 2. Contribute to economic, social, and environmental development. Companies operating in foreign countries not only should create jobs and wealth but should also foster human rights, better education, and social welfare. Multinational corporations have an obligation to enrich the world community through the wise use of resources, fair competition, and innovation.

Principle 3. Build trust by going beyond the letter of the law. Businesses ought to promote honesty, transparency, integrity, and keeping promises. These behaviors make it easier to conduct international business and to support a global economy.

Principle 4. Respect rules and conventions. Leaders of international firms must respect both international and local laws in order to reduce trade wars, to ensure fair competition, and to promote the free flow of goods and services. They also need to recognize that some behaviors may be legal but still have damaging consequences.

Principle 5. Support responsible globalisation. Firms should support international trading systems and agreements and eliminate domestic measures that undermine free trade.

Principle 6. Respect the environment. Corporations ought to protect and, if possible, improve the physical environment through sustainable development and by cutting back on the wasteful use of natural resources.

Principle 7. Avoid illicit activities. Global business managers must ensure that their organizations aren't involved in such forbidden activities as bribery, money laundering, supporting terrorism, and drug and arms trafficking.

After spelling out general principles, the Caux accord applies them to important stakeholder groups. Organizations following these standards seek to (a) treat customers and employees with dignity, (b) honor the trust of owners/investors, (c) create relationships with suppliers based on mutual respect, (d) interact fairly with competitors, and (e) work for reform and human rights in host communities.

Resolving Ethical Cross-Cultural Conflicts

So far, we've established that (1) there are significant differences between cultures in how they respond to ethical issues, and (2) there are universal moral principles that apply across cultural boundaries. Reconciling these two facts when making ethical decisions is not easy. How do we respect ethical diversity while remaining true to global moral principles, for example? What do we do when two competing ethical perspectives appear to be equally valid? What set of standards should have top priority—those of the host nation or those of the international organization? Business ethicists

Thomas Donaldson and Thomas Dunfee developed the integrated social contracts theory (ISCT) to help us answer questions like these.[46]

ISCT is based on the notion of social contracts, which are agreements that spell out the obligations or duties of institutions, communities, and societies. The model is integrative because it incorporates two kinds of contracts. The first kind of contract (*macrosocial*) sets the groundwork or standards for social interaction. Examples of ideal contracts include the requirement that governments respect the rights of people and help the poor. The second type of contract (*microsocial*) governs the relationships between members of particular communities (nations, regions, towns, professions, industries). These contracts are revealed by the norms of the group. Community contracts are considered authentic or binding if (a) members of the group have a voice in the creation of the norms, (b) members can exit the group if they disagree with prevailing norms, and (c) the norms are widely recognized and practiced by group members.

According to ISCT, universal principles (called *hypernorms*) act as the ultimate ethical standard in making choices. Communities have a great deal of latitude, or *moral free space*, to create their own rules, however, as long as these local norms do not conflict with hypernorms. Victim compensation provides one example of norms arising out of moral free space. In Japan (where the victim compensation system is unreliable), airline officials go in person to offer compensation to victims' families after an accident. In the United States (where the compensation system is more reliable), payments are determined through court decisions.

Dunfee and Donaldson offer a number of guidelines for determining which norms should take priority. Three of these rules of thumb are particularly important. One, determine if the local practice is authentic (widely shared) and legitimate (in harmony with hypernorms). If it's not, it should be rejected. Second, follow the legitimate local customs of the host community whenever possible. To return to our earlier compensation example, a U.S. airline official stationed in Japan should distribute compensation directly to crash victims' families instead of relying on the Japanese court system. Third, give more weight to norms generated by larger communities. A norm embraced by a nation as a whole, for instance, should generally take precedence over the norm of a region. The U.S. government followed this guideline in overturning laws promoting racial discrimination in the South. A similar argument can be made for choosing the norm of gender equality (which has broad international acceptance) over the norms of a particular nation that discriminates against women. (You can test the ISCT model and the one that follows by applying them to one or more of the scenarios in Case Study 10.3 at the end of the chapter.)

University of Louisiana professors J. Brooke Hamilton, Stephen B. Knouse, and Vanessa Hill offer an alternative strategy for resolving cross-cultural ethical conflicts, one specifically designed for use in multinational enterprises (MNEs).[47] They provide six questions (the HKH model) to guide managers in determining whether to follow the values of their firms or to adopt the practices of the host country instead. Decision makers don't have to completely answer one question before moving onto the next. Instead, they can move ahead, returning to reconsider earlier questions as needed in order to clarify the final course of action.

1. *What is the Questionable Practice (QP) in this situation?* The first question identifies the nature of the problem, which may or may not have an ethical component. To qualify as an ethical conflict, the norms and values of the host country and the business must clash. A firm then has to determine whether to comply with local customs or to follow its own standards, which may mean leaving the host country.

2. *Does the Questionable Practice violate any laws that are enforced?* Managers need to determine if the contested practice violates either the laws of their home country or the country where they are doing business. For example, the Foreign Corrupt Practices Act prevents U.S. firms from offering bribes anywhere in the world. Refusing to support government Internet censorship violates Chinese law.

3. *Is the QP simply a cultural difference, or is it also a potential ethics problem?* A questionable practice qualifies as an ethical issue if it seems to cause harm or violates widely accepted ethical principles like justice or human rights. For example, offering small gifts to show respect is standard business procedure in much of Asia. Gift giving doesn't become an ethical issue unless significant sums are offered to bribe recipients at the expense of other parties.

4. *Does the QP violate the firm's core values or code of conduct, an industrywide or international code to which the firm subscribes, or a firmly established hypernorm?* The answer to this question may differ based on whether a company is interested only in complying with the law or is also interested in living up to its values. For a compliance-only company, an action is ethical as long as it is legal. Managers are interested only in avoiding punishment or harm to the company. Corporations seeking both to comply with the law and to live out their values (compliance/integrity firms) follow a higher standard. They recognize that the law doesn't condemn all forms of unethical behavior, and at the same time, they empower their employees to base their decisions on core values. For example, workers at Motorola are encouraged to follow the firm's guidelines, called "Uncompromising Integrity and Constant Respect for People." Organizational decision makers can also base their choices on the widely accepted moral standards described earlier in the chapter.

5. *Does the firm have leverage (something of value to offer) in the host country that allows the firm to follow its own practices rather than the QP?* Companies with leverage have greater freedom to follow their own standards or to adapt their practices in a way that doesn't violate their central principles. Leverage comes from contributing to the local economy, offering jobs, supplying currency that can be used for international trade, providing training, purchasing local goods and services, transferring technology to the regional economy, and having an ethical reputation. McDonald's used its leverage to operate in Moscow without engaging in bribery and other forms of corruption endemic to the Russian economy. Of course, compliance-only companies don't have to worry about using leverage, since they automatically follow local regulations.

6. *Will market practices in the host country improve if the firm follows its own practices rather than the QP in the host country marketplace?* This question should be

considered only after determining the amount of leverage held by the firm. If the company has significant leverage, it has a responsibility to try to change prevailing practices by refusing to engage in the Questionable Practice. Improving the way business is done (by not offering bribes, for example) may encourage local firms to follow suit, and local residents will benefit as a result.

CHAPTER TAKEAWAYS

- Encourage your organization to act as a responsible citizen that acknowledges its obligations to outside communities, develops processes for anticipating and responding to societal pressures, and backs up its convictions with concrete actions. Make sustainability—doing business in a way that preserves the natural environment while creating long-lasting economic and social value—an important organizational objective.
- Determining your organization's stage of citizenship development can help you identify challenges and set objectives. Elementary organizations, which are at the lowest stage of development, don't understand corporate citizenship. Engaged organizations adopt social responsibility policies. Innovative organizations develop creative ways to improve and measure social performance. Integrated organizations incorporate citizenship into every operation. Transformative companies make citizenship central to their missions and reputations.
- Organizational citizenship rests largely on a commitment to stewardship. As an employee or manager, seek to meet the interests of the organization, followers, and external groups rather than your own needs.
- Your organization has a moral obligation to respond to groups affected by its policies and operations. Engage in stakeholder management by responding to five questions: (1) Who are our stakeholders? (2) What are our stakeholders' stakes? (3) What opportunities and challenges do our stakeholders present? (4) What responsibilities does the firm have to its stakeholders? (5) What strategies or actions should management take to best handle stakeholder challenges and opportunities?
- Whenever possible, seek to create value for all stakeholders, engaging in dialogue with supporters and critics alike. Track the progress of moral issues that might impact your organization.
- Recognize the dangers of globalization, which include the growing gap between the world's rich and poor, greed, the concentration of economic power in large corporations, and the destruction of local environments and cultures.
- Ethical diversity will make it more difficult for your organization to act as a responsible global citizen.
- Overcome ethnocentrism—the tendency to see the world from your cultural group's point of view—through dialogue, mindfulness, adoption of a pluralistic perspective, and the practice of personal virtues that promote global cooperation.
- Understanding the values that ethnic groups and nations hold in common helps explain ethical differences and better equips you to predict how members of other societies will respond to moral dilemmas. Common values orientations include power distance, individualism versus collectivism, masculinity versus femininity, uncertainty avoidance, performance orientation, future orientation, assertiveness, and humane orientation.
- Ethical differences between cultures can also be explained by the emphasis that various groups place on one or more of the following: harm/care, fairness/reciprocity, in-group/loyalty, authority/respect, purity/sanctity.
- Resist the temptation to practice cultural relativism. Instead, look for ethical common ground, found in such universal principles as the U.N. Universal Declaration of Human Rights, the eight global values, the Global Business Standards Codex, and the Caux Principles for Business.

- When making ethical decisions in global settings, balance universal principles with the need to honor local laws and values. Keep three key decision-making guidelines in mind: (1) local customs must conform to global standards or hypernorms; (2) give priority to the authentic, legitimate norms of the host country; (3) whenever possible, give more weight to norms generated by larger communities. In cases involving conflicts between your company's norms and those of the host country (questionable practices), empower employees to decide based on corporate values, and look for ways to leverage your firm's influence to change local business practices.

APPLICATION PROJECTS

1. In a group, identify the important stakeholders of your college or university. What ethical responsibilities does your institution have to each group?

2. How can you encourage you and your organization to adopt a stewardship mind-set?

3. Select an organization, and identify its stage of citizenship development. Explain your rating.

4. Identify the ethical issue that could pose a greatest challenge to your college or university or employer based on the Self-Assessment. Share your conclusions in a small group.

5. Select a culture, and write an analysis using the Hofstede and GLOBE dimensions. Determine how the culture rates on each dimension, and determine how this cultural profile shapes the ethical attitudes and behaviors of citizens. Write up your findings.

6. Is there a common morality that peoples of all nations can share? Which of the global codes described in the chapter best reflects these shared standards and values? If you were to create your own declaration of global ethics, what would you put in it?

7. Develop a case study based on the conflict between the ethical norms of different countries. Identify the values patterns that are contributing to this dilemma. Resolve the conflict using the guidelines provided by integrated social contracts theory or the HKH (questionable practices) model.

8. Select one of the diversity scenarios in Case Study 12.3, and reach a conclusion based on concepts presented in the chapter.

CASE STUDY 12.2

Nike Becomes a Global Citizen

In 1962, Stanford University student Phil Knight came up with the idea to create one of the world's first "virtual companies," a manufacturing firm with no physical assets. According to Knight's business plan, the company would cut costs by outsourcing all manufacturing and then pour the savings into marketing. Knight followed this formula to make Nike into the dominant athletic apparel manufacturer with an internationally recognized brand name.

Key to Nike's growth was the aggressive pursuit of low-cost labor. When labor costs began to rise, Nike urged its suppliers to move to lower-cost regions. The firm's first contracts were with Japanese manufacturers but then migrated to South Korea and Taiwan as production expenses increased. When costs in these nations soared, Nike contracted with facilities in China and Indonesia.

By the early 1990s, critics began to take note of conditions at Nike's suppliers. They documented inadequate pay (sometimes below legal minimums), dangerous working conditions, sexual harassment and physical abuse by supervisors, forced overtime, and the hiring of underage workers. The high-profile company made a tempting target for the Asian-American Free Labor Association and other human rights groups.

At first, Nike denied that it had any responsibility for conditions in its contractors' factories. One Nike manager responded to criticism in 1991 by claiming, "It's not within our scope to investigate. . . . I don't know that I need to know."[1] Pressure on the firm continued to increase, however. In 1992, *Harper's* magazine published a pay stub from an Indonesian factory, comparing workers' wages and Michael Jordan's Nike endorsement contract. It would have taken the average Indonesian worker 44,492 years to make what Jordan earned by promoting the company's sneakers. Later, CBS interviewed Indonesian workers who were paid 19 cents an hour and found that female employees could leave the company barracks only on Sunday afternoons with a special letter of permission from management. In 1996, *Life* magazine published a photo of a 12-year-old Pakistani boy stitching a Nike soccer ball.

Nike abandoned its hands-off policy in response to public criticism and began to address working conditions at its suppliers. The firm drafted a set of standards, hired Ernst & Young to conduct formal audits of overseas factories, sent former ambassador Andrew Young overseas to evaluate its code of conduct, and established a labor practices department. Activists and the public were skeptical about these efforts. In particular, they questioned the validity of the audits, which were sponsored by Nike. These evaluations were poorly designed and ignored key issues like factory wages.

The year 1998 was a watershed year for Nike. The company's earnings dropped dramatically due to changing tastes and anti-Nike campaigns. Knight announced a series of reforms, including (1) raising the minimum age of all sneaker workers to 18 and apparel employees to 16, (2) implementing OSHA (Occupational Safety and Health Administration) clean air standards in all of its factories, (3) expanding educational programs for workers, and (4) making micro loans to employees. Nike then helped create an oversight organization with other apparel groups (the Fair Labor Association), and Knight was the only U.S. CEO present at the formation of the U.N. Global Compact.

By 2004, Nike had made significant progress in its transition from corporate pariah to a socially responsible industry leader. That year, representatives from the human rights, international labor development, and environmental communities (often highly critical of the "swoosh" brand) gathered at the company's headquarters to discuss issues facing international workers. Nike's 2004 corporate responsibility report contained the names and addresses of 705 contract factories operating in 50 countries, along with audit results. This marked the first time that any major U.S. apparel company had released such details to the public.

Nike's experience since 2004 illustrates the difficulties the firm faces as a global citizen. After examining Nike's factory audit data, Richard Locke of MIT's Sloan School of Management found that, despite "significant efforts and investment by Nike . . . workplace conditions in almost 80% of its suppliers have either remained the same or worsened over time."[2] The problems seem to be greater in apparel factories than at shoe factories because Nike deals with many more apparel contractors on a short-term basis. Nike isn't about to give up its efforts to act responsibly, however. It is trying to convert suppliers from assembly lines to multitasking teams. Such a move would require that subcontractors provide more training and treat skilled workers better in order to retain them. Company managers are also trying to cut down last-minute design modifications and order changes, which result in greater demands for factory overtime. At the same time, Nike is adopting more sustainable manufacturing processes. The firm is considered a leader among top consumer brands in addressing climate change. Current shoe models produce 17% less waste and use 20% more green materials than previous models.

Discussion Probes

1. Does Nike's business model, which outsources shoe and apparel clothing manufacturing overseas, invite ethical abuses? Should it be abandoned as a result?

2. Why do you think Nike was so resistant at first to taking responsibility for working conditions at its factories?

3. Do you think Nike would have changed its policy towards its international workers if it hadn't suffered significant financial losses in 1998?

4. What risks did Nike take in meeting with its critics? In releasing the names and addresses of its overseas suppliers? Were these risks justified?

5. Do you think other apparel companies should follow Nike's lead and release details about their overseas manufacturing sites? Why or why not?

6. What additional steps can Nike take to increase the number of plants meeting its responsibility standards?

Notes

1. Paine, L. S. (2003). *Value shift: Why companies must merge social and financial imperatives to achieve superior performance.* New York: McGraw-Hill.
2. Levenson, E. (2008, November 24). Citizen Nike. *Fortune,* pp. 165–170.

Sources

Green, H. (2008, December 12). The greening of the corporation. *BusinessWeek Online,* p. 10.

Phatak, A. V., Bhagat, R. S., & Kashlak, R. J. (2005). *International management: Managing in a diverse and dynamic global environment.* Boston: McGraw-Hill Irwin, pp. 543–561.

Rafter, M. V. (2005, May). Nike opens a window on overseas factories. *Workforce Management, 84,* 17.

Ritson, M. (2005, April 20). Nike shows way to return from the wilderness. *Marketing* (UK), p. 21.

Zadek, S. (2004, December). The path to corporate responsibility. *Harvard Business Review,* pp. 125–132.

CASE STUDY 12.3

Scenarios for Analysis

The Penguin Project

Recently, Dai Schmidt was appointed general manager of the Chilean subsidiary of a large German-based conglomerate. When he assumed his position, Schmidt inherited responsibility for an aging canning factory. Rather than shut the plant down, the young manager came up with the Penguin Project to save the facility. If the plan succeeds, Schmidt will stay on track for future promotions. He believes that the aging plant could once again operate profitably if it were refurbished and began to process the meat and skins of Jackass Penguins. The meat would be shipped to another division of the company to be used in pet food, and the skins would be used locally for use in handbags and footwear. An estimated 100–250 million Jackass Penguins (which bray like donkeys when disturbed) live on the on the southern tip of South America and islands of Antarctica. Local fishermen blame the expanding penguin population for decimating the fish population and putting their livelihoods at risk. Experts believe that 100,000 birds could be killed and processed at the plant every week without damaging the overall penguin population. Jobs are scarce in southern Chile, and area residents support the penguin plan, which would keep 100 people working.

There is one serious drawback to the proposal. The conglomerate has recently been criticized for its poor performance on environmental issues, including waste disposal in Europe and a major chemical spill in Australia.

Schmidt believes that his supervisor in Germany will follow any recommendation he makes. *Should he recommend that the Penguin Project go forward?*

SOURCE: Condensed from: Roberts, K. E. (2001). Case: Anglo-German trading corporation. In M. H. Albrecht (Ed.), *International HRM: Managing diversity in the workplace* (pp. 360–361). Malden, MA: Blackwell.

Layoffs in Saudi Arabia

You're a British consultant sent to Saudi Arabia to have a look at a new joint venture your company has taken a stake in—a family-run, light manufacturing firm with 400 employees. You look at the books and mention that you think the workforce is terribly bloated. Output and revenue per employee are below average. You suggest laying off up to 20% of the workforce. The Saudi owners look at you in horror, saying that layoffs are downright unethical and that there is more to business than maximizing profits. You are equally horrified.

What will you do?

SOURCE: Mitchell, C. (2003). *International business ethics: Combining ethics and profits in global business.* Novato, CA: World Trade Press, p. 162.

The Warlord Tax*

You are the CEO of a small international relief agency. Your group's policy is never to pay bribes in any of the countries in which you operate, no matter how corrupt. The policy has not seriously hampered your operations until now. Severe famine has struck in the Horn of Africa, in an area controlled by armed warlords. In order for food to reach the 100,000 starving residents of the region, you must pay a "tax" to the local military commander in the form of money or foodstuffs. This "tax" is clearly a form of extortion and violates your anti-bribery policy and possibly U.S. law. Other international relief agencies pay the tax, so you know that food shipments won't be completely cut off if your organization decides to pull out of the area. On the other hand, stopping shipments would significantly reduce food supplies to the region and could contribute to malnutrition and starvation.

Will you pay the warlord tax and continue the food shipments?

*Loosely based on actual events.

Supporting Internet Censorship*

Your U.S. company supplies networking hardware for the Internet and operates in the United States and Europe. However, your executive team is anxious to expand into the Chinese Internet market, which is the largest and potentially most lucrative in the world. You have been assigned to lead this effort. Your preliminary research indicates that your firm could generate significant sales and profits in China. However, you know that your products will make it easier for the Chinese government to censor Internet activity and to locate and jail those accused of criticizing the government, supporting Tibetan independence, and other "subversive" activities. Members of Congress and human rights groups have been critical of Google, Yahoo!, Cisco, MSN, and other American companies that have participated in the communist government's censorship program.

Should your company enter the Chinese market?

*Loosely based on actual events.

ENDNOTES

1. Carroll, A. B., & Buchholtz, A. K. (2009). *Business and society: Ethics and stakeholder management* (7th ed.). Mason, OH: South-Western; Kottler, P., & Lee, N. (2005). *Corporate social responsibility.* Hoboken, NJ: John Wiley; Mirvis, P., & Googins, B. (2006). Stages of corporate citizenship. *California Management Review, 48,* 104–126; Neff, J. (2009, April 20). Green-marketing revolution defies economic downturn. *Advertising Age.*

2. Carroll & Buchholtz (2009); Carroll, A. B. (1979). A three-dimensional conceptual model of corporate performance. *Academy of Management Review, 4,* 497–508.

3. Wheeler, D., Colbert, B., & Freeman, R. E. (2003). Focusing on value: Reconciling corporate social responsibility, sustainability and a stakeholder approach in a network world. *Journal of General Management, 28,* 1–28.

4. Hart, S. L. (1997, January/February). Beyond greening: Strategies for a sustainable world. *Harvard Business Review,* pp. 66–76.

5. Mirvis & Googins.

6. Davis, J. H., Schoorman, F. D., & Donaldson, L. (1997). Toward a stewardship theory of management. *Academy of Management Review, 22,* 20–47; Yankelovich, D. (2006). *Profit with honor: The new stage of market capitalism.* New Haven, CT: Yale University Press.

7. Caldwell, C., & Karri, R. (2005). Organizational governance and ethical systems: A covenantal approach to building trust. *Journal of Business Ethics, 58,* 249–259; Caldwell, C., Bishchoff, S. J., & Karri, R. (2002). The four umpires: A paradigm for ethical leadership. *Journal of Business Ethics, 36,* 153–163; Barnett, T., & Schubert, E. (2002). Perceptions of the ethical work climate and covenantal relationships. *Journal of Business Ethics, 36,* 279–290.

8. Phillips, R. (2003). *Stakeholder theory and organizational ethics.* San Francisco: Berrett-Koehler.

9. See, for example: Freeman, E. (1984). *Strategic management.* Marshfield, MA: Pitman; Freeman, R. E. (1994). The politics of stakeholder theory: Some future directions. *Business Ethics Quarterly, 4,* 409–421; Freeman, R. E. (1995). Stakeholder thinking: The state of the art. In J. Nasi (Ed.), *Understanding stakeholder thinking* (pp. 35–73). Helsinki, Finland: LSR-Julkaisut Oy; Sims, R. R. (2003). *Ethics and corporate social responsibility: Why giants fall.* Westport, CT: Praeger; Agle, B. R., Donaldson, T., Freeman, R. E., Jensen, M. C., Mitchell, R. K., & Wood, D. J. (2008). Dialogue: Toward superior stakeholder theory. *Business Ethics Quarterly, 18,* 153–190; Laplume, A. O., Sonpar, K., & Litz, R. A. (2008). Stakeholder theory: Reviewing a theory that moves us. *Journal of Management 34*(6), 1152–1189.

10. Frederick, W. C. (1992). *Social issues in management: Coming of age or prematurely gray?* Paper presented at the Academy of Management annual meeting, Las Vegas, NV, p. 5.

11. Donaldson, T., & Preston, L. E. (1995). The stakeholder theory of the corporation: Concepts, evidence, and implications. *Academy of Management Review, 20,* 65–91; Cooper, S. (2004). *Corporate social performance: A stakeholder approach.* Burlington, VT: Ashgate; Goodpaster, K. E. (1991). Business ethics and

stakeholder analysis. *Business Ethics Quarterly, 1,* 53–72; Gibson, K. (2000). The moral basis of stakeholder theory. *Journal of Business Ethics 26,* 245–257.

12. Freeman (1994); Phillips (2003).

13. Buchholz, R. A., & Rosenthal, S. B. (2005). Toward a conceptual framework for stakeholder theory. *Journal of Business Ethics, 58,* 137–148.

14. Argandona, A. (1998). The stakeholder theory and the common good. *Journal of Business Ethics, 17,* 1093–1102.

15. Carroll & Buchholz (2009).

16. Carroll & Buchholz (2009).

17. Freeman, R. E., Harrison, J. S., & Wicks, A. C. (2007). *Managing for stakeholders: Survival, reputation, and success.* New Haven, CT: Yale University Press.

18. Carroll & Buchholz (2009).

19. Guth, D. W., & Marsh, C. (2006). *Public relations: A values-driven approach* (3rd ed.). Boston: Pearson; Heath, R. L. (1997). *Strategic issues management: Organizations and public policy challenges.* Thousand Oaks, CA: Sage; Seitel, F. P. (1997). *The practice of public relations* (7th ed.). Upper Saddle River, NJ: Prentice Hall.

20. Singer, P. (2002). *One world: The ethics of globalization.* New Haven, CT: Yale University Press; Lacey, M. (2003, September 10). Africans' burden: West's farm subsidies. *The New York Times,* p. A9; Muzaffar, C. (2002). Conclusion. In P. F. Knitter & C. Muzaffar (Eds.), *Subverting greed: Religious perspectives on the global economy* (pp. 154–172). Maryknoll, NY: Orbis Books; Harvesting poverty: Inching toward trade fairness [Editorial]. (2003, August 15). *The New York Times,* p. A28; Newton, L. H. (2005). *Business ethics and the natural environment.* Malden, MA: Blackwell.

21. Singer (2002).

22. Robinson, M. (2000). Internalizing human rights in corporate business practices. *UN Chronicle, 37,* 38–39.

23. Nielsen, S. (2003, November 2). At Wal-Mart, a world power runs the sale bins. *The Oregonian,* pp. E1–E2.

24. Examples of ethical diversity taken from: Mitchell, C. (2003). *A short course in international business ethics: Combining ethics and profits in global business.* Novato, CA: World Trade Press; Carroll, S. J., & Gannon, M. J. (1997). *Ethical dimensions of international management.* Thousand Oaks, CA: Sage.

25. Gudykunst, W. B., & Kim, Y. Y. (1997). *Communicating with strangers: An approach to intercultural communication* (3rd ed.). New York: McGraw-Hill.

26. Novak, M. (2003). A universal culture of human rights and freedom's habits: Caritapolis. In J. H. Dunning (Ed.), *Making globalization good: The moral challenges of global capitalism* (pp. 253–279). Oxford, UK: Oxford University Press.

27. Hofstede, G. (1984). *Culture's consequences.* Beverly Hills, CA: Sage; Hofstede, G. (1991). *Cultures and organizations: Software of the mind.* London: McGraw-Hill.

28. Hofstede, G. (2001). Difference and danger: Cultural profiles of nations and limits to tolerance. In M. H. Albrecht (Ed.), *International HRM: Managing diversity in the workplace* (pp. 9–23). Oxford, UK: Blackwell.

29. Husted, B. W. (1999). Wealth, culture and corruption. *Journal of International Business Studies, 30,* 339–359; Vitell, S. J., Nwachukwu, S. L., & Barnes, J. H. (1993). *Journal of Business Ethics, 12*(10), 753–760; Davis, J. H., & Ruhe, J. A. (2003). Perceptions of country corruption: Antecedents and outcomes. *Journal of Business Ethics, 43,* 275–288; Franke, G. P., & Nadler, S. S. (2007). Culture, economic development, and national ethical attitudes. *Journal of Business Research, 61,* 254–264; Williams, G., & Zinkin, J. (2008). The effect of culture on consumers' willingness to punish irresponsible corporate behaviour: Applying Hofstede's typology to the punishment aspect of corporate social responsibility. *Business Ethics: A European Review, 17,* 210–226.

30. Carroll & Gannon.

31. Javidan, M., & House, R. J. (2001). Cultural acumen for the global manager: Lessons from Project GLOBE. *Organizational Dynamics, 29,* 289–305; House, R. J., Hanges, P. J., Javidan, M., Dorfman, P. W., & Gupta, V. (Eds.). (2004). *Culture, leadership, and organizations: The GLOBE study of 62 societies.* Thousand Oaks, CA: Sage.

32. House et al., p. 239.

33. Quigley, N. R., Sully de Luque, M., & House, R. J. (2005). Responsible leadership and governance in a global context: Insights from the GLOBE study. In J. P. Doh & S. A. Stumpf (Eds.), *Handbook on responsible leadership and governance in global business* (pp. 352–379). Cheltenham, UK: Edward Elgar.

34. Haidt, J., & Bjorklund, F. (2008). Social intuitionists answer six questions about moral psychology. In W. Sinnott-Armstrong (Ed.), *Moral psychology. Vol. 2: The cognitive science of morality: Intuition and diversity* (pp. 182–217). Cambridge, MA: MIT Press; Haidt, J., & Graham, J. (2007). When morality opposes justice: Conservatives have moral intuitions that liberals may not recognize. *Social Justice Research, 20,* 98–116.

35. Jacobs, T. (2009, May). Morals authority. *Miller-McCune,* pp. 47–55.

36. Hauser, M. D. (2006). *Moral minds: How nature designed our universal sense of right and wrong.* New York: HarperCollins; Hauser, M. D., Young, L., & Cushman, F. (2008). Reviving Rawls's linguistic analogy: Operative principles and the causal structure of moral actions. In W. Sinnott-Armstrong (Ed.), *Moral psychology. Vol. 2: The cognitive science of morality: Intuition and diversity.* Cambridge, MA: MIT.

37. Humphrey, J. (1989). *No distant millennium: The international law of human rights.* Paris: UNESCO; Donnelly, J. (1989). *Universal human rights in theory and practice.* Ithaca, NY: Cornell University Press.

38. Mares, R. (Ed.). (2004). *Business and human rights: A compilation of documents.* Leiden, the Netherlands: Martinus Nijhoff, pp. 2–7.

39. Engardio, P. (2004, July 12). Global Compact, little impact. *BusinessWeek,* pp. 86–87; Engardio, P. (2004, July 20). Two views of the Global Compact. *BusinessWeek Online;* United Nations Global Compact: Participants and stakeholders. Retrieved from www.unglobalcompact.org/ParticipantsAndStakeholders/index.html

40. Kidder, R. M. (1994). *Shared values for a troubled world: Conversations with men and women of conscience.* San Francisco: Jossey-Bass; Kidder, R. M. (1994, July-August). Universal values: Finding an ethical common ground. *The Futurist,* pp. 8–13.

41. Kidder (1994, July-August), pp. 8–11.

42. Kidder (1994), p. 312.

43. Paine, L. S., Deshpande, R., Margolis, J. D., & Bettcher, K. E. (2005, December). Up to code. *Harvard Business Review,* pp. 122–133.

44. Caux Round Table. (2004). The Caux Round Table Principles for Business, 1994. In R. Mares (Ed.), *Business and human rights: A compilation of documents* (pp. 288–292). Leiden, the Netherlands: Brill; Caux Round Table. (2000). Appendix 26: The Caux Principles (pp. 384–388). In O. F. Williams, *Global codes of conduct: An idea whose time has come.* Notre Dame, IN: Notre Dame University Press.

45. Caux Round Table: Principles for business. (2010). Retrieved from http://www.cauxroundtable.org; Caux Round Table (2000), pp. 384–388.

46. Donaldson, T., & Dunfee, T. W. (1994). Toward a unified conception of business ethics: Integrative social contracts theory. *Academy of Management Review, 19,* 252–284; Donaldson, T., & Dunfee, T. W. (1999). *Ties that bind: A social contracts approach to business ethics.* Boston: Harvard Business School Press; Dunfee, T. W., & Donaldson, T. (1999). Social contract approaches to business ethics: Bridging the "is-ought" gap. In R. E. Frederick (Ed.), *A companion to business ethics* (pp. 38–52). Malden, MA: Blackwell.

47. Hamilton, J. B., Knouse, S. B., & Hill, V. (2009). Google in China: A manager-friendly heuristic model for resolving cross-cultural ethical conflicts. *Journal of Business Ethics, 86,* 143–157; Hamilton, J. B., & Knouse, S. B. (2001). Multinational enterprise decision principles for dealing with cross cultural ethical conflicts. *Journal of Business Ethics, 31,* 77–94.

References

Abate, T. (2009, January 6). High tech icon breaks silence of his health. *San Francisco Chronicle*, p. A1.

Abdolmohammadi, M. J., Read, W. J., & Scarbrough, D. P. (2003). Does selection-socialization help to explain accountants' weak ethical reasoning? *Business Ethics, 42*, 71–81.

Abrahams, J. (1999). *The mission statement book: 301 corporate mission statements from America's top companies.* Berkeley, CA: Ten Speed Press.

Adams, C. A., & Evans, R. (2004). Accountability, completeness, credibility and the audit expectations gap. *Journal of Corporate Citizenship, 14*, 97–115.

Adams, G. B., & Balfour, D. L. (1998). *Unmasking administrative evil.* Thousand Oaks, CA: Sage.

Adams, J. S., Tashchian, A., & Shore, T. H. (2001). Codes of ethics as signals for ethical behavior. *Journal of Business Ethics, 29*, 199–211.

Adams, W. L. (2010, May 10). Postcard: Halden. A look inside the world's most humane prison, *Time*, p. 14.

Adler, A., Underwood, A., Scelfo, J., Juarez, V., Johnson, D., Shenfeld, H., . . . Raymond, J. (2004, December 20). Toxic strength. *Newsweek*, pp. 44–52.

Agle, B. R., Donaldson, T., Freeman, R. E., Jensen, M. C., Mitchell, R. K., & Wood, D. J. (2008). Dialogue: Toward superior stakeholder theory. *Business Ethics Quarterly, 18*, 153–190.

Albrecht, T. L., & Bach, B. W. (1997). *Communication in complex organizations: A relational approach.* Fort Worth, TX: Harcourt Brace.

Alnuaimi, O. A., Robert, L. P., & Maruping, L. M. (2010). Team size, dispersion, and social loafing in technology-supported teams: A perspective on the theory of moral disengagement. *Journal of Management Information Systems, 27*(10), 203–230.

Amason, A. C. (1996). Distinguishing the effects of functional and dysfunctional conflict on strategic decision-making: Resolving a paradox for top management teams. *Academy of Management Journal, 39*(1), 123–148.

Amichai-Hamburger, Y. (2003). Understanding social loafing. In A. Sagie, S. Stashevsky, & M. Koslowsky (Eds.), *Misbehaviour and dysfunctional attitudes in organizations* (pp. 79–102). New York: Palgrave Macmillan.

Anand, V., Ashforth, B. E., & Joshi, M. (2004). Business as usual: The acceptance and perpetuation of corruption in organizations. *Academy of Management Executive, 18*, 39–53.

Anderson, J. (2010, August 2). Californians wonder how city officials got high pay. *The Washington Times*, p. A1.

Andersson, L. M., & Pearson, C. M. (1999). Tit for tat? The spiraling effect of incivility in the workplace. *Academy of Management Review, 24*, 452–471.

Andreoli, N., & Lefkowitz, J. (2008). Individual and organizational antecedents of misconduct in organizations. *Journal of Business Ethics, 85*, 309–332.

Apple CEO's prognosis 'excellent' surgeon says. *The Toronto Star*, p. B01.

Appleyard, B. (2009, August 16). The god of cool things. *The Sunday Times*, Magazine, pp. 40ff.

Aquino, K. (1998). The effects of ethical climate and the availability of alternatives on the use of deception during negotiation. *International Journal of Conflict Management, 9*, 195–217.

Archibold, R. C. (2010, January 14). Sweat lodge deaths not criminal, Guru's lawyer says. *The New York Times,* p. A22.

Archibold, R. C., & Berger, J. (2010, February 5). Sweat lodge leader is indicted in deaths. *The New York Times on the Web.*

Arens Bates, C., Bowes-Sperry, L., & O'Leary-Kelly, A. M. (2008). Sexual harassment in the workplace: A look back and a look ahead. In E. K. Kelloway, J. Barling, & J. J. Hurrell (Eds.), *Handbook of workplace violence* (pp. 381–415). Thousand Oaks, CA: Sage.

Argandona, A. (1998). The stakeholder theory and the common good. *Journal of Business Ethics, 17,* 1093–1102.

Argandona, A. (2003). Fostering values in organizations. *Journal of Business Ethics, 45,* 15–28.

Aristotle. (1962). *Nicomachean ethics* (Martin Ostwald, Trans.). Indianapolis, IN: Bobbs Merrill. (Original work published 350 B.C.E.)

Armour, S. (2005, June 15). Warning: Your clever little blog could get you fired. *USA Today,* p. 1B.

Arnett, R. C. (1986). *Communication and community: Implications of Martin Buber's dialogue.* Carbondale: Southern Illinois University Press.

Arnett, R. C., & Arneson, P. (1999). *Dialogic civility in a cynical age: Community, hope, and interpersonal relationships.* Albany: State University of New York Press.

Ashmos, D. P., & Duchon, D. (2000). Spirituality at work: A conceptualization and measure. *Journal of Management Inquiry, 9,* 134–145.

Associated Press. (2010, July 23). Pay czar will not fight banks over $1.6 billion in executive pay. *The Oregonian.*

Avolio, B. J. (1999). *Full leadership development: Building vital forces in organizations.* Thousand Oaks, CA: Sage.

Avolio, B. J., & Gardner, W. L. (2005). Authentic leadership development: Getting to the root of positive forms of leadership. *The Leadership Quarterly, 16,* 315–340.

Avolio, B. J., Gardner, W. L., Walumbwa, F. O., Luthans, F., & May, D. R. (2004). Unlocking the mask: A look at the process by which authentic leaders impact follower attitudes and behaviors. *The Leadership Quarterly, 15,* 801–823.

Avolio, B. J., & Luthans, F. (2006). *The high impact leader: Moments matter in accelerating authentic leadership development.* New York: McGraw-Hill.

Avolio, B. J., & Reichard, R. J. (2008). The rise of authentic followership. In R. E. Riggio, I. Chaleff, & J. Lipman-Blumen (Eds.), *The art of followership: How great followers create great leaders and organizations* (pp. 325–338). San Francisco: Jossey Bass.

Badger, T. A. (2005, May 3). Soldier says peers pressed for abuse. *The Oregonian,* pp. A1, A3.

Baker, S. (1997). Applying Kidder's ethical decision-making checklist to media ethics. *Journal of Mass Media Ethics, 12*(4), 197–210.

Baird, J. (2009, October 19). We are all getting lucky: But we are not all the boss. *Newsweek,* p. 26.

Banaji, M. R., Bazerman, M. H., & Clugh, D. (2003, December). How (un)ethical are you? *Harvard Business Review,* pp. 56–64.

Bandura, A. (1977). Self-efficacy: Toward a unifying theory of behavioral change. *Psychological Review, 84,* 191–215.

Bandura, A. (1999). Moral disengagement in the perpetration of inhumanities. *Personality and Social Psychology Review, 3,* 193–209.

Bardi, A., & Schwartz, S. H. (2003). Values and behavior: Strength and structure of relations. *Journal of Personality and Social Psychology, 29,* 1207–1220.

Barker, J. R. (1993). Tightening the iron cage: Concertive control in self-managing teams. *Administrative Science Quarterly, 38,* 408–437.

Barker, J. R. (1999). *The discipline of teamwork: Participation and concertive control.* Thousand Oaks, CA: Sage.

Barker, L., & Watson, K. (2000). *Listen up: How to improve relationships, reduce stress, and be more productive by using the power of listening.* New York: St. Martin's Press.

Barling, J. (1996). The prediction, experience, and consequences of workplace violence. In G. R. VandenBos & E. Q. Bulato (Eds.), *Violence on the job: Identifying risks and developing solutions* (pp. 29–49). Washington, DC: American Psychological Association.

Barnett, T., & Schubert, E. (2002). Perceptions of the ethical work climate and covenantal relationships. *Journal of Business Ethics, 36,* 279–290.

Baron, R. A. (2004). Workplace aggression and violence: Insights from basic research. In R. W. Griffin & A. M. O'Leary-Kelly (Eds.), *The dark side of organizational behavior* (pp. 23–61). San Francisco: Jossey-Bass.

Barry, J., Hirsh, M., & Isikoff, M. (2004, May 24). The roots of torture. *Newsweek,* pp. 26–34.

Barry, V. (1978). *Personal and social ethics: Moral problems with integrated theory.* Belmont, CA: Wadsworth.

Barth, S. R. (2003). *Corporate ethics: The business code of conduct for ethical employees.* Boston: Aspatore Books.

Bass, B. (1990). *Bass and Stogdill's handbook of leadership* (3rd ed.). New York: Free Press.

Bass, B. M. (1995). The ethics of transformational leadership. In J. Ciulla (Ed.), *Ethics: The heart of leadership* (pp. 169–192). Westport, CT: Praeger.

Bass, B. M. (1996). *A new paradigm of leadership: An inquiry into transformational leadership.* Alexandria, VA: Army Research Institute for the Behavioral and Social Sciences.

Bass, B. M., Avolio, B. J., Jung, D. I., & Berson, Y. (2003). Predicting unit performance by assessing transformational and transactional leadership. *Journal of Applied Psychology, 88,* 207–218.

Bass, B. M., & Steidlmeier, P. (1999). Ethics, character, and authentic transformational leadership behavior. *The Leadership Quarterly, 10,* 181–227.

Batson, C. D., Collins, E., & Powell, A. A. (2006). Doing business after the fall: The virtue of moral hypocrisy. *Journal of Business Ethics, 66,* 321–335.

Batson, C. D., & Thompson, E. R. (2001). Why don't people act morally: Motivational considerations. *Current Directions in Psychological Science, 10,* 54–57.

Batson, C. D., Thompson, E. R., & Chen, H. (2002). Moral hypocrisy: Addressing some alternatives. *Journal of Personality and Social Psychology, 83,* 330–339.

Batson, C. D., Thompson, E. R., Seuferling, G., Whitney, H., & Strongman, J. A. (1999). Moral hypocrisy: Appearing moral to oneself without being so. *Journal of Personality and Social Psychology, 77*(3), 525–537.

Batson, C. D., Van Lange, P. A. M., Ahmad, N., & Lishner, D. A. (2003). Altruism and helping behavior. In M. A. Hogg & J. Cooper (Eds.), *The Sage handbook of social psychology* (pp. 279–295). London: Sage.

Bazerman, M. H., Chugh, D., & Banaji, M. R. (2005, October). When good people (seem to) negotiate in bad faith. *Negotiation, 8,* pp. 3–5.

Becker, J. A. H., & O'Hair, H. D. (2007). Machiavellians' motives in organizational citizenship behavior. *Journal of Applied Communication Research, 35,* 246–267.

Beckford, M. (2010, December 6). Arrest warrant for website's founder 'a political stunt.' *The Daily Telegraph,* News, p. 18.

Beets, S. D. (2006). The vanishing AICPA code: Past, present, and future significance. In J. E. Ketz (Ed.), *Accounting ethics: Critical perspectives on business and management* (Vol. 1, pp. 270–306). London: Routledge.

Belknap, M. R. (2002). *The Viet Nam War on trial: The My Lai Massacre and the court-martial of Lieutenant Calley.* Lawrence: University of Kansas Press.

Benefiel, M. (2005). The second half of the journey: Spiritual leadership for organizational transformation. *The Leadership Quarterly, 16,* 723–747.

Benefiel, M. (2005). *Soul at work: Spiritual leadership in organizations.* New York: Seabury Books.

Bennett, R. J. (1998). Perceived powerlessness as a cause of employee deviance. In R. W. Griffin, A. O'Leary-Kelly, & J. M. Collins (Eds.), *Dysfunctional behavior in organizations: Violent and deviant behavior* (pp. 221–239). Stamford, CT: JAI.

Bennis, W. G., & Thomas, R. J. (2002). *Geeks and geezers: How era, values and defining moments shape leaders.* Boston: Harvard Business School Press.

Bentham, J. (1948). *An introduction to the principles of morals and legislation.* New York: Hafner.

Bernthal, P. R., & Insko, C. A. (1993). Cohesiveness without groupthink: The interactive effects of social and task cohesion. *Group & Organizational Management, 18,* 66–87.

Berry, J. (1995, February 24). My Lai Massacre was an American tragedy. *National Catholic Reporter,* pp. 10–11.

Beuchner, F. (1973). *Wishful thinking: A theological ABC.* New York: HarperCollins.

Beyer, J. M., & Trice, H. M. (1987). How an organization's rites reveal its culture. *Organizational Dynamics, 15,* 5–24.

Biemann, A. D. (Ed.). (2002). *The Martin Buber reader: Essential writings.* New York: Palgrave Macmillan.

Bird, F. B. (1996). *The muted conscience: Moral silence and the practice of ethics in business.* Westport, CT: Quorum Books.

Blasi, A. (2005). Moral character: A psychological approach. In D. K. Lapsley & F. C. Power (Eds.), *Character psychology and character education* (pp. 67–100). Notre Dame, IN: University of Notre Dame Press.

Blaskovich, J. L. (2008). Exploring the effect of distance: An experimental investigation of virtual collaboration, social loafing, and group decisions. *Journal of Information Systems, 22*(1), 27–46.

Blocker, H. G., & Smith, E. H. (Eds.). (1980). *John Rawls' theory of justice: An introduction.* Athens: Ohio University Press.

Blustein, J. (2007). Doctoring and self-forgiveness. In R. L. Walker & P. J. Ivanhoe (Eds.), *Working virtue: Virtue ethics and contemporary moral problems* (pp. 87–112). Oxford, UK: Clarendon.

Boatright, J. R. (1999). Finance ethics. In R. E. Frederick (Ed.), *A companion to business ethics* (pp. 153–163). Malden, MA: Blackwell.

Boatright, J. R. (2008). *Ethics in finance* (2nd ed.). Malden, MA: Blackwell.

Boatright, J. R. (2010). Ethics in finance. In J. R. Boatright (Ed.), *Finance ethics: Critical issues in theory and practice* (pp. 3–19). Hoboken, NJ: John Wiley.

Bobocel, D. R., & Meyer, J. P. (1994). Escalating commitment to a failing course of action: Separating the roles of choice and justification. *Journal of Applied Psychology, 79,* 360–363.

Boele, R., & Kemp, D. (2005, Spring). Social auditors: Illegitimate offspring of the audit family? Finding legitimacy through a hybrid approach. *Journal of Corporate Citizenship,* 109–119.

Bok, S. (1978). *Lying: Moral choice in public and private life.* New York: Pantheon Books.

Bok, S. (1980). Whistleblowing and professional responsibilities. In D. Callahan & S. Bok (Eds.), *Ethics teaching in higher education* (pp. 277–295). New York: Plenum Press.

Bok, S. (1989). *Secrets: On the ethics of concealment and revelation.* New York: Random House.

Borrus, A., McNames, M., Symonds, W., Byrnes, N., & Park, A. (2003, February 2). Reform: Business gets religion. *BusinessWeek,* pp. 40–41.

Boudreaux, G., & Steiner, T. (2005, Spring). Developing a code of ethics. *Management Quarterly,* pp. 2–19.

Bowes-Sperry, L., & O'Leary-Kelly, A. M. (2005). To act or not to act: The dilemma faced by sexual harassment observers. *Academy of Management Review, 30,* 288–306.

Bowes-Sperry, L., & Powell, G. N. (1996). Sexual harassment as a moral issue: An ethical decision-making perspective. In M. S. Stockdale (Ed.), *Sexual harassment in the workplace: Perspectives, frontiers, and response strategies* (Vol. 5, pp. 105–124). Thousand Oaks, CA: Sage.

Bowie, N. E. (2005). Kantian ethical thought. In J. W. Budd & J. G. Scoville (Eds.), *The ethics of human resources and industrial relations* (pp. 61–87). Champaign, IL: Labor Relations and Employment Association.

Boyce, N. (2001, August 20). Hugh Thompson. *U.S. News and World Report*, pp. 33–34.

Brandenberger, J. W. (2005). College, character, and social responsibility: Moral learning through experience. In D. K. Lapsley & F. C. Power (Eds.), *Character psychology and character education* (pp. 305–334). Notre Dame, IN: University of Notre Dame Press.

Brandl, P., & Maguire, M. (2002, Winter). Codes of ethics: A primer on their purpose, development and use. *Journal for Quality & Participation, 25,* 9–12.

Brasswell, M. K., Foster, C. M., & Poe, S. L. (2009, Summer). A new generation of corporate codes of ethics. *Southern Business Review,* pp. 1–10.

Bratton, V. K., & Kacmar, K. M. (2004). Extreme careerism: The dark side of impression management. In W. Griffin & K. O'Reilly (Eds.), *The dark side of organizational behavior* (pp. 291–308). San Francisco: Jossey-Bass.

Brehony, K. A. (1999). *Ordinary grace: Lessons from those who help others in extraordinary ways.* New York: Riverhead Books.

Brockner, J., Siegel, P. A., Daly, J. P., Tyler, T., & Martin, C. (1997). When trust matters: The moderating effect of outcome favorability. *Administrative Science Quarterly, 42,* 558–583.

Brooker, K. (2002, June 24). Fire the chairman of the bored. *Fortune,* pp. 72–73.

Brower, H. H., & Shrader, C. B. (2000). Moral reasoning and ethical climate: Not-for-profit vs. for-profit boards of directors. *Journal of Business Ethics, 26,* 147–167.

Brown, C. T., & Keller, P. W. (1994). Ethics. In R. Anderson, K. N. Cissna, & R. C. Arnett (Eds.), *The reach of dialogue: Confirmation, voice, and community* (pp. 284–290). Cresskill, NJ: Hampton Press.

Brown, K. W. (2007). Mindfulness: Theoretical foundations and evidence for its salutary effects. *Psychological Inquiry, 18*(4), 211–237.

Brown, K. W., & Ryan, R. M. (2003). The benefits of being present: Mindfulness and its role in psychological well-being. *Journal of Personality and Social Psychology, 84*(4), 822–848.

Brown, M. E., & Trevino, L. K. (2006). Ethical leadership: A review and future directions. *The Leadership Quarterly, 17,* 595–616.

Brown, M. E., Trevino, L. K., & Harrison, D. (2005). Ethical leadership: A social learning perspective for construct development and testing. *Organizational Behavior and Human Decision Processes, 97,* 117–134.

Brownell, J. (2002). *Listening: Attitudes, principles, and skills* (2nd ed.). Boston: Allyn & Bacon.

Brownell, J. (2003, November 22). *The skills of listening-centered communication.* Paper presented at the National Communication Association convention, Miami, FL.

Bruhn, J. G. (2001). *Trust and the health of organizations.* New York: Kluwer/Plenum.

Bryant, S. M., Albring, S. M., & Murthy, U. (2009). The effects of reward structure, media richness and gender on virtual teams. *International Journal of Accounting Information Systems, 10,* 190–213.

Buber, M. (1965). *The knowledge of man: Selected essays* (M. Friedman, Ed.). New York: Harper & Row, pp. 67–68.

Buber, M. (1970). *I and thou.* (R. G. Smith, Trans.). New York: Scribner's.

Buchholz, R. A., & Rosenthal, S. B. (2005). Toward a conceptual framework for stakeholder theory. *Journal of Business Ethics, 58*, 137–148.

Buechner, F. (1973). *Wishful thinking: A theological ABC.* New York: Harper & Row, p. 95.

Bugeja, M. (2007, January 26). Distractions in the wireless classroom. *Chronicle of Higher Education*, p. 1.

Bullis, C. (1991). Communication practices as unobtrusive control: An observational study. *Communication Studies, 42*(3), 254–271.

Bunkley, N., & Maynard, M. (2010, April 19). Toyota is expected to pay $16.4 million fine sought by U.S. over recall of sticking pedals. *The New York Times*, p. B3.

Burgoon, J. K., Berger, C. R., & Waldron, V. R. (2000). Mindfulness and interpersonal communication. *Journal of Social Issues, 56*(1), 105–127.

Burke, R. J., & Koyuncu, M. (2010). Developing virtues and virtuous behavior at workplace. *The IUP Journal of Soft Skills, IV*(3), 39–48.

Burling, S. (2005, August 21). Your blog could get you recruited—or fired. *The Philadelphia Inquirer*, p. A01.

Burns, J. F., & Somaiya, R. (2010, October 25). Amid disclosures, a quest for secrecy. *The International Herald Tribune*, p. 4.

Burns, J. M. (1978). *Leadership.* New York: Harper & Row.

Burns, J. M. (2003). *Transforming leadership: A new pursuit of happiness.* New York: Atlantic Monthly Press.

Buss, A. H. (1961). *The psychology of aggression.* New York: John Wiley.

Butterfield, K. D., Trevino, L. K., & Weaver, G. R. (2000). Moral awareness in business organizations: Influences of issue-related and social context factors. *Human Relations, 53*, 981–1018.

Byus, K., Deis, D., & Ouryang, B. (2010). Doing well by doing good: Corporate social responsibility and profitability. *SAM Advanced Management Journal, 75*(1), 44–55.

Caldwell, C., Bishchoff, S. J., & Karri, R. (2002). The four umpires: A paradigm for ethical leadership. *Journal of Business Ethics, 36*, 153–163.

Caldwell, C., & Karri, R. (2005). Organizational governance and ethical systems: A covenantal approach to building trust. *Journal of Business Ethics, 58*, 249–259.

Callahan, D. (2004). *The cheating culture.* Orlando, FL: Harcourt.

Carlson, D. S., Kacmar, K. M., & Wadsworth, L. L. (2009). The impact of moral intensity dimensions on ethical decision-making: Assessing the relevance of orientation. *Journal of Managerial Issues, 21*, 534–551.

Carney, J. (2005, May 2). Temper, temper, temper. *Time*, pp. 55–57.

Carroll, A. B. (1979). A three-dimensional conceptual model of corporate performance. *Academy of Management Review, 4*, 497–508.

Carroll, A. B., & Buchholtz, A. K. (2009). *Business and society: Ethics and stakeholder management* (7th ed.). Mason, OH: South-Western.

Carroll, R. (October 17, 2010). When the miners' leader met the president, two sides of Chile embraced. *The Observer*, p. 18.

Carroll, R., & Franklin, J. (2010, October 14). Chile's triumph. *The Guardian*, Home, p. 1.

Carroll, R., & Franklin, J. (2010, October 16). Chilean miners: Tales from the tomb. *The Guardian*, International, p. 30.

Carroll, S. J., & Gannon, M. J. (1997). *Ethical dimensions of international management.* Thousand Oaks, CA: Sage.

Carson, T. (2001). Deception and withholding information in sales. *Business Ethics Quarterly, 11*, 275–306.

Carter, B., & Stelter, B. (2009, October 3). Extortion case raises questions for Letterman and his network. *The New York Times*, p. A1.

Carter, S. L. (1998). *Civility: Manners, morals, and the etiquette of democracy.* New York: HarperCollins.

Caruso, D. R., Bien, B., & Kornacki, S. A. (2006). Emotional intelligence in the workplace. In *Emotional intelligence in everyday life* (2nd ed., pp.187–205). New York: Psychology Press.

Caruso, D. R., & Salovey, P. (2004). *The emotionally intelligent manager: How to develop and use the four key emotional skills of leadership.* San Francisco: Jossey-Bass.

Carver, C. S., & Scheier, M. F. (2005). Optimism. In C. R. Snyder & S. J. Lopez (Eds.), *Handbook of positive psychology* (pp. 231–243). Oxford, UK: Oxford University Press.

A case of Hurd labour. (2010, September 11). *The Economist*, p. 75.

Caux Round Table. (2000). Appendix 26: The Caux Principles. In O. F. Williams, *Global codes of conduct: An idea whose time has come* (pp. 384–388). Notre Dame, IN: Notre Dame University Press.

Caux Round Table. (2004). The Caux Round Table Principles for Business, 1994. In R. Mares (Ed.), *Business and human rights: A compilation of documents* (pp. 288–292). Leiden, the Netherlands: Brill.

CFA Institute. Retrieved from http://www.cfainstitute.org/learning/products/publications/ccb/pages/ccb.v2010.n14./aspx

Chaleff, I. (1995). *The courageous follower: Standing up to and for our leaders.* San Francisco: Berrett-Koehler.

Chaleff, I. (2003). *The courageous follower: Standing up to and for our leaders* (2nd ed.). San Francisco: Berrett-Koehler.

Chaleff, I. (2008). Creating new ways of following. In R. E. Riggio, I. Chaleff, & J. Lipman-Blumen (Eds.), *The art of followership: How great followers create great leaders and organizations* (pp. 67–92). San Francisco: Jossey-Bass.

Champoux, J. E. (2003). *Organizational behavior: Essential tenets* (2nd ed.). Mason, OH: South-Western.

Chan, A., Hannah, S. T., & Gardner, W. L. (2005). Veritable authentic leadership: Emergence, functioning, and impacts. In W. L. Gardner, B. J. Avolio, & F. O. Walumbwa (Eds.), *Authentic leadership theory and practice: Origins, effects and development* (pp. 3–41). Amsterdam: Elsevier.

Chan, G. K. Y. (2008). The relevance and value of Confucianism in contemporary business ethics. *Journal of Business Ethics, 77*, 347–360.

Chang, I. (1997). *The rape of Nanking: The forgotten holocaust of World War II.* New York: Basic Books.

Charan, R., & Tichy, N. (1988). *Every business is a growth business: How your company can prosper year after year.* New York: Random House.

Charity navigator (http://www.charitynavigator.org).

Chen, A., Lawson, R. B., Gordon, L. R., & McIntosh, B. (1996). Groupthink: Deciding with the leader and the devil. *Psychological Record, 46*, 581–590.

Chesebro, J. L. (1999). The relationship between listening styles and conversational sensitivity. *Communication Research Reports, 16*(3), 233–238.

Chidambaram, L., & Tung, L. L. (2005). Is out of sight, out of mind? An empirical study of social loafing in technology-supported groups. *Information Systems Research, 16*(2), 149–168.

Christians, C. G., Rotzell, K. B., & Fackler, M. (1990). *Media ethics* (3rd ed.). New York: Longman.

Christie, R., & Geis, F. L. (1970). *Studies in Machiavellianism.* New York: Academic Press.

Cialdini, R. B. (2001). *Influence: Science and practice* (4th ed.). Boston: Allyn & Bacon.

Cialdini, R. B., Petrova, P. K., & Goldstein, N. J. (2004, Spring). The hidden costs of organizational dishonesty. *MIT Sloan Management Review*, pp. 67–73.

Cissna, K. N., & Anderson, R. (1994). Communication and the ground of dialogue. In R. Anderson, K. N. Cissna, & R. C. Arnett (Eds.), *The reach of dialogue: Confirmation, voice, and community* (pp. 9–30). Cresskill, NJ: Hampton Press.

Cissna, K. N., & Sieburg, E. (1990). Patterns of interactional confirmation and disconfirmation. In J. Stewart (Ed.), *Bridges not walls: A book about interpersonal communication* (5th ed., pp. 237–246). New York: McGraw-Hill.

Ciulla, J. (2000). *The working life*. New York: Times Books.

Clapp-Smith, R., Vogelgesang, G. R., & Avey, J. B. (2009). Authentic leadership and positive psychological capital: The mediating role of trust at the group level of analysis. *Journal of Leadership & Organizational Studies, 15*(3), 227–240.

Cleary, T. (1992). *The essential Confucius: The heart of Confucius' teachings in authentic I Ching order*. San Francisco: HarperSanFrancisco.

Cloud, D. S., & Parker, N. (2010, October 23). Leaks focus on U.S. role in Iraq. *Los Angeles Times*, p. AA1.

Cohen, D. V. (1993). Creating and maintaining ethical work climates: Anomie in the workplace and implications for managing change. *Business Ethics Quarterly, 3*, 343–358.

Cohen, J. R. (2004). The ethics of respect in negotiation. In C. Menkel-Meadow & M. Wheeler (Eds.), *What's fair: Ethics for negotiators* (pp. 257–263). San Francisco: Jossey-Bass.

Cohen, M. (2010, August 2). A renegade site, now working with the news media. *The New York Times*, p. B3.

Cohen-Charash, Y., & Spector, P. E. (2001). The role of justice in organizations: A meta-analysis. *Organizational Behavior and Human Decision Processes, 86*(2), 278–321.

Colby, A., & Damon, W. (1992). *Some do care: Contemporary lives of moral commitment*. New York: Free Press.

Colby, A., & Damon, W. (1995). The development of extraordinary moral commitment. In M. Killen & D. Hart (Eds.), *Morality in everyday life: Developmental perspectives* (pp. 342–369). Cambridge, UK: Cambridge University Press.

Coldwell, D. A., Billsberry, J., van Meurs, N., & Marsh, P. J. G. (2008). The effects of person-organization ethical fit on employee attraction and retention: Towards a testable explanatory model. *Journal of Business Ethics, 78*, 611–622.

Coles, R. (2001). *Lives of moral leadership*. New York: Random House.

Collins, J. C., & Porras, J. I. (1994). *Built to last: Successful habits of visionary companies*. New York: HarperBusiness.

Collins, J. C., & Porras, J. I. (1996, September-October). Building your company's vision. *Harvard Business Review*, pp. 65–77.

Collins, M. H., Hari, J. F., & Rocco, T. S. (2009). The older-worker-younger-supervisor dyad. A test of the reverse Pygmalion effect. *Human Resource Development Quarterly, 20*(1), 21–41.

Company settles case in firing tied to Facebook. *The New York Times*, p. B7.

Confucius (2007). *The Analects of Confucius* (B. Watson, Trans.). New York: Columbia University Press.

Congo-Kinshasa: Peace campaigners turn up heat on Apple, Intel over conflict minerals. (2009, September 18). *Africa News*.

Cooper, S. (2004). *Corporate social performance: A stakeholder approach*. Burlington, VT: Ashgate.

Cooper, T. L. (1992). Prologue: On virtue. In T. L. Cooper & N. D. Wright (Eds.), *Exemplary public administrators: Character and leadership in government* (pp. 1–8). San Francisco: Jossey-Bass.

Cooper, T. L., & Wright, N. D. (1992). *Exemplary public administrators: Character and leadership in government.* San Francisco: Jossey-Bass.

Corporate Accountability International. (2011). Clowning with kids' health: The case for Ronald McDonald's retirement. Retrieved from http://www.RetireRonald .org

Cortina, L. M., Magley, V. I., Hunter Williams, J., & Langhout, R. D. (2001). Incivility in the workplace: Incidence and impact. *Journal of Occupational Health Psychology, 6,* 64–80.

Covey, S. R. (1989). *The seven habits of highly effective people.* New York: Simon & Schuster.

Covey, S. R. (2004). *The 8th habit: From effectiveness to greatness.* New York Free Press.

Craigie, F. C. (1999). The spirit and work: Observations about spirituality and organizational life. *Journal of Psychology and Christianity, 18,* 43–53.

Crano, W. D., & Seyranian, V. (2009). How minorities prevail: The context/comparison-lenience contract model. *Journal of Social Issues, 65*(2), 335–363.

Creswell, J. (2003, July 7). Scandal hits—now what? *Fortune,* pp. 127–129.

Cropanzano, R., Bowen, D. E., & Gilliland, S. W. (2007). The management of organizational justice. *Journal of Management Perspectives, 21*(4), 34–48.

Cropanzano, R., & Stein, J. H. (2009). Organizational justice and behavioral ethics: Promises and prospects. *Business Ethics Quarterly, 19*(2), 193–233.

Crossman, M. (2007, June 25). Lost. *The Sporting News,* p. 12.

Cruver, B. (2002). *Anatomy of greed: The unshredded truth from an Enron insider.* New York: Carroll & Graf.

Cullen, J. B., Parboteeah, K. P., & Victor, B. (2003). The effects of ethical climates on organizational commitment: A two-study analysis. *Journal of Business Ethics, 46,* 127–141.

The curse of HP. (2010, August 14). *The Economist,* p. 54.

Czubaroff, J. (2000). Dialogic rhetoric: An application of Martin Buber's philosophy of dialogue. *Quarterly Journal of Speech, 2,* 168–189.

D'Abate, C. P. (2005). Working hard or hardly working: A study of individuals engaging in personal business on the job. *Human Relations, 58,* 1009–1032.

Damon, W. (Ed.). (2002). *Bringing in a new era in character education.* Stanford, CA: Hoover Institution Press.

Daniels, C. (2003, April 14). Mr. Coffee. *Fortune,* pp. 139–140.

Danner, M. (2004). *Torture and truth: America, Abu Ghraib, and the War on Terror.* New York: New York Review Books.

Darley, J. M. (1996). How organizations socialize individuals into evildoing. In D. M. Messick & A. E. Tenbrunsel (Eds.), *Codes of conduct: Behavioral research into business ethics* (pp. 13–43). New York: Russell Sage Foundation.

Dash, E., & Sorkin, A. R. (2008, September 26). In largest bank failure, U.S. seizes, then sells. *The New York Times,* p. A1.

Davis, C. (2008, November 9). Pay package awarded to WHYY chief questioned. *The Philadelphia Inquirer,* p. A01.

Davis, J. H., & Ruhe, J. A. (2003). Perceptions of country corruption: Antecedents and outcomes. *Journal of Business Ethics, 43,* 275–288.

Davis, J. H., Schoorman, F. D., & Donaldson, L. (1997). Toward a stewardship theory of management. *Academy of Management Review, 22,* 20–47.

Day, L. A. (2003). *Ethics in media communications: Cases and controversies* (4th ed.). Belmont, CA: Thomson/Wadsworth.

De Clercq, S., Fontaine, J. R. J., & Anseel, F. (2008). In search of a comprehensive value model for assessing supplementary person-organization fit. *The Journal of Psychology, 142*(3), 277–302.

De Dreu, C. K. W., & Beersma, B. (2001). Minority influence in organizations: Its origins and implications for learning and group performance. In C. K. W. De Dreu & N. K. DeVries (Eds.), *Group consensus and minority influence: Implications for innovation* (pp. 258–283). Oxford: Blackwell.

De Dreu, C. K. W., & Gelfand, J. J. (2008). Conflict in the workplace: Sources, functions, and dynamics across multiple levels of analysis. In C. K. W. De Dreu & M. J. Gelfand (Eds.), *The psychology of conflict and conflict management in organizations* (pp. 3–54). New York: Lawrence Erlbaum.

De Dreu, C. K. W., & Weingart, L. R. (2003). Task versus relationship conflict, team performance, and team member satisfaction: A meta-analysis. *Journal of Applied Psychology, 88*(4), 741–749.

De George, R. T. (1995). *Business ethics* (4th ed.). Englewood Cliffs, NJ: Prentice Hall.

Denning, P. (2002, March). Internet time out. *Communications of the ACM,* pp. 15–18.

Depre, K. E., & Barling, J. (2003). Workplace aggression. In A. Sagie, S. Stashevsky, & M. Koslowsky (Eds.), *Misbehaviour and dysfunctional attitudes in organizations* (pp. 13–32). Hampshire, UK: Palgrave Macmillan.

DesJardins, J. (2011). *An introduction to business ethics* (4th ed.). New York: McGraw-Hill.

Dessler, G. (2008). *Human resource management.* Upper Saddle River, NJ: Pearson, p. 2.

Devettere, R. J. (2002). *Introduction to virtue ethics: Insights of the ancient Greeks.* Washington, DC: Georgetown University Press.

De Vise, D. (2010, March 9). Web of diversions evicts laptops from lecture halls. *The Washington Post,* p. A01.

Ding, H., & Ding, X. (2008). Project management, critical praxis, and process-oriented approach to teamwork. *Business Communication Quarterly, 71*(4), 456–471.

Dirks, K. T. (1999). The effects of interpersonal trust on work group performance. *Journal of Applied Psychology, 84,* 445–455.

Dirks, K. T., & Ferrin, D. L. (2002). Trust in leadership: Meta-analytic findings and implications for research and practice. *Journal of Applied Psychology, 87,* 611–628.

Divir, T., Eden, D., & Banjo, M. L. (1995). Self-fulfilling prophecy and gender: Can women be Pygmalion and Galatea? *Journal of Applied Psychology, 80,* 253–270.

Dolfsma, W. (2006). Accounting as applied ethics: Teaching a discipline. *Journal of Business Ethics 63,* 209–215.

Donaldson, T., & Dunfee, T. W. (1994). Toward a unified conception of business ethics: Integrative social contracts theory. *Academy of Management Review, 19,* 252–284.

Donaldson, T., & Dunfee, T. W. (1999). *Ties that bind: A social contracts approach to business ethics.* Boston: Harvard Business School Press.

Donaldson, T., & Preston, L. E. (1995). The stakeholder theory of the corporation: Concepts, evidence, and implications. *Academy of Management Review, 20,* 65–91.

Donnelly, J. (1989). *Universal human rights in theory and practice.* Ithaca, NY: Cornell University Press.

Dotinga, R. (2005, February 7). Office memo: 'Blogging' can get you bounced. *The Christian Science Monitor,* p. 13.

Dotlich, D. L., Noel, J. L., & Walker, N. (2004). *Leadership passages: The personal and professional transitions that make or break a leader.* San Francisco: Jossey-Bass.

Dougherty, J. (2009, October 12). Sweat lodge deaths: Bring soul-searching to area deep in seekers. *The New York Times,* p. A13.

Dougherty, J. (2009, October 22). A witness recalls a grim end to a quest for spiritual rebirth. *The New York Times,* p. A1.

Dougherty, J. (2009, October 23). New Age vibes strike tragic chord. *The International Herald Tribune,* p. 2.

Douglas, S. C., & Martinko, M. J. (2001). Exploring the role of individual differences in the prediction of workplace aggression. *Journal of Applied Psychology, 86,* 547–559.

Dowd, M. (2009, October 7). Men behaving madly. *The New York Times,* p. A29.

Drake, B., Yuthas, K., & Dillard, J. E. (2000). It's only words—Impacts of informational technology on moral dialogue. *Journal of Business Ethics, 23,* 41–59.

Drath, W. (2001). *The deep blue sea: Rethinking the source of leadership.* San Francisco: Jossey-Bass.

Drory, A., & Romm, T. (1990). The definition of organizational politics: A review. *Human Relations, 43*(11), 1133–1154.

Drummond, H. (1996). *Escalation in decision-making: The tragedy of Taurus.* New York: Oxford University Press.

Drummond, H. (2001). *The art of decision-making: Mirrors of imagination, masks of fate.* Chichester, UK: John Wiley.

Drumwright, M. E., & Murphy, P. E. (2004). How advertising practitioners view ethics: Moral muteness, moral myopia, and moral imagination. *Journal of Advertising, 33*(2), 7–24.

Duchon, D., & Plowman, D. A. (2005). Nurturing the spirit at work: Impact on work unit performance. *The Leadership Quarterly, 16,* 807–833.

Duin, S. (2002, April 28). Dead peasants may return to haunt PGE. *The Oregonian,* p. B01.

Duke, A. B., Goodman, J. M., Treadway, D. C., & Breland, J. W. (2009). Perceived organizational support as a moderator of emotional labor/outcomes relationships. *Journal of Applied Social Psychology, 39*(5), 1013–1034.

Dunfee, T. W., & Donaldson, T. (1999). Social contract approaches to business ethics: Bridging the "is-ought" gap. In R. E. Frederick (Ed.), *A companion to business ethics* (pp. 38–52). Malden, MA: Blackwell.

Duska, R. F., & Duska, B. S. (2003). *Accounting ethics.* Malden, MA: Blackwell.

Dwyer, J., & Flynn, K. (2005). *102 minutes: The untold story of the fight to survive inside the Twin Towers.* New York: Times Books.

Eden, D. (1984). Self-fulfilling prophecy as a management tool: Harnessing Pygmalion. *Academy of Management Review, 9,* 64–73.

Eden, D. (1990). *Pygmalion in management.* Lexington, MA: Lexington Books/D.C. Heath.

Eden, D. (1993). Interpersonal expectations in organizations. In P. D. Blanck (Ed.), *Interpersonal expectations: Theory, research, and applications* (pp. 154–178). Cambridge, UK: University of Cambridge Press.

Eden, D., & Shami, A. B. (1982). Pygmalion goes to boot camp: Expectancy, leadership, and trainee performance. *Journal of Applied Psychology, 67,* 194–199.

Edmundson, A. (1999). Psychological safety and learning behavior in work teams. *Administrative Science Quarterly, 44,* 350–383, p. 354.

Ehrhart, M. G. (2004). Leadership and procedural justice climate as antecedents of unit-level organizational citizenship behavior. *Personnel Psychology, 57*(1), 61–94.

Einarsen, S., Aasland, M. S., & Skogstad, A. (2007). Destructive leadership behavior: A definition and conceptual model. *The Leadership Quarterly, 18,* 207–216.

Einarsen, S., Skosgtad, A., & Aasland, M. S. (2010). The nature, prevalence, and outcomes of destructive leadership: A behavioral and conglomerate approach. In B. Schyns & T. Hansbrough (Eds.), *When leadership goes wrong: Destructive leadership, mistakes, and ethical failures.* Charlotte, NC: Information Age.

Eisenberg, D., Fonda, D., & Zagorin, A. (2002, June 17). Dennis the menace. *Time,* pp. 46–49.

Eisenberg, N. (2000). Emotion, regulation, and moral development. *Annual Review of Psychology, 51,* 665–697.

Ekman, P. (2003). *Emotions revealed: Recognizing faces and feelings to improve communication and emotional life*. New York: Times Books.

Elkind, P. (2004, June 14). The trials of Eliot Spitzer. *Fortune*, pp. 33–35.

Ellenwood, S. (2007). Revisiting character education: From McGuffey to narratives. *The Journal of Education, 187*(3), 21–43.

Ellis, K. (2000). Perceived teacher confirmation: The development of validation of an instrument and two studies of the relationship to cognitive and affective learning. *Human Communication Research, 26*, 264–291.

Ellis, K. (2004). The impact of perceived teacher confirmation on receiver apprehension, motivation, and learning. *Communication Education, 53*, 1–20.

Ellis, K. (2004). Perceived parental confirmation: Development and validation of an instrument. *Southern Communication Journal, 67*, 319–334

Emmons, R. A., & McCullough, M. E. (2003). Counting blessings versus burdens: An experimental investigation of gratitude and subjective well-being in daily life. *Journal of Personality and Social Psychology 84*(2), 377–389.

Engardio, P. (2004, July 12). Global Compact, little impact. *BusinessWeek*, pp. 86–87.

Engardio, P. (2004, July 20). Two views of the Global Compact. *BusinessWeek Online*.

Engelbrecht, A. S., Van Aswegen, & Theron, C C. (2005). The effect of ethical values on transformational leadership and ethical climate in organizations. *South Africa Journal of Business Management, 36*(2), 19–26.

Epley, N., & Dunning, D. (2000). Feeling "holier than thou": Are self-serving assessments produced by errors in self- or social prediction? *Journal of Personality and Social Psychology, 79*, 861–875.

Esser, J. K. (1998). Alive and well after 25 years: A review of groupthink research. *Organizational Behavior and Human Decision Processes, 73*, 116–141.

Estes, R. (1996). *Tyranny of the bottom line*. San Francisco: Berrett-Koehler.

Etzel, B. (2002, July 1). WorldCom's wrong number. *Investment Dealers' Digest*, pp. 9–12.

Evangelista, B. (2010, September 21). Oracle's Hurd cedes options, settling HP suit. *San Francisco Chronicle*, p. D1.

Ever farther, ever faster, ever higher? (2004, August 7). *The Economist*, pp. 20–22.

Expert or shill? (2008, November 30). *The New York Times*, p. WK7.

Fairholm, G. W. (1996). Spiritual leadership: Fulfilling whole-self needs at work. *Leadership & Organization Development Journal, 17*(5), 11–17.

Farmer, S. (2010, September 12). Concussions and the NFL: Hard knocks. *Los Angeles Times*, p. C1.

Fedor, D., Maslyn, J., Farmer, S., & Bettenhausen, K. (2008). The contribution of positive politics to the prediction of employee reactions. *Journal of Applied Social Psychology, 38*, 76–96.

Ferrell, O. C., & Gardiner, G. (1991). *In pursuit of ethics: Tough choices in a world of work*. Springfield, IL: Smith Collins.

Fineman, S. (1995). Stress, emotion and intervention. In T. Newton (Ed.), *Managing stress: Emotion and power at work* (pp. 120–136). London: Sage.

Finlayson, J. G. (2000). Modernity and morality in Habermas's discourse ethics. *Inquiry, 43*, 319–340.

Finlayson, J. G. (2005). *Habermas: A very short introduction*. Oxford, UK: Oxford University Press.

Fisher, R., Ury, W., & Patton, B. (1991). *Getting to yes: Negotiating agreement without giving in* (2nd ed.). New York: Bantam Books.

Fisk, M. C. (2008, December 24). Wal-Mart to settle 63 lawsuits over wages. *The Washington Post*, p. D01.

Fiske, S. T. (1993, June). Controlling other people: The impact of power on stereotyping. *American Psychologist, 48*, 621–628.

Fitzgerald, L. F. (1993). Sexual harassment: Violence against women in the workplace. *American Psychologist, 48*, 1070–1076.

Fitzgerald, L. F., Drasgow, F., Hulin, C. L., Gelfand, M. J., & Magley, V. (1997). Antecedents and consequences of sexual harassment in organizations: A test of an integrated model. *Journal of Applied Psychology, 82,* 578–589.

Flanagan, J., & Clarke, K. (2007). Beyond a code of professional ethics: A holistic model of ethical decision-making for accountants. *ABACUS, 43,* 488–518.

Fletcher, M. (2010, October 16). 'We decided to look for the miners as if they were our sons.' *The Times* (London), News, pp. 4, 5.

Flippen, A. R. (1999). Understanding groupthink from a self-regulatory perspective. *Small Group Research, 30,* 139–165.

Folger, J., Poole, M., & Stutman, R. (1993). *Working through conflict.* New York: HarperCollins.

Folger, R., & Baron, R. A. (1996). Violence and hostility at work: A model of reactions to perceived injustice. In G. R. VandenBos & E. Q. Bulato (Eds.), *Violence on the job: Identifying risks and developing solutions* (pp. 51–85). Washington, DC: American Psychological Association.

Fonda, D., & Kadlec, D. (2004, May 31). The rumble over executive pay. *Time,* pp. 62–64.

Foote, J., Gaffney, N., & Evans, J. R. (2010). Corporate social responsibility: Implications for performance excellence. *Total Quality Management, 21*(8), 799–812.

Forrester, R. (2000). Empowerment: Rejuvenating a potent idea. *Academy of Management Executive, 14,* 67–80.

Fortin, M. (2008). Perspectives on organizational justice: Concept clarification, social context, integration, time and links with morality. *International Journal of Management Reviews, 10*(2), 93–126.

Fouche, G. Where convicts lead the good life. *Globalpost.* Retrieved from http://www.globalppost.com

Fountain, H. (2010, October 13). Plan B turns out to be fastest path for rescue in Chile. *The New York Times,* p. A8.

Franke, G. P., & Nadler, S. S. (2007). Culture, economic development, and national ethical attitudes. *Journal of Business Research, 61,* 254–264.

Frederick, W. C. (1992). *Social issues in management: Coming of age or prematurely gray?* Paper presented at the Academy of Management annual meeting, Las Vegas, NV.

Freeman, E. (1984). *Strategic management.* Marshfield, MA: Pitman.

Freeman, R. E. (1994). The politics of stakeholder theory: Some future directions. *Business Ethics Quarterly, 4,* 409–421.

Freeman, R. E. (1995). Stakeholder thinking: The state of the art. In J. Nasi (Ed.), *Understanding stakeholder thinking* (pp. 35–73). Helsinki, Finland: LSR-Julkaisut Oy.

Freeman, R. E., Harrison, J. S., & Wicks, A. C. (2007). *Managing for stakeholders: Survival, reputation, and success.* New Haven, CT: Yale University Press.

French, R. P., & Raven, B. (1959). The bases of social power. In D. Cartwright (Ed.), *Studies in social power* (pp. 150–167). Ann Arbor: University of Michigan, Institute for Social Research.

Frey, B. F. (2000). The impact of moral intensity on decision making in a business context. *Journal of Business Ethics 26,* 181–195.

Fritzche, D. J. (2000). Ethical climates and the ethical dimension of decision making. *Journal of Business Ethics, 24,* 125–140.

Frymier, A. B., & Houser, M. L. (2000). The teacher-student relationship as an interpersonal relationship. *Communication Education, 49*(3), 207–219.

Fulmer, I. S., & Barry, B. (2009). Managed hearts and wallets: Ethical issues in emotional influence by and within organizations. *Business Ethics Quarterly, 12,* 155–191.

Gabarro, J. J., & Kotter, J. P. (2005, January). Managing your boss. *Harvard Business Review,* pp. 92–99.

Garcia-Zamor, J. C. (2003). Workplace spirituality and organizational performance. *Public Administration Review, 63,* 355–363.

Gardner, H. (2010, September 10). Stem cell financing ban ends, for now. *The New York Times*, p. 14.

Gardner, W. L. (1992). Lessons in organizational dramaturgy: The art of impression management. *Organizational Dynamics, 21,* 33–47.

Gardner, W. L., Avolio, B. J., Luthans, F., May, D. R., & Walumbwa, F. O. (2005). "Can you see the real me?" A self-based model of authentic leader and follower development. *The Leadership Quarterly, 16,* 343–372.

Gardner, W. L., Avolio, B. J., & Walumbwa, F. O. (2005). Authentic leadership development: Emergent themes and future directions. In W. L. Gardner, B. J. Avolio, & F. O. Walumbwa (Eds.), *Authentic leadership theory and practice: Origins, effects and development* (pp. 387–406). Amsterdam: Elsevier.

Garrett, R. K., & Danziger, J. N. (2008). On cyberslacking: Workplace status and personal Internet use at work. *CyberPsychology & Behavior, 11,* 287–292.

Gates, D. (2005, March 8). Boeing faces CEO dilemma. *The Seattle Times*, p. A1.

Gaudine, A., & Thorne, L. (2001). Emotion and ethical decision-making in organizations. *Journal of Business Ethics, 31,* 175–187.

Gellerman, S. W. (1989, Winter). Managing ethics from the top down. *Sloan Management Review*, pp. 73–79.

Gellis, H., Giladi, K., & Friedman, H. H. (2002). Biblical and Talmudic basis of accounting ethics. *CPA Journal, 72*(9), 11–13.

George, J. M. (1995). Asymmetrical effects of rewards and punishments: The case of social loafing. *Journal of Occupational and Organizational Psychology, 68,* 327–338.

Gergen, D. (2000). *Eyewitness to power: The essence of leadership.* New York: Simon & Schuster.

Giacalone, R. A., & Greenberg, J. (1997). *Antisocial behavior in organizations.* Thousand Oaks, CA: Sage.

Giacalone, R. A., & Jurkiewicz, C. L. (2003a). Right from wrong: The influence of spirituality on perceptions of unethical business activities. *Journal of Business Ethics, 46,* 85–97.

Giacalone, R. A., & Jurkiewicz, C. L. (2003b). Toward a science of workplace spirituality. In R. A. Giacalone & C. L. Jurkiewicz (Eds.), *Handbook of workplace spirituality and organizational performance* (pp. 3–28). Armonk, NY: M. E. Sharpe.

Gibb, J. R. (1961). Defensive communication. *Journal of Communication, 11–12,* 141–148.

Gibson, K. (2000). The moral basis of stakeholder theory. *Journal of Business Ethics, 26,* 245–257.

Gilligan, C. (1982). *In a different voice: Psychological theory and women's development.* Cambridge, MA: Harvard University Press.

Gillis, J., & Fountain, H. (2010, June 7). Rate of oil leak, still not clear, puts doubt on BP. *The New York Times*, p A1.

Gino, F., Moore, D. A., & Bazerman, M. H. (2008, January). See no evil: When we overlook other people's unethical behavior. *Harvard Business School Working Paper No. 08–045.* Retrieved from http://www.people.hbs.edu/mbazerman

Gino, F., Moore, D. A., & Bazerman, M. H. (2009). No harm, no foul: The outcome bias in ethical judgments. *Harvard Business School Working Paper 08–080.* Retrieved from http://www.people.hbs.edu/mbazerman

Gittell, J. H. (2003). *The Southwest Airlines way.* New York: McGraw-Hill.

Gladwell, M. (2005). *Blink: The power of thinking without thinking.* New York: Little, Brown.

Global Reporting Initiative. (2002). *The 2002 sustainability reporting guidelines.* Retrieved from http://www.globalreporting.org

Glomb, T. M., & Hui, L. (2003). Interpersonal aggression in work groups: Social influence, reciprocal, and individual effects. *Academy of Management Journal, 46,* 486–496.

Glomb, T. M., Steel, P. D. G., & Arvey, R. D. (2002). Office sneers, snipes, and stab wounds: Antecedents, consequences, and implications of workplace violence and aggression. In R. G. Lord, R. J. Klimoski, & R. Kanfer (Eds.), *Emotions in the workplace* (pp. 227–259). San Francisco: Jossey-Bass.

Goe, K. (2010, April 29). Dual report on Mike Belotti's Oregon settlement find no criminal wrongdoing or public expense. *The Oregonian*. Retrieved from Oregonlive.com.

Goffman, E. (1959). *The presentation of self in everyday life.* Garden City, NY: Doubleday.

Goldman, S. (2008). *Temptations in the office: Ethical choices and legal obligations.* Westport, CT: Praeger.

Goldsborough, R. (2000, January). Doing the right thing: Computers and ethics. *Tech Directions,* p 9.

Goleman, D. (1998). *Working with emotional intelligence.* New York: Bantam Books.

Goleman, D. (2001). An EI-based theory of performance. In C. Cherniss & D. Goleman (Eds.), *The emotionally intelligent workplace: How to select for, measure, and improve emotional intelligence in individuals, groups, and organizations* (pp. 27–44). San Francisco: Jossey-Bass.

Good, T., & Brophy, J. (1980). *Educational psychology: A realistic approach.* New York: Holt, Rinehart & Winston.

Goodboy, A. K., & Myers, S. A. (2008). The effect of teacher confirmation on student communication and learning outcomes. *Communication Education, 57*(2), 153–179.

Goodman, P. S., & Morgenson, G. (2008, December 28). Saying yes to anyone, WaMu built empire on shaky loans. *The New York Times,* p. A1.

Goodpaster, K. E. (1991). Business ethics and stakeholder analysis. *Business Ethics Quarterly, 1,* 53–72.

Goodwin, S. A. (2003). Power and prejudice: A social-cognitive perspective on power and leadership. In D. van Knippenberg & M. A. Hogg (Eds.), *Leadership and power: Identity processes in groups and organizations* (pp. 138–152). London: Sage.

Gordon, M. D. (2008). Management education and the base of the pyramid. *Journal of Management Education, 32*(6), 767–781.

Gottlieb, J., Vives, R., & Leonard, J. (2010, September 22). Crisis in Bell. *Los Angeles Times,* p. A1.

Gottlieb, J., Yoshino, K., & Vives, R. (2010, September 23). Fee hikes flowed to Rizzo's pay. *Los Angeles Times,* p. A1.

Gouws, D. J. (1995). The role concept in career development. In D. E. Super & B. Sverko (Eds.), *Life roles, values and careers: International findings of the Work Importance Study* (pp. 22–53). San Francisco: Jossey-Bass.

Graham, C. (2010, October 17). For 14 days we were all in pitch darkness. There was no night and no day. We begged God to help us. *London Mail.*

Graham, G. (2004). *Eight theories of ethics.* London: Routledge, Chap. 6.

Graham, J. (1995). Leadership, moral development, and citizenship behavior. *Business Ethics Quarterly, 5,* 43–54.

Greed is bad. (2004, May 29). *The Economist,* pp. 72–73.

Green, H. (2008, December 12). The greening of the corporation. *BusinessWeek Online,* p. 10.

Greenhouse, S. (2010, April 4). Unpaid internships worry state and federal officials. *The Oregonian,* p. E3.

Greenhouse, S. (2010, November 9). Labor board says rights apply on net. *The New York Times,* p. B1.

Greenleaf, R. K. (1977). *Servant leadership.* New York: Paulist Press.

Greenwald, J. (2009, November 2). Scandals put spotlight on workplace romance: Task for employers is finding balance of protection, privacy. *Business Insurance,* News, p. 3.

Grover, S. (1993). Lying, deceit, and subterfuge: A model of dishonesty in the workplace. *Organization Science, 4,* 478–494.

Grover, S. L. (1997). Lying in organizations: Theory, research, and future directions. In R. A. Giacalone & J. Greenberg (Eds.), *Antisocial behavior in organizations* (pp. 68–84). Thousand Oaks, CA: Sage.

Gudykunst, W. B., & Kim, Y. Y. (1997). *Communicating with strangers: An approach to intercultural communication* (3rd ed.). New York: McGraw-Hill.

Guglielmo, C. (2009, June 23). When Steve Jobs returns to his CEO job, experts disagree on whether Apple should reveal if he had a liver transplant. *The Houston Chronicle*, p. B7.

Guglielmo, C. (2010, May 12). A year after surgery, "He's the Jobs of old." *Edmonton Journal*, p. F9.

Gumbel, A. (2009, October 22). Death in Arizona. *The Guardian*, Features, p. 5.

Guth, D. W., & Marsh, C. (2006). *Public relations: A values-driven approach* (3rd ed.). Boston: Pearson.

Guyon, J. (2002, October 14). The king and I. *Fortune* (Europe), p. 38.

Habermas, J. (1970). Towards a theory of communicative competence. *Inquiry, 13,* 360–375.

Habermas, J. (1990). *Moral consciousness and communicative action* (C. Lenhardt & S. Weber Nicholsen, Trans.). Cambridge, MA: MIT Press.

Hackman, M. Z., & Johnson, C. E. (2009). *Leadership: A communication perspective* (5th ed.). Long Grove, IL: Waveland Press.

Haidt, J. (2003). The moral emotions. In R. J. Davidson, K. R. Scherer, & H. H. Goldsmith (Eds.), *Handbook of affective sciences* (pp. 852–870). Oxford: Oxford University Press.

Haidt, J., & Bjorklund, F. (2008). Social intuitionists answer six questions about moral psychology. In W. Sinnott-Armstrong (Ed.), *Moral psychology: Vol. 2. The cognitive science of morality: Intuition and diversity* (pp. 182–217). Cambridge, MA: MIT Press.

Haidt, J., & Graham, J. (2007). When morality opposes justice: Conservatives have moral intuitions that liberals may not recognize. *Social Justice Research, 20,* 98–116.

Hall, C. S., & Nordby, V. J. (1973). *A primer of Jungian psychology.* New York: New American Library.

Hamilton, J. B., & Knouse, S. B. (2001). Multinational enterprise decision principles for dealing with cross cultural ethical conflicts. *Journal of Business Ethics, 31,* 77–94.

Hamilton, J. B., Knouse, S. B., & Hill, V. (2009). Google in China: A manager-friendly heuristic model for resolving cross-cultural ethical conflicts. *Journal of Business Ethics, 86,* 143–157.

Hampson, R., & Dorell, O. (2010, October 14). Thrilling rescue made for TV. *USA Today,* pp. 1A, 5A.

Hanna, S. T., Lester, P. B., & Vogelgesang, G. R. (2005). Moral leadership: Explicating the moral component of authentic leadership. In W. L. Gardner, B. J. Avolio, & F. O. Walumbwa (Eds.), *Authentic leadership theory and practice: Origins, effects and development* (pp. 43–81). Amsterdam: Elsevier.

Hardy, L. (1990). *The fabric of this world: Inquiries into calling, career choice, and the design of human work.* Grand Rapids, MI: Eerdmans.

Hardy, S. A., & Carlo, G. (2005). Identity as a source of moral motivation. *Human Development, 48,* 232–256.

Hart, D. K. (1992). The moral exemplar in an organizational society. In T. L. Cooper & N. D. Wright (Eds.), *Exemplary public administrators: Character and leadership in government* (pp. 9–29). San Francisco: Jossey-Bass.

Hart, D. K. (1994). Administration and the ethics of virtue. In T. C. Cooper (Ed.), *The handbook of administrative ethics* (pp. 107–123). New York: Marcel Dekker.

Hart, S. L. (1997, January/February). Beyond greening: Strategies for a sustainable world. *Harvard Business Review,* pp. 66–76.

Hartman, E. (1996). *Organizational ethics and the good life.* New York: Oxford University Press.

Hartog, M., & Frame, P. (2004). Business ethics in the curriculum: Integrating ethics through work experience. *Journal of Business Ethics, 54,* 399–409.

Harvard Medical School conflict of interest policy receives approval from American Medical Student Association. Retrieved November 11, 2010, from http://www.amsa.org?AMSA/Homepage/About/News/072110.aspx

Harvesting poverty: Inching toward trade fairness [Editorial]. (2003, August 15). *The New York Times*, p. A28.

Harvey, J. (1988). *The Abilene Paradox and other meditations on management.* Lexington, MA: Lexington Books.

Harvey, J. (2001). The Abilene Paradox: The management of agreement. *Organizational Dynamics, 33,* 17–34.

Harvey, P., Martinko, M. J., & Gardner, W. L. (2006). Promoting authentic behavior in organizations: An attributional perspective. *Journal of Leadership and Organizational Studies, 12,* 1–11.

Harvey, S. J., Jr. (2000). Reinforcing ethical decision making through organizational structure. *Journal of Business Ethics, 28,* 43–58.

Hauerwas, S. (1981). *A community of character.* Notre Dame, IN: University of Notre Dame Press.

Hauser, M. D. (2006). *Moral minds: How nature designed our universal sense of right and wrong.* New York: HarperCollins.

Hauser, M. D., Young, L., & Cushman, F. (2008). Reviving Rawls's linguistic analogy: Operative principles and the causal structure of moral actions. In W. Sinnott-Armstrong (Ed.), *Moral psychology. Volume 2: The cognitive science of morality: Intuition and diversity.* Cambridge, MA: MIT.

Heames, J. T., & Service, R. W. (2003). Dichotomies in teaching, application, and ethics. *Journal of Education for Business, 79,* 118–122.

Heath, R. L. (1997). *Strategic issues management: Organizations and public policy challenges.* Thousand Oaks, CA: Sage.

Held, V. (2004). Taking care: Care as practice and value. In C. Calhoun (Ed.), *Setting the moral compass: Essays by women philosophers* (pp. 59–71). Oxford, UK: Oxford University Press.

Held, V. (2006). The ethics of care. In D. Copp (Ed.), *The Oxford handbook of ethical theory* (pp. 537–566). Oxford, UK: Oxford University Press.

Hempel, J., & Borrus, A. (2004, June 21). Now the nonprofits need cleaning up. *BusinessWeek,* pp. 107–108.

Henle, C. A., & Blanchard, A. L. (2008). The interaction of work stressors and organizational sanctions on cyberloafing. *Journal of Managerial Issues, 20,* 383–400.

Herbert, B. (2005, May 2). From "gook" to "raghead." *The New York Times*, p. A21.

Herper, M., & Langreth, R. (2006, September 4). Anti-ban billionaires. *Forbes,* pp. 124–130.

Hershcovis, M. S., & Barling, J. (2008). Preventing insider-initiated workplace violence. In E. K. Kelloway, J. Barling, & J. J. Hurrell (Eds.), *Handbook of workplace violence* (pp. 607–632). Thousand Oaks, CA: Sage.

Hershcovis, M. S., Turner, N., Barling, J., Arnold, K. A., Dupre, K. E., Inness, M., . . . Sivanathan, N. (2007). Predicting workplace aggression: A meta-analysis. *Journal of Applied Psychology, 92,* 228–238.

Hicks, D. A. (2003). *Religion and the workplace: pluralism, spirituality and leadership.* Cambridge, UK: Cambridge University Press.

Hiestand, M., & Mihoces, G. (2004, December 29). Apnea common for NFL linemen. *USA Today,* p. 1C.

Higgs, M. (2009). The good, the bad and the ugly: Leadership and narcissism. *Journal of Change Management, 9,* 165–178.

Hindo, B. (2008, February 16). Solving Tyco's identity crisis. *BusinessWeek*, pp. 62–66.

Hinken, T. R., & Schreisheim, C. A. (1989). Development and application of new scales to measure the French and Raven (1959) Bases of Social Power. *Journal of Applied Psychology, 74*, 561–567.

Hitchens, C. (2001, May 28). Leave no child behind? *The Nation*, pp. 9–10.

Hochschild, A. R. (1983). *The managed heart: Commercialization of human feeling*. Berkeley: University of California Press.

Hoffman, W. M., Neill, J. D., & Stovall, O. S. (2007). An investigation of ethics officer independence. *Journal of Business Ethics, 78,* 87–95.

Hoffman, W. M., & Rowe, M. (2007). The ethics officer as agent of the board: Leveraging ethical governance capability in the post-Enron corporation. *Business & Society Review, 112*(4), 553–572, p. 556.

Hofmann, P. B. (2006, March/April). The value of an ethics audit. *Healthcare Executive*, pp. 44–45.

Hofstede, G. (1984). *Culture's consequences*. Beverly Hills, CA: Sage.

Hofstede, G. (1991). *Cultures and organizations: Software of the mind*. London: McGraw-Hill.

Hofstede, G. (2001). Difference and danger: Cultural profiles of nations and limits to tolerance. In M. H. Albrecht (Ed.), *International HRM: Managing diversity in the workplace* (pp. 9–23). Oxford, UK: Blackwell.

Holland, J. L. (1997). *Making vocational choices* (3rd ed.). Odessa, FL: Psychological Assessment Resources.

Holmgren, M. R. (1998). Self-forgiveness and responsible moral agency. *The Journal of Value Inquiry, 32,* 75–91.

Holt, S. (2005, March 8). Personal lives of executives under scrutiny. *The Seattle Times*, p. C1.

Hoppen, D. (2002, Winter). Guiding corporate behavior: A leadership obligation, not a choice. *Journal for Quality & Participation, 25,* 15–19.

Hornstein, H. (1996). *Brutal bosses and their prey*. New York: Riverhead.

Hosmer, L. T. (1995). Trust: The connecting link between organizational theory and philosophical ethics. *Academy of Management Review, 20,* 279–403.

House, R. J., Hanges, P. J., Javidan, M., Dorfman, P. W., & Gupta, V. (Eds.). (2004). *Culture, leadership, and organizations: The GLOBE study of 62 societies*. Thousand Oaks, CA: Sage.

Hoyt, C. L., & Blascovich, J. (2003). Transformational and transactional leadership in virtual and physical environments. *Small Group Research, 34,* 678–715.

Huan, C-L., & Chang, B-G. (2010). The effects of manager's moral philosophy on project decision under agency problem conditions. *Journal of Business Ethics, 94,* 595–611.

Hudson Employment Index. (2005). *One in three workers witness ethical misconduct despite clearly communicated guidelines*. Washington, DC: Hudson.

Humphrey, J. (1989). *No distant millennium: The international law of human rights*. Paris: UNESCO.

Hunt, J. (April 6, 2010). The $2.3 million question: How Mike Belotti's buyout sets with Oregon donors. *The Oregonian*. Retrieved from Oregonlive.com.

Husted, B. W. (1999). Wealth, culture and corruption. *Journal of International Business Studies, 30,* 339–359.

ICT and Telecom: How technology is fueling conflict in the country. (2009, December 7). *The East African*.

Ilies, R., Hauserman, N., Schwochau, S., & Stibal, J. (2003). Reported incidence rates of work-related sexual harassment in the United States: Using meta-analysis to explain reported rate disparities. *Personnel Psychology, 56,* 607–651.

Ilies, R., Morgeson, F. P., & Nahrgang, J. D. (2005). Authentic leadership and eudemonic well-being: Understanding leader–follower outcomes. *The Leadership Quarterly, 16,* 373–394.

Inamori, T., & Analoui, F. (2010). Beyond Pygmalion effect: The role of managerial perception. *Journal of Management Development, 29*(4), 306–321.

Inch, E. S., & Warnick, B. (2002). *Critical thinking and communication: The use of reason in argument* (4th ed.). Boston: Allyn & Bacon.

Infante, D. A. (1988). *Arguing constructively.* Long Grove, IL: Waveland Press.

Inzie, S. (2010, March 13). Senators critical of salary expenses, perks at Boys & Girls Clubs. *The Washington Post,* p. A05.

Ip, P. K. (2009). Is Confucianism good for business ethics in China? *Journal of Business Ethics, 88,* 463–476.

Isenhart, M. W., & Spangle, M. (2000). *Collaborative approaches to resolving conflict.* Thousand Oaks, CA: Sage.

J&J loses its way with secret buy-up of defective drug. (2010, October 5). *USA Today,* p. 10A.

Jacobs, T. (2009, May). Morals authority. *Miller-McCune,* pp. 47–55.

Jaffee, S., & Shibley Hyde, J. (2000). Gender differences in moral orientation: A meta-analysis. *Psychological Bulletin, 126,* 703–726.

James, H. S. (2000). Reinforcing ethical decision making through organizational structure. *Journal of Business Ethics, 28,* 43–58.

Janis, I. (1971, November). Groupthink: The problems of conformity. *Psychology Today,* pp. 271–279.

Janis, I. (1982). *Groupthink* (2nd ed.). Boston: Houghton Mifflin.

Janis, I. (1989). *Crucial decisions: Leadership in policymaking and crisis management.* New York: Free Press.

Jaramillo, F., Grisaffe, D. B., Chonko, L. B., & Roberts, J. H. A. (2009a). Examining the impact of servant leadership on sales force performance. *Journal of Personal Selling & Sales Management, 29,* 257–275.

Jaramillo, F., Grisaffe, D. B., Chonko, L. B., & Roberts, J. A. (2009b). Examining the impact of servant leadership on salesperson's turnover intention. *Journal of Personal Selling & Sales Management, 29,* 351–365: 22.

Jarrett, J. L. (1991). *The teaching of values: Caring and appreciation.* London: Routledge.

Jaska, J. A., & Pritchard, M. S. (1994). *Communication ethics: Methods of analysis.* Belmont, CA: Wadsworth.

Javidan, M., & House, R. J. (2001). Cultural acumen for the global manager: Lessons from Project GLOBE. *Organizational Dynamics, 29,* 289–305.

Jehn, K. A. (1995). A multimethod examination of the benefits and detriments of intragroup conflict. *Administrative Science Quarterly, 40,* 256–282.

Jennings, M. M. (2006). *The seven signs of ethical collapse: How to spot moral meltdowns in companies. . .before it's too late.* New York: St. Martin's Press.

Johannesen, R. L. (2002). *Ethics in human communication* (5th ed.). Prospect Heights, IL: Waveland Press.

Johnson, C. E. (2000). Emerging perspectives in leadership ethics. *Proceedings of the International Leadership Association,* pp. 48–54. College Park, MD: International Leadership Association.

Johnson, C. E. (2000). Taoist leadership ethics. *Journal of Leadership Studies, 7,* 82–91.

Johnson, C. E. (2009). Book review: Followership and The Art of Followership. *International Leadership Journal, 1,* 107–109.

Johnson, C. E. (2012). *Meeting the ethical challenges of leadership: Casting light or shadow* (4th ed.). Thousand Oaks, CA: Sage.

Johnson, C. E., & Hackman, M. Z. (1995). *Creative communication: Principles and applications.* Prospect Heights, IL: Waveland Press.

Johnson, D. W. (1974). Communication and the inducement of cooperative behavior in conflicts: A critical review. *Speech Monographs, 41,* 64–78.

Johnson, D. W., & Johnson, F. P. (2006). *Joining together: Group theory and group skills* (9th ed.). Boston: Pearson.

Johnson, D. W., & Johnson, R. T. (1974). Instructional goal structure: Cooperative, competitive, or individualistic. *Review of Educational Research, 44,* 212–239.

Johnson, D. W., Maruyama, G., Johnson, R., Nelson, D., & Skon, L. (1981). Effects of cooperative, competitive, and individualistic goal structures on achievement: A meta-analysis. *Psychological Bulletin, 82,* 47–62.

Johnson, H. H. (2001). Corporate social audits—this time around. *Business Horizons, 44,* 29–37.

Johnson, R. A. (1993). *Owning your own shadow: Understanding the dark side of the psyche.* San Francisco: HarperSan Francisco.

Johnson, R. A. (2003). *Whistle-blowing: When it works—and why.* Boulder, CO: Lynne Rienner.

Johnson, S. (2007, September/October). SC Johnson builds business at the base of the pyramid. *Global Business and Organizational Excellence,* pp. 6–17.

Jones, P. E., & Roelofsma, P. H. M. P. (2000). The potential for social contextual and group biases in team decision-making: Biases, conditions and psychological mechanisms. *Ergonomics, 43,* 1129–1152.

Jones, T. M. (1991). Ethical decision making by individuals in organizations: An issue-contingent model. *Academy of Management Review, 16,* 366–395.

Joyce, A. (2005, February 11). Free expression can be costly when bloggers bad-mouth jobs. *The Washington Post,* p. A01.

Jurkiewicz, C. L., & Giacalone, R. A. (Eds.). (2003). *Handbook of workplace spirituality and organizational performance* (pp. 3–28). Armonk, NY: M. E. Sharpe.

Jurkiewicz, C. L., & Giacalone, R. A. (2004). A values framework for measuring the impact of workplace spirituality on organizational performance. *Journal of Business Ethics, 49,* 129–142.

Kant, I. (1964). *Groundwork of the metaphysics of morals* (H. J. Ryan, Trans.). New York: Harper & Row.

Kanter, R. M. (1977). *Men and women of the corporation.* New York: Basic Books.

Kanter, R. M. (1979, July-August). Power failure in management circuits. *Harvard Business Review,* pp. 65–75.

Kanter, R. M. (2001). An Abilene defense: Commentary one. *Organizational Dynamics, 33,* 37–40.

Kanungo, R. N., & Conger, J. A. (1993). Promoting altruism as a corporate goal. *Academy of Management Executive, 7,* 37–49.

Karakas, F. (2009). Spirituality and performance in organizations: A literature review. *Journal of Business Ethics, 94,* 89–106.

Karau, S. J., & Williams, K. D. (1993). Social loafing: A meta-analytic review and theoretical integration. *Journal of Personality and Social Psychology, 65,* 681–706.

Karau, S. J., & Williams, K. D. (2001). Understanding individual motivation in groups: The collective effort model. In Keil, M., Depledge, G., & Rai, A. (2007). Escalation: The role of problem recognition and cognitive bias. *Decision Science, 38(3),* 391–417.

Keil, M., Depledge, G., & Rai, A. (2007). Escalation: The role of problem recognition and cognitive bias. *Decision Science, 38*(3), 391–417.

Keil, M., & Montealegre, R. (2000, Spring). Cutting your losses: Extricating your organization when a big project goes awry. *Sloan Management Review,* pp. 55–58.

Kellerman, B. (2004). *Bad leadership: What it is, how it happens, why it matters.* Boston: Harvard Business School Press.

Kellerman, B. (2008). *Followership: How followers are creating change and changing leaders.* Boston: Harvard Business School Press.

Kelley, R. E. (1992). *The power of followership: How to create leaders that people want to follow and followers who lead themselves.* New York: Doubleday/Currency.

Kelley, R. E. (1998). Followership in a leadership world. In L. C. Spears (Ed.), *Insights on leadership* (pp. 170–184). New York: John Wiley.

Keltner, D., Langner, C. A., & Allison, M. L. (2006). Power and moral leadership. In D. L. Rohde (Ed.) *Moral leadership: The theory and practice of power, judgment, and policy* (pp. 177–194). San Francisco: Jossey-Bass.

Kernis, M. H. (2003). Toward a conceptualization of optimal self-esteem. *Psychological Inquiry, 14,* 1–26.

Kerr, N. A., Markus, M. J., & Stasson, M. F. (2001). Individual differences in social loafing: Need for cognition as a motivator in collective performance. *Group Dynamics: Theory, Research, and Practice, 5*(2), 150–158.

Kidder, R. M. (1994). *Shared values for a troubled world: Conversations with men and women of conscience.* San Francisco: Jossey-Bass.

Kidder, R. M. (1994, July-August). Universal values: Finding an ethical common ground. *The Futurist,* pp. 8–13.

Kidder, R. M. (1995). *How good people make tough choices.* New York: Simon & Schuster.

Kidwell, R. E. (2004). "Small" lies, big trouble: The unfortunate consequences of résumé padding, from Janet Cooke to George O'Leary. *Journal of Business Ethics, 51,* 175–184.

Kim, R. (2009, January 22). SEC reportedly looks at Jobs' health. *San Francisco Chronicle,* p. C1.

Kinz, H. (2010, March 10). Ex-producer pleads guilty in Letterman extortion case. *The Washington Post,* p. C01.

Kipnis, D., Schmidt, S. M., Swaffin-Smith, C., & Wilkinson, I. (1984). Patterns of managerial influence: Shotgun managers, tacticians, and bystanders. *Organizational Dynamics, 12,* 58–76.

Kirkman, B. L., & Rosen, B. (1999). Beyond self-management: Antecedents and consequences of team empowerment. *Academy of Management Journal, 42,* 58–74.

Kirkpatrick, W. K. (1992). Moral character: Story-telling and virtue. In R. T. Knowles & G. F. McLean (Eds.), *Psychological foundations of moral education and character development: An integrated theory of moral development* (pp. 169–184). Washington, DC: Council for Research in Values and Philosophy.

Klein Aguilar, M. (2010, February). CCO role is now a full-time job. *Compliance Week,* pp. 29–31.

Kohlberg, L. A. (1984). *The psychology of moral development: The nature and validity of moral stages* (Vol. 2). New York: Harper & Row.

Kohlberg, L. A. (1986). A current statement on some theoretical issues. In S. Modgil & C. Modgil (Eds.), *Lawrence Kohlberg: Consensus and controversy* (pp. 485–546). Philadelphia: Falmer Press.

Kolb, R. W. (2010). Ethical implications of finance. In J. R. Boatright (Ed.), *Finance ethics: Critical issues in theory and practice* (pp. 23–43). Hoboken, NJ: John Wiley.

Kosseff, J. (2004, March 14). Charity Inc. *The Oregonian,* pp. A1, A11.

Kottler, J. A. (2000). *Doing good: Passion and commitment for helping others.* Philadelphia: Brunner-Routledge.

Kottler, P., & Lee, N. (2005). *Corporate social responsibility.* Hoboken, NJ: John Wiley.

Kracher, B., & Wells, D. L. Employee selection and the ethic of care. In M. Schminke (Ed). *Managerial ethics: Management of people and processes* (pp. 81–97). Mahwah, NJ: Lawrence Erlbaum.

Kristof, A. L. (1996). Person-organization fit: An integrative review of its conceptualizations, measurement, and implications. *Personnel Psychology, 49*(1), 1–49.

Kristof, N. (2010, November 19). Becoming our own version of a banana republic. *The Oregonian,* p. B7.

Kristof, N. D. (2010, June 27). Death by gadget. *The New York Times,* p. WK11.

Kristof-Brown, A. L., Zimmerman, R. D., & Johnson, E. C. (2005). Consequences of individuals' fit at work: A meta-analysis of person-job, person-organization, person-group, and person-supervisor fit. *Personnel Psychology, 58,* 281–343.

Kung, H. (1998). *A global ethic for global politics and economics.* New York: Oxford University Press.

Kurchner-Hawkins, R., & Miller, R. (2006). Organizational politics: Building positive political strategies in turbulent times. In E. Vigoda-Gadot & A. Drory (Eds.), *Handbook of organizational politics* (pp. 328–351). Cheltenham, UK: Edward Elgar.

Kuzmits, F., Sussman, L., Adams, A., & Raho, L. (2002, October). Using information and e-mail for political gain. *The Information Management Journal,* pp. 76–80.

Lacey, M. (2003, September 10). Africans' burden: West's farm subsidies. *The New York Times,* p. A9.

Lacey, M. (2011, June 23). New age guru guilty in sweat lodge deaths. *The New York Times,* p. 16.

Lacoay, R., & Ripley, A. (2003, January 6). Persons of the year. *Time,* pp. 30–60.

Laczniak, G. R., & Murphy, P. E. (2006). Normative perspectives for ethical and socially responsible marketing. *Journal of Macromarketing, 26,* 154–177.

LaFasto, F., & Larson, C. (2001). *When teams work best.* Thousand Oaks, CA: Sage.

Laing, R. D. (1994). Confirmation and disconfirmation. In R. Anderson, K. N. Cissna, & R. C. Arnett (Eds.), *The reach of dialogue: Confirmation, voice, and community* (pp. 73–78). Cresskill, NJ: Hampton Press.

Langer, E. J. (1989). *Mindfulness.* Reading, MA: Addison-Wesley.

Langer, E. J. (1989). Minding matters: The consequences of mindlessness-mindfulness. *Advances in Experimental Social Psychology, 22,* 137–173.

Langer, E. J. (1997). *The power of mindful learning.* Reading, MA: Addison-Wesley.

Langer, E. J., & Burgoon, J. K. (1995). Language, fallacies, and mindlessness-mindfulness in social interaction. In B. Burleson (Ed.), *Communication yearbook 18* (pp. 83–104). Thousand Oaks, CA: Sage.

Laplume, A. O., Sonpar, K., & Litz, R. A. (2008). Stakeholder theory: Reviewing a theory that moves us. *Journal of Management 34*(6), 1152–1189.

Lapsley, D. K. (2008). Moral self-identity as the aim of education. In L. P. Nucci & D. Narvaez (Eds.), *Handbook of moral and character education* (pp. 30–52). New York: Routledge.

Larrabee, M. J. (Ed.) (1993). An ethic of care: Feminist and interdisciplinary perspectives. New York: Routledge.

Lau, D. C. (1970). *Mencius.* New York: Penguin Books.

Lau, D. C. (1979). *The Analects.* New York: Penguin Books.

Lavelle, L. (2002, June 17). When directors join CEOs at the trough. *BusinessWeek,* p. 57.

Lavelle, L. (2002, October 7). The best and worst boards. *BusinessWeek,* pp. 104–114.

Lavelle, L. (2002, November 11). Rebuilding trust in Tyco. *BusinessWeek,* pp. 94–96.

Lavoie, J. A. A., & Pychyl, T. A (2001). Cyberslacking and the procrastination superhighway: A web-based survey of online procrastination, attitudes and emotion. *Social Science Computer Review, 12,* 431–444.

Lax, D. A., & Sebenius, J. K. (2004). Three ethical issues in negotiation. In C. Menkel-Meadow & M. Wheeler (Eds.), *What's fair: Ethics for negotiators* (pp. 5–14). San Francisco: Jossey-Bass.

Leary, M. R., & Kowalski, R. M. (1990). Impression management: A literature review and two-component model. *Psychological Bulletin, 107,* 34–47.

Lee, M. R. (2008). E-ethical leadership for virtual project teams. *International Journal of Project Management, 27,* 456–463.

Leidner, R. (1991). Selling hamburgers and selling insurance: Gender, work, and identity in interactive service jobs. *Gender & Society, 5,* 154–177.

Leidner, R. (1993). *Fast food, fast talk: Service work and the routinization of everyday life.* Berkeley: University of California Press.

Lemonick, M. D., & Novak, V. (2005, July 11). The power broker. *Time,* pp. 30–33.

Leslie, L. Z. (2000). *Mass communication ethics: Decision-making in postmodern culture.* Boston: Houghton Mifflin.

Levenson, E. (2008, November 24). Citizen Nike. *Fortune,* pp. 165–170.

Levoy, G. (1997). *Callings: Finding and following an authentic life.* New York: Three Rivers Press.

Levy, A. C., & Paludi, M. A. (2002). *Workplace sexual harassment* (2nd ed.). Upper Saddle River, NJ: Prentice Hall.

Lewicki, R. J., & Bunker, B. B. (1996). Developing and maintaining trust in work relationships. In R. M. Kramer & T. R. Tyler (Eds.), *Trust in organizations: Frontiers of theory and research* (pp. 114–139). Thousand Oaks, CA: Sage.

Lewis, M. (1989). *Liar's poker.* New York: Norton.

Lincoln, N. D., Travers, C., Ackers, P., & Wilkinson, A. (2002). The meaning of empowerment: The interdisciplinary etymology of a new management concept. *International Journal of Management Reviews, 4,* 271–290.

Liopis, J., Gonzalez, M. R., & Gasco, J. L. (2007). Corporate governance and organizational culture: The role of ethics officers. *International Journal of Disclosure and Governance, 4*(2), 96–105.

Lipman-Blumen, J. (2005). *The allure of toxic leaders: Why we follow destructive bosses and corrupt politicians—and how we can survive them.* Oxford, UK: Oxford University Press, pp. 19–23.

Lipman-Blumen, J. (2008). Following toxic leaders: In search of posthumous praise. In R. E. Riggio, I. Chaleff, & J. Lipman-Blumen (Eds.), *The art of followership: How great followers create great leaders and organizations* (pp. 181–194). San Francisco: Jossey-Bass.

Lirbyson, F. (2009, October 24). Police probe deaths at 'sweat lodge.' *National Post,* p. A7.

Locke, E. A., Tirnauer, D., Roberson, Q., Goldman, B., Lathan, M. E., & Weldon, E. (2001). The importance of the individual in an age of groupism. In M. E. Turner (Ed.), *Groups at work: Theory and research* (pp. 501–528). Mahwah, NJ: Lawrence Erlbaum.

Lockwood, A. L. (2009). *The case for character education: A developmental approach.* New York: Teachers College Press.

Loe, T. W., Ferrell, L., & Mansfield, P. (2000). A review of empirical studies assessing ethical decision making in business. *Journal of Business Ethics, 25,* 185–204.

London, T., Anupindi, R., & Sheth, S. (2010). Creating mutual value: Lessons learned from ventures serving base of the pyramid producers. *Journal of Business Research, 63,* 582–594.

Lonergan, B. (1957). *Insight: A study of human understanding.* Longmans, Green.

Longnecker, J. G. (1985). Management priorities and management ethics. *Journal of Business Ethics, 4,* 65–70.

Loomis, C. J., & Kahn, J. (1999, January 11). Citigroup: Scenes from a merger. *Fortune,* pp. 76–83.

Lopes, P. N., Cote, S., & Salovey, P. (2006). An ability model of emotional intelligence: Implications for assessment and training. In V. J. Druskat, F. Sala, & G. Mount (Eds.), *Linking emotional intelligence and performance at work: Current research evidence with individuals and groups* (pp. 53–80). Mahwah, NJ: Lawrence Erlbaum.

Lowe, K. B., & Kroeck, K. G. (1996). Effectiveness correlates of transformational and transactional leadership: A meta-analytic review. *The Leadership Quarterly, 7,* 385–425.

Lubit, R. (2002). The long-term organizational impact of destructively narcissistic managers. *Academy of Management Executive, 18,* 127–183.

Lucadamo, L. (2010, April 1). Poll's got beef with Ronald. *Daily News,* News, p. 13.

Lumpkin, J. L. (2005, May 11). One-day halt called in Army recruiting. *Associated Press.*

Luthans, F., & Avolio, B. J. (2009). The "point" of positive organizational behavior. *Journal of Organizational Behavior, 30,* 291–307.

Luthans, F., Norman, S., & Hughes, L. (2006). Authentic leadership: A new approach for a new time. In R. J. Burke & C. L. Cooper (Eds.), *Inspiring leaders* (pp. 84–194). London: Routledge.

Luthans, F., Youssef, C. M., & Avolio, B. J. (2006). *Psychological capital: Developing the human competitive edge.* Cary, NC: Oxford University Press.

MacIntyre, A. (1984). *After virtue: A study in moral theory* (2nd ed.). Notre Dame, IN: University of Notre Dame Press.

Mahan, B. J. (2002). *Forgetting ourselves on purpose: Vocation and the ethics of ambition.* San Francisco: Jossey-Bass.

Malhotra, D. (2004, May). Some alternatives to lying in negotiation. *Negotiation, 7*(5), 3–5.

Malone, S. (2011, January 25). Trust in business tumbled in 2010: Survey. *Reuters.* Retrieved from http://www.reuters.com/article/2011/01/25/corporate-trust. Edelman Trust Survey Executive Summary 2011.

Mandleson, R. (2010, November 8). Why it pays to be a jerk. *Canadian Business,* pp. 28–34.

Manning, J. (2010, April 21). Melinda Grier, attorney at center of Mike Belotti scandal, on the way out. *The Oregonian.* Retrieved from Oregonlive.com.

Manz, C. C., & Neck, C. P. (1995). Teamthink: Beyond the groupthink syndrome in self-managing work teams. *Journal of Managerial Psychology, 10,* 7–15.

Mares, R. (Ed.). (2004). *Business and human rights: A compilation of documents.* Leiden, the Netherlands: Martinus Nijhoff.

Margolis, J. D., Grant, A. M., & Molinsky, A. L. (2007). Expanding the ethical standards of HRM: Necessary evils and the multiple dimensions of impact. In A. H. Pinnington, R. Macklin, & T. Campbell (Eds.), *Human resource management: Ethics and employment* (pp. 237–251). Oxford, UK: Oxford University Press.

Marshall, J., & Heffes, E. M. (2006, June). Roundtable survey finds clear trends. *Financial Executive,* p. 10.

Martin, J. (2002). *Organizational culture: Mapping the terrain.* Thousand Oaks, CA: Sage.

Martin, K. D., & Cullen, J. B. (2006). Continuities and extensions of ethical climate theory: A meta-analytic review. *Journal of Business Ethics, 69,* 175–194.

Martin, R. L. (2003). The virtue matrix: Calculating the return of corporate responsibility. *Harvard Business Review on corporate responsibility* (pp. 83–104). Boston: Harvard Business School Press.

Mason, J. (2002, October 2). Time runs out for bill to limit companies' secret life insurance polices. *The Houston Chronicle.*

Mass, A., & Clark, R. D. (1984). Hidden impact of minorities: Fifteen years of minority influence research. *Psychological Bulletin, 95,* 428–450.

Matthew 20:26 in *The Holy Bible: New International Version* (1973). Grand Rapids, MI: Zondervan.

Mattoon, M. A. (1981). *Jungian psychology in perspective.* New York: Free Press.

May, D. R., Chan, A. Y. L., Hodges, T. D., & Avolio, B. J. (2003). Developing the moral component of authentic leadership. *Organizational Dynamics, 32,* 247–260.

May, D. R., & Pauli, K. P. (2002). The role of moral intensity in ethical decision-making: A review and investigation of moral recognition, evaluation and intention. *Business & Society, 41,* 84–117.

Mayhall, C. W., & Mayhall, T. B. (2004). *On Buber.* Belmont, CA: Wadsworth-Thomson Learning.

Mayer, C. E. (2005, January 28). McDonald's makes Ronald a health ambassador. *The Washington Post*, p. E1.

Mayer, D. M., Bardes, M., & Piccolo, R. F. (2008). Do servant-leaders help satisfy follower needs? An organizational justice perspective. *European Journal of Work and Organizational Psychology, 17*(2), 180–197.

Mayer, J. D. (1986). How mood influences cognition. In N. Sharkey (Ed.), *Advances in cognitive science* (pp. 290–314). Chichester, UK: Ellis Horwood.

Mayer, J. D., Caruso, D. R., & Salovey, P. (2000). Emotional intelligence meets traditional standards for an intelligence. *Intelligence, 27,* 267–298.

Mayer, J. D., & Salovey, P. (1993). The intelligence of emotional intelligence. *Intelligence, 17,* 433–442.

Mayer, J. D., & Salovey, P. (1995). Emotional intelligence and the construction and regulation of feelings. *Applied and Preventive Psychology, 4,* 197–208.

Mayer, J. D., & Salovey, P. (1997). What is emotional intelligence? In P. Salovey & D. J. Sluyter (Eds.), *Emotional development and emotional intelligence: Educational implications* (pp. 3–31). New York: Basic Books.

Mayer, J. D., Salovey, P., & Caruso, D. R. (2004). Emotional intelligence: Theory, findings, and implications. *Psychological Inquiry, 15*(3), 197–215.

Mayer, J. D., Salovey, P., & Caruso, D. R. (2008). Emotional intelligence: New ability or eclectic traits? *American Psychologist, 63*(6), 503–517.

Mayer, R. C., & Davis, J. H. (1995). An integrative model of organizational trust. *Academy of Management Review, 29,* 709–734.

McAllister, D. J. (1995). Affect- and cognition-based trust as foundations for interpersonal cooperation in organizations. *Academy of Management Journal, 38,* 24–61.

McCabe, D., & Trevino, L. K.(1993). Academic dishonesty: Honor codes and other contextual influences. *Journal of Higher Education, 64,* 522–569.

McCall, J. J. (2003). A defense of just cause dismissal rules. *Business Ethics Quarterly, 13*(2), 151–175.

McCann, N. D., & McGinn, T. A. (1992). *Harassed: 100 women define inappropriate behavior in the workplace.* Homewood, IL: Business Irwin.

McCuddy, M. K., & Cavin, M. C. (2008). Fundamental moral orientations, servant leadership, and leadership effectiveness: An empirical test. *Review of Business Research, 8*(4), 107–117.

McFarlin, D. B., & Sweeney, P. D. (2000). *Where egos dare.* London, UK: Kogan Page.

McFarlin, D. B., & Sweeney, P. D. (2010). The corporate reflecting pool: Antecedents and consequences of narcissism in executives. In B. Schyns & T. Hansbrough (Eds.), *When leadership goes wrong: Destructive leadership, mistakes, and ethical failures* (pp. 247–283). Charlotte, NC: Information Age.

McGeary, J. (2004, May 24). Pointing fingers. *Time*, pp. 43–47, 50.

McGreal, C. (2010, April 10). Who watches WikiLeaks? *The Guardian*, Comment, p. 32.

McGuire, C. (2006, November 27). Managing a graceful bon voyage. *PR Week*, p. 18.

McKinnon, C. (1999). *Character, virtue theories, and the vices.* Peterborough, ON: Broadview Press.

McLean, B., & Elkind, P. (2003). *The smartest guys in the room: The amazing rise and fall of Enron.* New York: Portfolio.

McMahon, J. M, & Harvey, R. J. (2006). An analysis of the factor structure of Jones' moral intensity construct. *Journal of Business Ethics, 64,* 381–404.

McNamara, G., Moon, H., & Bromiley, P. (2002). Banking on commitment: Intended and unintended consequences of an organization's attempt to attenuate escalation of commitment. *Academy of Management Journal, 45,* 443–452.

McNatt, D. B. (2000). Ancient Pygmalion joins contemporary management: A meta-analysis of the result. *Journal of Applied Psychology, 85,* 314–322.

McNeil, Jr., D. G. (2010, October 14). Welcome to life. *The Oregonian,* pp. A1, A7.

McPhail, K. (2001). The other objective of ethics education: Re-humanising the accounting profession—A study of ethics education in law, engineering, medicine and accountancy. *Journal of Business Ethics, 34,* 279–298.

Meisenbach, R. J. (2006). Habermas's discourse ethics and principle of universalization as a moral framework for organizational communication. *Management Communication Quarterly, 20*(1), 39–62.

Melchin, K. R. (1998). *Living with other people: An introduction to Christian ethics based on Bernard Lonergan.* Collegeville, MN: The Liturgical Press.

Messick, D. M., & Bazerman, M. H. (1996, Winter). Ethical leadership and the psychology of decision making. *Sloan Management Review,* pp. 9–23.

Miceli, M. P., Near, J. P., & Dworkin, T. M. (2008). *Whistle-blowing in organizations.* New York: Routledge.

Miceli, M. P., Near, J. P., & Dworkin, T. M. (2009). A word to the wise: How managers and policy-makers can encourage employees to report wrongdoing. *Journal of Business Ethics, 86,* 379–396.

Michalos, A. C. (1995). *A pragmatic approach to business ethics.* Thousand Oaks, CA: Sage.

Mieszkowski, K. (2020, June 13). Stanford considers guideline for 'conflict minerals.' *The New York Times,* p. A31.

Miethe, T. D. (1999). *Whistleblowing at work: Tough choices in exposing fraud, waste, and abuse on the job.* Boulder, CO: Westview Press.

Mihoces, G. (2007, June 19). Concussions command NFL's attention. *USA Today,* p. 1C.

Milgram, S. (1974). *Obedience to authority.* New York: Harper & Row.

Miller, B. K., Rutherford, M. A., & Kolodinsky, R. W. (2008). Perceptions of organizational politics: A meta-analysis. *Journal of Business Psychology, 22,* 209–222.

Miller, W. A. (1981). *Make friends with your shadow.* Minneapolis, MN: Augsburg.

Milton, L. P., & Westphal, J. D. (2005). Identity confirmation networks and cooperation in work groups. *Academy of Management Journal, 48,* 191–212.

Mintzberg, H. (2004). *Managers, not MBAs.* San Francisco: Berrett-Koehler.

Mirvis, P., & Googins, B. (2006). Stages of corporate citizenship. *California Management Review, 48,* 104–126.

Mirvis, P. H. (1997). "Soul work" in organizations. *Organization Science, 8,* 193–206.

Mishra, A. K. (1996). Organizational responses to crisis: The centrality of trust. In R. M. Kramer & T. R. Tyler (Eds.), *Trust in organizations: Frontiers of theory and research* (pp. 261–287). Thousand Oaks, CA: Sage.

MissionStatements.com (2010). Retrieved from http://www.missionstatement.com/fortune_500_mission_statements.html

Mitchell, C. (2003). *A short course in international business ethics: Combining ethics and profits in global business.* Novato, CA: World Trade Press.

Moore, A. (2000). Employee monitoring and computer technology: Evaluative surveillance vs. privacy. *Business Ethics Quarterly, 10,* 697–709.

Moore, T. (1992). *Care of the soul: A guide to cultivating depth and sacredness in everyday life.* New York: HarperCollins.

Moore, T. (1995). Caring for the soul in business. In B. Defoore & J. Renesch (Eds.), *Rediscovering the soul of business: A renaissance of values* (pp. 341–356). San Francisco: Sterling & Stone.

Moorhead, G., Neck, C. P., & West, M. S. (1998). The tendency toward defective decision making within self-managing teams: The relevance of groupthink for the 21st century. *Organizational Behavior and Human Decision Processes, 73,* 327–351.

Morris, J. A., Brothridge, C. M., & Urbanski, J. C. (2005). Bringing humility to leadership: Antecedents and consequences of leader humility. *Human Relations, 58*(10), 1323–1350.

Mortenson, E. (2010, April 22). Unpaid internships may skirt rules. *The Oregonian,* p. B1.

Mortkowitz, L. (2010, April 25). Laptops and other devices in class? For more colleges, it doesn't compute. *The Washington Post,* p. G03.

Moscovici, S., Mucchi-Faina, A., & Mass, A. (1994). *Minority influence.* Chicago: Nelson-Hall.

Moscovici, S., Mugny, G., & Van Avermaet, D. (Eds.). (1985). *Perspectives on minority influence.* Cambridge, UK: Cambridge University Press.

Moxley, R. S. (2004). Hardships. In C. D. McCauley, R. S. Moxley, & E. Van Velsor (Eds.), *Handbook of leadership development* (2nd ed., pp. 183–204). San Francisco: Jossey-Bass.

Mugny, G., & Perez, J. A. (1991). *The social psychology of minority influence* (V. W. Lamongie, Trans.). Cambridge, UK: Cambridge University Press.

Mulhall, S., & Swift, A. (1992). *Liberals and Communitarians.* Oxford, UK: Blackwell.

Mundy, A. (2005, March 8). The board took 8 days to decide CEO had to go. *The Seattle Times,* p. A1.

Munrol, N. (2002). Patient-lobbyists divided over cloning. *National Journal, 34,* 1490–1491.

Murphy, D. (2004, June 4). Abu Ghraib holds mirror to Arabs. *The Christian Science Monitor,* p. 1C.

Muzaffar, C. (2002). Conclusion. In P. F. Knitter & C. Muzaffar (Eds.), *Subverting greed: Religious perspectives on the global economy* (pp. 154–172). Maryknoll, NY: Orbis Books.

Myerson, D. E. (2001). *Tempered radicals: How people use difference to inspire change at work.* Boston, MA: Harvard Business School Press.

Nagourney, A., & Cathcart, R. (2010, September 22). Well-paid officials arrested to cheers. *The New York Times,* p. A14.

Narvaez, D. (2006). Integrative ethical education. In M. Killen & J. G. Smetana (Eds.), *Handbook of moral development* (pp. 703–733). Mahwah, NJ: Lawrence Erlbaum.

Narvaez, D., & Lapsley, D. K. (2005). The psychological foundations of morality and moral expertise. In D. K. Lapsley & F. C. Power (Eds.), *Character psychology and character education* (pp. 140–165). Notre Dame, IN: University of Notre Dame Press, p. 151.

Nash, L. (1990). *Good intentions aside: A manager's guide to resolving ethical problems.* Boston: Harvard Business School Press.

Naughton, K., & Gimbel, B. (2004, March 14). Martha's fall. *Newsweek,* pp. 28–36.

Neff, J. (2009, April 20). Green-marketing revolution defies economic downturn. *Advertising Age.*

Nemeth, C. (1985). Dissent, group process and creativity: The contribution of minority influence research. In E. Lawler (Ed.), *Advances in group processes* (Vol. 2, pp. 57–75). Greenwich, CT: JAI.

Nemeth, C., & Chiles, C. (1986). Modeling courage: The role of dissent in fostering independence. *European Journal of Social Psychology, 18,* 275–280.

Neuman, J. H. (2004). Injustice, stress, and aggression in organizations. In R. W. Griffin & A. M. O'Leary-Kelly (Eds.), *The dark side of organizational behavior* (pp. 62–102). San Francisco: Jossey-Bass.

Neuman, J. H., & Baron, R. A. (1997). Aggression in the workplace. In R. A. Giacalone & J. Greenberg (Eds.), *Antisocial behavior in organizations* (pp. 37–67). Thousand Oaks, CA: Sage.

Newstrom, J. W., & Davis, K. (1993). *Organizational behavior: Human behavior at work* (9th ed.). New York: McGraw-Hill.

Newton, L. H. (2005). *Business ethics and the natural environment.* Malden, MA: Blackwell.

Nielsen, S. (2003, November 2). At Wal-Mart, a world power runs the sale bins. *The Oregonian,* pp. E1–E2.

Nocera, J. (2008, July 26). Apple's culture of secrecy. *The New York Times,* p. C1.

Nocera, J. (2010, September 11). H.P.'s blundering board. *The New York Times,* p. B1.

Noddings, N. (2003). *Caring: A feminine approach to ethics and moral education.* Berkeley: University of California Press.

Norman, W., & MacDonald, C. (2004). Getting to the bottom of "triple bottom line." *Business Ethics Quarterly, 14,* 243–262.

Norris, F. (2005, March 8). Moving from scandal to scandal, Boeing finds its road to redemption paved with affairs great and small. *The New York Times,* p. C5.

Novak, M. (2003). A universal culture of human rights and freedom's habits: Caritapolis. In J. H. Dunning (Ed.), *Making globalization good: The moral challenges of global capitalism* (pp. 253–279). Oxford, UK: Oxford University Press.

Nutt, P. (2002). *Why decisions fail.* San Francisco: Berrett-Koehler.

O'Connor, E. S. (1997). Compelling stories: Narrative and the production of the organizational self. In O. F. Williams (Ed.), *The moral imagination: How literature and films can stimulate ethical reflection in the business world* (pp. 185–202). Notre Dame, IN: University of Notre Dame Press.

O'Dwyer, D. (2010, April 3). Why online whistleblowers need protection from the powerful. *The Irish Times,* Weekend, p. 2.

Offermann, L. R., & Malamut, A. B. (2002). When leaders harass: The impact of target perceptions of organizational leadership and climate on harassment reporting and outcomes. *Journal of Applied Psychology, 87,* 885–893.

Offstein, E. H., & Dufresne, R. L. (2007). Building strong ethics and promoting positive character development: The influence of HRM at the United States Military Academy at West Point. *Human Resource Management, 46*(1), 95–114.

O'Leary-Kelly, A. M. (2001). Sexual harassment as unethical behavior: The role of moral intensity. *Human Resource Management Review, 11,* 73–92.

O'Leary-Kelly, A. M., Griffin, R. W., & Glew, D. J. (1996). Organization-motivated aggression: A research framework. *Academy of Management Review, 21,* 225–253.

O'Leary-Kelly, A. M., Paetzold, R. L., & Griffin, L. W. (2000). Sexual harassment as aggressive behavior: An actor-based perspective. *Academy of Management Review, 25,* 372–388.

Olson, E. (2008, December 30). A nonprofit for veterans is faulted on spending. *The New York Times,* p. B3.

Opotow, S. (1990). Deterring moral exclusion. *Journal of Social Issues, 46,* 173–182.

Opotow, S. (1990). Moral exclusion and injustice: An introduction. *Journal of Social Issues, 46,* 1–20.

Opotow, S. (1995). Drawing the line: Social categorization, moral exclusion, and the scope of justice. In B. B. Bunker & J. Z. Rubin (Eds.), *Conflict, cooperation, and justice: Essays inspired by the work of Morton Deutsch* (pp. 347–369). San Francisco: Jossey-Bass.

Opotow, S. (2005). Hate, conflict, and moral exclusion. In R. J. Sternberg (Ed.), *The psychology of hate* (pp. 121–154). Washington, DC: American Psychological Association.

Opotow, S., Gerson, J., & Woodside, S. (2005). From moral exclusion to moral inclusion: Theory for teaching peace. *Theory into Practice 44*(4), 303–318.

Opotow, S., & Weiss, L. (2000). Denial and the process of moral exclusion in environmental conflict. *Journal of Social Issues, 56*(3), 475–490.

Organ, D. W. (1988). *Organizational citizenship behavior: The good soldier syndrome.* Lexington, MA: Lexington Books.

Oswick, C. (2009). Burgeoning workplace spirituality? A textual analysis of momentum and directions. *Journal of Management, Spirituality & Religion, 6,* 15–25.

Oz, S., & Eden, D. (1994). Restraining the golem: Boosting performance by changing the interpretation of low scores. *Journal of Applied Psychology, 79,* 744–754.

Packer, D. J. (2009). Avoiding groupthink: Whereas weakly identified members remain silent, strongly identified members dissent about collective problems. *Psychological Science, 20*(5), 546–548.

Padded résumés: Fake laurels that went unnoticed for years. (2003, January 13). *BusinessWeek,* p. 1C.

Padilla, A., Hogan, R., & Kaiser, R. B. (2007). The toxic triangle: Destructive leaders, susceptible followers, and conducive environments. *The Leadership Quarterly, 18,* 176–194.

Paine, L. S. (1996, March-April). Managing for organizational integrity. *Harvard Business Review,* pp. 106–117.

Paine, L. S. (1996). Moral thinking in management: An essential capability. *Business Ethics Quarterly, 6*(4), 477–492, p. 477.

Paine, L. S. (2003). *Value shift: Why companies must merge social and financial imperatives to achieve superior performance.* New York: McGraw-Hill.

Paine, L. S., Deshpande, R., Margolis, J. D., & Bettcher, K. E. (2005, December). Up to code. *Harvard Business Review,* pp. 122–133.

Park, N., & Peterson, C. M. (2003). Virtues and organizations. In K. S. Cameron, J. E. Dutton, & R. E. Quinn (Eds.), *Positive organizational scholarship: Foundations of a new discipline* (pp. 33–47). San Francisco: Berrett-Koehler.

Park, W-W. (2000). A comprehensive empirical investigation of the relationships among variables of the groupthink model. *Journal of Organizational Behavior, 21,* 873–887.

Paulus, D. L., & Williams, K. M. (2002). The dark triad of personality: Narcissism, Machiavellianism, and psychopathy. *Journal of Research in Personality, 36,* 556–563.

Pearson, C. M., Andersson, L. M., & Porath, C. L. (2000). Assessing and attacking workplace incivility. *Organizational Dynamics, 29,* 123–137.

Pearson, C. M., & Porath, C. L. (2004). On incivility, its impact, and directions for future research. In R. W. Griffin & A. M. O'Leary-Kelly (Eds.), *The dark side of organizational behavior* (pp. 23–61). San Francisco: Jossey-Bass.

Pearson, C. M., & Porath, C. L. (2005). On the nature, consequences and remedies of workplace incivility: No time for "nice"? Think again. *Academy of Management Executive, 19,* 7–18.

Pearson, G. (1995). *Integrity in organizations: An alternative business ethic.* London: McGraw-Hill.

Perrewe, P. L., Ferris, G. R., Stoner, J. S., & Brouer, R. L. (2007). The positive role of political skill in organizations. In D. Nelson & C. L. Cooper (Eds.), *Positive organizational behavior* (pp. 117–128). London: Sage.

Peterson, C., Stephens, J. P., Park, N., Lee, F., & Seligman, M. E. P. (2010). Strengths of character and work. In P. A. Linley, S. Harrington, & N. Garcea (Eds.), *Oxford handbook of positive psychology and work* (pp. 221–231). Oxford, UK: Oxford University Press.

Peterson, D. K. (2002). The relationship between unethical behavior and the dimensions of the Ethical Climate Questionnaire. *Journal of Business Ethics, 41,* 313–326.

Petrick, J. A. (2008). Using the business integrity capacity model to advance business ethics education. In D. L. Swanson & D. G. Fisher (Eds.), *Advancing business ethics education* (pp. 103–124). Charlotte, NC: Information Age.

Petrick, J. A. (2011). The measured impact of the transtheoretical model of educational change on advancing business ethics education. In D. L. Swanson & D. G. Fisher (Eds.), *Toward assessing business ethics education* (pp. 335–360). Charlotte, NC: Information Age.

Pfeffer, J. (1998). *The human equation: Building profits by putting people first.* Boston: Harvard Business School Press.

Phatak, A. V., Bhagat, R. S., & Kashlak, R. J. (2005). *International management: Managing in a diverse and dynamic global environment.* Boston: McGraw-Hill Irwin.

Phillips, R. (2003). *Stakeholder theory and organizational ethics.* San Francisco: Berrett-Koehler.

Piliavin, J. A., & Charng, H-W. (1990). Altruism: A review of recent theory and research. *American Sociological Review, 16,* 27–65.

Pilkington, E. (2009, June 23). What's driving Steve Jobs? *The Guardian,* Features, p. 4.

Pillmore, E. M. (2003, December). How we're fixing up Tyco. *Harvard Business Review,* 96–97.

Piper, T. R., Gentile, M. C., & Parks, S. D. (1993). *Can ethics be taught? Perspectives, challenges, and approaches at Harvard Business School.* Boston: Harvard Business School Press.

Pogrebin, R. (2007, June 21). Smithsonian ex-chief criticized in report. *The New York Times,* p. E1.

Pogrebin, R., & Taylor, K. (2010, April 26). Pulling the reins (a bit) on hefty salaries for cultural executives. *The New York Times,* p. C1.

Polgreen, L. (2008, November 16). Congo's riches, looted by renegade troops. *The New York Times,* p. A1.

Ponemon, L. A. (1990). Ethical judgments in accounting: A cognitive-developmental perspective. *Critical Perspectives on Accounting, 1,* 191–215.

Ponemon, L. A. (1992). Ethical reasoning and selection-socialization in accounting. *Accounting, Organizations and Society, 17*(3/4), 239–258.

Pontin, J. (2000, July 3). Foul-mouthed genius—What did you expect Apple's Steve Jobs to be like? *The Scotsman,* p. 18.

Posner, B. Z. (2010). Another look at the impact of personal and organizational values congruency. *Journal of Business Ethics, 97,* 535–541.

Post, S. G. (2002). The tradition of agape. In S. G. Post, L. G. Underwood, J. P. Schloss, & W. B. Hurlbut (Eds.), *Altruism and altruistic love: Science, philosophy, and religion in dialogue* (pp. 51–64). Oxford, UK: Oxford University Press.

Post, S. G., Underwood, L. G., Schloss, J. P., & Hurlbut, W. B. (2002). General introduction. In S. G. Post, L. G. Underwood, J. P. Schloss, & W. B. Hurlbut (Eds.), *Altruism and altruistic love: Science, philosophy, & Religion in dialogue* (pp. 3–12). Oxford, UK: Oxford University Press.

Postmes, T., Spears, R., & Cihangir, S. (2001). Quality of decision-making and group norms. *Journal of Personality and Social Psychology, 80,* 918–930.

Prahalad, C. K., & Hammond, A. (2002, September). Serving the world's poor, profitably. *Harvard Business Review,* p. 48–57.

Puffer, S. M., & McCarthy, D. J. (2008). Ethical turnarounds and transformational leadership: A global imperative for corporate social responsibility. *Thunderbird International Business Review, 50,* 303–313.

Quigley, N. R., Sully de Luque, M., & House, R. J. (2005). Responsible leadership and governance in a global context: Insights from the GLOBE study. In J. P. Doh & S. A. Stumpf (Eds.), *Handbook on responsible leadership and governance in global business* (pp. 352–379). Cheltenham, UK: Edward Elgar.

Quinn, R. E. (1996). *Deep change.* San Francisco: Jossey-Bass.

Quinn, R. E. (2000). *Change the world: How ordinary people can achieve extraordinary results.* San Francisco: Jossey-Bass.

Radin, T. J., & Werhane, P. H. (2003). Employment-at-will, employee rights, and future directions for employment. *Business Ethics Quarterly, 13*(2), 113–130.

Radtke, J. M. (1998). *Strategic communications for nonprofit organizations: Seven steps to creating a successful plan.* New York: John Wiley.

Rafaeli, A., & Sutton, R. I. (1989). The expression of emotion in organizational life. In L. L. Cummings & B. M. Staw (Eds.), *Research in organizational behavior* (Vol. 2, pp. 1–42). Greenwich, CT: JAI.

Rafter, M. V. (2005, May). Nike opens a window on overseas factories. *Workforce Management, 84,* 17.

Rahim, M. A. (1983). A measure of styles of handling interpersonal conflict. *Academy of Management Journal, 26,* 368–376.

Rahim, M. A., Buntzman, G. F., & White, D. (1999). An empirical study of the stages of moral development and conflict management styles. *The International Journal of Conflict Management, 10,* 154–171.

Rahim, M. A., Garrett, J. E., & Buntzman, G. F. (1992). Ethics of managing interpersonal conflict in organizations. *Journal of Business Ethics 11,* 423–432.

Randolph, W. A. (2000). Re-thinking empowerment: Why is it so hard to achieve? *Organizational Dynamics, 29,* 94–107.

Rawls, J. (1971). *A theory of justice.* Cambridge, MA: Belknap Press.

Rawls, J. (1993). Distributive justice. In T. Donaldson & P. H. Werhane (Eds.), *Ethical issues in business: A philosophical approach* (4th ed., pp. 274–285). Englewood Cliffs, NJ: Prentice Hall.

Rawls, J. (1993). *Political liberalism.* New York: Columbia University Press.

Rawls, J. (2001). *Justice as fairness: A restatement* (E. Kelly, Ed.). Cambridge, MA: Belknap Press.

Rayburn, C. A. (1997). Vocation as calling. In D. P. Bloch & L. J. Richmond (Eds.), *Connections between spirit and work in career development* (pp. 162–183). Palo Alto, CA: Davies-Black.

Reddan, F. (2010, March 8). Taking a morbid approach to investment in workers. *The Irish Times,* Finance, p. 19.

Rego, A., & Pina e Cunha, M. (2008). Workplace spirituality and organizational commitment: An empirical study. *Journal of Organizational Change Management, 21*(1), 53–75.

Reina, D. S., & Reina, M. L. (2006). *Trust and betrayal in the workplace.* San Francisco: Berrett-Koehler.

Rest, J. R. (1979). *Development in judging moral issues.* Minneapolis: University of Minnesota Press.

Rest, J. R. (1986). *Moral development: Advances in research and theory.* New York: Praeger.

Rest, J. R. (1993). Research on moral judgment in college students. In A. Garrod (Ed.), *Approaches to moral development* (pp. 201–211). New York: Teachers College Press.

Rest, J. R. (1994). Background: Theory and research. In J. R. Rest & D. Narvaez (Eds.), *Moral development in the professions: Psychology and applied ethics* (pp. 1–25). Hillsdale, NJ: Lawrence Erlbaum.

Rest, J. R., & Narvaez, D. (1991). The college experience and moral development. In W. M. Kurtines & J. L. Gewirtz (Eds.), *Handbook of moral behavior and development. Vol. 2: Research* (pp. 229–245). Hillsdale, NJ: Lawrence Erlbaum.

Rest, J. R., Narvaez, D., Bebeau, M. J., & Thoma, S. J. (1999). *Postconventional moral thinking: A neo-Kohlbergian approach.* Mahwah, NJ: Lawrence Erlbaum.

Reynolds, D. (2007). Restraining Golem and harnessing Pygmalion in the classroom: A laboratory study of managerial expectations and task design. *Academy of Management Learning & Education, 6*(4), 475–483.

Reynolds, S. J., & Ceranic, T. L. (2007). The effects of moral judgment and moral identity on moral behavior: An empirical examination of the moral individual. *Journal of Applied Psychology, 92*(6), 1610–1624.

Rice, D., & Dreilinger, C. (1990, May). Rights and wrongs of ethics training. *Training and Development Journal,* pp. 103–108.

Ridberg, M. (2006, May 4). Professors want their classes 'unwired.'" *The Christian Science Monitor*, Currents, p. 16.

Risen, J. (2004, May 3). The struggle for Iraq: Prisoners. *The New York Times*, p. A1.

Ripley, A. (2004, June 21). Redefining torture. *Time*, pp. 49–50.

Ritson, M. (2005, April 20). Nike shows way to return from the wilderness. *Marketing* (UK), p. 21.

Roberto, M. A. (2002). Lessons from Everest: The interaction of cognitive bias, psychological safety, and system complexity. *California Management Review, 45*(1), 136–158.

Roberts, K. E. (2001). Case: Anglo-German trading corporation. In M. H. Albrecht (Ed.), *International HRM: Managing diversity in the workplace* (pp. 360–361). Malden, MA: Blackwell.

Robins, S. P., & Judge, T. A. (2011). *Organizational behavior* (14th ed.). Boston: Prentice Hall.

Robinson, M. (2000). Internalizing human rights in corporate business practices. *UN Chronicle, 37*, 38–39.

Rodriguez, J. (2010, April 3). Inside the cult of Apple. *The Star Phoenix*, p. E1.

Roesler, R. (2003, March 3). Lawmakers may tighten up "dead peasant" laws. *Spokesman Review*, p. A6.

Rogoway, M. (2010, June 25). Conflict minerals rule will affect Oregon's high-tech sector. *The Oregonian*, pp. B4, B5.

Roloff, M. E., & Paulson, G. D. (2001). Confronting organizational transgressions. In J. M. Darley, D. M. Messick, & T. R. Tyler (Eds.), *Social influences on ethical behavior in organizations* (pp. 53–68). Mahwah, NJ: Lawrence Erlbaum.

Romar, E. J. (2002). Virtue is good business: Confucianism as a practical business ethics. *Journal of Business Ethics, 38*, 119–131.

Romar, E. J. (2004). Globalization, ethics, and opportunism: A Confucian view of business relationships. *Business Ethics Quarterly, 14*, 663–678.

Rosenfeld, P., Giacalone, R. A., & Riordan, C. A. (1995). *Impression management in organizations: Theory, measurement, practice*. London: Routledge.

Rosenthal, R. (1993). Interpersonal expectations: Some antecedents and some consequences. In P. D. Blanck (Ed.), *Interpersonal expectations: Theory, research, and applications* (pp. 3–24). Cambridge, UK: Cambridge University Press.

Rosenthal, R., & Jacobson, L. (1968). *Pygmalion in the classroom*. New York: Holt, Rinehart & Winston.

Ross, J., & Staw, B. M. (1993). Organizational escalation and exit: Lessons from the Shoreham Nuclear Plant. *Academy of Management Journal, 36*, 701–732.

Ross, W. T., & Robertson, D. C. (2000). Lying: The impact of decision context. *Business Ethics Quarterly, 10*, 409–440.

Rost, J. (1991). *Leadership for the twenty-first century*. New York: Praeger.

Rost, J. (1993). Leadership in the new millennium. *Journal of Leadership Studies, 1*, 92–110.

Rost, J. C. (1995). Leadership: A discussion about ethics. *Business Ethics Quarterly, 5*(1), 129–142.

Rost, J. C. (2008). Followership: An outmoded concept. In R. E. Riggio, I. Chaleff, & J. Lipman-Blumen (Eds.), *The art of followership* (pp. 53–64). San Francisco: Jossey-Bass.

Rothwell, J. D. (1998). *In mixed company: Small group communication* (3rd ed.). Fort Worth, TX: Harcourt Brace.

Rousseau, D. M., Sitkin, S. B., Burt, R. S., & Camerer, C. (1998). Not so different after all: A cross-discipline view of trust. *Academy of Management Review, 23*, 393–404.

Rubin, J. Z., & Brown, B. R. (1975). *The social psychology of bargaining and negotiation*. New York: Academic Press.

Rubin, R. (2010, October 1). FDA says recall of adult Motrin 'took too long': company hired contractor to buy up affected product. *USA Today*, p. 4A.

Ruggieri, S. (2009). Leadership in virtual teams: A comparison of transformational and transactional leaders. *Social Behavior and Personality, 36*(8), 1017–1022.

Runde, C. E., & Flanagan, T. A. (2007). *Becoming a conflict competent leader.* San Francisco: Jossey-Bass.

Runde, C. E., & Flanagan, T. A. (2008, Winter). Conflict competent leadership. *Leader to Leader,* pp. 46–51.

Ruschman, N. L. (2002). Servant-leadership and the best companies to work for in America. In L. C. Spears & M. Lawrence (Eds.), *Focus on leadership: Servant-leadership for the twenty-first century* (pp. 123–139). New York: John Wiley.

Ryan, L. V., Buchholtz, A. K., & Kolb, R. W. (2010). New directions in corporate governance and finance: Implications for business ethics research. *Business Ethics Quarterly, 20*(4), 673–694.

Saillant, C., & Gottlieb, J. (2010, July 22). Huge pensions await Bell leaders. *Los Angeles Times,* p. AA1.

Salls, H. (2007). *Character education: Transforming values into virtue.* Lanham, MD: University Press of America.

Salovey, P., & Grewal, D. (2005). The science of emotional intelligence. *Current Directions in Psychological Science 14*(6), 281–285.

Salovey, P., Hsee, C. K., & Mayer, J. D. (1993). Emotional intelligence and the self-regulation of affect. In D. M. Wegner & J. W. Pennebaker (Eds.), *Handbook of mental control* (pp. 258–277). Englewood Cliffs, NJ: Prentice Hall.

Saraceno, J. (2004, December 29). White's death sends message to super-sized NFL. *USA Today,* p. 12C.

Scarpello, V. G. (2008). Parallel approaches to development of the HRM field and HRM education. In V. G. Scarpello (Ed.), *The handbook of human resource management education: Promoting an effective and efficient curriculum* (pp. 3–37). Thousand Oaks, CA: Sage.

Scelfo, J., & Nordland, R. (2004, July 19). Beneath the hoods. *Newsweek,* pp. 40–42.

Schafer, M., & Crichlow, S. (2010). *Groupthink versus high-quality decision making in international relations.* New York: Columbia University Press.

Schat, A. C. H., Frone, M. R., & Kelloway, E. K. (2006). Prevalence of workplace aggression in the U.S. workforce: Findings from a national study. In E. K. Kelloway, J. Barling, & J. J. Hurrell (Eds.) *Handbook of workplace violence* (pp. 47–89). Thousand Oaks, CA: Sage.

Schein, E. H. (1992). *Organizational culture and leadership* (2nd ed.). San Francisco: Jossey-Bass.

Schlegelmilch, B. B., & Oberseder, M. (2010). Half a century of marketing ethics: Shifting perspectives and emerging trends. *Journal of Business Ethics, 93,* 2–3.

Schlenker, B. R. (1980). *Impression management: The self-concept, social identity, and interpersonal relations.* Monterey, CA: Brooks/Cole.

Schminke, M. (Ed.). (1998). *Managerial ethics: Moral management of people and processes.* Mahwah, NJ: Lawrence Erlbaum.

Schrodt, P., Turman, P. D., & Soliz, J. (2006). Perceived understanding as a mediator of perceived teacher confirmation and students' rating of instruction. *Communication Education, 55*(4), 370–388.

Schwartz, M. (2001). The nature of the relationship between corporate codes of ethics and behaviour. *Journal of Business Ethics, 32,* 247–262.

Schwartz, S. H. (1994a). Are there universal aspects in the structure and contents of human values? *Journal of Social Issues, 50,* 19–45.

Schwartz, S. H. (1994b). Beyond individualism/collectivism: New cultural dimensions of values. In U. Kim, H. C. Triandis, C. Kagitcibasi, S. Choi, & G. Yoon (Eds.), *Individualism and collectivism: Theory, method and applications* (pp. 85–119). Thousand Oaks, CA: Sage.

Schwartz, S. H., & Sagiv, L. (1995). Identifying culture-specifics in the content and structure of values. *Journal of Cross-Cultural Psychology, 26,* 92–116.

Schwarz, A. (2007, May 31). Study of ex-N.F.L. players ties concussion to depression risk. *The New York Times,* p. A1.

Schwarz, A. (2009, December 3). New N. F. L. rule on concussions benches injured. *The New York Times,* p. A1.

Schwepker, C. H., & Good, D. J. (2010). Transformational leadership and its impact on sales force moral judgment. *Journal of Personal Selling & Sales Management, 30*(4), 299–317.

Scileppi, P. A. (2005). *Values for interpersonal communication: How then shall we live?* Belmont, CA: Star.

Scott, E. D. (2005). The ethics of human resource management. In J. W. Budd & J. G. Scoville (Eds.), *The ethics of human resources and industrial relations* (pp. 173–201). Champaign, IL: Labor Relations and Employment Association.

Seabright, M. A., & Moberg, D. J. (1998). Interpersonal manipulation: Its nature and moral limits. In M. Schminke (Ed.), *Managerial ethics: Moral management of people and processes* (pp. 153–175). Mahwah, NJ: Lawrence Erlbaum.

Seibert, S. E., Silver, S. R., & Randolph, W. A. (2004). Taking empowerment to the next level: A multiple-level model of empowerment, performance, and satisfaction. *Academy of Management Journal, 47,* 332–349.

Seitel, F. P. (1997). *The practice of public relations* (7th ed.). Upper Saddle River, NJ: Prentice Hall.

Seligman, M. E. P. (2002). *Authentic happiness: Using the positive psychology to realize your potential for lasting fulfillment.* New York: Free Press.

Sellers, P. (2005, August 22). Retire? No way! *Fortune,* p. 18.

Sequera, V. (2010, October 16). Calm engineer led rescue of miners. *The Register-Guard,* p. A6.

Sethi, S. P. (1975). Dimensions of corporate social performance: An analytical framework. *California Management Review, 17,* 58–64.

Shao, R., Aquino, K., & Freeman, D. (2008). Beyond moral reasoning: A review of moral identity research and its implications for business ethics. *Business Ethics Quarterly, 18*(4), 513–540.

Shaub, M. K., & Fisher, D. G. (2008). Beyond agency theory: Common values for accounting. In D. L. Swanson & D. G. Fisher (Eds.), *Advancing business ethics education* (pp. 305–328). Charlotte, NC: Information Age.

Shaw, R. B. (1997). *Trust in the balance: Building successful organizations on results, integrity and concern.* San Francisco: Jossey-Bass.

Shaw, W. H. (2011). *Business ethics: A textbook with cases* (7th ed.). Boston: Wadsworth.

Sheppard, J. A. (1993). Productivity loss in performance groups: A motivation analysis. *Psychological Bulletin, 113,* 67–81.

Sheppard, J. A. (2001). Social loafing and expectancy-value theory. In S. G. Harkins (Ed.), *Multiple perspectives on the effects of evaluation on performance: Toward an integration* (pp. 1–24). Boston: Kluwer.

Shockley-Zalabak, P., Ellis, K., & Winograd, G. (2000). Organizational trust: What it means, why it matters. *Organizational Development Journal, 18,* 35–47.

Shockley-Zalabak, P. S. (2006). *Fundamentals of organizational communication: Knowledge, sensitivity, skills, values* (6th ed.). Boston: Pearson.

Shu, L. L., Gino, F., & Bazerman, M. H. (2009). Dishonest deed, clear conscience: Self-preservation through moral disengagement and motivated forgetting. *Harvard Business School Work Paper No. 09–078.*

Sillars, A. L. (1986). *Procedures for coding interpersonal conflict* (rev.). University of Montana: Department of Communication Studies.

Sims, R. L. (2000). The relationship between employee attitudes and conflicting expectations for lying behavior. *Journal of Psychology, 134,* 619–633.

Sims, R. L., & Keon, T. L. (1997). Ethical work climate as a factor in the development of person-organization fit. *Journal of Business Ethics, 16,* 1095–1105.

Sims, R. R. (1992). Linking groupthink to unethical behavior in organizations. *Journal of Business Ethics, 11,* 651–662.

Sims, R. R. (1994). *Ethics and organizational decision making: A call for renewal.* Westport, CT: Quorum Books.

Sims, R. R. (2002). *Managing organizational behavior.* Westport, CT: Quorum Books.

Sims, R. R. (2003). *Ethics and corporate social responsibility: Why giants fall.* Westport, CT: Praeger.

Sims, R. R., & Brinkmann, J. (2002). Leaders as moral role models: The case of John Gutfreund at Salomon Brothers. *Journal of Business Ethics, 35,* 327–339.

Singer, M., Mitchell, S., & Turner, J. (1998). Consideration of moral intensity in ethicality judgments: Its relationship with whistle-blowing and need-for-cognition. *Journal of Business Ethics 17,* 527–541.

Singer, N. (2010, January 18). In recall, role model stumbles. *The New York Times,* p. B1.

Singer, N. (2010, May 28). F. D. A. weighs more penalties in drug recall by J.&J. unit. *The New York Times,* p. B1.

Singer, N. (2010, June 11). Johnson & Johnson seen as uncooperative on recall inquiry. *The New York Times,* p. B1.

Singer, N. (2010, June 12). More disputes over handling of drug recall. *The New York Times,* p. B3.

Singer, N., & Abelson, R. (2011, January 13). Oregon sues J. & J. in Motrin buyback. *The New York Times,* p. B3.

Singer, P. (2002). *One world: The ethics of globalization.* New Haven, CT: Yale University Press.

Singh, V., Kumra, S., & Vinnicombe, S. (2002). Gender and impression management: Playing the promotion game. *Journal of Business Ethics, 37,* 77–89.

Sison, A. J. G. (2003). *The moral capital of leaders: Why virtue matters.* Northampton, MA: Edward Elgar.

Sixel, L. M. (2010, January 7). 'Dead peasant' policies. *The Houston Chronicle,* Business, p. 1.

Sixel, L. M. (2010, January 9). Widow settles life insurance case. *The Houston Chronicle,* Business, p. 1.

Smith, B. N., Kerr, N. A., Markus, M. J., & Stasson, M. F. (2001). Individual differences in social loafing: Need for cognition as a motivator in collective performance. *Group Dynamics: Theory, Research, and Practice, 5*(2), 150–158.

Smith, E. E. (2010, February 3). National campaign against McDonald's mascot kicks off in Cedar Mill. *The Oregonian,* pp. B1 & B3.

Smith, N. C. (1993). Ethics and the marketing manager. In N. C. Smith & J. A. Quelch (Eds.). *Ethics in marketing* (pp.1–34). Burr Ridge, IL: Irwin.

Smith, P., & Lorentzon, M. (2005). Is emotional labour ethical? *Nursing Ethics, 12,* 638–642.

Smith, P. K., Jostmann, N. B., Galinsky, A. D., & van Dijk, W. W. (2008). Lacking power impairs executive function. *Psychological Science, 19,* 441–447.

Smithey Fulmer, I., & Barry, B. (2009). Managed hearts and wallets: Ethical issues in emotional influence by and within organizations. *Business Ethics Quarterly, 12,* 155–191.

Snow, N. E. (2003). Self-forgiveness. *The Journal of Value Inquiry, 27,* 75–80.

Soares, C. (2007, September 4). Norwegian prisoners do organic porridge in world's first "green jail." *Belfast Telegraph,* http://www.belfasttelegraph.co.uk

Social Accountability International. (2005). *Overview of SA8000.* Retrieved from http://www.sa-intl.org

Solomon, R. C. (1993). What a tangled web: Deception and self-deception in philosophy. In M. Lewis & C. Saarni (Eds.), *Lying and deception in everyday life* (pp. 30–58). New York: Guilford Press.

Sorokin, P. A. (1954). *The ways and power of love: Types, factors, and techniques of moral transformation.* Boston: Beacon Press.

Spangle, M. L., & Isenhart, M. W. (2003). *Negotiation: Communication for diverse settings.* Thousand Oaks, CA: Sage.

Spears, L. C. (2002). Introduction: Tracing the past, present and future of servant-leadership. In L. C. Spears & M. Lawrence (Eds.), *Focus on leadership: Servant-leadership for the twenty-first century* (pp. 1–18). New York: John Wiley.

Spector, M., & Banjo, S. (2009, March 27). Currents: Pay at nonprofits gets a closer look. *The Wall Street Journal,* p. A9.

Spreitzer, G. M. (1995). Psychological empowerment in the workplace: Dimensions, measurement, and validation. *Academy of Management Journal, 38,* 1442–1485.

Spreitzer, G. M. (1996). Social structural characteristics of psychological empowerment. *Academy of Management Journal, 39,* 483–504.

Spreitzer, G. M., Kizilos, M. A., & Nason, S. W. (1997). A dimensional analysis of the relationship between psychological empowerment and effectiveness, satisfaction, and strain. *Journal of Management, 23,* 679–705.

Staczek, J. J. (2008). An interview with Eric M. Pillmore: Hitting the CSR bull's-eye in a shifting corporate environment. *Thunderbird International Business Review, 50,* 295–301.

Stairs, M., & Galpin, M. (2010). Positive engagement: From employee engagement to workplace happiness. In P. A. Linley, S. Harrington, & N. Garcea (Eds.), *Oxford handbook of positive psychology and work* (pp. 155–172). New York: Oxford University Press.

Stansbury, J. (2009). Reasoned moral agreement: Applying discourse ethics within organizations. *Business Ethics Quarterly, 19,* 33–56.

Stanwick, P. A., & Stanwick, S. D. (2009). *Understanding business ethics.* Upper Saddle River, NJ: Pearson Education, p. 2.

Starr, M. (2004, August 16). A long jump. *Newsweek,* pp. 52–53.

Statman, D. (1997). Introduction to virtue ethics. In D. Statman (Ed.), *Virtue ethics* (pp. 1–41). Washington, DC: Georgetown University Press.

Staw, B. M. (1981). The escalation of commitment to a course of action. *Academy of Management Review, 6,* 577–587.

Steinberg, R. J., & Figart, D. M. (1999). Emotional labor since The Managed Heart. *Annals of the American Academy of Political and Social Sciences, 561,* 10–26.

Sternberg, R. J. (2000). Images of mindfulness. *Journal of Social Issues, 56*(1), 11–26.

Sternberg, R. J. (2002). Smart people are not stupid, but they sure can be foolish: The imbalance theory of foolishness. In R. J. Sternberg (Ed.), *Why smart people can be so stupid* (pp. 232–242). New Haven, CT: Yale University Press.

Stevens, B. (2007). Corporate ethical codes: Effective instruments for influencing behavior. *Journal of Business Ethics, 78,* 601–609.

Stevens, C. K., & Kristof, A. L. (1995). Making the right impression: A field study of applicant impression management during job interviews. *Journal of Applied Psychology, 80,* 587–606.

Stewart, J. (2008). Cosmopolitan communication ethics understanding and action: Religion and dialogue. In K. Glenister Roberts & R. C. Arnett (Eds.), *Communication ethics: Between cosmopolitanism and provinciality* (pp. 105–119). New York: Peter Lang.

Storr, A. (1983). *The essential Jung.* Princeton, NJ: Princeton University Press.

Street, M. D. (1997). Groupthink: An examination of theoretical issues, implications, and future research suggestions. *Small Group Research, 28,* 72–93.

Super, D. E. (1990). A life-span, life-space approach to career development. In D. Brown, L. Brooks, & Associates (Eds.), *Career choice and development: Applying contemporary theories to practice* (2nd ed.). San Francisco: Jossey-Bass.

Susskind, L., & Field, P. (1996). *Dealing with an angry public: The mutual gains approach to resolving disputes.* New York: Free Press.

Sussman, L., Adams, A. J., Kuzmits, F. E., & Raho, L. E. (2002). Organizational politics: Tactics, channels, and hierarchical roles. *Journal of Business Ethics, 40,* 313–329.

Sutton, R. I. (1991). Maintaining norms about expressed emotions: The case of bill collectors. *Administrative Science Quarterly, 36,* 245–268.

Sutton, R. I., & Rafaeli, A. (1988). Untangling the relationship between displayed emotions and organizational sales: The case of convenience stores. *Academy of Management Journal, 31,* 461–487.

Swanson, D. L., & Fisher, D. G. (Eds.). (2008). *Advancing business ethics education.* Charlotte, NC: Information Age.

Sweeney, B., & Costello, F. (2009). Moral intensity and ethical decision-making: An empirical examination of undergraduate accounting and business students. *Accounting Education: An International Journal, 18*(1), 75–97.

Tangney, J. P. (2005). Humility. In C. R. Snyder & S. J. Lopez (Eds.), *Handbook of positive psychology* (pp. 411–419). Oxford, UK: Oxford University Press.

Teather, D. (2005, June 9). Fatboy Ronald McDonald downsizes to head off critics. *The Guardian,* City, p. 19.

The Ten Commandments of Computer Ethics. Computer Ethics Institute. Retrieved January 17, 2010, from http://computerethicsinstitute.org

Tenbrunsel, A. E., Diekman, K. A., Wade-Benzoni, K. A., & Bazerman, M. H. (2009). The ethical mirage: A temporal explanation as to why we aren't as ethical as we think we are. *Harvard Business School Working Paper No. 08–012.* Available at http://www.people.hbs.edu/mbazerman

Tenbrunsel, A. E., Smith-Crowe, K., & Umphress, E. E. (2003). Building houses on rocks: The role of ethical infrastructure in organizations. *Social Justice Research, 16,* 285–307.

`T Hart, P. (1990*). Groupthink in government.* Amsterdam: Swets & Zeitlinger.

`T Hart, P. (1990). *Groupthink in government: A study of small groups and policy failure.* Baltimore, MD: Johns Hopkins University Press.

Thomas, E., Taylor, S., Jr., Murr, A., Wingert, P., Clift, E., & Meadows, S. (2005, July 11). Queen of the center. *Newsweek,* pp. 24–31.

Thomas, K. W., & Kilmann, R. (1977). Developing a forced-choice measure of conflict-handling behavior: The MODE instrument. *Educational and Psychological Measurement, 37,* 390–395.

Thomas, K. W., & Velthouse, B. A. (1990). Cognitive elements of empowerment: An "interpretive" model of intrinsic task motivation. *Academy of Management Review, 15,* 666–681.

Thompson, H. (1999, March 8). The massacre at My Lai. *Newsweek,* p. 64.

Tileaga, C. (2006). Representing the 'other': A discursive analysis of prejudice and moral exclusion in talk about Romanies. *Journal of Community & Applied Social Psychology, 16,* 19–41.

Timmons, H., Cohn, L., McNamee, M., & Rossant, J. (2002, August 5). CITI's sleepless nights. *BusinessWeek,* pp. 42–43.

Tjosvold, D. (1984). Cooperation theory and organizations. *Human Relations, 37,* 743–767.

Tjosvold, D. (1986). The dynamics of interdependence in organizations. *Human Relations, 39,* 517–540.

Tobias, A. (1976). *Fire and ice.* New York: William Morrow.

Toffler, B. L., & Reingold, J. (2003). *Final accounting: Ambition, greed, and the fall of Arthur Andersen.* New York: Broadway Books.

Tompkins, P. K., & Cheney, G. (1985). Communication and unobtrusive control in contemporary organizations. In R. D. McPhee & P. K. Tompkins (Eds.), *Organizational communication: Traditional themes and new directions* (pp. 179–210). Newbury Park, CA: Sage.

Toor, S., & Ofori, G. (2009). Ethical leadership: Examining the relationships with full range leadership model, employee outcomes, and organizational cultures. *Journal of Business Ethics, 90,* 533–547.

Top 10 reasons why David Letterman's sex saga is not funny. (2009, October 9). *The Christian Science Monitor,* Editorial, p. 8.

Tracy, S. J. (2000). Becoming a character for commerce: Emotion labor, self-subordination, and discursive construction of identity in a total institution. *Management Communication Quarterly, 14,* 90–128.

Tracy, S. J., & Tracy, K. (1998). Emotional labor at 911. *Journal of Applied Communication Research, 26,* 390–411.

Trenholm, S., & Jensen, A. (2004). *Interpersonal communication* (5th ed.). New York: Oxford University Press.

Trevino, L. K. (1986). Ethical decision making in organizations: A person-situation interactionist model. *Academy of Management Review, 11,* 601–607.

Trevino, L. K. (1990). A cultural perspective on changing and developing organizational ethics. In W. A. Pasmore & R. W. Woodman (Eds.), *Research in organizational change and development* (Vol. 4). Greenwich, CT: JAI.

Trevino, L. K., Butterfield, K. D., & McCabe, D. L. (1998). The ethical context in organizations: Influences on employee attitudes and behaviors. *Business Ethics Quarterly, 8,* 447–476.

Trevino, L. K., Hartman, L. P., & Brown, M. (2000). Moral person and moral manager: How executives develop a reputation for ethical leadership. *California Management Review, 42,* 128–142.

Trevino, L. K., & Nelson, K. A. (2004). *Managing business ethics: Straight talk about how to do it right* (3rd ed.). Hoboken, NJ: John Wiley.

Trevino, L. K., & Weaver, G. R. (2001). Organizational justice and ethics program "follow-through": Influences on employees' harmful and helpful behavior. *Business Ethics Quarterly 11*(4), 651–671.

Trevino, L. K., & Weaver, G. R. (2003). *Managing ethics in business organizations: Social scientific perspectives.* Stanford, CA: Stanford University Press.

Trevino, L. K., Weaver, G. R., Gibson, D. G., & Toffler, B. L. (1999). Managing ethics and legal compliance: What works and what hurts. *California Management Review, 41,* 131–151.

Trevino, L. K., & Youngblood, S. A. (1990). Bad apples in bad barrels: A causal analysis of ethical decision-making behavior. *Journal of Applied Psychology, 75,* 378–385.

Trice, H. M., & Beyer, J. M. (1984). Studying organizational cultures through rites and ceremonials. *Academy of Management Review, 9,* 653–699.

Tronto, J. C. (1993). *Moral boundaries: A political argument for an ethic of care.* New York: Routledge.

Troyer, J. (Ed.). (2003). *The classical utilitarians: Bentham and Mill.* Indianapolis, IN: Hackett.

Trumbull, M. (2009, October 8). Letterman didn't violate his company's harassment policy. *The Christian Science Monitor,* USA, p. 2.

Turman, P. D., & Schrodt, P. (2006). Student perceptions of teacher power as a function of perceived teacher confirmation. *Communication Education, 55*(3), 265–279.

Turner, N., Barling, J., Epitropaki, O., Butcher, V., & Milner, C. (2002). Transformational leadership and moral reasoning. *Journal of Applied Psychology, 87,* 304–311.

Tuuli, M. M., & Rowlinson, S. (2009). Empowerment in project teams: A multilevel examination of the job performance implications. *Construction Management and Economics, 27,* 473–498.

Ugboro, I. O., & Obeng, K. (2000). Top management leadership, employee empowerment, job satisfaction, and customer satisfaction in TQM organizations: An empirical study. *Journal of Quality Management, 5,* 247–272.

United Nations Global Compact: Participants and stakeholders. Retrieved from http://www .unglobalcompact.org/ParticipantsAndStakeholders/index.html

United Nations Global Compact: The ten principles. Retrieved from http://www.unglobal compact.org

Unruh, G. (2008). Should you manage ethics or corruption? *Thunderbird International Business Review, 50,* 287–293.

Useem, M. (1998). *The leadership moment.* New York: Times Business.

Useem, M. (2001). *Leading up: How to lead your boss so you both win.* New York: Crown Business.

Valentine, S., & Barnett, T. (2003). Ethics code awareness, perceived ethical values, and organizational commitment. *Journal of Personal Selling & Sales Management, 23,* 359–367.

Valle, M. (2006, May/June). The power of politics: Why leaders need to learn the art of influence. *Leadership in Action, 26*(2), 8–12.

Van Aswegen, A. S., & Engelbrecht, A. S. (2009). The relationship between transformational leadership, integrity, and an ethical climate in organizations. *South Africa Journal of Human Resource Management, 7*(1), 221–229.

Van Es, R., French, W., & Stellmaszek, F. (2004). Resolving conflicts over ethical issues: Face-to-face verses Internet negotiations. *Journal of Business Ethics 53,* 171–172.

Van Maanen, J. (1991). The smile factory: Work at Disneyland. In P. J. Frost, L. F. Moore, M. R. Louis, C. C. Lundberg, & J. Martin (Eds.), *Reframing organizational culture* (pp. 58–76). Newbury Park, CA: Sage.

Vance, A. (2010, August 7). Hewlett-Packard ousts chief for hiding payments to friend. *The New York Times,* p. A1.

Vance, A. (2010, December 21). S.E.C. is investigating Hurd's departure as chief of H.P. *The New York Times,* p. B4.

Vanderklippe, N. (2010, October 16). Chile's CEO moment. *The Globe and Mail,* p. F1.

Velasquez, M. G. (1992). *Business ethics: Concepts and cases* (3rd ed.). Englewood Cliffs, NJ: Prentice Hall.

Victor, B., & Cullen, J. B. (1988). The organizational bases of ethical work climates. *Administrative Science Quarterly, 33,* 101–125.

Victor, B., & Cullen, J. B. (1990). A theory and measure of ethical climate in organizations. In W. C. Frederic & L. E. Preston (Eds.), *Business ethics: Research issues and empirical studies* (pp. 77–97). Greenwich, CT: JAI.

Victor, B., Cullen, J. B., & Boynton, A. (1993). Toward a general framework of organizational meaning systems. In C. Conrad (Ed.), *Ethical nexus* (pp. 193–216). Norwood, NJ: Ablex.

Villaume, W. A., & Bodie, G. D. (2007). Discovering the listener within us: The impact of trait-like personality variables and communicator styles on preferences for listening style. *The International Journal of Listening, 21*(2), 102–123.

Vistica, G. L. (1997, November 24). A quiet war over the past. *Newsweek,* p. 41.

Viswesvaran, C., & Ones, D. S. (2002). Examining the construct of organizational justice: A meta-analytic evaluation of relations with work attitudes and behaviors. *Journal of Business Ethics, 38,* 193–203.

Vitell, S. J., Davis, J. H., & Ruhe, J. A. (2003). Perceptions of country corruption: Antecedents and outcomes. *Journal of Business Ethics, 43,* 275–288.

Vitell, S. J., Nwachukwu, S. L., & Barnes, J. H. (1993). *Journal of Business Ethics, 12*(10), 753–760.

Vogel, G. (2001, March 3). Nobel laureates lobby for stem cells. *Science, 291*(5509), 1683–1684.

Waddock, S. (2005). Hollow men and women at the helm . . . Hollow accounting ethics? *Issues in Accounting Education, 20*(2), 145–150.

Waldron, V. R. (1994). Once more, with feeling: Reconsidering the role of emotion at work. In S. A. Deetz (Ed.), *Communication yearbook 17* (pp. 388–428). Thousand Oaks, CA: Sage.

Walsh, A. J. (2007). HRM and the ethics of commodified work in a market economy. In A. H. Pinnington, R. Macklin, & T. Campbell (Eds.), *Human resource management: Ethics and employment* (pp. 102–116). Oxford, UK: Oxford University Press.

Walumbwa, F. O., Avolio, B. J., Gardner, W. L., Wernsing, T. S., & Peterson, S. J. (2008). Authentic leadership: Development and validation of a theory-based measure. *Journal of Management, 34*(1), 89–126.

Walumbwa, F. O., Hartnell, C. A., & Oke, A. (2010). Servant leadership, procedural justice climate, service climate, and organizational citizenship behavior: A cross-level investigation. *Journal of Applied Psychology, 95,* 517–529.

Watson, K. W., Barker, L. L., & Weaver, J. B., III (1995). The Listening Styles Profile (LSP-16): Development and validation of an instrument to assess four listening styles. *International Journal of Listening, 9,* 1–13.

Wayne, L. (2005, March 8). Boeing chief is ousted after admitting affair. *The New York Times,* p. A1.

Wayne, L. (2005, March 11). Ousted chief of Boeing gets $2.1 million bonus for 2004. *The New York Times,* p. C6.

Wayne, L. (2005, March 19). Executive involved with chief has resigned, Boeing says. *The New York Times,* p. C10.

Weatherbee, T., & Kelloway, E. K. (2005). A case of cyberdeviancy: Cyberaggression in the workplace. In E. K. Kelloway, J. Barling, & J. J. Hurrell, Jr. (Eds.), *Handbook of workplace violence* (pp. 445–487). Thousand Oaks, CA: Sage.

Weaver, G. R., Trevino, L. K., & Cochran, P. L. (1999). Corporate ethics practices in the mid-1990s: An empirical study of the Fortune 1000. *Journal of Business Ethics, 18,* 283–294.

Weaver, G. R., Trevino, L. K., & Cochran, P. L. (1999). Corporate ethics programs as control systems: Influence of executive commitment and environmental factors. *Academy of Management Journal, 42,* 41–57.

Weaver, G. R., Trevino, L. K., & Cochran, P. L. (1999). Integrated and decoupled corporate social performance: Management commitments, external pressures, and corporate ethics practices. *Academy of Management Journal, 42,* 539–552.

Weber, J. (2008, February 13). The new ethics enforcers. *BusinessWeek,* pp. 76–77.

Weber, J. (2009). Using exemplary business practices to identify Buddhist and Confucian ethical value systems. *Business and Society Review, 114*(4), 511–540.

Wente, M. (2010, July 27). When nothing is secret any more. *The Globe and Mail,* p. A13.

Werhane, P. H. (1985). *Persons, rights and corporations.* Englewood Cliffs, NJ: Prentice Hall.

Werhane, P. H. (1999). *Moral imagination and management decision-making.* New York: Oxford University Press.

West, H. R. (2004). *An introduction to Mill's utilitarian ethics.* Cambridge, UK: Cambridge University Press.

Westneat, D. (2005, March 11). Boeing's message puzzling. *The Seattle Times,* p. B1.

Wheeler, D., Colbert, B., & Freeman, R. E. (2003). Focusing on value: Reconciling corporate social responsibility, sustainability and a stakeholder approach in a network world. *Journal of General Management, 28,* 1–28.

Wheeler, M. (2004, March). Fair enough: An ethical fitness quiz for negotiators. *Negotiation,* pp. 3–5.

Whicker, M. L. (1996). *Toxic leaders: When organizations go bad.* Westport, CT: Quorum Books.

White, S. S., & Locke, E. A. (2000). Problems with the Pygmalion effect and some proposed solutions. *The Leadership Quarterly, 11,* 389–415.

Why your negotiating behavior may be ethically challenged—and how to fix it. (2008, April). *Negotiation, 11*(4), pp. 1–5.

Whyte, G. (1991). Diffusion of responsibility: Effects on the escalation tendency. *Journal of Applied Psychology, 76,* 408–415.

Wicks, A. C., Freeman, R. E., Werhane, P. H., & Martin, K. E. (2010). *Business ethics: A managerial approach.* Boston: Prentice-Hall.

Wieberg, S. (2005, August 8). Mascot policy will be tough to overcome. *USA Today,* p. 9C.

Wiener, R. L., & Gutek, B. A. (1999). Advances in sexual harassment research, theory, and policy. *Psychology, Public Policy and Law, 5*(3), 507–518.

Williams, G., & Zinkin, J. (2008). The effect of culture on consumers' willingness to punish irresponsible corporate behaviour: Applying Hofstede's typology to the punishment aspect of corporate social responsibility. *Business Ethics: A European Review, 17,* 210–226.

Williams, K. D., Harkins, S. G., & Karau, S. J. (2003). Social performance. In M. A. Hogg & J. Cooper (Eds.), *The Sage handbook of social psychology* (pp. 333–346). London: Sage.

Wilmot, W. W., & Hocker, J. L. (2001). *Interpersonal conflict* (6th ed.). New York: McGraw-Hill.

Wilson, D. (2009, March 3). Patching a wound. *The New York Times,* p. B1.

Wilson, D. (2009, March 3). Pfizer worker photographed student protest at Harvard. *The New York Times,* p. B6.

Wilson, D. (2009, March 4). Senator asks Pfizer to detail pay to Harvard. *The New York Times,* p. B3.

Wilson, D. (2009, September 2). Harvard backs off media policy. *The New York Times,* p. B4.

Wilson, D. (2010, July 22). A tougher conflict policy at Harvard Medical School. *The New York Times,* p. B4.

Wilson, F., & Thompson, P. (2001). Sexual harassment as an exercise of power. *Gender, Work and Organization, 8,* 61–83.

Wimbush, J. C., Shepard, J. M., & Markham, S. E. (1997). An empirical examination of the relationship between ethical climate and ethical behavior from multiple levels of analysis. *Journal of Business Ethics, 16,* 1705–1716.

Wiseman, P. (2005, December 9). On the train tracks in Sri Lanka, life does move on. *USA Today,* pp. 15A–16A.

Wrzesniewski, A., McCauley, C., Rozin, P., & Schwartz, B. (1997). Jobs, careers, and callings: People's relations to their work. *Journal of Research in Personality, 31,* 21–33.

Wood, W., Lundgren, S., Ouellette, J. A., Busceme, S., & Blackstone, T. (1994). Minority influence: A meta-analytic review of social influence processes. *Psychological Bulletin, 115,* 323–345.

Woods, K. C., & Buchanan, N. T. (2008). Sexual harassment in the workplace. In M. Paludi (Ed.), *The psychology of women at work: Challenges and solutions for our female workforce* (Vol. 1, pp. 119–132). Westport, CT: Praeger.

Wright, A. D. (2008, May). Survey: Nonnprofts fall short on ethics. *HR Magazine, 53* (5), 24.

Wright, J. P., Cullen, F. T., & Blankenship, M. B. (2002). Chained factory fire exits: Media coverage of a corporate crime that killed 25 workers. In M. D. Ermann & R. J. Lundman (Eds.), *Corporate and governmental deviance* (6th ed., pp. 262–276). New York: Oxford University Press.

Wusun, L. (2010). *Getting to know Confucius—A new translation of the Analects.* Beijing: Foreign Languages Press.

Yanay, N., & Sharar, G. (1998). Professional feelings as emotional labor. *Journal of Contemporary Ethnography, 27,* 345–373.

Yankelovich, D. (2006). *Profit with honor: The new stage of market capitalism.* New Haven, CT: Yale University Press.

Young, J. S., & Simon, W. L. (2005). *Icon: Steve Jobs, the greatest second act in the history of business.* Hoboken, NJ: John Wiley.

Yukl, G. (2002). *Leadership in organizations* (5th ed.). Upper Saddle River, NJ: Prentice Hall.

Yukl, G. (2006). *Leadership in organizations* (6th ed.). Upper Saddle River, NJ: Prentice Hall.

Zadek, S. (2004, December). The path to corporate responsibility. *Harvard Business Review, 82*(12), 125–132.

Zaitz, L. (2011, January 13). State sues the maker of Motrin. *The Oregonian,* p. A8.

Zajac, A. (2010, October 1). J&J chief sees lapses in quality. *Los Angeles Times,* p. B4.

Zand, D. E. (1972). Trust and managerial problem solving. *Administrative Science Quarterly, 17,* 229–239.

Zapf, D., & Holz, M. (2006). On the positive and negative effects of emotion work in organizations. *European Journal of Work and Organizational Psychology, 15*(1), 1–28.

Zernike, K. (2004, June 27). Defining torture: Russian roulette, yes. Mind-altering drugs, maybe. *The New York Times,* p. 7.

Zhu, W., May, D. R., & Avolio, B. J. (2004). The impact of ethical leadership behavior on employee outcomes: The roles of psychological empowerment and authenticity. *Journal of Leadership and Organizational Studies, 11,* 16–26.

Zinnbauer, B. J., & Pargament, K. I. (2005). Religiousness and spirituality. In R. F. Paloutzian & C. L. Park (Eds.), *Handbook of the psychology of religion and spirituality* (pp. 21–42). New York: Guilford.

Zyglidopoulos, S. C., & Fleming, P. J. (2007). Ethical distance in corrupt firms: How do innocent bystanders become guilty perpetrators? *Journal of Business Ethics, 78,* 265–274.

Index

About the Author

Craig E. Johnson (PhD, University of Denver) is Professor of Leadership Studies and Director of the Doctor of Business Administration program at George Fox University, Newberg, Oregon. He teaches undergraduate and graduate courses in ethics, leadership, and management. Previously, he served as chair of the university's Department of Communication Arts. Johnson is the author of *Meeting the Ethical Challenges of Leadership: Casting Light or Shadow* (also published by Sage), and is coauthor, with Michael Z. Hackman, of *Leadership: A Communication Perspective.* He has published research findings, instructional ideas, and book reviews in *The Journal of Leadership Studies, The Journal of Leadership and Organizational Studies, The Journal of Leadership Education, Academy of Management Learning and Education, The International Leadership Journal, Communication Quarterly, Communication Reports,* and other journals. When not writing or teaching, he enjoys reading, running, and fly-fishing.